W9-BMC-414

SALES, LEASES AND ELECTRONIC COMMERCE:

Problems and Materials on National and International Transactions

Second Edition

By

John E. Murray, Jr.
Chancellor and Professor of Law
Duquesne University

Harry M. Flechtner
Professor of Law
University of Pittsburgh

AMERICAN CASEBOOK SERIES®

THOMSON
———✶———™
WEST

Mat #40141011

West Group has created this publication to provide you with accurate and authoritative information concerning the subject matter covered. However, this publication was not necessarily prepared by persons licensed to practice law in a particular jurisdiction. West Group is not engaged in rendering legal or other professional advice, and this publication is not a substitute for the advice of an attorney. If you require legal or other expert advice, you should seek the services of a competent attorney or other professional.

American Casebook Series and West Group are
registered trademarks used herein under license.

ISBN 0–314–14608–3

 *TEXT IS PRINTED ON 10% POST
CONSUMER RECYCLED PAPER*

To Liz
      J.E.M.

To Joan
      H.M.F.

*

Preface to the Second Edition

The first edition of this book went to press after the American Law Institute (ALI) had approved an extensive 1999 revision to Article 2 of the Uniform Commercial Code (UCC), the essential statute governing the domestic law of Sales in the United States. It was assumed that this long-awaited product of almost a decade of drafts and redrafts would be approved subsequently by the ALI's partner, the National Conference of Commissioners on Uniform State Laws (NCCUSL). The first edition of this book contained pervasive and substantial references to that draft. To the surprise of many, it was not approved by NCCUSL. A new Committee was formed that ultimately produced the 2002 "proposed amendments" to Article 2. The amendments won NCCUSL approval and preliminary ALI approval. Instead of a major revision with new section numbers, the amendments retain original section numbers and are relatively modest in substance. This edition includes references to 2002 amendments instead of the 1999 draft.

While a new edition might be justified on this basis alone, it is not, by far, the most significant change in this edition. Important elaborations of Sales law in very recent cases are included in this edition. New text and new or modified problems also reflect the accelerating changes in this vital field. This edition is larger than its predecessor, reflecting coverage of additional topics and elaborations of other important topics. More cases are included in this edition, though the materials retain their problem-centered focus. Materials on leases have been revised and the revisions in UCC Article 2A are carefully noted. Related references to the revised Article 1 are also included as are references to revisions in Article 9 and other UCC Articles. Developments in electronic transactions under the Uniform Electronics Transaction Act (UETA and "E-Sign" law) and computer information transactions under the Uniform Computer Information Transactions Act (UCITA) are updated and otherwise elaborated. Developments in international transactions, including the most recent interpretations of the United Nations Convention on Contracts for the International Sale of Goods (CISG) by domestic courts and the courts of other countries, provide the most complete treatment of that subject currently available.

Beyond the comprehensive character of the materials, their utility to teacher and student has been further enhanced. The problems are interesting and challenging, but the student's ability to meet these challenges is enhanced by case and text material that surround the problems. An extensive index and tables provide easy reference to the materials throughout this edition.

Producing a comprehensive work in this extended ambience of dynamic change to allow students to develop a sophisticated appreciation of domestic and international Sales law and related areas is a worthy challenge. We joyfully present this response to that challenge.

JOHN E. MURRAY, JR.
HARRY M. FLECHTNER

Pittsburgh, Pennsylvania, 2003

Summary of Contents

_____

Page

PREFACE --- v

TABLE OF CASES -- xxv

TABLE OF STATUTES AND U.C.C. SECTIONS ----------------------------- xxxi

Chapter 1.   Introduction --------------------------------------- **1**

PART 1: OVERVIEW

A.   The Study of Commercial Law------------------------------------- 1
B.   The Uniform Commercial Code—History ------------------------- 2
C.   Summary of UCC Articles --------------------------------------- 3
D.   "Official" Comments--- 6
E.   Related Statutes --- 7

PART 2: SCOPE OF ARTICLE 2 AND RELATED STATUTES

A.   Questions of Scope—Transactions in Goods------------------- 11
B.   "Sale" and "Contract for Sale"—"Title" ------------------- 20
C.   Secured Transactions --- 21
D.   Leases and Secured Transactions—Article 2A----------------- 22
E.   Computer Information Transactions—UCITA--------------------- 26
F.   Scope and Structure of the United Nations Convention on
     International Sales of Goods (CISG) ------------------------- 27

**Chapter 2.   The Contract Law of the UCC—Electronic Con-
     tracts**-- **35**
A.   Radical Changes in Traditional Contract Law ----------------- 35
B.   Contract Formation—2–204, 2–206, 2–504 ------------------ 36
C.   The "Battle of the Forms"—2–207----------------------------- 37
D.   Confirmations (2–207(1)) ------------------------------------- 50
E.   The New (Amended) Section 2–207 (2002)-------------------- 51
F.   Contract Formation and Battle of the Forms—International
     Sales—CISG --- 52
G.   The Battle of the Leases --------------------------------------- 53
H.   UCITA and the Battle of the Forms----------------------------- 53
I.   The Operative Effect of Post–Purchase Terms—"Rolling" or
     "Layered" Contracts --- 54
J.   UCITA—"Layered" Contracts and "Mass Market Licenses"---- 61
K.   The "Reasonable Expectations" Doctrine---------------------- 62
L.   Electronic Contracts-- 63

Page

M. The Statute of Frauds—Scope—2–201, 8–113, 9–203, and Pre–
Amendment 1–206 --- 67
N. Statute of Frauds—Sufficient Writing --------------------------------- 67
O. Statute of Frauds—Confirmations -------------------------------------- 68
P. Statute of Frauds—Part Performance ---------------------------------- 69
Q. Amended Section 2–201—"Record," $5000, Reliance, Admis-
sions, and the One–Year Provision ----------------------------------- 70
R. Statute of Frauds—Leases -- 71
S. Statute of Frauds—UCITA and CISG --------------------------------- 72
T. Requirement and Output Contracts—2–306 ------------------------- 72
U. Contract Modifications and Waivers—2–209 ----------------------- 73
V. Contract Modifications—CISG & Leases ---------------------------- 79
W. Parol Evidence—Trade Usage, Course of Dealing, Course of
Performance --- 80
X. Parol Evidence and Interpretation—CISG -------------------------- 91
Y. Leases and the Parol Evidence Rule ---------------------------------- 99
Z. "Open" and Implied Terms—The "Anti–Technical" Environ-
ment --- 99
AA. Assignment and Delegation -- 103

Chapter 3. Warranties -- 104
A. Introduction: The Warranty Concept --------------------------------- 104
B. Express Warranty Under UCC Article 2—Facts vs. Commen-
dations, Value Or "Puff" --- 105
C. Express Warranty—"Basis of the Bargain" ------------------------ 108
D. Express Warranties—Samples & Models ---------------------------- 118
E. Express Warranties—Leases, CISG and UCITA ------------------ 119
F. The Implied Warranty of Merchantability—Scope—2–314 ------ 119
G. "Merchantability" Defined --- 120
H. Merchantability—Leases, CISG and UCITA ----------------------- 123
    1. The Implied Warranty of Merchantability in Article 2A ------ 123
    2. The Implied Obligation to Deliver Goods Fit for Ordinary
       Purposes Under the CISG --- 123
    3. Implied Warranties of Merchantability and on Information-
       al Content Under UCITA -- 124
I. Implied Warranty of Fitness for a Particular Purpose Under
UCC Article 2—2–315 --- 126
J. Particular Purpose—Leases, CISG, and UCITA -------------------- 129
    1. The Implied Warranty of Fitness for Particular Purpose
       Under Article 2A -- 129
    2. The Implied Obligation to Deliver Goods Fit for a Particu-
       lar Purpose Under CISG Article 35(2)(b) ------------------------- 129
    3. Implied Reliance Warranties Under UCITA–Fitness for
       Particular Purpose and Accuracy of Informational Con-
       tent --- 133
K. Cumulation and Conflict of Warranties ------------------------------- 133
    1. Cumulation and Conflict of Warranties Under UCC
       Article 2 -- 133

Page

    2. Cumulation and Conflict of Warranties Under UCC Article 2A ----- 139

    3. Cumulation and Conflict of Quality Obligations Under the CISG ----- 139

    4. Cumulation and Conflict of Warranties Under UCITA ----- 139

L. Finance Leases ----- 139

M. Warranty Disclaimers ----- 146

    1. Disclaimers Under UCC Article 2 ----- 146

    2. Warranty Disclaimers Under UCC Article 2A ----- 153

    3. Precluding Obligations of Quality Under the CISG ----- 153

    4. Warranty Disclaimers Under UCITA ----- 155

N. Ownership and Variations on the Theme ----- 156

O. Warranties of Title and Against Infringement Under UCC Article 2—Disclaimers ----- 162

P. Transferee's Right to Undisturbed Possession/Use Under UCC Article 2A, the CISG, And UCITA ----- 171

    1. Protection of Lessee's Rights to Leased Goods ----- 171

    2. Buyer's Protections Against Third–Party Claims Under the CISG ----- 172

    3. Warranty Against Infringements and Misappropriations, and Warranty Against Interference Under UCITA ----- 173

Q. Unconscionability ----- 173

R. Limitation of Remedy; Failure of Essential Purpose of Limited Remedies ----- 185

    1. Limited Remedies Under UCC Article 2 ----- 185

    2. Limited Remedies Under UCC Article 2A, the CISG, and UCITA ----- 194

S. Contract and Tort: Products Liability—Privity ----- 195

T. Proof and Causation in Products Liability Actions ----- 211

U. Products Liability—Article 2A, the CISG, and UCITA ----- 219

V. Consumer Protection—Magnuson Moss Et Al. ----- 221

Chapter 4. Nonconforming Tender and Prospective Non-performance ----- **236**

PART 1: THE RESPONSE TO TENDER

A. The Buyer's Courses of Action Upon Receipt of Goods Under UCC Article 2 ----- 236

    1. Rejection, Acceptance, and Revocation of Acceptance Under Article 2: An Overview ----- 236

    2. Rejection ----- 237

    3. Cure ----- 245

    4. Acceptance and Revocation ----- 254

    5. Revocation for Breach of Manufacturers' Warranties ----- 277

B. The Lessee's Courses of Action Upon Receipt of Goods Under UCC Article 2A ----- 288

    1. Rejection, Acceptance and Revocation of Acceptance under Article 2A–in General ----- 288

    2. Rejection and Revocation in Finance Leases ----- 288

Page

C. Refusing Computer Information Under UCITA ---------------------- 291
D. Refusing Goods Under the CISG—Avoidance of Contract -------- 292
   1. Avoidance in General -- 292
   2. Avoidance for Fundamental Breach ---------------------------- 293
   3. "Nachfrist" Avoidance -- 297
   4. Nonavoidance --- 299

PART 2: PROSPECTIVE NONPERFORMANCE

A. Adequate Assurances and Anticipatory Repudiation Under Article 2 of the UCC -- 300
B. Adequate Assurances and Anticipatory Repudiation Under Article 2A of the UCC and UCITA ---------------------------- 319
C. Prospective Nonperformance Under the CISG --------------------- 319

Chapter 5. Risk Allocation ------------------------------------- **324**
A. Basic Obligations: A Survey --------------------------------------- 324
B. Delivery Terms and Risk of Loss Under Pre–Amendment UCC Article 2: Basic Concepts -------------------------------------- 326
C. Other Delivery Terms Under Pre–Amendment UCC Article 2: F.O.B. Vessel—F.A.S.—C.I.F. ------------------------------------- 327
D. Delivery Terms Under Amended UCC Article 2; Incoterms ----- 328
E. Breach of Contract and Risk of Loss (2–510) -------------------- 340
F. Risk of Loss Under the CISG (Articles 66–70) ------------------- 344
G. Risk of Loss Under UCC Article 2A -------------------------------- 345
H. Risk of Loss Under UCITA -- 346
I. Identification and Casualty to Identified Goods ----------------- 346
J. Commercial Impracticability --------------------------------------- 348
K. Exemption Under CISG Article 79 ---------------------------------- 367
L. Excuse for Non–Performance Under Article 2A ------------------ 367
M. Excuse for Non–Performance Under UCITA ------------------------ 367
N. The Documentary Transaction -------------------------------------- 367
O. Negotiable or Non–Negotiable -------------------------------------- 376
P. Letters of Credit --- 380
   1. What Is a "Letter of Credit"? --------------------------------- 380
   2. "Commercial" and "Standby" Letters of Credit -------------- 381
   3. Law Governing Letters of Credit ------------------------------- 382

Chapter 6. Remedies -- **395**
A. Remedies Under UCC Article 2—In General --------------------- 395
B. UCC Remedies When the Buyer Does Not Receive or Retain the Goods --- 396
   1. Buyers' Damages Measured by Substitute Transactions or Market Prices --- 396
   2. Buyers' Recovery of the Goods -------------------------------- 405
   3. Seller's/Lessor's Damages Measured by Substitute Transactions or Market Prices --------------------------------------- 413
   4. Sellers' Lost Profit Recovery ---------------------------------- 415
   5. Sellers' Right to Specific Performance ----------------------- 421

Page

C. UCC Article 2 Remedies When the Buyer Retains the Goods 421
   1. Aggrieved Buyers' Damages When Goods Remain Accepted 421
   2. Sellers' Right to the Price for Accepted Goods 427
   3. Reclamation by Sellers 432
D. Other Remedies Under UCC Article 2 435
   1. Incidental and Consequential Damages 435
   2. Liquidated Damages 449
   3. Restitution for Breaching Buyers 454
E. Remedies Under UCC Article 2A 455
   1. Overview of Article 2A Remedies 455
   2. Lessees' Remedies under Article 2A 455
   3. Lessors' Remedies under Article 2A 460
   4. Liquidated Damages under Article 2A 462
F. Remedies Under the CISG 463
   1. Overview of CISG Remedies 463
   2. Buyers' Remedies Under the CISG 463
   3. Sellers' Remedies Under the CISG 466
   4. Incidental, Consequential and Liquidated Damages Under
      the CISG 471
G. Remedies Under UCITA 483

INDEX 485

*

Table of Contents

———

Page

PREFACE --- v
TABLE OF CASES -- xxv
TABLE OF STATUTES AND U.C.C. SECTIONS -- xxxi

Chapter 1. Introduction --- 1

PART 1: OVERVIEW

A. The Study of Commercial Law -- 1
B. The Uniform Commercial Code—History --- 2
C. Summary of UCC Articles -- 3
D. "Official" Comments --- 6
E. Related Statutes --- 7

PART 2: SCOPE OF ARTICLE 2 AND RELATED STATUTES

A. Questions of Scope—Transactions in Goods ----------------------------------- 11
    Loughridge v. Goodyear Tire & Rubber Co. -------------------------------------- 11
    Note --- 13
    Princess Cruises v. General Electric Company -------------------------------- 13
    Questions --- 18
    Problem 1 --- 18
    Problem 2 --- 19
    Problem 3 --- 19
    Problem 4 --- 20
B. "Sale" and "Contract for Sale"—"Title" --- 20
C. Secured Transactions -- 21
D. Leases and Secured Transactions—Article 2A ------------------------------- 22
    Problem 5 --- 26
E. Computer Information Transactions—UCITA ---------------------------------- 26
    Problem 6 --- 27
F. Scope and Structure of the United Nations Convention on
    International Sales of Goods (CISG) --- 27
    Problem 7 --- 27
    Questions --- 29
    Asante Technologies, Inc. v. PMC–Sierra, Inc. ------------------------------- 29
    Problem 7A -- 33
    Note --- 33

Chapter 2. The Contract Law of the UCC—Electronic Contracts ------- 35
A. Radical Changes in Traditional Contract Law ------------------------------- 35
B. Contract Formation—2–204, 2–206, 2–504 ---------------------------------- 36
    Problem 8 --- 36

Page

C. The "Battle of the Forms"—2–207 37
Coastal & Native Plant Specialties, Inc. v. Engineered Textile Products, Inc. 37
Problem 9 42
Reilly Foam Corp. v. Rubbermaid Corp. 43
Problem 9A 46
Southern Illinois Riverboat Casino Cruises, Inc. v. Triangle Insulation and Sheet Metal Company 46
Problem 9B 50
D. Confirmations (2–207(1)) 50
Problem 10 50
E. The New (Amended) Section 2–207 (2002) 51
F. Contract Formation and Battle of the Forms—International Sales—CISG 52
Problem 11 52
Problem 11A 53
G. The Battle of the Leases 53
Problem 12 53
H. UCITA and the Battle of the Forms 53
I. The Operative Effect of Post–Purchase Terms—"Rolling" or "Layered" Contracts 54
Hill v. Gateway 2000, Inc. 55
Notes 58
Questions 60
J. UCITA—"Layered" Contracts and "Mass Market Licenses" 61
K. The "Reasonable Expectations" Doctrine 62
L. Electronic Contracts 63
M. The Statute of Frauds—Scope—2–201, 8–113, 9–203, and Pre–Amendment 1–206 67
Problem 13 67
N. Statute of Frauds—Sufficient Writing 67
Problem 14 67
O. Statute of Frauds—Confirmations 68
Problem 15 68
P. Statute of Frauds—Part Performance 69
Problem 16 69
Q. Amended Section 2–201—"Record," $5000, Reliance, Admissions, and the One–Year Provision 70
R. Statute of Frauds—Leases 71
Problem 17 71
S. Statute of Frauds—UCITA and CISG 72
T. Requirement and Output Contracts—2–306 72
Problem 18 72
U. Contract Modifications and Waivers—2–209 73
Problem 19 73
BMC Industries, Inc. v. Barth Industries, Inc. 74
Problem 19A 78
Note 79
V. Contract Modifications—CISG & Leases 79
Problem 20 79

Page

V. Contract Modifications—CISG & Leases—Continued
    Problem 21 --- 79
W. Parol Evidence—Trade Usage, Course of Dealing, Course of
    Performance -- 80
    C-Thru Container Corporation v. Midland Manufacturing Company --- 80
    Note --- 83
    Puget Sound Financial, L.L.C. v. Unisearch, Inc. --------------------- 83
    Questions -- 89
    Problem 22 -- 90
    Questions -- 91
X. Parol Evidence and Interpretation—CISG ------------------------------ 91
    MCC–Marble Ceramic Center, Inc. v. d'Agostino, S.p.A., ----------- 91
Y. Leases and the Parol Evidence Rule ----------------------------------- 99
Z. "Open" and Implied Terms—The "Anti–Technical" Environ-
    ment --- 99
    Problem 23 -- 101
AA. Assignment and Delegation -- 103

Chapter 3. Warranties -- **104**
A. Introduction: The Warranty Concept ---------------------------------- 104
B. Express Warranty Under UCC Article 2—Facts vs. Commen-
    dations, Value Or "Puff" -- 105
    Web Press Services Corp. v. New London Motors, Inc. ------------- 105
    Problem 24 -- 107
    Note --- 108
    Problem 25 -- 108
C. Express Warranty—"Basis of the Bargain" -------------------------- 108
    Cipollone v. Liggett Group, Inc. ---------------------------------- 108
    Note --- 112
    In re Bridgestone/Firestone Inc. Tires Products Liability Litigation ----- 112
    Note --- 116
    Problem 26 -- 117
    Problem 27 -- 117
D. Express Warranties—Samples & Models ----------------------------- 118
    Problem 28 -- 118
E. Express Warranties—Leases, CISG and UCITA --------------------- 119
F. The Implied Warranty of Merchantability—Scope—2–314 ------- 119
    Problem 29 -- 119
G. "Merchantability" Defined --- 120
    Problem 30 -- 120
    Note --- 122
H. Merchantability—Leases, CISG and UCITA ----------------------- 123
    1. The Implied Warranty of Merchantability in Article 2A ----- 123
    2. The Implied Obligation to Deliver Goods Fit for Ordinary
       Purposes Under the CISG -- 123
       *Decision of March 8, 1995, Bundesgerichtshof (Supreme Court),
       Germany, Case No. VIII ZR 159/94* ------------------------ 123
    3. Implied Warranties of Merchantability and on Information-
       al Content Under UCITA -- 124
I. Implied Warranty of Fitness for a Particular Purpose Under
    UCC Article 2—2–315 -- 126
    Outlook Windows Partnership v. York International Corporation ------- 126

Page

I. Implied Warranty of Fitness for a Particular Purpose Under
    UCC Article 2—2–315—Continued
    Problem 31 128
J. Particular Purpose—Leases, CISG, and UCITA 129
    1. The Implied Warranty of Fitness for Particular Purpose
        Under Article 2A 129
        Problem 32 129
    2. The Implied Obligation to Deliver Goods Fit for a Particu-
        lar Purpose Under CISG Article 35(2)(b) 129
        Schmitz–Werke Gmbh & Co. v. Rockland Industries, Inc. 129
        Question 133
    3. Implied Reliance Warranties Under UCITA–Fitness for
        Particular Purpose and Accuracy of Informational Con-
        tent 133
K. Cumulation and Conflict of Warranties 133
    1. Cumulation and Conflict of Warranties Under UCC Article
        2 133
        The Singer Company v. E.I. du Pont de Nemours Company 133
        Problem 33 138
        Problem 34 138
    2. Cumulation and Conflict of Warranties Under UCC Article
        2A 139
        Problem 34A 139
    3. Cumulation and Conflict of Quality Obligations Under the
        CISG 139
        Problem 34B 139
    4. Cumulation and Conflict of Warranties Under UCITA 139
L. Finance Leases 139
    Dudley v. Business Express, Inc. 139
    Note 145
    Problem 35 146
M. Warranty Disclaimers 146
    1. Disclaimers Under UCC Article 2 146
        Problem 36 146
        Problem 37 147
        James River Equip. Co. v. Beadle County Equip., Inc. 148
        Notes 150
    2. Warranty Disclaimers Under UCC Article 2A 153
    3. Precluding Obligations of Quality Under the CISG 153
        Supermicro Computer Inc. v. Digitechnic, S.A. 153
        Questions 154
    4. Warranty Disclaimers Under UCITA 155
        Problem 37A 155
N. Ownership and Variations on the Theme 156
    Problem 38 156
    Inmi–Etti v. Aluisi 158
O. Warranties of Title and Against Infringement Under UCC
    Article 2—Disclaimers 162
    Problem 39 163
    Note 163
    Yttro Corp. v. X–Ray Marketing Assn., Inc. 165
    Note 170

Page

P. Transferee's Right to Undisturbed Possession/Use Under UCC Article 2A, the CISG, And UCITA 171
    1. Protection of Lessee's Rights to Leased Goods 171
        Problem 40 172
    2. Buyer's Protections Against Third–Party Claims Under the CISG 172
        Problem 40A 173
    3. Warranty Against Infringements and Misappropriations, and Warranty Against Interference Under UCITA 173
Q. Unconscionability 173
    Moscatiello v. Pittsburgh Contractors Equipment Co. 178
    Note 184
R. Limitation of Remedy; Failure of Essential Purpose of Limited Remedies 185
    1. Limited Remedies Under UCC Article 2 185
        Rheem Manufacturing Company v. Phelps Heating & Air Conditioning, Inc. 185
        Problem 41 193
    2. Limited Remedies Under UCC Article 2A, the CISG, and UCITA 194
        Problem 41A 194
        Note on Limitation of Remedies under UCITA 195
S. Contract and Tort: Products Liability—Privity 195
    UCC 2–318 "Third Party Beneficiaries" 197
    S & R Assocs. v. Shell Oil Co. 197
    Notes 199
    Stoney v. Franklin 200
    Note 205
    Problem 42 210
T. Proof and Causation in Products Liability Actions 211
    International Motors Inc. v. Ford Motor Company, Inc. 211
    Note 214
    Castro v. QVC Network, Inc. 215
    Note 218
U. Products Liability—Article 2A, the CISG, and UCITA 219
    Note: Statute of Limitations Applicable under Article 2A, the CISG, and UCITA 220
V. Consumer Protection—Magnuson Moss Et Al. 221
    Skelton v. General Motors Corporation 223
    Cunningham v. Fleetwood Homes of Georgia, Inc. 227
    Problem 43 234

Chapter 4. Nonconforming Tender and Prospective Nonperformance **236**

PART 1: THE RESPONSE TO TENDER

A. The Buyer's Courses of Action Upon Receipt of Goods Under UCC Article 2 236
    1. Rejection, Acceptance, and Revocation of Acceptance Under Article 2: An Overview 236
    2. Rejection 237
        Problem 44 237

Page

A. The Buyer's Courses of Action Upon Receipt of Goods Under UCC Article 2—Continued
    Questions 238
    Problem 45 238
    Problem 46 238
    Questions 238
    Note: Limitations on the Perfect Tender Rule 239
    Problem 47 240
    Neumiller Farms, Inc. v. Cornett 240
    Notes on Neumiller 242
    Problem 48 243
    Problem 49 244
    Question 245
   3. Cure 245
    Problem 50 245
    Problem 51 245
    Note on the Requirements For Cure After The Date For Delivery 245
    Problem 52 246
    Note on "Shaken Faith" and Cure by Replacement or Repair 247
    Note on Cure by Price Adjustment 248
    Problem 53 249
    Knic Knac Agencies v. Masterpiece Apparel, Ltd. 249
    Note: Cure and Good Faith 253
   4. Acceptance and Revocation 254
    Problem 54 254
    Cissell Mfg. Co. v. Park 254
    Questions 258
    Problem 55 258
    Problem 56 258
    Note on the Purpose and Content of Buyer's Notice of Breach 259
    Problem 57 260
    Problem 58 261
    Note: Consequences of Acceptance 261
    Problem 59 262
    Liarikos v. Mello 263
    Notes 266
    Problem 60 268
    Questions 268
    Note: Revocation and the Circumstances of Acceptance 268
    Champion Ford Sales, Inc. v. Levine 269
    Notes and Questions 274
    Note: Subjective vs. Objective Non–Conformity 275
   5. Revocation for Breach of Manufacturers' Warranties 277
    Seekings v. Jimmy GMC of Tucson, Inc. 277
    Notes 286
B. The Lessee's Courses of Action Upon Receipt of Goods Under UCC Article 2A 288
   1. Rejection, Acceptance and Revocation of Acceptance under Article 2A–in General 288
    Problem 60A 288
   2. Rejection and Revocation in Finance Leases 288
    Problem 61 288
    Questions 290
    Note—Finance Lessee's Notice of Revocation 290

Page

C. Refusing Computer Information Under UCITA 291
D. Refusing Goods Under the CISG—Avoidance of Contract 292
   1. Avoidance in General 292
   2. Avoidance for Fundamental Breach 293
     Problem 62 293
     Decision of April 3, 1996, Bundesgerichtshof (Supreme Court),
      Germany, Case No. VIII ZR 51/95 293
     Notes and Questions on Buyer's Course of Action following Funda-
      mental Breach 294
     Note on Retaining the Goods after Avoidance 295
     Problem 63 296
     Questions 296
     Note: Compensation for Benefits From Goods 296
     Problem 64 297
   3. "Nachfrist" Avoidance 297
     Problem 65 297
     Notes and Questions 298
     Problem 66 298
     Questions 299
     Note 299
   4. Nonavoidance 299
     Problem 67 299
     Note on Nonavoidance Remedies 299

PART 2: PROSPECTIVE NONPERFORMANCE

A. Adequate Assurances and Anticipatory Repudiation Under Ar-
   ticle 2 of the UCC 300
   Introductory Note 300
   Neptune Research & Development, Inc. v. Teknics Industrial Systems,
    Inc. 301
   Notes and Questions 309
   Problem 68 310
   Questions 311
   Problem 69 312
   Problem 70 312
   Universal Resources Corp. v. Panhandle Eastern Pipe Line Co. 312
   Problem 71 315
   Notes and Questions 316
   Problem 72 318
   Problem 73 319
   Questions 319
B. Adequate Assurances and Anticipatory Repudiation Under Ar-
   ticle 2A of the UCC and UCITA 319
   Note on Prospective Nonperformance Under Article 2A 319
   Note on Prospective Nonperformance Under UCITA 319
C. Prospective Nonperformance Under the CISG 319
   Problem 74 319
   Problem 75 320
   Questions 321
   Decision of September 30, 1992, Landgericht Berlin, Germany Case
    No. 99 O 123/92 321
   Note: Risks in Using Articles 71 and 72 322
   Problem 76 323
   Questions 323

		Page
Chapter 5. Risk Allocation		**324**
A.	Basic Obligations: A Survey	324
	Problem 77	324
B.	Delivery Terms and Risk of Loss Under Pre–Amendment UCC Article 2: Basic Concepts	326
	Problem 78	326
	Problem 79	327
C.	Other Delivery Terms Under Pre–Amendment UCC Article 2: F.O.B. Vessel—F.A.S.—C.I.F.	327
	Problem 80	327
	Problem 81	327
D.	Delivery Terms Under Amended UCC Article 2; Incoterms	328
	St. Paul Guardian Insurance Company v. Neuromed Medical Systems & Support	330
	Note	334
	Jason's Foods, Inc. v. Peter Eckrich & Sons, Inc.	335
	Note	339
	Problem 82	339
	Problem 83	339
E.	Breach of Contract and Risk of Loss (2–510)	340
	Problem 84	340
	Multiplastics, Inc. v. Arch Industries, Inc.	341
	Note	343
	Question	343
	Problem 84A	343
F.	Risk of Loss Under the CISG (Articles 66–70)	344
	Problem 85	344
G.	Risk of Loss Under UCC Article 2A	345
	Problem 86	345
	Problem 86A	346
H.	Risk of Loss Under UCITA	346
	Note	346
I.	Identification and Casualty to Identified Goods	346
	Problem 87	346
J.	Commercial Impracticability	348
	Specialty Tires of America, Inc. v. The CIT Group, Inc.	350
	Problem 88	357
	Note	357
	Cliffstar Corporation v. Riverbend Products, Inc.	357
	Problem 89	363
	Note	364
	Perlman v. Pioneer Limited Partnership	364
K.	Exemption Under CISG Article 79	367
	Problem 90	367
L.	Excuse for Non–Performance Under Article 2A	367
	Problem 90A	367
M.	Excuse for Non–Performance Under UCITA	367
N.	The Documentary Transaction	367
	I.C.C. Metals, Inc. v. Municipal Warehouse Co.	370
	Notes	375
O.	Negotiable or Non–Negotiable	376
	Problem 91	378
P.	Letters of Credit	380
	1. What Is a "Letter of Credit"?	380
	2. "Commercial" and "Standby" Letters of Credit	381

Page

P.   Letters of Credit—Continued
    3. Law Governing Letters of Credit 382
       Benetton Services Corporation v. Benedot, Inc. 382
       Note 386
       Courtaulds North America, Inc. v. North Carolina Nat. Bank 388
       Note 393
       Problem 92 393

Chapter 6. Remedies **395**
A. Remedies Under UCC Article 2—In General 395
B. UCC Remedies When the Buyer Does Not Receive or Retain
    the Goods 396
    1. Buyers' Damages Measured by Substitute Transactions or
       Market Prices 396
       Problem 93 396
       Dangerfield v. Markel 396
       Notes on Dangerfield 401
       Problem 94 402
       Note: Equivalency of Substitute Purchase for Purposes of Cover
         Damages 403
       Problem 95 403
       Problem 96 403
       Note: Measuring Buyer's Market Price Damages when Seller Re-
         pudiates 404
    2. Buyers' Recovery of the Goods 405
       Introductory Note on Buyers' Right to Reach the Goods under the
         UCC 405
       Problem 97 406
       Sedmak v. Charlie's Chevrolet, Inc. 407
       Question 410
       Note: Proof Problems and Specific Performance 410
       Note on Specific Performance in Requirement and Output Con-
         tracts 410
       Problem 98 412
       Problem 99 412
       Question 412
       Problem 100 412
    3. Seller's/Lessor's Damages Measured by Substitute Transac-
       tions or Market Prices 413
       Problem 101 413
       Problem 102 413
       Note: Types of Resales and Notice of Resale 414
       Problem 103 414
    4. Sellers' Lost Profit Recovery 415
       Problem 104 415
       Kenco Homes, Inc. v. Williams 415
       Note: The "Lost Volume Seller" and Other Theories for Sellers to
         Recover Lost Profits 419
       Problem 105 420
       Note on Accounting for the Proceeds of Resale in a Lost Profits
         Recovery 420
    5. Sellers' Right to Specific Performance 421
       Problem 106 421
       Note on Seller's Specific Performance 421

Page

C. UCC Article 2 Remedies When the Buyer Retains the Goods   421
    1. Aggrieved Buyers' Damages When Goods Remain Accepted   421
        Problem 107   421
        Note: Buyer's Damages for Non–Conforming Goods that Are Accepted   422
        Problem 108   424
        Holden Machinery v. Sundance Tractor & Mower   424
        Note on Using Repair Costs to Measure Damages for Breach of Warranty   427
        Question   427
    2. Sellers' Right to the Price for Accepted Goods   427
        Problem 109   427
        Question   428
        Siemens Energy & Automation, Inc. v. Coleman Electrical Supply Co.   428
        Problem 110   430
        Note on Ineffective vs. Wrongful Rejection   430
        Questions   431
        Problem 111   431
        Problem 112   431
    3. Reclamation by Sellers   432
        Problem 113   432
        Note on Sellers' Right to Recover Delivered Goods   432
        Problem 114   432
        Questions   433
        Problem 115   434
        Questions   434
        Note: Sellers' Reclamation Rights and Bankruptcy   434
D. Other Remedies Under UCC Article 2   435
    1. Incidental and Consequential Damages   435
        Introductory Note   435
        Problem 116   436
        City National Bank of Charleston v. Wells   436
        Problem 117   439
        Problem 118   440
        Problem 119   440
        Indiana Glass Company v. Indiana Michigan Power Company   441
        Problem 120   444
        Note on Recovering Finance Charges   445
        Problem 121   446
        Problem 122   446
        Remedies for Breach of Warranty to a "Remote Buyer" under Proposed Amended Article 2   446
        Note on Sellers' Incidental and Consequential Damages   447
        Problem 123   448
        Question   449
    2. Liquidated Damages   449
        Kvassay v. Murray   449
        Notes and Questions on Kvassay   452
        Problem 124   452
        Note on "Take-or-Pay" Contracts   453
    3. Restitution for Breaching Buyers   454
        Problem 125   454
        Problem 126   454
E. Remedies Under UCC Article 2A   455
    1. Overview of Article 2A Remedies   455

Page

E. Remedies Under UCC Article 2A—Continued
   2. Lessees' Remedies under Article 2A ------------------------------- 455
      Problem 127 --- 455
      Note: Equivalency of Substitute Lease for Purposes of Cover Damages -- 456
      Problem 128 --- 456
      Note: Lessees' Right to Recover Leased Goods from the Lessor ------ 456
      Note: Present Value Damages under UCC Article 2A --------------- 457
   3. Lessors' Remedies under Article 2A ------------------------------- 460
      Problem 129 --- 460
      Questions --- 461
      Problem 130 --- 461
      Note on Lessors' Right to Repossess ------------------------------ 461
      Note on Lessor's Recovery of the Full Rent ----------------------- 462
   4. Liquidated Damages under Article 2A ----------------------------- 462
      Note on Liquidated Damages under Article 2A --------------------- 462
      Problem 131 --- 463
F. Remedies Under the CISG --- 463
   1. Overview of CISG Remedies -------------------------------------- 463
   2. Buyers' Remedies Under the CISG -------------------------------- 463
      Problem 132 --- 463
      Problem 133 --- 464
      Note on Calculating Price Reduction under CISG Article 50 -------- 465
      Problem 134 --- 465
      Problem 135 --- 466
   3. Sellers' Remedies Under the CISG -------------------------------- 466
      Problem 136 --- 466
      Question --- 467
      Note: Avoidance of Contract under the CISG Compared to Cancellation under the UCC -- 467
      Decision of September 22, 1992, Oberlandesgericht Hamm, Germany --- 468
      Problem 137 --- 469
      Note on a Seller's Right to the Price under the CISG ------------- 469
      Problem 138 --- 470
      Problem 139 --- 470
      Question --- 471
      Problem 140 --- 471
      Note: Sellers' Right to Recover Delivered Goods under the CISG ---- 471
   4. Incidental, Consequential and Liquidated Damages Under the CISG --- 471
      Delchi Carrier SpA v. Rotorex Corp. ------------------------------ 471
      Zapata Hermanos Sucesores, S.A. v. Hearthside Baking Co. --------- 477
      Notes --- 481
      Note on Liquidated Damage Clauses under the CISG --------------- 482
G. Remedies Under UCITA --- 483
   Note on UCITA Remedies -- 483

I*NDEX* --- 485

*

Table of Cases

The principal cases are in bold type. Cases cited or discussed in the text are roman type. References are to pages. Cases cited in principal cases and within other quoted materials are not included.

Ace Equipment Co., Inc. v. Aqua Chem, Inc., 20 U.C.C.Rep.Serv. 392 (Pa.Com. Pl.1975), 407

Admae Enterprises, Ltd. v. 1000 Northern Blvd. Corp., 104 A.D.2d 919, 480 N.Y.S.2d 537 (N.Y.A.D. 2 Dept.1984), 459

Alamance County Bd. of Educ. v. Bobby Murray Chevrolet, Inc., 121 N.C.App. 222, 465 S.E.2d 306 (N.C.App.1996), 357

Alan Wood Steel Co. v. Capital Equipment Enterprises, Inc., 39 Ill.App.3d 48, 349 N.E.2d 627 (Ill.App. 1 Dist.1976), 150

Aluminum Co. of America v. Essex Group, Inc., 499 F.Supp. 53 (W.D.Pa.1980), 350

AMF, Inc. v. McDonald's Corp., 536 F.2d 1167 (7th Cir.1976), 317

Apex Oil Co. v. Belcher Co. of New York, Inc., 855 F.2d 997 (2nd Cir.1988), 414

Art Masters Associates, Ltd. v. United Parcel Service, 566 N.Y.S.2d 184, 567 N.E.2d 226 (N.Y.1990), 376

Art Masters Associates, Ltd. v. United Parcel Service, 153 A.D.2d 41, 549 N.Y.S.2d 495 (N.Y.A.D. 2 Dept.1989), 376

Asante Technologies, Inc. v. PMC–Sierra, Inc., 164 F.Supp.2d 1142 (N.D.Cal. 2001), **29**

Asciolla v. Manter Oldsmobile–Pontiac, Inc., 117 N.H. 85, 370 A.2d 270 (N.H. 1977), 247

Aubrey's R.V. Center, Inc. v. Tandy Corp., 46 Wash.App. 595, 731 P.2d 1124 (Wash. App. Div. 3 1987), 445

Automated Energy Systems, Inc. v. Fibers & Fabrics of Georgia, Inc., 164 Ga.App. 772, 298 S.E.2d 328 (Ga.App.1982), 317

Baker v. International Record Syndicate, Inc., 812 S.W.2d 53 (Tex.App.-Dallas 1991), 452

Barker v. Fleetwood Enterprises, Inc., 2002 WL 453931 (Cal.App. 1 Dist.2002), 222

Beard Plumbing and Heating, Inc. v. Thompson Plastics, Inc., 152 F.3d 313 (4th Cir.1998), 200

Benetton Services Corp. v. Benedot, Inc., 551 So.2d 295 (Ala.1989), **382,** 386

Bergkamp v. Carrico, 108 Idaho 476, 700 P.2d 98 (Idaho App.1985), 458

Beyond the Garden Gate, Inc. v. Northstar Freeze–Dry Mfg., Inc., 526 N.W.2d 305 (Iowa 1995), 446

Big Mac Mobile Homes, Inc. v. Cowgill, 31 U.C.C.Rep.Serv. 1619 (Ark.App.1981), 275, 276

Blankenship v. Northtown Ford, Inc., 95 Ill.App.3d 303, 50 Ill.Dec. 850, 420 N.E.2d 167 (Ill.App. 4 Dist.1981), 276, 287

BMC Industries, Inc. v. Barth Industries, Inc., 160 F.3d 1322 (11th Cir. 1998), **74**

Bridgestone/Firestone Inc. Tires Products Liability Litigation, In re, 205 F.R.D. 503 (S.D.Ind.2001), **112,** 116, 117

Brower v. Gateway 2000, Inc., 246 A.D.2d 246, 676 N.Y.S.2d 569 (N.Y.A.D. 1 Dept. 1998), 59, 185

California and Hawaiian Sugar Co. v. Sun Ship, Inc., 794 F.2d 1433 (9th Cir.1986), 453

Cardozo v. True, 342 So.2d 1053 (Fla.App. 2 Dist.1977), 125

Carl Beasley Ford, Inc. v. Burroughs Corp., 361 F.Supp. 325 (E.D.Pa.1973), 445

Carlson v. Rysavy, 262 N.W.2d 27 (S.D. 1978), 423, 427

Carnival Cruise Lines, Inc. v. Shute, 499 U.S. 585, 111 S.Ct. 1522, 113 L.Ed.2d 622 (1991), 60

Castro v. QVC Network, Inc., 139 F.3d 114 (2nd Cir.1998), **215**

Ceco Corp. v. Carson Concrete Corp., 691 F.Supp. 850 (E.D.Pa.1988), 18

Champion Ford Sales, Inc. v. Levine, 49 Md.App. 547, 433 A.2d 1218 (Md. App.1981), **269,** 274

Chandler v. Hunter, 340 So.2d 818 (Ala.Civ. App.1976), 243

Chase v. Kawasaki Motors Corp., 140 F.Supp.2d 1280 (M.D.Ala.2001), 214

Chatlos Systems, Inc. v. National Cash Register Corp., 670 F.2d 1304 (3rd Cir. 1982), 423

Cipollone v. Liggett Group, Inc., 893 F.2d 541 (3rd Cir.1990), **108,** 116

Cissell Mfg. Co. v. Park, 36 P.3d 85 (Colo.App.2001), **254,** 258

City Nat. Bank of Charleston v. Wells, 181 W.Va. 763, 384 S.E.2d 374 (W.Va. 1989), **436**

Clark v. Ford Motor Co., 46 Or.App. 521, 612 P.2d 316 (Or.App.1980), 286

Claudia v. Olivieri Footwear Ltd., 1998 WL 164824 (S.D.N.Y.1998), 334

Cliffstar Corp. v. Riverbend Products, Inc., 750 F.Supp. 81 (W.D.N.Y.1990), **357**

Coastal & Native Plant Specialties, Inc. v. Engineered Textile Products, Inc., 139 F.Supp.2d 1326 (N.D.Fla. 2001), **37**

Coast Trading Co. v. Cudahy Co., 592 F.2d 1074 (9th Cir.1979), 414

Cole v. Melvin, 441 F.Supp. 193 (D.S.D. 1977), 317

Colonial Dodge, Inc. v. Miller, 420 Mich. 452, 362 N.W.2d 704 (Mich.1984), 274

Colorado–Ute Elec. Ass'n, Inc. v. Envirotech Corp., 524 F.Supp. 1152 (D.Colo. 1981), 413

Columbus Trade Exchange, Inc. v. AMCA Intern. Corp., 763 F.Supp. 946 (S.D.Ohio 1991), 70

Connick v. Suzuki Motor Co., Ltd., 174 Ill.2d 482, 221 Ill.Dec. 389, 675 N.E.2d 584 (Ill.1996), 260

Continental Grain Co. v. McFarland, 628 F.2d 1348 (4th Cir.1980), 317

Continental Sand & Gravel, Inc. v. K & K Sand & Gravel, Inc., 755 F.2d 87 (7th Cir.1985), 423, 427

Cooper v. Lyon Financial Services, Inc., 65 S.W.3d 197 (Tex.App.-Hous. (14 Dist.) 2001), 290

Copylease Corp. of America v. Memorex Corp., 408 F.Supp. 758 (S.D.N.Y.1976), 410, 412

Cosden Oil & Chemical Co. v. Karl O. Helm Aktiengesellschaft, 736 F.2d 1064 (5th Cir.1984), 404

Courtaulds North America, Inc. v. North Carolina Nat. Bank, 528 F.2d 802 (4th Cir.1975), **388**

Courtesy Enterprises, Inc. v. Richards Laboratories, 457 N.E.2d 572 (Ind.App. 3 Dist.1983), 240

Creusot–Loire Intern., Inc. v. Coppus Engineering Corp., 585 F.Supp. 45 (S.D.N.Y. 1983), 317

Crume v. Ford Motor Co., 60 Or.App. 224, 653 P.2d 564 (Or.App.1982), 286

C–Thru Container Corp. v. Midland Mfg. Co., 533 N.W.2d 542 (Iowa 1995), **80**

Cunningham v. Fleetwood Homes of Georgia, Inc., 253 F.3d 611 (11th Cir. 2001), **227**

Dangerfield v. Markel, 278 N.W.2d 364 (N.D.1979), **396, 401**

Daniel v. Dow Jones & Co., Inc., 137 Misc.2d 94, 520 N.Y.S.2d 334 (N.Y.City Civ.Ct.1987), 125

Daughtrey v. Ashe, 243 Va. 73, 413 S.E.2d 336 (Va.1992), 112

David Crystal, Inc. v. Cunard S. S. Co., 223 F.Supp. 273 (S.D.N.Y.1963), 370

David Tunick, Inc. v. Kornfeld, 838 F.Supp. 848 (S.D.N.Y.1993), 248

Delchi Carrier SpA v. Rotorex Corp., 71 F.3d 1024 (2nd Cir.1995), **471**

Delgatti v. Cosmos, 1997 WL 193195 (Conn.Super.1997), 199

Design Plus Store Fixtures, Inc. v. Citro Corp., 131 N.C.App. 581, 508 S.E.2d 825 (N.C.App.1998), 266, 267

Dingley v. Oler, 117 U.S. 490, 6 S.Ct. 850, 29 L.Ed. 984 (1886), 300

Distco Laminating, Inc. v. Union Tool Corp., 81 Mich.App. 612, 265 N.W.2d 768 (Mich.App.1978), 445

Dorton v. Collins & Aikman Corp., 453 F.2d 1161 (6th Cir.1972), 60

Dresser Industries, Inc., Waukesha Engine Div. v. Gradall Co., 965 F.2d 1442 (7th Cir.1992), 41

Dudley v. Business Exp., Inc., 882 F.Supp. 199 (D.N.H.1994), **139**

Durfee v. Rod Baxter Imports, Inc., 262 N.W.2d 349 (Minn.1977), 287

Duval & Co. v. Malcom, 233 Ga. 784, 214 S.E.2d 356 (Ga.1975), 406

Eastern Air Lines, Inc. v. McDonnell Douglas Corp., 532 F.2d 957 (5th Cir.1976), 259

East River S.S. Corp. v. Transamerica Delaval, Inc., 476 U.S. 858, 106 S.Ct. 2295, 90 L.Ed.2d 865 (1986), 206

Federal Signal Corp. v. Safety Factors, Inc., 125 Wash.2d 413, 886 P.2d 172 (Wash. 1994), 108

First Nat. Bank of Chicago v. Jefferson Mortg. Co., 576 F.2d 479 (3rd Cir.1978), 404

Fitzner Pontiac–Buick–Cadillac, Inc. v. Smith, 523 So.2d 324 (Miss.1988), 274

Ford Motor Credit Co. v. Harper, 671 F.2d 1117 (8th Cir.1982), 287

Frantz Lithographic Service, Inc. v. Sun Chemical Corp., 38 U.C.C.Rep.Serv. 485 (E.D.Pa.1984), 276

Fullerton Aircraft Sales and Rentals, Inc. v. Page Avjet Corp., 818 F.2d 28 (4th Cir. 1987), 287

Gaha v. Taylor–Johnson Dodge, Inc., 53 Or.App. 471, 632 P.2d 483 (Or.App. 1981), 286

Gappelberg v. Landrum, 666 S.W.2d 88 (Tex.1984), 248, 274

Gardynski–Leschuck v. Ford Motor Co., 142 F.3d 955 (7th Cir.1998), 234

General Elec. Capital Corp. v. Munson Marine, Inc., 1991 WL 256680 (N.D.Ill. 1991), 150

Germantown Mfg. Co. v. Rawlinson, 341 Pa.Super. 42, 491 A.2d 138 (Pa.Super.1985), 175

Gibbs, Nathaniel (Canada) Ltd. v. International Multifoods Corp., 804 F.2d 450 (8th Cir.1986), 312

Government Street Lumber Co., Inc. v. AmSouth Bank, N.A., 553 So.2d 68 (Ala. 1989), 243

Great Plains Gasification Associates, United States v., 819 F.2d 831 (8th Cir. 1987), 317

Greene v. Boddie–Noell Enterprises, Inc., 966 F.Supp. 416 (W.D.Va.1997), 122

Hamada v. Far East Nat. Bank, 291 F.3d 645 (9th Cir.2002), 386

Hare, United States v., 269 F.3d 859 (7th Cir.2001), 176

Hemmert Agr. Aviation, Inc. v. Mid–Continent Aircraft Corp., 663 F.Supp. 1546 (D.Kan.1987), 276, 277

Henningsen v. Bloomfield Motors, Inc., 32 N.J. 358, 161 A.2d 69 (N.J.1960), 174, 175, 177, 206

Hill v. Gateway 2000, Inc., 105 F.3d 1147 (7th Cir.1997), **55,** 59, 60, 61, 90, 176

Holden Machinery v. Sundance Tractor & Mower, 218 B.R. 247 (Bkrtcy. M.D.Ga.1998), **424**

Hugo Boss Fashions, Inc. v. Sam's European Tailoring, Inc., 293 A.D.2d 296, 742 N.Y.S.2d 1 (N.Y.A.D. 1 Dept.2002), 49

I.C.C. Metals, Inc. v. Municipal Warehouse Co., 431 N.Y.S.2d 372, 409 N.E.2d 849 (N.Y.1980), **370**

Indiana Glass Co. v. Indiana Michigan Power Co., 692 N.E.2d 886 (Ind.App. 1998), **441**

Inmi–Etti v. Aluisi, 63 Md.App. 293, 492 A.2d 917 (Md.App.1985), **158**

In re (see name of party)

Inspec Foams, Inc. v. Claremont Sales Corp., 2002 WL 1765630 (N.D.Ill.2002), 49

Integrated Circuits Unlimited, Inc. v. E.F. Johnson Co., 691 F.Supp. 630 (E.D.N.Y. 1988), 430

International Motors, Inc. v. Ford Motor Co., Inc., 133 Md.App. 269, 754 A.2d 1115 (Md.App.2000), **211**

Iowa Elec. Light and Power Co. v. Atlas Corp., 467 F.Supp. 129 (N.D.Iowa 1978), 349, 350

James River Equipment Co. v. Beadle County Equipment, Inc., 646 N.W.2d 265 (S.D.2002), **148**

Jason's Foods, Inc. v. Peter Eckrich & Sons, Inc., 774 F.2d 214 (7th Cir.1985), **335,** 339

Johnson v. Mobil Oil Corp., 415 F.Supp. 264 (E.D.Mich.1976), 174

Kassab v. Central Soya, 432 Pa. 217, 246 A.2d 848 (Pa.1968), 199

Kee v. Campbell, 8 Kan.App.2d 561, 661 P.2d 831 (Kan.App.1983), 422

Kel–Keef Enterprises, Inc. v. Quality Components Corp., 316 Ill.App.3d 998, 250 Ill.Dec. 308, 738 N.E.2d 524 (Ill.App. 1 Dist.2000), 163

Kenco Homes, Inc. v. Williams, 94 Wash.App. 219, 972 P.2d 125 (Wash. App. Div. 2 1999), **415,** 419

Kinlaw v. Long Mfg. N. C., Inc., 298 N.C. 494, 259 S.E.2d 552 (N.C.1979), 287

Klocek v. Gateway, Inc., 104 F.Supp.2d 1332 (D.Kan.2000), 59

Knic Knac Agencies v. Masterpiece Apparel, 1999 WL 156379 (S.D.N.Y.1999), **249**

Kunian v. Development Corp. of America, 165 Conn. 300, 334 A.2d 427 (Conn. 1973), 317

Kvassay v. Murray, 15 Kan.App.2d 426, 808 P.2d 896 (Kan.App.1991), **449,** 452

Laclede Gas Co. v. Amoco Oil Co., 522 F.2d 33 (8th Cir.1975), 411

Lake River Corp. v. Carborundum Co., 769 F.2d 1284 (7th Cir.1985), 454

Landis and Staefa (UK) Ltd. v. Flair Intern. Corp., 60 F.Supp.2d 14 (E.D.N.Y.1999), 170

Lanham v. Solar America of Cincinnati, Inc., 28 Ohio App.3d 55, 501 N.E.2d 1245 (Ohio App. 12 Dist.1986), 276

Lawrance v. Elmore Bean Warehouse, Inc., 108 Idaho 892, 702 P.2d 930 (Idaho App. 1985), 364

Lee Oldsmobile, Inc. v. Kaiden, 32 Md.App. 556, 363 A.2d 270 (Md.App.1976), 448

Lemmer v. IDS Properties, Inc., 304 N.W.2d 864 (Minn.1980), 60

Liarikos v. Mello, 418 Mass. 669, 639 N.E.2d 716 (Mass.1994), **263,** 266, 267

Liebeck v. McDonald's Restaurants, P.T.S., Inc., 1995 WL 360309 (N.M. Dist.1994), 122

Lind Bldg. Corp. v. Pacific Bellevue Developments, 55 Wash.App. 70, 776 P.2d 977 (Wash.App. Div. 1 1989), 453

Look v. Werlin, 590 S.W.2d 526 (Tex.Civ. App.-Hous. (1 Dist.) 1979), 459

Loughridge v. Goodyear Tire and Rubber Co., 192 F.Supp.2d 1175 (D.Colo. 2002), **11,** 13

Lucien Bourque, Inc. v. Cronkite, 557 A.2d 193 (Me.1989), 60

MacPherson v. Buick Motor Co., 217 N.Y. 382, 111 N.E. 1050 (N.Y.1916), 196

M.A. Mortenson Co., Inc. v. Timberline Software Corp., 93 Wash.App. 819, 970 P.2d 803 (Wash.App. Div. 1 1999), 59

Management Assistance, Inc. v. Computer Dimensions, Inc., 546 F.Supp. 666 (N.D.Ga.1982), 243

Mantaline Corp. v. PPG Industries, Inc., 225 F.3d 659 (6th Cir.2000), 50

Martin v. American Medical Systems, Inc., 116 F.3d 102 (4th Cir.1997), 112

Martin v. Melland's Inc., 283 N.W.2d 76 (N.D.1979), 340

Matter of (see name of party)

Max True Plastering Co. v. United States Fidelity and Guar. Co., 912 P.2d 861 (Okla.1996), 63, 185

Maxwell v. Fidelity Financial Services, Inc., 184 Ariz. 82, 907 P.2d 51 (Ariz.1995), 184, 185

MCC–Marble Ceramic Center, Inc. v. d'Agostino, S.p.A., 144 F.3d 1384 (11th Cir.1998), **91**

McGinnis v. Wentworth Chevrolet Co., 295 Or. 494, 668 P.2d 365 (Or.1983), 401, 402

McKenzie v. Alla–Ohio Coals, Inc., 29 U.C.C.Rep.Serv. 852 (D.D.C.1979), 248

McLaughlin v. Watercraft Intern., Inc., 87 Wash.App. 1051 (Wash.App. Div. 1 1997), 152

McMahon v. Bunn–O–Matic Corp., 150 F.3d 651 (7th Cir.1998), 122

McNally Wellman Co. v. New York State Elec. & Gas Corp., 63 F.3d 1188 (2nd Cir.1995), 446

Melody Home Mfg. Co. v. Morrison, 502 S.W.2d 196 (Tex.Civ.App.-Hous. (1 Dist.) 1973), 423

Mineral Park Land Co. v. Howard, 172 Cal. 289, 156 P. 458 (Cal.1916), 349

Miron v. Yonkers Raceway, Inc., 400 F.2d 112 (2nd Cir.1968), 261

Missouri Public Service Co. v. Peabody Coal Co., 583 S.W.2d 721 (Mo.App. W.D. 1979), 350

Moscatiello v. Pittsburgh Contractors Equipment Co., 407 Pa.Super. 363, 595 A.2d 1190 (Pa.Super.1991), **178**

Mullan v. Quickie Aircraft Corp., 797 F.2d 845 (10th Cir.1986), 175

Multiplastics, Inc. v. Arch Industries, Inc., 166 Conn. 280, 348 A.2d 618 (Conn.1974), **341**

National Marking Mach. Co. v. Triumph Mfg. Co., 13 F.2d 6 (8th Cir.1926), 410

NEC Technologies, Inc. v. Nelson, 267 Ga. 390, 478 S.E.2d 769 (Ga.1996), 185

Neptune Research & Development, Inc. v. Teknics Indus. Systems, Inc., 235 N.J.Super. 522, 563 A.2d 465 (N.J.Super.A.D.1989), **301,** 309, 310, 312, 319

Neumiller Farms, Inc. v. Cornett, 368 So.2d 272 (Ala.1979), **240,** 242

Nobs Chemical, U.S.A., Inc. v. Koppers Co., Inc., 616 F.2d 212 (5th Cir.1980), 420

North American Lighting, Inc. v. Hopkins Mfg. Corp., 37 F.3d 1253 (7th Cir.1994), 268

North American Steel Corp. v. Siderius, Inc., 75 Mich.App. 391, 254 N.W.2d 899 (Mich.App.1977), 240

Northridge Co. v. W.R. Grace and Co., 162 Wis.2d 918, 471 N.W.2d 179 (Wis.1991), 207

Oloffson v. Coomer, 11 Ill.App.3d 918, 296 N.E.2d 871 (Ill.App. 3 Dist.1973), 404

O'Neal Ford, Inc. v. Earley, 13 Ark.App. 189, 681 S.W.2d 414 (Ark.App.1985), 287

Outlook Windows Partnership v. York Intern. Corp., 112 F.Supp.2d 877 (D.Neb.2000), **126**

Palmisciano v. Tarbox Motors, Inc., 39 U.C.C.Rep.Serv. 146 (R.I.Super.1984), 274

Parton v. Mark Pirtle Oldsmobile–Cadillac–Isuzu, Inc., 730 S.W.2d 634 (Tenn.Ct. App.1987), 175

Paul Blum Co. v. Daewoo Intern. (America) Corp., 2001 WL 1537687 (S.D.N.Y.2001), 334

Perlman v. Pioneer Ltd. Partnership, 918 F.2d 1244 (5th Cir.1990), **364**

Petroleo Brasileiro, S. A., Petrobras v. Ameropan Oil Corp., 372 F.Supp. 503 (E.D.N.Y.1974), 448

Plateq Corp. of North Haven v. Machlett Laboratories, Inc., 189 Conn. 433, 456 A.2d 786 (Conn.1983), 261

Prenalta Corp. v. Colorado Interstate Gas Co., 944 F.2d 677 (10th Cir.1991), 454

Princess Cruises, Inc. v. General Elec. Co., 143 F.3d 828 (4th Cir.1998), **13**

Printing Center of Texas, Inc. v. Supermind Pub. Co., Inc., 669 S.W.2d 779 (Tex. App.-Hous. (14 Dist.) 1984), 242

ProCD, Inc. v. Zeidenberg, 86 F.3d 1447 (7th Cir.1996), 54, 58, 59, 60, 61, 90

Procter & Gamble Distributing Co. v. Lawrence Am. Field Warehousing Corp., 266 N.Y.S.2d 785, 213 N.E.2d 873 (N.Y. 1965), 375

Proyectos Electronicos, S.A. v. Alper, 37 B.R. 931 (E.D.Pa.1983), 412

Puget Sound Financial, L.L.C. v. Unisearch, Inc., 146 Wash.2d 428, 47 P.3d 940 (Wash.2002), **83,** 177

Ramirez v. Autosport, 88 N.J. 277, 440 A.2d 1345 (N.J.1982), 239, 247

R.E. Davis Chemical Corp. v. Diasonics, Inc., 826 F.2d 678 (7th Cir.1987), 419, 420

Reid v. Key Bank of Southern Maine, Inc., 821 F.2d 9 (1st Cir.1987), 243

Reilly Foam Corp. v. Rubbermaid Corp., 206 F.Supp.2d 643 (E.D.Pa. 2002), **43**

Resource Management Co. v. Weston Ranch and Livestock Co., Inc., 706 P.2d 1028 (Utah 1985), 174

Rheem Mfg. Co. v. Phelps Heating & Air Conditioning, Inc., 746 N.E.2d 941 (Ind.2001), **185**

Rinaldi v. Iomega Corp., 1999 WL 1442014 (Del.Super.1999), 59

Sabine Corp. v. ONG Western, Inc., 725 F.Supp. 1157 (W.D.Okla.1989), 454

Salvador v. Atlantic Steel Boiler Co., 457 Pa. 24, 319 A.2d 903 (Pa.1974), 199

Sam & Mary Housing Corp. v. Jo/Sal Market Corp., 121 Misc.2d 434, 468 N.Y.S.2d 294 (N.Y.Sup.1983), 459

Santor v. A & M Karagheusian, Inc., 44 N.J. 52, 207 A.2d 305 (N.J.1965), 206

Schmitz–Werke Gmbh & Co. v. Rockland Industries, Inc., 37 Fed.Appx. 687 (4th Cir.2002), **129**

Scott v. Crown, 765 P.2d 1043 (Colo.App. 1988), 317

Sedmak v. Charlie's Chevrolet, Inc., 622 S.W.2d 694 (Mo.App. E.D.1981), **407**, 410

Seekings v. Jimmy GMC of Tucson, Inc., 130 Ariz. 596, 638 P.2d 210 (Ariz. 1981), 276, **277**, 286, 287

Seely v. White Motor Co., 63 Cal.2d 9, 45 Cal.Rptr. 17, 403 P.2d 145 (Cal.1965), 206

Siemens Energy & Automation, Inc. v. Coleman Elec. Supply Co., Inc., 46 F.Supp.2d 217 (E.D.N.Y.1999), **428**

Silivanch v. Celebrity Cruises, Inc., 171 F.Supp.2d 241 (S.D.N.Y.2001), 218

Simmons v. Taylor Childre Chevrolet–Pontiac, Inc., 629 F.Supp. 1030 (M.D.Ga. 1986), 234

Singer Co. v. E. I. du Pont de Nemours & Co., 579 F.2d 433 (8th Cir.1978), **133**

Skandia Ins. Co., Ltd. v. Star Shipping AS, 173 F.Supp.2d 1228 (S.D.Ala.2001), 334

Skelton v. General Motors Corp., 660 F.2d 311 (7th Cir.1981), 222, **223**

Snyder v. Herbert Greenbaum & Associates, Inc., 38 Md.App. 144, 380 A.2d 618 (Md.App.1977), 419

Southern Illinois Riverboat Casino Cruises, Inc. v. Triangle Insulation and Sheet Metal Co., 302 F.3d 667 (7th Cir.2002), **46**

Specht v. Netscape Communications Corp., 150 F.Supp.2d 585 (S.D.N.Y.2001), 58

Specialty Tires of America, Inc. v. CIT Group/Equipment Financing, Inc., 82 F.Supp.2d 434 (W.D.Pa.2000), **350**

SPS Industries, Inc. v. Atlantic Steel Co., 186 Ga.App. 94, 366 S.E.2d 410 (Ga.App. 1988), 316

S & R Associates, L.P. v. Shell Oil Co., 725 A.2d 431 (Del.Super.1998), **197**

Standard Alliance Industries, Inc. v. Black Clawson Co., 587 F.2d 813 (6th Cir. 1978), 259

Stephan's Mach. & Tool, Inc. v. D & H Machinery Consultants, Inc., 65 Ohio App.2d 197, 417 N.E.2d 579 (Ohio App. 6 Dist.1979), 406

Step–Saver Data Systems, Inc. v. Wyse Technology, 939 F.2d 91 (3rd Cir.1991), 59, 60, 61

Stock Shop, Inc. v. Bozell and Jacobs, Inc., 126 Misc.2d 95, 481 N.Y.S.2d 269 (N.Y.Sup.1984), 452

Stoney v. Franklin, 2001 WL 683963 (Va. Cir. Ct.2001), **200**, 206

St. Paul Guardian Ins. Co. v. Neuromed Medical Systems & Support, GmbH, 2002 WL 465312 (S.D.N.Y. 2002), **330**

Supermicro Computer, Inc. v. Digitechnic, S.A., 145 F.Supp.2d 1147 (N.D.Cal.2001), **153**

Tai Wah Radio Manufactory Ltd. v. Ambassador Imports Ltd., 3 U.C.C.Rep.Serv.2d 117 (S.D.N.Y.1987), 268

Taylor v. Caldwell, 32 L.J, Q.B. 164 (1863), 348, 349

Transatlantic Financing Corp. v. United States, 363 F.2d 312, 124 U.S.App.D.C. 183 (D.C.Cir.1966), 349

Trans World Metals, Inc. v. Southwire Co., 769 F.2d 902 (2nd Cir.1985), 420

T.W. Oil, Inc. v. Consolidated Edison Co. of New York, Inc., 457 N.Y.S.2d 458, 443 N.E.2d 932 (N.Y.1982), 245, 253

United Nuclear Corp. v. General Atomic Co., 96 N.M. 155, 629 P.2d 231 (N.M. 1980), 410

United States v. _____ (see opposing party)

Universal Resources Corp. v. Panhandle Eastern Pipe Line Co., 813 F.2d 77 (5th Cir.1987), **312**, 319

Viva Vino Import Corp. v. Farnese Vini, S.r.l., 2000 WL 1224903 (E.D.Pa.2000), 33

Voytovich v. Bangor Punta Operations, Inc., 494 F.2d 1208 (6th Cir.1974), 287

Weaver v. American Oil Co., 257 Ind. 458, 276 N.E.2d 144 (Ind.1971), 174

Web Press Services Corp. v. New London Motors, Inc., 203 Conn. 342, 525 A.2d 57 (Conn.1987), **105**

Westinghouse Elec. Corp. Uranium Contracts Litigation, Matter of, 517 F.Supp. 440 (E.D.Va.1981), 349

Wharton, Aldhizer & Weaver v. Savin Corp., 232 Va. 375, 350 S.E.2d 635 (Va. 1986), 424

Wille v. Southwestern Bell Tel. Co., 219 Kan. 755, 549 P.2d 903 (Kan.1976), 175

Williams v. Walker–Thomas Furniture Co., 350 F.2d 445, 121 U.S.App.D.C. 315 (D.C.Cir.1965), 174, 175, 176

Williams v. West Penn Power Co., 502 Pa. 557, 467 A.2d 811 (Pa.1983), 209

Wilson v. Scampoli, 228 A.2d 848 (D.C.App. 1967), 247

Winterbottom v. Wright, 152 Eng.Rep. 402 (1842), 195

W.L. Scott, Inc. v. Madras Aerotech, Inc., 103 Idaho 736, 653 P.2d 791 (Idaho 1982), 460

Wright Schuchart, Inc. v. Cooper Industries, Inc., 40 F.3d 1247 (9th Cir.1994), 446

Yazoo Mfg. Co. v. Lowe's Companies, Inc., 976 F.Supp. 430 (S.D.Miss.1997), 83

Yttro Corp. v. X–Ray Marketing Ass'n, Inc., 233 N.J.Super. 347, 559 A.2d 3 (N.J.Super.A.D.1989), **165,** 173

Zabriskie Chevrolet, Inc. v. Smith, 99 N.J.Super. 441, 240 A.2d 195 (N.J.Super.L.1968), 247

Zapata Hermanos Sucesores, S.A. v. Hearthside Baking Co., Inc., 313 F.3d 385 (7th Cir.2002), 481

Zapata Hermanos Sucesores, S.A. v. Hearthside Baking Co., Inc., 2001 WL 1000927 (N.D.Ill.2001), **477**

Table of Statutes and U.C.C. Sections

UNITED STATES

UNITED STATES CODE ANNOTATED

7 U.S.C.A.—Agriculture

Sec.	This Work Page
241—273	369
499a—s	369

11 U.S.C.A.—Bankruptcy

Sec.	This Work Page
365	461
546	435
546(c)	368

15 U.S.C.A.—Commerce and Trade

Sec.	This Work Page
2301(1)	235
7000	64

15 U.S.C.A.App.—Commerce and Trade

Sec.	This Work Page
52	1

46 U.S.C.A.—Shipping

Sec.	This Work Page
190—195	369
1300—1315	369

49 U.S.C.A.—Transportation

Sec.	This Work Page
20(11)	369
20(12)	369
81—124	369

POPULAR NAME ACTS

BRITISH SALES OF GOODS ACT

Sec.	This Work Page
22	156

ELECTRONIC SIGNATURES IN GLOBAL AND NATIONAL COMMERCE ACT

Sec.	This Work Page
101(b)(2)	65
101(c)	65
101(h)	66
102(a)(1)	64
103(a)(1)	65
103(a)(3)	65
106(5)	65
106(9)	64

FEDERAL BILLS OF LADING ACT

Sec.	This Work Page
81	369

FEDERAL TRADE COMMISSION ACT

Sec.	This Work Page
5	222

MAGNUSON–MOSS WARRANTY ACT

Sec.	This Work Page
101(1)	235
101(6)	234
102	235
102(b)(1)(A)	235
103	235
104	235
104(a)(2)	235
106	235
108	235
108(b)	235
110(d)(2)	222
110(f)	235

STATE STATUTES

———

NEW JERSEY STATUTES ANNOTATED

Sec.	This Work Page
12A:2–312	166
12A:2–725(2)	167

PENNSYLVANIA CONSOLIDATED STATUTES ANNOTATED

Tit.	This Work Page
73, § 1955	288

UTAH CODE ANNOTATED

Sec.	This Work Page
46–3–101 et seq.	65

———

UNIFORM COMMERCIAL CODE

Sec.	This Work Page
Art. 1	3
Art. 1	21
Art. 1	25
Art. 1	64
Art. 1	66
Art. 1	242
Art. 1	243
Art. 1	244
Art. 1	279
Art. 1	395
Art. 1	403
Art. 1	415
Art. 1	420
Art. 1	435
Art. 1	447
Art. 1	455
1–102(3)(f)	6
1–103	37
1–103	70
1–103	280
1–103(a)	3
1–103(b)	36
1–103(b)	69
1–103(b)	70
1–105	3
1–105	34
1–106	279
1–106	395
1–106	403
1–106	420
1–106	455
1–106(1)	415
1–106(1)	435
1–106(1)	447
1–201	3
1–201(2)	35
1–201(3)	21
1–201(3)	89
1–201(3)	99
1–201(6)	319

UNIFORM COMMERCIAL CODE

Sec.	This Work Page
1–201(11)	35
1–201(12)	35
1–201(16)	319
1–201(19)	3
1–201(23)	319
1–201(23)	412
1–201(26)	68
1–201(31)	64
1–201(35)	21
1–201(37)	21
1–201(37)	22
1–201(37)	25
1–201(37)	146
1–201(39)	67
1–201(46)	67
1–201(b)(2)	4
1–201(b)(2)	208
1–201(b)(3)	3
1–201(b)(3)	54
1–201(b)(3)	240
1–201(b)(6)	327
1–201(b)(6)	368
1–201(b)(9)	20
1–201(b)(9)	157
1–201(b)(10)	146
1–201(b)(12)	240
1–201(b)(15)	160
1–201(b)(15)	327
1–201(b)(16)	368
1–201(b)(16)	369
1–201(b)(16)	380
1–201(b)(20)	3
1–201(b)(20)	242
1–201(b)(29)	157
1–201(b)(29)	161
1–201(b)(35)	21
1–201(b)(35)	25
1–201(b)(35)	26
1–201(b)(42)	368
1–203	3
1–203	22
1–203	25
1–203	26
1–203	146
1–203	243
1–203, Comment 2	26
1–205	3
1–205	41
1–205	99
1–205(2)	84
1–205(3)	85
1–206	67
1–301	4
1–301	34
1–302	3
1–303	3
1–303	90
1–303	240
1–303	244
1–303(e)	90
1–303(e)(1)	91
1–304	3

UNIFORM COMMERCIAL CODE

Sec.	This Work Page
1–304	242
1–304	243
1–305	4
1–305	195
1–305	279
1–305	395
1–305	403
1–305	455
1–305(1)	435
1–305(a)	415
1–305(a)	420
1–305(a)	447
1–305(b)	243
2–101	20
2–101, Comment	21
2–102	11
2–102	18
2–102	20
2–102	21
2–102	450
2–103	66
2–103(1)(b)	3
2–103(1)(d)	279
2–103(1)(p)	446
2–104(2)	386
2–105	18
2–105(1)	11
2–105(2)	11
2–105(4)	254
2–105(5)	254
2–105(6)	254
2–105, Comment 1	11
2–106	20
2–106(2)	238
2–106(2)	275
2–106(3)	468
2–106(4)	246
2–106(4)	467
2–106(4)	468
2–107	11
2–107	18
2–201	67
2–201	69
2–201	70
2–201	71
2–201	91
2–201	325
2–201	408
2–201	427
2–201(2)	69
2–201(3)	71
2–201(3)(b)	69
2–201(3)(b)	71
2–201(3)(c)	69
2–201(4)	71
2–201, Comment 2	71
2–201, Comment 7	71
2–201, Comment 8	71
2–202	36
2–202	99
2–202	151
2–202, Comment 1(c)	84

UNIFORM COMMERCIAL CODE

Sec.	This Work Page
2–202, Comment 3	99
2–202, Comment 4	99
2–203	68
2–203	70
2–204	36
2–204	99
2–204(1)	35
2–204(1)	60
2–204(1)	100
2–204(2)	35
2–204(2)	100
2–204(3)	35
2–204(3)	100
2–206	36
2–206	37
2–206	51
2–206	100
2–206(1)(a)	35
2–206(1)(b)	37
2–206(2)	37
2–206(3)	51
2–207	18
2–207	36
2–207	37
2–207	43
2–207	47
2–207	50
2–207	51
2–207	52
2–207	53
2–207	54
2–207	59
2–207	60
2–207	61
2–207	89
2–207	90
2–207	99
2–207(1)	18
2–207(1)	51
2–207(1)	60
2–207(2)	18
2–207(2)	43
2–207(2)	46
2–207(2)	49
2–207(2)	50
2–207(2)	60
2–207(2)(b)	49
2–207(3)	41
2–207(a)	52
2–207(b)	52
2–207(c)	52
2–207, Comment 5	49
2–207, Comment 5	61
2–208	3
2–208	41
2–208	99
2–208	244
2–208(3)	79
2–209	73
2–209	74
2–209	79
2–209(1)	36

UNIFORM COMMERCIAL CODE

Sec.	This Work Page
2–209(1)	60
2–209(3)	73
2–209(3)	91
2–209(4)	74
2–209(4)	79
2–209(5)	74
2–209(5)	79
2–210	103
2–210(2)	103
2–210, Comment 3	103
2–211	66
2–212	66
2–213	66
2–301	100
2–301	324
2–301	325
2–301—2–319	41
2–302	173
2–302	174
2–302	175
2–302	178
2–302(1)	281
2–302(2)	174
2–302, Comment 1	174
2–304	18
2–304	67
2–304(1)	428
2–305	36
2–305	100
2–305, Comment 1	100
2–306	36
2–306	72
2–306	100
2–307	101
2–307—2–311	36
2–308	101
2–308	325
2–309	101
2–310	101
2–310	325
2–310, Comment 1	325
2–311	101
2–312	101
2–312	104
2–312	153
2–312	163
2–312	167
2–312	170
2–312	172
2–312(1)	104
2–312(1)	162
2–312(1)	163
2–312(1)	170
2–312(1)(a)	162
2–312(1)(a)	170
2–312(1)(b)	162
2–312(1)(b)	170
2–312(2)	101
2–312(2)	105
2–312(2)	153
2–312(2)	170
2–312(2)	171

UNIFORM COMMERCIAL CODE

Sec.	This Work Page
2–312(3)	101
2–312(3)	104
2–312(3)	153
2–312(3)	162
2–312(3)	163
2–312(3)	170
2–312(3)	171
2–312(3)	172
2–312(3)	173
2–312, Comment 4	170
2–312, Comment 6	101
2–312, Comment 6	163
2–312, Comment 6	170
2–312, Comment 9	105
2–313	104
2–313	116
2–313	119
2–313	148
2–313(1)	116
2–313(2)	116
2–313(2)	209
2–313(4)	116
2–313, Comment 4	148
2–313, Comment 7	118
2–313, Comment 7	151
2–313, Comment 10	108
2–313A	116
2–313A	209
2–313A	286
2–313A	446
2–313A	447
2–313A(1)	116
2–313A(2)	447
2–313A(4)	286
2–313A(4)	287
2–313A(4)(a)	117
2–313A(4)(b)	286
2–313A(4)(b)	447
2–313A(4)(c)	286
2–313A(4)(c)	447
2–313A, Comment 9	286
2–313A, Comment 9	447
2–313B	117
2–313B	209
2–313B	286
2–313B	446
2–313B	447
2–313B(2)	117
2–313B(2)	447
2–313B(4)	286
2–313B(4)	287
2–313B(4)(b)	286
2–313B(4)(b)	447
2–313B(4)(c)	286
2–313B(4)(c)	447
2–314	18
2–314	19
2–314	101
2–314	104
2–314	105
2–314	119
2–314	120

UNIFORM COMMERCIAL CODE

Sec.	This Work Page
2–314	121
2–314	123
2–314	126
2–314	145
2–314	209
2–314	289
2–314(2)	120
2–314(2)(c)	123
2–314, Comment 13	122
2–315	101
2–315	104
2–315	105
2–315	126
2–315	128
2–315	133
2–315	209
2–316	105
2–316	146
2–316	151
2–316	153
2–316	155
2–316	170
2–316	174
2–316	281
2–316	286
2–316(1)	148
2–316(1)	150
2–316(1)	151
2–316(2)	101
2–316(2)	105
2–316(2)	151
2–316(2)	152
2–316(2)	153
2–316(2)	170
2–316(3)	101
2–316(3)	105
2–316(3)	170
2–316(3)(a)	152
2–316(3)(b)	149
2–316(3)(b)	152
2–316(3)(c)	152
2–316(4)	152
2–316, Comment 5	152
2–316, Comment 7	152
2–317	138
2–317	139
2–317, Comment 3	138
2–318	19
2–318	105
2–318	117
2–318	120
2–318	121
2–318	122
2–318	197
2–318	199
2–318	200
2–318	205
2–318	210
2–318	214
2–318	219
2–318	260
2–318, Comment 3	199

UNIFORM COMMERCIAL CODE

Sec.	This Work Page
2–319	325
2–319	326
2–319	327
2–319—2–324	328
2–319(1)	37
2–319(2)	327
2–320	328
2–320	334
2–320, Comment 1	334
2–325(1)	386
2–325(3)	394
2–326	103
2–326	340
2–327	340
2–401	20
2–401	21
2–401	326
2–401	405
2–401(4)	238
2–401, Comment 1	21
2–403	20
2–403	160
2–403(1)	157
2–403(1)(a)	157
2–403(1)(b)	157
2–403(1)(d)	157
2–403(2)	157
2–403(2)	326
2–403(3)	157
2–403(3)	326
2–403, Comment 1	156
2–501	11
2–501	18
2–501	326
2–501	343
2–501	347
2–501(1)(b)	11
2–502	157
2–502	405
2–502	412
2–503	102
2–503	325
2–503	326
2–503	327
2–503(1)	236
2–503(4)(a)	339
2–503, Comment 5	37
2–503, Comments	102
2–503, Comments	326
2–504	36
2–504	37
2–504	244
2–504	325
2–504	326
2–507	325
2–507	434
2–507(2)	157
2–507(2)	434
2–508	237
2–508	247
2–508	248
2–508	249

UNIFORM COMMERCIAL CODE

Sec.	This Work Page
2–508	253
2–508	274
2–508	295
2–508(1)	245
2–508(1)	246
2–508(2)	245
2–508(2)	246
2–508(2)	249
2–509	102
2–509	325
2–509	326
2–509	327
2–509	340
2–509	347
2–509(1)	37
2–509(1)	326
2–509(2)	326
2–509(2)(b)	339
2–509(3)	325
2–509(3)	326
2–510	340
2–510	344
2–510	431
2–510(3)	343
2–510, Comment 3	343
2–511	325
2–511	434
2–511(3)	157
2–513	325
2–601	236
2–601	237
2–601	244
2–601	309
2–601	326
2–602	238
2–602(1)	237
2–602(1)	294
2–602(2)	238
2–602(2)	294
2–602(2)(a)	262
2–602(2)(b)	246
2–602(2)(b)	262
2–602(3)	239
2–602, Comment 3	239
2–603	238
2–603	294
2–604	266
2–604	294
2–605	238
2–605	252
2–605	258
2–605	294
2–605	344
2–606	42
2–606	207
2–606	236
2–606	254
2–606	261
2–606	294
2–606(1)(b)	237
2–606(1)(c)	262
2–606(c)	266

UNIFORM COMMERCIAL CODE

Sec.	This Work Page
2–607	207
2–607	422
2–607	431
2–607(1)	237
2–607(1)	238
2–607(1)	239
2–607(1)	261
2–607(1)	269
2–607(2)	237
2–607(2)	261
2–607(2)	310
2–607(3)(a)	27
2–607(3)(a)	207
2–607(3)(a)	208
2–607(3)(a)	254
2–607(3)(a)	259
2–607(3)(a)	260
2–607(4)	242
2–607(4)	261
2–607, Comment 1	238
2–607, Comment 4	259
2–607, Comment 5	208
2–607, Comment 5	260
2–608	237
2–608	254
2–608	255
2–608	271
2–608	276
2–608	279
2–608	281
2–608	282
2–608	283
2–608	288
2–608	296
2–608(1)	261
2–608(1)	274
2–608(1)	281
2–608(1)	283
2–608(1)(a)	268
2–608(1)(a)	274
2–608(1)(b)	268
2–608(1)(b)	274
2–608(2)	258
2–608(2)	284
2–608(3)	237
2–608(4)	262
2–608(4)	267
2–608(4)	268
2–608(4)(b)	268
2–608(4)(b)	297
2–608, Comment 2	274
2–608, Comment 4	258
2–608, Comment 6	296
2–609	301
2–609	312
2–609	315
2–609	317
2–609	319
2–609	321
2–609—2–611	319
2–609(1)	317
2–609(4)	317

UNIFORM COMMERCIAL CODE

Sec.	This Work Page
2–609(4)	318
2–609, Comment 3	315
2–609, Comment 3	316
2–609, Comment 4	315
2–609, Comment 4	321
2–609, Comment 6	318
2–610	300
2–610	309
2–610	311
2–610	315
2–610(2)	310
2–610(a)	310
2–610(a)	311
2–610(b)	312
2–610(c)	310
2–610, Comment 1	310
2–610, Comment 1	311
2–610, Comment 2	310
2–610, Comment 4	315
2–611	300
2–611(1)	468
2–611(2)	311
2–612	431
2–612(1)	244
2–612(2)	244
2–612(3)	244
2–612(3)	297
2–612(3)	468
2–612, Comment 4	244
2–612, Comment 5	248
2–612, Comment 6	297
2–612, Comment 6	315
2–613	325
2–613	326
2–613	347
2–615	348
2–615	349
2–615	350
2–615	357
2–615	359
2–615	363
2–615	364
2–615	367
2–615, Comment 3	349
2–615, Comment 4	349
2–615, Comment 5	357
2–615, Comment 8	349
2–615, Comment 9	347
2–616	364
2–702	368
2–702	433
2–702(1)	319
2–702(1)	434
2–702(2)	157
2–702(2)	368
2–702(2)	432
2–702(2)	433
2–702(2)	434
2–702(3)	157
2–702(3)	368
2–702(3)	432
2–702(3)	433

UNIFORM COMMERCIAL CODE

Sec.	This Work Page
2–702(3)	434
2–702, Comment 3	434
2–702, Comment 4	433
2–703	239
2–705	319
2–705	434
2–705(2)(d)	323
2–706	246
2–706	413
2–706	414
2–706	415
2–706	421
2–706	447
2–706	448
2–706(1)	312
2–706(1)	435
2–706(2)	414
2–706(3)	414
2–706(4)	414
2–706(4)(b)	414
2–706(6)	295
2–706(6)	296
2–706, Comment 2	258
2–706, Comment 2	431
2–706, Comment 4	414
2–706, Comment 5	414
2–706, Comment 8	414
2–708	246
2–708	416
2–708	447
2–708	467
2–708(1)	413
2–708(1)	414
2–708(1)	415
2–708(1)	420
2–708(1)	435
2–708(1)(a)	435
2–708(1)(b)	435
2–708(2)	415
2–708(2)	419
2–708(2)	420
2–708(2)	435
2–708, Comment 2	258
2–708, Comment 2	431
2–708, Comment 5	415
2–708, Comment 5	419
2–708, Comment 5	420
2–709	326
2–709	327
2–709	421
2–709	427
2–709	428
2–709	431
2–709	447
2–709(1)	435
2–709(1)(a)	239
2–709(1)(a)	246
2–709(1)(a)	269
2–709(1)(b)	421
2–709(2)	421
2–710	435
2–710	447

UNIFORM COMMERCIAL CODE

Sec.	This Work Page
2–710	448
2–710(2)	395
2–710(2)	435
2–710(3)	435
2–711	396
2–711(1)	268
2–711(1)	294
2–711(1)	468
2–711(3)	262
2–711(3)	295
2–712	72
2–712	396
2–712	398
2–712	402
2–712	404
2–712	456
2–712(2)	435
2–712(3)	396
2–712, Comment 2	403
2–712, Comment 4	403
2–713	396
2–713	398
2–713	403
2–713	404
2–713	436
2–713(1)	404
2–713(1)	435
2–713(1)(a)	404
2–713(1)(b)	404
2–713, Comment 4	404
2–713, Comment 5	403
2–713, Comment 7	403
2–714	128
2–714	422
2–714	424
2–714	427
2–714	445
2–714(1)	287
2–714(1)	422
2–714(1)	427
2–714(1)	446
2–714(1)	447
2–714(2)	422
2–714(2)	423
2–714(2)	424
2–714(2)	464
2–714(3)	427
2–714(3)	435
2–715	105
2–715	120
2–715	121
2–715	436
2–715	442
2–715	443
2–715	447
2–715(1)	435
2–715(2)	200
2–715(2)	435
2–715(2)	437
2–715(2)(a)	200
2–715(2)(a)	395
2–715(2)(b)	19

UNIFORM COMMERCIAL CODE

Sec.	This Work Page
2–715(2)(b)	205
2–715(2)(b)	214
2–715(2)(b)	260
2–716	406
2–716	421
2–716(1)	405
2–716(1)	407
2–716(1)	409
2–716(1)	410
2–716(1)	421
2–716(2)	435
2–716(3)	405
2–716(3)	412
2–716, Comment 2	406
2–716, Comment 2	410
2–716, Comment 3	407
2–717	422
2–718	153
2–718(1)	452
2–718(1)	453
2–718(2)	454
2–718(3)	454
2–718, Comment 1(b)	452
2–719	153
2–719	195
2–719	287
2–719(1)	105
2–719(1)	240
2–719(1)(b)	195
2–719(2)	105
2–719(2)	192
2–719(3)	435
2–723	396
2–724	396
2–725	19
2–725	208
2–725	209
2–725	220
2–725	259
2–725(1)	208
2–725(1)	209
2–725(2)	208
2–725(2)	209
2–725(2)(a)	209
2–725(2)(b)	209
2–725(2)(c)	209
2–725(2)(d)	209
2–725(3)	209
2–725(3)(a)	209
2–725(3)(b)	209
2–725(3)(c)	210
2–725(3)(d)	210
2–725(4)	210
2–725(5)	210
2A–101	22
2A–101	23
2A–101	319
2A–102	22
2A–103(1)(g)	123
2A–103(1)(g)	145
2A–103(1)(g)	146
2A–103(1)(g)(iii)(D)	145

UNIFORM COMMERCIAL CODE

Sec.	This Work Page
2A–103(1)(j)	22
2A–103(1)(j)	25
2A–103(1)(j)	26
2A–103(1)(j)	146
2A–103(1)(k)	99
2A–103(1)(k)	289
2A–103(1)(*l*)	289
2A–103(1)(s)	289
2A–103(1)(t)	289
2A–103(1)(u)	458
2A–103(1)(u)	459
2A–103(1)(u)	460
2A–201	71
2A–201	79
2A–202	99
2A–207	99
2A–208	79
2A–209	145
2A–209	289
2A–209(1)	289
2A–209, Comment 2	289
2A–210	119
2A–211	153
2A–211	171
2A–211(1)	171
2A–211(1)(a)	171
2A–211(2)	171
2A–211(2)(a)	171
2A–211(3)	171
2A–211(4)	153
2A–211(4)	172
2A–212	123
2A–212	146
2A–212(1)	289
2A–213	129
2A–214	153
2A–214	171
2A–214(2)	153
2A–214(3)(a)	153
2A–214(4)	153
2A–214(4)	171
2A–214(4)	172
2A–215	139
2A–216	146
2A–216	219
2A–219	345
2A–220	345
2A–221	346
2A–301, Comment 2	24
2A–303	172
2A–305	172
2A–307	172
2A–307	461
2A–401	319
2A–401—2A–403	319
2A–402	319
2A–405	367
2A–407	145
2A–407	146
2A–407	289
2A–407, Comment 2	289
2A–407, Comment 5	289

UNIFORM COMMERCIAL CODE

Sec.	This Work Page
2A–503	194
2A–504(1)	462
2A–504, Comments	462
2A–506	220
2A–506(2)	220
2A–507(2)	456
2A–507A	457
2A–507A	461
2A–508(1)(b)	268
2A–508(1)(b)	455
2A–508(5)	456
2A–508(6)	456
2A–508, Comment 2	268
2A–509	288
2A–509	289
2A–509—2A–517	288
2A–509(1)	289
2A–509(2)	288
2A–510	288
2A–511	288
2A–512	288
2A–514	288
2A–515	288
2A–516	288
2A–516	290
2A–516, Comment 1	289
2A–517	288
2A–517	289
2A–518	455
2A–518	459
2A–518	483
2A–518(2)	456
2A–518(2)	458
2A–518(3)	456
2A–518, Comment 4	456
2A–518, Comment 5	456
2A–519(1)	456
2A–519(1)	457
2A–519(2)	456
2A–519(3)	456
2A–519(4)	456
2A–521	457
2A–522	457
2A–523(1)	461
2A–523(3)(a)	461
2A–525(2)	23
2A–525(2)	461
2A–525(3)	461
2A–527	460
2A–527	462
2A–528	23
2A–528	462
2A–528(1)	460
2A–528(2)	461
2A–529(1)(a)	462
2A–529(1)(b)	461
2A–529(1)(b)	462
Art. 3	5
Arts. 3—9	9
Arts. 3—9	65
3–104(f)	378
3–302	377

UNIFORM COMMERCIAL CODE

Sec.	This Work Page
3–305	377
Art. 4	5
Art. 4A	5
Art. 5	3
Art. 5	5
Art. 5	242
Art. 5	380
Art. 5	381
Art. 5	382
Art. 5	387
Art. 5	393
5–102	381
5–102(4)	382
5–102(a)(2)	386
5–102(a)(3)	386
5–102(a)(9)	386
5–102(a)(10)	394
5–103(c)	382
5–103, Comment 2	382
5–104	394
5–105	386
5–106	386
5–106(a)	394
5–106(b)	394
5–106(c)	394
5–106(d)	394
5–106, Comment 1	394
5–108	386
5–108	387
5–108(a)	381
5–108(b)	394
5–108(f)(1)	381
5–108(i)(1)	386
5–108, Comment 1	387
5–109(a)	381
5–109(a)	393
5–109, Comment 1	393
5–111	394
5–115	393
Art. 6	5
Art. 7	5
Art. 7	369
Art. 7	370
7–102(1)(d)	368
7–103	369
7–104(1)	376
7–104(1)	378
7–104(1)(a)	378
7–104(1)(b)	378
7–104, Comment	378
Art. 7, Pt. 2	370
Art. 7, Pt. 3	370
7–303	380
7–309(2)	375
7–309(2)	376
7–403	379
7–403	380
7–403(1)	369
7–403(1)	379
7–403(3)	369
7–403(3)	379
7–403(4)	369

UNIFORM COMMERCIAL CODE

Sec.	This Work Page
7–403(4)	379
7–502	378
Art. 8	6
Art. 8	11
Art. 8	71
8–113	67
8–113	71
Art. 9	5
Art. 9	6
Art. 9	21
Art. 9	22
Art. 9	23
Art. 9	24
Art. 9	25
Art. 9	103
Art. 9	157
Art. 9	368
Art. 9	405
Art. 9	432
9–102(52)	368
9–203	67
9–318(4)	103
9–320(b)	157
9–406	103
9–406(d)	103
9–609	157

UNIFORM COMPUTER INFORMATION TRANSACTIONS ACT

Sec.	This Work Page
102(10)	346
102(a)(14)	483
102(a)(51)	119
102(a)(51)	125
102(a)(51)	133
102(a)(51)(A)	119
102(a)(51)(B)	119
104	7
112	61
112(e)	62
113	7
201	72
201(e)	72
204(b)	54
204(d)	54
208	61
209	61
209	62
211	62
301	99
401	173
401(a)	173
401(b)(1)	173
401(b)(2)	173
401(c)	173
401(d)	173
401(e)	173
402	119
402	125

UNIFORM COMPUTER INFORMATION TRANSACTIONS ACT

Sec.	This Work Page
402(c)	119
403	124
403(2)	124
403(a)(1)	124
403(a)(2)	124
403(a)(3)	124
404	119
404	124
404	125
404	133
404	155
404(a)	125
404(b)(1)	125
404, Comment 2	125
404, Comment 3	125
405(a)(1)	133
405(a)(2)	133
405(b)	133
405(c)	133
406	124
406(b)	155
406(b)(1)(A)	155
406(b)(1)(B)	155
406(b)(2)	155
406(b)(3)	155
406(b)(4)	155
406(c)	155
406(d)	155
406(e)	155
406(f)	155
406(g)	155
408	139
409(a)	219
409(b)	219
409(c)	219
409(d)	219
409, Comment 1	220
409, Comment 3	219
409, Comment 4	219
601	291
601, Comment 2	291
601, Comment 3	291
609	292
614	346
615	367
704(b)	291
708	292
708—710	319
801, Comment 2	483
803	195
803(a)	195
803(a)(2)	195
803(b)	195
803(c)	195
803(d)	195
805	220
807(a)	483
807(e)	484
808(b)(1)(B)	483
808(b)(1)(C)	483
809(a)(1)(B)(i)	483

UNIFORM COMPUTER INFORMATION TRANSACTIONS ACT

Sec.	This Work Page
809(a)(1)(B)(ii)	483
809(a)(1)(B)(iii)	483
809(a)(2)	483
811	483
813	483
814	483
816	483

UNIFORM ELECTRONIC TRANSACTIONS ACT

Sec.	This Work Page
2(6)	65
2(8)	65
2(13)	54
2(13)	64
2, Comment 7	65
3(a)	65
3(b)(1)	65
3(b)(2)	65
5(a)	65
5(b)	65
5(d)	65
5, Comment 4, Ex. B	65
9	65
10	65
10(1)	65
10(2)	65
13	66
14	66
14(2)	66
14, Comment 1	66
15	66

UNIFORM SALES ACT

Sec.	This Work Page
66	405
68	406

REVISED UNIFORM SALES ACT

Sec.	This Work Page
14	150
14, Comment 1	150
41(1)	150

CODE OF FEDERAL REGULATIONS

Tit.	This Work Page
12, § 32.2	382
16, § 700.1	235
16, § 700.3	234
16, § 700.4	235
16, § 700.7	235

CODE OF FEDERAL REGULATIONS

Tit.	This Work Page
16, § 700.11	235
16, § 701.3	235
16, § 702.3	235
16, § 702.3(c)	235

CONVENTION ON CONTRACTS FOR THE INTERNATIONAL SALE OF GOODS

Art.	This Work Page
1(1)	28
1(2)	28
2	29
2(a)	29
3(1)	28
3(2)	28
4	471
4	482
4(a)	29
5	29
5	219
6	9
6	194
7(1)	10
8	154
10(a)	28
11	72
12	72
14	52
16(1)	52
16(2)	52
18	53
18(1)	52
18(2)	52
19	53
19	154
22	52
25	293
25	298
25—26	296
26	293
26	294
28	300
28	466
28	470
28	471
29	79
34	295
35	154
35	293
35	296
35(1)	119
35(1)	139
35(2)	154
35(2)(a)	123
35(2)(b)	129
35(2)(c)	119
35(2)(c)	139
35(3)	154
37	295
38	296

CONVENTION ON CONTRACTS FOR THE INTERNATIONAL SALE OF GOODS

Art.	This Work Page
38—40	294
38—40	295
38—40	296
38—40	466
39	296
39(2)	296
41	172
42	172
42(1)	172
42(1)(a)	172
42(1)(a)	173
42(1)(b)	172
42(1)(b)	173
42(2)(a)	172
42(2)(b)	172
43(1)	172
43(2)	172
44	173
44	294
44	466
45	293
45	296
45	466
45(2)	466
46	466
46(1)	466
46(2)	292
46(2)	299
46(2)	300
46(2)	466
46(3)	299
46(3)	300
46(3)	466
47	298
47(1)	298
48	295
49	296
49	298
49(1)	464
49(1)(a)	293
49(1)(b)	298
49(2)	296
49(2)(b)(i)	294
50	464
50	465
51	298
51	299
51(1)	297
51(2)	297
51(2)	298
62	469
62	470
62	471
64(1)	467
64(1)	471
64(2)	467
66—70	344
67(1)	344
71	320
71	321
71	322

CONVENTION ON CONTRACTS FOR THE INTERNATIONAL SALE OF GOODS

Art.	This Work Page
71	323
71(2)	323
71(3)	321
71(3)	323
72	320
72	322
72	323
73	299
73(1)	297
73(2)	297
73(3)	297
74	464
74	466
74	467
74	481
74	482
75	464
75	467
75	470
76	464
76	467
77	464
77	466
77	467
77	470
79	367
81	293
81	464
81	467
81	468
81—84	296
81(1)	294
81(1)	299
81(2)	294
81(2)	295
81(2)	471

CONVENTION ON CONTRACTS FOR THE INTERNATIONAL SALE OF GOODS

Art.	This Work Page
82	294
82	296
82	299
82	300
82—83	466
82(2)(c)	296
83	296
84	293
84(1)	295
84(2)	296
84(2)	299
86	294
86—88	296
86—88	299
86—88	466
86(1)	292
86(1)	295
86(2)	292
87	294
88	294
88(1)	295
88(2)	470
88(3)	295
88(3)	296
88(3)	470
96	72

FEDERAL RULES OF CIVIL PROCEDURE

Rule	This Work Page
23(a)	113
23(b)	113
23(b)(3)	113

*

SALES, LEASES AND ELECTRONIC COMMERCE

Problems and Materials on National and International Transactions

Second Edition

*

Chapter 1

INTRODUCTION

PART 1: OVERVIEW

A. THE STUDY OF COMMERCIAL LAW

This book is designed to facilitate the study of a large segment of commercial law. Traditionally called the law of "Sales," for much of the last half century the focus was on the sale of tangible, moveable property (goods) as governed by Article 2 of the Uniform Commercial Code ("UCC"). While Article 2 continues as the central focus, the modern course in "Sales" law must consider a number of other important dimensions. The United States and some sixty other nations have agreed to surrender their domestic law and be governed by the United Nations Convention on Contracts for the International Sale of Goods (CISG) in the purchase and sale of goods between parties whose places of business are in CISG nations.[1] Fifteen years ago, a new Article was added to the UCC to deal with *leases* of goods.[2] Just as leases are not sales of goods, licenses of software or access to databases are not sales and what is licensed is not tangible property. It is intangible information in digitalized form. The Uniform Computer Information Transactions Act (UCITA), was designed to react to these challenges.[3] Meanwhile, the accelerating changes in electronic commerce required recognition of electronic signatures and electronic records on a par with traditional signatures and writings. The Uniform Electronic Transactions Act (UETA)[4] and the

---

1. United Nations Convention on Contracts for the International Sale of Goods, opened for signature April 11, 1980, S. Treaty Doc. No. 9, 98th Cong., 1st Sess. 22 (1983), *19 I. L. M. 671,* reprinted at *15 U.S.C. App. 52* (1997). Adopting nations are listed in E(3), *infra.* The CISG may be applicable even where one of the parties does not have its place of business in another CISG nation. See the materials in Part II F *infra.*

2. Article 2A, "Leases," was added in 1987.

3. At the time of this writing, UCITA has been enacted in Maryland and Virginia. The text may be found on the website of the National Conference of Commissioners on Uniform State Laws (NCCUSL) at *http://www.nccusl.org* along with other NCCUSL drafts, including proposed revisions of UCC Articles.

4. The text of UETA may be found on the NCCUSL website at *http://www.nccusl.org.*

federal "E–Sign" (Electronic Signatures in Global and National Commerce) Act[5] serve this purpose in facilitating electronic commerce. Finally, as this book goes to press, proposed amendments to UCC Article 2 itself are in the process of being approved by the two organizations responsible for revising UCC Articles. These proposed amendments must be included in any modern analysis of the subject.

The 21st century student is confronted with a more complex and challenging landscape, including new statutory designs that have yet to be subjected to their inevitable interpretation and construction by courts. While these important changes and developments will be considered, the dominant focus of this book continues to be Article 2 of the UCC. It is important to begin with a brief history of the UCC from its origins to its current status, followed by brief descriptions of the statutory additions that will become increasingly important in modern national and international transactions.

B.　THE UNIFORM COMMERCIAL CODE—HISTORY

The UCC is the product of two distinguished organizations: the National Conference of Commissioners on Uniform State Laws (NCCUSL), composed of Commissioners from each of the states as well as the District of Columbia and Puerto Rico, whose principal purpose is to promote uniformity in state laws; and the American Law Institute (ALI), a voluntary organization of judges, law professors and leading practitioners concerned with the improvement and clarification of American law. ALI is also widely known and respected for its production of Restatements of the law in various subjects.

What eventually became the Uniform Commercial Code began with the chief architect of the Code, Professor Karl Llewellyn and his associates, pursuing a long overdue revision of the 1907 Uniform Sales Act. Eventually, the desirability of a uniform law that would govern the great bulk of other commercial transactions as well as the sale of goods induced the monumental effort to create the first uniform law of commercial transactions.

In 1953, Pennsylvania became the first state to enact the Code when it adopted the 1952 "official text." In New York, the governor referred this comprehensive commercial law proposal to the New York Law Revision Commission, which applauded the concept of a uniform commercial code but decided that the 1952 official text required substantial revision. Pennsylvania was operating under the 1952 version. NCCUSL and the ALI carefully considered both the New York study and the Pennsylvania experience in preparing and promulgating a revised edition of the Code to be known as the 1958 Official Text of the Code.

Though fourteen states had enacted the Code prior to 1962, the enactment in New York in that year prompted enactment throughout the country. In 1963, eleven states adopted the Code, and by 1968, forty-

---

5.　15 USC § 7001 (2000).

nine states had done so. Finally, in 1974, Louisiana adopted parts of the Code.

In 1961, the Code sponsors established a Permanent Editorial Board to promote uniformity in state enactments and interpretation of the Code. The Board was also concerned with the evaluation of the Code experience in the various states, in order to fulfill its continuing duty to prepare proposals for revision of the official text. There have been numerous revisions of original Code Articles and new Articles have been added.

C. SUMMARY OF UCC ARTICLES

Article 1. This Article, which was revised in 2001 to harmonize its provisions with changes in other Articles, sets forth the underlying purposes and policies of the Code in Section 1–103(a)[6]: "(1) to simplify, clarify and modernize the law governing commercial transactions; (2) to permit the continued expansion of commercial practices through custom, usage and agreement of the parties; (3) to make uniform the law among various jurisdictions." Section 1–302 emphasizes freedom of contract by expressly allowing its provisions to be "varied by agreement" unless explicitly or implicitly prohibited (e.g, an oral waiver of the statute of frauds would be prohibited), or if they violate the pervasive obligations of good faith, diligence or reasonableness.[7] The vitally important definition of "agreement" continues to emphasize the "bargain of the parties in fact" as found not only in their language but in other circumstances including course of performance, course of dealing and usage of trade.[8] This definition is but one of forty-three definitions provided in the general definition section (1–201) of Article 1—a section that is invaluable to any student of the UCC. Original Section 1–205 defined "usage of trade" and "course of dealing," but "course of performance" was defined later—in Section 2–208. Amended Article 1 corrects this placement by including the definitions of all three in one section.[9] One of the more important provisions of amended Article 1 deals with the freedom of the parties to choose the law that will govern their transaction.[10] Finally,

---

6. The section numbers in the amended version of Article 1 have changed from its earlier version. Section number references in the text are to the amended version.

7. Original Section 1–201(19) defined "good faith" as "honesty in fact." Section 2–103(1)(b) defined good faith with respect to merchants as "honesty in fact *and* the observance of reasonable commercial standards of fair dealing in the trade." This definition only applied to merchants involved in transactions governed by Article 2 and, strictly construed, may have been said to apply only to uses of "good faith" in Article 2 sections. Thus there was a question as to the proper definition of good faith under original Section 1–203, which imposed an obligation of good faith in the performance and enforcement of every contract or duty governed by the UCC. Amended 1–201(b)(20) defines "good faith" as "honesty in fact and the observance of reasonable commercial standards of fair dealing," and this definition applies throughout the UCC (except for Article 5, which retains a subjective definition of good faith). The pervasive obligation of good faith in former 1–203 is now found in 1–304.

8. 1–201(b)(3) (2002).

9. 1–303 (2002).

10. Original Section 1–105 allowed parties to designate the law governing their transaction if the transaction bore a "reasonable relation" to that jurisdiction. The amended version of this provision (now

Section 1–305 illustrates the theme of liberal construction in providing that UCC remedies "must be liberally administered to the end that the aggrieved party [defined as "a party entitled to pursue a remedy" in 1–201((b)2)] may be put in as good a position as if the other party had fully performed. . . ."

Article 2, the principal focus of this book, deals with sales of goods and contracts for the sale of goods. It is a radical departure from its predecessor, the Uniform Sales Act, which was based largely on a property orientation focusing in great part on questions such as which party had "title" to the goods. As the chief architect of the entire UCC and the principal draftsman of Article 2, Professor Karl Llewellyn created a new paradigm focusing on the contract and its terms, rather than on rules of property law. By emphasizing the "agreement" of the parties, i.e., their "bargain-in-fact," he sought to remove technical barriers of the common law of contract in order to better effectuate the factual bargain representing the "true understanding" of the parties. Significant changes made by Article 2 in traditional rules governing contracts for the sale of goods have found their way into basic contract law through judicial decisions and through the influence of the Restatement (Second) of Contracts, whose author (the ALI) is one of the co-sponsors of the UCC.

Proposed Amendments to Article 2. In the late 1980's, a decision was made to create a revision of Article 2 with a target date of 1996. Several drafts were produced, but the ALI did not approve a revision draft until 1999. That draft, however, was not approved by the other UCC sponsoring body, NCCUSL. Recognizing that the original Article 2 continued to serve the needs of commercial society effectively, and also recognizing an inability to reach consensus on certain issues, it was decided to forego a true revision of Article 2 in favor of amending particular sections to deal with electronic commerce, developments in business practices, changes in other law, and the relatively few interpretive difficulties of practical significance that had arisen under Article 2. In August, 2002, the proposed amendments were approved by NCCUSL, and in October they were approved by the Council of the ALI, although final adoption would have to await approval by the ALI membership in May, 2003. A number of sections are subject to simple language changes designed to assure gender neutrality and to reflect modern business terminology. Any significant substantive change suggested by the pro-

numbered 1–301) no longer requires a showing of "reasonable relation" except in consumer transactions. Under the amended provision, commercial parties may designate the law of a state in domestic transactions, or the law of a state or country in international transactions, regardless of the jurisdiction's relation to the transaction. Such designation, however, may not be contrary to a fundamental policy of the State or country whose law would govern absent an agreement designating the governing law. The "reasonable relation" requirement, however, continues if one of the parties to the transaction is a consumer. Moreover, the consumer may not be deprived of any protective rule of law that would apply absent the designation of applicable law in the contract. If the parties do not designate the applicable law, the governing law will be selected by the conflict of law principles of the forum hearing the dispute.

posed amendments are reflected in appropriate places throughout this volume.

Article 2A was added to the UCC in response to the popular practice of leasing rather than buying goods. While Article 2 had been applied by analogy to leases of goods, the application could be cumbersome since Article 2 was not designed to deal with lease transactions. Issues such as the critical distinction between a true lease and a "lease" that was, in substance, a security interest in the goods that should be governed by Article 9 of the Code required clarification. "Finance leases," in which a commercial lender fills it financing role by acquiring a product and leasing it to the party who actually chose the product, also deserved separate treatment. A new governing statute with appropriate leasing terminology appeared to be desirable, and Article 2A was adopted in 1987. It was revised in 1990, and has been enacted in every state except Connecticut (where it has been introduced), Louisiana and South Carolina. A proposed revision of Article 2A, designed to coordinate with the proposed amendments to Article 2, was presented to NCCUSL in 2002. Where relevant, these proposed amendments to Article 2A are also reflected in the materials in this book.

Articles 3, 4 and 4A deal with negotiable instruments (checks, drafts, promissory notes, and certificates of deposit), bank deposits and collections (the rights and duties of banks and their customers), and wire transfers (electronic funds transfers involving huge sums) respectively. These Articles provide the central focus in separate courses analyzing payment systems. Articles 3 and 4 were revised in 1990 and have been adopted in all states except New York and South Carolina. Article 4A was introduced in 1989 and has been adopted in all states.

Article 5 is concerned with Letters of Credit, which assure sellers of payment through the credit of a party with reliable credit standing (a bank) when goods and their accompanying documents such as bills of lading are properly delivered. An introductory coverage of letters of credit is included in this book. A 1995 revised version of Article 5 has been adopted in all states except Wisconsin, where it was introduced for possible adoption in 2002.

Article 6 deals with "bulk transfers" and was designed to complement fraudulent conveyance and bankruptcy laws in protecting unsecured creditors against sales of major parts of their debtors' inventories outside the ordinary course of business. Because modern creditors are in a better position to make informed judgments about extending credit, in 1989 NCCUSL recommended the repeal of Article 6 but promulgated a revised version for those jurisdictions that may find benefits in its continuation. Forty-three states have repealed Article 6 and four states have adopted the revised version.

Article 7 deals with "documents of title," such as receipts issued by public warehouses where the owner of the goods chose to store them (warehouse receipts) and receipts from public carriers (trucking companies, railroads and airlines) called "bills of lading," issued when goods are placed with the carrier for transportation. These documents may take on great importance, particularly if they are "negotiable," because the document will control the disposition of the goods. The law surrounding documents of title and their operation is introduced in this book. A drafting committee has been appointed to produce a revised version of this Article.

Article 8 governs transactions in securities (stocks, bonds and other securities that serve as investment devices). It has sometimes been called a negotiable instruments law for investment securities. To reflect technological and other changes, Article 8 was revised in 1994. All states have adopted the revised version.

Article 9 governs arrangements that help assure creditors of payment by giving the creditor a "security interest" in personal property of the debtor (the collateral) which will allow the creditor to seize and sell the collateral if the debtor defaults. Article 9 replaced a series of disparate and sometimes-confusing pre-Code security devices (such as "conditional sales contracts" and "chattel mortgages"), whose requirements varied from state to state, with a unitary secured transaction concept that has succeeded in promoting uniformity and clarity over pre-existing law. Article 9 is typically pursued in separate courses involving secured transactions and bankruptcy law. A 1998 revision of Article 9 has been adopted by all states.

D. "OFFICIAL" COMMENTS

Each section of the UCC is followed by "official comments" that elaborate the purpose and application of the section. They vary in length, clarity, and sophistication. These "official" comments, however, are not part of the enacted law. The various legislatures enacted only the sections of the Code—not the comments. Moreover, the Permanent Editorial Board added or amended comments after the Code had been enacted in many states. The comments, therefore, do not have the weight of "legislative history" in the interpretation of Code sections. An early version of the Code contained a section stating that the comments "may be consulted in the construction and application of this Act." (1952 version, Section 1–102(3)(f)). However, that section was deleted in 1956, and no similar section was inserted in subsequent drafts. In theory, the comments may be ignored. Courts have, however, relied heavily upon the comments in their construction and application of the Code. Judicial adoption of the comments provides them with precedential force. The comments contain a wealth of material, but it must always be remembered that the comments are not legislation. Moreover, they are not exhaustive. One of the more useful features of the comments is their cross references to statutory definitions found in other Code sections. Since the comments are not part of the enacted law, should there be any conflict between the enacted section language and comment language, the section language controls.

E. RELATED STATUTES

(1) Uniform Consumer Information Transactions Act (UCI-TA).[1] In the last decade of the 20th century, it became abundantly clear that the revolution in information and communication has had an overwhelming effect on commerce. Indeed, the information industry is already larger than many manufacturing sectors, reflecting a major shift toward an information economy. Confronted with unfamiliar transactions involving software, courts resorted to their typical practice of applying existing law by analogy. It was not uncommon for a court to apply Article 2 to software transactions, although software is normally not purchased but licensed. Article 2, however, was not designed for such transactions. Contracts dealing with "access" to databases, and myriad electronic transactions involving "electronic agents" (computer programs) making contracts with other electronic agents with no human review raised new challenges. Earlier attempts to revise Article 2 to deal with these matters included a "hub and spoke" approach that contemplated a core of common general principles with separate "chapters" devoted to the specific issues of "sales" versus "licenses." This approach was rejected, giving rise to a proposal for a new and separate UCC Article 2B to govern in this area. The historic partners, ALI and NCCUSL, however, decided that the new concept should not become part of a revised Uniform Commercial Code. Instead, the proposed Article 2B became NCCUSL's *Uniform Computer Information Transactions Act* (UCITA).

UCITA focuses on *computer information transactions*—agreements to create, modify or distribute computer data (including software, multimedia interactive products, and other computer data and databases). The exclusive focus is computer information and not the tangible media that contains the information. A purchaser may own a diskette containing computer information, but that does not mean she owns the information thereon. Her use of the information is typically limited by a license contract. The Act, which (like the Uniform Commercial Code) may be varied by the parties' agreement,[2] covers contracts to access digitalized information through the Internet, other forms of distribution of computer information, as well as agreements to provide support for, maintain, or modify information related to such contracts. It deals with "mass

---

1. The text of and background information on this statute may be found on the website in note 3, *supra*. For an extensive analysis and critique of the predecessor of UCITA, proposed Article 2B of the UCC, see *Symposium: Intellectual Property and Contract Law for the Information Age: The Impact of Article 2B of the Uniform Commercial Code on the Future of Information and Commerce*, 87 CALIF. L. REV. 1 *et. Seq.* (1999). For an analysis of the effect on contractual relationships arising from the fundamental shift from a goods-based econ-

omy to an economy devoted in substantial part to the distribution of digital-based information, see Raymond T. Nimmer, *Images and Contract Law—What Law Applies in Information*, 36 HOUS. L. REV. 1 (1999).

2. UCITA § 113. A previous version included § 104, which provided express opt-in and opt-out provisions. They proved to be too complicated and unnecessary in light of § 113 allowing variation by agreement. Former § 104 is deleted in the most recent proposed amendments to UCITA.

market licenses"—standard form license agreements for software marketed to a consumer or the public in general, often found "inside the box" that contains the software and sometimes called "shrinkwrap" licenses because of the tight plastic or cellophane in which the box and license are covered. UCITA does not apply to a transaction merely because information related to the transaction is sent or recorded in digitalized form (for example, the electronic purchase of an airline ticket or other services), nor does it apply to print, motion picture, broadcast or sound recording transactions because the commercial practices relating to these transactions differ from those in the computer software, online and data industries. UCITA also does not apply to a computer program embedded in a product such as an ordinary television set or automobile. On the other hand, separately licensed software that enables a digital camera to be linked to a computer would be within the scope of the Act.

UCITA has proven controversial, with critics insisting that it favors producers of computer information and self-protective practices they have introduced into the software industry. At the time of this writing it has been enacted in only two states, Maryland and Virginia, though it has been introduced in a handful of other state legislatures.

(2) Uniform Electronic Transactions Act (UETA).[3] This Act is designed to address situations in which information, records and signatures are presented and retained electronically. Its limited objective is to recognize the validity of electronic records and signatures. An *electronic record* is a record created, generated, sent, communicated or stored by electronic means. An *electronic signature* is an electronic sound, symbol or process attached to or logically associated with an electronic record and executed or adopted by a person with intent to sign the electronic record. The UETA definition of *electronic record* is not limited to records intended for communication. It extends to any information contained or transferred in an electronic medium. Electronic means for creating, storing, generating, receiving or communicating electronic records include information processing systems, computer equipment and programs, electronic data interchange (EDI), electronic mail, voice mail, facsimile, telex, telecopying, scanning and other developing technologies.

The purpose of UETA with respect to electronic signatures is to avoid unwarranted biases against electronic methods of signing and authenticating records, and to promote equivalency between manual and electronic signatures. The spectrum of *electronic signature* covers one's name at the end of an e-mail message, a digital signature using public key encryption technology and even a webpage "click" as evidence that the party had the requisite intent to "sign."

UETA applies to electronic records and electronic signatures that relate to any transaction except those expressly excluded, such as those

---

3. The current 1999 draft may be found in some current compilations of commercial law statutes or on the NCCUSL website at *http://www.nccusl.org*. See also Kalama M. Lui–Kwan, *Article VI. Business Law: 1.* *Electronic Commerce: a) Digital Signatures: Recent Developments in Digital Signature Legislation and Electronic Commerce*, 14 Berkeley Tech. L. J. 463 (1999).

subject to a law governing the creation and execution of wills, codicils or testamentary trusts, or transactions within Articles 3 through 9 of the UCC (negotiable instruments, payments systems, letters of credit, investment securities and secured transactions), which contain their own rules for electronic transactions.

(3) United Nations Convention on Contracts for the International Sale of Goods (CISG). In the past, the traditional course in Commercial Law or Sales Law placed little emphasis on international transactions, which were viewed as the subject matter for specialized courses. International sales were governed by the national or "domestic" sales law of one of the involved nations, determined by applying choice-of-law ("private international law" or "conflict-of-law") principles. With the rise of multinational corporations and the increasing interdependency of world trade, the need for a uniform law for international contracts for the sale of goods grew. Visionaries had been attempting to develop such international uniformity even prior to 1930. In 1980, the United Nations Commission on International Trade Law (UNCITRAL) submitted a draft of a *Convention on Contracts for the International Sale of Goods* (hereinafter referred to as CISG or the Convention) to sixty-two nations at a diplomatic conference in Vienna. The Conference adopted the draft and the slow ratification process began.

The CISG displaces domestic sales law as the law applicable to international sales of goods. Consider, for example, a transaction involving parties who have their places of business in countries that have adopted the CISG ("Contracting States"). Instead of being governed by one country's domestic sales law chosen by using conflict of law rules (as would have been the case in the past), such sales are now subject to the CISG. The spirit of compromise pervading the monumental achievement that is the CISG led to numerous exceptions and limitations to its scope. Thus under Article 6, the buyer and seller may agree to "opt out" of the entire Convention or parts thereof. In addition, the CISG does not apply to consumer transactions, and issues of "validity" such as fraud, duress, mistake and unconscionability, are not within its coverage. Moreover, ratifying countries may make "declarations" or "reservations" under which they will not be bound by certain CISG Articles. To the extent an international sale of goods is not within the scope of the Convention, it remains subject to the domestic law applicable under a valid choice-of-law clause or, in the absence of such a clause, conflict of laws rules.

The United States formally ratified the CISG in 1986. The Convention became effective for the United States and the other original Contracting States on January 1, 1988, 12 months after at least 10 nations had ratified it. At the time of this writing 61 nations have adopted the CISG: Argentina, Australia, Austria, Bosnia and Herzegovina, Bulgaria, Burundi, Canada, Chile, China, Columbia, Croatia, Cuba, Czech Republic, Denmark, Ecuador, Egypt, Estonia, Finland, France, Georgia, Germany, Greece, Guinea, Hungary, Iceland, Iraq, Israel, Italy, Kyrgystan, Latvia, Lesotho, Lithuania, Luxembourg, Mauritania, Mexico, Moldova, Mongolia, Netherlands, New Zealand, Norway, Peru, Poland, Republic of Moldova, Romania, Russian Federation, Saint Vincent & Grenadines, Singapore, Slovakia, Slovenia, Spain, Sweden, Switzerland, Syria, Uganda, Ukraine, the United States of America, Uruguay, Uzbekistan, Venezuela, Yugoslavia and Zambia.

In some measure, the CISG reflects contract and commercial law similar to the UCC, but it is heavily influenced by the law of other countries. There is no separate court system to apply the Convention, nor is there a final authority to interpret it. The CISG is applied by regular courts within each of the adopting countries, which creates a major challenge. Article 7(1) of the Convention seeks to meet this challenge by requiring courts to interpret the CISG with regard for "its international character and . . . the need to promote uniformity in its application. . . ." It emphasizes the essential focus of uniformity by directing courts in many different nations to view the CISG through an international lens rather than the domestic law lens so familiar to such courts. This requires lawyers and judges confronted with CISG issues to become familiar with legislative history, as well as scholarly commentary and case law from other countries.

The views of commentators from other legal traditions are important aids in developing an international perspective concerning the CISG.[4] Foreign case law applying the Convention is a particularly valuable tool in the search for a uniform interpretation.[5] The modern commercial lawyer must be aware of the provisions of the CISG, and they will be reflected throughout these materials.[6]

4. English speakers are fortunate to have splendid commentary from the leading German CISG scholar, Peter Schlechtriem, whose COMMENTARY ON THE UN CONVENTION ON THE INTERNATIONAL SALE OF GOODS (CISG) (2d ed. 1998) is now available. The authoritative U.S. commentary is by John Honnold, UNIFORM LAW FOR INTERNATIONAL SALES UNDER THE 1980 UNITED NATIONS CONVENTION (3d ed. 1999).

5. UNCITRAL which was responsible for the CISG, publishes "Case Law on UNCITRAL Texts" (CLOUT), containing abstracts of CISG decisions in the official languages of the United Nations, including English. CLOUT is available online at *http://www.un.or.at/uncitral/en-index.htm.* CISG case summaries are also available through the Pace University Institute of International Commercial Law website at *http://www.cisg.law.pace.edu/cisg/text/caseschedule.html.* The Institute of Foreign and International Private Law at the University of Freiburg sponsors CISG On-line at *http://www.jura.uni-freiburg.de/ipr1/cisg/,* and Professor Claude Witz of the Centre Juridique Franco–Allemand posts CISG–France at http://www.jur.unsb.de/FB/LS/Witz/ cisg.htm. The Centre for Comparative and

Foreign Law Studies in Rome has created UNILEX, a database available at http://www.unilex.info/, containing texts of CISG cases in their original languages accompanied in many cases by English abstracts. Professor Michael Will of the University of Geneva (Switzerland) has published a series of books citing CISG cases from around the world, including INTERNATIONAL SALES LAW UNDER CISG, THE UN CONVENTION ON CONTRACTS FOR INTERNATIONAL SALE OF GOODS (1980): THE FIRST 555 OR SO DECISIONS.

6. Other important efforts to promote uniformity in transnational commercial law include the UNIDROIT PRINCIPLES OF INTERNATIONAL COMMERCIAL CONTRACTS (1994). The International Institute for the Unification of Private Law (UNIDROIT) was created in 1926 under the auspices of the League of Nations. Currently, it is an independent international organization composed of 56 members with a seat in Rome. The "father" of the Principles is Professor Michael Joachim Bonell of the University of Rome. Unlike the CISG, which is a treaty, the Principles are not binding. They function much more like a Restatement of the law. They are much broader in scope than the CISG, dealing with issues (including "validity") that are not covered by the CISG. See Joseph M. Perillo, *UNIDROIT Principles of*

PART 2: SCOPE OF ARTICLE 2 AND RELATED STATUTES

A. QUESTIONS OF SCOPE—TRANSACTIONS IN GOODS

It is logical to begin the study of "Sales Law" by defining the scope of the inquiry. Where the governing law is a statute, it is critically important to examine the statutory language with care. Section 2–102 of the UCC presents a broad framework—unless the context otherwise requires, Article 2 "applies to transactions in goods." " 'Goods' means all things (including specially manufactured goods) which are moveable at the time of identification[1] to the contract for sale other than the money in which the price is to be paid, investment securities (Article 8) and things in action" (2–105(1)). An interest in goods can only be passed if the goods are both existing and "identified." If goods are not both existing and identified, they are "future goods" (2–105(2)). Where the goods are attached to realty they may be "natural" to the realty, such as minerals, oil, gas or the like, or they may be wheat, corn, tomatoes or other growing crops planted by a farmer. 2–107 treats the "natural" things attached to realty as "goods" if they are to be severed by the seller, but as realty if they are to severed by the purchaser. Growing crops, however, are goods, regardless of whether the buyer or seller will sever them from the earth. In an earlier version of 2–107, timber was treated as one of the natural products. Trade usage, however, was to treat timber like growing crops, and the section was revised to provide for such treatment.

Other goods that are neither "natural" to the realty nor grown thereon may become attached to the realty. A water heater, air conditioning system, or a variety of other products that become attached to realty may become "fixtures." Article 2, however, avoids the use of the term "fixtures" because of "the diversity of definitions of that term" (Comment 1 to 2–105). Consider how a court may deal with goods that will become "fixtures."

LOUGHRIDGE v. GOODYEAR TIRE & RUBBER CO.

United States District Court for the District of Colorado, 2002.
192 F.Supp.2d 1175.

BABCOCK, C. J. Heatway sells parts for hydronic radiant heating systems. These systems circulate warm fluid under indoor flooring as an

---

International Commercial Contracts: The Black Letter Text and a Review, 63 FORDHAM L. REV. 281 (1994). The International Chamber of Commerce has produced INTERNATIONAL COMMERCIAL TERMS (1990), known throughout the commercial world as INCOTERMS, to further uniformity in transnational commercial transactions.

1. ["Identifying" goods is the means of referring certain goods to a particular con-

tract. (2–501). The typical means of identification occurs when goods are taken from inventory and marked, shipped or designated by the seller as goods to which the contract refers. Upon identification, the buyer has a special property and insurable interest in the goods. 2–501(1)(b). This concept will be explored in subsequent chapters.]

alternative to conventional heating systems, or under driveways and sidewalks to melt snow and ice. Goodyear manufactured and sold a hose, the Entran II, used in Heatway's radiant systems. Colorado was a major market for these systems. [A number of homeowners filed suits against Goodyear and Heatway claiming the Entran II was cracking and leaking.]

All Plaintiffs bring claims for breach of express warranty, breach of implied warranty of merchantability, and breach of implied warranty of fitness for a particular purpose against Goodyear. Each of these claims is based on the Colorado Uniform Commercial Code (UCC). Goodyear argues that all claims based on the UCC should be dismissed because the transaction did not involve a sale of goods but rather a fixture of real property. Article 2 of the UCC applies only to sales of goods. See Colo. Rev. Stat. § 4–2–102(1).

'Goods' means all things (including specially manufactured goods) which are movable at the time of identification to the contract for sale ... 'Goods' also includes ... other identified things attached to realty as described in the section on goods to be severed from realty (section 4–2–107). Colo. Rev. Stat. § 4–2–105(1). The terms of section 4–2–107 do not apply here.

Goodyear argues that because the Entran II was used in the construction of radiant systems which were then covered by flooring or cement, the hose became a fixture of real property and not a good for purposes of the UCC. I disagree. The Plaintiffs have made clear that they are suing as third-party beneficiaries to the contract between Goodyear and Heatway for sale of the hose. Thus, the Entran II was an existing and identifiable thing which was movable at the time of identification to the contract for sale, making it a "good" for purposes of the UCC. See Colo. Rev. Stat. § 4–2–105(1)-(2). Further, the Colorado Courts have held that separate units of goods which are later incorporated into a home or other building are still goods at the time that they are procured for installation. "The fact that [materials sold] might later be installed in the ... home and assume the character of fixtures does not undermine the primary purpose of the contract as one for a sale of goods." Colorado Carpet Installation, Inc. v. Palermo, 668 P.2d 1384, 1389 (Colo.1983); Thomas v. Bove, 687 P.2d 534 (Colo.Ct.App.1984) (installation of heating system in home); Regents of Univ. of Colo. v. Pacific Pump & Supply, Inc., 35 Colo. App. 36, 528 P.2d 941 (Colo.Ct. App.1974) (installation of standby emergency electric power plant, consisting of an engine and generator); Cherokee Inv. Co. v. Voiles, 166 Colo. 270, 443 P.2d 727 (Colo. 1968) (installation of a water softener in a home). I therefore conclude that the Entran II hose is a "good" for purposes of the Colorado UCC, and deny Goodyear's motion for summary judgment on Plaintiffs' contract claims.

Note

Beyond their contract claims under the Uniform Commercial Code to secure the protection of UCC warranties and remedies, the plaintiffs also sought recovery under tort theories including a count for products liability. As we will see in Chapter 3, courts are unwilling to allow recovery for loss-of-bargain damages under a tort theory since the buyer is suing for breach of contract. Recovery under a tort theory for losses caused by a defective product is recognized for personal injury or damage to other property. If the only property damaged is the product itself, the *Loughridge* court recognized a split of authority. While the court found that Colorado law would allow a tort recovery even if the only property damaged was the product itself, it found that the facts evidenced damage to other property. Absent such damage to other property in a jurisdiction denying tort recovery for damage to the product itself, a court's determination of whether a contract for a product that will become a fixture is a contract for the sale of goods to which the UCC applies takes on heightened importance.

Suppose the transaction involves not only goods but services—a "mixed" or "hybrid" sale. When you buy a new water heater, for example, the cost of labor to install the device (a service) may be a major component of the total price. Is this a contract for goods or services? Should Article 2 apply to such transactions, or should the common law of contracts govern? Moreover, what difference would it make?

PRINCESS CRUISES v. GENERAL ELECTRIC COMPANY

United States Court of Appeals for the Fourth Circuit, 1998.
143 F.3d 828.

Goodwin, District Judge: This suit arises out of a maritime contract between General Electric Company (GE) and Princess Cruises, Inc. (Princess) for inspection and repair services relating to Princess's cruise ship, the SS Sky Princess. In January 1997, a jury found GE liable for breach of contract and awarded Princess $4,577,743.00 in damages. On appeal, GE contends that the district court erred in denying its renewed motion for judgment as a matter of law, which requested that the court vacate the jury's award of incidental and consequential damages. Specifically, GE argues that the district court erroneously applied Uniform Commercial Code principles, rather than common law principles, to a contract primarily for services.

Princess scheduled the SS Sky Princess for routine inspection services and repairs in December 1994 and requested that GE, the original manufacturer of the ship's main turbines, perform services and provide parts incidental to the ship's inspection and repair. Princess issued a Purchase Order in October 1994. The Purchase Order included a proposed contract price of $260,000.00 and contained a brief description of services to be performed by GE. The reverse side of the Purchase Order listed terms and conditions which indicated that Princess intended the Purchase Order to be an offer. These terms and conditions also stated that GE could accept the Purchase Order through acknowledgment or performance; that the terms and conditions could not be changed unilaterally; and that GE would provide a warranty of workmanlike quality and fitness for the use intended.

On the same day that GE received the Purchase Order, GE faxed a Fixed Price Quotation to Princess. The Fixed Price Quotation provided a more detailed work description than Princess's Purchase Order and included a parts and materials list, an offering price of $201,888.00, and GE's own terms and conditions. When GE reviewed Princess's Purchase Order, it discovered that Princess requested work not contemplated by GE in its Fixed Price Quotation. GE notified Princess of GE's error. On October 28, 1994, GE faxed a Final Price Quotation to Princess. In the Final Price Quotation, GE offered to provide all services, labor, and materials for $231,925.00. Attached to both GE Quotations were GE's terms and conditions, which: (1) rejected the terms and conditions set forth in Princess's Purchase Order; (2) rejected liquidated damages; (3) limited GE's liability to repair or replacement of any defective goods or damaged equipment resulting from defective service, exclusive of all written, oral, implied, or statutory warranties; (4) limited GE's liability on any claims to not more than the greater of either $5000.00 or the contract price; and (5) disclaimed any liability for consequential damages, lost profits, or lost revenue. During an October 31, 1994 telephone call, Princess gave GE permission to proceed based on the price set forth in GE's Final Price Quotation.

On November 1, 1994, GE sent a confirmatory letter to Princess acknowledging receipt of Princess's Purchase Order and expressing GE's intent to perform the services. The letter also restated GE's $231,925.00 offering price from its Final Price Quotation and specified that GE's terms and conditions, attached to the letter, were to govern the contract.

When the SS Sky Princess arrived for inspection, GE noted surface rust on the rotor and recommended that it be taken ashore for cleaning and balancing. The parties agree that during the cleaning, good metal was removed from the rotor, rendering the rotor unbalanced. Although GE attempted to correct the imbalance, Princess canceled a ten-day Christmas cruise as a result of delays caused by the repair. At trial, Princess alleged that the continued vibration and high temperatures caused damage to the ship, forcing additional repairs and the cancellation of a ten-day Easter cruise. It was undisputed, however, that Princess paid GE the full amount of the contract: $231,925.00.

On April 22, 1996, Princess filed a four-count complaint against GE, alleging breach of contract, breach of express warranty, breach of implied maritime warranty, and negligence. The district court granted GE's motion for summary judgment as to the negligence claim. Following Princess's presentation of evidence at trial, GE made a motion for judgment as a matter of law, which the district court denied. In instructing the jury, the district court drew on principles set forth in U.C.C. § 2–207 and allowed the jury to imply the following terms as part of the contract: (1) the warranty of merchantability; (2) the warranty of fitness for a particular purpose; (3) the warranty of workmanlike performance; (4) Princess's right to recover damages for GE's alleged breach of the contact; and (5) Princess's right to recover incidental and consequential damages, as well as lost profits, proximately caused by GE's alleged breach. On January 24, 1997, the jury returned a $4,577,743.00 verdict in favor of Princess....

* * *

[T]he district court found it "unnecessary for the Court to determine whether the contract is primarily one for goods or services. In either case, the UCC is regarded as a source of admiralty law." We respectfully disagree.... [T]he district court correctly noted that U.C.C. principles inform admiralty law. However, we are unpersuaded that U.C.C. § 2–207 applies to maritime transactions regardless of the nature of the transaction. [A] court must first determine whether the predominant purpose of the transaction is the sale of goods. Once this initial analysis has been performed, the court then may properly decide whether the common law, the U.C.C., or other statutory law governs the transaction.

Although the U.C.C. governs the sale of goods, the U.C.C. also applies to certain mixed contracts for goods and services. Whether a particular transaction is governed by the U.C.C., rather than the common law or other statutory law, hinges on the predominant purpose of the transaction, that is, whether the contract primarily concerns the furnishing of goods or the rendering of services. In determining whether goods or services predominate in a particular transaction, we are guided by the seminal case of *Bonebrake v. Cox, 499 F.2d 951, 960 (8th Cir.1974).* In holding the U.C.C. applicable, the Bonebrake court stated:

> The test for inclusion or exclusion is not whether they are mixed but, granting that they are mixed, whether their predominant factor, their thrust, their purpose, reasonably stated, is the rendition of service, with goods incidentally involved (e.g., contract with artist for painting) or is a transaction of sale, with labor incidentally involved (e.g., installation of a water heater in a bathroom).

The Fourth Circuit has deemed the following factors significant in determining the nature of the contract: (1) the language of the contract, (2) the nature of the business of the supplier, and (3) the intrinsic worth of the materials. See *Coakley & Williams, 706 F.2d at 460* (applying Maryland law).

It is plain that the GE–Princess transaction principally concerned the rendering of services, specifically, the routine inspection and repair of the SS Sky Princess, with incidental—albeit expensive—parts supplied by GE. Although Princess's standard fine-print terms and conditions mention the sale of goods, Princess's actual purchase description requests a GE "service engineer" to perform service functions: the opening of valves for survey and the inspection of the ship's port main turbine.

GE's Final Price Quotation also contemplates service functions, stating in large print on every page that it is a "Quotation for Services." The Final Price Quotation's first page notes that GE is offering a quotation for "engineering services." GE's Quotation further specifies that the particular type of service offered is "Installation/Repair/Maintenance." The Final Price Quotation then lists the scope of the contemplated work—opening, checking, cleaning, inspecting, disassembling—in short, service functions. Although GE's materials list shows that GE planned to manufacture a small number of parts for Princess, Princess appeared to have had most of the needed materials on board. Thus, the language of both the Purchase Order and the Final Price Quotation indicates that although GE planned to supply certain parts, the parts were incidental to the contract's predominant purpose, which was inspection, repair, and maintenance services.

As to the second Coakley factor—the nature of the business of the supplier—although GE is known to manufacture goods, GE's correspondence and Quotations came from GE's Installation and Service Engineering Department. Evidence at trial showed that GE's Installation and Service Engineering division is comprised of twenty-seven field engineers who perform service functions, such as overhauls and repairs. Finally, the last Coakley factor—the intrinsic worth of the materials supplied—cannot be determined because neither Princess's Purchase Order nor GE's Final Price Quotation separately itemized the value of the materials. Instead, both the Purchase Order and the Final Price Quotation blend the cost of the materials into the final price of a services contract, thereby confirming that services rather than materials predominated in the transaction. Although not a Coakley factor, it is also telling that Princess's counsel admitted that the gravamen of Princess's complaint did not arise out of GE's furnishing of deficient parts, but rather out of GE's deficient services. Accordingly, we find as a matter of law that services rather than goods predominated in the GE–Princess contract.

The parties do not dispute that a contract was formed by their exchange of documents. And there is no dispute that the GE–Princess contract for ship inspection and repair is maritime in nature and governed by the substantive law of admiralty. However, the issue here—whether courts should draw on U.C.C. principles or on common-law doctrines when assessing the formation of a maritime services contract—is undecided. When no federal statute or well-established rule of admiralty exists, admiralty law may look to the common law or to state law, either statutory or decisional, to supply the rule of decision. Because the majority of states refer to common-law principles when assessing contracts predominantly for services, we choose to do the same.

Under the common law, an acceptance that varies the terms of the offer is a counteroffer which rejects the original offer. RESTATEMENT (SECOND) OF CONTRACTS § 59 (1981) ("A reply to an offer which purports to accept it but is conditional on the offeror's assent to terms additional to or different from those offered is not an acceptance but is a counter-offer."). Virginia follows the same rule. Here, GE's Final Price

Quotation materially altered the terms of Princess's Purchase Order by offering a different price, limiting damages and liability, and excluding warranties. Thus, GE's Final Price Quotation was a counteroffer rejecting Princess's Purchase Order. Although Princess could have rejected GE's counteroffer, Princess accepted the Final Price Quotation by giving GE permission to proceed with the repair and maintenance services, by not objecting to the confirmatory letter sent by GE, and by paying the amount set forth in GE's Final Price Quotation, $231,925.00, rather than the $260,000.00 price term set forth in Princess's Purchase Order. At common law, an offeror who proceeds under a contract after receiving the counteroffer can accept the terms of the counteroffer by performance. Although GE and Princess never discussed the Purchase Order's and the Final Price Quotation's conflicting terms and conditions, both Princess's actions and inaction gave GE every reason to believe that Princess assented to the terms and conditions set forth in GE's Final Price Quotation. See RESTATEMENT (SECOND) OF CONTRACTS § 19(1) (1981) ("The manifestation of assent may be made wholly or partly by written or spoken words or by other acts or by failure to act."). Accordingly, we find that the terms and conditions of GE's Final Price Quotation control liability and damages in the GE–Princess transaction.

For the reasons stated above, the jury could only have considered one contract in awarding damages: GE's Final Price Quotation. The Quotation restricted damages to the contract price, $231,925.00, and eliminated liability for incidental or consequential damages and lost profits or revenue. Moreover, GE's Final Price Quotation controlled the warranties available to its customers. Yet the jury awarded $4,577,743.00 in damages to Princess. This verdict demonstrates that the jury relied on Princess's Purchase Order or some other contract when awarding damages (district court opinion noting that "the jury either found that Princess'[s] Purchase Order governed or that neither parties' document established the complete contract"). As a matter of law, the jury could only have awarded damages consistent with the terms and conditions of GE's Final Price Quotation and could not have awarded incidental or consequential damages. By requesting that the Court award Princess the maximum amount available under the Final Price Quotation, GE concedes that it breached its contract with Princess and that damages consistent with its Final Price Quotation are appropriate. Accordingly, we find it unnecessary to remand for a new trial on this issue. We reverse the district court's decision denying GE's motion for judgment as a matter of law and remand for entry of judgment against GE in the amount of $231,925.00, interest to accumulate from the date of the original judgment.

REVERSED AND REMANDED.

Questions

Suppose the transaction had been characterized as one predominantly for the sale of goods. Would this change have supported a Princess recovery of over $4.5 million? Is there a difference between the contract formation process of the common law and the UCC with respect to different or additional terms?

The RESTATEMENT (SECOND) OF CONTRACTS, § 59 states that "a reply to an offer which purports to accept it but is conditional on the offeror's assent to terms additional to or different from those offered is not an acceptance but is a counter offer." Compare this statement with the last proviso of UCC 2–207(1). Suppose the reply to the offer is not expressly conditional on the offeror's assent to additional or different terms. It just contains additional or different terms. What does § 59 have to say about that situation? Section 61 of the RESTATEMENT (SECOND) OF CONTRACTS states that "an acceptance which requests a change or addition to the terms of the offer is not thereby invalidated unless the acceptance is made to depend on an assent to the changed or added terms." Suppose the "acceptance" does not request any changes or additions to the offer, but merely states different or additional terms. What does § 61 say about that situation?

There is preciously little case law comparing these two Restatement (Second) sections and UCC 2–207. Consider a statement from *Ceco Corp. v. Carson Concrete Corp.*, 691 F.Supp. 850, 859 (E.D.Pa.1988): "Significantly lacking from the Restatement formulations is the UCC specification that a reply purporting to agree to an offer but stating additional or different terms is treated as an acceptance unless the offeree's acceptance is 'expressly made conditional on [the offeror's] assent.'" Comment *a* to § 59 of the Restatement Second, however, states, "[b]ut a definite and seasonable expression of acceptance is operative despite the statement of additional or different terms if the acceptance is not made to depend on assent to the additional or different terms. See § 61; UCC § 2–207(1). The additional or different terms are then to be construed as proposals for modification of the contract. See UCC § 2–207(2)." If the contract were "between merchants," however, would the additional terms be a "mere proposal" under 2–207(2)?

Problem 1

With the assistance of 2–102, 2–105, 2–107, 2–304, 2–314 and 2–501 determine whether UCC Article 2 applies to the following:

(a) Contract for the sale of two acres of (i) grown or (ii) not-yet-planted asparagus.

(b) Contract for the sale of coal which the buyer must mine.

(c) Contract for the sale of a new Mercedes Benz automobile, the buyer to pay by conveying three acres of land.

(d) Contract to purchase a stand of timber.

(e) Contract to sell oil in the ground in exchange for oil drilling equipment.

(f) Contract to purchase an unborn Bengal tiger.

(g) Contract to sell a computer.

(h) Contract to sell computer information.

(i) Contract to sell disk copies of computer information.

(j) Contract to buy a McDonald's hamburger to be eaten in one's office.

(k) Contract to buy a McDonald's hamburger to be eaten at McDonald's.

(*l*) Assignment of a contract right to purchase goods.

(m) Sale of certificated or uncertificated shares of stock in a corporation.

(n) Sale of a radio station, including the FCC license, good will, real estate, transmission equipment and other furnishings where the goods constitute less than 20 percent of the purchase price.

(*o*) Aerial spraying of crops where the price of the herbicide is no more than 35 percent of the total contract price.

(p) A contract with a public utility to deliver natural gas or electricity to a factory.

Problem 2

Mrs. Newmark was advised against an advertised "special" permanent wave by her hair stylist who stated that she required a "good" permanent wave. The stylist applied a solution called "Candle Glow" manufactured by the Curtis Corporation. That evening, Mrs. Newmark experienced considerable hair loss and major scalp irritation later diagnosed as contact dermatitis caused by the "Candle Glow." Does she have a UCC cause of action against the Curtis Corporation? See 2–314 and 2–318.

Problem 3

Maryann was driving her new Hoyota car purchased from Jack's New Cars when the steering mechanism went out of control causing Maryann to smash into a nearby tree, resulting in injury to herself and three bystanders. The car was totaled. May Maryann bring an action for personal injury and property damage against Jack's or Hoyota under the UCC Article 2, or is she relegated to a tort action? See 2–715(2)(b), 2–314. What about the bystanders? See 2–318. Why would anyone sue under UCC Article 2 if § 402A of the Restatement of Torts were available? See UCC 2–725. Suppose there was no accident and no injury to Maryann or others. Only one month after Maryann took delivery of the new car and following just 1000 miles of normal driving, the car stopped working and could not be repaired. Could Maryann sue Jack's or Hoyota under a tort theory because the car will not function and cannot be repaired?

Problem 4

Owens' new car was stolen by Miller who, through fraud, obtained a clean certificate of title from the State Bureau of Motor Vehicles. Armed with the clean certificate, Miller sold the car to Hughes, who bought it for fair value and in good faith. Owens discovered the car and seeks to replevy it from Hughes. See §§ 1–201(b)(9), 2–102 and 2–403. Does the state certificate of title law preempt the UCC?

B. "SALE" AND "CONTRACT FOR SALE"—"TITLE"

While the Article 2 "scope" section, 2–102, refers to "transactions in goods," the "Short Title" of Article 2 is "Uniform Commercial Code— Sales" (2–101). Most of the substantive provisions of Article 2, further- more, apply only to "sales" or "contracts for sales" (defined in 2–106 as both a present sale of goods and a contract to sell goods in the future), or to "buyers" or "sellers." Thus it is critical to understand what a "sale" is. As defined in 2–401, a "sale" is the "passing of title from the seller to the buyer for a price." The reference to "title" here points up a dramatic change in the use of the "title" concept under the UCC.

For many years, the law dealing with sales of goods was considered to be a hybrid of property and contract law with a particular emphasis upon property law. The dominant concept in the prior law of sales was "title," a construct indicating which party had ownership of the goods at a given time. This concept was used as an analytical device to resolve many sales issues. For example, one of the more important sales ques- tions is the allocation of the risk that goods will be damaged or destroyed (risk of loss). Prior law placed that risk on the party who had "title." Professor Karl Llewellyn, the "father" of the UCC and principal drafts- man of Article 2, was particularly critical of the use of "title" to resolve such questions.

The law that preceded Article 2 of the UCC—the Uniform Sales Act—contained analytical constructs to determine which party had title at any given time in the transaction. Llewellyn considered these con- structs to be artificial because they did not reflect the commercial understanding of people in commerce—"merchants." A very important Comment to the first section of Article 2 reflects this concern in the use of the "title" concept:

> The arrangement of the present Article is in terms of *contract for sale* and the various steps of its performance. The legal conse- quences are stated as following directly from the contract and action taken under it without resorting to the idea of when property or title passed or was to pass as being the determining factor. The purpose is to avoid making practical issues between practical men turn upon the location of an intangible something, the passing of which no man can prove by evidence and to substitute for such abstractions proof of words and actions of a tangible character.

Paragraph 3 of the Comment to 2–101 (emphasis supplied).

Among the radical changes effected by Article 2, the move from a property to a contracts orientation is the most fundamental modification of pre-Code law. The rights and duties of the parties under the Code are determined by their contract so as to capture the intention of the parties—the "factual bargain" of the buyer and the seller (1–201(3)). In the American Legal Realist tradition, Llewellyn was obsessed with an emphasis upon effectuating the factual bargain between reasonable parties. The adoption of Article 2 marks a radical change. Title is no longer an important analytical construct in sales law. It is the contract between the parties that dominates.

Given the emphasis of contract principles over property concepts, why does the Code contain a separate section—2–401—dealing with the passage of title? The first Comment to 2–401 reiterates the emphasis upon contract in Article 2: "This Article deals with the issues between seller and buyer in terms of step by step performance or non-performance under the contract for sale and not in terms of whether or not 'title' to the goods has passed." Comment 1 to 2–401. The Code drafters nevertheless recognized that the law governing taxation, insurance or other non-UCC matters may require a determination of who had title to goods. The issues arising under such laws are beyond the scope of the UCC. It was, therefore, necessary to provide guidance as to the passage of title exclusively for these extra-Code questions.

C. SECURED TRANSACTIONS

The underlying desire of all creditors is to receive payment. To increase the likelihood of being paid, creditors often assume "secured" status. For example, banks and others who lend to purchasers of real estate often take mortgages on the property, allowing them to seize (foreclose) and sell the property if the borrower defaults. The UCC does not deal with transactions in real property. Creditors can, however, take mortgage-like rights in personal property such as goods (indeed, some such arrangements were called "chattel mortgages" prior to the UCC), which rights are governed by Article 9 of the UCC. The scope section of Article 2, 2–102, excludes any transaction "intended to operate only as a security transaction" because Article 9 is designed to deal with secured transactions. Consider a contract to sell goods on credit which includes a provision giving the seller a property interest in the goods and the right to repossess the goods should the buyer default in paying the purchase price. Prior to the UCC, such transactions were called "conditional sales contracts" or, again, "chattel mortgages." Now such a transaction would be called a "security agreement" giving the seller a "security interest" in the goods. A "security interest" is defined as "an interest in personal property or fixtures which secures payment or performance of an obligation" (1–201(b)(35)).[2] In such a transaction, the debtor not only agrees

---

2. The amended Article 1 defines "security interest" in Amended 1–201(35) (2002), but retains only the first paragraph of the original definition in 1–201(37). The re-to repay the loan plus interest, but also, in order to assure the loan's repayment, grants to the creditor a property interest in certain goods— the identified collateral—which can be repossessed if the debtor fails to repay the debt as promised. The seller has a property interest in the goods to assure the payment of the price. Other creditors of a buyer, including banks and other commercial lenders, may also acquire security interests in goods (collateral) that they did not sell. Thus, a bank loan given to permit the borrower to buy a car will invariably be attended by a security agreement whereby the borrower grants a security interest in the identified collateral (the car) to the lending bank. As a secured creditor, the bank has rights in the identified collateral and, upon default by the purchaser, it may repossess the car and resell it to receive payment of the outstanding loan balance. Whether there has been a default under the security agreement, giving the seller the right to repossess the goods, is only one of the many questions that may arise under a secured financing arrangement. Such questions are governed by Article 9 of the UCC. Article 2 deals only with a few tangential questions involving security for the sale of goods.

D. LEASES AND SECURED TRANSACTIONS—ARTICLE 2A

A lease of goods does not purport to transfer ownership of the goods. It merely allows a party other than the owner to possess and use the goods for a certain time. Thus Article 2, which generally deals with contracts for the sale of goods and consistently refers to "buyers" and "sellers," does not directly apply to true leases. Some transactions called "leases," however, may be disguised sales of goods to which Article 2 should apply. Even with respect to "true" leases, some courts have applied Article 2 concepts by analogy. The application of Article 2 to leases, however, has been neither uniform nor always clear. Thus, Article 2A was added to the UCC to govern lease transactions.

Article 2A "applies to any transaction, regardless of form, that creates a lease." 2A–102. The key word in this provision is "lease," defined in 2A–103(1)(j) as "a transfer of the right to possession and use of goods for a term in return for consideration...." Although "sales" are explicitly excluded from the definition of "lease," important aspects of leases resemble sales in that both transactions involve a transfer of rights in the subject property. It is not surprising, therefore, that the bulk of Article 2A is modeled on Article 2.[1] Indeed, "the official comments to those sections of Article 2 whose provisions were carried over [into Article 2A] are incorporated by reference in Article 2A ...; further, any case law interpreting those provisions should be viewed as persua-

mainder of the pre-amendment versions of 1–201(37), dealing with the distinction between leases and security interests, is found in Amended 1–203 (2002).

1. See the official comment to 2A–101, "Statutory Analogue."

sive but not binding on a court when deciding a similar issue with respect to leases."[2]

A lease differs from a sale in that the lessor transfers possession and use of the leased property to the lessee only for a term and the lessor retains title to the property. This means not only that a lessor can demand return of leased goods once the lease term ends, but that the lessor may be entitled to their return during the lease term if the lessee defaults on the lease agreement. 2A–525(2). The right of a lessor to retake the goods upon the lessee's default resembles the foreclosure right enjoyed by a party who has taken a security interest in goods to secure repayment of a debt. As earlier described, a security interest is a limited form of property interest (a "lien") taken by a creditor in specified property ("collateral") of the debtor to assure that the creditor will be paid. If the debtor fails to pay, the security interest permits the creditor to obtain possession of the collateral by foreclosing, much as a lessor can demand return of leased goods if the lessee fails to pay rent. After foreclosing, the secured creditor can sell the property and deduct the amount of the unpaid debt from the proceeds.[3] Security interests in goods are governed by Article 9 of the UCC and are frequently (but by no means always) included as a part of a sales transaction. For instance, a credit seller can reserve a security interest in the goods to secure the buyer's payment of the price.[4]

Because the rights of a lessor are similar to those of a secured party, what is in substance a sale of goods coupled with a grant of a security interest can be cast in the form of a lease. Consider the following.

Jordan Manufacturing Corporation (J) wishes to purchase a computerized lathe from Southern Equipment Corporation (SEC). SEC is willing to sell, but only if it can repossess the machinery if J fails to pay. SEC could sell the machinery to J and take a security interest in the goods to secure the payment of the price. The parties, however can achieve much the same result by using the form of a lease. For instance, SEC could "lease" the machinery to J for the entire useful life of the goods at a rent equal to the periodic payments it would demand in an outright sale. At the end of the lease term the machinery to be returned to SEC would be worn-out and valueless. SEC, however, would have

---

2. Official comment to 2A–101, "Relationship of Article 2A to Other Articles."

3. One difference between the rights of a lessor and a secured party is that the secured party *must sell* seized collateral and can retain the proceeds only up to the amount of the outstanding debt (plus recoverable costs); if there is a balance remaining, it must be remitted to the debtor. In contrast, a lessor who repossesses leased goods upon default by the lessee can retain the goods themselves; if the lessor sells the goods, he or she can keep all proceeds even if they exceed the remaining unpaid rental payments. Such a lessor, furthermore, may be entitled to additional damages if the rent reserved in the defaulted lease exceeds the market rent for the goods or if the lessor has lost profitable volume because of the default and repossession. See 2A–528.

4. Alternatively, a buyer may pay the price through a loan from a third party and grant the lender a security interest in the purchased goods to secure repayment. Note that a security interest arises only by consent of the owner of property and is not an automatic feature of sales transactions. For example, a seller who extends credit to the buyer does not obtain a security interest in the goods unless the buyer explicitly grants one in the manner required by Article 9. Absent such a security interest, a credit seller does not have any special right to seize the goods if the buyer fails to pay.

collected the full price, just as if the machinery had been sold outright, and J would have enjoyed the full economic value of the goods, just as if it had bought them. Why would such a transaction be cast in the form of a lease? As a "lessor," SEC would have had the right to repossess the machinery if J failed to make the "rental" payments—much as it could foreclose on the machinery for default if it had sold it outright while retaining a security interest. In an alternative arrangement, SEC might "lease" the machine to J for less than its useful life at a rent equal to the purchase price, at the same time giving J an option to purchase the lathe for a nominal amount at the end of the lease. In effect, this would mean that SEC has sold the machine because it is clear from the time the lease is formed that J will want to exercise the option to purchase. Until all "rent" is paid, SEC as a lessor again enjoys repossession rights that are superior to those of a secured party. The result is that the transaction is really the granting of a security interest in certain property though it is cast in the garb of a "lease," though no true lease has been created.

The problem with sale/security interest transactions masquerading as leases is that they can be used to circumvent the requirements of UCC Article 9. To be protected against competing claims by other creditors to J's collateral (the lathe), Article 9 requires a secured party such as SEC to "perfect" the security interest by some action designed to give third parties notice of the security interest. For many important kinds of collateral, the secured party can (or must) perfect by filing a notice of the security interest (a "financing statement") in public records.[5] Article 9 imposes perfection requirements because, without a means to learn that a debtor's property is encumbered with a security interest, third parties may be misled into thinking that the debtor has full ownership rights in the property.

Recording a real estate mortgage provides public notice to other potential creditors that the real property is subject to an outstanding security interest in the creditor named in the record. Similarly, to protect a third party from lending sums to a debtor such as J on the assumption that he owns a valuable computerized lathe which the third party will view as solid security for the new loan, Article 9 requires SEC to "perfect" the security interest by filing a public record to protect subsequent creditors from "secret liens." If the transaction is viewed as a true lease, a lessor such as SEC would have a right to reclaim the lathe upon default by J without any public notice of SEC's property interest in the lathe as contrasted with the requirements imposed on holders of security interests.[6] Thus the ability to disguise as a "lease" what is in reality a sale of goods coupled with a security interest for the purchase price creates the potential for abuse. If parties can avoid perfection

---

5. Different methods of perfection (such as taking possession of the collateral) are available or required in certain situations.

6. Except in the case of fixtures (personal property that becomes attached to real property), Article 2A continues the true lessor's traditional exemption from public notice requirements. See comment 2 to 2A–301.

requirements merely by disguising their secured transactions as leases, the Article 9 rules will be undermined. For this reason, even before the adoption of Article 2A, the UCC definition of "security interest"[7] was elaborated to become the longest definition by far, in order to assure that courts will distinguish between "true" leases and false leases that are really security agreements that must meet Article 9 standards. If a court found that a purported lease of goods created a "security interest" within this definition, the "lessor's" interest in the goods would be subject to Article 9. In that case, the "lessor" might well lose its rights in the leased goods, particularly if the "lessee" was in bankruptcy proceedings, unless the lessor had perfected as provided in Article 9.[8] On the other hand, a lessor's rights under a "true lease"—i.e., one that did not create a "security interest"—would be valid even if the lessor had not met the Article 9 requirements.

Article 2A added several dimensions to the issue of whether a purported lease is in fact a disguised security interest. The definition of "lease" in 2A–103(1)(j) specifically excludes "retention or creation of a security interest." Whether a given transaction is in fact a lease under 2A–103(1)(j), requires a determination of whether the transaction creates a "security interest" under 1–201(b)(35). If the transaction does create a "security interest," it is not within the scope of Article 2A. See the official comment to 2A–103(1)(j).

At the time Article 2A was added to the official text of the UCC, the definition of "security interest," now in 1–201(b)(35) and 1–203,[9] was significantly modified. Under the pre-Article 2A version, a purported lease created a security interest subject to Article 9 if the lease "was intended as security" as "determined by the facts of each case." The definition provided only minimal guidance for distinguishing "true leases" from disguised security interests and generated a substantial volume of litigation involving rights to property worth many millions of dollars.[10] The purpose of the amendments to the definition of security interest that accompanied Article 2A was to provide clear and specific guidance on the lease/security interest distinction. The new version abandons the "intent" approach, substituting a test based on the economics of the transaction and providing a detailed guide to relevant factors.

---

7. The Amended Article 1 includes a definition of "security interest" in 1–201(b)(35) (2002), but also devotes a separate section to the distinction between leases and security interests (Amended § 1–203 (2002), incorporating the distinctions found in former 1–201(37)).

8. Because of the possibility that a "lease" will be found to create a disguised security interest, lessors frequently file "precautionary" financing statements that satisfy the perfection requirements of Article 9.

9. These two sections are derived from former § 1–201(37).

10. "Virtually every commercial law advance sheet contains a case or two in which the key issue is whether a transaction labeled as a 'lease' is, in fact, a true lease or, instead, a hidden security interest." Cohen, McLaughlin & Zaretsky, "Lease" or "Security Interest"? Impending Clarification, 1 Comm. L. Rep. 199 (1987).

Problem 5

Foundry Corporation has just leased a new hydraulic stamping machine from Apex Machine Tools, Inc. The five-year lease calls for annual rent of $10,000 due at the start of each year of the lease. For purposes of amortizing the cost of such machines, the federal tax code provides that they have a useful life of eight years. Five-year-old used machines can currently be purchased for $8,000. Does Article 2A apply? See 2A–103(1)(j), 1–201(b)(35), 1–203 and the official comments to those sections. Would any of the following alternative additional facts change your answer?

(a) A new machine can be purchased for $30,000;

(b) Foundry agreed to pay for all maintenance, taxes and other expenses associated with the machine, and agreed to continue paying rent even if the machine was damaged or destroyed (provided the casualty was not the fault of the lessor). Such provisions create what is frequently called a "net lease"—see the eighth paragraph of comment 2 to 1–203.

(c) Foundry has an option to purchase the machine at the end of the lease term for $100.

(d) Same as (c), except the option price is $10,000.

(e) Foundry had an option to purchase the machine at any time during the term of the lease for $51,000 less any lease payments made.

(f) At the end of the lease term Foundry could renew the lease for another five years at an annual rent of $100.

E. COMPUTER INFORMATION TRANSACTIONS—UCITA

The intended scope of UCITA is "computer information transactions," which include the creation or distribution of computer software, multimedia or interactive products, and computer data, as well as Internet and online distribution of information. "Computer Information" does not include other intellectual property such as print books, magazines, newspapers, motion picture, broadcast or sound recording products. The core concept is information, its content or capability, rather than the tangible medium such as a disk by which the information is delivered. A party may be said to purchase the disk copy which is a necessary delivery medium of the information, but the owner of the copy does not own the information or rights associated with the information. The information is licensed and may be used only within the confines of the terms of such a license. The information on the typical disk is copied on the purchaser's computer and the disk is retained only as security in the event the copied version is no longer available.

The UCITA definition of "computer" is "an electronic device that can perform substantial computations, including numerous arithmetic operations or logic operations, without human intervention during the computation or operation." The proposed Act does not, however, apply to computers per se. Nor does it apply to various goods that may contain automated systems such as the typical television set, VCR or automobile with increasing reliance on computerization. The subject matter is relegated to acquiring, accessing or using computer information. An "access contract" with America On–Line or similar company allowing access to the Internet with e-mail and other features would be a transaction within its scope. Just because a transaction is in electronic form, however, does not necessarily activate UCITA. Thus, the electronic purchase of an airline ticket or various purchases recorded in digital form, providing information electronically to a bank to secure a loan, or similar transactions are not covered. Again, the subject matter must be the computer information, access to it or use of it for the Act to apply. Thus, a contract for the creation or development of computer information such as the creation of databases or software development is within the scope of UCITA.

Problem 6

(a) Unicom Corporation developed copyrighted management information software which it sold throughout the world. The Internal Revenue Service (IRS) was interested in the system but required changes for its purposes. Unicom customized the software for the IRS and supplied a copy of the disk to the IRS under a contract limiting the use of this software to the IRS which received the software and used it for five months before notifying Unicom that it was defective. Unicom brings an action for the contract price of $450,000 while the IRS counterclaims for damages of $300,000. The jurisdiction whose law applies to the transaction has not enacted UCITA. One intermediate appellate case in the jurisdiction has determined that customized software is a good, while another intermediate appellate case holds that it is a service. Unicom claims that Article 2 of the UCC governs and, since the IRS failed to notify Unicom of any defects within a reasonable time after the goods were accepted, the IRS is barred from any remedy under UCC 2–607(3)(a).[1] Analyze.

(b) Assume the contract price of $450,000 included technical support by Unicom personnel. This included two Unicom employees on sight at IRS offices for a period of one year and available technical support thereafter by telephone or other communications to the main offices of Unicom for three more years. While the cost of personnel was not segregated in the contract, the estimated value of these services is $250,000. Does UCC Article 2 apply?

F. SCOPE AND STRUCTURE OF THE UNITED NATIONS CONVENTION ON INTERNATIONAL SALES OF GOODS (CISG)

Problem 7

American Discounts, Inc. (ADI) is a U.S. Corporation (incorporated in Delaware) which owns and operates a chain of 57 retail stores selling a full

---

1. 2–607(3)(a) states that a buyer's failure to give timely notice of a breach where the goods have been accepted bars the buyer's remedies for the breach, although the proposed amended version of 2–607(3)(a) would limit this to situations where the seller has been prejudiced by the lack of notice.

line of products aimed at the consumer market. Ruhr Products, Ltd. (RPL) is a manufacturer of various products, including electric shavers, with its principal place of business in Germany, although it has operations in a variety of European countries. A vice-president of ADI met with the General Manager of RPL and entered into a contract for the sale of 5000 Ruhr electric shavers, payment due 60 days after delivery. The contract documents were signed in New York. The contract does not contain any clause dealing with choice of law or choice of forum. ADI was aware that RPL produced the shavers at its principal manufacturing facility in Germany. The United States has ratified the Convention with the reservation permitted by Article 95 and Germany has ratified without that reservation. Answer the following questions:

(a) Does the contract involve an "international" sale to which the CISG applies? See Arts. 1(1) and 10(a).

(i) Would your answer change if ADI neither knew nor had reason to know that it was dealing with a manufacturer with a place of business outside the United States? See Art. 1(2).

(ii) Assuming ADI knew it was dealing with a German manufacturer, would your answer change if RPL negotiated the contract through an office it maintains in a country that has not ratified the Convention?

(b) Suppose ADI ordered specially manufactured electric shavers— i.e., it supplied specifications to RPL for particular shavers to be marketed under the ADI brand name. Does the CISG apply? See Art. 3(1).

(i) Suppose ADI supplied RPL special materials for manufacturing the shavers. Does the CISG apply? See Art. 3(1).

(ii) Suppose the ADI/RPL contract was for computers that RPL agreed to install and maintain for the next 10 years. Does the CISG apply? See Art. 3(2).

(c) A dispute arises concerning the contract.

(i) Suit is filed in New York. Does the CISG apply?

(ii) Suit is filed in Germany. Does the CISG apply?

(iii) Suit is filed in England, where RPL has a subsidiary. England has not ratified the Convention. Does the CISG apply?

(d) Suppose the buyer was located in Brazil rather than the United States. At the time the contract was formed, Brazil had not ratified the CISG. A dispute arises and the buyer sues RPL. The conflicts rule applied by the court leads to the application of the law of the seller's jurisdiction—Germany. Does the CISG apply?

(e) Suppose the buyer, ADI, was located in the United States but the seller was located in Japan. At the time the contract was formed, Japan had not ratified the CISG. Applicable choice of law principles point to the law of the buyer's jurisdiction, the U.S. Does the CISG apply?

Questions

1) Are consumer sales subject to the CISG? Does Article 2(a) of the Convention mean that the CISG does not apply to the sale of the shavers in Problem 7? Consider the exclusions in each of the remaining subparts of CISG Article 2. What is the reason for each such exclusion?

2) Suppose a shaver manufactured by RPL malfunctions and injures an ADI customer. Does the CISG apply in an action brought by the consumer against RPL? See Art. 5.

3) Suppose either ADI or RPL claims that the contract is unenforceable because it is "unconscionable," "grossly unfair" or illegal. Does the CISG apply to these questions? See Art. 4(a).

ASANTE TECHNOLOGIES, INC. v. PMC–SIERRA, INC.

United States District Court for the Northern District of California, 2001.
164 F.Supp. 2d 1142.

WARE, J. This lawsuit arises out of a dispute involving the sale of electronic components [computer chips, which the plaintiff contends failed to meet certain designated technical specifications]. Plaintiff, Asante Technologies Inc., filed the action in the Superior Court for the State of California. Defendant, PMC–Sierra, Inc., removed the action to this Court, asserting federal question jurisdiction. Specifically, Defendant asserts that Plaintiff's claims for breach of contract and breach of express warranty are governed by the United Nations Convention on Contracts for the International Sale of Goods ("CISG"). Plaintiff is a Delaware Corporation. Defendant is also a Delaware corporation [but,] at all relevant times, its corporate headquarters, inside sales and marketing office, public relations department, principal warehouse, and most design and engineering functions were located in Burnaby, British Columbia, Canada. Defendant also maintains an office in Portland, Oregon, where many of its engineers are based. Defendant's products are sold in California through Unique Technologies, which is an authorized distributor of Defendant's products in North America. It is undisputed that Defendant directed Plaintiff to purchase Defendant's products through Unique, and that Defendant honored purchase orders solicited by Unique. Unique is located in California. Determining Defendant's "place of business" with respect to its contract with Plaintiff is critical to the question of whether the Court has jurisdiction in this case.

Plaintiff's Complaint focuses on five purchase orders. Four of the five purchase orders were submitted to Defendant through Unique. However, Plaintiff does not dispute that one of the purchase orders, dated January 28, 2000, was sent by fax directly to Defendant in British Columbia, and that Defendant processed the order in British Columbia. Defendant shipped all orders to Plaintiff's headquarters in California. Upon delivery of the goods, Unique sent invoices to Plaintiff, at which time Plaintiff tendered payment to Unique either in California or in Nevada.

Plaintiff asserts that acceptance of each of its purchase orders was expressly conditioned upon acceptance by Defendant of Plaintiff's "Terms and Conditions," which were included with each Purchase Order. Paragraph 20 of Plaintiff's Terms and Conditions provides "APPLICABLE LAW. The validity [and] performance of this [purchase] order shall be governed by the laws of the state shown on Buyer's address on this order." The buyer's address as shown on each of the Purchase Orders is in San Jose, California. Alternatively, Defendant suggests that the terms of shipment are governed by a document entitled "PMC–Sierra TERMS AND CONDITIONS OF SALE." Paragraph 19 of Defendant's Terms and conditions provides "APPLICABLE LAW: The contract between the parties is made, governed by, and shall be construed in accordance with the laws of the Province of British Columbia and the laws of Canada applicable therein, which shall be deemed to be the proper law hereof...."

The Convention on Contracts for the International Sale of Goods ("CISG") is an international treaty which has been signed and ratified by the United States and Canada, among other countries. The CISG was adopted for the purpose of establishing "substantive provisions of law to govern the formation of international sales contracts and the rights and obligations of the buyer and the seller." The CISG applies "to contracts of sale of goods between parties whose places of business are in different States ... when the States are Contracting States." 15 U.S.C. App., Art.1(1)(a). Article 10 of the CISG provides that "if a party has more than one place of business, the place of business is that which has the closest relationship to the contract and its performance." 15 U.S.C. App. Art. 10.

The parties do not dispute that the CISG properly creates a private right of action. (U.S. Ratification of 1980 United Nations Convention on Contracts for the International Sale of Goods: Official English Text, 15 U.S.C. App. at 52 (1997): "The Convention sets out substantive provisions of law to govern the formation of international sales contracts and the rights and obligations of the buyer and seller. It will apply to sales contracts between parties with their places of business in different countries bound by Convention, provided the parties have left their contracts silent as to applicable law."). Therefore, if the CISG properly applies to this action, federal jurisdiction exists.

The CISG only applies when a contract is "between parties whose places of business are in different States." [In the context of the CISG, "different States" refers to different countries.] If this requirement is not satisfied, Defendant cannot claim jurisdiction under the CISG. It is undisputed that Plaintiff's place of business is Santa Clara County, California, U.S.A. It is further undisputed that during the relevant time period, Defendant's corporate headquarters, inside sales and marketing office, public relations department, principal warehouse, and most of its design and engineering functions were located in Burnaby, British Columbia, Canada. However, Plaintiff contends that, pursuant to Article 10 of the CISG, Defendant's "place of business" having the closest relationship to the contract at issue is the United States. Article 10(a) of the CISG states: "For the purposes of this Convention, if a party has more than one place of business, the place of business is that which has the closest relationship to the contract and its performance, having regard to the circumstances known to or contemplated by the parties at any time before or at the conclusion of the contract." Plaintiff asserts that Unique acted in the United States as an agent of Defendant, and that Plaintiff's contacts with Unique establish Defendant's place of business in the U.S. for the purposes of this contract.

Plaintiff has failed to persuade the Court that Unique acted as the agent of Defendant. [A] distributor of goods for resale is normally not treated as an agent of the manufacturer. Restatement of the Law of Agency, 2d § 14J (1957) ("One who receives goods from another for resale to a third person is not thereby the other's agent in the transaction."). Agency results "from the manifestation of consent by one person to another that the other shall act on his behalf and subject to his control, and consent by the other so to act." Restatement of the Law of Agency, 2d, § 1 (1957). Plaintiff has produced no evidence of consent by Defendant to be bound by the acts of Unique. To the contrary, Defendant cites the distributorship agreement with Unique, which expressly states that the contract does not "allow Distributor to create or assume any obligation on behalf of [Defendant] for any purpose whatsoever." Furthermore, while Unique may distribute Defendant's products, Plaintiff does not allege that Unique made any representations regarding technical specifications on behalf of Defendant. Indeed, Unique is not even mentioned in the Complaint. To the extent that representations were made regarding the technical specifications of the ASICs, and those specifications were not satisfied by the delivered goods, the relevant agreement is that between Plaintiff and Defendant. Accordingly, the Court finds that Unique is not an agent of Defendant in this dispute. Plaintiff's dealings with Unique do not establish Defendant's place of business in the United States.

Plaintiff's claims concern breaches of representations made by Defendant from Canada. Moreover, the products in question are manufactured in Canada, and Plaintiff knew that Defendant was Canadian, having sent one purchase order directly to Defendant in Canada by fax. The Court concludes that contacts [with defendant in Oregon] are not sufficient to override the fact that most if not all of Defendant's alleged representations regarding the technical specifications of the products emanated from Canada. Moreover, Plaintiff directly corresponded with Defendant at Defendant's Canadian address. Plaintiff relies on all of these alleged representations at length in its Complaint. In contrast, Plaintiff has not identified any specific representation or correspondence emanating from Defendant's Oregon branch. For these reasons, the Court finds that Defendant's place of business that has the closest relationship to the contract and its performance is British Columbia, Canada. Consequently, the contract at issue in this litigation is between parties from two different Contracting States, Canada and the United States. This contract therefore implicates the CISG.

Plaintiff next argues that, even if the Parties are from two nations that have adopted the CISG, the choice of law provisions in the "Terms and Conditions" set forth by both Parties reflect the Parties' intent to "opt out" of application of the treaty. Article 6 of the CISG provides that "the parties may exclude the application of the Convention or, subject to Article 12, derogate from or vary the effect of any of its provisions." 15 U.S.C. App., Art. 6. Defendant asserts that merely choosing the law of a jurisdiction is insufficient to opt out of the CISG, absent express exclusion of the CISG. The Court finds that the particular choice of law provisions in the "Terms and Conditions" of both parties are inadequate to effectuate an opt out of the CISG.

Although selection of a particular choice of law, such as "the California Commercial Code" or the "Uniform Commercial Code" *could* amount to implied exclusion of the CISG, the choice of law clauses at issue here do not evince a clear intent to opt out of the CISG. For example, Defendant's choice of applicable law adopts the law of British Columbia, and it is undisputed that the CISG *is* the law of British Columbia. Furthermore, even Plaintiff's choice of applicable law generally adopts the "laws of" the State of California, and California is bound by the Supremacy Clause to the treaties of the United States. U.S. Const. art. VI, cl. 2 ("This Constitution, and the laws of the United States which shall be made in pursuance thereof; and all treaties made, or which shall be made, under the authority of the United States, shall be the supreme law of the land.") Thus, under general California law, the CISG is applicable to contracts where the contracting parties are from different countries that have adopted the CISG. In the absence of clear language indicating that both contracting parties intended to opt out of the CISG, and in view of Defendant's Terms and Conditions which would apply the CISG, the Court rejects Plaintiff's contention that the choice of law provisions preclude the applicability of the CISG.

The Court concludes that the expressly stated goal of developing uniform international contract law to promote international trade indicates the intent of the parties to the treaty to have the treaty preempt state law causes of action. The availability of independent state contract law causes of action would frustrate the goals of uniformity and certainty embraced by the CISG. Allowing such avenues for potential liability would subject contracting parties to different states' laws and the very same ambiguities regarding international contracts that the CISG was designed to avoid. As a consequence, parties to international contracts would be unable to predict the applicable law, and the fundamental purpose of the CISG would be undermined.

Plaintiff next claims that the CISG does not completely supplant state law, because the CISG is limited in scope to the formation of the contract and the rights and obligations of the seller and buyer arising from the contract. (Id.) Plaintiff's correct observation that the CISG does not concern the validity of the contract or the effect which the contract may have on the property in the goods sold fails to support Plaintiff's conclusion that the CISG does not supplant *any area* of state contract law. Although the CISG is plainly limited in its scope (15 U.S.C. App., Art. 4.), the CISG nevertheless can and does preempt state contract law to the extent that the state causes of action fall within the scope of the CISG.

Finally, Plaintiff appears to confuse the matter of exclusive federal jurisdiction with preemption. Plaintiff first asserts that "if . . . the CISG is 'state law' . . . then the California courts have jurisdiction to adjudicate a case arising under these laws." The matter of whether California courts may have jurisdiction to interpret the CISG is irrelevant to the determination of whether the CISG preempts state law and establishes federal jurisdiction over the case. Even where federal law completely preempts state law, state courts may have concurrent jurisdiction over the federal claim if the defendant does not remove the case to federal court. This Court does not hold that it has exclusive jurisdiction over CISG claims. Hence, the Court's conclusion that the CISG preempts state claims is not inconsistent with Plaintiff's examples of the adjudication of CISG-based claims in state court. Plaintiff's motion to remand is denied.

Problem 7A

Draft language that would insure the application of domestic law such as the UCC instead of CISG.

Note

Suppose the CISG does not apply to an international transaction. What are the criteria for determining the choice of law? In ***Viva Vino Import Corp. v. Farnese Vini, S.r.l.***, 2000 WL 1224903 (E.D.Pa.2000), even though the United States and Italy are both CISG "contracting states," the court held that CISG was inapplicable to an exclusive distributorship agreement between a Pennsylvania Corporation and an Italian Company because the agreement did not cover the sale of specific goods or set forth definite quantities and price. Because the CISG was inapplicable, the court indicated that the transaction was governed either by the law of Italy or the law of Pennsylvania, which differed with respect to the issues raised in the litigation. In deciding which domestic law applied, the opinion states:

> In determining which jurisdiction has the greater interest in a contract dispute, Pennsylvania courts consider the following factors: (1) the place of contracting; (2) the place of negotiation of the contract; (3) the place of performance; (4) the location of the subject matter of the contract; and (5) the domicile, residence, nationality, place of incorporation, and place of business of the parties. See Benevento v. Life USA Holding, Inc., 61 F.Supp. 2d 407, 414–15 (E.D.Pa.1999).

> Applying the foregoing factors to the contract-based claims, the Court concludes that Pennsylvania has the greater interest in the

application of its law. Although the parties disagree as to whether negotiation of the agreements took place in Pennsylvania or Italy, it is clear that performance of the agreements was centered in Pennsylvania. On this issue, the Court rejects defendant's argument that performance was in Italy because its wines were shipped F.O.B., and that, as a result, defendant was not responsible for the wines once they were delivered to the shipper in Italy. Such terms of shipment certainly affect liability issues, but they do not alter the fact that performance of the contracts was to be primarily in Pennsylvania.

Choice of Law under the UCC. In domestic transactions where the UCC applies, except where otherwise noted in specific sections of other Articles, original *Section 1–105* allows the parties to choose the applicable law of a state or nation where the transaction "bears a reasonable relation" to the chosen state or nation. *Amended Section 1–301 (2002)* replaces 1–105 with significant changes. Like its predecessor, the amended section is not applicable where other specific UCC sections specify the applicable law. Where the parties designate the applicable law, different rules are provided for consumer and non-consumer (business to business) transactions. In non-consumer domestic transactions, the parties may choose the law of a U.S. State whether or not the transaction bears a reasonable relation to the designated State, i.e., greater autonomy is permitted in choosing the governing law. They may not, however, choose the law of a foreign nation in a domestic transaction. In an international transaction, the parties may designate the law of the forum State or any other State or country, whether or not the transaction bears a relation to the State or country designated. In either domestic or international transactions, however, a designation that would otherwise be effective is not effective if the law of the designated jurisdiction is contrary to a fundamental policy of the State or country whose law would govern in the absence of an agreement to designate the applicable law. Where one of the parties to the transaction is a consumer, the transaction must bear a reasonable relation to the state or country whose law is designated and the consumer may not be deprived of any protective law (statutes, regulations or case law) that cannot be varied by agreement. Typically, that consumer protective law will be the law of the jurisdiction where the consumer resides. If, however, the transaction is a sale of goods, the protective consumer law will be the law of the state where the contract is made and the consumer takes delivery of the goods. Where the parties have *not* designated the applicable law in their contract, the governing law will be determined by the conflict of laws principles of the forum, except that, again, a consumer may not be deprived of a law that would protect the consumer and could not be varied by agreement.

Chapter 2

THE CONTRACT LAW OF THE UCC—
ELECTRONIC CONTRACTS

A. RADICAL CHANGES IN TRADITIONAL CONTRACT LAW

Long before the UCC was enacted, Karl Llewellyn was a well-known critic of traditional, monistic contract law. He yearned for an anti-technical, realistic contracts jurisprudence that would reflect the "true understanding" of the parties. The contract law of Article 2 reflects his radically different views.

The UCC sparse definition of "contract" reflects the realistic thrust: " 'Contract' as distinguished from 'agreement,' means the total legal obligation that results from the parties' agreement as determined by [the Uniform Commercial Code] as supplemented by any other applicable law."[1] The focus is on the *agreement* of the parties, defined as "the bargain of the parties in fact as found in their language, or inferred from other circumstances, including course of performance, course of dealing or usage of trade...."[2] The purpose is to discover, as accurately as the *ex ante* evidence will allow, the actual or presumed agreement of the parties. That search must not be fettered by technical rules. Thus, a general formation section allows a contract to be formed in any manner sufficient to show agreement (2–204(1)), even though it cannot be determined exactly when the contract was made (2–204(2)) and even though numerous terms are missing from the agreement. The absence of the price term as well as terms setting forth the time or place of delivery will not preclude the finding of a contract so long as the parties manifested their intention to form a contract and there is a reasonably certain basis for providing an appropriate remedy (2–204(3)).

Article 2 allows offers to be accepted in any reasonable manner and by any reasonable medium. It changes the presumption that offerors have a particular manner of acceptance in mind. Thus, the normal offer

---

1. 1–201(12) (2002). References are to the latest (revised) version of Article 1. A similar definition of "contract" appeared in 1–201(11) of the earlier version.

2. 1–201(2).

under the UCC may be accepted either by promising or performing. An offeror can dictate a particular manner of acceptance only by unambiguously demanding it or where reasonable parties would contemplate such a singular manner of acceptance (2–206(1)(a)). The sacred "matching acceptance" ("mirror image") rule is substantially modified to allow the factual bargain of the parties to dominate unread fine print in boilerplate provisions of standard forms (2–207). The Article 2 version of the parol evidence rule precludes prior or contemporaneous evidence of agreement only when such agreements "would certainly" be included in final or complete writings, and those writings are no longer subject to a "plain meaning rule" of interpretation. Evidence of trade usage, course of dealing and course of performance will be admitted regardless of the completeness of the writing (2–202). The pre-existing duty rule is modified to allow good-faith modifications to be enforced without consideration (2–209(1)). Missing terms in a factual bargain will be supplied (2–305 and 2–307 through 2–311), and requirement and output contracts that the parties intend to be binding will not fail for indefiniteness (2–306).

These and other departures and modifications of pre-Code contract law reflect the underlying philosophy of Article 2: modern contract law should reflect the bargain the parties made, unhampered by technical rules. The influence of these radical modifications to general contract law, particularly reflected in the Restatement (Second) of Contracts, has been so pervasive that the changes effected by "Karl's Code" no longer appear as radical departures. Modern contract law, however, clearly reflects this Llewellyn perspective.

B.   CONTRACT FORMATION—2–204, 2–206, 2–504[1]

Problem 8

Super Appliances, Inc. (SAI) sent a purchase order to its normal distributor of television sets, TVI, which stated, in pertinent part, "Ship 200 32–inch Sony model 374 television sets at $490 per set." Consider each of the following reactions to this purchase order by TVI and provide your analysis as to whether a contract was formed.

(a) TVI received the SAI purchase order within two days after it was mailed and immediately mailed its acknowledgment to SAI. SAI received the acknowledgment two days after it was sent.

(b) Same as (a) except the acknowledgment was never received. Does 2–206 incorporate the common law "mailbox" ("dispatch") rule? See 1–103(b).

(c) Assume that TVI faxed or e-mailed its acknowledgment on the same day the purchase order was received. Would either be a reasonable medium

---

1. When studying these and any other provisions of the UCC cited in this book, students should also consider the sections cited in the "definitional cross references" following the comments to each UCC section.

under 2–206? Should the "mailbox" rule apply to faxes, e-mails or the like? Does 1–103 provide any assistance?

(d) TVI sent no message of any kind to SAI but, upon receipt of the purchase order, TVI immediately shipped the sets by independent carrier. See 2–206 and 2–504.

(e) As soon as the purchase order was received, TVI immediately took the 200 sets of the correct model from its inventory and began to load them on its own TVI truck for delivery to SAI. As the loading operation was underway, TVI received a fax from SAI canceling the order. See 2–206(2).

(f) Assume that TVI shipped the correct model sets as soon as the purchase order was received. It took three days for the sets to arrive. On the first day after the sets were shipped by TVI, SAI sent a message to TVI "canceling" the order. That message was received on the same day it was sent. On the morning of the third day, before the sets arrived at SAI's store, TVI sent its acknowledgment to SAI which arrived on the fifth day, i.e., two days after arrival of the sets.

(g) TVI shipped the sets but they were never received by SAI. They were destroyed when the independent trucker transporting the sets was involved in a head-on collision with a drunk driver whose car crossed the median barrier. SAI learned of this situation in a message from TVI one week after the accident. See 2–206(1)(b), 2–319(1), 2–509(1) and 2–503, comment 5.

(h) Upon receipt of the purchase order, TVI immediately shipped 200 Sony 32–inch sets, but they were model 376 instead of 374 as required by the purchase order. The sets were received by SAI. See 2–206(1)(b).

(i) Same as (h) except that TVI sent an E-mail to SAI stating: "Sorry that we do not have Model 374's in stock. We are sending model 376 sets in the hope that they will be satisfactory."

C. THE "BATTLE OF THE FORMS"—2–207

Many courses in contract law provide the student with background and analysis of the "battle of the forms" governed by 2–207 of the UCC. Even those students who have spent time with these complex issues, however, benefit from further confrontation with the "battle." Consider the following materials, which provide a variety of such confrontations.

COASTAL & NATIVE PLANT SPECIALTIES, INC. v. ENGINEERED TEXTILE PRODUCTS, INC.

United States District Court for the Northern District of Florida, 2001.
139 F.Supp. 2d 1326.

[Coastal purchased ten polyvinyl chloride (PVC) liners from Engineered Textile Products (ETP), which had purchased the material to make the liners from Occidental Chemical Corporation (OxyChem). Coastal allegedly suffered damages because the liners shrank and leaked chemicals, and it sued ETP. ETP, in turn, brought a third-party claim against OxyChem based on OxyChem's breaches of implied and express warranties, and upon OxyChem's negligent misrepresentations. ETP claimed that it reasonably relied upon OxyChem's representations and warranties when it purchased PVC material from OxyChem and when it fabricated liners for Coastal using that material. ETP had ordered the material by sending its purchase orders to OxyChem, which responded with invoices expressly conditioning its acceptance of the order on the buyer's assent to the terms on OxyChem's invoice. Those terms disclaimed warranties and limited OxyChem's liability to a return of the purchase price for that portion of the product that allegedly caused damages.]

COLLIER, J. This case involves a classic "battle of the forms" situation which can only be resolved by section 2–207 of the UCC. The drafters of the UCC designed this section to "allow parties to enforce their agreement ... despite discrepancies between a written offer and a written acceptance." 1 JAMES J. WHITE & ROBERT S. SUMMERS, UNIFORM COMMERCIAL CODE § 1–3 n.1 (4th ed.). It states as follows:

(1) A definite and seasonable expression of acceptance or a written confirmation which is sent within a reasonable time operates as an acceptance even though it states terms additional to or different from those offered or agreed upon, unless acceptance is expressly made conditional on assent to the additional or different terms.

(2) The additional terms are to be construed as proposals for addition to the contract. Between merchants such terms become part of the contract unless:

(a) The offer expressly limits acceptance to the terms of the offer;

(b) They materially alter it;

(c) notification of objection to them has already been given or is given within a reasonable time after notice of them is received.

(3) Conduct by both parties which recognizes the existence of a contract is sufficient to establish a contract for sale although the writings of the parties do not otherwise establish a contract. In such case the terms of the particular contract consist of those terms on which the writings of the parties agree, together with any supplementary terms incorporated under any other provisions of this Act.

Thus, section 2–207 contemplates contract formation via three different routes. Under subsection (1), the parties may form a contract by satisfying the language up to the comma. The parties can also form a contract by satisfying the language after the comma (also known as the "proviso"). Subsection (3) provides the third and final method of forming a contract. Therefore, before the Court can decide what terms govern ETP and OxyChem's agreements, the Court must determine the manner in which the parties formed their contracts.

In the case sub judice, OxyChem never accepted ETP's purchase orders. OxyChem's invoices made its acceptance "subject to and expressly conditioned" upon ETP's assent to the terms and conditions printed on the reverse side of the invoices. The invoices also expressly rejected ETP's terms. Thus, under the UCC, each invoice did not operate as an acceptance. The record fails to show ETP assented to the additional terms. Consequently, the parties never formed legally binding contracts upon the exchange of their written documents. This conclusion remains true notwithstanding the language in OxyChem's invoices stating "Buyer shall be deemed to have assented to the provisions hereof in all respects by its acceptance of any goods shipped or by failure to give Seller written notice of objection within five business days of Buyer's receipt of this invoice." Once OxyChem made a counteroffer, a contract could only be formed by ETP's express acceptance of the terms. Acceptance of the goods or failure to object does not constitute "assent" within the meaning of section 2–207(1).

This does not mean, however, the parties failed to form a contract. OxyChem shipped the goods after receiving ETP's purchase orders. ETP accepted the goods and paid for them before any dispute arose. Without a doubt the parties acknowledged the existence of a contract every time they conducted business with each other. Therefore, section 2–207(3) governs and the terms of each contract "consist of those terms on which the writings of the parties agree, together with any supplementary terms incorporated under any other provision" of the UCC. This conclusion begs the question: Can a party utilize section 2–207(2) to provide additional terms to a contract formed pursuant to section 2–207(3)? Stated differently, can OxyChem use subsection (2) to incorporate the terms printed on the reverse side of its invoice into the contracts formed with ETP? For the reasons stated below, the Court answers this question in the negative.

In C. Itoh & Co. v. Jordan Int'l Co., 552 F.2d 1228, 1236 (7th Cir.1977), the Seventh Circuit asked the following question: "What are the terms of a contract created by conduct under Section 2–207(3) rather than by an exchange of forms under Section 2–207(1)?" The appellate court explained:

> The second sentence of Section 2–207(3) provides that where, as here, a contract has been consummated by the conduct of the parties, "the terms of the particular contract consist of those terms on which the writings of the parties agree, together with any supplementary terms incorporated under any other provisions of this Act.".... We have been unable to find any case authority shedding light on the question of what constitutes "supplementary terms" within the meaning of Section 2–207(3) and the Official Comments to Section 2–207 provide no guidance in this regard. We are persuaded, however, that the disputed additional terms (i.e., those terms on which the writings of the parties do not agree) which are necessarily excluded from a Subsection (3) contract by the language, "terms on which the writings of the parties agree,"

cannot be brought back into the contract under the guise of "supplementary terms." This conclusion has substantial support among the commentators who have addressed themselves to the issue. Accordingly, we find that the "supplementary terms" contemplated by Section 2–207(3) are limited to those supplied by the standardized "gap-filler" provisions of Article Two. . . .

We are convinced that this conclusion does not result in any unfair prejudice to a seller who elects to insert in his standard sales acknowledgment form the statement that acceptance is expressly conditional on buyer's assent to additional terms contained therein. Such a seller obtains a substantial benefit under Section 2–207(1) through the inclusion of an "expressly conditional" clause. If he decides after the exchange of forms that the particular transaction is not in his best interest, Subsection (1) permits him to walk away from the transaction without incurring any liability so long as the buyer has not in the interim expressly assented to the additional terms. Moreover, whether or not a seller will be disadvantaged under Subsection (3) as a consequence of inserting an "expressly conditional" clause in his standard form is within his control. If the seller in fact does not intend to close a particular deal unless the additional terms are assented to, he can protect himself by not delivering the goods until such assent is forthcoming. If the seller does intend to close a deal irrespective of whether or not the buyer assents to the additional terms, he can hardly complain when the contract formed under Subsection (3) as a result of the parties' conduct is held not to include those terms. Although a seller who employs such an "expressly conditional" clause in his acknowledgment form would undoubtedly appreciate the dual advantage of not being bound to a contract under Subsection (1) if he elects not to perform and of having his additional terms imposed on the buyer under Subsection (3) in the event that performance is in his best interest, we do not believe such a result is contemplated by Section 2–207. Rather, while a seller may take advantage of an "expressly conditional" clause under Subsection (1) when he elects not to perform, he must accept the potential risk under Subsection (3) of not getting his additional terms when he elects to proceed with performance without first obtaining buyer's assent to those terms. Since the seller injected ambiguity into the transaction by inserting the "expressly conditional" clause in his form, he, and not the buyer, should bear the consequence of that ambiguity under Subsection (3).

Itoh, 552 F.2d at 1236—37

Thus, the court held that "supplementary terms," within the meaning of section 2–207(3), are limited to the standard gap-filler provisions of the UCC. Recently, the Supreme Judicial Court of Massachusetts declared: The criteria in subsection (2) determine what "additional or different terms" will or will not be part of a contract that is formed by the exchange of writings. Where the writings do not form a contract, subsection (3) states its own criteria—"those terms on which the writings agree" plus any terms that would be provided by other Code sections. One cannot turn to subsection (2) as another Code section that would supply a term when, by its express provisions, subsection (2) simply does not apply to the transaction. Commerce & Indus. Ins. Co. v. Bayer Corp., 433 Mass. 388, 742 N.E.2d 567, 573—74 (Mass. 2001); cf. McCarty v. Verson Allsteel Press Co., 89 Ill. App. 3d 498, 411 N.E.2d 936, 945, 44 Ill. Dec. 570 (Ill. App. Ct. 1980) (stating "it is well established that under this provision terms contained only in one of the party's forms are not part of the contract"). But see JOM, 193 F.3d at 54 (stating "the terms of their agreement would then be determined under the 'default' test in § 2–207(3), which implicitly incorporates the criteria prescribed in § 2–207(2)").

Based on the foregoing authority, subsection (2) only becomes operative when a contract is formed under subsection (1). Therefore, the Court holds that a party cannot utilize section 2–207(2) to provide additional terms once a contract is formed pursuant to section 2–207(3). When a contract is formed pursuant to section 2–207(3), as here, the contract terms consist of the standard gap-filler provisions of the UCC as well as those sections relating to course of performance and course of dealing and usage of trade.

As stated in this Court's previous order denying ETP's motion for summary judgment, the record before the Court contains too many facts in dispute to resolve this matter on summary judgment. Because the Court has determined that the parties did not form a contract based on the exchange of their written documents, issues of fact as to the contract terms remain. A fact finder must decide what terms govern the parties' agreements by examining the parties' course of performance and course of dealing and usage of trade,[1] and by applying the standard gap-filler provisions of the UCC. See N.Y. U.C.C. LAW §§ 1–205, 2–208, 2–301 to–319. Issues of fact also remain with regard to when ETP received OxyChem's invoices. If OxyChem's invoice arrived after the goods arrived, then section 2–207 does not control. Case law suggests section 2–206(1)(b) forms the contract in accord with ETP's terms, as well as the standard UCC gap-filler provisions. See, e.g., Wheaton Glass Co. v. Pharmex, Inc., 548 F.Supp. 1242, 1244—45 (D.N.J.1982); G.W. White & Son, Inc. v. Gosier, 219 A.D.2d 866, 632 N.Y.S.2d 910, 912 (N.Y.App.Div. 1995) (noting that "a disclaimer or exclusion of warranties delivered to the buyer after consummation of the sale is not effective unless the parties have entered into a separate agreement pursuant to ... § 2–209"); Niagara Real Estate, Inc. v. Wollstein, 198 A.D.2d 913, 604 N.Y.S.2d 464, 464 (N.Y.App.Div.1993) (stating the "terms are not binding upon the purchaser because the invoice was not sent within a

---

1. [Ed Note.] The court had previously adopted the view of the Seventh Circuit in Dresser Industries, Inc., Waukesha Engine Division v. Gradall Co., 965 F.2d 1442, 1451–52 (7th Cir.1992), providing a liberal interpretation of 2–207(3) by not limiting "supplementary terms" to UCC gap-fillers (2–301–2–319) but, on the basis of the phrase, "any other provisions of this Act," also incorporating terms created by trade usage and course of dealing (1–205) as well as course of performance (2–208).

reasonable time within the meaning of UCC 2–207(1)" and citing Wiencken v. Mill–Rite Sash Door Co. (In re Empire Pac. Indus., Inc.), 71 B.R. 500 (Bankr.D.Or.1987));[2] cf. First Sec. Mortgage Co. v. Goldmark Plastics Compounds, Inc., 862 F.Supp. 918, 934 (E.D.N.Y.1994) (finding that a seller failed to prove the buyer "ever received or even saw the reverse side of the bills of lading or the relevant language in the invoices at issue" and concluding the buyer "could not be bound by such provisions"); WHITE & SUMMERS § 1–5 (stating "where the buyer sends a purchase order, the seller then ships the goods, and thereafter sends a form that arrives after the goods arrive, 2–207 does not control"). OxyChem's motion for summary judgment is DENIED.

Problem 9

Using one of its purchase order forms (P.O. #3345897), the Sims Corporation offered to purchase 300 computerized cash registers, Model 987, from the Hart Corporation, at a unit price of $1,400, total price of $420,000, to be delivered no later than 45 days from the date of the purchase order. Hart responded with its acknowledgment form, which repeated all the foregoing terms of the Sims' P.O. and indicated it would deliver the registers within the time set forth in the purchase order. The Hart form contained the following printed clause ("boilerplate") among 14 other clauses:

> 4.   The goods described herein are warranted against any defects in materials and workmanship for a period of 90 days from the date of delivery. Seller will repair or replace (at seller's option) any defective part under this warranty. THIS WARRANTY IS IN LIEU OF ANY OTHER WARRANTY, EXPRESS OR IMPLIED, INCLUDING, WITHOUT LIMITATION, THE IMPLIED WARRANTY OF MERCHANTABILITY. The warranty and remedy expressed herein are the sole and exclusive warranty and remedy of the buyer with respect to this contract for sale. Seller will not be liable for any other loss or damage of

2.   In In re Empire, the bankruptcy court concluded that invoices sent by a seller were not "written confirmations" within the meaning of Oregon Revised Statute 72.2070 (the uniform counterpart of section 2–207 of the UCC) because the seller did not send the invoices within a reasonable time after the parties made their contracts. See 71 B.R. at 503. Prior to sending its invoices, the seller sent the buyer a written confirmation in the form of a copy of its production order. See id. The bankruptcy court determined that this was "the reasonable time to include proposals for additional terms to the oral contract." Id. The court explained:

> Sending such a proposal with the goods or after the goods were sent, as they were in this case, is not within a reasonable time of the making of the oral agreement. At the time the invoice was sent, the [seller] had completely performed its obligations under the contract by sending the

goods. To allow the seller to make proposals for additions to a contract it has already completely performed would work an injustice on the buyer, who in this case had accepted the goods on the basis of the terms agreed to orally. While the Uniform Commercial Code places upon buyers an obligation to inspect goods prior to accepting them, and will deem that they have been accepted if objection is not timely made, [2–606], it nowhere places an obligation upon the buyer to inspect the invoice which accompanies the goods at the risk of being deemed to accept any terms on the invoice to which it does not object. Thus, the terms on the reverse side of the invoices are not part of the contracts between these two parties. The contracts contain the terms which were agreed to orally, plus whatever provisions of the UCC that are necessary to fill any gaps in the agreement.

whatsoever kind or nature, including but not limited to CONSEQUEN-TIAL DAMAGE, whether arising from alleged breach of contract or tort duty. Any dispute concerning the terms of this contract will be submitted to arbitration under the rules of the American Arbitration Association.

The Sims P.O. was silent with respect to any of the terms found in Clause 4 of the Hart acknowledgment. After Sims received the acknowledgment, Hart shipped the registers. Sims took delivery of the goods and began to use them. Ninety-three days later, the 300 registers no longer functioned properly although they had been used only in normal business transactions for which they had been designed.

(a) Assume that the situation arose prior to the enactment of the Uniform Commercial Code in the relevant jurisdiction. What is your analysis under pre-Code law?

(b) Assuming the applicable law is UCC 2–207, consider the following issues:

(1) Is the Hart acknowledgment "a definite and seasonable expression of acceptance?"

(2) Are the terms in clause 4 of the Hart acknowledgment different or additional terms? If they are "different" terms, does 2–207(2) have any application? Consider the following excerpt.

REILLY FOAM CORP. v. RUBBERMAID CORP.

United States District Court for the Eastern District of Pennsylvania, 2002.
206 F.Supp.2d 643.

[In this contract action, the court was required to predict how the Supreme Court of Pennsylvania would deal with *different* terms in an acceptance that formed a contract under UCC 2–207. The court analyzed this issue as follows.]

SCHILLER, J. Frequently, businessmen do not set forth all of the terms of their agreements in a single, comprehensive document. Rather, deals are made on the basis of conversations and letters exchanged between the parties. Ultimately, one party reduces the terms of a proposed deal to writing, which is deemed an offer. Under the common law, a document qualifying as an offer could only be 'accepted' by a second document expressing acceptance on terms identical to the offer.

The rule changed with the enactment of the Battle of the Forms provision of the Pa.U.C.C., which permits an expression of acceptance to operate as an acceptance even if it contains *additional* or *different* terms. See Pa.U.C.C. § 2207(a). The *additional* terms become part of the contract unless: (1) the offer expressly limits acceptance to the terms of the offer; (2) the inserted term materially alters the offer; or (3) notification of objection to the inserted terms has been given or is given within a reasonable time. Pa.U.C.C. § 2207(b)(1)-(3).

The fate of *different* terms is less clear. Section 2207(b) does not directly address different terms in an acceptance, and the question remains: if the offer is accepted on different terms, should the terms of the offer control or should the acceptance be followed, or should the conflicting terms cancel each other out, to be replaced by gap fillers provided by the U.C.C.? The question has divided courts and scholars.

One approach considers any expression of acceptance with differing terms as actually a rejection and counter-offer. Thus, the terms outlined in the acceptance would govern. This view has been widely discredited as a revival of the common law rule, and the Court is not aware of any jurisdiction in which it is currently in force.

The minority view permits the terms of the offer to control. Because there is no rational distinction between additional terms and different terms, both are handled under § 2207(b). For support, advocates of this position point to Official Comment 3: "Whether or not *additional or different* terms will become part of the agreement depends upon the provisions of subsection [b]." *See Steiner v. Mobil Oil Corp.*, 20 Cal. 3d 90, 569 P.2d 751, 759–60 n. 5, 141 Cal. Rptr. 157 (Cal. 1977); *Boese-Hilburn Co. v. Dean Mach. Co.*, 616 S.W.2d 520, 527 (Mo.Ct.App.1981); *see also Mead Corp. v. McNally–Pittsburg Mfg. Corp.*, 654 F.2d 1197, 1204 & n. 11 (6th Cir.1981) (implicitly assuming, without holding, that different terms in acceptance would be subject to analysis under Ohio's version of § 2207(b)).[1] Professor Summers, the leading advocate of the minority rule, reasons that offerors have more reason to expect that the terms of their offer will be enforced than the recipient of an offer can hope that its inserted terms will be effective. *See* James J. White & Robert S. Summers, UNIFORM COMMERCIAL CODE § 1–3 at 35 (5th ed. 2000). The offeree at least had the opportunity to review the offer and object to its contents; if the recipient of an offer objected to a term, it should not have proceeded with the contract. *See id.* Following this approach, Reilly Foam urges that the terms of its March 26, 1999 letter and price list, as the offer, would control. Because each of Rubbermaid's new terms posed material alterations to the parties contract, they would have no effect.

The final approach, held by a majority of courts, is now known as the "knockout rule." Under this approach, terms of the contract include those upon which the parties agreed and gap fillers provided by the U.C.C. provisions. This approach recognizes the fundamental tenet behind U.C.C. § 2207: to repudiate the "mirror-image" rule of the common law. One should not be able to dictate the terms of the contract merely because one sent the offer. Indeed, the knockout rule recognizes that merchants are frequently willing to proceed with a transaction even though all terms have not been assented to. It would be inequitable to lend greater force to one party's preferred terms than the other's. As one court recently explained, "An approach other than the knock-out rule for

---

1. Judge Posner, speaking for himself, has advocated a similar rule: that the terms of the offer prevail over different terms set forth in the acceptance only if the different terms do not materially alter the contract. *See Northrop Corp. v. Litronic Indus.*, 29 F.3d 1173, 1178 (7th Cir.1994). However, as noted below, he predicted that Illinois would adopt the knockout rule.

conflicting terms would result in ... any offeror always prevailing on its terms solely because it sent the first form. That is not a desirable result, particularly when the parties have not negotiated for the challenged clause." *Richardson v. Union Carbide Indus. Gases Inc.*, 347 N.J. Super. 524, 790 A.2d 962, 968 (N.J.Super.Ct.App.Div.2002). Support for this view is also found in the Official U.C.C. Comments:

> Where clauses on confirming forms sent by both parties conflict each party must be assumed to object to a clause of the other conflicting with one on the confirmation sent by himself. As a result the requirement that there be notice of objection which is found in subsection [b] is satisfied and the conflicting terms do not become a part of the contract. The contract then consists of the terms originally expressly agreed to, terms on which the confirmations agree, and terms supplied by this Act, including subsection [b].

U.C.C. § 2207 cmt. 6.

Advocates of the knockout rule interpret Comment 6 to require the cancellation of terms in both parties' documents that conflict with one another, whether the terms are in confirmation notices or in the offer and acceptance themselves. A majority of courts now favor this approach. *See JOM, Inc. v. Adell Plastics, Inc.*, 193 F.3d 47, 54 (1st Cir.1999) (ascribing knockout rule to law of Maine and Maryland); *Ionics v. Elmwood Sensors, Inc.*, 110 F.3d 184, 189 (1st Cir.1997) (applying Massachusetts law); *Northrop Corp. v. Litronic Indus.*, 29 F.3d 1173, 1178 (7th Cir.1994) (describing this approach as "majority rule" and predicting Illinois would adopt it); *Daitom, Inc. v. Pennwalt Corp.*, 741 F.2d 1569, 1578–79 (10th Cir.1984)(applying Pennsylvania law); *Westinghouse Elec. Corp. v. Nielsons, Inc.*, 647 F.Supp. 896 (D.Colo.1986) (applying Colorado law); *Owens-Corning Fiberglas Corp. v. Sonic Dev. Corp.*, 546 F.Supp. 533 (D.Kan.1982) (applying Kansas law); *Armco Steel Corp. v. Isaacson Structural Steel Co.*, 611 P.2d 507, 518 & n. 30 (Alaska 1980); *Southern Idaho Pipe & Steel Co. v. Cal–Cut Pipe & Supply, Inc.*, 98 Idaho 495, 567 P.2d 1246, 1254–55 (Idaho 1977); *Uniroyal, Inc. v. Chambers Gasket & Mfg. Co.*, 177 Ind. App. 508, 380 N.E.2d 571, 578 (Ind.Ct.App.1978); *S.C. Gray, Inc. v. Ford Motor Co.*, 92 Mich. App. 789, 286 N.W.2d 34 (Mich.App.1979); *St. Paul Structural Steel Co. v. ABI Contracting, Inc.*, 364 N.W.2d 83 (N.D.1985) (applying Minnesota law); *Richardson*, 790 A.2d at 968 (applying New Jersey law); *Gardner Zemke Co. v. Dunham Bush, Inc.*, 115 N.M. 260, 850 P.2d 319, 325–26 (N.M. 1993); *Lory Fabrics, Inc. v. Dress Rehearsal, Inc.*, 78 A.D.2d 262, 434 N.Y.S.2d 359, 363 (N.Y.App.Div.1980); *Superior Boiler Works v. R.J. Sanders, Inc.*, 711 A.2d 628, 635 (R.I.1998); *Hartwig Farms, Inc. v. Pacific Gamble Robinson Co.*, 28 Wn.App. 539, 625 P.2d 171 (Wash.App. 1981).

[The court predicted that the Pennsylvania Supreme Court would adopt the "knockout" rule.]

Problem 9A

(a) The majority "knockout" rule applies where the offer and acceptance contain terms that *expressly* conflict. In Problem 9 *supra*, the Sims purchase order was silent concerning warranties and remedies. Does the "knockout" rule apply in that situation, or would the absence of any expressly conflicting terms in the Sims purchase order result in characterizing the terms in the Hart acknowledgment as *additional* terms to which 2–207(2) applied?

(b) Suppose the Sims P.O. in Problem 9 had contained a printed clause stating that all U.C.C. express and implied warranties and all remedies of the U.C.C. applied to the sale. Would the terms of clause 4 of the Hart acknowledgment then be converted to *different* terms to which 2–207(2) would not apply under the "knockout" rule?

(c) Are the terms of Hart's clause 4 acknowledgment in Problem 9 "material" terms? Consider the following case:

SOUTHERN ILLINOIS RIVERBOAT CASINO CRUISES, INC. v. TRIANGLE INSULATION AND SHEET METAL COMPANY

United States Court of Appeals for the Seventh Circuit, 2002.
302 F.3d 667.

MANION, CIRCUIT JUDGE. Southern Illinois Riverboat Casino Cruises, Inc. d/b/a Players Island Casino ("Players") owns and operates a casino river boat in Metropolis, Illinois. In March 2000, Players installed new exterior air conditioning unit ducts on the outside stern of its motor vessel, Players II, which operates as a gaming casino. [Players claims that Gary Holder, a representative of Triangle Co., recommended the type of sealant the casino should use to seal the ducts, and gave advice regarding the proper application of the product. Players ordered the recommended sealant which came in containers. The label on the containers included the following disclaimer of warranties and remedy limitation:]

> IMPORTANT: Childers [the manufacturer of the sealant] warrants that the materials herein contained, when shipped, conform to specifications and are of first class materials and workmanship. This product is sold upon the condition and agreement that there have been no representations or undertakings made by or on behalf of manufacturer and/or seller, and that there are no guarantees or warranties, express or implied in fact or by law, except as contained herein. Manufacturer and/or seller shall not be responsible, obligated or liable for any application or use of or to which the products may be put, either singly or in combination with other products or ingredients. It being expressly understood and agreed that manufacturer's and/or seller's liability shall in no event exceed the purchase price.

[The sealant was applied by Players personnel. Later that day, guests and employees of Players complained that they felt ill from air inside the vessel. Holder was summoned and, after inspecting, recommended that the sealant be removed. It was removed and discarded. The casino was closed for two or three business days. Players claimed that the air quality was affected by the sealant's fumes, and the cleanup, which "involved virtually the entire vessel, including air conditioning coils and fan motors on all of the air handlers on the boat," cost thousands of dollars. Players sought recovery for breach of warranty. The district court granted Triangle's summary judgment on this count and Players appealed.]

Players contends that the remedy limitation is not included in the parties' sales contract because it was an "additional term" under 810 ILCS § 5/ 2–207 (i.e., the "battle of the forms" section) that "materially altered" the agreement. [Here, the court quotes Section 2–207]. Players argues that the remedy limitation on the Encacel V container label is a per se material alteration of the parties' sales contract because any limitation on the right to recover consequential damages causes a significant and substantial shift in the ordinary allocation of risk. In support of this argument, Players relies heavily on the case of Album Graphics, Inc. v. Beatrice Foods Co., 87 Ill.App.3d 338, 408 N.E.2d 1041, 42 Ill.Dec. 332 (Ill.App.Ct. 1st Dist., 4th Div. 1980). In Album Graphics, a cosmetics company sued a glue manufacturer for breach of warranty when a weak adhesive that it purchased from the manufacturer caused its packages to come undone. 408 N.E.2d at 1043. The glue manufacturer defended the suit by contending that the warranty disclaimers and remedy limitations included on the glue container labels, as well as the shipping invoices, limited the cosmetic company's damages to the purchase price of the glue. 408 N.E.2d at 1044. The Album Graphics court held, after assuming the parties formed their contract prior to delivery of the product, that under § 5/2–207, "[a] term disclaiming warranties, and we might add a term limiting remedies, is undoubtedly a term that materially alters a contract ... [and] thus ... we necessarily conclude that ... the limitation of remedies language could [not] become part of the contract under section 2–207(2)". 408 N.E.2d at 1048 (emphasis added).

The holding of Album Graphics was, however, recently called into question by a different division of the same Illinois district appellate court in Intrastate Piping & Controls, Inc. v. Robert–James Sales, Inc., 315 Ill. App. 3d 248, 733 N.E.2d 718, 248 Ill. Dec. 43 (Ill.App.Ct. 1st Dist., 3d. Div. 2000). In Intrastate Piping, a pipe installation company sued a pipe manufacturer and "middleman" distributor for the cost of removing and replacing allegedly defective pipe. 733 N.E.2d at 720. As in Album Graphics, the Intrastate Piping parties disputed whether a disclaimer of warranties and remedy limitation were included in their sales contract by arguing over the time the agreement was made. The Intrastate Piping court held that regardless of the time of contract formation, "the remedy limitation—became part of the contracts by operation of statute'' because the buyer failed to seasonably object to it. In reaching this conclusion, the Intrastate Piping court rejected the Album Graphics court's determination that a remedy limitation is a per se material alteration of a sales contract, noting that in Album Graphics the court "ignored" Comment 5 to § 5/2–207, id., which provides, in pertinent part, that "examples of clauses which involve no element of unreasonable surprise and which therefore are to be incorporated in the contract unless notice of objection is seasonably given are . . . a clause . . . otherwise limiting remedy in a reasonable manner (see Sections 2–718 and 2–719)." § 5/2–207, U.C.C. cmt. 5. Not surprisingly, Triangle argues that Intrastate Piping controls our decision in this case.

The Supreme Court of Illinois has not yet addressed the issue before us: whether a remedy limitation may constitute a material alteration of a sales contract under § 5/2–207. In the absence of a decision by the state's highest court, "federal courts treat decisions by its intermediate appellate courts as authoritative, unless . . . a split among those courts makes such treatment impossible, or unless there is a compelling reason to doubt that the courts have got the law right." As we have already noted, there are only two intermediate appellate court decisions that have specifically addressed this issue, Album Graphics and Intrastate Piping. These decisions were made by different divisions of the First District Appellate Court of Illinois, and their holdings are clearly not consistent. We must, therefore, determine whether this split of authority makes it impossible for us to give authoritative effect to either decision.

At the outset of our analysis, we note that the Album Graphics court and the Intrastate Piping court both concluded that whether a remedy limitation materially alters a contract under § 5/2–207 is purely a question of law. The Album Graphics court held that a remedy limitation is a per se material alteration of a contract under the statute. The Intrastate Piping court, however, established a per se rule against treating any remedy limitation as a material alteration under § 5/2–207. Having carefully considered the holdings of both cases, we believe there is a compelling reason to doubt the correctness of the Album Graphics decision, at least as it pertains to remedy limitations, given the plain meaning of Comment 5 to § 5/2–207. On the other hand, the plain meaning of Comment 5 does support the Intrastate Piping decision. As explained by the court in re Chateaugay Corp., 162 B.R. 949 (Bankr. S.D.N.Y.1994), a case relied upon by the Intrastate Piping court:

> The literal provisions of the UCC appear to provide a straightforward basis for analyzing the inclusion of a remedy or damage limitation clause in a battle of the forms between merchants. Section 2–207, Official Uniform Comment No. 5 renders such clauses reasonable, *and directs the parties and the court to § 2–719.* Under the latter provision, limitations on remedies, including consequential damages, are reasonable *as a matter of law*, and do not materially alter the parties' agreement, unless the limitation on the remedy, such as to repair or replacement, fails of its essential purpose, or the limitation on consequential damages is unconscionable. . . . *This*

approach looks to § 2–719 rather than § 2–207 for the result in the case.

Id. at 956 (emphasis added).

We recognize that other courts "analyze the question of material alteration on a case-by-case basis as purely a factual one," see, e.g., Chateaugay Corp., 162 B.R. at 956, and that this circuit has utilized such an approach in prior U.C.C. cases, see, e.g., Union Carbide Corp. v. Oscar Mayer Foods Corp., 947 F.2d 1333, 1336–37 (7th Cir.1991). However, to date, no Illinois court has adopted such an approach with respect to remedy limitations. As such, Intrastate Piping is the controlling case on the issue before us, and we are required to give the decision preclusive effect because it is a permissible interpretation of § 5/2–207. We, therefore, conclude that after Intrastate Piping a remedy limitation cannot, as a matter of Illinois law, constitute a material alteration of a sales contract under § 5/2–207.

In sum, we conclude that the remedy limitation was not a material alteration of the parties' sales contract and became part of the agreement by operation of law, i.e., § 5/2–207, when Players failed to seasonably object to it. Having concluded that the remedy limitation is part of the parties' sales contract, we will now address the reasonableness of the clause under 810 ILCS § 5/2–719. Section 5/2–719(1)(a) provides that a sales contract "may provide for remedies in addition to or in substitution for those provided in this Article and may limit or alter the measure of damages recoverable under this Article, as by limiting the buyer's remedies to return of the goods and repayment of the price or to repair and replacement of nonconforming goods or parts." Id. If parties to a sales contract expressly agree for a remedy to be the exclusive remedy, it is the sole remedy available to the buyer, see § 5/2–719(1)(b), unless it fails of its essential purpose, § 5/2–719(2), or is unconscionable. See § 5/2–719(3).

As previously noted, the remedy limitation in this case confines Players's recovery to the "purchase price" of the Encacel V. This is clearly the type of exclusive remedy contemplated by § 5/2–719(1). The only question then is whether this remedy failed of its essential purpose or is unconscionable. Players does not, however, challenge the validity of the remedy limitation on either of these grounds, and therefore has waived this issue as well. We, therefore, AFFIRM the district court's grant of summary judgment on that basis.[1]

---

1. [Ed. Note.] Consider these other decisions dealing with the materiality issue. In Inspec Foams, Inc. v. Claremont Sales Corp., 2002 WL 1765630, (N.D.Ill.2002) Foams, supplied insulation products to Claremont at a price of $871,000. The Foams invoice stated, "net 45 days from date of invoice; 1.25% per month finance charge on late payments." Claremont claimed that the 1.25% finance charge was not enforceable because it was an additional term that did not become part of the contract under 2–207(2)(b). The court held that the finance charge was an immaterial term that became part of the contract between merchants under 2–207(2). See Comment 5 to 2–207.

In Hugo Boss Fashions, Inc. v. Sam's European Tailoring, 293 A.D.2d 296, 742 N.Y.S.2d 1 (2002), a California buyer ordered goods via telephone and fax from a New York seller. The seller's invoices con-

Problem 9B

(a) Assume the Hart acknowledgment form in Problem 9 contained, in addition to Clause 4, the following clause:

"7. This acceptance is expressly conditioned on buyer's assent to any different or additional terms contained on the front or reverse side of this form."

(i) After sending this acknowledgment, Hart refused to ship any registers to Sims unless Sims would agree to pay $1600 per unit. Sims alleges that Hart is breaching its contract. Analyze.

(ii) Having sent the acknowledgment containing clause 7, assume that Hart did not seek additional consideration but shipped the registers which Sims received and accepted. Is there a contract? If a contract exists, what are its terms?

(b) Assume that, prior to the sending of its P.O., Sims had inquired concerning Hart's price for 300 Model 987 cash registers. Hart replied with a detailed "quotation," which contained the exact terms of the deal. It also contained the clause 4 material. Assume that this "quotation" was an offer, i.e., it contained promissory language to convert it from a mere quotation to an offer. Consider the effect of the following responses from Sims:

(i) A purchase order that is silent concerning warranties and remedies.

(ii) A purchase order expressly limiting acceptance to the terms of the purchase order.

(iii) A purchase order that contained the following statement: "This purchase order is effective and expressly conditional on supplier's assent to all terms and conditions in this purchase order that are additional to or different from those stated in supplier's quotation or other offering documents. Supplier's assent to this provision will be manifested by delivery of any portion of the goods designated herein." See Mantaline v. PPG Industries, Inc., 225 F.3d 659 (6th Cir.2000).

D.   CONFIRMATIONS (2–207(1))

Problem 10

Apex Corporation placed a telephone order to the Daniels Company to purchase a computerized lathe, model X–35 at a price of $170,000. Daniels agreed to ship the lathe within 30 days. To confirm the agreement, Daniels sent an acknowledgment form containing an arbitration clause that had not been discussed on the telephone. Apex later alleged certain defects in the lathe and sued Daniels in court. Daniels made a motion to compel arbitration of the dispute, and Apex resisted. Analyze under 2–207. Would it matter if Daniels could prove that arbitrating disputes was an established usage in the relevant trade?

tained a clause stating that any disputes would be governed by New York Law and the buyer waived a trial by jury in any such litigation. When a dispute arose, the buyer claimed it was not bound by the forum selection clause in the seller's invoices. The court held that the clause was a material alteration that did not become part of the contract under 2–207(2).

E.   THE NEW (AMENDED) SECTION 2–207 (2002)

The 2002 Proposed Amendments to Article 2 contain a restructured Section 2–207. Issues of whether a contract has been formed on the basis of an acceptance that does not match the offer are no longer within the scope of proposed amended 2–207. The well-known language of pre-amendment 2–207(1) designed to reject the "last shot" principle is found in the proposed amended version of 2–206 (the offer and acceptance section):

> A definite and seasonable expression of acceptance in a record operates as an acceptance even if it contains terms additional to or different from the offer. Section 2–206(3) (2002).

Proposed amended 2–207 is called *Terms of Contract—Effect of Confirmation*, and it reads:

> If (i) conduct by both parties recognizes the existence of a contract although their records do not otherwise establish a contract, (ii) a contract is formed by an offer and acceptance, or (iii) a contract formed in any manner is confirmed by a record that contains terms additional to or different from those in the contract being confirmed, the terms of the contract, subject to Section 2–202 [the parol evidence rule], are:
>
>> (a) terms that appear in the records of both parties;
>>
>> (b) terms, whether in a record or not, to which both parties agree; and
>>
>> (c) terms supplied or incorporated under any provision of this Act.

Analysis: To avoid not only the "last shot" principle that was the evil at which the pre-amendment version of 2–207 was aimed, but also the "first shot" principle that could result by focusing exclusively upon the offer as controlling (as occurs in some situations under the pre-amendment version of 2–207), the rules on contract terms in the amended section avoid offer and acceptance terminology. Instead, if a court determines that a contract exists and the only issue is to define the terms of the contract, a term is deemed part of the contract only if it fits into one of the three rules stated in subparts (a), (b) or (c). Under subpart (a), if the same term appears in the records of both parties, it becomes part of the contract. The result obviously makes sense because both parties clearly intended to include the term in their contract. The rule means that conflicting terms in the parties' records, whether express or implied, are "knocked out." In fact, the former reporter for the revision of Article 2 calls the new 2–207 "a giant knockout" rule. In addition, terms that appear in only one party's record are not incorporated under subpart (a). The parties could, however, agree to a term even though it does not appear in either record or it appears in only one record. In that case, the term becomes part of the contract under subpart (b). Agreement to a term not found in a record can be manifested not only expressly, but also by trade usage, course of dealing or course of performance.[1] Finally, UCC gap-filling terms not displaced by the parties' agreement are incorporated into the contract under subsection (c).

Unlike the pre-amendment version of 2–207, proposed amended 2–207 does not attempt to distinguish "different" from "additional" terms. If a term is *either* different *or* additional, it by definition does not appear in both records and thus would not be incorporated into the contract under proposed amended 2–207(a). Unless such a different or additional term can be shown to have been agreed to under (b) or it replicates an implied term of the UCC under (c), it will not become part of the contract. Nor does the proposed amended section distinguish material and immaterial terms. Any term—material, immaterial, different or additional—will not become part of the contract unless it finds its way into subparts (a), (b) or (c).

F. CONTRACT FORMATION AND BATTLE OF THE FORMS— INTERNATIONAL SALES—CISG

Problem 11

(a) The Universal Power Company (UPC) is a United States public utility firm. In need of a new generator, UPC negotiated with several domestic and foreign suppliers. It finally chose Swiss Power, Ltd. (SPL), a firm located in a country that has ratified the CISG. UPC sent a letter to SPL offering to purchase an SPL generator, model 3600–X, at a price of $30 million. Upon receipt of this letter, SPL immediately mailed a letter accepting the offer. Is there a contract between the parties? See CISG Articles 14, 18(1) and 18(2). Suppose SPL's letter got lost in the mail and was never delivered?

(b) Assume the same facts as (a) except that, prior to dispatching its letter of acceptance, SPL received a fax from UPC revoking the offer. See Art. 16(1). Would it matter if the offer specified a date for acceptance? See Art. 16(2).

(c) Assume the same facts as (a) except that SPL received a revocation of the UPC offer after SPL had dispatched the acceptance.

(d) Assume the same facts as (a) except that, after dispatching its letter of acceptance, SPL changed its mind and dispatched a withdrawal of its acceptance. The withdrawal reached UPC at the same time the acceptance was received. See Arts. 18(2) and 22.

---

1. Of course a term in one record that reflects trade usage or course of dealing does not become an operative contract term because it appeared in a party's record. Such a term was an implied part of the original contract and of any record unless it was "carefully negated." A course of performance term can also become part of the parties' contract as a modification or as a waiver of an original term. Such a course of performance term could not have been part of the original agreement because it was created only after the contract was in the performance stage.

(e) Assume that SPL immediately dispatched a letter of acceptance that was promptly delivered to UPC, but SPL's acceptance included an arbitration term that was not part of UPC's offer. Is there a contract between the parties at this point and, if so, does it include SPL's arbitration term? Suppose that, after exchanging this correspondence, SPL shipped the generator to UPC, which accepted delivery. Is there a contract between the parties at this point and, if so, does it include SPL's arbitration term? Would any of your analysis change if the only difference between UPC's offer and SPL's letter of acceptance was that SPL proposed using a different shipping company to deliver the goods, although the delivery date would remain the same? Suppose that, after receiving SPL's letter, UPC had emailed SPL that it objected to the change, and then had refused to accept delivery of the generator SPL shipped, even though SPL used the shipping company UPC had originally proposed in its offer? See Art. 19.

Problem 11A

In a transaction governed by the CISG, Cool, Inc. (CI) sent an offer to World Products (WP) to purchase 1000 fabricated parts for use in the manufacture of refrigerators. The purchase order specified a price of $50 per unit and included the phrase "for immediate delivery." It also sufficiently identified the goods to be purchased. Upon receipt of the purchase order, WP immediately shipped the 1000 parts precisely as ordered. Before the goods reached CI, the freighter carrying the parts sank and the goods were lost. Assume that, if the parties have a contract, CI bears risk of loss (a matter explored in Chapter 5) and would have to pay for the goods. Do the parties have a contract? See Art. 18.

G.   THE BATTLE OF THE LEASES

Problem 12

The Monmouth Corporation (M) wished to lease a crane for use in installing the limestone sides of a skywalk between two buildings. The installation of the limestone sides required closing a city street, and M had to employ a special crew. It was, therefore, imperative that the installation occur on schedule. M contacted Leases, Inc. (L) and explained its special time-sensitive requirements. M then sent L a form captioned "Equipment Lease" covering the lease of specified crane for certain dates. L sent an acknowledgment which recited the same terms as M's form but added a clause excluding all consequential damages. L delivered a crane, but it was not the kind M had ordered nor did it meet M's needs. Waiting for a replacement crane delayed the installation work, costing M an additional $23,000. Analyze. Note that there is no counterpart to 2–207 in Article 2A on the footing that the typical leasing pattern does not involve a "battle of the forms."

H.   UCITA AND THE BATTLE OF THE FORMS

UCITA claims it follows original UCC Article 2 with respect to the "battle of the forms," but it presents a solution highly reminiscent of the

CISG analysis. The "battle of the records"[1] section of UCITA states, "[A] definite and seasonable expression of acceptance operates as an acceptance even if the acceptance contains terms that vary from the terms of the offer *unless the acceptance materially alters the offer*" UCITA 204(b) (emphasis supplied). Thus, unlike the result under UCC 2–207, if there is a materially variant term in the response to an offer, the response cannot be an acceptance under UCITA. The pre-UCC "mirror image" principle (leading to the "last shot" problem) is clearly evident in this structure, as it is under CISG. However, nonmatching terms in an acceptance which are not material do not preclude formation of a contract under the UCITA provision. Such additional terms are treated as proposals, but, between merchants, the proposed nonmaterial additional terms become part of the contract unless the offeror gives notice of objection before or within a reasonable time after receiving the proposed terms. UCITA 204(d).

I. THE OPERATIVE EFFECT OF POST–PURCHASE TERMS— "ROLLING" OR "LAYERED" CONTRACTS

When a buyer opens a package containing goods he has previously purchased, he may discover additional or different terms "inside the box." The original judicial reaction was to deny the operative effect of such terms since they were not part of the factual bargain of the parties and, therefore not part of their "agreement" as defined in UCC 1–201(b)(3). The inclusion of such new terms in packages of software containing software license terms (a "shrinkwrap license") which the buyer had not seen prior to purchase has become common in "mass marketing" transactions involving consumers or the general public. In *ProCD v. Zeidenberg*, 86 F.3d 1447 (7th Cir.1996), a customer purchased a copy of software in a retail computer store. There was an inconspicuous notice on the outside of the box about license terms contained inside. When the purchaser began to run the program, the license appeared on the screen as a condition to the use of the program. The purchaser used the program to create a new commercial venture, violating a" single-user" restriction in the license. When the licensor sought relief, the purchaser claimed that the sale was completed and all contract terms were settled when he paid for and took delivery of the software at the store before he had any opportunity to review the license terms. Reversing the lower court, the Seventh Circuit Court of Appeals broke new ground by enforcing the terms "inside the box." It was not long thereafter, that the same court confronted a similar question of the enforcement of post-purchase terms where not even an inconspicuous notice appeared on the outside of the box.

---

1. The broad (and now preferred) term "record" covers traditional writings and documents as well as electronic files. "Record" is defined in UETA § 2(13) as "information that is inscribed on a tangible medium or that is stored in an electronic or other medium and is retrievable in perceivable form." The shorthand term,"retrievable perceivable," is probable if not inevitable.

HILL v. GATEWAY 2000, INC.

United States Court of Appeals for the Seventh Circuit, 1997.
105 F.3d 1147.

EASTERBROOK, CIRCUIT JUDGE. A customer picks up the phone, orders a computer, and gives a credit card number. Presently a box arrives, containing the computer and a list of terms, said to govern unless the customer returns the computer within 30 days. Are these terms effective as the parties' contract, or is the contract term-free because the order-taker did not read any terms over the phone and elicit the customer's assent?

One of the terms in the box containing a Gateway 2000 system was an arbitration clause. Rich and Enza Hill, the customers, kept the computer more than 30 days before complaining about its components and performance. They filed suit in federal court. Gateway asked the district court to enforce the arbitration clause; the judge refused, writing that "the present record is insufficient to support a finding of a valid arbitration agreement between the parties or that the plaintiffs were given adequate notice of the arbitration clause." Gateway took an immediate appeal, as is its right.

The Hills say that the arbitration clause did not stand out: they concede noticing the statement of terms but deny reading it closely enough to discover the agreement to arbitrate, and they ask us to conclude that they therefore may go to court. Terms inside Gateway's box stand or fall together. If they constitute the parties' contract because the Hills had an opportunity to return the computer after reading them, then all must be enforced.

ProCD, Inc. v. Zeidenberg, 86 F.3d 1447 (7th Cir.1996), holds that terms inside a box of software bind consumers who use the software after an opportunity to read the terms and to reject them by returning the product. Likewise, *Carnival Cruise Lines, Inc. v. Shute*, 499 U.S. 585, 113 L.Ed.2d 622, 111 S.Ct. 1522 (1991), enforces a forum-selection clause that was included among three pages of terms attached to a cruise ship ticket. ProCD and Carnival Cruise Lines exemplify the many commercial transactions in which people pay for products with terms to follow; ProCD discusses others. 86 F.3d at 1451–52. The district court concluded in ProCD that the contract is formed when the consumer pays for the software; as a result, the court held, only terms known to the consumer at that moment are part of the contract, and provisos inside the box do not count. Although this is one way a contract could be formed, it is not the only way: "A vendor, as master of the offer, may invite acceptance by conduct, and may propose limitations on the kind of conduct that constitutes acceptance. A buyer may accept by performing the acts the vendor proposes to treat as acceptance." *Id.* at 1452. Gateway shipped computers with the same sort of accept-or-return offer ProCD made to users of its software.

Plaintiffs ask us to limit ProCD to software, but where's the sense in that? ProCD is about the law of contract, not the law of software. Payment preceding the revelation of full terms is common for air transportation, insurance, and many other endeavors. Practical considerations support allowing vendors to enclose the full legal terms with their products. Cashiers cannot be expected to read legal documents to customers before ringing up sales. If the staff at the other end of the phone for direct-sales operations such as Gateway's had to read the four-page statement of terms before taking the buyer's credit card number, the droning voice would anesthetize rather than enlighten many potential buyers. Others would hang up in a rage over the waste of their time. And oral recitation would not avoid customers' assertions (whether true or feigned) that the clerk did not read term X to them, or that they did not remember or understand it. Writing provides benefits for both sides of commercial transactions. Customers as a group are better off when vendors skip costly and ineffectual steps such as telephonic recitation, and use instead a simple approve-or-return device. Competent adults are bound by such documents, read or unread. For what little it is worth, we add that the box from Gateway was crammed with software. The computer came with an operating system, without which it was useful only as a boat anchor. Gateway also included many application programs. So the Hills' effort to limit ProCD to software would not avail them factually, even if it were sound legally—which it is not.

For their second sally, the Hills contend that ProCD should be limited to executory contracts (to licenses in particular), and therefore does not apply because both parties' performance of this contract was complete when the box arrived at their home. This is legally and factually wrong: legally because the question at hand concerns the formation of the contract rather than its performance, and factually because both contracts were incompletely performed. ProCD did not depend on the fact that the seller characterized the transaction as a license rather than as a contract; we treated it as a contract for the sale of goods and reserved the question whether for other purposes a "license" characterization might be preferable. All debates about characterization to one side, the transaction in ProCD was no more executory than the one here: Zeidenberg paid for the software and walked out of the store with a box under his arm, so if arrival of the box with the product ends the time for revelation of contractual terms, then the time ended in ProCD before Zeidenberg opened the box. But of course ProCD had not completed performance with delivery of the box, and neither had Gateway. One element of the transaction was the warranty, which obliges sellers to fix defects in their products. The Hills have invoked Gateway's warranty and are not satisfied with its response, so they are not well positioned to say that Gateway's obligations were fulfilled when the motor carrier unloaded the box. What is more, both ProCD and Gateway promised to help customers to use their products. Long-term service and information obligations are common in the computer business, on both hardware and software sides. Gateway offers "lifetime service" and has a round-the-clock telephone hotline to fulfil this promise. Some vendors spend more money helping customers use their products than on developing and manufacturing them. The document in Gateway's box includes promises of future performance that some consumers value highly; these promises bind Gateway just as the arbitration clause binds the Hills.

Next the Hills insist that ProCD is irrelevant because Zeidenberg was a "merchant" and they are not. Section 2–207(2) of the UCC, the infamous battle-of-the-forms section, states that "additional terms [following acceptance of an offer] are to be construed as proposals for addition to a contract. Between merchants such terms become part of the contract unless . . .". Plaintiffs tell us that ProCD came out as it did only because Zeidenberg was a "merchant" and the terms inside ProCD's box were not excluded by the "unless" clause. This argument pays scant attention to the opinion in ProCD, which concluded that, when there is only one form, "§ 2–207 is irrelevant." 86 F.3d at 1452. The question in ProCD was not whether terms were added to a contract after its formation, but how and when the contract was formed—in particular, whether a vendor may propose that a contract of sale be formed, not in the store (or over the phone) with the payment of money or a general "send me the product," but after the customer has had a chance to inspect both the item and the terms. ProCD answers "yes," for merchants and consumers alike. Yet again, for what little it is worth we observe that the Hills misunderstand the setting of ProCD. A "merchant" under the UCC "means a person who deals in goods of the kind or otherwise by his occupation holds himself out as having knowledge or skill peculiar to the practices or goods involved in the transaction", § 2–104(1). Zeidenberg bought the product at a retail store, an uncommon place for merchants to acquire inventory. His corporation put ProCD's database on the Internet for anyone to browse, which led to the litigation but did not make Zeidenberg a software merchant.

At oral argument the Hills propounded still another distinction: the box containing ProCD's software displayed a notice that additional terms were within, while the box containing Gateway's computer did not. The difference is functional, not legal. Consumers browsing the aisles of a store can look at the box, and if they are unwilling to deal with the prospect of additional terms can leave the box alone, avoiding the transactions costs of returning the package after reviewing its contents. Gateway's box, by contrast, is just a shipping carton; it is not on display anywhere. Its function is to protect the product during transit, and the information on its sides is for the use of handlers ("Fragile!" "This Side Up!") rather than would-be purchasers.

Perhaps the Hills would have had a better argument if they were first alerted to the bundling of hardware and legal-ware after opening the box and wanted to return the computer in order to avoid disagreeable terms, but were dissuaded by the expense of shipping. What the remedy would be in such a case—could it exceed the shipping charges?—is an interesting question, but one that need not detain us because the

Hills knew before they ordered the computer that the carton would include some important terms, and they did not seek to discover these in advance. Gateway's ads state that their products come with limited warranties and lifetime support. How limited was the warranty—30 days, with service contingent on shipping the computer back, or five years, with free onsite service? What sort of support was offered? Shoppers have three principal ways to discover these things. First, they can ask the vendor to send a copy before deciding whether to buy. The Magnuson–Moss Warranty Act requires firms to distribute their warranty terms on request, *15 U.S.C. § 2302*(b)(1)(A)[1]; the Hills do not contend that Gateway would have refused to enclose the remaining terms too. Concealment would be bad for business, scaring some customers away and leading to excess returns from others. Second, shoppers can consult public sources (computer magazines, the Web sites of vendors) that may contain this information. Third, they may inspect the documents after the product's delivery. Like Zeidenberg, the Hills took the third option. By keeping the computer beyond 30 days, the Hills accepted Gateway's offer, including the arbitration clause.

The decision of the district court is vacated, and this case is remanded with instructions to compel the Hills to submit their dispute to arbitration.

Notes

"Rolling" or "Layered" Contract Theory. The United States Court of Appeals for the Seventh Circuit created the "rolling or "layered" contract theory in *ProCD v. Zeidenberg*, 86 F.3d 1447 (7th Cir.1996), and in the principal case, which was handed down six months later. In *ProCD*, the defendant purchased the plaintiff's software by removing the package containing the diskette from a display shelf in a retail computer store and paying the $150 price at the checkout counter. The software contained millions of telephone numbers taken from the white pages of telephone books. The information could not be copyrighted. *ProCD* made two versions of the software, a commercial version that sold for a much higher price and the retail version. On the outside of the package purchased by Zeidenberg, a fine print statement indicated that the sale was subject to license terms that were inside the box.[2] The terms were printed in a manual and splashed on

---

1. [Ed. Note.] The Magnuson–Moss Warranty Act provides protection for buyers of consumer products where the supplier makes a written warranty as defined in the Act. The Act and its interpretation are reviewed in Chapter 3.

2. The term "shrinkwrap license" is derived from the packaging used for commercial software–i. e., software packages are covered in tight plastic or cellophane "shrinkwrap." The entire license may be printed on the outside of the package in very fine print with a statement indicating that tearing the shrinkwrap constitutes an acceptance of the license terms. In Specht v. Netscape Communications, Corp., 150 F.Supp. 2d 585 (S.D.N.Y.2001), the court distinguished "shrinkwrap" licenses such as those in *ProCD* from "click-wrap" licenses that require a party to click on an icon indicating agreement to license terms before the software can be downloaded, and from "browse-wrap" licenses that allow but do not require the user to discover license terms before the software can be downloaded. The court held that "click-wrap" licenses manifest the mutual assent required to incorporate terms into a contract, but

the monitor screen when the program was run. They limited the program to non-commercial purposes. Zeidenberg copied the information, and used it to create his own commercial software that he marketed. *ProCD* sued to enjoin such use.

Zeidenberg argued that the contract was made when he took the product from the shelf and paid for it, thereby accepting the offer impliedly made by the store when it displayed the product on the shelf and invited customers to buy it. Thus, Zeidenberg argued, he was unaware of the terms "inside the box" when the contract was formed. The trial court agreed and found that the terms were not part of the contract. Its analysis was similar to that a *Step–Saver Data Systems, Inc. v. Wyse Technology,* 939 F.2d 91 (3d Cir. 1991), which involved software license terms printed on the outside of the box containing the software, with the admonition that, by opening the box, the purchaser agreed to the license terms. That court held that the contract had been formed prior to the delivery of the disks, and the terms printed on the box constituted an attempt to incorporate different or additional terms. They did not become part of the contract under 2–207, the *Step–Saver* court held, since they were material alterations of the terms of the already-formed contract.

On appeal in the *ProCD* case, however, the Seventh Circuit, in an opinion by Judge Easterbrook (who also wrote the opinion in the principal case), held that the terms of ProCD's license were enforceable even though Zeidenberg saw them for the first time only after he had purchased the software. The court asserted that "[n]otice on the outside, terms on the inside, and a right to return the software for a refund if the terms are unacceptable (a right that the license expressly extends), may be a means of doing business valuable to buyer and sellers alike."[3] According to the *ProCD* opinion, the contract is not formed when the parties presumably think it is— i.e., when the buyer takes the goods from the shelf and pays for them. It is a "rolling" formation process. The contract is not formed until the buyer has an opportunity to learn of the terms inside the box and decide whether to accept them. If the buyer either uses the product with actual or presumed knowledge of the terms or, as in *Hill v. Gateway*, does not object to the

"browse-wrap" licenses fail to demonstrate such assent. The plaintiffs, therefore, were not bound to the terms of a "browse-wrap" license. In Rinaldi v. Iomega Corp., 1999 WL 1442014 (Del.Super.1999), the court held that a disclaimer of the implied warranty of merchantability in a shrinkwrap license placed inside the packaging of a "Zip" drive was enforceable under the "rolling" contract analysis.

3. The court noted the efficiency of "standardized" contracts, which reduce the seller's transaction costs, resulting theoretically in lower prices for buyers. The buyer also saves transaction costs by not having to hire a lawyer to advise the buyer in such transactions. This analysis carries the huge assumption that the standardized terms will be fair. Supporters of the theory argue that competition helps assure fair terms. Moreover, courts have the power to police

against any bizarre or oppressive terms in standardized, unread and incomprehensible boilerplate through the doctrine of unconscionability. See M. A. Mortenson Co. v. Timberline Software Corp., 93 Wash.App. 819, 970 P.2d 803 (1999), where a court applied the "rolling" contract theory but found an arbitration provision in the previously unseen terms to be unconscionable. The *ProCD* analysis has also been followed in Brower v. Gateway 2000, Inc., 246 A.D.2d 246, 676 N.Y.S.2d 569 (1st Dep't 1998). In Klocek v. Gateway, Inc., 104 F.Supp.2d 1332 (D.Kan.2000), however, the court rejected the *ProCD* analysis on the footing that the Seventh Circuit had mistakenly interpreted 2–207. The court also indicated that it could not discern how the Seventh Circuit concluded that Gateway was the offeror in *Hill v. Gateway.*

terms inside the box for the stated period of time, the use of the product or the silence of the buyer constitutes an acceptance of the offer made by the seller. At that point, the "rolling" contract has come to the end of its journey or, if you will, the final "layer" of the formation process has been laid down.

In *ProCD,* the court sought to "distinguish" *Step-Saver* and two similar cases by suggesting that they were not "consumer transactions," and that *Step–Saver* was a "battle of the forms" case involving two forms whereas the *ProCD* case involved only one form (the terms inside the box).

Questions

(i) Does 2–207 apply only to "merchants"? Consider the first and second sentences of 2–207(2). See also Lucien Bourque, Inc. v. Cronkite, 557 A.2d 193 (Me.1989) and Lemmer v. IDS Properties, Inc., 304 N.W.2d 864 (Minn. 1980). Notwithstanding that *ProCD* distinguished *Step–Saver* on the basis that *Step–Saver* was not a consumer case, what does Judge Easterbrook say about the application of the "rolling" or "layered" contract theory in *Hill*?

(ii) Does 2–207 apply only where there are "two forms" as suggested by *ProCD* and *Hill*? Consider the language of 2–207(1) and the opening language of Comment 1 concerning the term "confirmation." Also consider a well-known 2–207 case in which a telephone offer or contract was made, followed by the sending of a confirmation that included different or additional terms. Dorton v. Collins & Aikman Corp., 453 F.2d 1161 (6th Cir.1972).

(iii) Was there any notice on the outside of the box in *Hill*? What happened to the "notice on the outside, terms on the inside" analysis from *ProCD*? According to the court, where were the Hills supposed to learn about the terms "inside the box" before they received and opened the box?

(iv) In a self-service transaction such as that in *ProCD*, there is authority for finding that the seller made the offer in displaying the goods on shelves and inviting customer to take the goods from the shelves and pay for them. In a telephone (800 number) transaction such as *Hill*, who is the offeror? Having determined that 2–207 was not applicable, the *Hill* opinion relies on 2–204(1), the general formation section that allows a contract to be "made in any manner sufficient to show agreement." The court emphasizes that the UCC continues the common law view that the offeror is "master of the offer" and that Gateway could, therefore, make any offer it chose to make. Was Gateway the offeror in the *Hill* case as suggested by the court? Are sellers who induce buyers through advertising to "order" goods through 800 (or similar) telephone numbers "offerors"?

(v) Can you conceive of a way in which a telephone operator in a transaction like *Hill* could alert a buyer of terms without reading "four page statements"?

(vi) Assuming, arguendo, that 2–207 does not apply in a situation like *Hill*, does Section 2–209(1) apply to "inside-the-box" terms? If it does apply, would such terms be enforceable?

(vii) In *ProCD* and *Hill*, the court refers to a United States Supreme Court case, Carnival Cruise Lines v. Shute, 499 U.S. 585 (1991), where a divided court upheld a forum selection clause printed on the back of a cruise line ticket. While the majority insisted that its decision rested upon the assumption that the "respondents had sufficient notice of the forum clause before entering the contract," can you make an effective argument, consistent with UCC provisions, that certain printed clauses not communicated at the time of the original transaction are binding? Could such an argument have been made in *ProCD* concerning the term at issue in that case–i.e., a term limiting used of the software to non-commercial use?

The Proposed Amendment to Section 2–207. Comment 5 to proposed amended 2–207 takes no position on the question of whether a court should follow the reasoning of the *Hill* case (i.e., the "rolling contract" theory) or should follow Step–Saver Data Systems v. Wyse Technology, 939 F.2d 91 (3d Cir.1991) (contract to purchase software was made orally at the time of ordering, and the terms printed on the container or otherwise inside the box become part of the contract only if they comply with pre-amendment 2–207). It is interesting to note that, unlike Judge Easterbrook, the drafters of the amendment see a clear conflict between these two approaches, i.e., there is no possibility of "distinguishing" the cases.

J.   UCITA—"LAYERED" CONTRACTS AND "MASS MARKET LICENSES"

The committees charged with revising Article 2 and with drafting the Uniform Computer Information Transactions Act (UCITA) had been attempting to address the issue of the binding effect of post-formation terms in only one record (the seller's record) prior to the *ProCD* and *Hill v. Gateway* opinions from the Seventh Circuit. The appearance of these opinions emphasized the need for statutory guidance since an earlier draft of revised Article 2 had indicated a highly favorable response to the *Step-Saver* opinion–an opinion which, although allegedly distinguished in *ProCD*, clearly suggests a contrary analysis. The revisers of Article 2, however, finally decided to take no position with respect to these issues. The UCITA drafters, however, adopted the *ProCD* analysis.

Under UCITA Section 208 (Adopting the Terms of Records), a party may adopt the terms of a record by agreeing to such terms through a manifestation of assent, which requires an "opportunity to review" (Section 112). Section 208 "rejects the idea that a contract and all terms must be formed at a single point in time." Rather, a party may adopt the terms of a contract "after beginning performance or use under the agreement, if the parties had reason to know that their agreement would be represented in whole or in part by a later record to be agreed on and there would be no opportunity to review the record or a copy of it before performance or use began." Thus, the Act adopts the "layered contracting" theory, i.e., formation of the contract does not occur at one time such as when the disk on which the software is recorded is purchased. "Layered" or "rolling" contract formation can also encompass terms later discovered, as when the buyer finds the terms "inside the box" or splashed on the computer screen. Section 209 ("Mass–Market License") then allows a party to assent to terms after the initial agreement, but it must occur no later than during the initial use of the information. The terms of the agreement must be such that a reasonable person ought to have noticed them, which would be the case, e.g., if the terms of the information license are displayed on the screen and the party must manifest assent before using the information through a keyboard or mouse signal. UCITA Section 211 provides guidance for *pretransaction disclosures in Internet transactions*, which are designed to create an opportunity for the licensee to review license terms before the initial agreement. If the party does not agree to license terms that it receives after acquiring computer information, Sections 112(e) and 209 allow for a return of the purchase price as well as any other reasonable expenses or foreseeable costs associated with attempts to use the information. The fact that the license terms are non-negotiable, i.e., a contract of adhesion, does not invalidate them, although an argument that they are unconscionable is not precluded. If, however, a party has had an opportunity to review a record containing such terms and manifests assent thereto, such facts strongly suggest that such terms are not unconscionable.

K. THE "REASONABLE EXPECTATIONS" DOCTRINE

The issue of the binding effect of boilerplate terms where the transaction involves only a single form is one that has challenged courts for much of the twentieth century. The essential question is whether one is bound by what he signs or to which he otherwise assents, whether he read or understood such terms. Unless parties are bound by terms to which they appear to have assented, the stability of contracts is threatened. Yet, it is abundantly clear that reasonable parties often sign or otherwise manifest assent to standardized agreements that they do not read or understand. If the ignored boilerplate in such agreements turns out to contain bizarre or oppressive terms, the party who seemed to assent will be unfairly surprised by such terms. Attempts to deal with the tension of binding a party to unread boilerplate while not oppressing the party with unfair terms that have not truly been assented to has proven to be a major challenge.

Section 211 of the Restatement (Second) of Contracts suggests that where the provider of a standardized form has "reason to believe" that the other party would not assent to certain boilerplate terms, they are not binding; otherwise they are binding. Three decades ago, Professor, later Judge, Robert Keeton wrote a two part article in which he suggested two basic principles in relation to insurance contracts: (1) that an insurer should be denied any unconscionable advantage in such contracts, and (2) that the "reasonable expectations" of insureds and beneficiaries should be preserved. Robert E. Keeton, *Insurance Law Rights at Variance With Policy Provisions*, 83 HARV. L. REV. 961 (1970); Robert E. Keeton, *Insurance Law Rights at Variance with Policy Provisions: Part Two*, 83 HARV. L. REV. 1281 (1970). The second principle is now widely known as the "doctrine of reasonable expectations." The test would bind a party to boilerplate terms that are "reasonably expected," but not to those that are not reasonably expected The "reasonable expectations" doctrine has been widely accepted, but only with respect to insurance contracts. (See Max True Plastering Co. v. United States Fidelity & Guar. Co., 912 P.2d 861 (Okla.1996), where the court states that 32 of 36 jurisdictions have adopted it.) While there is "reasonable expectation" language in comment *f* to Restatement (Second) of Contracts Section 211 that might render form terms inoperative, this will occur under Section 211(3) only if the party who created the language had "reason to believe that the party manifesting assent would not do so if he knew that the writing contained a particular term...." For an analysis, see MURRAY ON CONTRACTS § 97A & B (4th ed. 2001). The Section 211 test has seen only limited application outside of insurance contracts. Such applications have occurred primarily in Arizona courts, which appear to equate the Restatement approach with the "reasonable expectation" test, without regard for the "reason to believe" language in the Restatement.

L. ELECTRONIC CONTRACTS

Karl Llewellyn and friends were hard at work using foolscap, pens and typewriters to assemble the Uniform Commercial Code when the first programmable computer, the Electronic Numerical Integrator and Computer (ENIAC), was unveiled in 1946. It was ten feet tall, a hundred and fifty feet wide, and cost millions. It was a marvel at the time because it could perform 5000 operations per second. Twenty five years later, by which time the UCC was firmly established, 12 times the power of ENIAC could be pressed into an electronic chip costing $200. Today, a personal computer (PC) can accommodate more than 400 million instructions per second (MIPS). Within a few years, such a PC will appear primitive as ordinary computers will perform over a billion instructions per second.

In the 1960's when the UCC was in the process of being enacted throughout the country, the information technology part of business investment hovered around 3 percent. Today, for the typical business, it often consumes 45 percent of investment, and for businesses in the computer information industry, the percentage is considerably higher.

The computer information industry or, simply, IT (information technology), is already a sizeable portion of U.S. Gross Domestic Product (GDP). In 1994, 3 million people, mostly Americans, used the Internet. In 1998, 100 million people used the Internet and within a very short time, one billion people will use the Internet. History does not record any technological development resembling this digitalized revolution in terms of total immersion and reliance by society, or the incredible speed at which it has invaded the lives of everyone on the planet. The "law industry" was caught off guard by the accelerated pace of these developments. Our statutes and judicial decisions requiring "writings" and "signatures" instantly became antediluvian. The notion of "electronic agents" (computer programs) making contracts with no human intervention was far removed from any legislative or judicial contemplation. The reality dawned on legislators just a few years ago, and they scrambled to react effectively to the felt needs of this digitalized society.

The flurry of state legislative activity to produce statutes recognizing the validity of electronic transactions is revealing. Many of these efforts focused exclusively on electronic signatures, often failing to distinguish between an ordinary electronic signature and a secured digitalized signature. This disparate legislative production, ranging from a statute that only recognized the validity of an electronic signature on a tax form to those that recognized electronic signatures and documents in almost any form, posed a dire threat to uniformity and functionality. NCCUSL was at the ready with what became the 1999 *Uniform Electronic Transactions Act.* The Congress of the United States had been quite willing to leave commercial law matters to the states, but the tsunami of electronic commerce induced the Congress to create the *Electronic Signatures in Global and National Commerce Act*, ("E–Sign"), which was signed by the President on June 30, 2000 and became effective on October 1, 2000.[1]

Both UETA and E–Sign have the same limited objective, i. e., to facilitate electronic transactions by removing barriers to electronic commerce.[2] Since both statutes have the same purpose and often use the same language, E–Sign provides that state law will supercede it if the state has enacted UETA without modification.[3] Given the importance of uniformity in this area and the incentive to comply with the federal E–Sign law, it is not remarkable that, at the time of this writing, UETA has already been enacted in 41 states and introduced in five others. A number of international efforts relating to the legal infrastructure for e-commerce have also appeared in recent years, including the United Nations Commission on International Trade Law (UNICITRAL) *Model Law on Electronic Commerce*,[4] which recognizes that the CISG was deficient in this area upon its birth in 1980.

Electronic Contracting and the UCC. Under E–Sign or UETA, where a rule such as the statute of frauds requires a contract to be evidenced by a "signed" writing, an electronic *record*[5] and an *electronic*

---

1.   15 USCS § 7000 (2000).

2.   The preamble to E–Sign describes the legislation as "[a]n Act to facilitate the use of electronic records and signatures in interstate or foreign commerce." According to UETA § 6, the statute "must be construed and applied to facilitate electronic transactions consistent with other law."

3.   E–Sign, § 102(a)(1).

4.   36 I. L. M. 197 (1997). Among many other thrusts, the International Chamber of Commerce has issued guidelines for Internet commerce through the *General Usage*

for International Digitally Ensured Commerce (GUIDEC) (see www./iccwbo.org/guidec2/htm). In general, see Jack L. Goldsmith, *Against Cyberanarchy*, 65 U. CHI. L. REV. 1199 (1998).

5.   UETA defines "record" in § 2(13) as "information that is inscribed on a tangible medium or that is stored in an electronic or other medium and is retrievable in perceivable form." The identical language is found in the E–Sign definition of "record" at § 106(9), and it also appears in amended Article 1 of the UCC at Section 1–201(31).

signature[6] will meet that requirement. No specific technology is required to create a valid signature. A voice on an answering machine may suffice if the requisite intention is present. Inserting one's name into an electronic mail communication may also suffice, as may including a firm's name on a facsimile.[7] Both statutes emphasize that no one is *required* to use or accept electronic records or signatures,[8] and UETA insists that parties must agree to conduct their transactions by electronic means.[9] "Agreement" or "consent" is, however, defined broadly to include conduct. A business card with an E-mail address may, for example, allow a reasonable inference that such a party is willing to transact business electronically.[10] The ordering of goods from an online vendor is an obvious manifestation of willingness to contract electronically.[11] Where a statute or regulation requires that information be made available to *consumers*, an electronic record will meet this requirement only if certain procedures are followed to assure the consumer's assent to such use.[12] While E–Sign and UETA include business, commercial, governmental and consumer transactions within their scope, both statutes expressly exclude wills, codicils, testamentary trusts, and transactions subject to UCC Article 3 through 9 (which contain their own electronic transaction rules).[13] Neither statute deals with substantive state law matters. Both pursue a minimalist and procedural approach with the simple purpose of allowing electronic records and signatures to enhance electronic commerce.

While the statutes are very similar and often use identical language, UETA is more comprehensive. It allows the parties to vary its provisions by agreement.[14] E–Sign does not mention *attribution*, but UETA provides that where a signature appears on an electronic record, the named party is not bound unless she produced the signature, ratified it, or is responsible for the agent who produced the signature.[15] UETA also sets forth rules for changes or errors in electronic records.[16] It also expressly

6. UETA, § 2(8) defines "electronic signature" as "an electronic sound, symbol or process attached to or logically associated with a record and executed or adopted by a person with the intent to sign the record." The identical language is found in the E-sign definition at § 106(5).

7. UETA § 2, comment 7. Some earlier state legislation had required the use of particular technology, such as dual key encryptions and third party certifiers. See, e.g., Utah Stat. Ann. S46–3–101 *et. seq.* UETA avoids any such requirement, recognizing that technology is always developing.

8. UETA § 5(a); E–Sign § 101(b)(2).

9. UETA § 5(b).

10. See Comment 4 and Example B to UETA § 5.

11. *Id.*

12. UETA § 3(a); E–Sign § 101(c).

13. UETA §§ 3(b)(1) & (2); E–Sign §§ 103(a)(1) & (3).

14. UETA § 5(d).

15. UETA § 9.

16. UETA § 10. Where the parties have agreed upon a security procedure to detect changes or errors and one party has conformed to the procedure while the other has not, if the nonconforming party would have detected the change or error had it conformed, the conforming party may avoid the effect of the change or of the erroneous record (§ 10(1)). Section 10(2) allows a party dealing with an "electronic agent" (§ 2(6)—a computer program or other automated means used independently to initiate an action or respond to electronic records or performance without review by an individual) to avoid the effect of an error if the agent did not provide an opportunity for prevention or correction of the error and, upon learning of the error, the individual

provides that electronic records are not to be denied admissibility into evidence solely because they are in electronic form.[17] There are no comparable provisions in E–Sign. Nothing in E–Sign deals with the time and place of sending and receipt of electronic records, but UETA confronts these issues.[18]

Both statutes recognize contracts between electronic agents[19] or between an individual and an electronic agent.[20] The notion of two computer programs making a contract with no human intervention may seem contrary to the requirement that the parties to a contract must intend to contract, but a moment's reflection cures that concern because electronic agents have been programmed with that intention.[21] Where an individual and an electronic agent interact, the contract will be formed when the individual perform actions that she is free to refuse to perform and which she knows or has reason to know will cause the electronic agent to complete the transaction or performance.[22] Thus, in an online transaction, where the individual is advised that a contract will be formed by her clicking the "agree" button, her clicking action will create an enforceable agreement.

Proposed Amendments to UCC Article 2 include definitions of "electronic," "electronic agent" and "record" in proposed amended Section 2–103. Each of these definitions replicate the definitions in UETA and E–Sign. These definitions may be moved to amended Article 1 of the UCC. The proposed amendments to Article 2 also contain three *new* sections on electronic contracting: 2–211, Legal Recognition of Electronic Contracts and Signatures; 2–212, Attribution; and 2–213, Electronic Communication (effect of receipt of electronic communication). Each of these sections conforms to and is based upon UETA.

---

promptly notifies the other party and takes reasonable steps to return or destroy the consideration received and has not used or received any benefit or value.

17. UETA § 13.

18. UETA § 15. The electronic record is *sent* when it is properly addressed to an information system designated by the recipient for the purpose of receiving the record, it is in a form capable of being processed by the recipient system, and it enters an information processing system outside the control of the sender or someone acting on his behalf, or it enters a region of the information processing system designated by the recipient. An electronic record is *received* when the information enters a processing system designated for that purpose by the recipient and from which the recipient is able to retrieve the record in a form capable of being processed by that system. As to

place, unless otherwise expressly agreed, an electronic record is deemed to be sent from the sender's place of business and received at the recipient's place of business. If either has more than one place of business, the one having the closest relationship to the underlying transaction is the place of business. If either party has no place of business, the place of business is the party's residence. An electronic record is received even if no individual is aware of its receipt. If either party is aware that an electronic record that purportedly was sent or received was not actually sent or received, the legal effect of sending or receiving is determined by other applicable law.

19. See the definition of "electronic agent" in note 16, *supra*.

20. UETA § 14; E–Sign § 101(h).

21. UETA § 14, Comment 1.

22. UETA § 14(2).

M. THE STATUTE OF FRAUDS—SCOPE—2–201, 8–113, 9–203, AND PRE–AMENDMENT 1–206

Problem 13

Which of the following transactions require evidence in a *record* under the U.C.C.?

(a) A contract for the sale of contract rights.

(b) A contract covering the sale of both real estate and personal property.

(c) A contract for the sale of investment securities.

(d) A contract for the sale of patents.

(e) A contract for the sale of advertising flyers where the printer had completed 25 percent of the flyers with the buyer's name thereon before the buyer "canceled" the order.

(f) A contract for the sale and installation of blackboards in a school.

(g) A contract for the sale of trademarks.

(h) A contract to exchange a used riding mower for a used 32–inch direct projection television set. See 2–304.

(i) A contract to exchange a tract of land for an automobile.

(j) A contract for the sale of false teeth.

(k) A contract for the sale of a painting valued at $800.

(*l*) A contract to supply two million units of E–27 plastic at a price of $2 million, delivery to be in monthly shipments of 100,000 units with the first shipment to occur one month after the contract was made.

N. STATUTE OF FRAUDS—SUFFICIENT WRITING

Problem 14

Which of the following constitute a record sufficient to satisfy the requirements of U.C.C. 2–201?

(a) A letter from a buyer canceling its previous purchase order for ordinary equipment priced at $10,000. The cancellation letter was sent before the seller shipped the goods.

(b) Same as (a) except that the cancellation letter was sent after seller had shipped the goods.

(c) A letter from a buyer repudiating a previously negotiated oral contract.

(d) A letter evidencing a contract for the sale of goods at a price of $25,000 which the buyer never sent but which remains in the buyer's files.

(e) Same as (d) except that the letter was addressed to a third person rather than the seller.

(f) A tape recording or electronic file or E-mail or voice mail containing a recital of the terms of a contract. See 1–201(46). How does one "sign" a tape recording? Consider 1–201(39).

(g) A will containing the terms of a contract.

(h) A seller's invoice showing the terms of a contract.

(i) Corporate minutes containing the terms of a contract.

(j) A writing that shows a contract was made for the purchase and sale of 100 office desks of a specified model, identifies the parties, and is initialed by both parties, but which does not indicate which party is buyer or seller and which contains no information concerning price, time or place of delivery.

(k) Assume the same record states the price at $30,000, the time and place of delivery and identifies each party as buyer and seller as well as the subject matter (office desks) and model the parties have agreed upon. The record does not, however, state the quantity term.

(*l*) A record sufficient to satisfy the statute also contains a seal. Five years later the seller claims that buyer failed to make all necessary payments under the contract. The statute of limitations for sealed instruments in the jurisdiction is fourteen years. Analyze. See 2–203.

O. STATUTE OF FRAUDS—CONFIRMATIONS

Problem 15

(a) The Pizza Factory, Inc. (PFI) is a restaurant owned by George Haber, who had lunch with Bill Armstrong, the sales manager of Dairyland Cheese (DC). The parties discussed PFI's purchase of 300 pounds of cheese per months for the next 12 months at $3.00 per pound. At the conclusion of the discussion, Armstrong departed believing that a deal had been made. Haber, however, did not believe he had made a firm commitment. Two days later, PFI received a DC confirmation form describing a contract to supply 300 pounds of certain kinds of cheese for each of the next 12 months at a price of $3.00 per pound. Haber decided to ignore this communication since he intended to discuss PFI's cheese requirements with other suppliers. Two weeks later, Haber signed a contract with another supplier for the same quantity and types of cheese at $2.75 per pound. DC contends it has an enforceable contract with PFI. Analyze.

(b) Assume the facts of (a) except that, upon receiving the confirmation from DC, Haber immediately sent a notice of objection which stated that no contract had been formed. Haber's notice of objection, however, was not received. What result? See 1–201(26).

(c) On the facts of (b), would it matter if Haber's notice of objection to the confirmation were addressed to DC's corporate offices rather than to the particular agent of the seller with whom Haber had dealt?

(d) Pastor Henry McNulty chaired the committee that was organizing a "Family Day" picnic sponsored by churches of all denominations in a major city. As part of his duties, Pastor McNulty began serious bargaining with various food distributors. After meeting several times with Pastor McNulty, one of the distributors, Food, Inc. (FI), concluded that it had an exclusive contract to provide all food for the city-wide picnic at a price of $25,000. FI sent Pastor McNulty a sufficient memorandum confirming its assumption.

Pastor McNulty did not believe that he had made a contract with FI, and he ignored the confirmation. Three weeks later, FI came forward claiming it had a contract with the affiliated churches. Analyze.

(e) Suppose that Pastor McNulty left the meeting with FI concluding that he had a contract with FI. He sent a confirmation to FI, which did not object to the confirmation. Consider 2–201(2).

(f) What is the significance of the fact that George Haber in (a) and Pastor McNulty in (d) did not believe they had made a contract with the other party? Suppose no confirmations had been sent in (a) and (d) but the sellers nevertheless sued to enforce the alleged agreements. The answers filed by the buyers denied that contracts were made. Should a court permit the plaintiffs to depose the buyers, or should it dismiss the cases? Suppose depositions were permitted. Haber and McNulty, while continuing to deny that contracts had been formed, admitted facts sufficient to establish the existence of contracts. What result? Would it matter if, at the time the depositions were taken, Haber or McNulty were no longer officers or agents of their respective organizations? Consider 2–201(3)(b). Proposed amended 2–201(3)(b) recognizes admissions made in court or out of court (depositions and affidavits).

P. STATUTE OF FRAUDS—PART PERFORMANCE

Problem 16

(a) Mars, Inc. (M) of Cincinnati, Ohio placed a telephone order with United Almond Corporation (UAC) in Tampa, Florida for 50,000 pounds of almonds at $2 per pound. Mars immediately sent a check to UAC with a notation on the check which read, "Payment for Almonds." Is there sufficient evidence to satisfy 2–201?

(b) Assume M had not sent a check to UAC, but UAC sent a confirmation of the contract to M setting forth the quantity at 5000 pounds of almonds. Analyze. Is there a remedy that might be considered pursuant to amended 1–103(b)?

(c) Assume that no writings or records or any kind were sent by either party. Mars informed UAC that it needed the almonds immediately. UAC shipped 5000 pounds, which were received and used by M. When M inquired as to the remaining 5000 pounds, UAC indicated that it had completed the contract with M. The market price of almonds had risen sharply since the original shipment. See 2–201(3)(c).

(d)) Assume that UAC had not shipped any almonds, but M had sent a check in the amount of $10,000 to UAC which the latter cashed. Analyze.

(e) Suppose that M required its almonds to be processed in a unique fashion. Upon receipt of the telephone order, UAC immediately began the special processing. The entire 10,000 pounds were being processed and could no longer be reclaimed for sale to others when M notified UAC that M was canceling the order. Analyze.

(f) Assume that M and UAC orally agreed that UAC would supply M with all of the almonds it required up to 1000 pounds per month for the next eighteen months at a price of $2 per pound. Neither party confirmed this agreement in any form. After this oral agreement was formed, UAC received a written offer from another customer for a similar long-term contract. UAC sent a letter stating its regret in not being able to perform this contract because it had just concluded the deal with M. Before the first shipment was due, UAC received a telephone call from M canceling the order. In UAC's action against M, the answer to the complaint raises both the UCC 2–201 statute of frauds and the provision in the state statute of frauds that requires contracts not performable within one year from the time they are made to be evidenced by a writing. Analyze.

(g) Assume that M and UAC entered into a contract under which UAC agreed to supply M with its requirements of almonds each month for a period of one year. M agreed to purchase a minimum of 1000 pounds per month and UAC agreed to supply a maximum of 2000 pounds per month. The price was based on a well-known index in the trade. The contract was evidenced by an electronic record containing the encrypted signatures of both parties. After each signature the phrase *locus sigilli* appeared. After six months, the parties had a disagreement and UAC stopped shipments. Seven years later, UAC brought an action against M. Analyze. See 2–203.

Q. AMENDED SECTION 2–201—"RECORD," $5000, RELIANCE, ADMISSIONS, AND THE ONE–YEAR PROVISION

Early drafts of proposed revisions to UCC Article 2 eliminated the statute of frauds for sales of goods over a specified price, but it reappeared in later drafts. There was never any doubt that the threshold price of $500 to trigger the writing requirement in pre-amendment 2–201 had to be raised, and the amount finally settled upon was $5000 (somewhat belatedly justified as an appropriate amount due to inflation). It was also necessary to recognize that an electronic record would suffice as a "writing" and an electronic signature would fulfill the "signed" requirement. Proposed amended 2–201 incorporates these changes.

Proposed amended 2–201 also resolves a dispute in the case law concerning judicial recognition of another exception to the "record" requirement. There is a split of authority over whether promissory estoppel can be used to avoid the UCC Article 2 statute of frauds. See *Columbus Trade Exchange, Inc. v. AMCA International Corp.*, 763 F.Supp. 946 (S.D.Ohio 1991), where the court lists jurisdictions that recognize and those that do not recognize a promissory estoppel exception to the statute. Courts holding that promissory estoppel should be permitted to satisfy the statute often point to 1–103,[1] which recognizes the continuing applicability of supplementary general principles of law—including "estoppel"—if they are not displaced by particular provisions of the UCC. Courts refusing to recognize promissory estoppel to satisfy the statute may emphasize the opening phrase of pre-amendment 2–201, which states that a writing is required "[e]xcept as otherwise provided in

---

1. This section now appears in Amended Section 1–103(b) (2002).

this Section...." Three exceptions are found in pre-amendment 2–201(3): (a) specially manufactured goods, (b) admissions, and (c) part performance. Proposed amended 2–201 eliminates the opening phrase "Except as otherwise provided in this Section" and, in Comment 2, explains that the removal is intended to allow for judicially-crafted exceptions such as one based on promissory estoppel.

Proposed amended Section 2–201 also resolves another disputed matter relating to pre-amendment 2–201(3)(b), which creates an exception from the signed writing requirement if the party against whom enforcement is sought admits in a pleading, testimony or otherwise *in court* that a contract was made. The language of the proposed amended provision recognizes both admissions "in court" and admissions "under oath but not in court." This change allows for admissions made through testimony in a deposition or by an affidavit filed with a motion (see proposed amended 2–201, comment 7).

Proposed amended Section 2–201(4) is a new subsection that insulates sales contracts from provisions of a general statute of frauds imposing writing requirements on contracts not performable within one year (or some other specified period) from their making. The one-year provision of the typical state statute of frauds is not confined to sales of goods. It is, therefore, somewhat odd for a statute limited to such contracts to repeal the one-year provision for contracts within its scope. Comment 8 to proposed amended Section 2–201 explains that new subsection (4) was added because of "the confused and contradictory interpretations under the so-called 'one-year' clause as illustrated in *C. R. Klewin, Inc. v. Flagship Properties, Inc.,* 600 A.2d 772 (Conn.1991)." In the cited case, Chief Justice Peters makes a compelling case for elimination of the one-year provision and, in lieu thereof, suggests the narrowest application of that provision. Proposed amended Section 2–201(4) is also consonant with UCC 8–113, which eliminates the statute of frauds in Article 8 (governing investment securities) and makes the one-year provision of general statutes of frauds inapplicable to the sale or purchase of a security.

R. STATUTE OF FRAUDS—LEASES

Problem 17

A principal of the Bolt Construction Company (B) telephoned Lease Equipment, Inc. (LEI) indicating that, because another equipment supplier had failed to meet its obligations, Bolt required two back-hoes for one of its construction projects. The principal stated that B needed the back-hoes for three months, and would pay the going rent of $1000 per month for each machine. B immediately sent a check to LEI for $2,000. The check was received and cashed by LEI. LEI failed to deliver the equipment to B, contending that no lease contract had been formed. LEI returned B's payment of $2000. Analyze under Article 2A. See 2A–201.

S. STATUTE OF FRAUDS—UCITA AND CISG

UCITA. Under Section 201 of UCITA, a license contract requiring payment of $5000 or more (as contrasted with the mere possibility of reaching that amount through, e.g., royalties or options) with a duration of one year or more must be evidenced by a sufficient record. No particular formalities are required of the record. If it indicates that a contract was formed and reasonably identifies the copy, it will be sufficient even if it omits or incorrectly states a term. The contract, however, is not enforceable beyond the number of copies or subject matter shown in the record. Full performance, an admission in court that the contract was made or a confirming record not objected to within ten days of its receipt will satisfy the statute. UCITA 201(e) allows parties to agree in an authenticated record to conduct business without additional authenticated records.

CISG. Article 11 of the CISG states that a contract for the sale of goods governed by the CISG need not be evidenced by any writing or be in any particular form. Since the Statute of Frauds has, with only two exceptions, been repealed in England where it was born,[1] has been the subject of considerable criticism in the United States, was excised entirely in earlier drafts of revisions to Article 2 before being restored in more recent drafts, and has no counterpart in continental law, it is not remarkable that the CISG does not require written evidence of a contract for the sale of goods. It should be noted, however, that under CISG Articles 12 and 96 a Contracting State whose domestic law requires a contract of sale to be evidenced by a writing can make Article 11 inapplicable to contracts governed by the CISG. Several nations, including Argentina, China and Hungary but not the United States, have done so by making the declaration permitted under Article 96.

T. REQUIREMENT AND OUTPUT CONTRACTS—2–306

Problem 18

(a) The Stylette Corporation agreed to purchase from Resin, Inc. one year's requirements of the resin Stylette used to manufacture its plastic products. Before making any deliveries, Resin informed Stylette that it would not perform under the contract absent a price increase. Stylette refused to pay a higher price and acquired replacement resin from a new supplier, Miles, Inc., at a price higher than Resin's original contract price but lower than the increased price Resin had demanded. Stylette sued for its "cover" remedy pursuant to 2–712. Resin argued that its contract with Stylette lacked consideration, was too indefinite to be enforced, and violated the statute of frauds. Analyze.

(b) Assume that Stylette had been making consumer plastic products for the last 20 years and its resin requirements had remained relatively stable

---

1. By the Law Reform Act of 1954, England repealed the Statute of Frauds except for the sections dealing with suretyship and contracts for the sale of land.

for the last 5 years. Resin, Inc. had performed its contractual duties for six months when Stylette suddenly increased its demand by more than forty percent after negotiating a contract with the United States Department of Defense to supply an expensive part for military aircraft. Must Resin supply Stylette's additional requirements at the contract price for the remainder of the year?

(c) Assume that Stylette's forty percent increase emanated from an increase in the demand for its regular consumer products. Analyze.

(d) Suppose that, because of new environmental regulations, Stylette decides to reduce its production by 40 percent in order to insure the same average corporate profit it has earned over the last 5 years. Does Resin, which has been making deliveries under the contract for three months, have a cause of action?

(e) Assume the facts of (d) except that Stylette's reduction is necessary to allow the firm to avoid filing for bankruptcy. Analyze.

(f) Assume that Stylette had agreed to become the exclusive supplier of plastic lawn furniture to the X–Mart chain of retail stores over a five year period. To meet that demand, Stylette expanded its facilities and increased its workforce based on the estimates of past demand from X–Mart. After two years of sales, X–Mart chose not to advertise these products for sale. The result was a 90 percent reduction in X–Mart's requirements of Stylette products. Analyze.

U. CONTRACT MODIFICATIONS AND WAIVERS—2–209

Problem 19

(a) In 1983, Navistar and Zemco formed a sales contract, renewable on a yearly basis, under which Navistar would purchase all of its requirements of certain components from Zemco. This practice continued until 1995 when Navistar began to purchase its requirements from another supplier. The parties had renewed their agreement in writing through 1987, but no written extension occurred thereafter. Navistar now claims that it is not bound to any extension with Zemco since modifications must be evidenced by a writing under 2–209(3). Analyze.

(b) Suppose the parties to a written contract for the sale of goods at a price of $50,000 orally agree to modify the time or place of delivery, or merely to postpone or to accelerate delivery of the goods. Is the modification enforceable?

(c) Alpha Corporation (A) contracted with Pulsar Printing (P) for 40,000 copies of its corporate report at a total cost of $25,000. The design of A's report required a special graphic on the cover. After the contract was formed, P notified A that this special effect would be more costly than expected, and that the contract price would be increased to $30,000. A did not object. P then sent A a confirmation of the change in price. After 40,000 copies of the report were delivered to A, A refused to pay more than $25,000. Analyze.

(d) The Zonex Corporation (Z) purchased a used airplane from Deer, Inc. (D). The sale was made on an "as is" basis—i.e., without any warranties. After receiving the aircraft Z discovered engine problems and D agreed to perform major engine repairs without charge. The repairs were more costly than D had contemplated. D now seeks the reasonable value of the repairs. Analyze.

(e) The Frank Corporation (F) agreed to purchase 100 computers from the Vax Corporation (V) at $5000 each in 1997. The following day, F telephoned V and asked V to ascertain that the computers would not encounter Y2K problems. V said that it would modify the computers to meet F's concerns. The computers were delivered and used by F which, in 1998, discovered that the modifications had not occurred, and the cost of performing the modifications at this point would be $50,000. Applying 2–209, what result?

(f) Same as (e) except that the written contract between F and V contains the following clause: "The parties hereby agree that no modification of this contract shall be of any effect unless that modification is evidenced by a writing signed by both parties to this contract." Should 2–209(4) and (5) apply to this situation? Consider the following case.

BMC INDUSTRIES, INC. v. BARTH INDUSTRIES, INC.

United States Court of Appeals for the Eleventh Circuit, 1998.
160 F.3d 1322.

[BMC's Vision–Ease Division manufactures lenses for eyeglasses using a production-line process requiring personnel to perform various functions. To compete more effectively with competitors using low cost foreign labor, BMC pursued the automation of many of these functions under a contract with Barth at a price of $515,200.00. The contract required delivery of the automated lines by June, 1987 and stated that time was of the essence. The parties amended the contract to extend the delivery date to October, 1987. There were, however, many delays thereafter. Barth was required to expend additional sums in overcoming technical problems. While the parties did not execute further amendments, BMC cooperated with Barth and otherwise acted as if the contract continued, though it protested the delays. Finally, in May, 1989, Barth notified BMC that it was ready to deliver the completed product. BMC refused to accept, and filed an action against Barth in early June of 1988. The court found that the UCC applied because the contract was predominantly a contract for the sale of goods. Among other issues, the court addressed Barth's waiver claim under UCC 2–209.]

TJOFLAT, CIRCUIT JUDGE. The Contract included a provision requiring all modifications to be in writing. Although the parties therefore did not successfully modify the Contract, we apply chapter 672.209 to determine whether BMC's conduct constituted a waiver of the October 1987 delivery date. Although the UCC does not specifically lay out the elements of waiver, we have stated that waiver requires "(1) the existence at the time of the waiver a right, privilege, advantage, or benefit which may be waived; (2) the actual constructive knowledge thereof; and (3) an intention to relinquish such right, privilege, advantage, or benefit." Dooley v.

Weil (In re Garfinkle), 672 F.2d 1340, 1347 (11th Cir.1982). Conduct may constitute waiver of a contract term, but such an implied waiver must be demonstrated by clear evidence. Waiver may be implied when a party's actions are inconsistent with continued retention of the right.

As an initial matter, we must determine whether, under the UCC, waiver must be accompanied by detrimental reliance. Although it is settled that waiver under Florida common law must be supported by valid consideration or detrimental reliance, see Masser v. London Operating Co., 106 Fla. 474, 145 So. 72 (1932), courts disagree on whether the UCC retains this requirement. We conclude, however, that the UCC does not require consideration or detrimental reliance for waiver of a contract term.

Our conclusion follows from the plain language of subsections 672.209(4) and (5). While subsection (4) states that an attempted modification that fails may still constitute a waiver, subsection (5) provides that the waiver may be retracted unless the non-waiving party relies on the waiver. Consequently, the statute recognizes that waivers may exist in the absence of detrimental reliance—these are the retractable waivers referred to in subsection (5). Only this interpretation renders meaning to subsection (5), because reading subsection (4) to require detrimental reliance for all waivers means that waivers would never be retractable. See Wisconsin Knife Works v. National Metal Crafters, 781 F.2d 1280, 1291 (7th Cir.1986) (Easterbrook, J., dissenting) (noting that reading a detrimental reliance requirement into the UCC would eliminate the distinction between subsections (4) and (5)). Subsection (5) would therefore be meaningless.

At least one Florida court implicitly agrees with this conclusion; in Linear Corp. v. Standard Hardware Co., 423 So. 2d 966 (Fla. 1st DCA 1982), the court held that a contract term had been waived despite the absence of any facts showing detrimental reliance. The court in Linear addressed a contract between a manufacturer and a retailer for the sale of electronic security devices. The contract included a provision stating that the manufacturer would not repurchase any devices the retailer was unable to sell, and another term providing that contract modifications must be in writing. Despite this contractual language, the retailer filed suit claiming that the manufacturer subsequently made an oral agreement to repurchase unsold devices, but failed to adhere to this oral agreement.

Citing chapter 672.209(4), the court concluded that the parties' conduct demonstrated that they had waived the requirement that modifications be in writing, and therefore gave effect to the oral modification. See id. at 968. The court recognized this waiver despite the apparent absence of any detrimental reliance by the retailer—in fact the court never even mentioned any reliance requirement for waiver under the UCC. Consequently, the court implicitly held that a contract term could be waived without the existence of detrimental reliance by the non-waiving party.

Although other courts have held that waiver requires reliance under the UCC, those courts have ignored the UCC's plain language. The leading case espousing this view of waiver is Wisconsin Knife Works v. National Metal Crafters, 781 F.2d 1280 (7th Cir.1986) (addressing section 2–209 of the model version of the UCC, from which Florida adopted section 672.209 verbatim), in which a panel of the Seventh Circuit addressed a contract that included a term prohibiting oral modifications, and considered whether an attempted oral modification could instead constitute a waiver. Writing for the majority, Judge Posner concluded that the UCC's subsection (2), which gives effect to "no oral modification" provisions, would become superfluous if contract terms could be waived without detrimental reliance. Judge Posner reasoned that if attempted oral modifications that were unenforceable because of subsection (2) were nevertheless enforced as waivers under subsection (4), then subsection (2) is "very nearly a dead letter." Id. at 1286. According to Judge Posner, there must be some difference between modification and waiver in order for both subsections (2) and (4) to have meaning. This difference is waiver's detrimental reliance requirement.[1]

Judge Posner, however, ignores a fundamental difference between modifications and waivers: while a party that has agreed to a contract modification cannot cancel the modification without giving consideration for the cancellation, a party may unilaterally retract its waiver of a contract term provided it gives reasonable notice. The fact that waivers may unilaterally be retracted provides the difference between subsections (2) and (4) that allows both to have meaning. We therefore conclude that waiver under the UCC does not require detrimental reliance. Consequently, without reaching the issue of detrimental reliance, we consider whether BMC waived the Contract's October 1987 delivery date.

Applying the elements of waiver to the facts before us, we hold as a matter of law that BMC waived the October 1987 delivery date. The October 1987 delivery date was a waivable contract right, of which BMC had actual knowledge. We also conclude that BMC's conduct impliedly demonstrated an intent to relinquish that right. [The court found that BMC's waiver was evidenced by its express reliance on assurances from the parent company of Barth, Nesco, that the contract would be performed.] Furthermore, BMC's course of dealing with Barth evidenced BMC's waiver of the October 1987 delivery date, because BMC failed

---

1. Contrary to our reasoning above, Judge Posner claims that reading a reliance requirement into waiver under subsection (4) is not inconsistent with subsection (5). According to Judge Posner, subsection (5) is broader than subsection (4), covering waivers other than mere attempts at oral modification. Judge Posner argues as an example that subsection (5) covers express waivers that are written and signed. See id. at 1287. In dissent, however, Judge Easterbrook convincingly dissects this argument. As Judge Easterbrook explains, subsection (5) is narrower than subsection (4)—limiting the effect of waivers that are not detrimentally relied upon—not the reverse as Judge Posner claims. Furthermore, Judge Easterbrook demonstrates that subsection (5) cannot cover express written and signed waivers because such writings are not waivers, but rather effective written modifications under subsection (2). See id. at 1291 (Easterbrook, J., dissenting).

timely to demand compliance with that contract term or terminate the Contract and file suit. When a delivery date passes without the seller's delivery, the buyer must object within a reasonable time and warn the seller that it is in breach. See Harrison v. City of Tampa, 247 F.569, 572 (S.D.Fla.1918) ("I do not recognize any principle by which one party to a contract, after a breach by the other party, may continue acting under such contract to some future time, and then abrogate the contract by reason of such former breach.").

Although BMC maintained at trial that Barth breached the contract as of October 1987, BMC did not tell Barth it intended to terminate the contract and hold Barth liable for the breach until May 1989. In fact, the earliest indication from BMC that it was considering termination was August 1988, when BMC executives met with Tomsich to seek assurance that Barth would perform. As we have already stated, however, the result of that meeting was a waiver of the October 1987 delivery date, not a timely exercise of BMC's right to terminate the Contract. BMC did not warn Barth in earnest of its intent to terminate until February 1989, when BMC sent Barth a letter along with $100,000 of the $250,000 payment Tomsich had requested at the August 1988 meeting. This letter warned Barth that BMC was not waiving its rights and remedies for Barth's failure to meet contractual delivery dates. BMC warned Barth again in March when it sent a letter advising of its intent to "hold [Barth] responsible, both for the initial breach and for all failures to meet subsequently promised dates."

Until 1989, however, BMC continued to act as though both parties were bound by the Contract and that Barth was not in default of its obligations: the October 1987 delivery date passed without comment from BMC; engineers from BMC frequently provided advice or assistance to help Barth personnel overcome technical problems; BMC executives frequently visited Barth's production facilities and encouraged Barth to continue working to complete the equipment; BMC even continued to spend money on the project—in December 1987, over one month after the October 1987 delivery date had passed, BMC purchased an additional $71,075 worth of springs and tooling for the machines. In sum, rather than terminating the Contract, or at least warning Barth that it was in breach after the October 1987 delivery date had passed, BMC continued to act as though the Contract remained in effect.

This is not to say that BMC never complained that Barth had missed deadlines; BMC executives frequently expressed their concern and disappointment that the project was so far behind schedule. On April 5, 1988, for example, the Chairman, President, and CEO of BMC sent a letter to Barth in which he stated: "The project is well behind schedule, and each day of delay represents lost savings for Vision–Ease. I hope that Barth will exert every effort to ensure the speedy completion and installation of the equipment and avoid any further delay." But while BMC complained of delays, it never declared Barth in default or terminated the contract—instead, BMC told Barth to keep working. After Barth had spent an additional eighteen months of time and money and, according to Barth, was prepared to deliver the machines, however, BMC suddenly decided to terminate the Contract. This BMC could not do.

The UCC states that when a contractual delivery date is waived, delivery must be made within a reasonable time. Consequently, because BMC waived the October 1987 delivery date, Barth was only obligated to deliver the machines within a reasonable time period. We remand this case to the district court for a new trial on the question of whether Barth tendered the machines within a reasonable time period.[2]

———

Problem 19A

(a) Appliances, Inc. (A) is a national chain of discount stores selling name-brand appliances. A had ordered 4000 model 946 refrigerators from the Everfreeze Corporation (E). The written contract between A and E called for delivery to A no later than March 15. E was preparing to deliver by that date when it received a call from A requesting that delivery be delayed until April 5 because A had a storage problem. E agreed to delay the shipment. E later shipped 4000 refrigerators, which arrived on April 5. A refused to accept the refrigerators because of late delivery. Assume the contract contained an NOM clause such as that found in problem 19(f). Analyze. Assume the contract did not contain an NOM clause. Analyze.

(b) Assume a contract between A and E for 4000 refrigerators, model 946, at $300 per unit. A telephones E and requests a price change to $275 per unit and E agrees. Later, E insists on the original price of $300 per unit. Again, would your analysis be affected by the presence or absence of an NOM clause in the contract?

(c) E contracts to sell A 4000 refrigerators, model 946, at $300 per unit. After signing the contract, both parties agree that a different model, 837, will be substituted for the model 946's. The contract price was not changed. Model 837 is substantially different from model 946. Later, E insists on shipping model 946 refrigerators and A insists that it is entitled to the model 837 units. Analyze this situation with and without a no oral modification clause.

(d) Same facts as (c) except there is no model change. Rather, the parties orally agree to reduce the shipment by 500 units, i.e., E will ship 3500 refrigerators instead of 4000. Later, A insists on 4000 units. Analyze this situation with and without a no oral modification clause.

(e) Suppose that in (c) and (d) litigation was started and depositions were taken. In the deposition of its vice president, E admitted the oral modifications in (d) and (e). Analyze this situation with and without a no oral modification clause.

---

2. On remand, if the jury concludes that Barth did not deliver the machines within a reasonable time period, then BMC will prevail on its breach of contract claim against Barth. BMC's damages should then be calculated according to Fla. Stat. ch. 672.713 (1997). If instead, however, the jury finds that BMC terminated the contract before a reasonable time had passed, then Barth will prevail on its counterclaim. BMC has stipulated that Barth is entitled to recover $1.13 million if it prevails.

(f) Assume that A orders computer hardware and software from the Computerex Corporation over the Internet. Computerex responds by Internet that it will ship the software at the price offered by A. A then authorizes payment through its Visa card. The goods arrive accompanied by a record containing additional terms that A ignores without notice to Computerex. Does 2–209 apply?

(g) Assume that North signs a standard form contract provided by West containing a no oral modification clause. Is the clause enforceable against North?

(h) A contract contains an express condition of ten days notice of shipment by the seller. Seller fails to notify but the buyer accepts the shipment and uses the goods. Later, the buyer seeks to return the goods because of seller's failure to notify. Analyze. See 1–303(f)[1] and 2–209(4). See also Restatement (Second) of Contracts Section 229. Suppose buyer had informed the seller prior to shipment that notice was not essential. Analyze See 2–209(5).

Note

Except for slight language changes (such as substituting "record" for "writing"), proposed amended 2–209 replicates the pre-amendment version.

V. CONTRACT MODIFICATIONS—CISG & LEASES

Problem 20

(a) An oral contract was formed between corporations located in countries that have adopted the CISG. The contract covered the purchase of 10,000 units of X–35 plastic at $10 per unit. Prior to the shipment date, the buyer telephoned the seller and requested an increase in the quantity to 12,000 at the same unit price. Seller agreed. Seller then shipped 10,000 units and refused to ship the additional units unless the buyer agreed to pay $14 per unit. What result? See CISG Art. 29.

(b) Assume the facts of (a) except the original contract was evidenced by a writing. The modification, however, was oral. What result?

(c) Assume the facts of (b) except the written contract contained a clause requiring all modifications to be evidenced by a writing. What result?

(d) Assume the facts of (c) except that, after the oral modification, the buyer rejected an offer from another supplier to ship 2,000 units of the same plastic at $10 per unit. What result?

Problem 21

(a) Bart Corporation (B) contacted the Xonex Equipment Corporation (X) by telephone offering $900 for the lease of certain road equipment for one month. X agreed. The next day, X telephoned B requesting that the rent be increased to $1050 and B agreed. Two days later, B telephoned X to "cancel the order." Analyze. See 2A–201 and 208.

---

1. Pre-amendment 2–208(3).

(b) Assume that the original lease contract in (a) was evidenced by a writing. Does the analysis change?

(c) Assume the facts of (b) except that the written lease contained a clause excluding modification except by a signed writing. Does the analysis change?

W. PAROL EVIDENCE—TRADE USAGE, COURSE OF DEALING, COURSE OF PERFORMANCE

C-THRU CONTAINER CORPORATION v. MIDLAND MANUFACTURING COMPANY

Supreme Court of Iowa, 1995.
533 N.W.2d 542.

TERNUS, JUSTICE. This case requires us to interpret and apply the trade-usage exception to the parol evidence rule embodied in Iowa's Uniform Commercial Code (U.C.C.). The trial court held that parol evidence of trade usage was inadmissible and granted summary judgment to the defendant, Midland Manufacturing Company.

C–Thru Container Corporation entered into a contract with Midland Manufacturing Company in March of 1989. In this contract, Midland agreed to purchase bottle-making equipment from C–Thru and to make commercially acceptable bottles for C–Thru. Midland was to pay for the equipment by giving C–Thru a credit against C–Thru's bottle purchases. The contract stated that C–Thru expected to order between 500,000 and 900,000 bottles in 1989. Finally, the contract also provided that if Midland failed to manufacture the bottles, C–Thru could require Midland to pay the entire purchase price plus interest within thirty days.

Midland picked up the equipment as agreed and later sent a notice to C–Thru that it was ready to begin production. C–Thru never ordered any bottles from Midland, but instead purchased its bottles from another supplier at a lower price. C–Thru claims that in numerous phone conversations between the parties Midland indicated that it was unable to produce commercially acceptable bottles for C–Thru.

C–Thru notified Midland that Midland had failed to comply with the terms of the contract and that the full purchase price plus interest was due and payable within thirty days. When Midland failed to pay C–Thru the amount requested, C–Thru filed a petition alleging that Midland had breached the contract by being incapable of producing the bottles as agreed to in the contract.

Midland filed a motion for summary judgment. It contended that the contract did not require that it demonstrate an ability to manufacture commercially acceptable bottles as a condition precedent to C–Thru's obligation to place an order. Midland asserted that the contract merely required that it manufacture commercially acceptable bottles in response to an order from C–Thru. Because C–Thru never placed an order,

Midland argued that it had not breached the contract by failing to manufacture any bottles.

C–Thru resisted Midland's motion. It argued that a material issue of fact existed on whether Midland was unable to manufacture the bottles, thereby excusing C–Thru's failure to place an order. As proof that Midland could not manufacture the bottles, C–Thru pointed to Midland's failure to provide sample bottles. C–Thru relied on deposition testimony that the practice in the bottle-making industry was for the bottle manufacturer to provide sample bottles to verify that it could make commercially acceptable bottles before the purchaser placed any orders.

In ruling on Midland's motion for summary judgment, the trial court found no sample container requirement in the written contract. The court also held that the parol evidence rule precluded consideration of any evidence that the practice in the trade was to provide sample bottles before receiving an order. It concluded that no genuine issue of material fact existed and granted Midland summary judgment. The court of appeals reversed the district court's ruling, concluding that evidence regarding the trade practice should have been considered. We granted Midland's application for further review.

Under the common law of Iowa, parol evidence is admissible to shed light on the parties' intentions but it may not be used to modify or add to the contract terms. Nevertheless, sale-of-goods contracts, such as the agreement here, are governed by the Iowa Uniform Commercial Code. Section 554.2202 contains the applicable U.C.C. parol evidence rule and it states:

> Terms with respect to which the confirmatory memoranda of the parties agree or which are otherwise set forth in a writing intended by the parties as a final expression of their agreement with respect to such terms as are included therein may not be contradicted by evidence of any prior agreement or of a contemporaneous oral agreement but may be explained or supplemented
>
> a. by course of dealing or usage of trade (section 554.1205) or by course of performance (section 554.2208); and
>
> b. by evidence of consistent additional terms unless the court finds the writing to have been intended also as a complete and exclusive statement of the terms of the agreement.

Thus, unlike the common law, parol evidence may be used to supplement a fully integrated agreement governed by the U.C.C. if the evidence falls within the definition of usage of trade.

The Iowa U.C.C. includes the following definition of usage of trade:

> 2. A usage of trade is any practice or method of dealing having such regularity of observance in a place, vocation or trade as to justify an expectation that it will be observed with respect to the transaction in question. The existence and scope of such a usage are to be proved as facts. . . .

Section 554.1205 goes on to provide that any usage of trade of which the parties are or should be aware supplements their agreement. Id. § 554.1205(3)

Midland does not dispute that a trier of fact could find that the alleged practice in the bottling industry of providing samples to a prospective purchaser is a usage of trade. However, Midland argues usage-of-trade evidence may not be used to add a new term to a contract that is complete and unambiguous.

We first reject Midland's argument that evidence of trade usage is admissible only when the contract is ambiguous. There is no such requirement in section 554.2202. Moreover, the official comment to section 2–202 of the Uniform Commercial Code, which is identical to section 554.2202, states that this section "definitely rejects" a requirement that the language of the contract be ambiguous as a condition precedent to the admission of trade-usage evidence. U.C.C. § 2–202 cmt.1 (1977).

We also hold that even a "complete" contract may be explained or supplemented by parol evidence of trade usages.[1] As the official comment to section 2–202 states, commercial sales contracts "are to be read on the assumption that the course of prior dealings between the parties and the usages of trade were taken for granted when the document was phrased." U.C.C. § 2–202 cmt. 2 (1977). Therefore, even a completely integrated contract may be supplemented by practices in the industry that do not contradict express terms of the contract.

That brings us to the remaining argument made by Midland—that C–Thru may not use parol evidence to add a new term to the agreement. Section 554.2202 says that when parol evidence shows a usage of trade that does not contradict a contract term the evidence is admissible to "supplement" the contract. We look to the common meaning of the word "supplement" (we give words used in a statute their ordinary meaning, including reference to the dictionary definition). "Supplement" means "to add ... to." Webster's Third New Int'l Dictionary 2297 (1993). Consequently, the trade-usage evidence upon which C–Thru relies is admissible even though it adds a new term to the contract. White & Summers, § 3–3 (usage of trade may itself constitute a contract term).

The usage-of-trade evidence offered by C–Thru does not contradict any explicit contractual term. It supplements the written agreement which is permitted under section 554.2202. Taking this evidence in a light most favorable to C–Thru, we conclude there exists a genuine issue of fact concerning the performance required of Midland as a prerequisite to C–Thru's obligation to place an order. Therefore, summary judgment is not appropriate. We affirm the decision of the court of appeals, reverse the judgment of the district court and remand for further proceedings.

---

1. The contract here stated that "this agreement constitutes the entire agreement between C–Thru and Midland and super-   sedes any and all prior agreements between them."

Note

In ***Yazoo Mfg. Co. v. Lowe's Companies, Inc.***, 976 F.Supp. 430 (S.D.Miss.1997), the court states:

> Ordinarily, under Mississippi law, in the absence of ambiguous terms, the intention of the parties should be gleaned solely from the wording of the contract. Usually, the court looks to other sources to determine the intent of the parties only when the terms and/or wording of the contract are unclear. However, the instant case involves the UCC. As such, a different standard applies. Under Mississippi law, an agreement that falls within the purview of UCC "does not require that the agreement in question first be found to be incomplete or ambiguous before evidence of course of dealing and usage of trade may be considered." J.O. Hooker & Sons v. Roberts Cabinet, 683 So.2d 396, 396 (Miss.1996).

PUGET SOUND FINANCIAL, L.L.C. v. UNISEARCH, INC.

Supreme Court of Washington, 2002.
146 Wash.2d 428, 47 P.3d 940.

BRIDGE, J. Between 1993 and 1996, Puget Sound Financial L.L.C., (Factors), routinely contacted Unisearch, Inc. (Unisearch) by telephone to request that Unisearch search for specified Uniform Commercial Code (U.C.C.) filings in Washington. Unisearch would conduct the requested searches and then send the search results in a report to Factors. All of the search reports included the statement, "The responsibility for maintaining public records rests with the filing officer, and Unisearch, Inc. will accept no liability beyond the exercise of reasonable care." Unisearch charged $25 for each search, and every invoice contained the statement "Liability Limited to Amount of Fee." Unisearch completed 47 such searches prior to the present dispute. We are now asked to determine whether limitations on consequential damages presented in regular invoices for the purchase of commercial services can be enforced against a business purchaser.

In July 1996, Factors contacted Unisearch requesting a search for "The Benefit Group, Inc." Unisearch produced a search report for "The Benefit Group, Inc." indicating that no U.C.C. filings were found. Unisearch charged Factors $25 for this service. Upon receiving the report, Factors loaned The Benefit Group $100,000, secured by existing and future accounts receivable and other business assets. A year later, The Benefit Group defaulted on the loan. When Factors attempted to realize on the collateral, it discovered that Travelers Insurance Co. (Travelers) had a preexisting priority lien. Travelers' lien was filed under the name, "The Benefits Group, Inc." Unisearch had failed to locate this plural spelling of Factors' requested search.

Factors filed a lawsuit against Unisearch. Unisearch claimed that if found liable, Factors' recovery for damages would be limited to $25. The trial court granted Unisearch's motion for summary judgment on damages, finding that " '[i]f plaintiff were to establish liability . . . arising either in contract or in tort, the measure of damages . . . would be limited to the cost of the services rendered, viz., $25.00.' " Factors appealed. The Court of Appeals held that the trial court had abused its discretion in granting Unisearch's motion for summary judgment as to damages and remanded to proceed to trial on both liability and damages. The court stated, "Summary judgment would only be proper if Unisearch is able to show that Factors undisputedly agreed to include the limitations clause in their agreement for subsequent transactions." The court disagreed with Unisearch's argument that the invoices created a course of dealing warranting summary judgment, stating "Unisearch has not shown that Factors unequivocally agreed to be bound by the terms of the invoice."

Factors and Unisearch entered into an oral contract when Factors contacted Unisearch requesting its services. The terms of the oral contract are not in dispute. The parties do dispute whether the language in the search report and the invoices modified this oral contract, or were part of the contract itself. Factors asserts that it never accepted the liability limitation clause. Unisearch contends that the course of dealing between the parties established the liability limitation clause as part of the contract. As Unisearch emphasized, and we agree in part, "The invoice stated the price and quantity terms. Without **both** the search report and the invoice, there was no contract." We hold that the language in the search reports and invoices was part of the contract.

Trade usage and course of dealing are relevant to interpreting a contract and determining the contract's terms. Ambiguity is not required before evidence of trade usage or course of dealing can be used to ascertain the terms of a contract. RESTATEMENT (SECOND) OF CONTRACTS §§ 222 cmt. b, 223 cmt. b (1981). [See UCC 2–202, *cmt.* 1(c)]

Section 222 of the *Restatement* pertaining to trade usage states:

> (1) A usage of trade is a usage having such regularity of observance in a place, vocation, or trade as to justify an expectation that it will be observed with respect to a particular agreement. It may include a system of rules regularly observed even though particular rules are changed from time to time.

> (2) The existence and scope of a usage of trade are to be determined as questions of fact. If a usage is embodied in a written trade code or similar writing the interpretation of the writing is to be determined by the court as a question of law.

> (3) Unless otherwise agreed, a usage of trade in the vocation or trade in which the parties are engaged or a usage of trade of which they know or have reason to know gives meaning to or supplements or qualifies their agreement.

[See UCC 1–205(2).]

Unisearch has presented numerous examples of liability exclusions on invoices from other states as evidence of trade usage.[1] Unisearch has also presented examples of search firms who claimed that they would reimburse the search fees paid, if they made a mistake. Additionally, Unisearch produced an expert who declared that, "It is a standard practice in the UCC search industry to disclaim any liability resulting from the use of the information provided, and to provide a limitation of damages equal to the fee paid for the service."[2] Furthermore, amicus curiae, the National Public Records Research Association (NPRRA), notes:

> The industry practice is to place liability limitations on the invoices accompanying search results. This practice is born of customers' need for searches to be completed as quickly as possible. With customers expecting search results within the day and companies processing a multitude of searches, companies simply do not have time to negotiate the terms of all search orders received.

We find this unrebutted evidence persuasive of trade usage, supporting the inclusion of the limiting language in the contract between Factors and Unisearch.

Section 223 of the *Restatement* regarding course of dealing states:

> (1) A course of dealing is a sequence of previous conduct between the parties to an agreement which is fairly to be regarded as establishing a common basis of understanding for interpreting their expressions and other conduct.

> (2) Unless otherwise agreed, a course of dealing between the parties gives meaning to or supplements or qualifies their agreement. "Course of dealing may become part of an agreement either by explicit provision or by tacit recognition, or it may guide the court in supplying an omitted term."

[See UCC 1–205(3).]

Unisearch sent 47 search results and invoices to Factors prior to the transaction before this court. Unisearch contends that, after the first invoice was sent and Factors did not reject it, a course of dealing was

---

1. All–Search & Inspection, Inc., UT: "[W]e accept no liability for errors or omissions." Bay Area Search, FL: "[W]e accept no liability for error or omission." Delany Corporate Services, Ltd., NY: "[W]e accept no liability for the report contained herein." Docu–Search California, CA: "We accept no liability for errors or omissions." Harbor City Research, Inc., MD: "[W]e accept no liability for errors or omissions." JM Search Services, Inc., FL: "[W]e accept no responsibility for error or omission." Kaufman Information Resources, Inc., NJ: "Although meticulous care has been taken in conducting this service, no liability is assumed." National Corporate Research, Ltd., DL: "[W]e accept no liability for the report contained herein." Northshore Paralegal Services, Inc., MA: "We cannot accept liability for error or omission." The Research Connection, Inc., NH: "Reasonable Care Is Taken In Every Search. We Accept No Liability." Search Company International, CO: "[W]e accept no liability for errors or omissions." U.C.C. Filing & Search Services, Inc., FL: "[W]e will accept no liability for errors and omissions."

2. Unisearch's expert, William J. Stokes, was the President of the National Public Records Research Association when he wrote his declaration.

established. We need not determine the impact of the first invoice to decide that, after 48 transactions, a course of dealing was clearly established. According to the *Restatement* a course of dealing can be established when there is "a common basis of understanding." We find a factually analogous Ninth Circuit case persuasive in determining that a common basis of understanding was achieved between Factors and Unisearch.

The Ninth Circuit held that a shipper's receipt of invoices containing language limiting the shipper's liability to $50 on 47 occasions prior to the disputed transaction was sufficient to presume knowledge of the term and that the limitation was enforceable. *Ins. Co. of N. Am. v. NNR Aircargo Serv. (USA), Inc.*, 201 F.3d 1111, 1114–15 (9th Cir.2000). A manufacturer and distributor of sporting goods had contracted with NNR for the transportation of golf balls and other sporting goods by ocean carriage. The court held that the provision was enforceable as a course of dealing, even though the shipper did not receive the invoice for the stolen shipment until two weeks after the shipment was stolen. Significantly, the court held that the invoice terms and conditions could supplement the shipping agreement if there was sufficient course of dealing. The court then determined that 47 prior transactions were sufficient to establish a course of dealing.

Additionally, a recent decision from this court supports a conclusion that Unisearch's agreement with Factors could be interpreted as a "layered" contract, which incorporates the search reports and sales invoices. *See M.A. Mortenson Co. v. Timberline Software Corp.*, 140 Wash. 2d 568, 998 P.2d 305 (2000). In *Mortenson*, we addressed a shrinkwrap license on software and held that the original purchase order was not an integrated contract, that the licensing agreement in the software packaging and instruction manual was part of the contract, and that the provision limiting damages to the recovery of the purchase price was not unconscionable. We applied UCC § 2–204 pertaining to contract formation, to reach this conclusion: "[B]ecause RCW 62A.2–204 allows a contract to be formed 'in any manner sufficient to show agreement ... even though the moment of its making is undetermined,' it allows the formation of 'layered contracts'....". Under either analysis, by trade usage and course of dealing, Factors and Unisearch incorporated the liability limitation provisions into their contract for services.

Enforceability of Liability Limitation

Having determined that the liability limitation is included in the contract between Factors and Unisearch, we must now determine whether these liability limitations are enforceable. The liability limitations will not be enforceable if they are unconscionable.

Thirty years ago this court set the standard for applying warranty disclaimers in transactions involving a noncommercial entity. According to the decision in *Berg*, warranty disclaimers in a contract must be both (1) explicitly negotiated and (2) set forth with particularity. The presumption leans against the warranty disclaimer, and the burden lies on the party seeking to include the disclaimer to prove its legality.

Berg involved the sale of a car from a car dealer to a consumer. The car had numerous mechanical problems, but the dealer claimed that the purchaser could not recover because the purchase contract contained warranty disclaimers. The *Berg* court noted that "printed disclaimers of warranty in the purchase of new automobiles are now regarded with increasing disfavor by the courts." Accordingly, the court stated, "unless there is proof of explicit departure, ... the presumption is that the dealer intended to deliver and the buyer intended to receive a reasonably safe, efficient and comfortable brand new car."

A few years later this court held that *Berg* applied in commercial transactions, but with some modifications to the original *Berg* analysis. In *Schroeder*, we shifted the presumption from the party seeking to validate the disclaimer to the party seeking to invalidate the liability limitation by presuming that the limitation was prima facie conscionable in a commercial transaction. 86 Wash. 2d at 262–63. We stated, "It is readily apparent that both 'conspicuousness' and 'negotiations' are factors, albeit not conclusive, which are certainly relevant when determining the issue of conscionability in light of *all the surrounding circumstances.*"

Thus, in *Schroeder* we adopted a totality of the circumstances approach for interpreting the permissibility of exclusionary clauses in a commercial setting, instead of the two-prong approach applied to warranty disclaimers in *Berg* for a consumer transaction. The nonexclusive factors for assessing the totality of the circumstances include: (1) the conspicuousness of the clause in the agreement; (2) the presence or absence of negotiation regarding the clause; (3) the custom and usage of the trade; and (4) any policy developed between the parties during the course of dealing. *Id.* at 259–61. By extending part of *Berg* to commercial transactions, we expressed the intent to prevent unfair surprise in business dealings.

In *American Nursery* this court made another modification and extension of the *Berg/Schroeder* analysis. In that case we confirmed the use of the two-prong *Berg* analysis for consumer transactions involving warranty disclaimers and in commercial transactions for the sale of goods where there is sufficient evidence of unfair surprise. We thus also confirmed the *Schroeder* totality of the circumstances analysis for clauses excluding (or limiting) liability for consequential damages in commercial transactions for services where there is insufficient evidence of unfair surprise. Finding no indicia of unfair surprise, this court then specifically applied the *Schroeder* analysis to a contract for services between commercial parties. In applying the *Schroeder* totality of the circumstances analysis to determine conscionability, we referenced RCW 62A.2–719(3), which states, "Limitation of other consequential damages is valid unless it is established that the limitation is unconscionable." We have previously applied this U.C.C. section to service contracts, and we apply it by analogy here.

The Court of Appeals in this case stated that the exclusionary clause would not be valid if it was not explicitly bargained for. This consideration comes from *Berg* and is, therefore, not controlling in these circumstances. *Berg* involved a consumer transaction for a warranty disclaimer, which has been distinguished from a liability limitation clause in a commercial transaction, such as that presented by Factors and Unisearch. In a commercial transaction, as *Schroeder* and *American Nursery* make clear, whether the liability limitations clause was negotiated (or bargained for) is merely a factor and it is not necessarily the determinative factor in assessing the enforceability of the clause.

Significantly, in *American Nursery*, we limited the application of the *Berg* rule for explicit policy reasons:

> In consumer sales transactions, intervention is warranted to counteract the inherent inequality of bargaining power and the resultant inequities. Parties to a commercial contract, however, generally have equal bargaining power and an equal ability to seek advice and alternative offers. As a result, commercial contracts are less subject to the type of unfair surprise which may be found in consumer sales transactions. This being so, only those commercial transactions with sufficient indicia of unfair surprise in the negotiations should be subject to the *Berg* rule.

As a threshold matter, we conclude that there were no indicia of unfair surprise under these circumstances. Unlike the concern for unfair surprise, most commonly associated with a maze of fine print in warranty disclaimers, the search reports and invoices in this case were brief. The liability limitation clause printed on the invoice did not alter or change during any of the 48 transactions. Additionally, the invoices were directed to the attention of Factors' principals and Factors' president testified that he contemporaneously examined the invoices. Factors had received and paid numerous invoices prior to this dispute. We find all of these factors conclusive that there was no unfair surprise in this case.

Next, by evaluating the totality of the circumstances, we further conclude that the liability limitation clause in the contract for services between Factors and Unisearch is not unconscionable and is therefore enforceable. In *Schroeder* we recognized the following nonexclusive factors to consider in assessing the unconscionability of a liability exclusionary clause: (1) the conspicuousness of the clause in the agreement; (2) the presence or absence of negotiations regarding the clause; (3) the custom and usage of the trade; and (4) any policy developed between the parties during the course of dealing. Additionally, in *American Nursery*, we noted that "[u]nconscionability is determined in light of all the surrounding circumstances, including (1) the manner in which the parties entered into the contract, (2) whether the parties had a reasonable opportunity to understand the terms of the contract, and (3) whether the important terms were hidden in a maze of fine print."

In *American Nursery*, this court recognized that, "[t]he party defending [a limitation of liability clause] may prove the clause is conscionable regardless of the surrounding circumstances if the general commercial setting indicates a prior course of dealing or reasonable usage of trade as to the exclusionary clause." Unisearch provided numerous examples of invoices limiting liability from other states. Unisearch also presented an expert who testified that liability exclusions were common industry practice. Furthermore, the amicus reveals that it is industry practice to limit liability in the U.C.C. search context. Factors did not contest the validity of this evidence. Consistent with our previous analysis of trade usage, we find this evidence supportive of the enforceability of the liability limiting clause. Also consistent with our previous analysis, we find the course of dealing supportive of enforcing the liability limiting clause. Unisearch sent Factors 48 invoices, and at least as many search reports, with identical disclaimers on each respective form. The parties present no evidence regarding whether the invoices were ever discussed, but Factors did in fact receive the invoices and search reports. Therefore, we conclude that the general commercial setting establishes a prior course of dealing.

We thus hold, as a matter of law, that the totality of the circumstances support the conscionability and enforceability of the liability limitation clause in the contract for services between Factors and Unisearch. We reverse the Court of Appeals' decision and affirm the trial court's grant of summary judgment limiting Unisearch's liability, if any, to the amount of the fee charged for its service.

Questions

1. If course of dealing or usage of trade establishes a limitation of liability to the price of the service (or presumably, a product), is it necessary to discover a clause in some document–an invoice or other document—in order to recognize this understanding as part of the contract? See the definition of "agreement" in UCC 1–201(3).

2. If the evidence of trade usage in the instant case was insufficient to create an agreement limiting liability, would courts generally agree that course of dealing can be established through the repeated sending of printed ("standardized") forms containing a limitation of liability clause? Recall illustration 5 in the discussion of proposed amended Section 2–207, *supra*. Several courts have refused to accept the simple repeated sending of standardized terms as constituting prior course of dealing.

3. Consider the court's analysis of the evolution of warranty disclaimers and liability exclusions in the state of Washington, in particular the change to the presumption of conscionability concerning such clauses, at least in commercial transactions. Do you agree that commercial parties "generally have equal bargaining power"?

4. If there was no evidence of trade usage or course of dealing, does the court suggest that the same result may have been achieved through a

"layered" contract theory, which it had adopted (following the *ProCD* and *Hill v. Gateway* analyses) a few years earlier?

Problem 22

(a) Peck Industries, Inc. (P) sent a purchase order to Weiscz Graphics (W) for certain advertising materials at a price of $400,000. The purchase order required the materials to be delivered under a "release program"—i.e. W would produce the material and then store it to be shipped as needed by P. The W acknowledgment contained terms identical to those of the purchase order except for a statement that the contract was to be completed within twelve months. The clear trade usage was that "release program" contracts were to be completed within 12 months. P was not ready to complete the contract within 12 months. At the end of the 12 months period W demanded the balance of the contract price ($125,000) and refused to continue storing the remaining material for P without additional compensation. What result? See amended 1–303. Quaere: is this a "battle of the forms" problem under 2–207? Would your analysis change if the acknowledgment had not contained the 12 month limitation?

(b) Southland Farms, Inc. (S) alleged that it suffered consequential damages in the form of crop losses because of defects in agricultural chemicals supplied by Ciba Corporation (C). S had signed a C form which contained a clause excluding consequential damages. S claims that the clause is unconscionable. C argues that the same printed clause was found in fifty prior contracts between the parties, and that S had never complained. What result?

(c) Luedtke Engineering, Inc. (L) contracted to purchase all of the limestone it would require for a particular project from Portland Limestone, Inc. (P). The contract provided for delivery of 150 tons of limestone each day of the contract. The parties had five similar contracts in the past, each of which required deliveries of 150 tons per day although, in fact, P had never delivered exactly 150 tons. The daily deliveries ranged from 90 tons to 160 tons. After three daily deliveries of 100, 95 and 155 tons, L claimed a breach of contract. P sought to introduce evidence of the parties prior course of dealing. L argued that admitting such evidence would violate amended 1–303(e) of the UCC. Evaluate L's argument.

(d) Shelton (S) borrowed 90 percent of the purchase price of a new truck from Westinghouse Credit Corporation (W). Shelton was to repay the loan over five years in 60 monthly payments. One clause in the contract required payments no later than the 10th of each month. Another clause stated, "The waiver or indulgence of any default by the buyer of any provision of this agreement shall not operate as a waiver of any subsequent default by the buyer or as a waiver of any of the other rights of [W] herein. Time shall be deemed the essence of this agreement." S made 41 consecutive payments, each of which was late from three days to 19 days. When the 42nd payment was 14 days late, W refused to accept it and attempted to foreclose on its collateral. What result?

Questions

(1) If course of performance is proven, is it always a modification of the contract terms?

(2) What is the relationship between course of performance "waivers" and the parol evidence rule?

(3) If course of performance operates as a modification or "waiver," why does 1–303(e)(1) state that "express terms prevail over course of performance . . ."?

(4) Is a course of performance "waiver" subject to the 2–201 statute of frauds via 2–209(3)?

(5) If a writing evidencing a contract contains a no oral modification clause, may the contract be modified through course of performance not evidenced by any writing?

X. PAROL EVIDENCE AND INTERPRETATION—CISG

MCC–MARBLE CERAMIC CENTER, INC. v. d'AGOSTINO, S.p.A.,

United States Court of Appeals for the Eleventh Circuit, 1998.
144 F.3d 1384.

BIRCH, CIRCUIT JUDGE: This case requires us to determine whether a court must consider parol evidence in a contract dispute governed by the United Nations Convention on Contracts for the International Sale of Goods ("CISG"[1]). The district court granted summary judgment on behalf of the defendant-appellee, relying on certain terms and provisions that appeared on the reverse of a pre-printed form contract for the sale of ceramic tiles. The plaintiff-appellant sought to rely on a number of affidavits that tended to show both that the parties had arrived at an oral contract before memorializing their agreement in writing and that they subjectively intended not to apply the terms on the reverse of the contract to their agreements. The magistrate judge held that the affidavits did not raise an issue of material fact and recommended that the district court grant summary judgment based on the terms of the contract. The district court agreed with the magistrate judge's reasoning and entered summary judgment in the defendant-appellee's favor.

The plaintiff-appellant, MCC–Marble Ceramic, Inc. ("MCC"), is a Florida corporation engaged in the retail sale of tiles, and the defendant-appellee, Ceramica Nuova d'Agostino S.p.A. ("d'Agostino") is an Italian corporation engaged in the manufacture of ceramic tiles. In October 1990, MCC's president, Juan Carlos Mozon, met representatives of d'Agostino at a trade fair in Bologna, Italy and negotiated an agreement

---

1. United Nations Convention on Contracts for the International Sale of Goods, opened for signature April 11, 1980, S. Treaty Doc. No. 9, 98th Cong., 1st Sess. 22 (1983), 19 I.L.M. 671, reprinted at, 15 U.S.C. App. 52 (1997)

to purchase ceramic tiles from d'Agostino based on samples he examined at the trade fair. Mozon, who spoke no Italian, communicated with Gianni Silingardi, then d'Agostino's commercial director, through a translator, Gianfranco Copelli, who was himself an agent of d'Agostino. The parties apparently arrived at an oral agreement on the crucial terms of price, quality, quantity, delivery and payment. The parties then recorded these terms on one of d'Agostino's standard, pre-printed order forms and Mozon signed the contract on MCC's behalf. According to MCC, the parties also entered into a requirements contract in February 1991, subject to which d'Agostino agreed to supply MCC with high grade ceramic tile at specific discounts as long as MCC purchased sufficient quantities of tile. MCC completed a number of additional order forms requesting tile deliveries pursuant to that agreement.

MCC brought suit against d'Agostino claiming a breach of the February 1991 requirements contract when d'Agostino failed to satisfy orders in April, May, and August of 1991. In addition to other defenses, d'Agostino responded that it was under no obligation to fill MCC's orders because MCC had defaulted on payment for previous shipments. In support of its position, d'Agostino relied on the pre-printed terms of the contracts that MCC had executed. The executed forms were printed in Italian and contained terms and conditions on both the front and reverse. According to an English translation of the October 1990 contract, the front of the order form contained the following language directly beneath Mozon's signature:

> The buyer hereby states that he is aware of the sales conditions stated on the reverse and that he expressly approves of them with special reference to those numbered 1–2–3–4–5–6–7–8.

> Default or delay in payment within the time agreed upon gives d'Agostino the right to ... suspend or cancel the contract itself and to cancel possible other pending contracts and the buyer does not have the right to indemnification or damages.

d'Agostino also brought a number of counterclaims against MCC, seeking damages for MCC's alleged nonpayment for deliveries of tile that d'Agostino had made between February 28, 1991 and July 4, 1991. MCC responded that the tile it had received was of a lower quality than contracted for, and that, pursuant to the CISG, MCC was entitled to reduce payment in proportion to the defects.[4] d'Agostino, however, noted that clause 4 on the reverse of the contract states, in pertinent part:

> Possible complaints for defects of the merchandise must be made in writing by means of a certified letter within and not later than 10 days after receipt of the merchandise....

Although there is evidence to support MCC's claims that it complained about the quality of the deliveries it received, MCC never submitted any written complaints. MCC did not dispute these underlying

---

4. Article 50 of the CISG permits a buyer to reduce payment for nonconforming goods in proportion to the nonconformity under certain conditions.

facts before the district court, but argued that the parties never intended the terms and conditions printed on the reverse of the order form to apply to their agreements. As evidence for this assertion, MCC submitted Mozon's affidavit, which claims that MCC had no subjective intent to be bound by those terms and that d'Agostino was aware of this intent. MCC also filed affidavits from Silingardi and Copelli, d'Agostino's representatives at the trade fair, which support Mozon's claim that the parties subjectively intended not to be bound by the terms on the reverse of the order form. The magistrate judge held that the affidavits, even if true, did not raise an issue of material fact regarding the interpretation or applicability of the terms of the written contracts and the district court accepted his recommendation to award summary judgment in d'Agostino's favor. MCC then filed this timely appeal.

The parties to this case agree that the CISG governs their dispute because the United States, where MCC has its place of business, and Italy, where d'Agostino has its place of business, are both States Party to the Convention.[5] See CISG, art. 1. Article 8 of the CISG governs the interpretation of international contracts for the sale of goods and forms the basis of MCC's appeal from the district court's grant of summary judgment in d'Agostino's favor.[7] MCC argues that the magistrate judge and the district court improperly ignored evidence that MCC submitted regarding the parties' subjective intent when they memorialized the terms of their agreement on d'Agostino's pre-printed form contract, and that the magistrate judge erred by applying the parol evidence rule in derogation of the CISG.

Contrary to what is familiar practice in United States courts, the CISG appears to permit a substantial inquiry into the parties' subjective intent, even if the parties did not engage in any objectively ascertainable means of registering this intent. Article 8(1) of the CISG instructs courts to interpret the "statements … and other conduct of a party … according to his intent" as long as the other party "knew or could not have been unaware" of that intent. The plain language of the Convention, therefore, requires an inquiry into a party's subjective intent as long as the other party to the contract was aware of that intent.[8]

5. The United States Senate ratified the CISG in 1986, and the United States deposited its instrument of ratification at the United Nations Headquarters in New York on December 11, 1986. See Preface to Convention, reprinted at *15 U.S.C. app. 52* (1997). The Convention entered into force between the United States and the other States Parties, including Italy, on January 1, 1988. See id.; *Filanto S.p.A. v. Chilewich Int'l Corp.*, 789 F.Supp. 1229, 1237 (S.D.N.Y.1992).

7. CISG, Article 8: (1) For the purposes of this Convention statements made by and other conduct of a party are to be interpreted according to his intent where the other party knew or could not have been unaware what that intent was.

(2) If the preceding paragraph is not applicable, statements made by and conduct of a party are to be interpreted according to the understanding a reasonable person of the same kind as the other party would have had in the same circumstances.

(3) In determining the intent of a party or the understanding a reasonable person would have had, due consideration is to be given to all relevant circumstances of the case including the negotiations, any practices which the parties have established between themselves, usages and any subsequent conduct of the parties.

8. In the United States, the legislatures, courts, and the legal academy have voiced a preference for relying on objective manifes-

In this case, MCC has submitted three affidavits that discuss the purported subjective intent of the parties to the initial agreement concluded between MCC and d'Agostino in October 1990. All three affidavits discuss the preliminary negotiations and report that the parties arrived at an oral agreement for d'Agostino to supply quantities of a specific grade of ceramic tile to MCC at an agreed upon price. The affidavits state that the "oral agreement established the essential terms of quality, quantity, description of goods, delivery, price and payment." The affidavits also note that the parties memorialized the terms of their oral agreement on a standard d'Agostino order form, but all three affiants contend that the parties subjectively intended not to be bound by the terms on the reverse of that form despite a provision directly below the signature line that expressly and specifically incorporated those terms.

The terms on the reverse of the contract give d'Agostino the right to suspend or cancel all contracts in the event of a buyer's non-payment and require a buyer to make a written report of all defects within ten days. As the magistrate judge's report and recommendation makes clear, if these terms applied to the agreements between MCC and d'Agostino, summary judgment would be appropriate because MCC failed to make any written complaints about the quality of tile it received and d'Agostino has established MCC's non-payment of a number of invoices amounting to $108,389.40 and 102,053,846.00 Italian lira.

Article 8(1) of the CISG requires a court to consider this evidence of the parties' subjective intent. Contrary to the magistrate judge's report, which the district court endorsed and adopted, article 8(1) does not focus on interpreting the parties' statements alone. Although we agree with the magistrate judge's conclusion that no "interpretation" of the contract's terms could support MCC's position, article 8(1) also requires a court to consider subjective intent while interpreting the conduct of the parties. The CISG's language, therefore, requires courts to consider evidence of a party's subjective intent when signing a contract if the other party to the contract was aware of that intent at the time. This is precisely the type of evidence that MCC has provided through the Silingardi, Copelli, and Mozon affidavits, which discuss not only Mozon's intent as MCC's representative but also discuss the intent of d'Agostino's representatives and their knowledge that Mozon did not intend to

tations of the parties' intentions. For example, Article Two of the Uniform Commercial Code, which most states have enacted in some form or another to govern contracts for the sale of goods, is replete with references to standards of commercial reasonableness. See e.g., U.C.C. § 2–206 (referring to reasonable means of accepting an offer); see also *Lucy v. Zehmer*, 196 Va. 493, 503, 84 S.E.2d 516, 522 (1954) ("Whether the writing signed ... was the result of a serious offer ... and a serious acceptance ... , or was a serious offer ... and an acceptance in secret jest ... , in either event it consti-

tuted a binding contract of sale between the parties."). Justice Holmes expressed the philosophy behind this focus on the objective in forceful terms: "The law has nothing to do with the actual state of the parties' minds. In contract, as elsewhere, it must go by externals, and judge parties by their conduct." Oliver W. Holmes, The Common Law 242 (Howe ed. 1963) quoted in John O. Honnold, Uniform Law for International Sales under the 1980 United Nations Convention § 107 at 164 (2d ed. 1991) (hereinafter Honnold, Uniform Law).

agree to the terms on the reverse of the form contract. This acknowledgment that d'Agostino's representatives were aware of Mozon's subjective intent puts this case squarely within article 8(1) of the CISG, and therefore requires the court to consider MCC's evidence as it interprets the parties' conduct.[11]

Given our determination that the magistrate judge and the district court should have considered MCC's affidavits regarding the parties' subjective intentions, we must address a question of first impression in this circuit: whether the parol evidence rule, which bars evidence of an earlier oral contract that contradicts or varies the terms of a subsequent or contemporaneous written contract, plays any role in cases involving the CISG. We begin by observing that the parol evidence rule, contrary to its title, is a substantive rule of law, not a rule of evidence. The rule does not purport to exclude a particular type of evidence as proving a fact, but prevents a litigant from attempting to show the fact. As such, a federal district court cannot simply apply the parol evidence rule as a procedural matter—as it might if excluding a particular type of evidence under the Federal Rules of Evidence, which apply in federal court regardless of the source of the substantive rule of decision. See II Farnsworth on Contracts, § 7.2 at 196 (1990).[13]

The CISG itself contains no express statement on the role of parol evidence. It is clear, however, that the drafters of the CISG were comfortable with the concept of permitting parties to rely on oral contracts because they eschewed any statutes of fraud provision and expressly provided for the enforcement of oral contracts. Compare CISG, art. 11 (a contract of sale need not be concluded or evidenced in writing) with U.C.C. § 2–201 (precluding the enforcement of oral contracts for the sale of goods involving more than $500). Moreover, article 8(3) of the CISG expressly directs courts to give "due consideration . . . to all relevant circumstances of the case including the negotiations . . ." to determine the intent of the parties. Given article 8(1)'s directive to use the intent of the parties to interpret their statements and conduct, article 8(3) is a clear instruction to admit and consider parol evidence regarding the negotiations to the extent they reveal the parties' subjective intent.

11. Without this crucial acknowledgment, we would interpret the contract and the parties' actions according to article 8(2), which directs courts to rely on objective evidence of the parties' intent. On the facts of this case it seems readily apparent that MCC's affidavits provide no evidence that Mozon's actions would have made his alleged subjective intent not to be bound by the terms of the contract known to "the understanding that a reasonable person . . . would have had in the same circumstances." CISG, art 8(2).

13. An example demonstrates this point. The CISG provides that a contract for the sale of goods need not be in writing and that the parties may prove the contract "by any means, including witnesses." CISG, art. 11. Nevertheless, a party seeking to prove a contract in such a manner in federal court could not do so in a way that violated in the rule against hearsay. See Fed. R. Evid. 802 (barring hearsay evidence). A federal district court applies the Federal Rules of Evidence because these rules are considered procedural, regardless of the source of the law that governs the substantive decision. Cf. Farnsworth on Contracts § 7.2 at 196 & n. 16 (citing cases).

Despite the CISG's broad scope, surprisingly few cases have applied the Convention in the United States,[14] see *Delchi Carrier SpA v. Rotorex Corp.*, 71 F.3d 1024, 1027–28 (2d Cir.1995) (observing that "there is virtually no case law under the Convention"), and only two reported decisions touch upon the parol evidence rule, both in dicta. One court has concluded, much as we have above, that the parol evidence rule is not viable in CISG cases in light of article 8 of the Convention. In *Filanto*, a district court addressed the differences between the UCC and the CISG on the issues of offer and acceptance and the battle of the forms. See 789 F.Supp. at 1238. After engaging in a thorough analysis of how the CISG applied to the dispute before it, the district court tangentially observed that article 8(3) "essentially rejects ... the parol evidence rule." *Id.* at 1238 n.7. Another court, however, appears to have arrived at a contrary conclusion. In *Beijing Metals & Minerals Import/Export Corp. v. American Bus. Ctr., Inc.*, 993 F.2d 1178 (5th Cir.1993), a defendant sought to avoid summary judgment on a contract claim by relying on evidence of contemporaneously negotiated oral terms that the parties had not included in their written agreement. The plaintiff, a Chinese corporation, relied on Texas law in its complaint while the defendant, apparently a Texas corporation, asserted that the CISG governed the dispute. Without resolving the choice of law question, the Fifth Circuit cited *Filanto* for the proposition that there have been very few reported cases applying the CISG in the United States, and stated that the parol evidence rule would apply regardless of whether Texas law or the CISG governed the dispute. The opinion does not acknowledge *Filanto*'s more applicable dictum that the parol evidence rule does not apply to CISG cases nor does it conduct any analysis of the Convention to support its conclusion. In fact, the Fifth Circuit did not undertake to interpret the CISG in a manner that would arrive at a result consistent with the parol evidence rule but instead explained that it would apply the rule as developed at Texas common law. As persuasive authority for this court, the *Beijing Metals* opinion is not particularly persuasive on this point.

Our reading of article 8(3) as a rejection of the parol evidence rule, however, is in accordance with the great weight of academic commentary on the issue. As one scholar has explained:

> The language of Article 8(3) that "due consideration is to be given to all relevant circumstances of the case" seems adequate to override any domestic rule that would bar a tribunal from considering the relevance of other agreements.... Article 8(3) relieves tribunals from domestic rules that might bar them from "considering" any evidence between the parties that is relevant. This added flexibility for interpretation is consistent with a growing body of

---

14. Moreover, the parties have not cited us to any persuasive authority from the courts of other States Party to the CISG. Our own research uncovered a promising source for such decisions at http://www.cisg.law.pace.edu>, but produced no cases that address the issue of parol evidence.

opinion that the "parol evidence rule" has been an embarrassment for the administration of modern transactions.

Honnold, Uniform Law § 110 at 170.[17]

One of the factors motivating the negotiation and adoption of the CISG was to provide parties to international contracts for the sale of goods with some degree of certainty as to the principles of law that would govern potential disputes and remove the previous doubt regarding which party's legal system might otherwise apply. Courts applying the CISG cannot, therefore, upset the parties' reliance on the Convention by substituting familiar principles of domestic law when the Convention requires a different result.[18] We may only achieve the directives of good faith and uniformity in contracts under the CISG by interpreting and applying the plain language of article 8(3) as written and obeying its directive to consider this type of parol evidence.

This is not to say that parties to an international contract for the sale of goods cannot depend on written contracts or that parol evidence regarding subjective contractual intent need always prevent a party relying on a written agreement from securing summary judgment. To the contrary, most cases will not present a situation (as exists in this case) in which both parties to the contract acknowledge a subjective intent not to be bound by the terms of a pre-printed writing. In most cases, therefore, article 8(2) of the CISG will apply, and objective evidence will provide the basis for the court's decision. See Honnold, Uniform Law § 107 at 164–65. Consequently, a party to a contract governed by the CISG will not be able to avoid the terms of a contract and force a jury trial simply by submitting an affidavit which states that he or she did not have the subjective intent to be bound by the contract's terms. Cf. Klopfenstein v. Pargeter, 597 F.2d 150, 152 (9th Cir.1979)

17. See also Louis F. Del Duca, et al., Sales Under the Uniform Commercial Code and the Convention on International Sale of Goods, 173–74 (1993); Henry D. Gabriel, A Primer on the United Nations Convention on the International Sale of Goods: From the Perspective of the Uniform Commercial Code, 7 Ind. Int'l & Comp. L. Rev. 279, 281 (1997) ("Subjective intent is given primary consideration.... [Article 8] allows open-ended reliance on parol evidence...."); Herbert Berstein & Joseph Lookofsky, Understanding the CISG in Europe 29 (1997) ("The CISG has dispensed with the parol evidence rule which might otherwise operate to exclude extrinsic evidence under the law of certain Common Law countries."); Harry M. Fletchner, Recent Developments: CISG, 14 J.L. & Com. 153, 157 (1995) (criticizing the Beijing Metals opinion and noting that "commentators generally agree that article 8(3) rejects the approach to the parol evidence questions taken by U.S. domestic law.") (collecting authority); John E. Murray, Jr., An Essay on the Formation of

Contracts and Related Matters Under the United Nations Convention on Contracts for the International Sale of Goods, 8 J.L. & Com. 11, 12 (1988) ("We are struck by a new world where there is ... no parol evidence rule, among other differences."); Peter Winship, Domesticating International Commercial Law: Revising U.C.C. Article 2 in Light of the United Nations Sales Convention, 37 Loy. L. Rev. 43, 57 (1991).

18. Article 7 of the CISG provides, in pertinent part,

(1) In the interpretation of this Convention, regard is to be had to its international character and to the need to promote uniformity in its application and the observance of good faith in international trade."

(2) Questions concerning matters governed by this Convention which are not expressly settled in it are to be settled in conformity with the general principles on which it is based.

(affirming summary judgment despite the appellant's submission of his own affidavit regarding his subjective intent: "Undisclosed, subjective intentions are immaterial in [a] commercial transaction, especially when contradicted by objective conduct. Thus, the affidavit has no legal effect even if its averments are accepted as wholly truthful."). Moreover, to the extent parties wish to avoid parol evidence problems they can do so by including a merger clause in their agreement that extinguishes any and all prior agreements and understandings not expressed in the writing.[19]

Considering MCC's affidavits in this case, however, we conclude that the magistrate judge and the district court improperly granted summary judgment in favor of d'Agostino. Although the affidavits are, as d'Agostino observes, relatively conclusory and unsupported by facts that would objectively establish MCC's intent not to be bound by the conditions on the reverse of the form, article 8(1) requires a court to consider evidence of a party's subjective intent when the other party was aware of it, and the Silingardi and Copelli affidavits provide that evidence. This is not to say that the affidavits are conclusive proof of what the parties intended. A reasonable finder of fact, for example, could disregard testimony that purportedly sophisticated international merchants signed a contract without intending to be bound as simply too incredible to believe and hold MCC to the conditions printed on the reverse of the contract. Nevertheless, the affidavits raise an issue of material fact regarding the parties' intent to incorporate the provisions on the reverse of the form contract. If the finder of fact determines that the parties did not intend to rely on those provisions, then the more general provisions of the CISG will govern the outcome of the dispute.

MCC asks us to reverse the district court's grant of summary judgment in favor of d'Agostino. The district court's decision rests on pre-printed contractual terms and conditions incorporated on the reverse of a standard order form that MCC's president signed on the company's behalf. Nevertheless, we conclude that the CISG, which governs international contracts for the sale of goods, precludes summary judgment in this case because MCC has raised an issue of material fact concerning the parties' subjective intent to be bound by the terms on the reverse of the pre-printed contract. The CISG also precludes the application of the parol evidence rule, which would otherwise bar the consideration of evidence concerning a prior or contemporaneously negotiated oral agreement. Accordingly, we REVERSE the district court's grant of summary judgment and REMAND this case for further proceedings consistent with this opinion.

19. See Ronald A. Brand & Harry M. Fletchner, *Arbitration and Contract Formation in International Trade: First Interpretations of the U.N. Sales Convention*, 12 J.L. & Com. 239, 252 (1993) (arguing that article 8(3) of the CISG will not permit the consideration of parol evidence when the parties have expressly excluded oral modifications of the contract pursuant to article 29); see also I Albert Kritzer, Guide to Practical Applications of the United Nations Convention on Contracts for the International Sale of Goods 125 (1989) (counseling the use of a merger clause to compensate for the absence of a parol evidence rule in the CISG).

Y. LEASES AND THE PAROL EVIDENCE RULE

The parol evidence provision of Article 2A, 2A–202, replicates 2–202, thus making the familiar approach to parol evidence in Article 2 applicable to leases. Article 2A contains no separate section(s) concerning trade usage or course of dealing since the definitions of these terms in 1–205 apply to all U.C.C. articles. The treatment of course of performance in 2–208, in contrast, applies only under Article 2. To close this gap, pre-amendment Article 2A includes its own course of performance provision, 2A–207[1], which is virtually identical to the course of performance section of Article 2. Finally, the definition of "lease agreement" in 2A–103(1)(k) repeats the emphasis on "factual bargain" found in the definition of "agreement" in 1–201(3). Thus a "lease agreement" is to be discovered in the language of the parties "or by implication from other circumstances including course of dealing or usage of trade or course of performance." 2A–103(1)(k).

Proposed amended Section 2A–202 carries the same section number but differs from its predecessor as well as pre-amendment 2–202 and UCITA section 301, because it includes within the statutory language the test to be used by a court in deciding whether evidence of an additional term may be admitted: "terms in such a record may be supplemented by evidence of (1) consistent additional terms, unless the court finds that . . . the additional terms if agreed upon *would certainly have been included in the record* . . ." (emphasis supplied). There is no disagreement between the parol evidence rules in Articles 2 and 2A concerning this test: it is found in comment 3 to pre-amendment 2–202 and comment 4 to proposed amended Section 2–202.

Z. "OPEN" AND IMPLIED TERMS—THE "ANTI–TECHNICAL" ENVIRONMENT

The Basic Philosophy—2–204. Much of Part 3 of Article 2 is concerned with missing or implied terms, i.e., terms that the parties have not expressly addressed in their contract. Parties often intend to form a contract despite leaving "gaps" in their expression of agreement. Professor Llewellyn and the other drafters of Article 2 were compelled to make a policy decision concerning the level of indefiniteness that could exist in an enforceable contract. The basic approach of Article 2 to this issue is found in an often-overlooked but critical section. Section 2–204 establishes three significant policies concerning indefiniteness in contracts.

---

1. It should be recalled that Article 2A does not contain a "battle of the forms" section like 2–207 in Article 2.

First, as we saw earlier in this Chapter, the *manner* in which a contract for the sale of goods is formed is irrelevant if the outward manifestations of the parties are sufficient to demonstrate "agreement." 2–204(1). Section 2–206 dealing with offer and acceptance in contract formation and allowing any reasonable manner or medium of acceptance, is an elaboration of this general policy of 2–204(1). The focus, again, is the "agreement," the factual bargain of the parties, which must be effectuated notwithstanding the former technical barriers of monistic, pre-Code contract law.

Second, 2–204(2) rejects any notion that the precise moment of contract formation be identified. If the manifestations of the parties evidence their factual bargain, their agreement must be enforced even if the exact moment of its making cannot be determined. This again evidences the "anti-technical" nature of the Code. It is one more way in which Article 2 encourages courts to effectuate the factual bargain of the parties by ignoring outmoded doctrine.

Finally, 2–204(3) directly addresses the question of "open terms" and the extent to which courts should fill gaps in order to effectuate the agreement of the parties. Again, the central focus is the agreement of the parties: "Even though one or more terms are left open a contract for sale does not fail for indefiniteness if the parties have intended to make a contract and there is a reasonably certain basis for giving an appropriate remedy." Once the two critical elements have been found—intention to make a contract and a reasonably certain basis for an appropriate remedy—even numerous "gaps" will not be fatal.[1]

Part 3 of Article 2 supplies terms that the parties leave open. It does so by effectuating, and in some cases going beyond, pre-Code law. Section 2–301 states the general obligations of the parties: the seller must transfer and deliver the goods, and the buyer must accept and pay for them, in accordance with the contract. The comment to this section stresses the modern analysis of these basic obligations in terms of constructive "conditions."

Section 2–305 deals with open price terms. It emphasizes the enforceability of agreements with a missing price term, provided the parties intend to "conclude a contract for sale," and it goes well beyond pre-Code notions in enforcing "agreements to agree" on price.[2]

As we saw earlier in this Chapter, 2–306 governs the enforceability of requirement and output contracts. The section deals with the uncertainty of the quantity term in such agreements by imposing an obligation of good faith on the party determining quantity. Notwithstanding the somewhat nebulous character of this gap-filler, 2–306 emphatically

---

1. This policy is pursued in UCITA Section 306, which deals with "open terms" in a basic fashion: "A performance obligation that cannot be determined from the agreement or from other provisions of this Act requires the party to perform in a manner and in a time that is reasonable in light of the commercial circumstances existing at the time of agreement."

2. Comment 1 to 2–305 is abundantly clear: "This article rejects in these instances the formula that 'an agreement to agree is unenforceable.' "

rejects arguments that requirement and output contracts are fatally indefinite.

Where the parties have failed to specify whether the seller must deliver the goods in a single lot or in multiple installments, 2–307 provides a workable solution by rejecting overly-technical pre-Code holdings. Sections 2–308 and 2–309 supply appropriate terms where the parties have failed to specify the place or time of delivery. Section 2–310 fills the gap left when parties have not designated a time for payment, and it also deals with ambiguities relating to documentary transactions (e.g., delivery using a bill of lading), shipment under reservation, and sales on credit.

In some cases parties intend to be presently bound by an agreement that permits one of them to specify particulars of performance at a later date. For example, the buyer and seller may leave details concerning the selection or assortment of goods to be decided by one of them at the time of shipment. Although pre-Code law was split on the question, 2–311 permits the enforcement of such agreements. The section also fills gaps in agreements containing such arrangements.

Parties to a sale often fail to specify the standard of quality of the goods being sold. In those cases the quality standards are supplied by the critically important implied warranties of merchantability, 2–314, and fitness for a particular purpose, 2–315. While the warranties of title and against infringement created by 2–312 are not designated "implied" warranties, these warranties are in fact implied when an agreement does not expressly protect the buyer's expectation of ownership and use of the goods.[3] Warranty questions are sufficiently important to require separate treatment in Chapter 3. It should not be forgotten, however, that, like many other provisions in Part 3 of Article 2, the warranty sections frequently operate to fill gaps in the parties' agreement.

For a supplementary treatment of the law governing implication of missing terms, see Restatement of Contracts, Second, § 204, Comment d, which refers to UCC gap-filling sections.

Problem 23

(a) North Airlines, Inc. (N) entered into a contract with Continental Oil, Inc. (C) whereby C agreed to supply N with all of the jet fuel it would require for one year. The price was to be determined by reference to prices published weekly in the Jet Fuel Market Index (JFMI). Three months into the contract year, JFMI ceased publication. C insisted that the next delivery would

---

3. The drafters refused to characterize the warranties in 2–312 as "implied" because the section contains its own provisions for disclaimers (see 2–312(2) & (3)). Thus the other provisions of Article 2 dealing with disclaimers of "implied warranties," 2–316(2) & (3), were not intended to apply to the warranties in 2–312. To provide for this result, the 2–312 warranties are not labeled "implied." See comment 6 to 2–312. Note again, however, that the warranties of title and against infringement in 2–312 are in fact "implied" (although not designated as such) where the parties' agreement fails to address the question of the buyer's title or freedom from claims of third parties.

require a 20% increase over the last invoice price. N argued for only a five percent increase. What result?

(b) Assume that the parties in (a) had not agreed on an indexed price. Rather, they had signed the contract with an understanding that they would agree upon a price by one month before the first delivery of jet fuel. The first delivery is now due and the parties have yet to agree on a price. Analyze.

(c) Hanes Corporation (H) agreed to purchase three fork lift trucks from Lift, Inc. (L). As to price, the written contract stated, "Price in effect at time of delivery of equipment." After delivering the trucks the seller sent an invoice showing a 25 percent increase over its former list price. Other fork lift manufacturers had not raised their prices beyond 5 percent, and the national and world economies demonstrated extremely low inflation rates. Analyze.

(d) Mildred Wright owned an original painting by the famous artist, Utrillo. In need of funds, Wright offered to sell the painting to Charles Miller if the price was established by a well-known art critic and appraiser, Catherine Dumont. Miller accepted after Ms. Dumont agreed to appraise the painting and establish the price Miller would pay. A week before she was scheduled to inspect the painting Ms. Dumont was killed in an auto accident. Wright now refuses to sell the painting to Miller. What result?

(e) Arch Enterprises (A) sent an "RFP" (request for proposal) to King Thermostats, Inc. (K) for 1000 computerized thermostats to be shipped within three months. K replied with a letter stating "We will sell 1000 computerized thermostats to you on the following terms: X–35 thermostats each at $200; X–37 thermostats each at $250; X–41 thermostats each at $300." A responded by fax, "Accept offer for 1000 thermostats. We will notify you of model(s) we want before shipment." Prior to shipment, A had a change of heart and notified K that the order was canceled. Analyze.

(f) Assuming a contract was formed in (e), where was the place of delivery? What was the time for delivery?

(g) Assume the facts of (e) except that A did not have a change of heart. It notified K of the model it required and K shipped 1000 units of that model. The shipment was by an independent carrier, Transnational. Transnational's truck and the thermostats it carried were destroyed in an accident while en route to A. As we will see in Chapter 5, the party who bears the risk of such occurrences will vary depending upon the delivery term included in the contract. If a "shipment" term is specified, the risk of loss would pass to the buyer upon delivery of the thermostats to the carrier, and A would have to pay for the destroyed thermostats. If the contract contained a "destination" term, the risk would remain with the seller until the goods reached the buyer (2–509), and K would not be entitled to payment from A. Suppose the contract between A and K contained no delivery term. Which kind of term is implied? Consider 2–503 and the comments thereto.

(h) West University contracted with Scientific Products, Inc. (SPI) to deliver an X–3000 NMR to West at a price of $700,000. The contract required the product to be satisfactory to the buyer. The NMR was delivered and used under the direction of Professor Harold Davis. Ten days later,

Davis said that he was dissatisfied with the NMR and told a university official to "send it back." NMR can prove that there is no defect in the NMR and other scientists, including professors doing work similar to Davis', would find it acceptable. Consider 2–326.

AA. ASSIGNMENT AND DELEGATION

UCC 2–210(2) recognizes the free assignability of contract rights unless the assignment would materially change the obligor's duty, materially increase the burden or risk imposed upon him, or materially impair his chance of obtaining return performance. This principle is, however, prefaced by the phrase, "Unless otherwise agreed," suggesting that by their agreement, the parties could include an enforceable anti-assignment clause. This language may be seen as conflicting with UCC 9–406(d) (pre-amendment 9–318(4)), which makes anti-assignment clauses ineffective when applied to the assignment of accounts. While these sections can be reconciled by emphasizing that Article 9 does not apply to assignments that have nothing to do with commercial financing, proposed amended Section 2–210 continues the free assignability concept, "except as otherwise provided in Section 9–406." Comment 3 to proposed amended Section 2–210 explains that UCC 9–406 "makes rights for goods sold ('accounts'), whether or not earned, freely alienable by invalidating anti-assignment terms in agreements between account debtors and seller-assignors, and also by invalidating terms that render these assignments a breach." Except for reorganizing the provision, this is the only significant change made by proposed amended Section 2–210.

Chapter 3

WARRANTIES

A. INTRODUCTION: THE WARRANTY CONCEPT

The term "warranty" has been used in several distinct senses over the years. Karl Llewellyn, the principal draftsman of Article 2, once suggested that the "sane course is to discard the word from one's thinking" because to "say 'warranty' is to say nothing of legal effect."[1] Consider a factual statement about a product by the seller. It could be viewed as a promise of indemnity, i.e., one to save the buyer harmless if the product fails to conform to the seller's representation. That promise would be performed if the seller repaired or replaced the product or if the seller refunded payments on the price and canceled the debt for any unpaid balance. On the other hand, contract law could characterize the seller's statement as a representation that created a condition to the buyer's duty to pay for the product. When the representation proved to be false, the condition would not be met and the buyer's duty to pay for the mower would be discharged.

Whether warranties should be characterized as promises or conditions, however, is no longer significant. They have taken on a life of their own, and Llewellyn felt compelled to use the term in his new Code though he insisted on significant changes from the way the term had been used in the old Sales Act. Under UCC Article 2, four warranty sections are critical. Three are concerned with the *quality* of the goods, and these warranties of quality have clearly captured the center stage of judicial attention. In this chapter, therefore, *express* warranties (2–313), and the *implied* warranties of merchantability (2–314) and fitness for a particular purpose (2–315) will occupy most of our attention. The remaining warranties—the warranties of title and against infringement (2–312(1) & (3))—have played far smaller roles in litigation and will be explored later in this chapter in connection with related concepts concerning the ownership of goods.[2]

1. K. Llewellyn, Cases and Materials on the Law of Sales 210 (1930).

2. The warranty of title is not called an implied warranty because the section that governs it (2–312) contains its own dis-

This chapter will also consider how warranties are disclaimed under 2–316 and the effect of such disclaimers—a topic that is connected with remedies for breach of warranty. Except for a breach of an express warranty, if all implied warranties are effectively disclaimed, the buyer has no remedy for defects in the goods because there is no breach. Conversely, if the buyer retains warranty protection but agrees to severely limit remedies for breach (2–719(1)), the existence of the warranties may give the buyer little actual benefit. Parties are free to substitute their own remedies for breach in place of UCC remedies. Problems arise, however, when the substitute remedy fails to achieve its essential purpose (2–719(2)). A given disclaimer of warranty or exclusion of consequential damages, furthermore, may prove to be unconscionable.

Beyond these matters, it is important to consider the law of products liability, which first arose under a warranty theory and remains a part of sales law (2–318 and 2–715) notwithstanding the later development of a parallel tort theory of strict products liability in Restatement of Torts 2d § 402A. The unfolding complex relationship between warranty and tort theories requires careful analysis.

All of these and related issues must be examined under Article 2 and the CISG. The same issues arising in relation to leases under Article 2A will also be explored, along with relevant dimensions of the UCITA.

B. EXPRESS WARRANTY UNDER UCC ARTICLE 2—FACTS vs. COMMENDATIONS, VALUE OR "PUFF"

WEB PRESS SERVICES CORP. v. NEW LONDON MOTORS, INC.

Supreme Court of Connecticut, 1987.
203 Conn. 342, 525 A.2d 57.

DANNEHY, J. [T]he plaintiff alleged that in July, 1984, the defendant sold to the plaintiff a used 1980 model Ford Bronco (the vehicle), to be used for off-the-road driving. The plaintiff paid the purchase price and took delivery of the vehicle. Mechanical defects developed in the vehicle almost immediately, substantially impairing the vehicle's value to the plaintiff. The defendant several times attempted to remedy those defects, but without success. In October, 1984, the plaintiff tendered back the vehicle to the defendant and notified the defendant that it was revoking its acceptance pursuant to General Statutes sec. 42a–2–608.[1] The plain-

claimer provision (see 2–312(2), whereas the implied warranties of *quality* in 2–314 and 2–315 are subject to separate provisions (2–316(2) & (3)) governing disclaimers of "implied warranties." See comment 9 to 2–312. The warranty of title, however, is in fact "implied" in the sense that it automatically becomes part of a sale of goods unless disclaimed. Since cases dealing with the warranty of title usually focus on whether

the warranty has been disclaimed, discussion of the warranty is postponed until later in this chapter.

1. [General Statutes] Sec. 42a–2–608. Revocation of Acceptance in Whole or in Part. (1) The buyer may revoke his acceptance of a lot or commercial unit whose nonconformity substantially impairs its value to him if he has accepted it (a) on the

tiff requested the return of the purchase price. The defendant refused to return the purchase price.

At trial, there was evidence to show that during the time the plaintiff possessed the vehicle, it experienced various mechanical problems. These problems included leakage and a noise from the left rear of the vehicle and problems with the brakes, muffler, power steering and air conditioning. Most of these difficulties were remedied by ordinary repairs which the defendant performed without cost to the plaintiff. The trial court, in fact, characterized these problems as "mostly minor." Clearly, however, a structural defect in the rear axle was hardly minor. The vehicle continued to present problems to the plaintiff, especially on the left rear side. The defect was not detected by the defendant, but was later discovered upon inspection by a certified mechanic.

The court's basic finding was that the plaintiff had failed to prove that the defendant had breached any express [warranty].

According to the plaintiff, the defendant's repeated statements to the effect that the vehicle was an "excellent" and "unusual" one, and that it was in "mint" and "very good" condition, amounted to an express warranty under General Statutes § 42a–2–313 (a). That section provides that an express warranty is created by "[a]ny affirmation of fact or promise made by the seller to the buyer which relates to the goods and becomes part of the basis of the bargain. . . ." Subsection (b) provides that "[a]ny description of the goods which is made part of the basis of the bargain creates an express warranty that the goods conform to the description." In concluding that the defendant's statements did not amount to an express warranty, the trial court relied on Mikula v. Lucibello, 17 Conn.Sup. 360 (1951). There, the court held that words such as "[t]his car is in A–1 condition" did not create an express warranty but were merely "seller's talk." Id., 361.

The plaintiff bears the burden of proving the existence of an express warranty. The question of whether an express warranty exists is one of fact and we will not reverse a court's finding on this matter unless it is clearly erroneous. We are hard pressed to find that the court's conclusion in this case was clearly erroneous.

The Uniform Commercial Code recognizes that some statements of sellers are merely "puffing" and do not create express warranties. Section 42a–2–313 (2), for example, provides that "an affirmation merely of the value of goods or a statement purporting to be merely the seller's opinion or commendation of the goods does not create a warranty." Drawing the line between puffing and the creation of a warranty is often difficult, but several factors have been identified as helpful in making that determination. See generally J. White & R. Summers, Uniform Commercial Code (2d Ed.) Sec. 9–3. One such factor is the specificity of

reasonable assumption that its nonconformity would be cured and it has not been seasonably cured; or (b) without discovery of such nonconformity if his acceptance was reasonably induced either by the difficulty of discovery before acceptance or by the seller's assurances.

the statements made. A statement such as "this truck will give not less than 15.1 miles to the gallon when it is driven at a steady 60 miles per hour" is more likely to be found to create an express warranty than a statement such as "this is a top-notch car." Id., p. 329. Statements to the effect that a truck was in "good condition" and that a motor was in "perfect running order" have been held not to create express warranties. See Pell City Wood, Inc. v. Forke Bros. Auctioneers, Inc., 474 So.2d 694 (Ala.1985); Miller v. Lentine, 495 A.2d 1229 (Me.1985). Another factor to be considered in determining whether a statement creates an express warranty is whether it was written or oral, the latter being more likely to be considered puffing.

The defendant in the present case made various oral statements to the effect that the vehicle was "excellent," in "mint" condition and that it was an "unusual" one. These statements certainly cannot be considered specific in nature. Moreover, the plaintiff was allowed to examine and test drive the vehicle prior to purchase. Under the facts of this case the trial court's failure to find an express warranty ... cannot be considered clearly erroneous.

Problem 24

Which of the following constitute affirmations of fact as opposed to statements of commendation, value, opinion or "puff?"

(a) "These explosives are of good quality and you will be pleased with the breakage and the whole operation."

(b) "This bulldozer is in A–1 condition—just out of the woods from loading two loads of logs a day."

(c) "Big Red #1 is good seed."

(d) "This camper is totally compatible with your truck—you will have no difficulty towing the camper with your truck."

(e) "Ford school bus chassis have been designed to provide utmost safety and reliability for carrying the nation's most precious cargo—school children."

(f) "This car has a rebuilt carburetor and is a good runner."

(g) "Mechanically, this oil rig is a 9 on a scale of 10."

(h) "The new Mazda 929 is a wonderful car."

(i) "America's most complete line of reliable, economical gas-heating appliances."

(j) "You will find this product to be of high quality and it will deliver substantial profits."

(k) "Supreme tires are what you need when you hit a pothole at 50 miles an hour—when it's three in the morning and you're in a hurry. They have a brute of a carcass that's so strong, you can practically forget about blowouts."

(*l*) "The equipment is in perfect condition and only one year old."

(m) "This thing will last a lifetime—it's in perfect condition."

(n) "This car has been driven only 23,460 miles."

(o) "This is a 1989 Volkswagen Jetta."

(p) "Rollaway shutters lock automatically when fully closed."

Note

Fact vs. Puff. Comment 10 to the proposed amended Section 2–313 lists 8 factors that are relevant in drawing the line between representations and puffing: (1) whether the statements were oral rather than written, (2) general rather than specific, (3) related to the consequences of buying rather than the goods themselves, (4) were "hedged" in some fashion, (5) related to experimental rather than standard goods (6) concerned some aspects of the goods but not a hidden or unexpected nonconformity; (7) were phrased in terms of opinion rather than fact, or (8) were not capable of objective measurement. A similar list of factors is found in *Federal Signal Corp. v. Safety Factors, Inc.,* 125 Wash.2d 413, 886 P.2d 172, 179 (1994).

Problem 25

(a) Siebenmann (S) sold a painting entitled "Self Portrait," supposedly painted by the well-known English artist Francis Bacon, to Rogath (R) for $570,000. In the written contract, S warranted the painting as authentic. R then resold the painting to an art dealer (A) for $950,000. When A learned of a challenge to the painting's authenticity prior to R's purchase, it demanded the return of the purchase price and R complied. R then sued S for breach of warranty. S claims that in the light of common knowledge that the authenticity of the painting was in doubt, R could not have believed S's statement of authenticity. Assume that R was aware of doubts by others that the painting was authentic. Analyze.

(b) Michael and Karla Weng bought a ten-year old car which had been driven 96,000 miles from defendant Allison for $800 after Allison told them that the car was "mechanically sound," "in good condition," "a good, reliable car," "a good car," and had "no problems." On the drive home, the Wengs discovered that the car failed to operate properly. They took it to an auto dealership for inspection and learned that the car needed substantial repairs costing $1500. Do the Wengs have a cause of action for breach of warranty in light of the age and mileage of this car?

C. EXPRESS WARRANTY—"BASIS OF THE BARGAIN"

CIPOLLONE v. LIGGETT GROUP, INC.

United States Court of Appeals for the Third Circuit, 1990.
893 F.2d 541.

BECKER, CIRCUIT JUDGE. This appeal is from a final judgment in a protracted products liability case in which the plaintiff, Antonio Cipollone, seeks to hold Liggett Group, Inc., Lorillard, Inc., and Philip Morris,

Inc., three of the leading firms in the tobacco industry, liable for the death from lung cancer of his wife, Rose Cipollone, who smoked cigarettes from 1942 until her death in 1984. Both sides have appealed. Liggett's appeal on the express warranty claim presents an abstruse question about the nature of the reliance interest required by U.C.C. section 2–313, N.J.S.A. § 12A:2–313.

We conclude that the express warranty charge was flawed. Primarily, the district court erred to the extent that it prevented Liggett from proving, by a preponderance of the evidence, that Mrs. Cipollone did not believe the advertisements. The advertisements constitute an express warranty as long they constitute a basis of the bargain, that is, as long as Mr. Cipollone can prove that Mrs. Cipollone was aware of the advertisements and as long as Liggett does not prove that she disbelieved them.

Authority on the question whether reliance is a necessary element of section 2–313 is divided. Although a few courts have held that reliance is not a necessary element of section 2–313, the more common view has been that it is, and that either a buyer must prove reliance in order to recover on an express warranty or the seller must be permitted to rebut a presumption of reliance in order to preclude recovery.

The history of section 2–313(1)(a), although informative, fails to give a clear answer as to whether reliance is required. Section 2–313(1)(a) is an adaptation of section 12 of the Uniform Sales Act.[1] A comparison of the two sections reveals that they are substantially the same except for the replacement of section 12's express reliance requirement with section 2–313(1)(a)'s basis of the bargain requirement. The district court reasoned that the omission of the word "reliance" from section 2–313(1)(a), in light of section 12's use of that word, implied that reliance was no longer an element of express warranties. Liggett contends that "if U.C.C. § 2–313 wrought the radical change in New Jersey warranty law that the trial court has read into it," then "one would think that the New Jersey Study Comments would have at least made reference to it." There is no reference to the reliance issue.

Liggett argues that reliance must have some place in the "basis of the bargain" determination. Thus, even if reliance should be assumed, based on what "would reasonably induce the purchase of a product," a defendant must have an opportunity to prove non-reliance. This position finds some support in the U.C.C. comments. U.C.C. Official Comment 3 states:

> In actual practice affirmations of fact made by the seller about the goods during a bargain are regarded as part of the description of those goods; hence no particular reliance on such statements need

---

1. Section 12 of the Sales Act provides:
Any affirmation of fact or any promise by the seller relating to the goods is an express warranty if the natural tendency of such affirmation or promise is to induce the buyer to purchase the goods, and if the buyer purchases the goods relying thereon. No affirmation of the value of the goods, nor any statement purporting to be a statement of the seller's opinion only shall be construed as a warranty.

be shown in order to weave them into the fabric of the agreement. Rather, any fact which is to take such affirmations, once made, out of the agreement requires clear affirmative proof. The issue normally is one of fact.

Moreover, comment 8 states that "all of the statements of the seller [become part of the basis of the bargain] unless good reason is shown to the contrary." (Emphasis added) The plain language of these comments supports Liggett's position, at least to the extent it indicates that a defendant must be given some opportunity to show that the seller's statements were not meant to be part of the basis of the bargain.

[Yet], it is possible to read the "basis of the bargain" requirement as requiring some subjective inducement of the buyer, without requiring a reliance finding. Requiring that the buyer rely on an advertisement, whether by imposing this burden initially on the buyer bringing suit, or by allowing the seller to rebut a presumption of reliance, puts a heavy burden on the buyer—a burden that is arguably inconsistent with the U.C.C. as a whole, with other comments to section 2–313.

The reliance requirement does not comport well with U.C.C. Official Comment 7 to section 2–313. Comment 7 states that "if language is used after the closing of the deal ... the warranty becomes a modification, and need not be supported by consideration if it is otherwise reasonable and in order...." If a post-closing promise—on which, by definition, a seller cannot rely in deciding to make a purchase—can create a warranty, then it is difficult to see why a pre-closing promise can create a warranty only if relied upon.

Additionally, a reliance requirement seems inconsistent with U.C.C. Official Comment 4 to section 2–313. Comment 4 states that "the whole purpose of the law of warranty is to determine what it is that the seller has in essence agreed to sell." Reliance is irrelevant to what a seller agrees to sell.[2]

[It] is foolish to try to reconcile what is patently inconsistent. We reject this suggestion however, because we find it feasible to reconcile the competing arguments, and we believe that the New Jersey Supreme Court would want us to try. We believe that the most reasonable construction of section 2–313 is neither Liggett's reliance theory, which fails to explain how reliance can be relevant to "what a seller agreed to sell," or the district court's purely objective theory, which fails to explain

---

2. For example, imagine a tire merchant describing a tire to three different prospective purchasers, each listening to his sales talk at the same time. The seller guarantees that the tire will (1) be safe for use even in heavily loaded vehicles; (2) last at least 20,000 miles; and (3) be the same style tire sold with a Rolls Royce. The first purchaser buys the tire relying on the seller's safety warranty. The second buys the tire relying on the seller's durability warranty. The third buys the tire relying on the seller's style warranty. None of the purchasers communicates to the seller the reason why he or she is purchasing one of the tires, although the reason for the purchase is communicated to the buyer's spouse, who will later come forward to testify truthfully regarding what the buyer relied on when making the purchase. It is implausible that each buyer has a different warranty, and that the second buyer, but not the first or third buyers, can sue if the tire wears out before 20,000 miles.

how an advertisement that a buyer never even saw becomes part of the "basis of the bargain." Instead, we believe that the New Jersey Supreme Court would hold that a plaintiff effectuates the "basis of the bargain" requirement of section 2–313 by proving that she read, heard, saw or knew of the advertisement containing the affirmation of fact or promise Such proof will suffice "to weave" the affirmation of fact or promise "into the fabric of the agreement," U.C.C. Comment 3, and thus make it part of the basis of the bargain. We hold that once the buyer has become aware of the affirmation of fact or promise, the statements are presumed to be part of the "basis of the bargain" unless the defendant, by "clear affirmative proof," shows that the buyer knew that the affirmation of fact or promise was untrue. We believe that by allowing a defendant to come forward with proof that the plaintiff did not believe in the warranty, we are reconciling, as the New Jersey Supreme Court would want us to, the U.C.C. comments, the U.C.C. case law, and traditional contract principles, which serve as the background rules to the U.C.C.

We emphasize that we are not adopting Liggett's rebuttable presumption of reliance theory. Reliance only comes into play if, after the defendant has proved non-belief, the plaintiff then tries to prove reliance despite non-belief. The burden is on the plaintiff to prove reliance despite non-belief, and if she meets that burden she can collect economic damages.

As indicated above, Comment 4 and Comment 7, as well as the largely dominant objective theory of contracts, militate in favor of an interpretation of express warranty that ignores the buyer's subjective state of mind. Under the extreme version of this theory apparently adopted by the district court, all the buyer should have to show is what the seller agreed to sell. In other words, an express warranty would be created when a seller makes statements to the public at large that would induce a reasonable buyer to purchase the product, even if the actual buyer never heard those statements. We find this result untenable, however. First, as mentioned above, this interpretation drains all substantive meaning from the phrase "basis of the bargain," and would allow a seller [sic—'buyer"?] to collect even if that seller [sic] was unaware of the warranty until she walked into her attorney's office to file suit. Second, this interpretation is difficult, if not impossible, to square with other comments to the U.C.C. As discussed above, Comment 3 states that "no particular reliance on such statements need be shown ... Rather, any fact which is to take such affirmations, once made, out of the agreement requires clear affirmative proof." Comment 8 states that "all of the statements of the seller [become part of the basis of the bargain] unless good reason is shown to the contrary." Clearly, both Comment 3 and Comment 8 envision some mechanism for overcoming the presumption that the seller's statements, even if heard by the actual buyer, are a basis of the bargain.

Much of the case law supports this "belief" principle. A statement in the bill of sale that the goods are new does not constitute an express warranty when both the buyer and the seller knew that the statement was false. *See Coffee v. Ulysses Irrigation Pipe Co.*, 501 F.Supp. 239 (N.D.Tex.1980). When a buyer has operated trucks before and knows that they need repairs, he cannot sue in express warranty on the seller's statement that the trucks were in good condition. *See Janssen v. Hook*, 1 Ill.App. 3d 318, 272 N.E.2d 385 (1971). "The same representation that could have constituted an express warranty early in the series of transactions, might not have qualified as an express warranty in a later transaction if the buyer had acquired independent knowledge as to the fact asserted." *Royal Business Machines v. Lorraine Corp.*, 633 F.2d 34, 44 (7th Cir.1980). Although these cases reject, to a certain extent, one traditional contract principle, that terms should be construed objectively, they embrace another traditional contract principle, that of looking at the intention of the parties in light of the surrounding circumstances.

Applying our interpretation of section 2–313 to the case at bar, we conclude that the district court's jury instructions were erroneous for two reasons. First, they did not require the plaintiff to prove that Mrs. Cipollone had read, seen, or heard the advertisements at issue. Second, they did not permit the defendant to prove that although Mrs. Cipollone had read, seen, or heard the advertisements, she did not believe the safety assurances contained therein. We must therefore reverse and remand for a new trial on this issue.

Note

Knowledge of Express Warranty. John M. Martin, Sr. v. American Medical Systems, Inc., 116 F.3d 102, 105 (4th Cir.1997), recognizes a contrary view in Virginia concerning whether a buyer must have read or otherwise learned of a seller's express warranty if it is to become "part of the basis of the bargain." Describing another express warranty case–*Daughtrey v. Ashe*, 243 Va. 73, 413 S.E.2d 336 (1992)–the *Martin* court states:

> [A] jeweler had described a gem as being of higher quality than it actually was.... [T]he jeweler asserted that the buyer had not been aware of the description and had not relied upon it. The Virginia Supreme Court held that it did not matter. The express warranty inquiry focuses on what it is that the seller agreed to sell, and, absent clear proof that the parties did not intend their bargain to include the seller's description of the goods, that description is an express warranty.

Consider, however, the distinction the court makes in the following case.

IN RE BRIDGESTONE/FIRESTONE INC. TIRES PRODUCTS LIABILITY LITIGATION

United States District Court of the Southern District of Indiana, 2001.
205 F.R.D. 503.

[The plaintiffs are residents of 27 states who seek to represent two classes of plaintiffs: a class of "tire" plaintiffs and a class of "Explorer" plaintiffs. Together, the classes would comprise all persons in the United

States who have owned or leased Ford Explorer sport-utility vehicles or vehicles equipped with certain Firestone brand tires. The tire claimants allege that design or manufacturing defects in the Firestone tires caused an unreasonably dangerous propensity for the tires to suffer tread or "belt" separation. The Explorer claimants allege handling and stability defects in certain models of the Ford Explorer created a substantial risk of rollovers and other safety problems. The plaintiffs allege that Ford and Firestone agreed to lower the recommended tire pressure on the Firestone tires that were used as original equipment on the Explorer in order to compensate for the vehicle's stability defects. Although this had the effect of lowering rollover accidents, plaintiffs allege that it also exacerbated the tire defects by substantially increasing the risk of tread separation and other catastrophic tire failures. The plaintiffs filed their Master Complaint and a motion for class certification that was resisted by the defendants.[1] The actions were predicated on the plaintiff's economic loss rather than on personal injury. The plaintiffs asserted, *inter alia*, express warranty claims.]

Defendants argue that, under both Tennessee and Michigan law, in order to prevail on the breach of express warranty claims, each individual Plaintiff will have to prove that he or she relied upon the terms in the warranty when deciding to purchase the vehicle or Tires. As far as the Defendants' written warranties are concerned, the Court disagrees.[2] The relevant U.C.C. provision, § 2–313(1)(a), does not require a showing of reliance by the buyer; rather, it provides that "any affirmation of fact or promise made by the seller to the buyer which relates to the goods and

---

1. [Ed. note] A class is appropriate for certification only if it meets the four prerequisites for a class action under Rule 23(a) of the Federal Rules of Civil Procedure: numerosity, commonality, typicality, and adequacy of representation. Once this hurdle is cleared, the court also must ensure that the proposed class satisfies one of the three standards established by Rule 23(b). Plaintiffs claimed certification under Rule 23(b)(3) because their claims were essentially claims for damages. This standard requires that common questions predominate, and that a class action be superior to other available methods for the fair and efficient adjudication of the controversy. Common questions predominate when they "present a significant aspect of the case and they can be resolved for all members of the class in a single adjudication." Thus the plaintiffs had to establish that common questions of law or fact predominate with respect to the elements of their claims. The court found that Plaintiffs met this burden. The court also found that the plaintiffs met the additional Rule 23(b)(3) requirement that a class action would be the "superior" method in which to resolve the controversy. The court determined that the law of Michigan applied to the claims against Ford and the law of Tennessee applied to the claims against Firestone.

2. Ford cites to Monte v. Toyota Motor Corp., 2001 WL 1152901 (Mich.Ct.App. Sept.28, 2001), for the general proposition that, under Michigan law, reliance is an element of an express warranty claim. The court in Monte held that the plaintiff could not base an express warranty claim on descriptions of his vehicle's Supplemental Restraint System contained in the Owner's Manual and Owner's Guide because the plaintiff received those documents "after the bargain was already struck" and therefore could not have relied on any statements therein. The court cited no authority for this holding, and did not discuss whether it believed that reliance was synonymous with the U.C.C.'s "basis of the bargain" requirement. The court also did not address the official comments to the U.C.C., discussed below, which address the creation of express warranties via post-sale statements. In any event, we are not bound by this unpublished decision, see Mich. Ct. R. 7.215 ("An unpublished opinion is not precedentially binding under the rule of stare decisis."), and in light of its conclusory nature, we do not find it persuasive precedent.

becomes part of the basis of the bargain creates an express warranty that the goods shall conform to the affirmation or promise." Defendants have cited no case in which a court has ruled that an express written warranty provided to a consumer upon the purchase of a product was unenforceable by the consumer because it was not part of the basis of the bargain.[3] Whether the consumer was aware of the terms of the written warranty before the purchase or not, it was certainly part of the bargain, in that the warranty was part of what the seller sold to the buyer.[4]

The official comments to U.C.C. § 2–313 support this holding. Official Comment 7 provides:

> The precise time when words of description or affirmation are made or samples are shown is not material. The sole question is whether the language or samples or models are fairly to be regarded as part of the contract.

A buyer certainly cannot prove that she relied upon an affirmation made after the closing of the deal in deciding whether to consummate the deal; however, the U.C.C. clearly contemplates that such post-sale affirmations can be enforced as warranties, as long as they "are fairly to be regarded as part of the contract". See Murphy, 582 N.Y.S.2d at 531 (holding that a written warranty given to plaintiffs at time of delivery of motor home, after purchase price had been paid, was part of basis of bargain). Accordingly, we determine that Plaintiffs need not demonstrate reliance on the written warranties in order to enforce the terms of those written warranties against Defendants, and, further, no individual proof that the written warranties received by Plaintiffs (or, more likely, a subclass of Plaintiffs) were part of the basis of each Plaintiff's bargain will be required.

The same is not true of Plaintiffs' express warranty claim based upon the Defendants' advertising, however. Even assuming that Plaintiffs will be able to demonstrate that each Defendant conducted extensive, nationwide advertising campaigns about its respective products, and that those advertising campaigns contained statements sufficiently specific to create a warranty that the products were safe, or that the products had some other quality they did not actually have, the existence of such advertising, is not sufficient, in and of itself, to demonstrate that the statements in the ads were part of the basis of the bargain when each Plaintiff purchased his or her Tires or Explorers. Unlike a written warranty given to a consumer as part of that individual consumer's

3. Indeed, such an interpretation of the law "would, in effect, render almost all consumer warranties an absolute nullity," inasmuch as it is common practice for warranty booklets to be provided to consumers inside the sealed box in which a product is packaged, or, in the case of vehicles, in the glove box of a new car upon delivery. Murphy v. Mallard Coach Co., 179 A.D.2d 187, 582 N.Y.S.2d 528, 531 (N.Y.App.Div.1992).

4. Defendants themselves rely upon the durational limitations contained in their written warranties; Defendants cannot seriously suggest that the terms of the written warranties favorable to them are enforceable, while the terms favorable to the Plaintiffs are not enforceable.

purchase transaction, advertisements are simply put out for public consumption by a company in the hopes that they will be seen (or heard) and considered by potential buyers, who will then be induced to become actual buyers, in whole or in part because of the advertisements. For some Plaintiffs, the advertisements likely were successful, and those Plaintiffs may well demonstrate that statements in Defendants' ads were part of the basis of their bargain. For other Plaintiffs, however, this will not be the case, and those Plaintiffs will not have a breach of warranty claim based upon Defendants' advertising. See, e.g., Masters v. Rishton, 863 S.W.2d 702, 706 (Tenn.Ct.App.1992) (breach of express warranty not available to plaintiff who had never seen any advertisements for or heard any representations about the safety of the product at issue); Fargo Machine & Tool Co. v. Kearney & Trecker Corp., 428 F.Supp. 364, 370 (E.D.Mich.1977) ("It is clear that advertisements and promotional literature can be a part of the basis of the bargain where they are prepared and furnished by a seller to induce purchase of its product and the buyer relies on the representations."); Omega Engineering, Inc. v. Eastman Kodak Co., 30 F.Supp.2d 226, 246 (D.Conn.1998) ("While advertisements can be part of the basis of the bargain, the plaintiff must show, at a minimum that he or his agent knew of and relied on the statement.") (citing 1 J. White & R. Summers, Uniform Commercial Code § 9–5, at 494–95 (1995)); American Tobacco Co., Inc. v. Grinnell, 951 S.W.2d 420, 436–37 (Tex.1997) (plaintiff could not prevail on express warranty claim based on advertisements when he could not show that he saw or relied upon the defendant's advertisements).

While the Court need not, and thus will not, delve into the issue of precisely what type of proof would be required for a Plaintiff to prevail on an express-warranty-created-by-advertising claim, it is clear that the claim cannot be established by classwide proof. Rather, an examination of each Plaintiffs' exposure to, and consideration of, Defendants' various ads would be required. It is also clear that this inquiry will not fall into the same simple and straightforward category as proof of when and from whom a class member purchased the Tires and/or Explorer; rather, it almost certainly will require credibility determinations and other individual, unwieldy factual and legal determinations. We determine that these substantial individual issues preclude a finding that common issues will predominate in the resolution of Plaintiffs' claim for breach of express warranty based upon advertising, and therefore we decline to certify classes as to that claim.

For the same reasons that Plaintiffs' advertising-related warranty claims are not amenable to class certification, to the extent that some Plaintiffs assert express warranty claims based upon oral representations made to them at the time of sale, those claims clearly are not common to the class as a whole, and therefore are not appropriate for class certification. Accordingly, no classes are certified as to those claims.

Note

Amended Article 2: "Immediate" vs. "Remote" Buyers—Remedial Promises, "Pass Through" and Advertising Warranties. In both the *Cipollone* and *Bridgestone* cases, the court grappled with warranties made to "remote" purchasers. Express warranties may be made by a seller of goods directly to its immediate buyer. Yet, the typical chain of distribution of goods that begins with a manufacturer and ends with the purchaser who will use the goods involves intermediate parties that purchase and then resell the goods. Between the manufacturer-seller and the user, there may be a wholesaler who buys the goods from the manufacturer and resells them to a retailer who resells them to the ultimate user who may assert a claim for breach of express warranty against the manufacturer-seller with whom it has not dealt. There is no direct bargain or contract between the manufacturer and the ultimate "remote purchaser." A manufacturer, however, may make certain affirmations or promises contained on documents that are packaged with the goods, intending them to be "passed through" to the remote purchaser. The manufacturer may also "pass through" certain *remedial promises*—undertaking that do not represent that the goods are of any particular quality, but that promise to remedy defects should any appear in the goods. Whether or not any such "pass through" warranties or remedial promises are included with the goods, the manufacturer may have made affirmations or promises concerning the goods in advertising designed to induce parties to buy the product.

The proposed amendments to Article 2 add two new sections and make other changes designed to clarify the rights and obligations between a seller and a remote purchaser with respect to warranties and remedial promises of the "pass through" and "advertising" varieties. Among the changes are proposed amendments to 2–313 that would restrict the provision to express warranties and remedial promises made to the *immediate buyer*, i.e., a "buyer who enters into a contract with the seller" (2–313(1)). See proposed amended Section 2–313(2).[1] Otherwise, proposed amended Section 2–313 would be virtually identical to pre-amendment 2–313.

Where affirmations of fact, descriptions or promises relating to the goods, or remedial promises, are made in a "record" that is packaged with or accompanies goods sold to a remote purchaser ("pass through" warranties and remedial promises), new proposed Section 2–313A would govern. It provides that the "pass through" statements and promises create *obligations* of the seller rather than warranties, although the criteria for determining whether such an obligation exists are substantively identical to the criteria for finding an express warranties in 2–313. The Section is limited to "new goods and goods sold or leased as new goods in a transaction of purchase in the normal chain of distribution" (Proposed 2–313A(1)). Proposed Section 2–313A permits the seller to limit the remedies available to a remote purchaser, provided it does so no later than the time of purchase or if the

---

1. Proposed amended Section 2–313(4) recognizes *remedial promises* made to the immediate buyer as creating "an obligation that the promise will be performed upon the happening of the specified event."

limitation is contained in the record containing the affirmation, promise or description (Proposed 2–313A(4)(a)).

If a seller makes affirmations, promises or descriptions relating to the goods, or remedial promises, *in advertising or similar communications to the public*, proposed new Section 2–313B provides that they create obligations to a remote purchaser, but only if such a remote purchaser *"enters into a transaction of purchase with knowledge of and with the expectation that the goods will conform to the affirmation of fact, promise or description or that the seller will perform the remedial promise"* (proposed 2–313B(2), emphasis supplied). Compare this solution with the *Bridgestone* analysis.

It is important to note that these sections create obligations exclusively to *purchasers*, i.e., either immediate buyers or remote purchasers. They do not create obligations to other parties who may use, consume or be affected by the goods if such parties have not actually purchased the goods. If, for example, a member of the family or household of the purchaser, a guest in the purchaser's home, or an employee of the purchaser is injured by a product because the product does not conform to the seller's affirmation, promise or description of the goods, any obligation to such a remote, non-purchasing party is determined under Section 2–318—a provision that will be discussed in a later part of this chapter dealing with product liability issues.

Problem 26

Martin Davis was delighted with the new car he had purchased a month ago. A friend, Al Edwards, was so taken with the car that he purchased the identical automobile. When Davis asked whether Edwards was satisfied, Edwards said that he was more than pleased and, in particular, mentioned the automatic headlight feature that turned the lights on when necessary and shut them off automatically. Davis was surprised to learn of this feature since he had been operating the headlights manually. Davis's car does not have this feature. Advise Davis under the following alternatives:

(a) Referring to his owner's manual for the first time, Davis discovered the headlight feature was listed as standard equipment on the model that he and Edwards now owned.

(b) There was no mention of the automatic headlight feature in the owner's manual or in any other record delivered with Davis' or Edwards' cars. The feature had, however, been included in the manufacturer's television advertisements, although Davis had not seen them.

Problem 27

Abex manufactures airplane passenger loading bridges (Jetways). A ball-screw assembly allowed the Jetway to be raised and lowered to accommodate different airplane heights. Abex purchased such assemblies from GM. When a Jetway collapsed causing personal injuries, the injured parties sued Abex which filed a third-party complaint against GM alleging that a defect in the GM part allowed the Jetway to fall. Abex introduced evidence that on three occasions *after* the sale, GM represented that its ball-screw assemblies contained a fail-safe feature that would preclude the collapse of a Jetway. Analyze. See comment 7 to 2–313.

D.   EXPRESS WARRANTIES—SAMPLES & MODELS

Problem 28

(a) The Island Co. (IC) wanted to assure the supply of its coal requirements for the next 12 months. The President of IC, Charles Mays, possessed considerable expertise concerning coal and other minerals. He contacted the Kopper Co. (K) and personally discussed the quality of coal being mined by K. Officers of K showed Mays a sample of coal recently taken from the K mine, along with an accurate chemical analysis of the sample coal. Mays was impressed and agreed to purchase IC's coal requirements for the next year from K. Three months into the contract it became clear that the coal K was shipping, although taken from the same mine that produced the sample, was of lower quality than the sample. IC accepted the remainder of the coal but insisted that it was entitled to a price discount for the inferior coal. What result?

(b) Margo Heming, sales manager of the Triple Pane Corporation (TP), demonstrated TP's replacement windows to the Zile Corporation (Z). In her demonstration Ms. Heming used miniature versions of the windows, emphasizing a special feature that made the windows easily removable for cleaning. Z purchased and installed 74 TP replacement windows. Z now complains that the windows are not as represented because the weight of the full-sized windows makes them much more difficult to remove for cleaning than those in the demonstration. Analyze.

(c) The Arnold Corporation required steel cones to use in manufacturing equipment. Fenn Corporation, a fabricator, agreed to perform a "test run" to determine whether it could supply cones suitable for Arnold. Arnold supplied cold-rolled steel from which Fenn would make the cones. The product of the test run was approved by Arnold, and Fenn began full production. The full production cones proved unsatisfactory. Instead of supplying cold-rolled steel for the production cones as it had for the test run, Arnold supplied hot-rolled steel, which contained a greater concentration of oxides and caused Fenn to experience difficulties in the conversion process. Arnold claims a breach of warranty. Analyze.

(d) Plumbing Contractors, Inc. (PC) required 72 valves for parts of a plumbing "tree" in a new office building. A representative of PC went to the offices of Suppliers, Inc. (S) where he saw a large container of valves that met the specifications. The valves in the box had red handles. Through its representative, PC agreed to purchase 72 valves from S. The valves that were later delivered were perfect in every way except that the handles were green. PC wanted red handles because other valves in the plumbing tree were green and PC was eager to distinguish the 72 valves purchased from S. PC had not informed S that it required red handles. Instead, the PC representative had pointed to the container of valves at the S store and said, "We need 72 valves like these." Analyze.

E. EXPRESS WARRANTIES—LEASES, CISG AND UCITA

UCC Article 2A on leases contains an express warranty provision, 2A–210, that replicates the express warranty section of UCC Article 2 (2–313) except for the substitution of "lessor" and "lessee" for "seller" and "buyer."

In international sales governed by the **CISG**, Article 35(1) of the Convention requires the seller to "deliver goods which are of the quantity, quality and description required by the contract and which are contained or packaged in the manner required by the contract." The reach of this CISG article, which avoids using the term warranty, is potentially broader than that of the UCC express warranty section because the CISG provision does not limit the manner in which a contract can require goods of a particular quality (for example, the CISG does not impose a "basis of the bargain" requirement). Although CISG Article 35(1) does not specifically refer to "affirmations" or "representations" by the seller, such statements would come within the broad language of the provision. A separate subsection of the CISG, Article 35(2)(c), requires that the goods conform to samples or models that the seller has held out to the buyer.

For licenses of computer information, **UCITA** § 402 replicates the express warranty provision of Article 2 (2–313) except with respect to "published informational content" of the licensed information, for which UCITA § 402(c) preserves current common law standards and does not subject such content to express warranty concepts. "Published informational content" is defined in UCITA § 102(a)(51) as information "prepared for or made available to recipients generally or to a class of recipients, in substantially the same form," and is to be distinguished from information "customized" for a particular recipient (UCITA 102(a)(51)(A)) or "provided in a special relationship of reliance between the provider and the recipient" (UCITA 102(a)(51)(B)). An implied warranty relating to the informational content of licensed computer information—which also does not extend to "published informational content"—is provided in UCITA § 404, and is discussed *infra*.

F. THE IMPLIED WARRANTY OF MERCHANTABILITY— SCOPE—2–314

Problem 29

(a) NDM Corporation and Novamedix (N) competed in the sale of medical footpumps that increased blood circulation. N brought an action against NDM for patent infringement. Under a settlement agreement, NDM admitted infringement and turned over its inventory of foot pumps to N. N now brings an action for breach of the implied warranty of merchantability against NDM after learning that the foot pumps do not meet FDA specifications and cannot be resold. Analyze.

(b) Margaret Williams was injured while grocery shopping when she removed a six pack of cola from a supermarket shelf and one of the bottles exploded. In her action against the supermarket, she claimed breach of the implied warranty of merchantability. What result?

(c) Mike Brewster, vice president in charge of purchasing for the Beck Corporation, an investment company, purchased 100 air conditioning units from AirCool for a Beck building. The units were delivered, but before they could be unpacked the CEO of Beck decided that the building should be centrally air conditioned and directed Brewster to return the units to AirCool. Unfortunately, AirCool had declared bankruptcy and was in the process of liquidation. The CEO told Brewster, "Sell them to somebody." Brewster found four different buyers, each of whom agreed to purchase 25 units (still in their sealed cartons) at a price that was fifteen percent lower than the price Beck had paid for them. The units were installed in each of the buyer's four buildings. Within two weeks, the units did not function and were not repairable. Each of the buyers has sued Beck Corporation for breach of the implied warranty or merchantability. Analyze.

(d) The St. Anselm church picnic was a well-known annual community activity designed to raise funds to support the St. Anselm soup kitchen. For the last 10 years Pastor Albert Sims has organized the successful picnic. At 11 a.m. on the day of this year's picnic, the Pastor was informed that the grills were malfunctioning. He hurried to a nearby "Superburger" chain restaurant, one of 230 throughout the country, operated by a member of his flock, Miles Clark. When informed of the problem, Clark volunteered to supply to the church all of the hamburgers needed for the picnic at his cost. He suggested that Pastor Sims enjoy a superburger while he waited for the other 150 burgers to be prepared for the picnic. At the picnic, all 150 superburgers were all purchased and consumed. The burger wrappers displayed the well-known name "superburger" in conspicuous print. Later that day, Pastor Sims and all who had eaten the superburgers became ill because of bacteria in the superburger sauce. Consider the potential warranty liability of Pastor Sims, St. Anselm, Clark and Superburger, Inc. In addition to 2–314, see 2–318 and 2–715.

G. "MERCHANTABILITY" DEFINED

Problem 30

Is there a breach of the implied warranty of merchantability in the following situations? If so, indicate which specific subsection(s) of 2–314(2) have been violated.

(a) Hardware, Inc. (H) sold Edgar Thompson (T) a new lawn mower with a bag attachment for collecting the grass clippings. The mower adequately cut the grass but T was dissatisfied with the bag attachment because it was cumbersome to remove and replace. T wishes to return the mower to H and recover the purchase price.

(b) The Mann Corporation (M) purchased 100,000 units of plastic from Plastics, Inc. When the plastic arrived, M inspected it and determined that 1.5% of the units were defective. M refused to accept the shipment.

(c) Stilbestrol is a feed additive used to fatten cattle for slaughter. If stilbestrol is added to the feed of breeding cattle, it causes the cows to abort and the bulls to lose interest in breeding. For seven years Kassab, Inc. (K) had purchased feed for its breeding cattle from Soya, Inc. (S). The arrangement was quite satisfactory until S made a single delivery of feed containing stilbestrol. Unaware that the feed contained the additive because the feed bags failed to list stilbestrol as an ingredient, K fed the product to its breeding cattle. The K herd suffered the usual consequences of the additive, and K brought an action for breach of warranty against S. What result?

(d) Margaret Downs (D) was diagnosed as having lung cancer. There is a clear medical opinion that her cancer was caused by smoking, and the only brand of cigarettes she has ever smoked are Marvel cigarettes. D brought an action against Marvel for breach of warranty. What result?

(e) The husband of Margaret Downs, Harry Downs, suffered a heart attack. Clear medical opinion attributed Harry's condition to the consumption of butter with a typical high cholesterol count. Harry has always used butter manufactured by the Minnesota Dairy Cooperative. Does Harry have a cause of action against the Cooperative?

(f) Elbert Hayes was injured when his new car was struck by a truck crossing a median barrier. The new car did not have an airbag to protect the driver. Hayes seeks advice as to whether he has a cause of action against the car manufacturer for failure to include an airbag as standard equipment.

(g) Norm Abrams was injured while operating a lathe as an employee of Miller Manufacturing, Inc. Norm has discovered that the lathe lacked a safety device required by the Federal Occupational Safety and Health Act. Norm seeks to recover for his injuries under a breach of warranty theory. Analyze. In addition to 2–314, see 2–318 and 2–715.

(h) A public transit bus took a wrong turn and plunged down a steep hill, coming to rest in a place from which it could not escape without assistance. The transit authority used a log chain to attach the bus to another vehicle to pull it up the hill. When the bus was half way to the top of the hill, the chain broke and the bus was damaged. Does the transit authority have a cause of action against the chain supplier?

(i) Albert Mars ordered a martini before dinner in his favorite restaurant. As he held the martini glass in a normal manner, the glass broke and severely lacerated Mars' hand. Mars sues for breach of the implied warranty of merchantability. Analyze.

(j) Edward Houston was a new employee in an automobile repair shop. His supervisor directed him to unpack a large carton of replacement body panels. When Edward reached into the container to extract the panels he severely lacerated his hand. The particular panels are necessarily manufactured with sharp edges. Does Edward have a cause of action for breach of warranty? See, *inter alia*, 2–318.

(k) Assume the facts of (j) except that the container was clearly and conspicuously marked as follows: "WARNING: CONTENTS HAVE VERY SHARP EDGES—COULD CAUSE SEVERE INJURY." Edward saw the warning and carefully reached into the container to remove the parts, but he suffered the injury anyway. Analyze.

(*l*) Marilyn Harris purchased a new device called the "Golfing Gizmo" for her 12 year old son, George. Television ads for the device depicted a golf ball attached to a cord which pulled the ball back after it was struck. The ad promoted the product as a means to permit novice golfers to practice their golf stroke. The container, which Marilyn opened with George's assistance, clearly and conspicuously stated: "Perfectly safe—will not injure player." While using the device, George was seriously injured when the ball whipped back and struck him in the head. Does George have a cause of action for breach of warranty? See, *inter alia*, 2–318.

(m) Marian Webster, a resident of Utah, visited the city of Boston for the first time and she had lunch at the quaint Blue Ship Tea Room. Marian ordered "authentic New England fish chowder." The chowder was milky in appearance and, although Marian stirred the chowder, she detected no bones. After enjoying several spoonfuls, Marian suddenly discovered that something was stuck in her throat. Emergency surgery revealed a fish bone lodged in her esophagus. She sued the Tea Room for breach of the implied warranty of merchantability. The restaurant defended by producing evidence that "authentic" fish chowder recipes going back as far as Daniel Webster's favorite recipe invariably included fish bones, and that chowder without bones would not taste the same. The Tea Room also argued that fish bones are normal or natural ingredients in fish chowder, i.e., they are not foreign substances such as a mouse in a cola bottle or a decomposed toe or fish hook in chewing tobacco. Marian responded that, as a citizen of Utah, she was unfamiliar with "authentic" fish chowder. What result? Suppose the injury had been caused by a chicken bone in chicken pie, or a cherry stone in cherry pie? What of a bar patron who cracked a tooth on an olive pit in a martini olive?

(n) Martha Cross was driving the new family car when its steering mechanism failed and the car crashed into a concrete abutment. Martha and her husband Stephen, a passenger in the car, were seriously injured. A careful examination of the wreckage failed to disclose any defect in the steering mechanism. Both Martha and Stephen, however, will testify that the car was clearly uncontrollable. Can the Crosses prove a breach of warranty by the dealer and/or manufacturer of the automobile in these circumstances? See, in particular, comment 13 to 2–314.

Note

If coffee is hot enough to burn a part of the body if spilled, is it necessarily unmerchantable? In Greene v. Boddie–Noell Enterprises, 966 F.Supp. 416 (W.D.Va.1997), the answer given was "no." Merchantable coffee is "hot." Indeed, if coffee is not sufficiently hot, it would be unmerchantable. Other "coffee-burn" cases have been tried under a products liability (tort) rubric. See, e.g., McMahon v. Bunn–O–Matic Corp., 150 F.3d 651 (7th Cir.1998) (holding that requiring a seller of coffee to advise customers that its coffee is hot and could burn if spilled is unnecessary because the customers are already aware of that fact). In general, plaintiffs have been unsuccessful in spilled coffee cases. The celebrated verdict of $160,000 compensatory damages and $2,700,000 punitive damages in Liebeck v. McDonald's Restaurants P.T.S., Inc., 1995 WL 360309 (N.M.1995) was settled prior to an appeal without a published opinion.

H. MERCHANTABILITY—LEASES, CISG AND UCITA

1. *The Implied Warranty of Merchantability in Article 2A*

UCC 2A–212 replicates the implied warranty of merchantability provision in Article 2 (2–314), except for changes to reflect leasing terminology. The Article 2A implied warranty of merchantability, however, does not arise in "finance leases," even if the lessor is a merchant with respect to goods of the kind. This exception reflects the fact that the sole role of the finance lessor is to provide financing to allow the finance lessee to acquire the goods, and under the definition of "finance lease" in 2A–103(1)(g) the specific goods leased must in fact be selected by the lessee. Finance leases are discussed later in this chapter.

2. *The Implied Obligation to Deliver Goods Fit for Ordinary Purposes Under the CISG*

For international sales, the CISG establishes something akin to the implied warranty of merchantability when it specifies that, unless otherwise agreed, goods do not conform to the sales contract unless that are "fit for the purposes for which goods of the same description would ordinarily be used." CISG Art. 35(2)(a). Compare UCC 2–314(2)(c), which requires that goods be "fit for the ordinary purposes for which such goods are used" in order to conform to the implied warranty of merchantability. Consider the following decision

DECISION OF MARCH 8, 1995, BUNDESGERICHTSHOF (SUPREME COURT), GERMANY, CASE NO. VIII ZR 159/94[1]

English Abstract from the Unilex Data Base

A Swiss seller and a German buyer concluded a contract for the sale of New Zealand mussels. The buyer refused to pay the purchase price after the mussels were declared "not completely safe" because of the quantity of cadmium they contained, which quantity was significantly greater than the advised cadmium levels published by the German Federal Health Department. The buyer gave notice to the seller of the contamination and asked it to take back the mussels.... The seller commenced an action claiming payment and interest. At first instance the Court decided in favor of the seller, and the buyer's subsequent appeals were unsuccessful.

The Supreme Court confirmed the decisions of the lower courts, stating that the contract between the parties was governed by CISG according to Art. 1(1)(a) CISG.

---

1. Reprinted with the permission of the Centre for Comparative and Foreign Studies—UNIDROIT, Rome, Italy. The Unilex English abstract of the decision, as well as the original German text, is available through the Unilex website, <*http://www.unilex.info*>. The full German text of this decision is also available online at <http://www.jura.uni-freiburg.de/ ipr1/cisg/urteile/text/ 144.htm>. An English-language summary of the case appears as Abstract No. 123 in Case Law on UNCITRAL Texts ((CLOUT). The CLOUT summary and a full English translation are available online at <http://www.cisgw3.law.pace.edu/ cases/ 950308g3.html>.

The Court held that the buyer had to pay the purchase price.... The Court confirmed the findings of the lower courts, according to which the mussels were conforming to the contract since they were fit for the purposes for which goods of the same description would ordinarily be used (Art. 35(2)(a) CISG). The Court did find that the fact that the mussels contained a greater quantity of cadmium than the advised cadmium levels could well affect the merchantability of the goods, provided that the corresponding public law requirements were relevant. However, like the lower courts, the Supreme Court excluded that the seller can generally be expected to observe special public law requirements of the buyer's state; it could only be expected to do so: (1) where the same rules also exist in the seller's country; (2) where the buyer draws the seller's attention to their existence; (3) or, possibly, where the seller knows or should know of those rules due to "special circumstances", such as (i) when the seller has a branch in the buyer's country, (ii) when the parties are in a longstanding business relationship, (iii) when the seller regularly exports in the buyer's country, or (iv) when the seller advertises its own products in the buyer's country....

---

3. *Implied Warranties of Merchantability and on Informational Content Under UCITA*

UCITA § 403 provides for an implied warranty of merchantability for computer programs. Under this provision, if the licensor is "a merchant with respect to computer programs of the kind," the licensor impliedly warrants to the end user that the computer program is "fit for the ordinary purpose for which such computer programs are used." UCITA § 403(a)(1). In such cases, the licensor also impliedly warrants to the distributor of the program that it is adequately packaged and labeled, and in the case of multiple copies that the copies are of even kind, quality and quantity within the variations permitted by the agreement. UCITA § 403(a)(2), A merchant licensor also impliedly warrants to both end users and distributors that the program conforms to any promises or affirmations of fact made on the program's container or label. UCITA § 403(a)(3). The implied warranty of merchantability, however, may be disclaimed pursuant to UCITA § 406, and in any event does not extend to the "informational content" of a computer program, which encompasses aesthetics ("artistic character, tastefulness, beauty or pleasing nature of informational content" according to a comment to UCITA § 403), market appeal, accuracy, and subjective quality.[1]

The informational content of licensed computer information, however, may be subject to an implied warranty under UCITA § 404, which is based on Restatement (Second) of Torts § 552. Under the UCITA

---

1. According to UCITA § 403(2), other implied warranties relating to computer programs beyond the implied warranty of merchantability may arise from course of dealing or usage of trade, although such warranties can also be disclaimed or modified under UCITA § 406.

provision, unless the warranty is disclaimed, a merchant licensor warrants against inaccuracies in informational content that are caused by the merchant's failure to collect, compile, process, provide or transmit the information with *reasonable care*, but only if the merchant is *in a special relationship of reliance with the licensee.* UCITA § 404(a). Informational content is said to be accurate "if, within applicable understandings of the level of permitted errors, the information content correctly portrays the objective facts to which it relates." Comment 2 to UCITA § 404. The "special relationship" requirement is met only if the provider knows or should know that the licensee intends to rely on the data. According to comment 3 to UCITA § 404, the provider must possess specialized expertise and must be in a special position of confidence and trust with the licensee. Like express warranties under UCITA § 402, however, the implied warranty provided in UCITA § 404 does not apply to "published informational content," which by the definition of that term in UCITA § 102(a)(51) is information made available to the public as a whole or to a range of subscribers on a standardized rather than custom-tailored basis, and does not include information transferred in a reliance relationship. See UCITA § 404(b)(1).

UCITA's treatment of a licensor's liability for informational content in general, and published informational content in particular, reflects prior law designed to protect the free flow of information from the burden that would be created by a substantial risk of liability based on content. For example, where a plaintiff subscribed to a premium service for instantaneous transmission of news by computer, the service was found not liable to the subscriber for alleged misleading statements regarding a stock price on which plaintiff relied to his detriment. *Daniel v. Dow Jones & Co., Inc.,* 137 Misc.2d 94, 520 N.Y.S.2d 334 (N.Y.City Civ.Ct. 1987). The court treated the plaintiff as if he were a subscriber to a traditional newspaper which does not create a "special relationship" giving rise to liability. The First Amendment to the U.S. Constitution precludes liability for nondefamatory, negligently untruthful news, in order to serve the more important interest of maintaining a free press and avoiding the potential stifling effect that the imposition of liability might have on the dissemination of speech.

Consider also *Cardozo v. True,* 342 So.2d 1053 (Fla.Ct.App.1977), a case decided under UCC Article 2. Ingrid Cardozo purchased a copy of "Trade Winds Cookery" from Ellie's book store in Sarasota, Florida. While following a recipe in the book for the preparation and cooking of the Dasheen plant (commonly known as "elephant's ears), Ingrid ate a small slice of the plant and immediately experienced burning sensations of the lips, mouth, throat and tongue, coughing and gasping, and intense stomach cramps. These conditions persisted over several days despite medical care. Ingrid learned that the uncooked Dasheen plant can cause such reactions, and she brought an action against Ellie's for breach of the implied warranty of merchantability because the recipe contained no warning. The court held that while the sale of a book was the sale of goods within UCC 2–314, the warranty made by the retail book store did not extend to the ideas (informational content) in the book:

> The common theme running through these decisions is that ideas hold a privileged position in our society. They are not equivalent to commercial products. Those who are in the business of distributing the ideas of other people perform a unique and essential function. To hold those who perform this essential function liable, regardless of fault, when an injury results would severely restrict the flow of the ideas they distribute. We think that holding Ellie's liable under the doctrine of implied warranty would have the effect of imposing liability without fault not intended by the Uniform Commercial Code.

342 So.2d at 1056–57.

I. IMPLIED WARRANTY OF FITNESS FOR A PARTICULAR PURPOSE UNDER UCC ARTICLE 2—2–315

OUTLOOK WINDOWS PARTNERSHIP v. YORK INTERNATIONAL CORPORATION

United States District Court, D.Nebraska, 2000.
112 F.Supp.2d 877.

KOPF, J. The parties' dispute concerns the heating system at Outlook's manufacturing facility. [Outlook's wood-fired boiler used to heat its manufacturing facility suffered a "melt-down." Outlook claims that Natkin led Outlook to believe that the cost of operating a gas-fired heating system supplied by Natkin would be about equal to the cost of operating the old wood-fired system]. Outlook seeks to recover the difference between the actual and estimated cost of operation of the gas-fired system over its useful life or, alternatively, the cost of installing a new wood-fired system.

Outlook and Natkin agree that Outlook's cause of action, for "breach of implied warranty," arises under Neb. Rev. Stat. Ann. (Uniform Commercial Code) § 2–315 which pertains to implied warranties of fitness for a particular purpose. The elements of such an implied warranty claim are stated in Stones v. Sears, Roebuck & Co., 251 Neb. 560, 569, 558 N.W.2d 540, 547 (1997):

> A plaintiff relying on the implied warranty of fitness for a particular purpose must prove that (1) the seller had reason to know of the buyer's particular purpose in buying the goods, (2) the seller had reason to know that the buyer was relying on the seller's skill or judgment to furnish appropriate goods, and (3) the buyer, in fact, relied upon the seller's skill or judgment. Ordinarily, whether or not the implied warranty of fitness for a particular purpose arises in any individual case is a question of fact to be determined by the circumstances of the contracting between the parties. In this regard, a buyer proceeding under this implied warranty must first provide some evidence that the seller knew of the buyer's

particular purpose for which the goods are acquired. A "particular purpose" differs from the ordinary purpose for which the goods are used in that it envisages a specific use by the buyer which is peculiar to the nature of his or her business whereas the ordinary purposes for which goods are used are those envisaged in the concept of merchantability and go to uses which are customarily made of the goods in question. § 2–315, comment 2.

Natkin argues that there is no evidence that Outlook purchased the gas-fired boilers for a specific use peculiar to the nature of Outlook's business, and notes that Outlook has not even alleged a particular use in its petition. Natkin thus analogizes this case to Stones in which the evidence indicated that a gas grill (which caused a house fire) was used for its customary purpose of grilling food, such that § 2–315 did not apply. Because the gas-fired boilers are used by Outlook for their ordinary purpose of heating a building, Natkin concludes that the breach of warranty claim must be dismissed.

Nebraska case law does not support Natkin's narrow interpretation of U.C.C. § 2–315. In Mennonite Deaconess Home & Hosp. v. Gates Eng., 219 Neb. 303, 363 N.W.2d 155 (1985), for example, the plaintiff hospital had explored various options for repairing or replacing its old roof, and it was concerned about water leakage around various projections on the roof. The defendant's representative assured the hospital that the Gates one-ply roofing system would handle the problem. It, of course, did not. The Nebraska Supreme Court held that the evidence in the case would support a breach of either an implied warranty of merchantability under U.C.C. § 2–314 or an implied warranty of fitness for a particular purpose under U.C.C. § 2–315, or a breach of both sections. As to the § 2–315 claim, the Court stated:

> Certainly, the jury could find that Gates had reason to know of the hospital's particular purpose for the roof. Likewise, the jury could find that Gates had reason to know that the hospital was relying on Gates' skill or judgment to furnish the appropriately installed roof. Indeed, the hospital told Gates it was. And, finally, the jury could certainly find that the hospital relied upon Gates' skill or judgment. It was only after the hospital was contacted by the representatives of Gates and assured of the quality of the roof that it purchased the Gates roof rather than another one-ply roof.

Similarly, in Larutan Corp. v. Magnolia Homes Mfg. Co. of Neb., 190 Neb. 425, 209 N.W.2d 177 (1973), a soil compaction substance was applied around the outside of a factory for the purpose of eliminating muddy conditions, especially in areas where forklifts were driven and mobile homes, which were manufactured at the facility, were parked. Considering that the sales representative for the product was aware of the use of the area, and had given assurances that the product could do the job, the Nebraska Supreme Court affirmed the trial court's finding that there was an implied warranty of fitness for a particular purpose. In Shotkoski v. Standard Chemical Mfg. Co., 195 Neb. 22, 237 N.W.2d 92

(1975), a dairy farmer was assured that the defendant's cattle feed supplement would increase milk production. Using the product in the manner directed, however, milk production actually decreased. The Nebraska Supreme Court held that the evidence was sufficient to present a jury question as to the breach of an implied warranty under U.C.C. § 2–315. El Fredo Pizza, Inc. v. Roto–Flex Oven Co., 199 Neb. 697, 261 N.W.2d 358 (1978), involved a pizza oven which did not heat evenly. The Nebraska Supreme Court held that a jury question was presented as to whether the oven had been sold subject to an implied warranty of fitness for a particular purpose.[1]

As the above cases demonstrate, it is not necessary that the buyer put the goods to an abnormal use. Because there is evidence that Natkin was aware that Outlook wanted a heating system which would provide the same amount of heat for the same fuel cost as the old system, and that Outlook was relying upon Natkin's expertise in making the selection, Natkin's motion for summary judgment on this breach of warranty claim will be denied.

Problem 31

(a) Hiram Lewis purchased hydraulic equipment to operate his plant. Lewis asked one of his long-time suppliers, the Mobil Corporation, to advise him as to the proper lubricant for the new equipment. Mobil told Lewis that he should use a lubricant called Ampex 210, which contained an additive. Lewis purchased Ampex 210 from Mobil and used it in the equipment. The equipment suffered a series of breakdowns, requiring replacement of various parts. Lewis asked Mobil to reconsider its recommendation and Mobil suggested a different product that did not contain additives. Lewis adopted the new recommendation and the equipment thereafter performed without problems. Lewis seeks to recover from Mobil his losses for equipment repairs and loss of profits because of plant shutdowns. What result? See 2–315 and 2–714.

(b) Albert Young (Y) informed a clerk at Appliances, Inc. (A) that he wanted to purchase a model X–3500 General Electric air conditioner. The clerk asked Y for information concerning the space Y wanted to cool. Y replied, "I don't have time for that. Do you have what I want or do I have to go elsewhere?" The clerk apologized and completed the sale for the X–3500

---

1. The disputed issue in El Fredo Pizza was not whether baking pizzas is a particular purpose of a pizza oven, but, rather, whether the plaintiff actually relied upon the defendant's skill to furnish suitable goods for the plaintiffs business. In this connection, the Nebraska Supreme Court stated: "Comment 1 to section 2–315, U.C.C., provides that whether or not the warranty of fitness for a particular purpose arises in any particular case 'is basically a question of fact to be determined by the circumstances of the contracting. Under this section the buyer need not bring home to the seller actual knowledge of the particular purpose for which the goods are intended or of his reliance on the seller's skill and judgment, if the circumstances are such that the seller has reason to realize the purpose intended or that the reliance exists. The buyer, of course, must actually be relying on the seller'."

G.E. conditioner. A day later, Y returned to the store with the conditioner and informed the same clerk that the appliance would not cool the room in which Y installed it—a 20 x 15 space with four windows (allowing the sun to pour in all afternoon) and an eight-foot ceiling on the third floor of a three story house. The clerk explained that the X–3500 had insufficient capacity for such a room. Y shouted at the clerk, "That's too bad. This doesn't work and I want my money back." Analyze.

(c) Assume that in (b) Y had not originally asked to purchase the X–3500 but, at the clerk's request, Y had provided complete information about the space to be air conditioned and the clerk then recommended the X–3500. Y purchased on that recommendation. Analyze.

J.   PARTICULAR PURPOSE—LEASES, CISG, AND UCITA

1.   *The Implied Warranty of Fitness for Particular Purpose Under Article 2A*

Problem 32

The Mack Construction Company (M) had contracted to "rehab" an old campus building into a facility for a modern school of health sciences. Part of the contract involved the removal of a 32' brick smokestack—a project that required a crane. M was unsure of the type of crane needed, and sought the advice of Cranes Inc. (C) which leased and sold cranes. C recommended the Harbison Model 39 crane and M leased that equipment. The Harbison 39 proved inadequate for the job, causing the stack to fall and crush the newly completed mechanical room which housed heating, air conditioning and water equipment. The loss was major. M seeks your advice as to the proper cause of action. Advise. See 2A–213.

2.   *The Implied Obligation to Deliver Goods Fit for a Particular Purpose Under CISG Article 35(2)(b)*

SCHMITZ–WERKE GMBH & CO. v. ROCKLAND INDUSTRIES, INC.

United States Court of Appeals for the Fourth Circuit, 2002.
37 Fed.Appx. 687, 2002 WL 1357095.

Per Curiam: Rockland is a Maryland corporation that manufactures drapery lining fabric. In the early to mid 1990s, Rockland manufactured a type of drapery fabric called Trevira. Schmitz is a German company that manufactures, prints, and sells finished decorative fabrics in Germany and in other countries. A Rockland representative introduced the Trevira fabric to Schmitz, and during their negotiations Rockland's representatives stated that the fabric was particularly suited to be a printing base for transfer printing. Transfer printing is a process for imprinting the base fabric with dyes of particular colors or patterns.

[Schmitz placed several orders for Trevira and experienced some problems in transfer printing on the fabric. It continued to use Trevira at the urging of Rockland, but finally informed Rockland that it wanted to return some 8,000 meters of the product. Settlement discussions were not fruitful, and this suit followed.]

.... The district court found that Rockland gave Schmitz a warranty of fitness for a particular purpose (transfer printing) under Article 35(2)(b) of the CISG. The court also found that the Trevira fabric sold by Rockland had latent defects which were not detectable before the fabric was transfer printed, and that Schmitz' continued printing of the fabric even after it began to discover problems was reasonable since it was at the express urging of Rockland and was in any event the best way to mitigate its damages. The court specifically held that the goods did not conform to the warranty Rockland had given Schmitz, and that Schmitz had met its burden of proving that the defect existed at the time the fabric left Rockland's plant. [T]he court held that Schmitz need not prove the exact mechanism of the defect, and that showing that the transfer printing process used on the fabric was ordinary and competent was enough to establish that the Trevira fabric was unfit for the purpose of transfer printing. Having found for Schmitz, the court awarded damages in dollars and converted those dollars to Deutche Marks using the exchange rate as of the time Schmitz discovered the defects. Rockland appeals.

* * *

Both parties agree that this case is governed by the CISG, but there is some disagreement concerning how this Court should interpret that treaty.... When two nations are signatories to the CISG, the treaty governs contracts for the sale of goods between parties whose places of business are in those two nations, unless the contract contains a choice of law clause. CISG Art.1(1)(a). Courts interpreting the CISG should look to the language of the CISG and to the general principles on which the Convention is based. The CISG directs that "its interpretation be informed by its 'international character and ... the need to promote uniformity in its application and the observance of good faith in international trade.' "(CISG Art. 7(1)).

Rockland claims that the law of Maryland also governs this case. The CISG provides that private international law is the default law to apply to a question governed by the Convention that is not settled under its own terms. CISG Art. 7(2) The parties agree that private international law would apply the choice of law rules of the forum state (Maryland), which in this case would choose to apply the law of the contracting state. However, a court should only reach private international law if the CISG's text, interpreted in conformity with the general principles on which the CISG is based, does not settle the issue at hand. *See* CISG Art. 7(2). Schmitz agrees that Maryland law applies to issues on which the CISG is silent, but notes that Maryland law should not be reached unless the CISG fails to provide a resolution of the issue.

Rockland argues that Schmitz must demonstrate both the existence and the nature of the defect in the fabric before it can recover for breach of warranty—and that to show the nature of that defect, expert testimony is required. Article 35 of the CISG governs the duty of the seller to deliver goods that conform with the contract. Article 35(2) lists various reasons why goods may not conform with the contract, including goods which were expressly or impliedly warranted to be fit for a particular purpose. In response, Schmitz argues that all it need show is that the goods were unfit for the particular purpose warranted—transfer printing—and that it need not show precisely why or how the goods were unfit if it can show that the transfer printing process the goods underwent was performed competently and normally. Rockland is correct that Schmitz did not provide any evidence at trial that would establish the exact nature of the defect in the Trevira fabric. The text of the CISG is silent on this matter. *See* CISG, 15 U.S.C. App., Art. 35(2).[3]

Under Maryland law, Rockland is correct that a plaintiff in a products liability case must show that the product in question is defective, even if the cause of action is for breach of an express or implied warranty.... However, Rockland's resort to Maryland law does not aid its argument—there is no support in Maryland law for Rockland's claim that the plaintiff in such a case must *always* provide expert testimony describing the exact nature of the defect.[5] The district court in this case did not rule that expert testimony was not required to show the nature of the problem with the Trevira fabric. Instead, the district court held that since Schmitz had submitted sufficient evidence of the competence of [the] transfer printing process, it was proper to infer that the fabric was not suited for that process, even without direct evidence of the precise nature of the fabric's unsuitability. Schmitz argues that since it did submit expert testimony regarding the transfer printing process, even if such testimony is required, Schmitz has satisfied its burden, and the district court's ruling in their favor is supported by the evidence. We agree with Schmitz.

Under either the CISG or Maryland law, Schmitz may prevail on a claim that the fabric was unfit for the purpose for which it was warranted (transfer printing) by showing that when the fabric was properly used for the purpose Rockland warranted, the results were shoddy—even if Schmitz has introduced no evidence as to just *why* or how the fabric was unfit. Schmitz has shown that the fabric was defective—the fabric's defect was that it was unfit for transfer printing.

---

3. CISG, 15 U.S.C. App., Art. 35(2)(b). Under Article 35(2)(b) goods are unfit unless they "are fit for any particular purpose expressly or impliedly made known to the seller at the time of the conclusion of the contract, except where the circumstances show that the buyer did not rely, or that it was unreasonable for him to rely, on the seller's skill and judgment."

5. ... [T]he Maryland Special Court of Appeals rejected a claim that expert testimony was necessary to establish the existence of a defect in that case, and noted that "the general rule is well established that expert testimony is only required when the subject of the inference is so particularly related to some science or profession that it is beyond the ken of the average layman." *See Virgil v. "Kash 'N' Karry" Service Corp.*, 61 Md. App. 23,31, 484 A.2d 652 (1984) 31. Expert testimony is not required on matters of which the jurors would be aware by virtue of common knowledge. *Babylon v. Scruton*, 215 Md. 299, 307, 138 A.2d 375 (1958).

Rockland attempts to counter this argument by claiming that this improperly shifts the burden of proof. Rockland's concerns are misplaced—Schmitz still must prove that the transfer printing process was ordinary and competently performed, and still must prove that the fabric was defective—it just permits Schmitz to do so without proving the exact nature of the defect.

* * *

Rockland also argues that even if the court properly found that the Trevira fabric was not particularly well suited for transfer printing as warranted, Schmitz cannot recover on such a warranty because it did not in fact rely on Rockland's advice as required under CISG Article 35(2)(b). Rockland is correct that Article 35(2)(b) of the CISG requires that the buyer reasonably rely on the representations of the seller before liability attaches for breach of a warranty for fitness for a particular purpose. The district court explicitly found that Schmitz relied on the statements of Rockland's representative that the Trevira fabric was particularly well suited for transfer printing. The court also found that Schmitz continued to print the fabric with the express consent of Rockland after it discovered and reported problems with the fabric. The district court's finding that Schmitz relied on Rockland's statements proclaiming the Trevira fabric's suitability for transfer printing is supported by the evidence and was not clearly erroneous. . . .

Rockland also argues that the district court erred . . . in [using] the exchange rate as of the date Schmitz learned of the problems with the Trevira fabric. In contrast, the general rule is that the exchange rate as of the date of the award should be used. The CISG is silent on this issue, and it is proper for courts to resort to private international law in such situations. As discussed above, the parties agree that private international law would apply the choice of law rules of the forum, Maryland, and that since Maryland's choice of law rules apply the law of the place of contract, Maryland substantive law should apply.

* * *

There is no clear resolution of this issue that is dictated by the CISG or by Maryland law. And, we can discern no particular equitable advantage to either of the two rules—it is not clear that either position more fairly compensates an injured party or does so under the discrete facts here. Under these particular circumstances, the district court's decision to use the exchange rate as of the date of breach was not an abuse of discretion and we decline to disturb it. . . .

[T]he judgment of the district court is affirmed.

Question

If "Maryland law" (Maryland's version of the UCC, particularly UCC 2–315) applied in this case, would the analysis change?

---

3. Implied Reliance Warranties Under UCITA–Fitness for Particular Purpose and Accuracy of Informational Content

Unless the warranty is disclaimed, UCITA § 405 (a)(1) creates an implied warranty of fitness for the licensee's particular purpose if the licensee relies on the skill and judgment of the licensor to select, develop, or furnish suitable information. Where, however, the licensor was to be paid for his services regardless of the fitness of the resulting information, the implied warranty is that the information will not fail to achieve the licensee's particular purpose as a result of the licensor's lack of reasonable effort. UCITA § 405(a)(2). Under UCITA § 405(b), however, the fitness warranty does not apply to aesthetics, market appeal or subjective quality of the informational content, nor does it apply to "published informational content" as defined in UCITA § 102(a)(51) unless an individual acting on the licensor's behalf has selected among published informational content from different providers. UCITA § 405(c) creates a new warranty where an agreement requires the licensor to provide or select a system that combines computer programs and goods, and the licensor has reason to know that the licensee is relying on the licensor's skill and judgment to select the components. In such a case, there is an implied warranty that the components provided or selected will function together as a system.

As was noted previously, UCITA § 404 creates a new implied warranty by a merchant licensor "that there is no inaccuracy in the informational content caused by the merchant's failure to perform with reasonable care." The warranty only applies, however, where there is a special relationship of reliance with the licensee, and it can be disclaimed. For more information on the warranty in UCITA § 404, see the discussion in part H(3) *supra*.

K. CUMULATION AND CONFLICT OF WARRANTIES

1. Cumulation and Conflict of Warranties Under UCC Article 2

THE SINGER COMPANY v. E.I. du PONT de NEMOURS COMPANY

United States Court of Appeals for the Eighth Circuit, 1978.
579 F.2d 433.

HANSON, SENIOR DISTRICT JUDGE. In this diversity contract action, the Singer Company sued to recover losses incurred when the E.I. du Pont de Nemours and Company allegedly breached both an express warranty and an implied warranty of fitness in failing to provide plaintiff with suitable industrial paint for its plant operations at Red Bud, Illinois. The case was submitted to a jury only on the implied warranty theory, and judgment was returned for Singer in the amount of $108,367.00. Defendant was awarded no recovery on either of its two attendant counterclaims. Du Pont unsuccessfully moved for judgments notwithstanding the verdict and for new trial, contending that the trial court improperly instructed the jury and that there was insufficient evidence to support the jury verdicts. Du Pont appeals from those rulings.

Singer became interested during late 1972 in obtaining an electro deposition paint system for its Red Bud, Illinois plant, where until this time the metal, or ware, used in the manufacture of air-conditioners and furnaces had been painted in a spray system. Electro deposition is a method of painting by which pretreated ware is conveyed through an electrically charged paint tank and the ware, serving as an anode, is coated with paint in an electroplating type of process. After a period of negotiation between representatives from the two parties, Du Pont, in September and October of 1972, was contracted to provide Singer with paint for its approximately 22,000 gallon tank. Three additional companies were contracted to provide other interrelated steps in the overall finishing process, steps such as pretreatment of the ware and conveyance of the ware through the entire system.

From the beginning, in October of 1973, Singer experienced problems with the electro deposition system. Ware frequently emerged from the paint tank with "blotches" and "streaks." Repainting was necessary. Du Pont, which supervised the installation and starting up of this electro deposition system, tried unsuccessfully for six months to correct this problem. Finally, in April of 1974, the Du Pont paint was removed from the tank and replaced with paint supplied by the Sherwin–Williams Company. This lawsuit was filed the following year.

The nub of the factual controversy in the trial court was the cause for the blotches and streaks on the painted ware. Du Pont maintained that the problem was with the substrate, pretreated ware; Singer, however, insisted that the paint was at fault. In countering Singer's claim, Du Pont argued that the paint provided to plaintiff met contract specifications until the substrate was altered in February of 1974, at which time Du Pont could no longer be held to have expressly warranted its product. Singer contends that even if the specifications of this express warranty were met, Du Pont had given an implied warranty of fitness for a particular purpose by representing throughout the period in question that its paint would satisfy plaintiff's needs. Over Du Pont's objection, the trial court instructed the jury on implied warranty for a particular purpose. The issue of express warranty was not submitted.

.... There is ... no dispute that the "all tests" provision of the contract, which specified such set standards as color and texture that the paint was to satisfy upon pretreated laboratory test panels, was an express warranty pursuant to Section 2–213(1)(b) of the U.C.C. But Singer claims that the contract further preserved an implied warranty of fitness, a warranty that pursuant to Section 2–315 assured plaintiff the paint supplied would satisfactorily cover its substrate. A paragraph in the contract provided:

> None of the provisions or remedies herein are in lieu of any claims for damages Buyer may have at law or equity under the Uniform Commercial Code or otherwise, for the breach of any contracts or warranties with Buyer, which rights are specifically reserved by Buyer.

Du Pont contends that parties who have an express warranty regarding a contracted for item cannot also have an implied warranty of fitness for that same item. The warranty of fitness for a specific purpose is alleged to have been limited by expressly defining it in a set of specifications, and Du Pont claims that to find otherwise would permit Singer to escape the parties' true contractual bargain.

Pertinent sections of the U.C.C., and the comments pursuant thereto, lend inferential support to Singer's position that the implied warranty of fitness was cumulative to and not excluded by the express warranty. Section 2–316(2), with regard to the exclusion or modification of such warranties, states:

> ... [To] exclude or modify any implied warranty of fitness the exclusion must be a writing and conspicuous.

(Emphasis added.) Comment 9 to that section provides in part:

> The situation in which *the buyer* gives precise and complete *specifications to the seller* is not explicitly covered in this section, but this is a frequent circumstance by which the *implied warranties must be excluded*. The warranty of fitness for a particular purpose would not normally arise since in such a situation there is usually *no reliance on the seller by the buyer*.

(Emphasis added.) See also U.C.C. § 2–315, comment 2. Because the evidence in this case fully indicates that it was not the buyer but the seller who in fact recommended and supplied the paint specifications, and remained in control of the paint tank, it would appear that the trial court did not err in its determination that an implied warranty of fitness was at issue. This is especially so in view of the purported exclusion of this warranty, which could be scarcely termed "conspicuous."

A reading of the U.C.C. to suggest that an express warranty and an implied warranty of fitness are not necessarily mutually exclusive, as Singer has argued, receives support from Code authority.

> The fact that a warranty of fitness for a particular purpose does or does not exist has no bearing on any other warranty or theory of product liability. Conversely, the fact that there may be some other basis for liability of the defendant does not preclude the existence of a warranty for a particular purpose. *Thus the fact that there is a*

warranty of conformity to sample [an express warranty] does not preclude the existence of a warranty for a particular purpose.

(Emphasis added.) Anderson, Uniform Commercial Code § 2–315:5 (1970). Relevant case law, in the balance, further indicates that an express warranty would not control under the circumstances of this case.

Du Pont, in arguing the law upon appeal, relies principally upon two types of cases that have arisen under the U.C.C.: those in which there has been a showing that the buyer, in possession or control of the item, failed to follow the express warranty specifications; and those where an enforceable disclaimer of an implied warranty has been established. With respect to the first type of case, it is clear that the trial court did not confront a situation where a buyer in possession or control of an item failed to follow seller's specifications, used the item in a manner for which it was not intended, lost that for which he had contracted, and then erroneously claimed a breach of an implied warranty for fitness. Here, Du Pont, as the seller, was in control of the disputed item. No one denies that Du Pont was throughout this time in control of Singer's paint tank, directing its operation and determining its contents.

The disclaimer cases are likewise inapplicable. Even without a paragraph in the contract reserving all further warranties under the U.C.C., Du Pont would have difficulty in arguing that an express warranty of the paint effected a disclaimer of any further warranty. It is clear from these cases that disclaimers under the Code are not favored and are limited whenever possible. Du Pont also argues in general that to permit Singer to assert an implied warranty of fitness would be to allow utilization of the U.C.C. in avoidance of the parties' true bargain. The true bargain, though, is less than apparent from the face of the contract. This was not a situation where a buyer ordered according to specifications and then claimed an implied warranty of fitness when the product failed to measure up to expectations. In this instance, the buyer approached the seller describing the results desired and the seller professed to be able to supply it, thereby inducing a reliance that created the possibility of an implied warranty of fitness. Notwithstanding the express warranty contained within the specifications particularly defining and describing the item to be supplied, there may have been a further warranty that an item with those specifications would accomplish certain results or be adequate for the specified purpose. That is, the accomplishment of the purpose might be viewed as the essence of the contractual undertaking, and not the mere furnishing of the specified item. Nothing within this contract, or in writings or statements subsequent to it, indicate whether the end of the agreement was the specified item or the use for which the item was intended.

Du Pont simply failed to negotiate a contract that clearly delineated and limited allocation of risk. This case would never have arisen had defendant, as a party to and a scrivener of the contract, either inserted a specific disclaimer or demanded that the warranty savings clause be deleted.

Having left the contract ambiguous, the question as to whether use rather than supply of the product was intended to be of the essence, as well as questions regarding buyer's reliance and seller's knowledge of that reliance, are for jury determination. Such were submitted to the jury in this case under the trial court's following instruction:

Your verdict on the plaintiff's claim must be for the plaintiff if you believe:

First: The defendant sold paint to the plaintiff.

Second: The defendant knew the use for which plaintiff purchased the paint, and

Third: Plaintiff reasonably relied upon defendant's judgment for the suitability of the paint for such use, and,

Fourth: The paint was not suitable for such use, and

Fifth: As a direct result plaintiff was damaged.

Du Pont contends on appeal, as it did below, that the trial court was in error giving an instruction which allowed the jury to determine the construction of the contract. The question regarding the presence of an implied warranty, defendant maintains, constituted a question of law that should have been determined by the trial judge.

The better rule, when there remains an issue of contractual intent, is to submit the issue to the jury unless the evidence is so clear that no reasonable person would determine the issue but one way. Du Pont fails to offer any sustaining reason as to why the construction of an ambiguous contract, which involves the existence or nonexistence of an implied warranty of fitness under the U.C.C., should also not be left to a jury determination. The question of buyer's reliance and seller's knowledge of that reliance is a factual inquiry particularly well-suited for jury deliberation. U.C.C. §§ 2–316, 2–317.

Once having determined that the issue of implied warranty was properly submitted to the jury, sufficiency of the evidence becomes the controlling inquiry. We review the evidence to determine whether there was sufficient evidence for the jury to find that Singer reasonably relied upon Du Pont's judgment regarding the suitability of the paint, that Du Pont knew the use for which Singer purchased the paint, and that the paint was not suitable for such use.

In reviewing the evidence pursuant to the judgment n.o.v. standards, we cannot conclude that Singer failed to offer the necessary evidence to sustain a jury verdict against Du Pont for a breach of an implied warranty of fitness. Clearly, Du Pont, which reviewed the entire finishing system, knew at the time of contracting the particularized use for which plaintiff purchased the paint, and Singer reasonably relied upon Du Pont's judgment that its paint was suitable for the electro deposition system. Du Pont makes some argument that the change in substrate affected the suitability, but it was an argument not pressed upon appeal. In any event, if defendant did not consider itself bound by warranty to do anything more than furnish a paint of particular specifications, we find it difficult to explain not only why Du Pont supervised the installation of the system, but worked to alleviate the problems during the entire period its paint was in the tank.

Finally, in satisfaction of the last element necessary to an implied warranty of fitness, the evidence was sufficient to show that Du Pont's paint was not suitable for Singer's use. The evidence here presents a close question. Yet giving the "jury verdict the benefit of all reasonable inferences to be drawn from the evidence," this Court, though we might have cast our verdict otherwise, cannot say there was no more than a scintilla of evidence to support the jury verdict. The testimony of Singer employees and De Vittorio, and such evidence as the unexplained blotches and streaks upon the laboratory test panels, sufficiently takes this case from the undeterminative equipoise for which defendant argues.

The judgment appealed from is affirmed.

Problem 33

The Weise Company (W) submitted a prototype device to a prospective customer, Stewart, Inc. (S). S tested the prototype and was pleased with the results. S dispatched its form offering to purchase 1560 production line models of the prototype. The S form provided that the devices were to be "as per prototype and have input speeds of 1590 r.p.m." W accepted the offer and delivered the 2000 devices which, like the prototype, had input speeds of 3200 r.p.m. When it discovered the discrepancy between the actual input speeds and the r.p.m. set forth in its offer, S rejected the entire shipment. Litigation ensued. Analyze. See 2–317 and comment 3 thereto.

Problem 34

Richard Beck coached the Oak Hill High School baseball team. He refused to allow his players to use sunglasses because he thought them dangerous. Before the last season began, however, he saw an advertisement in the *Sporting News* that read:

> PLAY BALL—and *flip* for instant eye protection with Rayex baseball sunglasses—Professional Flip–Specs. These are scientific lenses which protect your eyes with a flip from sun and glare anywhere—baseball, beach, boat, driving, golfing, fishing—just perfect for active and spectator sports. These are the world's finest sunglasses.

Impressed with the ad, Beck bought six pairs of the sunglasses, which he distributed to his outfielders and infielders. Michael Filler was a 16 year-old outfielder who used a pair of the glasses to field "fungoes"—practice fly balls lofted to an outfielder by a teammate. While using the sunglasses at practice one day, Michael momentarily lost sight of a fungo. The ball struck the sunglasses, shattering the right lens which splintered into Michael's eye. The eye was damaged beyond help. In an action against Rayex Corporation, Michael sued for breach of the implied warranty of merchantability as well as breach of the implied warranty of fitness for a particular purpose. Analyze.

2. Cumulation and Conflict of Warranties Under UCC Article 2A

Problem 34A

Suppose that the transaction between S and W in Problem 33 *supra* had been a lease rather than a sale. How, if at all, would your analysis change? See 2A–215.

3. Cumulation and Conflict of Quality Obligations Under the CISG

Problem 34B

The Lee Corporation manufactured pantyhose in the United States, which it marketed under the L'Eggs brand name. It also manufactured pantyhose in Mexico (a country that has ratified the CISG), but the Mexican products were marketed under different brand names. Ames Corporation, located in Canada (which also has ratified the CISG), agreed to purchase 400,000 units produced in Mexico after Lee represented that the Mexican product was identical to the L'Eggs produced in the U.S., and presented a sample of the Mexican product. Lee shipped the pantyhose, but Ames rejected the shipment on the ground that the product it received was not the equivalent of L'Eggs. Conclusive evidence indicates that it was not the equivalent of L'Eggs, but the 400,000 units were identical to the sample of the Mexican product presented to Ames. Analyze. Consider Articles 35(1) and 35(2)(c).

---

4. Cumulation and Conflict of Warranties Under UCITA

The UCITA provision governing cumulation and conflict of warranties (UCITA § 408) closely tracks the language of UCC 2–317.

L. FINANCE LEASES

DUDLEY v. BUSINESS EXPRESS, INC.

United States District Court for the District of New Hampshire, 1994.
882 F.Supp. 199.

SHANE DEVINE, SENIOR JUDGE. While boarding Business Express flight #4526, scheduled for service between Logan Airport in Boston, Massachusetts, and Lebanon Municipal Airport in West Lebanon, New Hampshire, Terri Dudley allegedly struck her head on either the top of the aircraft's door frame or on the fuselage itself and suffered injury as a result. In addition to a loss of consortium claim asserted by Roger Dudley, Terri's husband, plaintiffs further asserted claims of negligence, strict liability, and breach of implied warranties against Business Express,[1] CCC, MCA, and Beech Aircraft Corporation (Beech), the manufacturer of the aircraft at issue.

Business Express is a third-tier subsidiary of MCA[2]. As a business, MCA "is primarily in the business of providing marketing consulting." By and through it subsidiaries, however, MCA "is involved or has been involved in developing real estate, developing computer software, selling newspaper coupon services/space, car sales, and advertising." "Other than as an accommodation to its subsidiary to assist the subsidiary in purchasing and financing its aircraft," MCA "is not in the business of purchasing and selling aircraft."

Similarly, CCC asserts that it "is in the business of providing financing to companies purchasing equipment. [CCC] is not in the business of selecting or selling aircraft."

A company desiring to finance its equipment purchase through Concord Commercial makes its own decision of what equipment it will purchase. Concord Commercial does not make that decision. The equipment is then purchased in the name of Concord Commercial and then is leased by Concord Commercial to the company that wanted the equipment in the first place. Consistent with its stated position as a finance lessor, CCC "never selected the aircraft [at issue] or had possession of it." Moreover, CCC "does not and did not control or direct the operations of Business Express or have anything to do with boarding of passengers."

With respect to the Beech Model 1900 aircraft presently at issue (N809BE), the interactions between the Business Express–MCA–CCC triumvirate are alleged as follows: Business Express, then known as Atlantic Aviation, Inc., d/b/a Business Express, selected N809BE based on the particular route it was to service. MCA, "as an accommodation to its subsidiary, Business Express, purchased the aircraft in its name on or about July 12, 1985 and obtained third party financing." On that same day, Business Express took possession of the aircraft directly from the manufacturer, Beech, and executed a lease of same with MCA.

Citing financial reasons, MCA subsequently transferred title to the N809BE to Business Express. On March 17, 1989, Business Express made its own decision to finance the aircraft through Concord Commercial. To carry out that financing, Business Express, without ever releasing possession, sold the aircraft to Concord Commercial which in turn immediately leased the aircraft to Marketing Corporation of America (an affiliate of Business Express)[3] with the understanding and expectation

1. The strict liability (Counts III, IV, and V) and breach of implied warranty (Counts VI and VII) claims brought against Business Express were dismissed by the court pursuant to its October 11, 1994, order

2. The precise business relationship between Business Express and MCA proceeds as follows: Business Express is a subsidiary of Northeast Aviation, Inc. (Northeast). Northeast is a subsidiary of Market Corp. Wings, Inc. (Market Corp.). Market Corp. is a subsidiary of MCA.

3. With respect to the terms and conditions of this particular leasing arrangement, defendants allege that "the lease between Concord Commercial and Marketing Corpo-

that Marketing Corporation of America would lease it back to Business Express. The rental rate for the CCC–MCA lease and the MCA–Business Express sublease is identical. At all relevant times since July 12, 1985, the date the aircraft was first purchased, "Business Express ... maintained possession and operational control of the aircraft."

Plaintiffs contend that defendants CCC and MCA are businesses that engage in the purchase and lease of aircraft. Plaintiffs further allege that by virtue of the purchase/lease arrangements employed to acquire N809BE, defendants have placed the aircraft into the stream of commerce and can thus be subject to liability on the basis of negligence, strict liability, and breach of implied warranty. Defendants CCC and MCA, however, contend that their role in the transaction merely constituted that of finance-lessor, and as such, liability under each of the above-noted theories does not attach.

The distinction between a customary chattel lease and a finance/security lease is illustrated as follows:

The true lease is what is commonly meant by the term "lease." In theory, the lessor allows the lessee to use the equipment for some fraction of its useful life, but "fully expects to retake the chattel at the end of the lease term and either resell or release it." The right to the possession of the equipment upon default or expiration of the lease may be termed the "equipment reversion."

The security lease may be thought of as a "disguised" security agreement, a secured installment sales contract, or a lease "intended as a security." Although the security leasing agreement is written in lease form, the security lessor does not expect to retake the goods at the end of the lease period but instead to transfer full ownership to the "lessee" for a minimal sum.

In simple terms, "[a] finance lease is the functional equivalent of an extension of credit." *Dominguez Mojica v. Citibank, N.A. (Citibank II), 853 F.Supp. 51, 54 (D.P.R. 1994).* The transaction, however, is usually " 'a three party relation. The lessor is a financial middleman between the supplier and the lessee.' " Id. Finance lessors thus "include banks, insurance companies and other financial institutions that provide funds to help businesses acquire products and equipment for commercial use. Instead of financing the purchase directly and accepting a security interest, the finance lessor obtains title to the property and 'leases' it to the actual user.... Finance companies have the merely tangential function of providing money to make the purchase of a product possible.... The finance lessor rarely ever takes physical possession of it." Citibank II, supra, 853 F.Supp. at 54[4]

ration of America expressly acknowledges that Concord Commercial did not select the equipment, is not a manufacturer or a dealer of such property, and that it leased the aircraft without any warranties, express or implied."

4. Appropriate in light of the facts at bar, the following is an illustration of a "classic" finance lease transaction: Assume that an airline selects a 747 and negotiates over its particular configuration with Boeing. Instead of purchasing the 747, the air-

The evidence before the court indicates that neither CCC nor MCA either selected the aircraft at issue or exercised physical control over same. Moreover, to the extent the parties entered into a sale-leaseback arrangement, such an arrangement was no more than a mere "business happenstance on the part of the lessor." *Brescia v. Great Road Realty Trust*, 117 N.H. 154, 157, 373 A.2d 1310, 1312 (1977). In consequence thereof, the court hereby finds and rules that at the time of the alleged incident, both CCC and MCA occupied the position of finance lessor and are entitled to all rights and defenses relevant thereto.

NEGLIGENCE

According to the Supreme Court of the State of New Hampshire,

"One who leases a chattel as safe for immediate use is subject to liability ... if the lessor fails to exercise reasonable care to make it safe for such use or to disclose its actual condition to those who may be expected to use it." Restatement (Second) of Torts § 408 (1965). The duty imposed is operationally related to the real life circumstances of the lessor, and thus the inspection required varies with "the length of time during which [the chattel] has been in the lessor's possession and use." Id., comment a, at 367.

Brescia, supra, 117 N.H. at 159, 373 A.2d at 1313.

Here, as in Brescia, the undisputed facts in the record fail to indicate any genuine issue of material fact which would support plaintiffs' claim that CCC or MCA, either independently or in concert, breached their duty to exercise reasonable care to plaintiffs.[5] Rather, their sole purpose was to provide the financial means whereby Business Express could consummate its agreement with Beech for the acquisition of N809BE. At no time did either CCC or MCA have possession of the aircraft, nor did they participate to any degree in the design, maintenance, manufacture, operation, or inspection of same.

Therefore, defendants' motion for summary judgment on the negligence claim (Count I) brought against defendants CCC and MCA must be and herewith is granted.

STRICT LIABILITY

Strict tort liability in New Hampshire is governed by section 402A of the RESTATEMENT (SECOND) OF TORTS. However, as the New Hampshire Supreme Court has chastened, "strict liability is not a no-fault system of compensation." *Thibault v. Sears, Roebuck & Co., 118 N.H. 802, 806, 395 A.2d 843, 845–46 (1978).* Moreover, "to the extent the

---

line then arranges for a bank to purchase it and for the bank to lease the aircraft to the airline. Although the document between the bank and the airline would be a true lease and not a security agreement, this transaction between the airline and the bank is first and last a financing transaction. Citibank II, supra, 853 F.Supp. at 54 n.5 (citation omitted).

5. "A plaintiff claiming negligence must show that the defendant owed the plaintiff a duty, that the duty was breached, that the plaintiff suffered an injury, and that the defendant's breach was the proximate cause of the injury." *Ronayne v. State*, 137 N.H. 281, 284, 632 A.2d 1210, 1212 (1993).

doctrine is applicable to a lease arrangement, it would seem to be applicable only where the lease in question represents something more than business happenstance on the part of the lessor." Brescia, supra, 117 N.H. at 157, *373 A.2d at 1312* (citing *Cintrone v. Hertz Truck Leasing, 45 N.J. 434, 212 A.2d 769 (N.J. 1965))*.

Since Brescia, decisions from other states and United States jurisdictions have echoed the reasoning of the New Hampshire Supreme Court in denying strict liability actions against finance lessors. See 1 FRUMER & FRIEDMAN § 3.03[4], at 3–432, and cases cited therein ("recent cases dealing with finance lessors ... have refused to apply strict tort liability ... reasoning that the finance lessor is merely a money lender and/or is not in the business of supplying products").

Although not specifically expressed in Brescia, exempting financial lessors from strict products liability is congruent with the politics inherent in the strict liability scheme. Put differently, "the policies served by applying Section 402A to conventional, commercial lessors would not be served when the lessor is not marketing or supplying the product, but rather is merely a financier." *Nath v. Nat'l Equip. Leasing Corp., 282 Pa.Super. 142, 422 A.2d 868, 875 (Pa.Super.Ct. 1981)*.

The Nath court indicated four rationales for this liability exception.

1) The finance lessor, in most cases, "is not the only member of the marketing chain available to the plaintiff for recovery," 2) imposing strict liability on a finance lessor will not increase safety, because "the finance lessor does not take actual possession of the equipment leased, and generally lacks the expertise necessary to detect or prevent product defects;" 3) the lessee is in a far better position "to detect and prevent use of a defective product than is the finance lessor, for it is the lessee who selects the product, takes actual possession of it, maintains it, and in general has expertise with respect to it;" and 4) while the finance lessor can increase the amount of rent charged to compensate for strict liability for injuries, the extra charges "would appear to penalize the finance lessee, a consumer of the product, rather than the parties who manufactured or sold the product."

Citibank I, supra, 830 F.Supp. at 672 (quoting Nath, supra, 422 A.2d at 875–76).

This court is persuaded by Nath. First, although some of plaintiffs' strict liability claims have been dismissed, the claim against Beech, the primary party in the chain of distribution, still remains viable. Second, financial lessors are not involved in the design, selection, or manufacture of the defective items and thus are not in a position to detect a possibly defective condition. Finally, the imposition of strict liability on financial lessors would adversely impact the leasing market as a whole, forcing the lessors to charge enhanced fees so as to protect themselves from liability claims for defective products whose condition they are unable to detect and powerless to correct.

In the present case, it is undisputed that CCC and MCA each lacked "dominion and control" over the aircraft in question. Further, in light of the evidence before the court, plaintiffs are unable to prove that CCC and/or MCA were a part of the original chain of production, marketing, or distribution of the aircraft. Under the instant facts, therefore, the court hereby grants summary judgment as it relates to the strict liability claims (Counts III, IV, and V) filed against defendants CCC and MCA.

IMPLIED WARRANTIES

"In this state, the statutory implied warranties of the Commercial Code are deemed to afford a complete remedy, and no common law cause of action in contract based on implied warranty is recognized." Brescia, supra, 117 N.H. at 157, 373 A.2d at 1312. Plaintiffs in their amended complaint allege violations of both the warranty of merchantability, New Hampshire Revised Statutes Annotated (RSA) 382–A:2–314, and the warranty of fitness for a particular purpose, RSA 382–A:2–315, contained in Article 2 of the Uniform Commercial Code (Code).[6]

The warranty of merchantability is applicable "only if the seller is a merchant with respect to goods of that kind." A "merchant", as defined by the Code, is "one who deals in goods of that kind or otherwise by his occupation holds himself out as having knowledge or skill peculiar to the goods involved." (RSA 382–A:2–104(1)). In light of their limited role as finance lessors, defendants CCC and MCA fail to satisfy the Code's "merchant" definition, a prerequisite to RSA 382–A:2–314 liability. The court therefore finds and rules that the warranty of merchantability embodied in RSA 382–A:2–314 is inapplicable to either CCC or MCA.

It is on the foundation of such reasoning that the corollary claim of warranty of fitness for a particular purpose is likewise inapplicable to either CCC or MCA. "By its terms, RSA 382–A:2–315 (1961) applies only if, at the time of sale, a seller knows or has reason to know of the particular purpose for which the goods are required, and that the buyer is relying on the seller's skill or judgment." *Dalton v. Stanley Solar & Stove, Inc.*, 137 N.H. 467, 471, 629 A.2d 794, 797 (1993) As indicated [earlier], one of the hallmarks of a finance-lease transaction is that the finance lessor serves merely as a source of capital, not advice or skilled judgment. Indeed, the finance lessor does not enter the transaction until after the lessee has already selected the item to be financed. As the New Hampshire Supreme Court noted in Brescia, "to speak of 'reliance' in these circumstances would be to indulge in an absurdity." Brescia,

---

6. The court notes that since the time of the alleged incident, the New Hampshire Legislature has adopted Article 2A (Leases) of the Code, effective January 1, 1994. See RSA 382–A:2A–101 (Supp. 1993). Although the provisions of Article 2A do not govern the resolution of the instant matter, they do inform this court's discussion. Of significant note is the fact that the drafters of Article 2A specifically exempted finance lessors from the warranties of merchantability and fitness for a particular purpose. See RSA 382–A:2A–212, 2A–213 (Supp. 1993). The rationale for this exemption is that "due to the limited function usually performed by the [finance] lessor, the lessee looks almost entirely to the supplier for representations, covenants, and warranties. If a manufacturer's warranty carries through, the lessee may also look to that." RSA 382–A:2A–103, cmt. g (Supp. 1993).

supra, 117 N.H. at 158, 373 A.2d at 1313 (citation omitted). Therefore, the court hereby finds and rules that, under the present set of facts, the implied warranty of fitness for particular purpose (RSA 382–A:2–315) is inapplicable to finance lessors such as CCC and MCA.

The court grants defendants' motion for summary judgment with respect to the breach of implied warranty claims (Counts VI and VII) alleged against CCC and MCA.

Note

Warranties—Finance Leases. The only warranty of quality a finance lessor can make under current Article 2A is an express warranty, and the typical finance lessor gives no such warranty. The finance lessee looks to the supplier rather than the finance lessor for warranty protection, even though the lessee is not in "privity" with the supplier. Under 2A–209 a finance lessee receives the benefit of and can enforce all warranties in the supply contract.

Suppose, for example, that a supplier who is a merchant in goods of the kind sells goods to a bank, which then leases them in a finance lease to the lessee. Absent an effective disclaimer, the supply contract—a contract of sale—includes an implied warranty of merchantability (2–314). The supply contract may also include express warranties from the supplier. Under 2A–209 the finance lessee is the beneficiary of all the warranties in the supply contract. If the goods prove unmerchantable or breach a supplier's express warranty, the finance lessee has a cause of action against the supplier.

Since a finance lessee is going to rely on the warranties in the supply contract rather than on warranty protections in the finance lease, the definition of "finance lease" in 2A–103(1)(g) requires *one* of the following alternatives: (a) before signing the finance lease, the lessee receives a copy of the supply contract between the finance lessor and the supplier; (b) the finance lease becomes effective only upon the lessee's approval of the supply contract; (c) before signing the finance lease, the lessee receives a complete and accurate statement of all warranties and remedies in the supply contract; or (d), before signing, the finance lessee is given specific opportunities to communicate with the supplier concerning the warranties in the supply contract.[1] The definition of "finance lease" also requires that the lessor not select, manufacture or supply the goods, and that the finance lessor acquire the goods from the supplier for the sole purpose of leasing them to the lessee.

There is another unique feature of finance leases. Under 2A–407, the finance lessee's obligations become "irrevocable and independent" when the lessee accepts the goods.[2] Upon accepting the goods, therefore, a finance lessee becomes obligated to continue paying rent to the lessor even if the goods are destroyed or turn out not to conform to warranties—although the

---

1. The last alternative will not satisfy the requirements for a consumer finance lease. 2A–103(1)(g)(iii)(D).

2. This rule is subject to the finance lessee's very limited right to revoke acceptance of goods. This situation is explored in the next Chapter.

lessee can claim damages for any breach suffered. Thus 2A–407 creates a statutory equivalent to the "hell or high water" clauses common in equipment leases.

Problem 35

Ann Murphy was an employee in a paper factory who was injured on the job while operating a machine. Her employer, Paper, Inc.(P), had acquired the machine in the following fashion: it negotiated the price of the machine with its manufacturer, Zeno Corporation (Z), then sought financing from Capital Finance (C), which purchased the machine from Z and then leased it to P. The agreement required P to pay C monthly rent for 60 months. Murphy was injured during the first year of the five-year lease term. C specialized in financing equipment acquisitions in the paper industry, and had engaged in similar lease transactions for this kind of machinery many times. Assume Murphy was injured because the machinery was unmerchantable. Can Murphy recover from C? From Z? See 2A–103(1)(g), 2A–212, and 2A–216. Suppose that the lease between C and P provided that, at the end of the lease term, P was entitled to purchase the machine for one dollar. Would that change your analysis? Consider 2A–103(1)(j) and 1–203.[1]

M.   WARRANTY DISCLAIMERS

1.   Disclaimers Under UCC Article 2

Problem 36

The Grauer Corporation (G) agreed to sell a computerized robotic assembly system to the Mandere Corporation (M). M intended to use the system to produce motorcycles. The price was $1,739,000.00. The written contract, which both parties signed, contained the following clause:

> The assembly system described herein is warranted against defects in workmanship for a period of 120 days from the date of delivery. Grauer will repair or replace any defective part during this warranty period. This warranty is the sole and exclusive warranty in this contract. *There is no other warranty express or implied, including the implied warranty of merchantability, under this contract.*

(a) Is the italicized disclaimer clause effective? See 2–316 and 1–201(b)(10).

(b) Assume the clause was not italicized. What result?

(c) Assume the clause was in capital letters.

(d) Assume the clause was in boldface print.

(e) Assume the clause was in red print while the remainder of the clause was in black print.

(f) Suppose the clause *was* italicized, but the entire clause was on the reverse side of a form with 19 other printed clauses that were not italicized.

---

1. Before Article 1 was amended in 2001, the material in current 1–203 was   part of the definition of "security interest" in pre-amendment 1–201(37).

(g) Assume the facts of (f) except that, on the front of the form, above the buyer's signature line, there was a clause reading, "This is the entire agreement of the parties, including the clauses on the reverse side of this form."

(h) Assume the written contract between G and M did not contain the clause set forth above, but after signing the contract the parties orally agreed to the terms of that clause. Is the disclaimer effective?

Problem 37

(a) Sam Edwards purchased a one year old used truck from Honest Bill's Auto Sales. At the time of the sale the truck had recorded only 14,000 miles on the odometer. The contract was evidenced by a writing on Honest Bill's letterhead. The document contained the following language: "Buyer purchases this truck in its present condition." Sam signed this writing. Sam had repeated problems with the truck and eventually discovered that it was worthless and had to be scrapped. The truck, in fact, had only been driven 14,000 miles before Sam purchased it. Sam brings an action for breach of the implied warranty of merchantability. What result?

(b) George Harris operated a service that cleared land for housing developments. Harris' principal problem in any clearing project was the removal of trees. He saw an ad for a used "tree spade" device which could be attached to his tractor. The ad stated, "Has removed only 400 trees." The seller was the Equipment Supply Company (ESC), operated by its owner, Cliff Hill. Harris inspected the spade at ESC's storage facility. Hill was quite accommodating. He told Harris to take the spade with him and "try it out." Harris declined, although he spent more than an hour inspecting the device. During this inspection, Harris noticed that two of the several blades on the spade appeared to be bent. He assumed that the blades were so designed, and was reluctant to question Hill for fear that he might raise the price. Harris had heard that, when new, these devices could cost up to $30,000. Hill was asking only $12,500. Seeking no further information from the seller, Harris agreed to take the device. When he attempted to use the spade, he discovered that it did not operate effectively. Moreover, as Harris later learned, the blades were *not* designed to be bent, and using the device with bent blades in effect destroyed it. Has Hill breached any warranties made to Harris?

(c) Burt Adams, a vegetable farmer, had purchased onion seed from Seed, Inc. for the last 15 years. Adams had been pleased with his results using this seed. Adams would typically take delivery of the seed at the Seed, Inc. supply house. For 15 years, the onion seed bags included a tag with the following statement:

> SEED, INC. DOES NOT WARRANT THIS SEED. THERE ARE NO WARRANTIES EXPRESS OR IMPLIED, INCLUDING BUT NOT LIMITED TO THE IMPLIED WARRANTY OF MERCHANTABILITY.

This year, as usual, Adams went to the supply house and picked 10 bags of seed from the piles on the floor. The bags had tags, but the print thereon was small and read: "There are no express or implied warranties given with this seed." Adams paid for the seed and later planted it. The entire crop failed because the seed was defective. Adams sued Seed, Inc. for breach of the implied warranty of merchantability. Analyze.

(d) Assume the facts of (c) except the tags on the bags of defective seed read as follows:

> THIS SEED IS WARRANTED AGAINST DEFECTS FOR A PERIOD OF 20 DAYS. THERE ARE NO OTHER WARRANTIES, EXPRESS OR IMPLIED, INCLUDING BUT NOT LIMITED TO THE IMPLIED WARRANTY OF MERCHANTABILITY.

It takes much longer than 20 days for the seed to germinate, and it is impossible to determine whether the seed is defective before that time. Analyze.

(e) Assume the facts of (c) except that the tags on the seed bags continued to read as they had for the previous 15 years. When Adams opened the bags, they contained sand. Can Adams get a refund? See 2–313 and comment 4 thereto. Also consider 2–316(1) and the following case.

JAMES RIVER EQUIP. CO. v. BEADLE COUNTY EQUIP., INC.

Supreme Court of South Dakota, 2002.
646 N.W.2d 265.

WILBUR, J. On February 23, 1994, the parties entered into a written agreement for James River to purchase Beadle County Equipment for approximately $1,800,000. As part of the transaction, James River purchased all used equipment inventory held by Seller as of the date of the agreement. The used equipment was valued at $1,361,000. Seller identified the used equipment inventory on a separate schedule attached to the purchase agreement. Seller made various representations regarding the listed equipment. Among other things, those representations included descriptions regarding the number of hours the equipment had been used.

The purchase agreement provided that "all representations and warranties by Seller set forth in the Agreement shall be true and correct in all material respects as of the Closing." The agreement also provided that "Buyer acknowledges that the Purchased Assets to be purchased hereunder are being conveyed to Buyer in an 'AS IS' condition and that neither Seller nor Seller's agents or employees have made any representation to Buyer concerning the condition of the Purchased Assets, or any of them, except as specifically provided in this Agreement." After the closing, James River learned that five of the used John Deere combines had substantially more hours of use than Seller had represented. James River testified that the differences in the hours between what was represented and what he actually found after closing affected the value of the combines. Seller agreed that the amount of time a machine has actually been operated as indicated by the hours of usage is a factor in determining its value. The trial court found in favor of James River on several smaller claims [but not] on its claim for breach of express warranty.

Seller argues, and the trial court agreed in its bench decision, that James River had the opportunity to and did inspect the used equipment inventory before closing, and that opportunity and inspection negated any express warranties. With respect to implied warranties, the Uniform Commercial Code provides that when the buyer before entering into the contract has examined the goods or the sample or model as fully as he desired, or has refused to examine the goods, there is no implied warranty with regard to defects which an examination ought in the circumstances to have revealed to him [§ 2–316(3)(b)]. But with regard to express warranties the situation is different. Under the Code, the real test of whether an express warranty exists is whether the warranty became a part of the basis of the bargain, and *the Code does not exclude an express warranty where the buyer has the opportunity for inspection, or does inspect the goods.*

Seller claimed that he sold the used equipment inventory to James River on an "as is" basis, and that the "as is" clause of the purchase agreement disclaimed any express warranties made. The trial court agreed in its bench decision that "there is an express provision in the agreement as well that the properties are being sold as is...." The UCC contemplates that only implied warranties can be disclaimed by use of "as is" clauses. The only UCC provision addressing "as is" clauses provides that "unless the circumstances indicate otherwise, all implied warranties are excluded by expressions like 'as is,' 'with all faults' or other language which in common understanding calls the buyer's attention to the exclusion of warranties and makes plain that there is no implied warranty" UCC § 2–316(3)(a). The official comment to that section confirms its plain meaning, i.e., that "only implied—not express—warranties are excluded in 'as is' transactions."

In view of the principle that the whole purpose of the law of warranty is to determine what it is that the seller has in essence agreed to sell, the policy is adopted of those cases which refuse except in unusual circumstances to recognize a material deletion of the seller's obligation. Thus, a contract is normally a contract for a sale of something describable and described. A clause generally disclaiming "all warranties, express or implied" cannot reduce the seller's obligation with respect to such description and therefore cannot be given literal effect under Section 2–316, UCC § 2–313 cmt 4 (1989). Regardless, "whether implied warranties have been excluded is immaterial when the buyer sues on an express warranty." Therefore, the UCC does not permit "as is" clauses to disclaim express warranties.

The South Dakota Supreme Court, interpreting North Dakota's UCC provisions, which are identical to SDCL 57A–2–316, stated in Husky Spray Service, Inc. v. Patzer, 471 N.W.2d 146, 151 (SD 1991): Section 2–316 of the UCC protects buyers from disclaimers inserted into written contracts or similar forms which are inconsistent with express warranties. Thus, where an express warranty and a disclaimer of the express warranty exist in the same sale, there is an irreconcilable conflict and the disclaimer is ineffective. (citations omitted)

The trial court's judgment as to breach of express warranty is reversed and this matter is remanded to the trial court for a determination of damages caused by the Seller's breach.

Notes

May express warranties be disclaimed? The earliest version of 2–316(1) appeared in 1944, when Karl Llewellyn and friends were attempting to revise the Uniform Sales Act. Subsection (1) of Section 41 of the 1944 draft of the proposed *Revised Uniform Sales Act* (forerunner to Article 2 of the Uniform Commercial Code) read as follows: "If the agreement creates an express warranty, words disclaiming it are inoperative." Even earlier, in 1941, the Llewellyn view of the non-disclaimable nature of description of goods is found in what was then Section 14 of the *Revised* Uniform Sales Act proposal:

> (1) Where there is a contract to sell or a sale of goods by description, there is a warranty that the goods shall correspond with the description.

> (2) The effect of this section is not subject to abrogation or modification by contract.

Professor Charles Heckman, who has analyzed these and other forerunners of the UCC warranty provisions, mentions another Llewellyn statement: "What the bargain can do, is to define the contract: as by a limitation of warranty, like 'as is;' but even then, sawdust in boxes does not conform to 'boxed grapes, as is.'" REVISED UNIF. SALES ACT § 14, comment 1 (National Conference of Commissioners on Uniform State Laws (Report and Second Draft 1941)), as quoted in Heckman, *"Reliance" or "Common Honesty of Speech": The History and Interpretation of Section 2–313 of the Uniform Commercial Code,* 38 CASE W RES. L. REV. 1, 9 (1987).

Some courts, attempting to deal with disclaimers of express warranties, have created confusion by first deciding that no express warranty existed, and then finding that a clause disclaiming express warranties was valid. See the discussion of Alan Wood Steel Co. v. Capital Equipment Enterprises, Inc., 39 Ill.App.3d 48, 349 N.E.2d 627 (1976) in John E. Murray, Jr., *"Basis of the Bargain": Transcending Classical Concepts,* 66 MINN. L. REV. 283, 298–301 (1982).

General Electric Capital Corp. v. Munson Marine, Inc., 1991 WL 256680 (N.D.Ill.1991), may suggest an effective way to exclude express warranties. The buyer in that case alleged breaches of implied and express warranties. With respect to implied warranties, paragraph 11 of the contract provided:

> [Convergent, the seller,] warrants that the equipment and Licensed Programs, at the time installed, will be in good working order. THE FOREGOING WARRANTY IS IN LIEU OF ALL OTHER WARRANTIES AND THERE ARE NO OTHER WARRANTIES, EXPRESS OR IMPLIED, INCLUDING, BUT NOT LIMITED TO, THE IMPLIED

WARRANTIES OF MERCHANTABILITY AND FITNESS FOR A PARTICULAR PURPOSE.

With respect to express warranties, paragraph 12 of the contract provided:

> This Agreement constitutes the entire agreement between the parties and there are no representations, warranties, covenants or obligations except as set forth herein. This Agreement ... supersedes all prior and contemporaneous agreements, understandings, negotiations, and discussions, written or oral between the parties ... (and) may be amended only in writing executed by the parties. . . .

The court concluded:

> The sales contract warranty exclusion is written in larger type with bold-faced capital letters. This warranty exclusion is both conspicuous and enforceable under § 2–316. Consequently, all Convergent's implied warranties have been excluded by the sales agreement. Furthermore, any extrinsic evidence of Convergent's alleged express warranties to Munson Marine is inadmissible because of the integration clause at paragraph 12 and the parol evidence rule. Ill.Ann.Stat. ch. 29, §§ 2–316(1), 2–202.

Reconsider Problem 27, *supra*, where statements concerning a fail-safe feature on ball-screw sockets that the manufacturer claimed would prevent the jetway from collapsing were made *after* the contract had been formed. Under Comment 7 to 2–313, the fact that the statements were made after the contract was formed would not prevent them from becoming part of the basis of the bargain between the parties. In the case on which the problem was based, the same statements were made prior to the formation of the contract but were not part of the record evidencing the contract. Assume the record was a complete and final (fully integrated) record of the parties' agreement, and that no statements concerning the fail-safe feature were made after the contract was formed. What result? What would you advise a client to do if some of the seller's statements of fact concerning the goods were inadvertently missing from the complete and final record of the agreement? See 2–316(1) and 2–202.

Proposed Amendments to Section 2–316. Proposed amended Section 2–316 would make no change in subsection (1) (disclaimers of express warranties). For disclaimers of implied warranties in consumer contracts, however, proposed amended 2–316(2) would require the following conspicuous language in a record: "The seller undertakes no responsibility for the quality of the goods except as otherwise provided in this contract."[1] In a commercial (merchant) contract, a disclaimer of the implied warranty of merchantability could be oral, but it would have to mention "merchantability." A disclaimer in a record would be required to be conspicuous. A disclaimer of the implied warranty of fitness in either a commercial or consumer contract would have to be in a record and conspicuous. To exclude all implied warranties of fitness in a consumer contract, the language would be required to state, "The seller assumes no responsibility that the goods will be fit for any particular purpose for which you may be buying these goods, except as otherwise provided in the contract." In a non-consumer

---

1. This rule, however, is "subject to subsection (3)."

contract, language such as, "There are no warranties which extend beyond the description on the face hereof" would be sufficient. Language that satisfies the requirements of proposed amended 2–316(2) for consumer contracts would also satisfy the disclaimer requirements for other contracts.

Subsection (3)(a) would continue to permit the exclusion of all implied warranties through the use of the familiar "as is" or "with all faults" trade language, as well as other language (such as "as they stand," according to comment 5 to proposed amended 2–316) which in common understanding calls the buyer's attention to such exclusion. Such disclaimer language could be oral, but in a consumer contract evidenced by a record the language would have to be set forth conspicuously in that record.

Proposed amended Section 2–316(3)(b) would continue the exclusion of implied warranties as to defects that a buyer ought to have discovered if the buyer, before entering into the contract, has examined the goods or the sample or model as fully as desired or has refused to examine the goods after a demand by the seller. The comments explain that where a buyer has not voluntarily examined the goods, the requirement that the buyer "refused to examine" the goods would not be met simply by making the goods available for inspection. There would have to be either an actual examination by the purchaser or a demand by the seller that the buyer examine the goods fully, i. e., the seller's demand would have to place the buyer on notice that the buyer is assuming the risk of defects that an examination ought to reveal. If the buyer has examined the goods but the seller has made statements concerning the merchantability or specific attributes of the goods that would otherwise amount to an express warranty, comment 7 to proposed amended 2–316 indicates that a court could find an express warranty, an implied warranty of merchantability or both. McLaughlin v. Watercraft Int'l, 87 Wash.App. 1051 (1997), adopts this approach when the court states,

> A seller may demand that the buyer examine the goods before entering into the contract. If the buyer examines the goods as fully as she desires, or ignores the seller's demand to examine the goods, then the implied warranty of merchantability is disclaimed [2–316(3)(b)]. In other words, there is no implied warranty of merchantability with regard to defects that the examination ought to have revealed. Furthermore, the seller receives the same protection if the buyer voluntarily examines the goods as fully as he wishes. McLaughlin admitted that he took the boat for a test run in early January 1993, and noted defects. After returning from the test run, "I told Richard we'd purchase the boat subject to the things that we had identified being repaired and fixed." [A] jury could find that McLaughlin voluntarily examined the boat prior to the contract and that no implied warranty exists with regard to defects that the examination did or ought to have revealed to him. [T]o the extent that McLaughlin received promises relating to the boat that became part of the basis of the bargain, a jury could also find, however, that the test run created express warranties.

Proposed amended Section 2–316(3)(c) would retain the possibility of excluding implied warranties by course of dealing, course of performance or usage of trade, and proposed amended Section 2–316(4) would retain the reminder that remedies for breach of warranty may be limited in accordance with the provisions on liquidated damages (2–718) and contractual modification of remedy (2–719).

2. *Warranty Disclaimers Under UCC Article 2A*

The Article 2A provision governing disclaimers of warranties, 2A–214, replicates the analogous section of the pre-amendment sales article (2–316) with certain differences. Section 2A–214(2) does not recognize an oral disclaimer of the implied warranty of merchantability in leases, although 2–316(2) permits such a disclaimer in a sale of goods. 2A–214(3)(a) also requires the "as is" or "with all faults" types of disclaimers to be in writing and "conspicuous." Proposed amended 2A–214 would conform to the proposed amendments to the UCC Article 2 disclaimer provision.[1]

3. *Precluding Obligations of Quality Under the CISG*

SUPERMICRO COMPUTER INC. v. DIGITECHNIC, S.A.

United States District Court for the Northern District of California, 2001.
145 F.Supp.2d 1147.

Legge, J. [The plaintiff is a California corporation that manufactured and sold computer parts to the defendant, a French corporation that makes computer network systems. Alleging that the parts were defective, the defendant brought an action demanding $200,400.00 in replacement costs and $6 million in consequential damages.] Plaintiff rejected the demand and claimed that, based on the limited warranty contained in the sales invoices and the consequential damages waiver found in the user's manual, defendant's sole remedy was the repair and replacement of any malfunctioning parts.

In December 1998 defendant filed an action in France in the Tribunal de Commerce de Bobginy (the "French Commercial Court.") The French case has been ongoing since that time and plaintiff has been participating in it. Plaintiff filed this [declaratory judgment] action on January 20, 2000, more than a year after the French action began. The complaint seeks a declaration that: (1) the computer parts were not defective; (2) the parts failed as a result of defendant's misuse, and (3) even if plaintiff were at fault, defendant's sole remedy is for repair or replacement. [The court held that it had discretion to decline to exercise jurisdiction under the Declaratory Judgment Act in order to avoid forum shopping and duplicative litigation. It then proceeded to a discussion of the CISG.]

---

1. There is one organizational difference between the disclaimer provisions of Articles 2 and pre-amendment Article 2A. For leases, the pre-amendment rules governing attempts to exclude or modify the 2A–211 warranties against interference and infringement are located in the general disclaimer provision, 2A–214 (see subsection (4)). The disclaimer rules for the analogous Article 2 warranties of title and against infringements are found in the section dealing with those specific warranties, 2–312 (see subsections (2) & (3)). In the proposed amendments to Article 2A, this organizational difference is eliminated—the proposed amendments would move the disclaimer rules for the warranties against interference and infringement to the section governing those warranties (proposed amended 2A–211(4)).

The parties agree that the United Nations Convention on Contracts for the International Sale of Goods ("CISG") governs their transactions. When two foreign nations are signatories to the CISG, as are the United States and France, the CISG governs contracts for the sale of goods between parties whose places of business are in these different nations. See CISG, Art. 1. A contract governed by the CISG may include a choice of law provision. If, as here, the agreement is silent as to choice of law, the CISG applies if both parties are located in signatory nations. Thus, the provisions of the CISG directly control. The case law interpreting and applying the CISG is sparse.

Application of the CISG here requires a court to resolve an issue of first impression. To wit, the court must determine whether a warranty disclaimer in a purchase order is valid under the CISG. The court has no controlling authority on this issue. Plaintiff contends that Article 35 of the CISG permits warranty disclaimers such as the one at issue. Article 35 however, deals with a seller's obligation to deliver conforming goods. It does not discuss disclaimers. If anything, a disclaimer in this case might not be valid because the CISG requires a "mirror-image" approach to contract negotiations that allows the court to inquire into the subjective intent of the parties. See CISG, Art. 8. Here, defendant has submitted evidence that it was not aware of the disclaimer and that it would not have purchased the goods had it been aware of the disclaimer. If the defendant was not aware of the disclaimer, then it may not have been valid. Given that this issue of law is unsettled, this factor weighs against this court exercising its discretion to hear the matter in favor of the French court that already has the issue before it.

Plaintiff does not explain why, after participating in the French proceeding for more than one year, a declaratory relief action here is necessary. Defendant has adduced evidence which demonstrates that it does not intend to bring an action in the United States. Moreover, there is additional evidence that plaintiff filed this action after receiving an adverse preliminary ruling in the French case. All of this indicates that plaintiff, after participating in the foreign action, initiated this proceeding in the hopes of obtaining a more favorable result in its home forum.

[Plaintiff's motion for partial summary judgment was denied.]

Questions

(1) The court states that CISG Article 35 "does not discuss disclaimers." Do you agree? Consider the opening phrase of Article 35(2). Is there a concept in the UCC comparable to Article 35(3)?

(2) The court wonders whether a disclaimer would be effective under the CISG, which requires the "mirror image" approach. Can you elaborate this concern? See CISG, Article 19.

(3) Consider the court's statement that a disclaimer may not be valid if the party against whom it is designed to operate is not aware of it. The court cites CISG Article 8 in support of this proposition. Do you agree?

4. *Warranty Disclaimers Under UCITA*

UCITA § 406(b) adheres to pre-amendment UCC 2–316 in not requiring a disclaimer of the implied warranty of merchantability to be evidenced by a record—although if the disclaimer is in a record, the UCITA provision requires that it mention either "merchantability," "quality" or words of similar import (UCITA § 406(b)(1)(A)). To disclaim the implied warranty of "accuracy" (UCITA § 404), language in a record must mention "accuracy" or words of similar import (406(b)(1)(B)). UCITA § 406(b)(2), however, requires a disclaimer of the implied warranty of fitness for a particular purpose to be in a record and provides the following safe harbor language: "There is no warranty that this information or efforts will fulfill any of your particular purposes or needs." UCITA § 406(b)(3) also provides safe harbor language sufficient to disclaim *all* implied warranties, and UCITA § 406(b)(4) allows any disclaimer sufficient to disclaim an implied warranty under Article 2 or 2A to be sufficient for UCITA purposes. UCITA § 406(c) allows for disclaimers through the use of "as is," "with all faults," or other language that calls the licensee's attention to the disclaimer. Under UCITA § 406(d), a licensee's examination of the information in question (or of a sample or model), as well as the licensee's refusal to so examine, excludes implied warranty protection for defects that such an examination ought to have revealed under the circumstances. UCITA § 406(e) allows a disclaimer through trade usage, course of dealing or course of performance, and § 406(f) treats warranties as disclaimed with respect to ongoing performances or a series of performances by the licensor if the contract meets the disclaimer provisions of this section. Finally, UCITA § 406(g) contains a reminder that remedies may be limited for breach of warranty.

Problem 37A

George Young was interested in accessing two computer programs available on the Computerex website. The first program was "Taxease," which George decided to download. Before downloading Taxease was possible, the license terms for the program were splashed on George's computer screen along with the amount of the license fee. George had to click the "I agree" buttons with respect to the license terms and the fee before the downloading process would begin. George clicked both "I agree" buttons and downloaded "Taxease." He then decided to download another Computerex program called "Artease," which provided access to images of some of the great paintings in the world. George was not required to agree to license terms before downloading this program. The Artease license terms could be seen only if he scrolled down to a button labeled "License Terms–Artease." George did not bother scrolling down. Instead, he merely clicked the "I agree" button for the fee, which activated the downloading of Artease. Computerex later claimed that George violated the license terms of both "Taxease" and "Artease." Analyze.

N.   OWNERSHIP AND VARIATIONS ON THE THEME

The Sacred Principle Requires Modification. One of the sacred principles of the common law was expressed in the maxim *"Nemo dat quod non habet,"* to the effect that you cannot give what you do not have. At first glance, to invoke this maxim and insist that one cannot transfer a better title to property than he possesses seems eminently fair. Yet, when the property ends up in the hands of an innocent buyer who, in good faith, has purchased the property from a nefarious seller lacking good title, the sacred principle become questionable.

You are walking down the street when a stranger appears. The stranger offers to sell you a diamond necklace for what appears to be a very low price. You buy it. You may be an innocent buyer, but if you do not recognize the risk that you may be purchasing stolen property you are a stupid one. Thus if the true owner of the necklace, from whom it was stolen, discovers you in possession and manages to recover it from you, you deserve little sympathy. Suppose, however, that you enter a highly reputable jewelry store and see the same necklace, which you purchase at a normal retail price, later to lose the necklace to someone who can prove superior title to the jewelry. Do these circumstances suggest an exception to *Nemo dat quod non habet* ?

Pre–Code law recognized an exception to the sacred principle where the true owner of goods had clothed the seller with apparent authority to dispose of the property and the innocent buyer had relied upon that authority. This concept is continued and expanded under the UCC. See comment 1 to 2–403. *The problem is to decide upon a fair allocation of the risk between the true owner and the innocent, good faith purchaser for value.* It is an international problem. Section 22 of the British Sales of Goods Act codified a concept called "market overt," which could result in a buyer enjoying rights exceeding those of the owner. Later, influenced by the approach in France and Germany, the English Law Reform Committee attempted to enlarge the protection of good-faith buyers. See the Twelfth Report of the English Law Reform Committee, captioned "Transfer of Title to Chattels" (1966). It is important to understand how our law deals with ownership of goods as between the "true owner" and an innocent purchaser for value.

Problem 38

(a) Margaret Huber left for her month-long European vacation. A week after her departure, in broad daylight, a truck with a large sign on its side, "Barton Piano Co.," arrived at Margaret's home. Three men were seen moving Margaret's twenty-five year old Steinway grand piano from her house to the truck. Two neighbors who observed this operation assumed Margaret had authorized it, although she had not. When Margaret returned from her vacation, she discovered that her piano was missing and called the police. Barton, which sells new and used pianos, sold the piano to Dr. Charles Good, a buyer in the ordinary course of business as defined in

1–201(b)(9). See also the definition of "purchase" in 1–201(b)(29). May Margaret recover the piano from Dr. Good? See 2–403(1).

(b) Suppose the piano had been removed from Margaret's house because she had arranged for it to be reconditioned by the Barton Piano Co. Barton also bought and sold pianos. When Margaret returned from her vacation, she discovered that Barton was out of business. She also discovered that Barton's owners (who cannot now be found) had sold Margaret's piano to Dr. Good. May Margaret recover her piano from Dr. Good? See 2–403(2) and (3).

(c) Suppose that Margaret had purchased the piano from Barton and had given Barton a security interest in the instrument (see Article 9 of the U.C.C.) to secure payment of the purchase price. Before leaving on her vacation Margaret missed five installments on the price. The security agreement allowed Barton to repossess the piano. Before her departure, Margaret had informed Barton that the key was under the mat at the entrance to her front door. May Margaret recover her piano from Barton? See 9–609.

(d) Assume the facts of (c) except that, before Barton repossessed the piano, Margaret sold it to her neighbor, Dr. Charles Good. Dr. Good was unaware of Margaret's dealings with Barton. May Barton recover the piano from Dr. Good? See 9–320(b).

(e) Suppose Margaret had "paid" for the piano with a check that was later dishonored. May Barton recover the piano from Margaret? See 2–507(2) and 2–511(3).

(f) Assume the facts of (e) except that, before Margaret's check was dishonored, she sold the piano to Dr. Good who was, again, innocent. May Barton recover the piano from Dr. Good? See 2–403(1)(b).

(g) Suppose that, three days after delivering the piano to Margaret on credit, Barton discovered that Margaret was insolvent. May Barton recover the piano from Margaret? 2–702(2).[1]

(h) Assume the facts of (g) except that, on the second day after delivery, Margaret had sold the piano to innocent Dr. Good. May Barton recover the piano from Dr. Good? See 2–702(3).

(i) Suppose that when Margaret purchased the piano from Barton she had misrepresented herself as Mrs. Charles Good, the wife of the well-known and-respected Dr. Good. The deception worked, and Barton delivered the piano to Margaret on credit. She immediately sold the piano to innocent Dr. Good at a fair price, then she disappeared. May Barton recover the piano from Dr. Good? See 2–403(1)(a) and (d).

(j) Suppose that an innocent and good faith Margaret had inspected a particular Steinway in the Barton showroom, then decided to purchase it. She paid $1,000 down on the $10,000 purchase price, with the balance due on delivery. Three days later, Barton became insolvent and refused to deliver the piano. May Margaret recover the piano? See 2–502.[2]

---

1. Proposed amended Section 2–702(2) would eliminate the 10–day and three-month deadlines in pre-amendment 2–702(2) for demanding return of the goods.

2. For consumer buyers, amendments made to 2–502 in 1999 eliminate the requirement that the seller become insolvent in order for the buyer to recover goods on which it has made payments.

INMI–ETTI v. ALUISI

Court of Special Appeals of Maryland, 1985.
63 Md.App. 293, 492 A.2d 917.

KARWACKI, J. Adeorike Ogunsanya Duros Inmi–Etti, the appellant, purchased a new automobile for $8,500 in cash, but much to her chagrin, lost both the car and her purchase price. . . .

The appellant, a native and resident of Nigeria came to the United States in June of 1981 to visit with her sisters, Adesola Dawodu of Takoma Park, Maryland and Tite Claxton of Hyattsville, Maryland. While, here, the appellant decided to buy a car and have it shipped back to Nigeria. An acquaintance of the appellant's family, David E. Butler, offered to assist the appellant in her purchase. With his aid the appellant placed an order for a new 1981 Honda Prelude on June 15, 1981, with Wilson Pontiac and Honda, Inc. of Silver Spring, Md. (hereinafter "Wilson Pontiac"). The purchase order, accompanied by appellant's deposit of $200, called for a purchase price of $8,500. Almost immediately thereafter the appellant returned to Nigeria, entrusting the cash balance of the purchase price to her sister, Ms. Claxton, with directions to complete the purchase when the automobile was available for delivery. On June 24, 1981, the sale was completed, and the automobile was delivered by Wilson Pontiac to the appellant's sisters who were accompanied by Butler. The automobile was driven by Butler to Ms. Dawodu's home. Within a few weeks a certificate of title for the automobile issued by the Motor Vehicle Administration in the name of the appellant was delivered to Butler by Wilson Pontiac. On August 18, 1981, Butler drove the automobile from Ms. Dawodu's home to a location in Marlow Heights, Maryland. Ms. Dawodu communicated with the appellant and learned that Butler's removal of the automobile was not authorized. She then applied for an arrest warrant charging Butler with theft. The warrant issued but was later quashed before it was executed.

While the arrest warrant was still outstanding, on October 1, 1981, Butler instituted a suit in the District Court of Maryland for Prince George's County and, at the same time, filed an application for an attachment on original process against the appellant's Honda, on the ground that the appellant was an absconding debtor. In the underlying suit, Butler complained that at the appellant's request he had purchased various items, including the 1981 Honda, for the appellant, but that the appellant had left this country without reimbursing him for the money he advanced on her behalf. The appellant received mailed notice of the suit in Nigeria in late November of 1981 and asked Ms. Dawodu to protect her interests. When no appearance was entered on behalf of the appellant in the district court action, however, that court granted Butler's motion for summary judgment on January 6, 1982 and rendered judgment absolute in his favor on January 11, 1982. When Ms. Dawodu learned that judgment had been entered, she finally retained counsel for the appellant. A motion filed on the appellant's behalf on February 4,

1982 to set aside the judgment was granted. The case was then set for trial and ultimately dismissed.

Meanwhile, Butler's application for the attachment on original process had been granted, and the district court authorized the attachment of the 1981 Honda to issue on October 26, 1981. A deputy sheriff from Prince George's County located the vehicle in a driveway to a single family dwelling at 4306 Tounsley Avenue, Marlow Heights, Maryland on October 29, 1981. Finding no one at home within the dwelling, the deputy sheriff placed a copy of the writ of attachment and other related documents under the windshield wiper of the vehicle and left. The instructions given the deputy by Butler by means of a preprinted district court form were to levy upon the vehicle and "leave such property with the person in whose custody or possession it was found." At no time was a judicial sale conducted. The district court docket entries indicate that a motion to quash this attachment was granted on May 27, 1982.

On January 18, 1982, after summary judgment had been entered in favor of Butler in the district court, but before that judgment was set aside, Butler offered to sell the 1981 Honda owned by the appellant to Pohanka [Pontiac]. He represented to the used car manager at Pohanka that he owned the automobile. Notwithstanding Butler's inability to produce a certificate of title for the car, Pohanka's manager agreed to purchase it for $7,200. That same day, Pohanka issued its check for $2,000 to Butler and agreed to pay him the $5,200 balance when Butler produced a certificate of title. The car was apparently left on Pohanka's lot in the meantime. Soon thereafter, Butler applied for a certificate of title for the appellant's automobile from the Motor Vehicle Administration. Butler solely supported his application with his sworn affidavit [filled with lies].... Amazingly, the Motor Vehicle Administration issued a certificate of title for the automobile to Butler based upon that affidavit. Armed with that certificate, Butler was paid the $5,200 balance of the agreed purchase price by Pohanka on February 8, 1982. Interestingly, Pohanka had already sold the automobile for $8,200 to another purchaser a week earlier.

The appellant sued Butler for conversion, malicious abuse of process, and wrongful attachment. She also sued Pohanka for conversion, and Aluisi [Sheriff] for negligence. The lower court, as noted earlier, granted a default judgment against Butler because of his failure to plead to the appellant's declaration but granted summary judgments in favor of the two remaining defendants.

In this Court the appellant contends that:

> The lower court erred when it denied her motion for summary judgment against Pohanka and instead entered summary judgment in favor of Pohanka because the undisputed material facts established Pohanka's liability to her for conversion, and that [t]he lower court erred in entering summary judgment in favor of Aluisi because there exists a material question of fact as to the negligence of Aluisi in the manner of the levy....

At common law the maxim was: "He who hath not cannot give (nemo dat qui non habet)." Black's Law Dictionary 935 (5th ed. 1979). Although at times the Uniform Commercial Code may seem to the reader as unintelligible as the Latin phrases which preceded it, we find in § 2–403 of the Code a definite modification of the above maxim. That section states: [The court quotes 2–403.] . . .

[T]he answer to the appellant's claim against Pohanka depends on whether Butler had "void" or "voidable" title at the time of the purported sale to Pohanka. If Butler had voidable title, then he had the power to vest good title in Pohanka. If, on the other hand, Butler possessed void title (i.e., no title at all), then Pohanka received no title and is liable in trover for the conversion of the appellant's automobile. Preliminarily, we note that there was no evidence that Butler was a "merchant who deals in goods of that kind" (i.e. automobiles). Md.Code, supra, § 2–403(2) and 2–104(1). Therefore the entrustment provisions of § 2–403(2)–(3) do not apply.

It has been observed that,

> Under 2–403, voidable title is to be distinguished from void title. A thief, for example, "gets" only void title and without more cannot pass any title to a good faith purchaser. 'Voidable title' is a murky concept. The Code does not define the phrase. The comments do not even discuss it. Subsections (1)(a)-(d) of 2–403 clarify the law as to particular transactions which were 'troublesome under prior law.' Beyond these, we must look to non-Code state law.

J. White & R. Summers, Handbook of the Law Under the Uniform Commercial Code § 3–11 (2d ed. 1980) (footnote omitted). White and Summers further explain that:

> subsection (a) of § 2–403(1) deals with cases where the purchaser impersonates someone else; subsection (b) deals with "rubber checks"; subsection (c) deals with "cash sales"; and subsection (d) deals with cases of forged checks and other acts fraudulent to the seller.

Id. None of these subsections apply to the facts of the present case and we, therefore, must turn to "non-Code state law" to determine whether Butler had voidable title.

Hawkland, § 403:04, suggests that "voidable title" may only be obtained when the owner of the goods makes a voluntary transfer of the goods. He reaches that conclusion from the Code definitions of the words "delivery" and "purchase" and summarizes:

> Section 2–403(1)(d) does not create a voidable title in the situation where the goods are wrongfully taken, as contrasted with delivered voluntarily because of the concepts of 'delivery' and 'purchaser' which are necessary preconditions. 'Delivery' is defined by section 1–201(14)[3] 'with respect to instruments, documents of title, chattel

---

3. [Ed. Note: This definition is now found in amended 1–201(b)(15).]

paper or securities' to mean 'voluntary transfer of possession.' By analogy, it should be held that goods are not delivered for purposes of section 2–403 unless they are voluntarily transferred. Additionally, section 2–403(1)(d) is limited by the requirement that the goods 'have been delivered under a transaction of purchase.' 'Purchase' is defined by section 1–201(32)[4] to include only voluntary transactions. A thief who wrongfully takes goods is not a purchaser within the meaning of this definition, but a swindler who fraudulently induces the victim to voluntarily deliver them is a purchaser for this purpose. This distinction, reminiscent of the distinction between larceny and larceny by truck made by the common law, is a basic one for the understanding of the meaning of section 2–403(1)(d)."

Hawkland later states that the above language applies generally to § 2–403(1) and not merely to subsection (1)(d)....

Under the undisputed facts of the present case Butler possessed void title when Pohanka dealt with him. Although the record simply is not sufficient for us to decide whether Butler actually stole the appellant's vehicle, it is undisputed that the appellant at no time made a voluntary transfer to Butler. Thus, Pohanka obtained no title, and its sale of the vehicle constituted a conversion of the appellant's property. We believe the above analysis sufficient to impose liability upon Pohanka.

We reject any notion that Butler obtained voidable title to the vehicle as a result of the attachment on original process carried out pursuant to former Maryland District Rules.... [The] district court never entered a judgment of condemnation nisi or absolute against the appellant's Honda and consequently never ordered a sale of the automobile. Therefore, although the automobile was in custodia legis at all times during the transaction between Butler and Pohanka, the appellant's title thereto had not been divested, and no title thereto had been acquired by Butler.... [A] judicial sale ... clearly never occurred.

Implicit in all that we have said so far is the fact that Butler did not obtain title (voidable or otherwise) merely from the fact that he was able to convince the Motor Vehicle Administration to issue a certificate of title for the automobile to him. Although "[a] certificate of title issued by the Administration is prima facie evidence of the facts appearing on it," Md.Code (1977, 1984 Repl.Vol.), § 13–107 of the Transportation Article, the erroneous issuance of such a certificate cannot divest the title of the true owner of the automobile.

Likewise, we find unpersuasive Pohanka's argument that since Butler had possession of the automobile and a duly issued certificate of title in his name, Pohanka should be protected as a "good faith purchaser for value" under § 2–403 of the Commercial Law Article, supra. Such status under that section of the Uniform Commercial Code is relevant in situations where the seller (transferor) is possessed of voidable title. It

4. [Ed. Note: This definition is now found in amended 1–201(b)(29).]

does not apply to the situation presented by the instant case where the seller had no title at all.

Finally, whether Pohanka converted the vehicle with innocent intent is immaterial. The Restatement (Second) of Torts § 229 (1979) provides: One who receives possession of a chattel from another with the intent to acquire for himself or for a third person a proprietary interest in the chattel which the other has not the power to transfer is subject to liability for conversion to a third person then entitled to the immediate possession of the chattel.

Comment e to § 299 explains:

Under the rule stated in this Section, one receiving a chattel from a third person with intent to acquire a proprietary interest in it is liable without a demand for its return by the person entitled to possession although he takes possession of the chattel without knowledge or reason to know that the third person has no power to transfer the proprietary interest. The mere receipt of the possession of the goods under such circumstances is a conversion.

Accordingly, we shall reverse the summary judgment in favor of Pohanka and enter judgment in favor of the appellant against Pohanka for $8,200, an amount representing the agreed fair market value of the appellant's automobile at the time of its conversion, plus interest at 10 percent per annum from February 1, 1982, the date when Pohanka sold the automobile. [The Court affirmed the summary judgment in favor of Sheriff Aluisi.]

O. WARRANTIES OF TITLE AND AGAINST INFRINGEMENT UNDER UCC ARTICLE 2—DISCLAIMERS

Having just explored the concept of ownership and the tension between a good faith purchaser for value and other claimants to goods, we now consider the obligations respecting ownership that arise in a contract for sale—the seller's duty to give the buyer good title to and undisturbed use of the goods purchased. The seller's obligations include (but are not limited to) the warranty of title described in 2–312(1) of the UCC. The warranty of title requires the seller to make a "rightful" transfer of "good" title to the goods (2–312(1)(a)), and to deliver goods free from security interests and other liens or encumbrances that were not revealed to the buyer before the contract was made (2–312(1)(b)). The warranty against infringements (2–312(3)) obliges merchant sellers who "regularly" deal in goods of the kind to protect their buyers against "rightful" claims that the goods infringe intellectual property rights of a third party. The warranty against infringements is unusual in also placing an obligation on the *buyer*. The last proviso of 2–312(3) requires the buyer to indemnify the seller against infringement claims if the seller was merely following the buyer's specifications in manufacturing the goods.

The Code does not refer to the warranties of title and against infringement as "implied" warranties. Yet, they automatically attach to sales of goods unless they have been disclaimed. Carefully consider comment 6 to 2–312, and then consider how the warranty against infringement in 2–312(3) may be disclaimed.

Problem 39

(a) Bill McGovern purchased a new Harley Davidson motorcycle from Cycle Sales, Inc. Three months later, Bill parked his Harley at a roadside tavern. When he left the tavern he was stopped by state police, who asked him to display his registration certificate. It seems a cycle fitting the description of Bill's Harley had just been stolen. Bill displayed the certificate but the registration numbers did not match the numbers engraved on the cycle. The police confiscated the cycle. Bill hired a lawyer who managed to replevy the cycle for Bill. The numbers on Bill's registration certificate had been erroneously copied by Cycle Sales, Inc. Does Bill have a claim under 2–312 against Cycle Sales?

(b) George Haig operated "Haig's Guitars," where he bought, sold, repaired and refinished used guitars. William Deavers claimed that a certain used "Martin" guitar on display in George's store actually belonged to Deavers. George carefully reviewed his files and reasonably concluded that the guitar in question did not belong to Deavers. The disgruntled Deavers told George, "You haven't heard the end of this." The following week, George sold the Martin guitar to Red Acres, an up and coming country and western musician and singer. A month later Deavers brought an action to recover the guitar from Red, claiming it had been stolen. A guitar similar to the one Red purchased from George had in fact been stolen from Deavers but, as was later proved, it was a different instrument. Red prevailed and retained the guitar. Does Red have an action against Haig's Guitars?

(c) Sanders, Inc. sold used equipment to the Morris Corporation under a contract containing the following clause: "WARRANTIES. Buyer purchases the equipment 'AS IS' and no representations or statements have been made by seller except as herein stated. No warranty, express or implied, arises from the purchase or this writing." Later, the true owner of the equipment, from whom it had been stolen, recovered it from Morris. Analyze Morris' action against Sanders for breach of the 2–312(1) warranty.

Note

In Kel–Keef Enters. v. Quality Components Corp., 316 Ill.App.3d 998, 250 Ill.Dec. 308, 738 N.E.2d 524, 535–36 (2000), the court stated:

> A warranty of title may be excluded or modified by specific language giving the purchaser reasons to know that the vendor is only selling what title he possesses. Very "precise and unambiguous language must be used to exclude a warranty so basic to the sale of goods as is title." Jones v. Linebaugh, 34 Mich.App. 305, 191 N.W.2d 142, 144–45 (Mich. App.1971). Furthermore, where the language in a purported disclaimer expresses how the seller's liability will be limited rather than what title (or lack thereof) the seller purports to transfer, the purported disclaimer is ineffective. In Sunseri v. RKO–Stanley Warner Theatres, Inc., 248

Pa.Super. 111, 374 A.2d 1342, 1344 (Pa.Super.1977), the court found language stating that the seller "shall in nowise be * * * liable * * * upon or under guaranties [sic] or warranties * * * including, but not limited to, the implied warranty of title" insufficiently specific to disclaim the warranty of title. The court reasoned that the language used was ineffective because it was "couched in negative terminology, expressing what the seller will not be liable for rather than what the buyer is or is not receiving." The court suggested that the 2–312 warranty of title could effectively be disclaimed by language stating that "the seller does not warrant that he has any right to convey the title to the goods." See also Rockdale, 97 Ill.App.3d at 757, 423 N.E.2d at 558 (finding language stating that the seller purports to transfer only such "right, title and interest" as he may possess insufficient to disclaim the implied warranty of title).

The language in the side letter in the case at bar is insufficiently specific to disclaim the implied warranty of title. The letter merely references a lawsuit and states that the vendor is "making no representations or warranties with regard to" that lawsuit. Like the language rejected by the court in Sunseri, the letter is too vague and general; it does not focus on the title to any of the assets which the purchaser may or may not be receiving in the transaction, but rather focuses on the liability of the seller.

We also disagree with [the] argument that there were circumstances sufficient to exclude the 2–312 warranty of title. A warranty of title may be excluded by circumstances which give the buyer reason to know that the seller does not claim title in himself or that the seller is purporting to sell only the title which he has. Circumstances may be sufficient to exclude the 2–312 warranty of title even if it has not been excluded by sufficiently specific language. See, e.g., Rockdale, 97 Ill. App. 3d at 757, 423 N.E.2d at 558 (where language in the bill of sale was insufficient to disclaim the implied warranty of title, evidence of a conversation between the parties which put the buyer on notice that the seller was selling only what right he possessed in the subject matter constituted sufficient circumstances to exclude the warranty of title). In this case there are no such circumstances.

Although the 2–312 warranty of title does function like an implied warranty, it is technically not considered an "implied" warranty under the UCC, 2–312(1) cmt. 6. It appears from committee comment six that the 2–312 warranty of title was not designated as an implied warranty to prevent the 2–316 disclaimer provisions from applying to it in place of the internal disclaimer provisions provided by 2–312(2), cmt. 6 ("The warranty of subsection (1) is not designated as an 'implied' warranty, and hence is not subject to Section 2–316(3). Disclaimer of the warranty of title is governed instead by subsection (2) which requires either specific language or the described circumstances").

YTTRO CORP. v. X–RAY MARKETING ASSN., INC.

Superior Court of New Jersey, Appellate Division, 1989.
233 N.J.Super. 347, 559 A.2d 3.

Ashbey, J. This appeal involves the interpretation of the Uniform Commercial Code (UCC) provisions concerning the seller's warranty against patent infringement. Plaintiff seller Yttro Corporation (Yttro) brought suit for breach of contract by defendant buyer X–Ray Marketing Association, Inc. (XMA). XMA defended, claiming Yttro violated the warranty against patent infringement provided for in the U.C.C. The court granted XMA summary judgment. Yttro appeals and we reverse and remand for trial.

The July 2, 1985 contract between the parties provided for Yttro to sell exclusively to XMA "Yttro™ filters."[1] XMA would distribute and market the filters through distributorships established by Yttro. Under the contract XMA was obligated to purchase each year for three years, beginning July 2, 1985, a minimum of 600 filters at a price of $135 per filter, or a minimum of 1,000 filters at a price of $125 per filter.

During the first year XMA elected to purchase 1,000 filters but refused to accept delivery of 738 of them. Apparently XMA took no further delivery at any time and whether delivery was tendered is not in the record on appeal. Yttro ultimately brought suit for its contract purchase price and XMA defended on grounds unrelated to patent infringement, the issue in this appeal.

On February 2, 1987, after Yttro commenced this suit, Jerry Hoyt, President of XMA wrote Gilbert Zweig, Vice President of Yttro Corporation: "[o]n behalf of X–Ray Marketing Associates, Inc., I am writing to you to formally repudiate the contract between X–Ray Marketing Associates, Inc. and Yttro Corporation which was signed by us on or about July 2, 1985.... We hereby tender back to you all remaining filters in our possession." This repudiation was based on the filters' performance, its compatibility with conventional X-ray equipment and the "master" distributorships Yttro had represented it had established.

While the litigation was in progress, on or about September 4, 1987, Yttro received a letter from the University of Virginia Alumni Patents Foundation (Foundation) demanding that Yttro cease selling these yttrium filters in violation of the Foundation's patent. Yttro responded that the Yttro filter was not covered by the Foundation's patent but sought to obtain a license.

On January 26, 1988, XMA wrote Yttro:

It has recently come to my client's attention that Yttro Corporation is not and never was the patent holder for the yttrium filter.

---

1. Yttro manufactured "filters" which, when used with conventional X-ray cameras, reduced a patient's exposure to radiation when X-ray pictures were taken. The filters are made out of yttrium, a rare earth element.

Moreover, my client has informed me that the patent holder has never granted a license to Yttro Corporation to sell the yttrium filter. Therefore, this letter will serve as notice to you that my client is rescinding its contract with Yttro Corporation based on Yttro Corporation's defective title with respect to the filters. This letter is not meant to obviate the [Hoyt to Zweig letter of February 2, 1987].

On March 17, 1988, Yttro and the Foundation entered into a licensing agreement which provided that Yttro would have the non-exclusive license to make and to sell the patented filters retroactively to February 12, 1985, the date of the issuance of the patent.

When the motion judge granted summary judgment in favor of XMA, he found that the contract between Yttro and XMA was void because Yttro did not have a valid patent, that Yttro had no right to cure this defect by a subsequent licensing agreement, and that if there was such a right Yttro had not cured its contract defect within a reasonable time.

Section 2–312 of the U.C.C., as adopted in New Jersey, provides in relevant part as follows:

(1)   ... there is in a contract for sale a warranty by the seller that

> (a) the title conveyed shall be good, and its transfer rightful; and ...

(3) Unless otherwise agreed a seller who is a merchant regularly dealing in goods of the kind warrants that the goods shall be delivered free of the rightful claim of any third person by way of infringement....

[N.J.S.A. 12A:2–312].

The New Jersey Study Comment to this section states:

> 312(3) makes a significant addition to the title warranties listed in U.S.A. sec. 13 (N.J.S.A. 46:30–19) [repealed]. It extends the statutory warranty of title to include claims by any third party by way of infringement. The subsection imposes a duty on the seller to make certain that no claim of infringement or patent will cloud or mar the buyer's title....

By failure to support its factual claim that the Yttro filters did not breach the Foundation patent in response to the summary judgment motion, Yttro conceded a breach of § 2–312(3). There are no New Jersey cases and the very few out-of-state cases interpreting the consequences of such a breach. American Container Corp. v. Hanley Trucking Corp., 111 N.J.Super. 322 (Ch.Div.1970), cited by the trial judge, interpreted § 2–312(1). There rescission was granted the buyer of a stolen truck for a breach of title warranty. The Court said,

> The purchaser of goods warranted as to title has a right to rely on the fact that he will not be required, at some later time, to enter into a contest over the validity of his ownership. The mere casting of a substantial shadow over his title, regardless of the ultimate

outcome, is sufficient to violate a warranty of good title. The policy advanced here has found expression in the past in cases where courts of equity have refused to order specific performance of contracts for the sale of land.

[Citations omitted].

Breach of a warranty of good title results in a failure of consideration and generally gives the purchaser the right to rescind the transaction. [Id. at 331–332]. In American Container, however, the goods were stolen and no cure was at issue.

We are first satisfied that Yttro may not assert that its breach did not occur until the patent infringement notice to the buyer. Section 2–312(3) provides specifically that the warranty against infringement attaches at the time of delivery. Section 2–725(2) also provides: A cause of action accrues when the breach occurs, regardless of the aggrieved party's lack of knowledge of the breach. A breach of warranty occurs when tender of delivery is made, except that where a warranty explicitly extends to future performance of the goods and discovery of the breach must await the time of such performance the cause of action accrues when the breach is or should have been discovered. [N.J.S.A. 12A:2–725(2).] Yttro's breach of warranty occurred when its product delivery was required by the contract. Only XMA's obligation to reject the goods was delayed until XMA's discovery of its infringement grounds. American Container, 111 N.J.Super. at 333.

Yttro's assertion that the warranty against infringement can only be breached where a direct claim of infringement is asserted against the buyer is similarly meritless. As the court in American Container said, "[t]he mere casting of a substantial shadow over his title, regardless of the ultimate outcome, is sufficient to violate a warranty of good title." 111 N.J.Super. at 331. The Uniform Commercial Code Comment states:

> This section [2–312] rejects the cases which recognize the principle that infringements violate the warranty of title but deny the buyer a remedy unless he has been expressly prevented from using the goods. Under this Article "eviction" is not a necessary condition to the buyer's remedy since the buyer's remedy arises immediately upon receipt of notice of infringement; it is merely one way of establishing the fact of breach.

In White and Summers, supra, the authors said of § 2–312(3):

> Although this section has yet to be litigated, there are two issues that deserve notice.... A second question is related to the quiet possession problem involved with the warranty of title. Is the warranty against infringement breached when the buyer incurs litigation expenses in successfully defending against an infringement claim? One commentator has opined: "A rightful claim is one where the buyer or seller reasonably believes that a third party's infringement charge would probably be upheld by the courts." In any event,

both of these problems will have to be worked out by the courts, which have hardly been inundated with 2–312(3) cases.

White and Summers, supra, § 9–12 at 490, quoting Dudline, "Warranties Against Infringement under the Uniform Commercial Code," 36 N.Y.S.B.F. 214, 219 (1964).

Yttro's main assertion on appeal however is that if it breached the warranty against infringement, it was entitled to cure that defect retroactively.

The trial judge held:

Therefore, we are brought to the issue of whether or not the plaintiff had the right to quote, "cure," end quote, its defect in title. . . . To now say we can cure that two and a half years into the contract, three years into the contract and then sue you for damages for the period of time prior to it seems unreasonable. The defendant did not have the obligation to have receipt of a warranty guarantee or right of or assurance from the plaintiff. There's nothing in the contract that would require them to now depend upon the final wording of the claimant to reimburse them for any damages that would have occurred had they marketed the product. . . . As I've said, the right to, quote, "cure this" did not exist once the contract was declared void and under the circumstances of this case even if there was such a right to cure it was not one that could be exercised reasonably under the circumstances since two and a half years had gone by before any cure was obtained. I think it's two and a half years, three-year contract. For those reasons the Motion for Summary Judgment will be granted.

In Ramirez v. Autosport, 88 N.J. 277 (1982), the Supreme Court extensively analyzed a buyer's and seller's rights under the UCC respecting delivery of non-conforming goods. The Court there held that the UCC's remedies replaced "rescission," and that a buyer may reject nonconforming goods or revoke its acceptance of non-conforming goods without necessarily having a right to cancel the contract. Id. at 285–286, 288. Before acceptance a buyer may reject goods for non-conformity (N.J.S.A. 12A:2–601). If the rejection occurs within the time set for delivery, the seller's right to cure is unconditional until that time occurs (N.J.S.A. 12A:2–508(1)). If rejection occurs after the time set for delivery, the seller has a further reasonable time to cure if the seller reasonably believes that the goods would be acceptable with or without a money allowance (N.J.S.A. 12A:2–508(2)). After acceptance the buyer may revoke its acceptance only if the non-conformity substantially impairs the value of the goods. (N.J.S.A. 12A:2–608). Id. at 285–286.

The motion judge did not apply the *Ramirez* analysis. For the first year of the contract XMA accepted delivery of 262 filters, refused 738, and in effect repudiated the contract before the time set for delivery of the remainder. As to those filters XMA accepted, there was no finding that the infringement defect (which was never asserted) substantially impaired the value of the goods. Moreover, even if found to be a substantial defect, Yttro was arguably still entitled to a reasonable time in which to cure. The court's finding was that Yttro was not entitled to cure the title defect respecting all of the filters regardless of time for delivery and that if it was so entitled, the cure attempted was unreasonable, but there was no differential analysis based on Ramirez or the UCC.

Professor Hawkland describes the seller's right to cure a title defect as follows:

A nonconforming delivery is curable if it does not subject the aggrieved party to any great inconvenience, risk or loss. . . .

Under this test, it is necessary to distinguish between cases in which the goods have been accepted before the title defect is discovered and those in which the goods are rejected initially because of such a defect. . . .

If the buyer takes possession before either party knows of the title defect, he is a converter and not even a prompt surrender of the goods, upon learning of the outstanding claim of ownership, will purge him of this tort. Whether or not cure should be permitted in this circumstance, therefore, does not turn on whether the buyer is exposed to the risk of an action for a conversion. It should depend on his possible inconvenience and loss.

Suppose a buyer purchases a car from a seller for $6,000 and drives it a year before discovering that it is a stolen vehicle, still owned by O. Suppose, additionally, that the car has depreciated in value to $4,000 and that O will sell his interest in it for $5,000. Can the seller cure this defective title by negotiating this settlement with O if the buyer objects and insists on revoking his acceptance on the basis of breach of warranty of title? The answer should be in the affirmative. If the seller clears the title, the buyer will suffer no loss, no risk and no inconvenience.

[Hawkland, supra, § 2–312:07 at 281–282.]

XMA urges that it had a right to rescind the entire contract, including its obligation to accept filters for which no delivery was called for prior to cure, because the contract was illegal and therefore void from its inception. We reject this reasoning. While there is no question that the first Yttro filter delivery violated the federal patent statutes, see 35 U.S.C.A. § 271(a) ("whoever without authority makes, uses or sells any patent invention, within the United States during the term of the patent, therefore, infringes the patent"), plaintiff did not violate any criminal provisions of the patent laws, see 35 U.S.C.A. § 292 (false markings). The statute provides only civil remedies against a patent infringer, see 35 U.S.C.A. § 281. XMA's reliance on cases respecting breaches of contract by violating a statute with criminal penalties is misplaced. While even absent criminal penalties contracts which violate public policy have been declared void and certain contracts which violate a statutory scheme have been declared void as against public policy, the motion judge did not rely on this authority and we do not regard it as applicable. We conclude that the contract was not void at inception based upon the patent infringement and that the summary judgment in XMA's favor must be reversed. Yttro was entitled to a hearing to resolve issues of fact under a Ramirez analysis. Respecting goods actually delivered in violation of the warranty against infringement, the reasonableness of Yttro's cure must be judged in the light of the absence of loss, risk or inconvenience to XMA.

Reversed and remanded for hearing.

Note

Disclaiming the Warranty against Infringements. The warranty against infringements in UCC 2–312(3) is not subject to the disclaimer provision of 2–312(2) (see comment 6 to 2–312), but subsection (3) begins with the phrase, "Unless otherwise agreed ...," clearly indicating that the warranty therein may be excluded by the parties. If a disclaimer of the 2–312(3) warranty need not meet the standard of 2–312(2), what standard should be applied? Although the warranties provided for in 2–312 are not called "implied" warranties (so as to remove them from the application of the implied warranty disclaimer rules in UCC 2–316), in Landis & Staefa (UK) Ltd. v. Flair Int'l Corp., 60 F.Supp. 2d 14 (E.D.N.Y.1999), the court held that general language disclaiming implied warranties was effective to disclaim a 2–312(3) warranty against infringements because the language met the disclaimer standards of 2–316(2) and (3) (dealing with the disclaimer of "implied warranties").

Proposed Amendments. Proposed amended Section 2–312(1)(a) would continue to provide that the warranty of title requires that the title conveyed shall be good and the transfer rightful, and it would expand the protection of the buyer against colorable claims or interests in the goods that unreasonably expose the buyer to litigation, regardless of the outcome of such litigation. Proposed amended 2–312(1)(b) would continue to provide that the warranty of title requires that the goods shall be free from any security interest, lien or encumbrance of which the buyer, at the time of contracting had no knowledge. Like pre-amendment 2–312, the amended version would not expressly provide for a separate warranty of quiet possession because disturbance of quiet possession is simply one of many ways in which the warranty of title may be breached. Proposed amended Section 2–312(2) would replicate the warranty against infringement found in pre-amendment 2–312(3).

The disclaimer provision in pre-amendment 2–312(2) provided only for disclaimer of the 2–312(1) warranty of title. As suggested *supra*, this meant that there was no guidance for disclaimers of the warranty against infringement, even though the opening phrase of 2–312(3) ("Unless otherwise agreed") clearly indicated that disclaiming the warranty was possible. Proposed amended 2–312(3) would overcome this curiosity by providing disclaimer rules that apply to both the warranty of title and the warranty against infringements. Comment 4 to 2–312, however, states that, unlike the implied warranty disclaimer rules in proposed amended 2–316, the rules in proposed amended 2–312(3) do not specifically require that disclaimers or modifications of the warranties of title and against infringements be contained in a record or be conspicuous. Pre-amendment 2–312(2) also did not require a disclaimer of the warranty of title to be in a record or be conspicuous. In light of the case law, explored earlier, that demanded specific, precise and unambiguous language in order to disclaim such a basic warranty, there was an argument for a record and conspicuousness requirement in proposed amended 2–312(3), but obviously that argument did not prevail.

P. TRANSFEREE'S RIGHT TO UNDISTURBED POSSESSION/USE UNDER UCC ARTICLE 2A, THE CISG, AND UCITA

1. Protection of Lessee's Rights to Leased Goods

Article 2A protects a lessee's right to possession and use of leased goods by implying in the lease a warranty that no third party has a claim to or interest in the goods that will interfere with the lessee's enjoyment of its leasehold interest. 2A–211(1). Under the pre-amendment version of this provision, the warranty is limited to protection against claims or interests arising from the lessor's acts or omissions, although the proposed amended version would eliminate this limitation except in the case of finance leases (proposed amended 2A–211(1)((a) & (2)(a)).[2] The proposed amendments would also explicitly protect against colorable claims to or interests in the goods that unreasonably expose the lessee to litigation even if those claims or interest are ultimately found invalid, although in the case of finance leases the protection would again be limited to colorable claims or interests arising from the lessor's acts or omissions. Except in finance leases, a merchant lessor who regularly deals in goods of the kind also warrants delivery of the goods free of the rightful claim of any person for infringement (e.g., violation of patent or trademark rights). Pre-amendment 2A–211(2); proposed amended 2A–211(3). As under the analogous Article 2 warranty against infringement (2–312(3)), a lessee must hold the lessor harmless against an infringement claim that arises out of compliance with specifications provided by the lessee. 2A–211(3).

Pre-amendment 2A–211 does not contain provisions governing disclaimers of the warranties against interference and against infringement, in contrast to the warranty of title section in Article 2, which includes a subsection governing disclaimer of the warranty (see pre-amendment 2–312(2) and proposed amended 2–312(3)). Pre-amendment Article 2A deals with disclaimers of the warranties of quiet possession and against infringement in its general warranty disclaimer provision, 2A–214. Subsection (4) of pre-amendment 2A–214, like its analogue in Article 2 (2–312(2)), requires such disclaimers to be specific. Unlike its

2. Proposed amended Section 2A–211(1)(a) provides that the warranty protection for non-finance lessee's does not extend to claims or interests attributable to the lessee's own acts or omissions.

counterpart in the sales article, however, pre-amendment 2A–214(4) requires the disclaimer to be in writing and conspicuous, unless course of dealing, usage of trade, course of performance or other circumstances gave the lessee reason to know that the goods were leased subject to the claim or interest of a third person. The proposed amendments to Article 2A would move the disclaimer section in pre-amendment 2A–214(4) to new 2A–211(4), in order to be consistent with the organization in the analogous Article 2 provision (2–312).

Problem 40

The Bond Corporation leased nine portable welding units from Leasing, Inc. Before the lease contract was signed, Bond discovered that the welding units were subject to a perfected security interest held by Finance Company of America (FCA), a creditor of Leasing. After using the equipment for the first two months of the one year lease, Bond required funds and sold three of the units to the Finney Corporation. Finney was completely unaware of the lease arrangement and thought that Bond owned the welding units. The sale to Finney constituted a default under Bond's lease contract with Leasing. Leasing has defaulted on its payments to FCA, which seeks to repossess the six welding units retained by Bond as well as the three units in the possession of Finney. Analyze. See 2A–303, 2A–305 and 2A–307.

2. Buyer's Protections Against Third–Party Claims Under the CISG

CISG Article 41 obligates a seller to deliver goods that are "free from any right or claim of a third party, unless the buyer agreed to take the goods subject to that right or claim." Thus if the buyer's ownership, possession or use of the goods is disturbed by such rights or claims, the seller has violated its obligations and is liable to the buyer. If the third party's right or claim is based on "industrial property or other intellectual property," however, the buyer's protections are governed by Article 42, which makes the seller liable to the buyer if all of the following requirements are met: 1) the seller "knew or could not have been unaware" of the third party's right or claim at the time the contract was concluded (Art. 42(1)); 2) the third party's right or claim arose under the law of a particular country, as determined under Article 42(1)(a) or (b), whichever is applicable; 3) the buyer is not disqualified from protection because it "knew or could not have been unaware of the right or claim" at the time the contract was concluded (Art. 42(2)(a)). Under Article 42(2)(b), furthermore, the seller is not liable if the third party's right or claim arose "from the seller's compliance with technical drawings, designs, formulae or other such specifications furnished by the buyer," although–unlike the UCC Article 2 rule dealing with this situation in 2–312(3)—CISG Article 42 does not expressly make the buyer liable for infringement claims brought against the seller for its compliance with the buyer's specifications. Article 43(1) of the CISG imposes notice requirements on a buyer seeking the protections of Articles 41 or 42, but Article 43(2) excuses a buyer's lack of notice if the seller was aware of the third party's claim and its nature, and Article 44 preserves certain remedies for a buyer that has failed to give the required notice but has "a reasonable excuse" for such failure.

Problem 40A

(a) Suppose that the CISG rather than UCC Article 2 applied in Problem 39(a), (b) and (c). Analyze.

(b) Suppose that the CISG rather than UCC Article 2 applied in the *Yttro v. X–Ray Marketing* case *supra*. Assume that the claim of patent infringement arose under the law of the country designated by the applicable provision of Article 42(1)(a) or (b). What result?

3. Warranty Against Infringements and Misappropriations, and Warranty Against Interference Under UCITA

Claims for violations of intellectual property rights assume center stage in transactions involving computer information. UCITA § 401(a) provides that a "merchant regularly dealing in information of the kind" warrants to a licensee of computer information that the information "will be delivered free of the rightful claim of any third person by way of infringement or misappropriation." Much like the rule in the UCC Article 2 warranty against infringements (2–312(3)), however, UCITA § 401(a) provides that the licensee must hold the licensor harmless if the third party's claim arose from the licensor's compliance with "detailed specifications ... and the method required for meeting the specifications" furnished by the licensee. UCITA § 401(b)(1) creates a warranty against rightful third party claims or interests that interfere with a licensee's "enjoyment of its interest," provided the third party's claim arose from an act or omission of the licensor, and UCITA § 401(b)(2) creates a warranty protecting *exclusive* rights granted under a license. The § 401 warranties are subject to a variety of limitations in UCITA § 401(c), and to the disclaimer rules in UCITA § 401(d). Finally, if both the licensor and the licensee are merchants, UCITA § 401(e) permits the licensee's warranty protections to be eliminated by the use of "quit-claim" language in the license–an approach that departs from the case law construing attempts to limit a buyer's warranty of title under UCC Article 2.

Q. UNCONSCIONABILITY

UCC 2–302 empowers a court to strike down contract clauses, or even entire contracts, that the court finds "unconscionable." As with any aspect of the UCC, it is important to begin the analysis of unconscionability by reviewing the relevant statutory language. Your reaction to the text, however, might be similar to that of Professor Arthur Leff, who suggested that the language of 2–302 amounts to nothing more than "an emotionally satisfying incantation" which demonstrates that "it is easy to say nothing with words."[1] We might paraphrase the statute (always a dangerous course) as follows: "Unconscionability is bad or evil; conscionability is good." After this paraphrase, the question remains: what is unconscionability?

The text of 2–302 merely states that, once a court has determined that a clause or an entire contract is unconscionable, it may refuse to enforce the clause or the contract. The provision clearly grants the court rather than the jury exclusive power to find unconscionability, although 2–302(2) insists that the parties must have a reasonable opportunity to present evidence of the commercial setting, purpose and effect of the alleged unconscionable clause. Again, however, the section language provides no guidance to a court in making the determination. Only a few questions have been settled in four decades of analysis: unconscionability must be determined as of the time the contract was made;[2] courts will rarely recognize the unconscionability defense in a contract between merchants, unless the defendant is only a technical merchant with the functional sophistication and bargaining power of a consumer buyer,[3] and, if language disclaiming implied warranties meets the threshold requirements of UCC 2–316, it remains subject to the unconscionability standard.[4]

Although the enacted statutory text is unhelpful, the unenacted language from comment (1) to 2–302 supports the view that unconscionability involves two critical elements: "The principle is one of the prevention of oppression and unfair surprise." If a party with little bargaining power must accept a burdensome clause dictated by the stronger side, the situation involves "oppression"—the contract of adhesion or "take-it-or-leave-it" deal. In the more common situation where one party inserts an unfair term into a maze of boilerplate where it will probably not be read, the other party will be "unfairly surprised" to later discover the unexpected provision.

Both the *unexpected* ("unfair surprise") and *no choice* ("oppression") types of unconscionability are recognized in the classic cases applying the doctrine. Justice Francis' famous opinion in Henningsen v. Bloomfield Motors, Inc., 32 N.J. 358, 161 A.2d 69 (1960), emphasized that consumer buyers of a new automobile either would not read or would not understand a warranty disclaimer in the contract of sale. Even if they did read and understand the disclaimer, Justice Francis opined, consumers would encounter virtually the same clause in any automobile purchase contract: they would be forced either to accept the disclaimer or forego buying one of the necessities of modern life. An equally well-known opinion by Judge Skelly Wright in Williams v. Walker–Thomas

---

1. Leff, *Unconscionability and the Code—The Emperor's New Clause*, 115 U. PA.L. REV. 485, 558–60 (1967).

2. See Resource Mgt. Co. v. Weston Ranch, 706 P.2d 1028, 1043 (Utah 1985).

3. See Johnson v. Mobil Oil Corp., 415 F.Supp. 264 (E.D.Mich.1976); Weaver v. American Oil Co., 257 Ind. 458, 276 N.E.2d 144 (1971).

4. *Id.*

Furniture Co., 350 F.2d 445 (D.C.Cir.1965), discussed both unexpected and no (reasonable) choice unconscionability.

Courts have used various labels for the different types of unconscionability. What has become the prevailing analysis distinguishes "procedural" from "substantive" unconscionability—a nomenclature suggested by Professor Leff in his early work.[5] Professor Leff used the "procedural" label to describe "bargain naughtiness" (i.e., defects in the bargaining process, such as inconspicuous boilerplate), while "substantive" unconscionability denoted terms that were one-sided and oppressive, unreasonably favoring one party. The "procedural" and "substantive" labels have surface appeal because they suggest a neat distinction between two types of unconscionability. Yet, to paraphrase Professor Leff's own criticism of section 2–302, the labels may only deceive courts into believing that they are engaged in a genuine analysis when, in fact, they have developed nothing more than another "emotionally satisfying incantation." Courts sometimes display confusion over what is included under each rubric. There have been more elaborate efforts to identify the elements of unconscionability. Thus, one court found seven elements,[6] while another found ten.[7] Yet another analysis focused upon the parties' actual or presumed "circle of assent," which is an elaboration of the Llewellyn analysis of assent to boilerplate terms.[8]

Professor Llewellyn regarded 2–302 "as perhaps the most valuable section in the entire Code."[9] He was well aware of the sins often cloaked under the rubric, "freedom of contract." That ringing phrase could not dispel the fact that there is no freedom of contract where bargaining power is unequal. Superior bargaining power allows one party to dictate terms to which the other party must adhere—the "contract of adhesion." Inferior bargaining power leaves no choice but to accede to the wishes of the superior party. It is difficult to call the resulting transaction an agreement or a bargain since it lacks the quintessential element of volition. It was, therefore, relatively easy to discern one manifestation of unconscionability, which may be called the "no choice" variety.

The prototype judicial descriptions of unconscionability emphasized this "take-it-or-leave-it" element as indispensable. For example, the Francis opinion in *Henningsen* (a classic analysis of unconscionability even though it did not use the term), describes the "standardized form designed for mass use" that was "imposed upon the automobile consumer. He takes it or leaves it, and he must take it to buy an automobile." The Skelly Wright description in *Williams v. Walker–Thomas* requires

---

5. See Leff, *Unconscionability and the Code—The Emperor's New Clause*, 115 U. Pa. L. Rev. 485, 487.

6. See Mullan v. Quickie Aircraft Corp., 797 F.2d 845, 850 (10th Cir.1986).

7. See Wille v. Southwestern Bell. Tel. Co., 219 Kan. 755, 549 P.2d 903, 906–07(1976).

8. See Parton v. Mark Pirtle Oldsmobile–Cadillac–Isuzu, 730 S.W.2d 634, 637 (Tenn.App.1987); Germantown Mfg. Co. v. Rawlinson, 341 Pa.Super. 42, 491 A.2d 138, 146 (1985).

9. Statement of K. Llewellyn in 1 State of New York 1954 Law Revision Commission Report, Hearings on the Uniform Commercial Code at 57.

an *absence of meaningful choice*.[10] There has, however, been a marked change in the judicial attitude towards this element of unconscionability. This change was dramatically evidenced in a recent opinion by Judge Easterbrook for the United States Court of Appeals for the Seventh Circuit, which remarked: "But what's wrong with a contract of adhesion, anyway? Many contracts have standard terms that are not open to negotiation yet are routinely enforced." United States v. Hare, 269 F.3d 859, 862 (7th Cir.2001), citing Hill v. Gateway 2000, Inc., 105 F.3d 1147 (7th Cir.1997).

A staunch defender of the "layered" contract concept adopted in UCITA confirms this "reality" in an answer to the charge that software licenses to which the licensee will be presumed to have assented are long and incomprehensible:

> [T]he criticism that some licenses can be lengthy and incomprehensible is accurate, but so are mortgages, credit card contracts, car rental contracts, insurance policies, brokerage agreements, and the myriad of other standard form contracts that we all encounter in our daily lives. The law is not always transparent and vendors who stray from statutorily required or judicially blessed wording often encounter unexpected results. So the criticism is logical but applies to all contracts. It is not reasonable to expect UCITA to change a *universal reality*."[11]

The common scenario of the seller's lawyer creating a document containing standardized, non-negotiable terms to which the buyer must assent or to which the buyer will be deemed to have assented so dominates commerce that it is no longer objectionable. The "standardized plan" of the UCC—which provides the buyer of goods with implied warranties, remedies protecting the expectation and other interests, and the right to sue in a court of law—has been overcome by sellers' boilerplate designed to emasculate UCC norms. Those norms, which are relegated to the status of "default" terms, never become operative because the seller's boilerplate, at least unread and typically incomprehensible to the ordinary consumer or merchant buyer, prevails. Karl Llewellyn recognized that since standardized forms are neither read nor understood, there is no genuine assent to the boilerplate terms. He suggested that one should be bound only to "decent" boilerplate terms, although he did not provide a test for distinguishing decent from indecent terms. Almost a half century later, courts are now confronted with distinguishing "good" or decent contracts of adhesion from "bad"

---

10. 350 F.2d 445, 449 (D.C.Cir.1965) (emphasis supplied).

11. Holly K. Towle, *Understanding the Uniform Computer Information Transactions Act and the Uniform Electronic Transactions Act*, 38 Duq. L. Rev. 371, 416 (2000) (emphasis supplied). The author is elsewhere identified as a lawyer representing a software trade association in connection with UCITA. See another article by the same author, *The Politics of Licensing Law*, 36 Hous. L. Rev. 121 (1999). The statement that only "some" licenses are incomprehensible seems euphemistic, and the justification that the law demands language that creates obtuseness is less than persuasive.

or indecent contracts of adhesion while the contract of adhesion, by itself, is now regarded as neutral.

The characterization of which terms are "bad" or "indecent" has also evolved. While a boilerplate term disclaiming the implied warranty of merchantability raised considerable concern in 1960,[12] its ubiquity has made it acceptable. A seller's form without a warranty disclaimer, an exclusion of consequential damages, and a limitation on the buyer's direct damages would excite collectors of rare documents. With emphatic support from the United States Supreme Court, arbitration has become the apotheosis of dispute settlement and the inclusion of arbitration clauses in the boilerplate is no longer surprising, unexpected or perhaps even "material." While there is authority for the idea that the repeated sending of unread and un-acted-upon standardized terms is not sufficient to constitute a prior course of dealing,[13] there are contrary views.[14] The *pièce de résistance* is the enforceability of standardized terms that appear only inside the box containing a product that a reasonable buyer would think he had contracted to purchase before having an opportunity to view the terms—the *rolling contract* theory discussed earlier in this volume.

The search for a workable unconscionability analysis has not succeeded, and there is an apparent absence of desire to pursue the task. Courts will continue to struggle with the evolving standard of unconscionability because, as 2–302(2) suggests, the defense is fundamentally a question of fact. Karl Llewellyn was particularly suspicious of "an approach by statute" which, to him, was "both dubious and awkward in manner and deficient and spotty in scope."[15] He designed 2–302 to be a judicial catalyst that would require courts to confront the diverse fact patterns that may suggest unconscionability. The result would be instructive (but not dispositive) "precedent." To restrain judges' "untutored imagination," subsection (2) would permit "all kinds of [business] background to be presented to instruct the court."[16] The overall effect of 2–302 would be to "greatly advance certainty in a most baffling, most troubling and almost unreckonable situation."[17] In summary, Llewellyn believed it was both impossible to achieve and counterproductive to attempt a highly adumbrated statute dealing with a vague standard of fairness. He envisioned the elaboration of the concept through the common law process to which he was unalterably committed.

The Llewellyn view has been justified by various unsuccessful efforts over more than a decade to restate the language of the unconscionability provision of UCC Article 2. Proposed amended Section 2–302 would

---

12. Henningsen v. Bloomfield Motors, 32 N.J. 358, 161 A.2d 69 (1960).

13. This view is supported by comment 4 to proposed amended Section 2–207.

14. See Puget Sound Financial v. Unisearch, 146 Wash.2d 428, 47 P.3d 940 (2002).

15. K. LLEWELLYN, THE COMMON LAW TRADITION: DECIDING APPEALS 370 (1960).

16. Statement of K. Llewellyn in 1 STATE OF NEW YORK 1954 LAW REVISION COMMISSION REPORT, HEARINGS ON THE UNIFORM COMMERCIAL CODE at 57.

17. Id.

replicate the pre-amendment language. The problem is not with the language of 2–302, which merely states a principled goal. The disappointment is in the stunted growth of the precedent that was supposed to elaborate the principle into a highly workable and reliable analysis. The absence of that kind of analysis has limited the application of the doctrine. Courts are not comfortable with invoking the unconscionability concept except in the most egregious cases, many if not most of which might have been resolved through traditional doctrines such as fraud or the occasional use of "covert tools." The current judicial understanding of unconscionability does not augur its extensive application in the 21st century. This background is important in recognizing that an application of the unconscionability standard in a commercial setting, as occurs in the following case, is particularly rare.

MOSCATIELLO v. PITTSBURGH CONTRACTORS EQUIPMENT CO.

Superior Court of Pennsylvania, 1991.
407 Pa.Super. 363, 595 A.2d 1190.

HESTER, J. This action arises out of a contract entered between appellant, PCEC, and appellee, Franco Moscatiello, I/a, t/d/b/a Moscatiello Construction Company ("Moscatiello"), for the purchase of a concrete paving machine ("paver") manufactured by Curbmaster, Inc.

Mr. Palino, Moscatiello's superintendent, executed a contract on a form provided by PCEC for the purchase from PCEC of a Curbmaster concrete spreader-finisher machine for a total price of $85,125.42. PCEC's purchase agreement stated on the reverse side that no warranties were offered on equipment sold and that any implied warranties were excluded in favor of the manufacturer's offer of warranties. The contract also contained a provision which limited a buyer's remedy solely to return of the purchase price, less wear and use of the machine. In addition, all consequential and incidental damages were expressly excluded.

Moscatiello had no previous dealing with PCEC and was not on notice that the sales agreement relinquished warranties and limited damages. During the contract negotiations, neither PCEC's vice president nor the salesman in attendance directed Moscatiello's attention to the reverse side of the contract where the warranty exclusions were printed.

When the paver arrived, it contained no warranty information from the manufacturer. It was alleged during trial that Curbmaster's warranty information was attached to Curbmaster's operations and parts manual, which was delivered to PCEC following execution of the sales contract between Curbmaster and PCEC. However, the trial court found that the manual which ultimately was delivered to Moscatiello did not contain Curbmaster's warranty exclusions and disclaimers. A Curbmaster employee was present when the paver arrived, assisted Moscatiello employees in assembling it, instructed Moscatiello employees on how to operate the machine, and was present when the machine was used for the first time. The Curbmaster representative never informed Moscatiello employees that the machine's warranties were limited or excluded.

According to the testimony of four witnesses during trial, from the time it was first used in June, 1987, to on or about November 12, 1987, when it was used last, the paver failed to lay concrete evenly. Furthermore, the product which resulted was unacceptable to PennDot [The Pennsylvania Department of Transportation which had contracted with Moscatiello]. During the five-month period of the paver's operation, Moscatiello made numerous complaints to PCEC about the paver's failure to produce an acceptable product. During this period, PCEC and Curbmaster unsuccessfully attempted numerous times to remedy the defects in the machine. The machine finally was returned to Curbmaster in December, 1987. As a result of the paver's failure to perform its functions properly, Moscatiello incurred increased labor costs in order to produce a product acceptable to PennDot.

Moscatiello filed a complaint against PCEC asserting breach of contract, breach of express warranty, breach of implied warranty of merchantability, and breach of implied warranty of fitness for a particular purpose. PCEC joined Curbmaster as an additional defendant, asserting breach of express warranty [and] breach of implied warranties of merchantability and fitness for a particular purpose.

[T]he trial court issued an opinion awarding $146,811.43 in damages, plus interest, to Moscatiello against PCEC and Curbmaster jointly. Both PCEC and Curbmaster filed timely post-trial motions, and on August 21, 1990, the trial court issued an opinion and order denying Curbmaster's post-trial motions and granting PCEC's post-trial motion only insofar as it related to PCEC's right to indemnification from Curbmaster. PCEC filed this timely appeal from the portion of the order which denied its post-trial motions.

PCEC first argues that the trial court erred in concluding that the disclaimer of warranties contained in the sales agreement was not conspicuous.

The exclusionary clause involved herein is located on the reverse side of a standard sales contract. The front of the form contains blank lines in which are typed a customer's name, shipping instructions, detailed description of the machine, price breakdown, and payment terms. All of the information is individually typed on separate lines at least one quarter of an inch wide. Toward the bottom of the form, inside the margins for the price breakdown, is the phrase in capital letters: "TERMS AND CONDITIONS ON REVERSE SIDE ARE AN INTEGRAL PART OF THIS ORDER." Immediately below is a sentence containing the clause, in smaller type, "subject to the provisions hereof and conditions contained on reverse side hereof." By contrast, the reverse side of the form contains eighteen numbered paragraphs which fill the page, top to bottom and side to side, in extremely small type, approximately one-sixteenth inch in height and one-fourth the size used on the front. The capital letters are slightly larger, but of the same color and in the same type style as the rest of the printing. The type used on the front of the contract is much larger and bolder than that used on the reverse side. The warranty disclaimer is buried in paragraph number sixteen at the bottom of the page. Though the operative language of the disclaimer is set forth in capital letters, the size of the type of even the capital letters is so minute that it simply does nothing to attract attention to the clause. As Moscatiello aptly observes, "to say that the print is 'fine' is an understatement." Appellee's brief at 12.

Upon our review of the agreement, we have no doubt, as the trial court stated, that PCEC's warranty disclaimer "did not adequately put Moscatiello on notice that substantial rights of theirs were being relinquished." Trial court opinion at 5.[1] The disclaimer was set forth in some of the "finest" print this court ever has read. Even the language on the front of the contract referring to terms and conditions on the reverse side of the contract was inconspicuous as well as misleading. The letters are capitalized but are buried in the middle of the contract within the margins of the price breakdown of the goods. In addition, reference is made only to the "terms" and "conditions" on the reverse side rather than to the limitation on warranties and remedies available to the buyer. This language clearly does not meet the letter or the spirit of the U.C.C. requirements.

The evidence during trial was unequivocal that PCEC was fully familiar with the terms of the agreement, having employed it for many years, and had numerous opportunities throughout the purchase negotiations to notify Moscatiello of the exclusion of warranties and the limitation on potential remedies set forth on the reverse side of the contract. It is clear that PCEC failed to take advantage of those opportunities. Instead, as the trial court noted, PCEC "utilized a boiler-plate provision in a standard sales agreement to exclude important warranties that naturally arise in the course of any sale." Trial court opinion at 5. Section 2316 of the U.C.C. protects buyers such as Moscatiello from this type of disclaimer hidden deep within the illegible fine print on the reverse side of a standard sales contract, and that section invalidates such exclusionary language. Thus, we agree with the trial court's finding that the warranty disclaimer was ineffective, and we find no error in the trial court's decision to allow Moscatiello to pursue its cause of action for breach of implied warranty of merchantability.

We also concur with the trial court's finding that PCEC, in fact, did breach its implied warranty of merchantability. Our review of the record in accordance with our standard compels the conclusion that the machine in question could not "pass without objection in the trade under

---

1. While it is true that the location of a disclaimer on the reverse side of a contract alone does not render the disclaimer inconspicuous, the disclaimer itself must be conspicuous and the front of the document must contain noticeable reference to the terms on the reverse side. Jaskey Finance and Leasing v. Display Data Corp., 564 F.Supp. 160 (E.D.Pa.1983).

the contract description," nor was it "fit for the ordinary purposes for which such goods are used." 13 Pa. C.S.A. sec. 2314(b).

PCEC contends that Moscatiello is bound by the limitation of remedies provisions in the contract regardless of whether such provisions were conspicuous "inasmuch as any limitation is a term set forth in a contract executed by [Moscatiello]." Appellant's brief at 22. Moscatiello responds that the provisions in the contract which prohibit recovery of incidental and consequential damages are unconscionable, and therefore, the trial court was correct in refusing to enforce those provisions. We concur and consequently, find no error in the trial court's ruling.

Our examination begins with a review of the applicable sections of the U.C.C. Section 2714(c) provides that incidental or consequential damages may be recovered in an action for breach of contract or breach of warranty. 13 Pa. C.S.A. § 2714(c). Consequential damages include "any loss resulting from general or particular requirements and needs of which the seller at the time of contracting had reason to know ..." 13 Pa. C.S.A. § 2715(b)(1). Consequential damages may be limited or excluded unless the limitation or exclusion is unconscionable. 13 Pa. C.S.A. § 2719(c). Section 2302 of the U.C.C. allows the court to refuse to enforce the contract as a whole or any single clause or group of clauses if permeated by unconscionability. 13 Pa. C.S.A. § 2302(a). The principle upon which this section rests is one of prevention of oppression and unfair surprise. 13 Pa. C.S.A. § 2302, Comment 1.

[P]aragraphs seventeen and eighteen in the parties' sales contract ... provide the following:

> 17. If the goods covered by this Order are new, Buyer and Vendor agree that there is no failure of an essential purpose of Buyer's exclusive and limited remedy so long as Vendor is willing and able to repair or replace any part which is not as warranted. If Vendor is not willing and able to repair or replace any such part or if for any reason it is determined that Buyer's exclusive and limited remedy has failed of its essential purpose, Buyer's sole and exclusive remedy shall then be to have its purchase price returned in exchange for the goods, less a reasonable charge for any use by Buyer.

> 18. It is agreed that Vendor shall not be liable for any incidental or consequential damages occasioned by the sale, possession, operation, maintenance or use of the goods or for any failure of the goods to operate under any claim of breach of warranty or contract, negligence, strict liability or otherwise.

A clause in a contract is considered unconscionable and unenforceable if there is "an absence of meaningful choice on the part of one of the parties together with contract terms which are unreasonably favorable to the other party." Germantown Manufacturing Co. v. Rawlinson, 341 Pa.Super. 42, 55, 491 A.2d 138, 145 (1985), quoting E.A. Farnsworth Contracts 314 (1982). In Germantown, we were asked to determine the enforceability of a confession of judgment clause which was buried, as were the contract provisions at issue here, within the fine print of boilerplate language of a standard form. In finding the clause unenforceable, we were guided by the following analysis contained in section 353 of J. Murray, Murray on Contracts, (2d ed., 1974).

> Parties to a contract rarely consciously advert to any number of terms which are binding upon them. If such terms allocate the risks of the bargain in a manner which the parties should have reasonably expected, they are enforceable—they are, to use the expression of Karl Llewellyn, decent terms. If the terms of the contract suggest the reallocation of material risks, an attempted reallocation may be so extreme that regardless of apparent and genuine assent, a court will not enforce it.... The parties will not be found to have agreed to an abnormal allocation or risk if the only evidence thereof is an inconspicuous provision on the boilerplate of a standard form. At a minimum, the reallocation must be physically manifested in a fashion comprehensive to the party against whom it is sought to be enforced. Finally, such party must have had a reasonable choice in relation to such reallocation.

Germantown Manufacturing Company v. Rawlinson, 341 Pa.Super. at 56–57, 491 A.2d at 146.

The question presented in the instant sales agreement, therefore, is whether Mr. Moscatiello and his superintendent reasonably should have expected that if the paver failed to perform as promised, they, rather than the seller, would be responsible for the economic losses which resulted. We cannot agree with appellant that appellee harbored any such expectation.

First, paragraphs seventeen and eighteen of the sales contract are, as appellee aptly states in his brief, "classic examples of physically inconspicuous provisions in the boilerplate of a standard form." Appellee's brief at 21. Neither Mr. Moscatiello nor Mr. Palino understood that buried in the fine print on the reverse side of the contract was a term that shifted to Moscatiello the risk of loss resulting from the purchase of a machine which was unable to perform the operations that it was designed to perform. Neither man was a dealer in concrete-spreader finishers or heavy equipment of any kind. Neither individual had ever dealt with PCEC on any previous occasion, and neither had any knowledge of the standard contracts or business practices of PCEC.

Thus, Moscatiello qualified as neither a merchant, as the term is defined in 13 Pa. C.S.A. § 2104, nor a substantial business concern skilled in the negotiation of sales contracts for goods. It is undisputed that PCEC was both. Courts have upheld limitation of damage provisions in sales contracts between merchants or experienced business concerns because there is no disparity between such entities in either bargaining power or sophistication. See K & C, Inc. v. Westinghouse Electric Corp., 437 Pa. 303, 263 A.2d 390 (1970) (buyers were an experienced attorney and the owner of a used furniture business who dealt with the renovation and sale of the type of machines being purchased); Chatlos Systems, Inc. v. National Cash Register Corp., 635 F.2d 1081 (3d Cir.1980) (buyer was a manufacturer of complex electronic equipment who purchased a defective computer system).[2]

Appellant places great reliance on S. M. Wilson and Co. v. Smith International, Inc., 587 F.2d 1363 (9th Cir.1978), in support of its argument that the limitation of damages provisions were reasonable. However, just as in K & C, Inc. and Chatlos, the parties in Wilson held equal bargaining positions as experienced business concerns. Moreover, the limitation of damages provision in Wilson was agreed to specifically by the buyer during purchase negotiations between the parties, and the damage provision as well as the warranty disclaimer were conspicuously set forth in the contract between the parties.

Similarly, the limitation of damages provision upheld by the court in Marr Enterprises, Inc. v. Lewis Refrigeration Co., 556 F.2d 951 (9th Cir.1977), also was set forth conspicuously in the contract between the parties. The contract provision at issue in the final case cited by appellant, FMC Finance Corp. v. Murphree, 632 F.2d 413 (5th Cir.1980), was a warranty disclaimer rather than a limitation of damage provision and therefore, is inapposite to the facts before us.

The contract provisions at issue in the cases cited by appellant are clearly distinguishable from the provisions contained in the contract between the parties herein. Each contract either involved experienced business concerns holding equal bargaining positions or the provision at issue was displayed in a very conspicuous manner in the contract. Appellee was not a dealer or manufacturer of heavy equipment of any kind, and he lacked any prior experience negotiating a contract for the purchase of this type of equipment with PCEC. He had no reason to expect that the contract he signed contained a clause that was buried in the fine print on the reverse side which shifted to him the risk of economic loss resulting from the purchase of a machine which was incapable of performing the job that it was designed to do.

In contrast, PCEC was a well-established dealer engaged in the sale, service, and support of construction equipment to area contractors. It had negotiated many other contracts for the purchase of this type of equipment and was familiar with the "conditions" on the reverse side of its own form which disclaimed warranties and limited damages. PCEC clearly held superior bargaining position with respect to Moscatiello. Moreover, the limitation of damages provisions were classic examples of physically inconspicuous provisions in the boilerplate language of a standard form. Thus, we find the numerous cases cited in appellant's brief inapplicable to the case at bar. Accordingly, we concur with appellee's contention that the limitation of damages provisions contained

---

2. Even in commercial contracts between merchants, courts have recognized that the signer may be theoretically and technically a merchant but functionally a consumer in terms of education, business acumen and experience. The operative factors are the legal expertise of the parties and/or their conscious awareness of the burdens assumed. See Johnson v. Mobil Oil, 415 F.Supp. 264 (E.D.Mich.1976).

in its contract with PCEC are unconscionable, and we affirm the trial court's refusal to give effect to those provisions.

The fourth error which appellant attributes to the trial court is its failure to find the manufacturer, Curbmaster, directly and solely liable to appellee. Appellant contends that there is no justification for imposing liability on it since its role was limited to a mere seller or conduit in the marketplace for Curbmaster. We disagree.

Appellant cites Klages v. General Ordnance Equipment Co., 240 Pa.Super. 356, 367 A.2d 304 (1976), and Walasavage v. Marinelli, 334 Pa.Super. 396, 483 A.2d 509 (1984), in support of its theory that a seller cannot be held liable for breach of contract or warranty in the sale of defective goods when the manufacturer is a party to the action. Appellant misstates the law. In both Klages and Walasavage, suit was brought against the seller and the manufacturer of a defective product which caused personal injuries to a consumer. In both cases, the seller was merely a "conduit" in the transaction between the purchaser and the manufacturer. We held that the seller's status as a mere conduit did not relieve it of liability to the purchaser but did entitle it to indemnification from the manufacturer, since the manufacturer was primarily responsible for the defective product.

In the present action, the trial court found that PCEC was a mere "conduit" in the transaction resulting in the sale of the paver to appellee. Our rulings in Klages and Walasavage do not relieve PCEC of liability to Moscatiello but entitle it to indemnification from Curbmaster, which primarily was responsible for the defective condition of the machine. Accordingly, we find that the trial court correctly ruled that PCEC was liable to Moscatiello for breach of contract and warranties.

Judgment affirmed.

Note

Maxwell v. Fidelity Financial Services, 184 Ariz. 82, 907 P.2d 51 (1995), provides a modern example of unconscionability in an egregious situation. A door-to-door salesman sold a solar water heater to the Maxwells for a purchase price of over $6,500. With compound interest charges over the course of the time payments, the amount the Maxwells would actually pay totaled just under $15,000, which was more than a third of the value of their home. To secure payment of this amount, the lender took a lien on the Maxwells' house. The water heater that the seller delivered never functioned, and in fact was eventually condemned so that the Maxwells were forced to pay to have it removed. Mrs. Maxwell sued to have the contract declared unconscionable.

Thus the court was confronted with a case involving gross disparity between price and value, together with abundant evidence of overreaching by the defendant in requiring that the buyer execute oppressive documents. The court of appeals found the contract enforceable because Mrs. Maxwell did not produce sufficient evidence that the agreement was beyond her "reasonable expectations" or unconscionable. The Supreme Court of Arizona, however, emphasized the distinction between the "reasonable expectations" doctrine (which, except in Arizona, is generally relegated to insurance contracts) and unconscionability[1]. The court stated that even if contract provisions are consistent with a party's reasonable expectations, the provisions may still be unconscionable.

In discussing unconscionability, the Arizona Supreme Court emphasized the distinction between "procedural unconscionability," which involves unfairness in the manner in which the contract terms were agreed to, and "substantive unconscionability," which involves terms that are not commercially reasonable and thus are without reasonable connection to the risks and needs of business. The court catalogued the factors to be considered in determining "procedural" unconscionability: (1) the age, education and intelligence of the parties; (2) their business acumen and experience; (3) their relative bargaining power; (4) which party drafted the contract; (5) whether the terms were explained to the weaker party; (6) whether alterations of a term were permitted; (7) whether there were alternative sources of supply. While it is common for courts to state that a finding of unconscionability requires a certain quantum of both the procedural and substantive varieties (see, e.g., NEC Technologies, Inc. v. Nelson, 267 Ga. 390, 478 S.E.2d 769 (1996)), the Arizona Supreme court found that a claim of unconscionability can be established with a showing of substantive unconscionability alone, particularly in cases involving either a price-value disparity (as in the *Maxwell* case) or limitation of a buyer's remedies.

See also Brower v. Gateway 2000, Inc., 246 A.D.2d 246, 676 N.Y.S.2d 569 (1998), where, in determining whether an arbitration clause should be struck down as unconscionable, the court found that substantive unconscionability alone would be sufficient if a clause is "egregiously oppressive." The opinion suggests a sliding scale of unconscionability: the more substantively oppressive the clause, the less procedural unconscionability (or "bargain naughtiness," to use Professor Leff's description) will be required.

R. LIMITATION OF REMEDY; FAILURE OF ESSENTIAL PURPOSE OF LIMITED REMEDIES

1. *Limited Remedies Under UCC Article 2*

RHEEM MANUFACTURING COMPANY v. PHELPS HEATING & AIR CONDITIONING, INC.

Supreme Court of Indiana, 2001.
746 N.E.2d 941.

SULLIVAN, J. Rheem Manufacturing Company ("Rheem") makes furnaces for use in homes and offices. During the late 1980s and early

---

1. For an example of the "reasonable expectations" doctrine being applied to insurance contracts, see Max True Plastering Co. v. United States Fidelity & Guaranty Co., 912 P.2d 861 (Okla.1996). See also § 211 of the Restatement (Second) of Contracts, particularly comment *f*, and MURRAY ON CONTRACTS § 97B (4th ed. 2001).

1990s, Rheem sold its furnaces through a distributor, Federated Supply Corporation ("Federated"). Federated in turn sold Rheem furnaces to Phelps Heating and Cooling ("Phelps"), a central Indiana contractor.

The box in which every furnace was shipped contained the following warranty: "Manufacturer, RHEEM AIR CONDITIONING DIVISION, warrants ANY PART of this furnace against failure under normal use and service within the applicable periods specified below, in accordance with the terms of this warranty." This express warranty was limited by three clauses that are at the heart of this appeal. First, Rheem limited the remedies available for breach of the warranty to replacement of parts: "Under this Warranty, RHEEM will furnish a replacement part that will be warranted for only the unexpired portion of the original warranty ..." Second, Rheem disclaimed consequential and incidental damages: "ANY CLAIMS FOR INCIDENTAL OR CONSEQUENTIAL DAMAGES ARE EXPRESSLY EXCLUDED." Finally, Rheem disclaimed any liability for the cost of servicing the furnaces: "This Warranty does not cover any labor expenses for service, nor for removing or reinstalling parts. All such expenses are your responsibility unless a service labor agreement exists between you and your contractor." On its face, it is unclear if this remedy is exclusive, but this ambiguity is clarified by a subsequent term: "RHEEM'S SOLE LIABILITY WITH RESPECT TO DEFECTIVE PARTS SHALL BE AS SET FORTH IN THIS WARRAN-TY...."

During the early 1990s, several types of Rheem furnaces malfunctioned after Phelps installed them. Phelps requested between $40,000 and $65,000 to compensate it for the cost involved in servicing the furnaces. Rheem rejected this request. Phelps brought suit against Rheem and Federated claiming that Rheem breached its express and implied warranties [and was negligent]. Phelps described its damages as including "but not limited to, lost customers, lost profits, and the additional cost of servicing the defective furnaces and remedying the defects therein."

Rheem moved for summary judgment on all of these claims. Rheem's brief in support of its motion asserted that the damages Phelps sought on the warranty theories were precluded by the limitations in the express warranty and by lack of privity on the implied warranties. Rheem also argued that Phelps could not claim tort damages for the purely economic injuries that resulted from the failure of the furnaces to operate as intended. The trial court granted Rheem's motion for summary judgment in regards to negligence, but denied it as to the warranties. The Court of Appeals affirmed the denial of summary judgment. As for the express warranties, the Court of Appeals found a genuine issue of material fact as to "whether the cumulative effect of Rheem's actions was commercially reasonable." On the implied warranty claims, the court stated that the evidence establishing privity was "slight." The court nevertheless held that "perfect vertical privity is not necessary in this case" and then found a genuine issue of material fact as to whether Rheem breached its implied warranties and whether its conduct in doing so was "reasonable."

Rheem first argues that the trial court should have granted summary judgment as to Phelps's claim for lost profits under the express warranty because the warranty excluded consequential damages. This argument requires us to examine the interplay between Indiana Code §§ 26–1–2–719(2) and (3), the UCC subsections pertinent to damage exclusions and remedy limitations in express warranties.

Rheem and Phelps present conflicting constructions of these subsections. Both parties appear to accept that the remedy provided by Rheem failed of its essential purpose and that Phelps is entitled to the benefits of the express warranty. Phelps argues that because Rheem's repair attempts failed for roughly four years, the limited remedy of replacement of parts failed of its essential purpose and Phelps could claim all buyer's remedies provided by the UCC, including consequential damages. Rheem counters that its exclusion of consequential damages is controlled by § 2–719(3). Rheem argues that despite the failure of the limited remedy under § 2–719(2), § 2–719(3) allows an exclusion of consequential damages to operate unless it is unconscionable. [Phelps does not argue that the limited remedy was unconscionable.]

These arguments pose the question of whether an exclusion of consequential damages survives when a separate contract provision limiting a buyer's remedies has failed of its essential purpose. The courts that have faced this issue have fallen into two camps that are divided along the lines of the parties' arguments in this case. One group takes what is known as the "dependent" view and reads § 2–719(2)'s reference to remedies "provided in [the UCC]" as overriding a contract's consequential damage exclusion. See, e.g., Middletown Concrete Prod. v. Black Clawson Co., 802 F.Supp. 1135, 1151 (D.Del.1992) (collecting cases). This gloss on § 2–719 makes an exclusion of consequential damages dependent on whether a limited remedy fails of its essential purpose. See Adams v. J.I. Case Co., 125 Ill.App.2d 388, 261 N.E.2d 1, 8 (Ill.App. 1970). Other courts take an "independent" view and reason that because 2–719(2) and (3) are separate subsections with separate language and separate standards, the failure of a limited remedy has no effect on an exclusion of consequential damages. See Waters v. Massey–Ferguson, Inc., 775 F.2d 587, 592–93 (4th Cir.1985) (collecting cases).

The Court of Appeals accepted the independent view. However, the court also grafted onto § 2–719 a requirement of "commercial reasonableness" and affirmed the denial of summary judgment on the ground that a triable issue existed as to whether Rheem's consequential damages exclusion and limited remedy were commercially reasonable.

We hold that Indiana Code § 26–1–2–719(2) does not categorically invalidate an exclusion of consequential damages when a limited remedy fails of its essential purpose. See Schurtz v. BMW of North America, Inc.,

814 P.2d 1108, 1112 (Utah 1991) (using tools of statutory interpretation in applying independent view). Our first step in interpreting any Indiana statute is to determine whether the legislature has spoken clearly and unambiguously on the point in question. In light of the depth of disagreement among the courts that have faced this issue, it is evident that the UCC is ambiguous on this point.

Faced with an ambiguous statute, we turn next to other applicable canons of construction. First, we note that "our main objective in statutory construction is to determine, effect and implement the intent of the legislature." In ascertaining this intent, we "presume that the legislature did not enact a useless provision" such that "where statutory provisions are in conflict, no part of a statute should be rendered meaningless but should be reconciled with the rest of the statute." ("Where possible, every word must be given effect and meaning, and no part is to be held meaningless if it can be reconciled with the rest of the statute.").

Several aspects of Indiana Code §§ 26–1–2–719(2) and (3) point to a legislative intent consistent with the independent view. First, as many independent courts have noted, the drafters of the UCC inserted distinct legal standards into each provision. A limited remedy will be struck when it fails of its essential purpose; an exclusion of consequential damages fails when it is unconscionable. Moreover, these subsections are distinct in who applies the standards they set out. Whether a limited remedy fails of its essential purpose is an issue of fact that a jury may determine. Conversely, an exclusion of consequential damages stands unless it is unconscionable, and unconscionability is determined by a court as a matter of law. These facial distinctions between §§ 2–719(2) and (3) suggest a legislative intent that the provisions should function independently of one another.[1]

Second, the independent view is consistent with the principle of statutory interpretation that "where possible, we interpret a statute such that every word receives effect and meaning and no part is rendered 'meaningless if it can be reconciled with the rest of the statute.'" The dependent view renders § 2–719(3) inoperative by deleting an exclusion of consequential damages without any analysis of its unconscionability. On the other hand, the independent view allows both provisions to operate: § 2–719(2) will strike a failed limited remedy, allowing the buyer to claim damages, but not consequential damages if a valid clause excludes them under § 2–719(3). This construction harmon-

---

1. The two sections also aim at distinct contractual functions: A contract may well contain no limitation on breach of warranty damages but specifically exclude consequential damages. Conversely, it is quite conceivable that some limitation might be placed on a breach of warranty award, but consequential damages would expressly be permitted. The limited remedy of repair and consequential damages exclusion are two discrete ways of attempting to limit recovery for breach of warranty. The Code, moreover, tests each by a different standard.... We therefore see no reason to hold, as a general proposition, that the failure of the limited remedy provided in the contract, without more, invalidates a wholly distinct term in the agreement excluding consequential damages. The two are not mutually exclusive. Chatlos Systems v. National Cash Register Corp., 635 F.2d 1081, 1086 (3d Cir. 1980).

izes the language in § 2–719(2) that "remedy may be had as provided in IC 26–1" with the unconscionability test imposed by § 2–719(3). The "remedy" clause in § 2–719(2), which is crucial to the dependent argument, must be taken in its fullest sense. On its face, the phrase refers to all of the UCC, not merely its remedy provisions. Therefore "remedy may be had" under subsection (2) only to the extent that it is not limited by subsection (3), which is part of "IC 26–1."

Third, the UCC instructs us to construe its provisions with three specific legislative purposes in mind, all of which comport with the independent view: (1) IC 26–1 shall be liberally construed and applied to promote its underlying purposes and policies (2) Underlying purposes and policies of IC 26–1 are: (a) to simplify, clarify, and modernize the law governing commercial transactions; (b) to permit the continued expansion of commercial practices through custom, usage, and agreement of the parties; (c) to make uniform the law among the various jurisdictions. The independent view serves all of the enumerated purposes. The independent view supplies simplicity and clarity by allowing a clearly expressed agreement to control a transaction. The independent view is also the modern trend. The independent view aids sound commercial practice by allowing the parties to anticipate clearly the results of their transaction, while the dependent view retains the specter of unknown damages for the seller despite the parties' explicit understanding to the contrary. The fact that courts are divided on this issue indicates that precise uniformity is impossible. However, as we have noted, the modern trend is towards the independent view.

Finally, the legislature's intent to follow the independent view is also supported by the UCC's general policy favoring the parties' freedom of contract. The UCC tells us that one of its paramount concerns is enabling contracting parties to control their own relationships. Ind. Code § 26–1–1–102(3) (1993) ("The effect of provisions of IC 26–1 may be varied by agreement, except as otherwise provided in IC 26–1 . . . ."); Id. cmt. 2 ("Subsection (3) states affirmatively at the outset that freedom of contract is a principle of the [UCC]. . . ."). Official Comment One to Indiana Code § 26–1–2–719 states that "under this section parties are left free to shape their remedies to their particular requirements and reasonable agreements limiting or modifying remedies are to be given effect." However, the dependent view ignores the intent of the parties and allows a buyer to recover consequential damages despite an explicit contract term excluding them. The dependent courts essentially presume that the parties intended the exclusion of consequential damages to depend on the limited remedy. On the other hand, the independent view refuses to override categorically an exclusion of consequential damages and will give effect to the terms of the contract. Indeed, consistent with the principle of freedom of contract, the independent view allows the parties to agree to a dependent arrangement.

This freedom to set contract terms is especially important in the context of a commercial transaction. Sophisticated commercial actors should be free to allocate risks as they see fit, and courts should not interfere simply because such risks have materialized. This is the view shared by Professors White and Summers:

> In general we favor the [independent] line of cases. Those cases seem most true to the Code's general notion that the parties should be free to contract as they please. When the state intervenes to allocate the risk of consequential loss, we think it more likely that the loss will fall on the party who cannot avoid it at the lowest cost. This is particularly true when a knowledgeable buyer is using an expensive machine in a business setting. It is the buyer who operates the machine, adjusts it, and understands the consequences of its failure. Sometimes flaws in such machines are inherent and attributable to the seller's faulty design or manufacture. But the fault may also lie in buyer neglect, in inadequate training and supervision of the operators or even in intentional use in ways forbidden by the seller. Believing the parties to know their own interests best, we would leave the risk allocation to the parties.

White & Summers, Uniform Commercial Code § 12–10, at 605 (3rd ed. 1988).

Phelps attempts to escape this conclusion by arguing that the furnace sales were not a sophisticated commercial transaction worthy of such deference. Phelps notes that the warranties were simply found inside of the furnace box and were not the product of detailed negations. Phelps's argument here may prove too much, i.e., that only the ultimate customer, and not Phelps at all, was to benefit from the warranty. If Phelps is a beneficiary of the warranty (as we have noted both parties appear to assume), Phelps cannot escape the conclusion that these goods were relatively sophisticated and flowed between businesses entities. This context is far different than those confronted in the many dependent cases that focus on losses suffered by consumers at the hands of large commercial entities.

The Court of Appeals applied the independent view, but found a genuine issue of material fact as to whether "the cumulative effect of Rheem's actions was commercially reasonable." The court pointed to no statutory authority that requires these exclusions or limitations to be "commercially reasonable," nor did it define this term. The court did make some passing references to Official Comment One to § 2–719, which assures a buyer an "adequate" remedy in the face of a breach of warranty. This comment, however, makes no reference to commercial reasonableness. Indeed, the court stated frankly that its primary concern was with the "fairness of the outcome" and reaching an "equitable result." In light of our conclusion that the legislature intended the independent view to apply to these circumstances, we are constrained to reject the commercial reasonableness test applied by the Court of Appeals and to reverse the trial court's denial of summary judgment on Phelps's claims for incidental and consequential damages.

Rheem next argues that the trial court erred by denying summary judgment on Phelps's claims for labor expenses incurred in fixing its customers' furnaces. The record shows that Phelps lost nearly $100,000 by servicing Rheem furnaces under a service labor warranty that Phelps gave to its customers. Rheem argues that a "service labor exclusion" found in the express warranty prevents Phelps from claiming damages in this form: "This Warranty does not cover any labor expenses for service, nor for removing or reinstalling parts. All such expenses are your responsibility unless a service labor agreement exists between you and your contractor." Phelps counters by arguing that this remedy clause failed of its essential purpose and therefore Phelps could claim all UCC damages. [The UCC applies because the predominant thrust of the contract was the sale of goods.]

The first step in determining whether a limited remedy failed of its essential purpose is to parse out exactly what purpose the remedy was to serve. [B]oth the terms of the warranty and the record illuminate the remedy's purpose. The limitation is addressed to the end-user, warning them that they must look to the contractor for repairs: "All such expenses are your responsibility unless a service labor agreement exists between you and your contractor." Further, a Rheem officer testified that the "custom, practice and standard method of dealing in the gas furnace industry is that the manufacturer's warranty is for parts only and excludes reimbursement for labor expenses for service or for removing or installing parts, consequential and incidental damages." Similarly, the president of Phelps testified that "standard procedure throughout the industry was that a dealer would supply a one-year warranty for labor. And then the parts, depending on the manufacture[r] . . . usually had a one-year warranty. . . ." In addition, Phelps at one time marketed extended service warranties as part of its business.

These facts demonstrate that the limited remedy was intended to maintain a reasonable division of responsibilities between the manufacturer and the contractor when customers experienced problems. Rheem's parts-only warranty worked in tandem with Phelps's labor warranties to let customers know that they had to seek repair service from the local contractor, not the distant manufacturer. Phelps benefited from this relationship by marketing extended warranties on top of its one-year service warranty. If the warranty held Rheem liable for repairs, Rheem would naturally skip over Phelps and sell extended service warranties directly to the customer. For its part, the limited remedy gave Rheem the reassurance that it would not be liable for repairs on its furnaces at distant locations around the country. With this limitation in place, customers could rely on local repair service, Phelps could market extended warranties, and Rheem could be sure it would not be obligated to make repairs. Thus the apparent purpose of this limited remedy was to facilitate the manufacturer/contractor distinction for the benefit of all parties.

Commentators have suggested that § 2–719, as it relates to failure of essential purpose, is not concerned with arrangements which were oppressive at the inception which is a question of unconscionability, but with the application of an agreement to "novel circumstances not contemplated by the parties." White & Summers, § 10–12. In addition, they have suggested that this provision should be triggered when the remedy fails of its essential purpose, not the essential purpose of the UCC, contract law, or of equity. Id. One author suggests that the method used to decide whether a particular limitation fails of its essential purpose is to identify the purpose underlying the provision and determine whether application of the remedy in the particular circumstances will further that purpose. If not, then, and only then, is there a failure of essential purpose. Jonathan A. Eddy, *On The "Essential" Purposes of Limited Remedies: The Metaphysics of UCC § 2–719(2)*, 65 Cal. L. Rev. 28, 36–40 (1978).

Using this analysis, we hold that the remedy served its purpose. Rheem, as the manufacturer, had technical expertise in the functioning of its product. It was reasonable for Phelps to expect Rheem to use this expertise to supply replacement parts and technical guidance in the event of malfunctions. Phelps, as the contractor, had the manpower and facilities to implement these fixes in the field. It was reasonable for Rheem to expect Phelps to use these tools to go into local homes and offices to fix the furnaces. With the extended warranties, Phelps could even profit through this process. By supplying technical guidance and replacement parts, Rheem's limited remedy lived up to the purpose it was designed to serve.

Phelps main argument as to the failure of essential purpose is that the furnaces experienced problems for roughly four years. However, the purpose of the limited remedy was not to guarantee that every furnace would be easily fixed, but to guarantee that the most logical party would be charged with making the repairs. Phelps was that party, and under this limitation it accepted the risk that repairs would be difficult and labor intensive. In *Martin Rispens*, we stated that a limited remedy fails only in the face of " 'novel circumstances not contemplated by the parties.' " 621 N.E.2d at 1085. As Comment One to Indiana Code § 26–1–2–719 puts it, a limited remedy fails when its application "operates to deprive either party of the substantial value of the bargain." Thus a limited remedy fails of its essential purpose when an unexpected circumstance arises and neither party accepted the risk that such circumstance would occur. See Osgood v. Medical, Inc., 415 N.W.2d 896, 902 (Minn.App.1987) ("This case involves the allocation of risks between two merchant manufacturers. That is exactly the intended effect of the Special Terms. We will not apply [2–719(2)] to overturn that result when the case involves the allocation of risk between two merchant manufacturers."); V.M. Corp. v. Bernard Distributing Co., 447 F.2d 864, 865 (7th Cir.1971) ("§ 2–719 was intended to encourage and facilitate consensual allocations of risk associated with the sale of goods. This is particularly true where commercial, rather than consumer sales are involved. Even where the defects of the goods cause substantial difficulties to those involved in wholesale and resale distribution, § 2–719(2) need not automatically require disregard of the particular limitation. . . .").

Even if we were to find that this remedy failed of its essential purpose, Phelps would not be entitled to the damages it seeks under the warranty. The parties characterize these service repair costs as either consequential damages or direct damages. In either event, Phelps is not entitled to recovery under the warranty and summary judgment should be entered.

The parties characterize the service labor as a form of consequential damage because Rheem should have foreseen that its failure to provide functioning furnaces would have caused Rheem to make multiple repairs under its service warranty. See Ind. Code § 26–1–2–715 (1993). To the extent these repair costs were consequential damages, they are excluded by Rheem's warranty as [previously] discussed.

The parties also characterize the repair costs as a form of direct damages. A buyer's remedy for breach of warranty is typically the difference between the goods as warranted and the goods as accepted. See Ind. Code § 26–1–2–714(2) (1993). However, the cost of repair may serve as a proxy for direct damages. See. e.g., Jones v. Abriani, 169 Ind. App. 556, 350 N.E.2d 635, 646 (1976) ("In this case, one reasonable way of measuring the difference in the value of the goods between what was actually delivered (a defective mobile home) and what was warranted (a mobile home with the defects repaired) is the cost of repairing the defects."), Schroeder v. Barth, Inc., 969 F.2d 421, 424 (7th Cir.1992) (applying Indiana law). Phelps argues that it should be able to recover the cost of repairing the furnaces in the event that the limited remedy failed of its essential purpose. Typically, a buyer claiming repair damages is suing its immediate seller. Recovering the repair cost replicates the typical warranty damages—value of goods as warranted minus value of goods as delivered—by awarding the amount spent to put the goods in the warranted condition. This measure of damages reflects the fact that a properly functioning market would deduct from the price of the item the cost of repairs a purchaser would have to make. The repair costs that Phelps seeks to recoup serve no such purpose because Phelps is not in possession of the goods.

We conclude by noting that, while Phelps, as an intermediate seller, is not entitled to these direct warranty damages, it may have a claim sounding in indemnity or subrogation for damages suffered by those with which it shared privity. See. e.g., Black v. Don Schmid Motor, Inc., 232 Kan. 458, 657 P.2d 517, 529 (Kan. 1983) ("A right of indemnity exists where a party is compelled to pay damages that rightfully should have been paid by another party. Thus, a seller that is liable for damages to a purchaser of defective goods may seek indemnity from the manufacturer where the damages were the proximate result of the manufacturer's breach of warranty."). Whether or not Phelps can recover on an indemnity theory is an issue to be decided on remand.

Problem 41

(a) The Midwest Power Company (M) contracted to have Westinghouse Corporation (W) deliver and install a new generator for a price of $30 million. Page four of the W contract form that the parties signed contained the following clauses:

14. Seller warrants this equipment against any defects in material or workmanship for a period of six months from the date the equipment is first installed and operating. This is the sole and exclusive warranty under this contract and is in lieu of any other warranty, express or implied, INCLUDING BUT NOT LIMITED TO THE IMPLIED WARRANTY OF MERCHANTABILITY.

15. In the event of a breach by seller of the sole and exclusive warranty under this contract, seller will repair or replace any defective part at no cost to Buyer. Such repair or replacement shall be the buyer's sole and exclusive remedy for breach of the warranty. Under no circumstances shall seller be liable, in contract, warranty or tort, for any other loss or damage of whatsoever kind or nature, INCLUDING BUT NOT LIMITED TO CONSEQUENTIAL DAMAGES.

W installed the generator, which operated perfectly for one month but then broke down. Upon receiving notice of the problem, W immediately sent a crew to repair the generator. This crew was unsuccessful and W sent its premier repair group. After the crew examined the equipment and analyzed tests performed to that point, its leader was heard to say, "I've never seen one like this before." The crew then disassembled the entire generator and rebuilt much of it. Five months after it broke down the generator had been totally repaired and was again operational. W notified M that all the repair work was covered under the warranty. M responded with a letter thanking W for its splendid effort, but adding: "Unfortunately, during the five months the generator was down we had to purchase substitute power which cost our company an extra $342,000. Please remit that amount in full satisfaction of our claim against you." W has refused to pay. M seeks your advice.

(b) Consider whether your advice in (a) would change if the following language were added at the end of clause 15: "In the event this sole and exclusive remedy fails of its essential purpose, the parties hereby agree and understand that seller shall still not be responsible for any consequential damages."

2. Limited Remedies Under UCC Article 2A, the CISG, and UCITA

Problem 41A

(a) Suppose that in Problem 41 M had leased rather than purchased the generator from W. How would that affect your analysis of (a) or (b)? See 2A–503.

(b) Suppose that the transaction in Problem 41 had been an international sale governed by the CISG. How would that affect your analysis of (a) or (b)? Consider CISG Art. 6.

Note on Limitation of Remedies under UCITA

UCITA § 803, which governs "contractual modification of remedy" in computer information transactions, largely replicates the approach and language of UCC 2–719. Thus UCITA § 803(a) permits parties to agree on remedies in addition to or in substitution for those provided by UCITA,[2] UCITA § 803(b) provides a failure of essential purpose limitation on exclusive agreed remedies, and UCITA § 803(d) permits the parties to limit or exclude liability for incidental and consequential damages. The one innovation is UCITA § 803(c), which provides:

> Failure or unconscionability of an agreed exclusive or limited remedy makes a term disclaiming or limiting consequential or incidental damages unenforceable unless the agreement expressly makes the disclaimer or limitation independent of the agreed remedy.

How would this provision impact the analysis if it applied in a situation like Problem 41(a)? Problem 41(b)?

S. CONTRACT AND TORT: PRODUCTS LIABILITY—PRIVITY

Origins. Products liability law is a curious admixture of tort and contract law with a history that defies uniformity. Tort law focuses on unreasonable risks that prove to be the proximate cause of injury to parties within the orbit of risk. Contract law requires an agreement of the parties, a more or less voluntary relationship in which the parties induce expectations of future performance. If a contract is breached, contract law seeks to place the aggrieved party in the position she would have been in had the contract been performed, thereby fulfilling her reasonable expectations (UCC 1–305). If a wrongful act causes injury, tort law seeks to restore the aggrieved party to the position he occupied as if no tort had occurred.

Injury caused by a defective product may induce a tort action alleging negligence by the seller. If, however, the seller was not the manufacturer but a distributor or retailer who resold the defective product to the buyer, may the buyer succeed in a negligence action against the manufacturer although the buyer had no contractual relationship with the manufacturer? In the famous case of *Winterbottom v. Wright*, 10 M. & W. 109, 152 Eng. Rep. 402 (1842), the driver of a stage coach was injured when it broke down and upset. The driver brought an action against a party who had contracted with the postmaster general to keep the coach in good repair to assure mail delivery. The court denied recovery on the footing that there was no ***privity of contract*** between the parties, i.e., the driver was not a party to any contract with the defendant. The court felt compelled to deny the recovery to the driver on the footing that otherwise any passenger or even stranger injured by the defective coach could state an actionable claim.

---

2. As is also the case under UCC 2–719(1)(b), UCITA provides that agreed remedies are presumed to be optional un-less there is express agreement that they are to be exclusive. See UCITA § 803(a)(2).

Exceptions to such holdings involving "inherently dangerous products" were subsequently determined on a case-by-case basis until "the quietest of revolutionary manifestos"[1] appeared in the famous opinion by Judge Benjamin Nathan Cardozo for the New York Court of Appeals in *MacPherson v. Buick Motor Company*, 217 N.Y. 382, 111 N.E. 1050 (1916). When the new automobile he had purchase from a retail dealer collapsed due to a defect in a wheel, McPherson sued the manufacturer instead of the dealer with whom he had contracted. The court did not attempt to create another exception to the *privity* requirement by labeling an automobile an inherently defective product (like an exploding coffee urn, defective scaffolding, or an ingested toxic substance, all of which had been recognized as falling into exceptions from the privity requirement under the rubric of "inherently dangerous products"). Instead, Cardozo unearthed the underlying principle by insisting upon "a rule which imposes upon A, who has contracted with B, a duty to C and D and others according as he knows or does not know that the subject-matter of the contract is intended for their use." 217 N.Y. at 393, 111 N.E. at 1054.

Warranty Theory—"Privity." While aggrieved parties could now sue negligent manufacturers with whom they had not contracted, proving that a manufacturer was negligent in the production of a product would often present insuperable obstacles. The promising alternative theory was an action for breach of warranty, which only required proof that the unmerchantable product was the proximate cause of the injury regardless of how the defect occurred, if the product left the manufacturer's control in defective condition. While proof of negligence could be avoided under this theory, breach of warranty is a contract action, and *privity of contract* reappeared to preclude actions against remote parties such as the manufacturer (as opposed to the dealer with whom the buyer had contracted).

This privity issue is often described as one of *vertical privity*, since the buyer is attempting to bring an action against a remote party who is "higher" (upstream) in the chain of distribution. Vertical privity deals with the question, **who can be sued?** There is another challenge that is often discussed under the label of *horizontal privity*. Buyers often purchase goods that are used by others. If, for example, a parent or spouse purchases food or other products that prove to be unmerchantable and cause injury to a member of the household other than the immediate buyer of the product, a breach of warranty claim against the seller could be met with the defense that such a plaintiff is not a party to *any* contract and, therefore, there is no *privity of contract* between the injured plaintiff and the seller defendant. Similarly, an employer may purchase equipment that is used by employees who may be injured if the equipment is unmerchantable. These employees are on the same horizontal line as the buyer. How can they be brought into *privity* with the

---

1. Richard A. Posner, CARDOZO: A STUDY IN REPUTATION 109 (1990).

seller-defendant? Horizontal privity deals with the question, **who can sue?**

Another contract law concept has become involved in resolving the privity issues arising in products liability actions based on warranty theory. Contract law allows two parties to form a contract that is intended to benefit a third party who would otherwise not be in *privity*. Such *third party beneficiaries* are allowed to enforce the contract in order to effectuate the intention of the immediate parties to the contract. Indeed, whenever the sole or main purpose of the promisee in such a contract is to benefit the third party, such an intended beneficiary becomes a "party" to the contract, i.e., *privity* has been extended to that third party whose rights are derivative. He "stands in the shoes" of the buyer who made the contract. Article 2 adopted the third party beneficiary concept as the basis for its provision dealing with privity issues in products liability actions–2–318. Consider the following case.

UCC 2–318 "THIRD PARTY BENEFICIARIES"

S & R ASSOCS. v. SHELL OIL CO.

Delaware Superior Court, 1998.
725 A.2d 431.

QUILLEN, J. [The plumbing in the plaintiff's apartment complex had been constructed with polybutylene pipe. The raw material for the pipe had been manufactured by the defendant, who urged its application in plumbing. When the pipes allegedly failed and caused damage to the complex, the plaintiff, a limited partnership sought to recover against the defendant even though it had not purchased the pipe from the defendant. The court considered the proper construction of UCC 2–318.]

Even without the statute of limitations issue, S & R, as a limited partnership, lacks standing to bring a warranty claim under 6 *Del. C.* § 2–318.[1] The plain language of the statute states that "a seller's warranty, whether express or implied, extends to any *natural person who* may reasonably be expected to use, consume or be affected by the goods...." The determination of exactly who is a "natural person" begins with an analysis of the statute and its history.

Prior to the adoption of the Uniform Commercial Code ("Code"), an injured party was required to establish privity with the defendant to recover under a breach of warranty claim. This was often difficult to accomplish when the ultimate user of a defective product was not the direct purchaser. To counter the harsh result of this rule, the legislature enacted Section 2–318, abolishing the privity requirement and granting standing to those likely to be injured by defective products. When the

---

1. Since S & R lacks direct privity with Shell, they must seek standing as a third party beneficiary under 6 Del. C. § 2–318. S & R lacks direct privity because Shell only manufactured the resin used in the production of polybutylene pipes; it did not manufacture or sell the final product.

Code was amended by the American Law Institute in 1966, Section 2–318 was changed to offer three distinct alternatives. The three alternatives were as follows:

> Alternative A. A seller's warranty whether express or implied extends to *any natural person* who is in the family or household of his buyer or who is a guest in his home if it is reasonable to expect that such person may use, consume or be affected by the goods and who is injured in person by breach of the warranty. A seller may not exclude or limit the operation of this section.

> Alternative B. A seller's warranty whether express or implied extends to *any natural person* who may reasonably be expected to use, consume or be affected by the goods and who is injured in person by breach of the warranty. A seller may not exclude or limit the operation of this section.

> Alternative C. A seller's warranty whether express or implied extends to *any person* who may reasonably be expected to use, consume or be affected by the goods and who is injured by breach of the warranty. A seller may not exclude or limit the operation of this section with respect to injury to the person of an individual to whom the warranty extends.

> As amended 1966.

Delaware adopted Alternative B, in a somewhat modified form, by omitting the words "in person" before the words "by breach." The American Law Institute's Official Comment to Section 2–318 states:

> [Alternative A] expressly includes as beneficiaries within its provisions the family, household, and guests of the purchaser.... [Alternative B] is designed for states where the case law has already developed further and for those that desire to expand the class of beneficiaries. [Alternative C] goes further, following the trend of modern decisions as indicated by Restatement of Torts 2d § 402A (Tentative Draft No. 10, 1965) in extending the rule beyond injuries to *the person.* It appears that when the legislature decided on a modified Alternative B, as opposed to Alternative C, the legislature expressed an intention to exclude legal entities from protection. Alternative C, the most liberal of the alternatives, applies to all "persons," while Alternatives A and B extend only to "natural persons."

Additionally, the Official Comment states that only Alternative C would extend protection beyond injuries to "the person." It would appear that our legislature did extend recovery to "natural persons" beyond injuries to the person and, to that extent, adopted Alternative C.

The case law also provides additional guidance on the subject. In *Dover Downs, Inc. v. Koppers Co. Inc.,* Del. Super., this Court stated that absent privity, § 2–318 does not extend warranty protection to corporations. Further evidence of the distinction between "persons" and "natural persons" is found in various Delaware cases and legal reference material. In talking about a corporation's need to be represented by counsel, the Supreme Court has stated that "a corporation, though a legally recognized entity, is regarded as an artificial or fictional entity, and not a natural person."

To hold that Section 2–318 applies to legal entities such as corporations and limited partnerships would nullify the legislature's decision in choosing Alternative B over Alternative C on this very point. While it may be desirable to extend warranty protection beyond natural persons, this change in policy should be made by the Legislature rather than the Court. Accordingly, S & R, being a limited partnership, lacks standing to bring a claim under § 2–318 and Shell's Motion for Summary Judgment on counts one through three must be granted.

Notes

The majority of states have enacted Alternative A of 2–318, the most conservative alternative. Beyond the "natural person" limitation, Alternative A relaxes privity requirements only for those who suffer personal injury as contrasted with property damage. Its further limitation to members of the buyer's family or household or a guest in the buyer's home who may be expected to use, consume or be affected by the goods, would exclude employees in a manufacturing plant injured by defects in machines purchased by the employer or other third parties. Comment 3 to this section, however, insists that it does not seek to freeze the categories of potential third party beneficiaries, i. e., it "is not intended to enlarge or restrict the developing case law on whether the seller's warranties, given to his buyer who resells, extend to other persons in the distributive chain."

A court could accept that invitation and enlarge the category of those in *horizontal* privity to include employees or even bystanders, i. e., to simply eliminate *horizontal* privity requirements. None of the 2–318 alternatives expressly address *vertical* privity, i.e., a party standing in the shoes of the buyer bringing an action against the remote manufacturer. Based on comment 3 to 2–318, however, a court might eliminate vertical as well as horizontal privity requirements. For example, although Alternative A was enacted in Pennsylvania, through judicial extension[2] parties such as employees and, theoretically, even bystanders can bring actions as "third party beneficiaries" of sellers' warranties, in effect, making Pennsylvania an Alternative B jurisdiction because it protects any natural person who may be affected by the goods. Other jurisdictions, however, strictly construe the limitations of their version of 2–318. See, e. g., Delgatti v. Cosmos, 1997 WL 193195 (Conn.Super.1997). If a court would allow recovery for injury to property as well as personal injury, the jurisdiction would, in effect, be an Alternative C jurisdiction, at least with respect to the type of injury contemplated under 2–318. If the Delaware court in the principal case had extended protection to artificial as well as natural persons, it would have judicially converted Alternative B to Alternative C since its Alternative B had already been modified to allow recovery for property damage. It is, therefore,

2. See, e.g., Kassab v. Central Soya, 432 Pa. 217, 246 A.2d 848 (1968) and Salvador v. Atlantic Steel Boiler Co., 457 Pa. 24, 319 A.2d 903 (1974).

important to consider not only the statutory language of 2–318 in a given jurisdiction, but possible judicial extension of that language.

Beyond the three alternatives and the possibility of judicial extensions of 2–318, other jurisdictions have altered their versions of 2–318. Massachusetts amended its 2–318 in 1971 to convert it to an "anti-privity" statute, legislatively removing the privity barrier, although Massachusetts courts have more recently held that privity remains necessary in actions seeking recovery for economic loss as contrasted with personal injury or property damage. Another example of an anti-privity version of 2–318 was the basis for the dispute in Beard Plumbing & Heating, Inc. v. Thompson Plastics, Inc., 152 F.3d 313 (4th Cir.1998), involving an action to recover consequential damages. The court recognized Virginia's anti-privity version of 2–318, but certified two questions to the Supreme Court of Virginia. The first question was whether the UCC definition of "consequential damages" in 2–715(2) requires privity to recover consequential damages? The Virginia Supreme Court answered yes, because the language in 2–715(2)(a) ("at the time of contracting") assumes that there is a contract between the parties, i.e., that the parties are in privity. The second certified question asked, as between the Virginia version of 2–318, which eliminates privity requirements, and 2–715(2), which (the Virginia Supreme Court found) contemplates parties in privity, which provision prevails? The Virginia Court held that 2–715(2) takes precedence because its requirement of a contract for the recovery of consequential damages is more specific than 2–318. A more recent Virginia case provides further elaboration on this issue, as well as an interesting construction of the definition of "goods."

STONEY v. FRANKLIN

Virginia Circuit Court, 2001.
44 UCC Rep Serv 2d 1211, 2001 WL 683963.

KELSEY, J. The plaintiffs, Archie and Nancy Stoney, hired a contractor to build a house for them. Claiming that the contractor used defective building materials, the plaintiffs seek to impose liability on the manufacturers and assemblers of these building materials. The plaintiffs assert claims against Dryvit Systems, Inc. (the manufacturer of the exterior insulation finish systems (EIFS)), MW Manufacturing, Inc. (the manufacturer of the window sashes) and Lowe's Home Centers, Inc., Thomasville Millwork Division (the manufacturer and assembler of the window frames).

The plaintiffs' negligence claims against these parties allege nothing more than disappointed economic expectations. The effect of the failure of the substandard parts to meet the bargained for level of quality was to cause a diminution in the value of the whole, measured by the cost of repair. This is a purely economic loss, for which the law of contracts provides the sole remedy. The Court sustains the demurrers to [the] negligence claims.

The plaintiffs also assert claims against Dryvit, MW, and Lowe's under the Uniform Commercial Code, i.e., that these defendants violated

UCC implied warranties of merchantability and fitness for a particular purpose both in their design and manufacture of their respective building supplies. Each of these claims fail, the defendants argue, because (i) the economic loss rule bars any implied warranty claims just as effectively as it bars negligent design and manufacture causes of action, and (ii) in any event, the UCC does not apply because the contract to build the residence involved a services contract (rather than a sale of goods) and, to make matters worse, the residence constitutes an immovable fixture of realty outside the reach of the UCC.

On the first point, the defendants contend that the economic loss rule cuts off implied warranty claims for the same reason it acts as a bar to the plaintiffs' negligence claims. No Virginia case directly addresses this issue. The Fourth Circuit certified this issue to the Virginia Supreme Court in Beard Plumbing & Heating, Inc. v. Thompson Plastics, Inc., 152 F.3d 313, 319 (4th Cir.1998), with the commentary that "it would be odd if economic losses, which result from the frustration of bargained-for expectations, could not be recovered for breach of warranty, notwithstanding the lack of privity, given the especially broad reach of Virginia's § 8.2–318."

In reply to the certified question in Beard, the Virginia Supreme Court conspicuously avoided any discussion of the reach of the economic loss rule into implied warranty law. Instead, the Virginia Supreme Court confined its analysis to the statutory privity requirement implicit in the UCC's definition of consequential damages. Beard Plumbing & Heating, Inc. v. Thompson Plastics, Inc., 254 Va. 240, 244–45, 491 S.E.2d 731, 733 (1997) (interpreting Va. Code Ann. § 8.2–715(2)(a)). This privity requirement, the Virginia Supreme Court noted, stems entirely from the UCC and was "not a privity requirement imposed by the common law." The observation that the common law would *not* impose a privity requirement in implied warranty claims seeking consequential economic losses undermines the existence of a common law privity requirement generally applicable to all economic loss claims (even those asserting direct damages) in implied warranty cases. In any event, the specific holding in Beard neither endorses nor forbids the application of the economic loss rule to implied warranty claims seeking direct damages. See Directors of Bay Point Condo. Ass'n. Inc. v. RML Corp., 52 Va. Cir. 432, 439 (Norfolk 2000) (Beard "expressly limited its discussion to breach of warranty claims for consequential economic loss damages, stating, 'we assume that the Court of Appeals concluded that the economic loss damages claimed by Beard were consequential damages rather than direct damages'.").

The debate draws us back to first principles. The economic loss rule exists, in large part, to guard "one of the last hilltops on the boundary between tort and contract." Tort law involves public policy concerns over safety, both to persons and property, that carry with them the nonconsensual imposition of duties. A manufacturer may choose to build a product and sell it. But whether the manufacturer agrees to or not, he must use reasonable care or be held responsible if his product injures either persons or property. Tort law imposes duties upon the otherwise unwilling. That is, no consent-of-the-governed concepts apply to tortfeasors. On the other hand, contract law involves an entirely different set of principles. Contract law itself imposes few, if any, duties in the first instance. As a general rule, contractual duties stem only from the consensual dealings of the parties. Based upon the expressed (or, in the case of implied warranties, the presumed) intention of the parties, contract law merely recognizes—rather than imposes—legal duties and permits the parties wide latitude to limit their liability and to disclaim implied warranties when the protected interests are purely economic.

Framed this way, the question is whether UCC implied warranty claims should be characterized as a sub-species of tort or contract for purposes of the economic loss rule. The best answer to this question comes from East River S.S. Corp. v. Transamerica Delaval, 476 U.S. 858, 90 L.Ed. 2d 865, 106 S.Ct. 2295 (1986), a unanimous U.S. Supreme Court decision relied upon by the Virginia Supreme Court. In distinguishing tort law concepts from those with a contractual pedigree, East River S.S. Corp. pointed out that disappointed customer expectations about product value "is precisely the purpose of express and implied warranties" (citing UCC § 2–313 (express warranty), § 2–314 (implied warranty of merchantability), and § 2–315 (warranty of fitness for a particular purpose)). "Contract law, and the *law of warranty in particular,* is well suited to commercial controversies of the sort involved in this case because the parties may set the terms of their own agreements." Unlike most tort duties, a "manufacturer can restrict its liability, within limits, by disclaiming warranties or limiting remedies."

These characteristics sufficiently distinguish UCC implied warranty claims from pure tort claims—when the remedy sought is purely economic—making it both unnecessary and unwise to treat them alike. As a result, the extent of liability and the remedies available in a warranty action are often quite different from the remedies available in tort. By precluding recovery of economic losses in actions for tort, the economic loss rule preserves the balance of rights and remedies established by warranty law. The economic loss rule barring negligence claims, therefore, does not apply to the plaintiffs' claims for breach of implied warranty of merchantability and fitness for a particular purpose.

The defendants also argue that, as a matter of statutory construction (rather than the application of the common law economic loss rule), no buyer of goods can ever seek direct damages from an upstream supplier. That result cannot be reconciled with the breadth of Virginia's anti-privity statute. The UCC offered three versions of anti-privity statutes to accompany Article 2's warranty provisions. Virginia adopted a paraphrase of Alternative C, the most expansive version. Under Va. Code Ann. § 8.2–318, lack of privity cannot be asserted as a bar to *"any action* brought against the manufacturer or seller of goods to *recover damages* for breach of warranty, express or implied, or for negligence, although the plaintiff did not purchase the goods from the defendant, if the plaintiff was a person whom the manufacturer or seller might reasonably have expected to use, consume, or be affected by the goods. . . ." (emphasis added). A claim for direct damages fits within the scope of "any action" to "recover damages" for breach of an implied warranty.

Unlike the built-in privity requirement of consequential damages, Beard Plumbing & Heating, Inc., 254 Va. at 244–45, no similar privity requirement can be interpolated into the statutory definition of direct damages. See Directors of Bay Point Condo. Ass'n. Inc., 52 Va. Cir. at 440 ("As opposed to the statute governing consequential damages considered by the Court in Beard, the UCC's provision governing the measure of direct damages in a breach of warranty claim does not condition the award of damages on the existence of a contract."). Indeed, if one were in fact found by the courts, the legislature's inclusion of implied warranties in the anti-privity statute would be essentially repealed by the judiciary.

Those jurisdictions that have retained a privity requirement for direct economic losses do not have the broad anti-privity statute adopted in Virginia. The Illinois Supreme Court, for example, held that privity must be established given its limited anti-privity statute (Alternative A), Szajna v. General Motors Corp., 115 Ill. 2d 294, 303, 503 N.E.2d 760, 762, 104 Ill. Dec. 898 (1986), but acknowledged that the broadest version of the anti-privity statute (Alternative C) arguably "eliminates any vertical-privity requirement." Id., 115 Ill. 2d at 308; see generally William L. Stallworth, An Analysis of Warranty Claims Instituted by Non–Privity Plaintiffs in Jurisdictions That Have Adopted Uniform Commercial Code Section 2–318 (Alternatives B & C), 27 Akron L. Rev. 197, 203 (1993) (Nonprivity plaintiffs "who have sustained only property damage or economic loss may have standing to sue under Alternative C."). The Virginia anti-privity statute, therefore, defeats the defendants' argument that direct economic damages can never be recovered in the absence of privity.

Even so, the defendants also contest the application of any UCC theory of recovery against them. The UCC, they correctly point out, applies only to transactions involving the "sale of goods," § 8.2–102 ("this title applies to transactions in goods"). If a contract involves both goods and services, it qualifies as a UCC contract only if its "predominant thrust" is the purchase of goods "with labor incidentally involved." Palmetto Linen Service v. U.N.X., Inc., 205 F.3d 126, 129 (4th Cir.2000). According to the Fourth Circuit, the seminal case applying this standard explains: The test for inclusion or exclusion is not whether they are mixed but, granting that they are mixed, whether their predominant factor, their thrust, their purpose, reasonably stated, is the rendition of service, with goods incidentally involved (e.g., contract with artist for painting) or is a transaction of sale, with labor incidentally involved (e.g., installation of a water heater in a bathroom). Princess Cruises, Inc. v. General Elec. Co., 143 F.3d 828, 833 (4th Cir.1998) (quoting Bonebrake v. Cox, 499 F.2d 951, 960 (8th Cir.1974)).

In this case, the plaintiffs contracted for the construction of a house. As the defendants correctly contend, the plaintiffs did not purchase stocks of two-by-fours, roof trestles, electrical conduit, window units, and plywood floor boards with the ancillary benefit of having these materials fashioned into a residential building. The contract called for a turn-key delivery of the house after a walk-through inspection. Nothing in the allegations of the motion for judgment or its exhibits suggests the plaintiffs contracted for specific personal property outside the scope of the "Contract for Construction." It is for this reason that "most courts find construction contracts to be primarily for services." 1 James J. White & Robert S. Summers, Uniform Commercial Code § 9–2, at 482 (4th ed. 1995).

For similar reasons, the defendants assert that the UCC also does not apply to sales of immovable improvements to real estate. The term "goods" includes things "which are movable at the time of identification to the contract for sale" and can include fixtures to realty if they are intended "to be severed from realty." Va. Code Ann. § 8.2–105(1). The building supplies complained about in the motion for judgment were all incorporated into the residential building. They did not *at that time* involve movable goods, or for that matter, identifiable goods intended later to be severed from the realty. The building itself constitutes an improvement to realty, a fixture qualifying for the status of real property every bit as much as the land itself.

This analysis is certainly right, as far as it goes—but it only goes so far. It proves that the UCC does not apply to the sale of the residence because it constitutes both a services contract and a sale of an improvement to realty. And, for that reason, the plaintiffs cannot sue the builder for breach of any UCC implied warranties. In this case, however, no such claim has been asserted. Instead, the plaintiffs seek to enforce the implied warranties made by the manufacturers and assemblers of the building products. Those transactions clearly involved sales of goods, not contracts for services or real estate. Under Va. Code Ann. § 8.2–105(1), goods exist if they "are movable at the time of identification to the contract of sale." In context, the "contract of sale" identifying the goods refers to the sale involving the seller that made the implied warranty— not simply the party with whom the claimant contracted.

Unless disclaimed, implied warranties accompanying goods extend under Virginia's antiprivity statute to any "person whom the manufacturer or seller might reasonably have expected to use, consume, or be affected by the goods." Va. Code Ann. § 8.2–3 18. Nothing in the UCC's definition of goods addresses, much less trumps, the broad reach of Virginia's antiprivity statute.

It seems an obvious *non sequitur* to say, as the defendants do, that (a) because the plaintiffs cannot sue the builder, then (b) they likewise cannot sue the manufacturers and assemblers of the building materials. The conceptual error becomes even clearer by carrying it to its logical conclusion. Consider the situation where no sale of goods occurs or, for that matter, where no sale of anything occurs (either services or goods), as when a plaintiff borrows a lawn mower from a friend. True, the plaintiff cannot sue the friend under implied warranty law when the mower explodes and causes injury. But that truism has no bearing on whether the plaintiff can sue the manufacturer of the lawn mower. He can, of course, by virtue of being a "person whom the manufacturer or seller might reasonably have expected to use, consume, or be affected by the goods." Va. Code Ann. § 8.2–318. The sole inquiry should be whether the plaintiff fits within the class of persons "whom the manufacturer or seller might reasonably have expected to use, consume, or be affected by the goods." Va. Code Ann. § 8.2–318.

The logical consequences of the defendants' argument go far beyond the circumstances of this case. If a claimant loses his implied warranty claims against upstream defendants because an intervening contract for services took place, then personal injury or death claims (no less than claims for economic losses) would be barred. For example, if a repairman tuned up the boiler and in the process replaced a piece of the equipment (with the predominant thrust of the transaction still being a services contract), no implied warranty claims could be asserted against the part maker if that same part, because of an inherently defective design, caused the boiler to explode and fatally injure the homeowner who hired the repairman. Likewise, under the defendants' argument, a person killed when a defectively manufactured elevator drops to the bottom of the shaft would have no implied warranty claims against the elevator manufacturer if, as will almost always be the case, the elevator was installed in the building during its construction. These examples cannot be dismissed as an exaggerated parade of horribles. They demonstrate how the position advocated by the defendants would unsettle settled principles of product liability law.

The Court holds that the UCC applies to the implied warranty claims by the plaintiffs against Dryvit, MW, and Lowe's.

Note

Contract (Warranty) or Tort Choices. When Karl Llewellyn and his colleagues were developing what was to become Article 2 of the UCC, Llewellyn had precociously included a products liability structure. That effort preceded the later products liability development of the Restatement (Second) of Torts § 402A by two decades. Criticism of what appeared to be a radical products liability thrust in a "sales" law statute, however, led to its removal from the sales article. Article 2, however, continued to recognize a recovery by "third party beneficiaries" for personal injury in 2–318; indeed, under Alternative C to 2–318, the beneficiary's recovery could encompass property damage. The Article 2 section defining consequential damages, furthermore, included "injury to person or property proximately resulting from any breach of warranty" (2–715(2)(b)). Thus, the enacted UCC allowed for what appeared to be "tort" actions under the caption "breach of warranty."

When courts throughout the country adopted Section 402A of the Restatement (Second) of Torts, and thus accepted the theory that a manufacturer should be held strictly liable in tort for defects in products that caused injury, products liability plaintiffs found themselves with an abundance or riches. They could bring actions under either a tort or contract (warranty) theory. Judicial reconciliation of the tort/contract dichotomy has, however, been anything but uniform or clear.

(a) Injury to Person or Property vs. "Economic Loss." As the *Stoney* case indicates, one of the celebrated products liability issues relates to the kind of injury the claimant has suffered. Since the UCC expressly allows recovery for personal injuries caused by defective products, courts have felt compelled to permit redress for such injuries under either a warranty or a tort theory. Suppose, however, the aggrieved party's injury is contractual in nature—i.e., the defective product causes an *economic loss* arising out defeated expectations, rather than a personal injury or injury to property that is normally associated with a tort. Courts confronted with such situations had to decide whether an action for "contract" injuries would lie under a tort products liability theory. In particular, if the only injury were to the product itself, could the aggrieved party bring a tort action, thereby escaping the limitations of contract theories (such as privity requirements)?

Where installed carpeting was found to be defective, the New Jersey Supreme Court allowed recovery on a tort products liability theory in *Santor v. A & M Karagheusian, Inc.*, 44 N.J. 52, 207 A.2d 305 (1965). The court's opinion was authored by Justice Francis, who had earlier written the landmark opinion in *Henningsen v. Bloomfield Motors, Inc.*, 32 N.J. 358, 161 A.2d 69 (1960), celebrated not only for its unconscionability analysis, but also for its rejection of vertical privity requirements—the decision allowed a buyer and his wife to bring an action directly against the manufacturer (as opposed to the direct seller) of a defective automobile that caused personal injury. However, a distinguished jurist from California, Justice Roger Traynor, disagreed with *Santor*. In Seely v. White Motor Co., 63 Cal.2d 9, 45 Cal.Rptr. 17, 403 P.2d 145 (1965), Justice Traynor insisted on preserving a proper role for warranty law by refusing to allow recovery in tort for purely economic injury to the defective product itself.

Just over two decades later, the United States Supreme Court, exercising its admiralty jurisdiction, confronted the same issue in *East River Steamship Corp. v. Transamerica Delaval, Inc.*, 476 U.S. 858 (1986). The court sided with the *Seely* position, which had become the prevailing view: "[W]e adopt an approach similar to *Seely* and hold that a manufacturer in a commercial relationship has no duty under either a negligence or strict products-liability theory to prevent a product from injuring itself." *Id.* at 871. The court also resisted distinctions suggested by other courts concerning the manner in which the product is injured:

> We realize that the damage may be qualitative, occurring through gradual deterioration or internal breakage. Or it may be calamitous [e.g., a defect in the product may cause the product to incinerate or explode]. But either way, since by definition no person or other property is damaged, the resulting loss is purely economic. Even when the harm to the product itself occurs through an abrupt, accident-like event, the

resulting loss due to the repair costs, decreased value, and lost profits is essentially the failure of the purchaser to receive the benefit of its bargain—traditionally the core concept of contract law.

Id. at 870.

In a more recent opinion, another court provides the following analysis:

The gist of a strict products liability tort case is that the plaintiff has suffered personal injury or property damage caused by a defective product that posed an unreasonable risk of injury to person or property. *Tort law is premised on safety.* Public policy demands that the manufacturer and seller bear the responsibility for such injury to person or property. * * * The principle of *economic loss*, on the other hand, is derived from the law of contract. Recovery for economic loss is intended to protect purchasers from losses suffered because a product failed in its intended use. Recovery for economic loss necessarily focuses on the bargain struck between the parties. . . . Economic loss is defined . . . as damages for inadequate value, because the product is inferior and does not work for the general purpose for which it was manufactured or sold. Liability for economic loss is based on express or implied representations manifesting the manufacturer's or seller's intent to guarantee the products. . . . *Thus defects of suitability and quality are redressed through contract actions and safety hazards through tort actions.*

Northridge Company v. W. R. Grace & Company, 162 Wis.2d 918, 933–34, 471 N.W.2d 179, 185 (1991) (emphasis supplied).

This "economic loss doctrine" obviously produces differences in the operation and scope of tort and warranty products liability theories. There are a number of other significant differences between the two types of theories, as the following materials suggest.

(b) Privity Limitations. Section 402A of the Restatement (Second) of Torts does not require any contractual relationship between the injured party and the defendant in order to permit recovery for injuries caused by unreasonably dangerous and defective products. Depending upon the jurisdiction, we have seen that warranty theory may encounter the horizontal and/or vertical privity limitations as discussed above.

(c) Warranty Disclaimers. The UCC validates warranty disclaimers in the agreement between the parties. If, therefore, a manufacturer and retailer agree upon a disclaimer of implied warranties, the ultimate buyer or third parties injured by the product may be left with no warranty recovery. A few states preclude such limitations with respect to consumers, but the overwhelming majority permit such disclaimers. An action under § 402A of the Restatement (Second) of Torts, however, is not limited by disclaimers.

(d) Notice Requirements. Under UCC 2–607(3)(a), a buyer who has accepted goods (see 2–606) must notify the seller of any claimed breach of warranty within a reasonable time after he discovers or should have discovered the breach. Under the pre-amendment version of 2–607, failure to give the required notice will bar the buyer from *any* remedy.[1] A beneficiary

1. Under proposed amended Section 2–607(3)(a), a buyer that fails to give the required notice would be barred from remedies "only to the extent that the seller is prejudiced by the failure."

standing in the shoes of the buyer, however, has nothing to do with the acceptance of the goods and is unlikely, therefore, to give notice of breach of warranty within the time frame imposed by 2–607(3)(a). Such a beneficiary, therefore, is in danger of unfairly losing its right to seek compensation under warranty law for injury from defective products. Comment 5 to 2–607 recognizes this dilemma and suggests that such a beneficiary "does not fall within the reason of the present section...." A court could alleviate the notice problem if it chooses to rely upon this comment and not insist on 2–607(3)(a) notice from someone other than the immediate buyer. Nonetheless, a party suing under warranty theory must be concerned with the 2–607(3)(a) notice requirement. That notice obligation, however, does not apply in an action based on tort theory.

(e) Statute of Limitations. The statute of limitations provision in pre-amendment UCC Article 2 provides that a cause of action *accrues* when the breach occurs, "regardless of the aggrieved party's lack of knowledge of the breach," and "[a] breach of warranty occurs when tender of delivery is made...." 2–725(2).[2] Since "[a]n action for breach of any contract for sale must be commenced within four years after the cause of action has accrued" (2–725(1)), a buyer typically has four years from tender of delivery to discover a breach of warranty and bring an action based on such breach. Thus, except in actions for breach of a warranty that "explicitly extends to future performance," the UCC statute of limitations is a statute of repose. A typical torts statute of limitations, however, runs from the time of the injury—a "discovery" statute of limitations. Since a products liability action for personal injury or property damage can be brought under either a tort or warranty theory, and might well be brought by someone other than the direct buyer of the product, should the designation of the action as one based on tort or contract–a matter of little more than the caption atop the complaint—determine which statute of limitations applies? Some courts searched for symmetry between tort and warranty theories, and applied a tort statute of limitations to claims for personal injuries no matter which type of theory was used, relegating UCC 2–725 to actions for economic losses based on loss of bargain (i.e., defeated expectations). Other courts, however, have insisted on applying the UCC 2–725 four year statute of repose to all actions captioned "breach of warranty," even if the action is to recover for personal injury, on the footing that 2–725 cannot be ignored.[3]

---

2. If, however, "a warranty explicitly extends to future performance of the goods and discovery of the breach must await the time of such performance the cause of action accrues when the breach is or should have been discovered." 2–725(2),

3. UCC 2–725 appears to have been designed exclusively for buyers of goods in a contract setting—the principal focus of Article 2. The express terms of the 2–725 state that a cause of action accrues when the breach occurs and the breach occurs upon tender of delivery, regardless of the aggrieved party's lack of knowledge of the breach. This can only apply to a buyer of the goods, since only the buyer can possibly be an "aggrieved party" (defined in UCC 1–201(b)(2) as a party entitled to assert a claim) at the time of tender, before any breach is discovered. A third party will not become "aggrieved" until he or she is injured by the product. Perhaps the premier illustration of confusion in this area is

(f) Statute of Limitations—Amended Article 2. Proposed amended Section 2–725 would make significant changes to and clarifications of pre-amendment 2–725:

When a buyer discovers a breach during the fourth year after its cause of action accrued, proposed amended 2–725(1) would supplement the basic four-year limitations period with a rule that permits an action to be brought within one year after discovery of the breach (but no later than five years after the cause of action accrued). The proposed amended provision would continue to allow the parties, by agreement, to reduce the statute of limitations to not less than one year, but it would preclude such reduction in consumer contracts.

Proposed amended 2–725(2) would clarify the time a cause of action accrues for statute of limitations purposes in situations not involving breach of warranty or obligations to remote buyers. While retaining the general rule that a right of action accrues for breach of contract when the breach occurs, regardless of the aggrieved party's lack of knowledge of the breach (2–725(2)(a)), the proposed amendments would specify when accrual occurs if the breach is by repudiation ("at the earlier of when the aggrieved party elects to treat the repudiation as a breach or when a commercially reasonable time for awaiting performance has expired" (2–725(2)(b)), if there has been a breach of a *remedial* promise ("when the remedial promise is not performed when due" ((2–725(2)(c)), and if there is an action by the buyer against a person answerable over to the buyer for a claim asserted against the buyer ("at the time the claim was originally asserted against the buyer" (2–725(2)(d)).

Proposed amended Section 2–725(3) would address when a cause of action accrues for breach of the various warranties provided for in Article 2. In actions by an immediate purchaser for breach of an express warranty (2–313(2)) or breach of an implied warranty of merchantability (2–314) or fitness for a particular purpose (2–315), the cause of action would accrue when the seller has tendered delivery to the immediate buyer *and* has completed performance of any agreed installation or assembly of the goods (2–725(3)(a)). An action for breach of an obligation to a remote purchase under 2–313A or 2–313B (other than a remedial promise) would accrue when the remote purchaser receives the goods (2–725(3)(b)). Where, however, a seller's express warranty to an immediate buyer or its obligation to a remote purchaser *explicitly extends to future performance of the goods* and discovery of the breach must await the time for performance, the cause of action accrues when the immediate buyer or remote purchaser "discovers or should

found in a case where the court recognized the logic of applying a torts (discovery) statute of limitations to third parties suing for personal injuries on a warranty theory, but refused to follow the logic because the case involved both a buyer and a third party injured by a defective product at the same time. The court concluded that it must treat the parties equally. It reasoned that, since 2–725 necessarily refers to the buyer, it must allow the buyer four years from the time of delivery to bring an action, and it then felt compelled to do the same for the third party. See *Williams v. West Penn Power Co.*, 502 Pa. 557, 467 A.2d 811 (1983). The court failed to consider that there is no evidence the drafters of 2–725 had products liability actions in mind when they provided that contract actions for defeated expectations should be subject to a four-year statute of repose, thereby putting a final time limit on the concerns of the seller. The dilemma illustrated by the *Williams* case has caused several jurisdictions to create separate statutes of limitations for products liability cases.

have discovered the breach" (2–725(3)(c)). With respect to breaches of the warranty of title and against infringement, the cause of action accrues when the aggrieved party discovers or should have discovered the breach; this rule recognizes that a buyer will typically not discover such breaches until it is sued by a party asserting title to or infringement by the goods, and this may not occur for many years after the buyer acquired the goods. Because a period of repose for actions based on the warranty against infringements was deemed desirable, however, such actions may not be commenced more than six years after tender of delivery of goods to the aggrieved party (2–725(3)(d)).

Proposed amended Section 2–725(4) would create a saving provision akin to provisions in many state limitations statutes allowing an additional short period for bringing new actions where an earlier action based on the same breach has been terminated. This rule is designed to preserve a remedy when litigation that was commenced in timely fashion is terminated after or shortly before the usual limitations period has run. In this situation, proposed amended 2–725(4) would allow the new action to be commenced within six months after the termination of the first action unless the termination resulted from voluntary discontinuance or from dismissal for failure or neglect to prosecute.

Proposed amended Section 2–725(5) emphasizes that the section does not purport to alter or modify any state law on the tolling of the statute of limitations.

Problem 42

(a) During her lunch hour Cecile Mendel walked to the nearby First National Bank to deposit a check in her account, as she had done many times in the past. She pushed open the thick glass door of the bank in a normal fashion and was instantly covered with broken glass, resulting in numerous lacerations. The shattering of the glass door was cause by a latent defect in the glass that had not appeared prior to this time. The bank doors were manufactured and installed by the Pittsburgh Plate Glass Company (PPG) seven years prior to Cecile's accident. The jurisdiction does not recognize § 402A of the Restatement of Torts (Second). Cecile brings an action against PPG for breach of the implied warranty of merchantability. The jurisdiction has adopted Alternative A of UCC 2–318. Analyze.

(b) Ahmed Salvador was injured when a boiler at his place of employment exploded. The boiler was purchased by his employer from the Atlantic Boiler Corporation three years prior to the explosion. The jurisdiction had adopted § 402A of the Restatement of Torts (Second) five years before the explosion. The torts personal injury statute of limitations in the jurisdiction is two years from the time of the injury. Three years later, Ahmed sought to recover for his injuries against Atlantic claiming negligence, strict liability in tort, and breach of warranty. The jurisdiction has enacted Alternative A of UCC 2–318. Analyze

(c) Ann Harris purchased a new car three years ago. While driving in a normal manner, Harris saw flames shooting from under the hood of the car. Though alarmed, she managed to bring the car to a stop and jump free as the entire car was engulfed in fire. Harris escaped unscathed, and there were no injuries to surrounding persons or property. The car was totally destroyed. Later examination revealed a latent defect in the wiring system that was present when Harris purchased the car. The same defect is present in all cars of that model and year. Does Harris have a cause of action to recover the value of the car under a warranty theory? A tort theory?

(d) Assume the facts of (c) except that the defect did not result in the car bursting into flames. Instead, the defect caused the car to stop working, and Harris had the car towed to the dealer that sold her the car. The defect could have caused the car to burst into flames as in (c), but luckily it did not. Instead, the entire wiring system and other parts of the car now require replacement at huge expense. Does Harris have a cause of action under a warranty theory? A tort theory?

(e) Southern Properties, Inc. (S) discovered that certain fireproofing material sold to S's general contractor by Coteproof (C), which the contractor used in constructing S's new shopping center, contained asbestos. S brought an action against C asserting that the asbestos contamination caused S to suffer damages by incurring expenses for inspection, testing and removal of the Coteproof material, and by diminishing the resale value of the property. There is no evidence of personal injury or damage to other property, although personal injury might have resulted if the asbestos was not removed. The material had been sold by C to the general contractor more than four years prior to S's discovery of asbestos in the material. S brings an action against C alleging a claim based on strict liability in tort. Analyze.

T. PROOF AND CAUSATION IN PRODUCTS LIABILITY ACTIONS

INTERNATIONAL MOTORS INC. v. FORD MOTOR COMPANY, INC.

Maryland Court of Appeals, 2000.
133 Md.App. 269, 754 A.2d 1115.

MURPHY, C. J. On March 15, 1995, Ford sold a 1995 F–350 chassis cab truck (the truck) to Homer Skelton Ford, Inc., a Ford dealership in Olive Branch, Mississippi. The truck came with an express "bumper to bumper" warranty that, in pertinent part, provided:

Authorized Ford Motor Company dealers will repair, replace or adjust all parts on your vehicle (except tires) that are defective in factory-supplied materials or workmanship for 3 years or 36,000 miles (whichever occurs first).

This express warranty, however, was limited by its terms: It stated that Ford would not be responsible for damage caused by "alteration, misuse, or damage caused by accident," or for any consequential damages.

On May 16, 1995, Elzenheimer Chevrolet, located in New York, purchased the truck from Homer Skelton Ford and converted it into a tow truck. To do so, Elzenheimer added many parts including a towing apparatus and strobe lights. On August 4, 1995, International Motors t/a Montrose Towing ("Montrose") purchased the truck from Elzenheimer, and insured it with General. The truck caught fire while its operator was preparing to tow another vehicle. [At the time of the fire, the truck had been driven approximately 27,600 miles.] After determining that the truck was a total loss and paying Montrose for its value, General sued Ford for breach of express warranty [and] breach of implied warranties of fitness and merchantability. We agree with the circuit court's resolution of the express warranty claim.

The express "bumper to bumper" warranty was a valid agreement entered into by sophisticated parties who knew and understood its contents. Both the buyer and the seller of the truck were "merchants" under the Commercial Code. Thus, both parties are charged with knowledge of the provisions of the contract, and equal bargaining power to arrive at mutually agreeable terms. An express warranty is breached when "a product fails to exhibit the properties, characteristics, or qualities specifically attributed to it by its warrantor, and therefore fails to conform to the warrantor's representations." *McCarty v. E.J. Korvette, Inc.*, 28 Md.App. 421, 437, 347 A.2d 253 (1975). The test of defectiveness in a breach of express warranty action is "whether the product performs in accordance with the express warranty given." The terms of the express warranty required that General prove a defect in the materials and/or workmanship upon leaving Ford's control. *See McCarty*, 28 Md.App. at 437 (where the court held that "had the tire here involved been warranted only against defects in material and workmanship, the consumers, in order to establish a breach of warranty, would have had to show that the blowout was caused by such a defect existing at the time the tire left the warrantor's control.").

The express warranty at issue in this case only protects against "parts ... that are defective in factory-supplied materials and workmanship." Thus, in order for General to succeed on a breach of the express warranty claim, General had to prove that a particular part in the chassis cab was "defective." The circuit court found that General was unable to prove that the fire was caused by a defective part. Because the circuit court was not clearly erroneous in concluding that General was unable to prove a defect, we affirm the judgment entered in favor of Ford on General's express warranty claims.

[Implied warranty claims.] Ford presented expert testimony that "the fire which resulted in the damage to the 1995 Ford truck on or about August 19th, 1997, was the result of an electrical malfunction within the heating and air-conditioning plenum at the right rear corner of the engine compartment." The circuit court rejected that testimony, finding instead that "this fire did originate under the hood area," rather than in the "cab area." On the basis of that not clearly erroneous factual finding, we are persuaded that the circuit court should not have entered judgments in favor of Ford on the implied warranties of fitness and merchantability claims. The circuit court did so on the ground that

General did not prove "by a preponderance of the evidence that it was either a defect or negligence by the—by the defendant." It is not necessary, however, to prove a particular (manufacturing or design) defect to prevail on an implied warranty claim.

The warranty of merchantability imposes upon sellers the obligation to warrant that the goods are "merchantable," i.e., "fit for the ordinary purposes for which such goods are used." Md.Code Ann., Commercial Law § 2–314(2)(c).[1] The words "defect" or "defective condition" do not appear anywhere in this section of the code, and Maryland case law does not require such proof.

General was also provided protection under the implied warranty of fitness for a particular purpose, defined as follows in Md.Code Ann., Commercial Law, § 2–315. The words "defect" or "defective conditions" do not appear in this section of the code, and Maryland case law does not require such proof. Ford manufactures chassis cabs with knowledge that they will be modified in some form or another. Ford was aware that Elzenheimer had, in the past, purchased Ford chassis cabs for the purpose of turning them into tow trucks. Thus, Ford impliedly warranted that the truck would be fit for usage as a tow truck.

Here, the evidence showed that Ford breached its implied warranty of fitness for a particular purpose when (1) General's insured was using the truck as a tow truck, and (2) the truck unexpectedly caught on fire. The circuit court was persuaded that the fire started in the engine compartment of the truck while the truck was idling. The truck was being used "normally" at that time, and trucks do not normally catch on fire while idling.

Implied warranties exist so consumers can recover in cases like this one without having to prove the particular defect that caused the problem. The circuit court was entitled to reject Ford's explanation of how the accident occurred. It was not, however, entitled to impose upon General the burden of proving the particular manufacture or design defect that caused the fire.

Ford alleges that it is relieved from liability because the fire was caused by modifications made to the truck after leaving its hands. While a post-sale modification may constitute a valid defense to a warranty claim, Ford—not General—has the burden of persuasion on this issue. Ford did present evidence of post-sale modifications and alterations to the truck. The record, however, does not indicate that the circuit court resolved the issue of whether the fire was caused by alterations or modifications after Ford had sold the truck. It is therefore necessary for the circuit court to determine whether the fire was caused by post-sale modifications to the truck.

---

1. Applied to vehicles, this warranty requires that the vehicle be reasonably safe when used in its normal manner. *Mercedes-* *Benz of N. Am., Inc. v. Garten*, 94 Md. App. 547, 562, 618 A.2d 233 (1993).

On remand the circuit court must decide whether Ford has an alteration or modification defense specific to the area where the fire originated; i.e. "under the hood area." Any other modifications or alterations are not relevant. This determination must be made on the evidence already presented to the circuit court. Neither party is entitled to a second "bite at the apple" on this issue. Unless persuaded that the fire started because of alterations to the truck after it left Ford's control, the circuit court shall enter judgment in favor of General on the implied warranty claims.

Note

In *Chase v. Kawasaki Motors Corp.*, 140 F.Supp. 2d 1280 (M.D.Ala. 2001), the plaintiff alleged a breach of the implied warranty of fitness for a particular purpose by a dealer selling all-terrain-vehicles (ATV) manufactured by the Kawasaki Corporation. The manufacturer provided information stating that the ATV was not suitable for children under 16. The plaintiff (mother) alleged that the dealer said it was suitable for her children, ages 14 and 12. An accident occurred when the brakes failed. The court recognized that the plaintiff had introduced evidence supporting the creation of an implied warranty of fitness for a particular purpose and its breach by the dealer if the ATV was not suitable for her children. The plaintiff, however, failed to produce any evidence that this breach was the proximate cause of the "wreck." The accident occurred through brake failure that could have resulted in injury to a driver and passenger regardless of age. The defendant, dealer, was entitled to summary judgment on this count since the plaintiff failed to prove proximate causation.

"Defect" vs. "Unmerchantable." Products liability cases are now dominated by the tort theory of strict liability. Restatement (Second) of Torts § 402A has been widely adopted by courts. Warranty theory, with its privity, notice, statute of repose, and disclaimer limitations, is typically a poor second choice for plaintiffs seeking a recovery for personal injury or damage to other property caused by product defects. Although warranty theory may used as a last resort by plaintiffs who have failed to file an action within the torts (discovery) statute of limitations, this possibility may, itself, suggest another reason for removing personal injury and property damage actions from the scope of Article 2. It is clear that all the UCC limitations on a products liability recovery result from the attempt to squeeze a tort concept into a statute dealing with breaches of contract. Why not, then, amend Article 2 by eliminating the references to recovery for personal injury (2–715(2)(b) and 2–318) and relegate the Code exclusively to those cases in which a product causes defeated expectation (bargain) losses, leaving personal injury and property damage cases to tort law? One possible response to this argument is that the standards for determining when a product gives rise to liability might be different under tort law and the UCC. In other words, goods might be free of defect from the view of tort law, yet still breach a UCC warranty. That certainly is a possibility with respect to express warranties or the implied warranty of fitness for a particular purpose. Is it possible, however, for a product to violate the implied warranty of merchantability notwithstanding a finding that the product is not defective under principles of tort law? Consider the next case.

CASTRO v. QVC NETWORK, INC.

United States Court of Appeals for the Second Circuit, 1998.
139 F.3d 114.

CALABRESI, CIRCUIT JUDGE: In this diversity products liability action, plaintiffs-appellants alleged, in separate causes of action for strict liability and for breach of warranty, that defendants-appellees manufactured and sold a defective roasting pan that injured one of the appellants. The United States District Court for the Eastern District of New York rejected appellants' request to charge the jury separately on each cause of action and, instead, instructed the jury only on the strict liability charge. The jury found for appellees and the court denied appellants' motion for a new trial. This appeal followed. We hold that, under New York law, the jury should have been instructed separately on each charge, and, accordingly, reverse and remand for a new trial on the breach of warranty claim.

In early November 1993, appellee QVC Network, Inc. ("QVC"), operator of a cable television home-shopping channel, advertised, as part of a one-day Thanksgiving promotion, the "T–Fal Jumbo Resistal Roaster." The roaster, manufactured by U.S.A. T–Fal Corp. ("T–Fal"), was described as suitable for, among other things, cooking a twenty-five pound turkey. Appellant Loyda Castro bought the roasting pan by mail and used it to prepare a twenty-pound turkey on Thanksgiving Day, 1993. Mrs. Castro was injured when she attempted to remove the turkey and roasting pan from the oven. Using insulated mittens, she gripped the pan's handles with the first two fingers on each hand (the maximum grip allowed by the small size of the handles) and took the pan out of the oven. As the turkey tipped toward her, she lost control of the pan, spilling the hot drippings and fat that had accumulated in it during the cooking and basting process. As a result, she suffered 116 second and third degree burns to her foot and ankle, which, over time, has led to scarring, intermittent paresthesia, and ankle swelling. It is uncontested that in their complaint appellants alleged that the pan was defective and that its defects gave rise to separate causes of action for strict liability and for breach of warranty. Moreover, in the pre-charge conference, appellants' counsel repeatedly requested separate jury charges on strict liability and for breach of warranty. The district court, nevertheless, denied the request for a separate charge on breach of warranty. Judge Wexler stated that "you can't collect twice for the same thing," and deemed the warranty charge unnecessary and "duplicative." The court, therefore, only gave the jury the New York pattern strict products liability charge. The jury returned a verdict for appellees QVC and T–Fal. Appellants moved that the jury verdict be set aside and a new trial be ordered for various reasons including that the court had failed to charge the jury on appellants' claim for breach of warranty. [T]he district court denied appellants' motion, reasoning that the breach of warranty and strict products liability claims were "virtually the same." This appeal followed.

Products liability law has long been bedeviled by the search for an appropriate definition of "defective" product design. Over the years, both in the cases and in the literature, two approaches have come to predominate. The first is the risk/utility theory, which focuses on whether the benefits of a product outweigh the dangers of its design. The second is the consumer expectations theory, which focuses on what a buyer/user of a product would properly expect that the product would be suited for.

Not all states accept both of these approaches. Some define design defect only according to the risk/utility approach [while others define it] solely in terms of the consumer expectations theory. Still others apply a "modified consumer expectations test" that incorporates risk/utility factors into the consumer expectations analysis. One of the first states to accept both approaches was California, which in Barker v. Lull Engineering Co., 20 Cal.3d 413, 143 Cal.Rptr. 225, 573 P.2d 443 (1978), held that "a product may be found defective in design, so as to subject a manufacturer to strict liability for resulting injuries, under either of two alternative tests"—consumer expectations and risk/utility. Id. at 430–32, 143 Cal.Rptr. at 237, 573 P.2d at 455. Several states have followed suit and have adopted both theories.

Prior to the recent case of Denny v. Ford Motor Co., 87 N.Y.2d 248, 639 N.Y.S.2d 250, 662 N.E.2d 730 (1995), it was not clear whether New York recognized both tests. In Denny, the plaintiff was injured when her Ford Bronco II sports utility vehicle rolled over when she slammed on the brakes to avoid hitting a deer in the vehicle's path. See Denny v. Ford Motor Co., 42 F.3d 106, 108 (2d Cir.1994), certifying questions to Denny, 87 N.Y.2d 248, 639 N.Y.S.2d 250, 662 N.E.2d 730. The plaintiff asserted claims for strict products liability and for breach of implied warranty, and the district judge—over the objection of defendant Ford—submitted both causes of action to the jury. The jury ruled in favor of Ford on the strict liability claim, but found for the plaintiff on the implied warranty claim. On appeal, Ford argued that the jury's verdicts on the strict products liability claim and the breach of warranty claim were inconsistent because the causes of action were identical. This court certified the Denny case to the New York Court of Appeals to answer the following questions: (1) "whether, under New York law, the strict products liability and implied warranty claims are identical"; and (2) "whether, if the claims are different, the strict products liability claim is broader than the implied warranty claim and encompasses the latter." Id. at 111–12. In response to the certified questions, the Court of Appeals held that in a products liability case a cause of action for strict liability is not identical to a claim for breach of warranty. Moreover, the court held that a strict liability claim is not per se broader than a breach of warranty claim such that the former encompasses the latter. Thus, while claims of strict products liability and breach of warranty are often used interchangeably, under New York law the two causes of action are definitively different. The imposition of strict liability for an alleged design "defect" is determined by a risk-utility standard. The notion of "defect" in a U.C.C.—based breach of warranty claim focuses, instead, on consumer expectations.

Since Denny, then, it has been settled that the risk/utility and consumer expectations theories of design defect can, in New York, be the bases of distinct causes of action: one for strict products liability and one for breach of warranty. This fact, however, does not settle the question of when a jury must be charged separately on each cause of action and when, instead, the two causes are, on the facts of the specific case, sufficiently similar to each other so that one charge to the jury is enough. While eminent jurists have at times been troubled by this issue, the New York Court of Appeals in Denny was quite clear on when the two causes of action might meld and when, instead, they are to be treated as separate. It did this by adding its own twist to the distinction—namely, what can aptly be called the "dual purpose" requirement. [T]he Court of Appeals pointed out that the fact that a product's overall benefits might outweigh its overall risks does not preclude the possibility that consumers may have been misled into using the product in a context in which it was dangerously unsafe. And this, the New York court emphasized, could be so even though the benefits in other uses might make the product sufficiently reasonable so that it passed the risk/utility test.

In Denny, the Ford Bronco II was not designed as a conventional passenger automobile. Instead, it was designed as an off-road, dual purpose vehicle. But in its marketing of the Bronco II, Ford stressed its suitability for commuting and for suburban and city driving. Under the circumstances, the Court of Appeals explained that a rational fact finder could conclude that the Bronco's utility as an off-road vehicle outweighed the risk of injury resulting from roll-over accidents (thus passing the risk/utility test), but at the same time find that the vehicle was not safe for the "ordinary purpose" of daily driving for which it was also marketed and sold (thus flunking the consumer expectations test). Indeed, as Ford argued, the design features that appellant complained of—high center of gravity, narrow track width, short wheel base, and a specially tailored suspension system—were important to preserve the vehicle's utility for off-road use. But, it was these same design features that made the vehicle susceptible to rollover accidents during evasive maneuvers on paved roads. That is precisely the situation before us. The jury had before it evidence that the product was designed, marketed, and sold as a multiple-use product. The pan was originally manufactured and sold in France as an all-purpose cooking dish without handles. And at trial, the jury saw a videotape of a QVC representative demonstrating to the television audience that the pan, in addition to serving as a suitable roaster for a twenty-five pound turkey, could also be used to cook casseroles, cutlets, cookies, and other low-volume foods. The court charged the jury that "[a] product is defective if it is not reasonably safe[,] [t]hat is, if the product is so likely to be harmful to persons that a reasonable person who had actual knowledge of its potential for producing injury would conclude that it should not have been marketed in that condition." And, so instructed, the jury presumably found that the pan, because it had many advantages in a variety of uses, did not fail the risk/utility test. In such circumstances, New York law is clear that a general charge on strict products liability based on the risk/utility approach does not suffice. The jury could have found that the roasting pan's overall utility for cooking low-volume foods outweighed the risk of injury when cooking heavier foods, but that the product was nonetheless unsafe for the purpose for which it was marketed and sold—roasting a twenty-five pound turkey—and, as such, was defective under the consumer expectations test. That being so, the appellants were entitled to a separate breach of warranty charge. Accordingly, we reverse the order of the district court denying the motion for a new trial, and remand the case for a new trial on the breach of warranty claim, consistent with this opinion.

Note

In ***Silivanch v. Celebrity Cruises, Inc.***, 171 F.Supp. 2d 241 (S.D.N.Y. 2001), the plaintiff claimed he contracted Legionnaire's disease proximately caused by defendant Essef's defectively designed filter. After finding the defendant liable for negligence and strict products liability, the court turned to the plaintiff's claim for breach of the implied warranty of merchantability:

> The Essef Defendants next argue that they may not be held liable for breach of implied warranty because that cause of action is duplicative of the plaintiffs' design defect claim. However, "in a products liability case a cause of action for strict liability is not identical to a claim for breach of warranty." Castro v. QVC Network, Inc., 139 F.3d 114, 117 (2d Cir.1998). First, "the core element 'defect' is subtly different in the two causes of action." While the strict products concept of a product that is "not reasonably safe" requires a weighing of the product's dangers against its over-all advantages, the ... concept of a "defective" product [for warranty purposes] requires an inquiry only into whether the product in question was "fit for the ordinary purposes for which such goods are used." Second, as a result of this conceptual distinction, the elements that must be proven for each cause of action differ. In order to establish a breach of implied warranty, the plaintiff must show: "(1) that the product was defectively designed or manufactured; (2) that the defect existed when the manufacturer delivered it to the purchaser or user; [and] (3) that the defect is the proximate cause of the accident." Thus, on an implied warranty claim, the injured party need not demonstrate that safer designs were available. The jury's verdicts on design defect and implied warranty are therefore not redundant.

U. PRODUCTS LIABILITY—ARTICLE 2A, THE CISG, AND UCITA

Leases. With appropriate changes to reflect leasing terminology, UCC 2A–216, entitled "Third–Party Beneficiaries of Express and Implied Warranties," replicates the three alternatives of the Article 2 provision governing relaxed privity requirements (2–318).

The CISG. Article 5 of the CISG attempts to exclude products liability issues from the scope of the Convention by providing, "This Convention does not apply to the liability of the seller for death or personal injury caused by the goods to any person." Whether this provision will in fact make the CISG irrelevant to products liability issues remains to be seen.

UCITA. As comment 3 to UCITA § 409 suggests, the statute does not attempt to deal with "product liability or other tort issues," and courts have seldom attached products liability to transactions in information. UCITA, however, includes a provision that, like UCC 2–318, permits third parties to enforce warranties. UCITA § 409(a) provides,

> Except for published informational content, a warranty to a licensee extends to persons for whose benefit the licensor intends to supply the information or informational rights and which rightfully use the information in a transaction or application of the kind in which the licensor intends the information to be used.

For this provision to apply, the information provider must have clearly intended to have an effect on specific third parties, i. e., more is required than that the third party is within the general classification of those whom might use the information. "There must be a closer and more clearly known connection to a particular third party." Comment 4 to UCITA § 409.

Under UCITA § 409(b), furthermore, a warranty to a consumer-licensee extends to members of the licensee's immediate family or household if such member's use was reasonably expected by the licensor. As comment 4 to UCITA § 409 indicates, this expansion of the benefit of warranties to consumer licensees "covers both personal injury and economic losses." Thus, for example, a provider of a mass-market computer program designed to control household lighting would presumably expect family or household members of the licensee to use the software, and would incur liability for personal injury caused by a breach of warranty.

UCITA § 409(c) permits a licensee to exclude or limit third parties to whom warranty protection extends, except for members of a consumer licensee's immediate family or household covered under § 409(b). In addition, disclaimers of warranties or limitations of remedies valid against the immediate licensor are also effective against beneficiaries of warranties (UCITA § 409(d)).

According to comment 1 to UCITA § 409, the section is expressly based on contract third party beneficiary law and Restatement (Second) of Torts § 552 concerning the liability of a provider of information to third parties.

Note: Statute of Limitations Applicable under Article 2A, the CISG, and UCITA

Leases. UCC 2A–506 adopts a four-year statute of limitations, but it does not copy the time of accrual rules in the Article 2 statute of limitations (2–725) The four-year limitations period for actions for breach of warranty in a lease begins to run when the default or breach of warranty is or should have been discovered, or when the default occurs, whichever is later (2A–506(2)).

International Sales. The CISG does not include a statute of limitations provision. As of December 1, 1994, however, a protocol known as the *Convention on the Limitation Period in the International Sale of Goods*[1] became effective in the United States, having been approved by the United States Senate in 1993 (Senate Treaty Doc. No. 10, 103d Cong., 1st Sess. (1993) (139 Cong. Rec. S16,213 (daily ed. Nov. 18. 1993)). The "Limitations Convention" is sometimes called the "first born" of the United Nations Commission on International Trade (UNCITRAL), which also sponsored the CISG. The Limitations Convention was promulgated on June 14, 1974 to promote uniformity and certainty in statutes of limitation applicable to international sales. Article 8 of the Limitations Convention provides for a uniform limitation period of four years from the time a claim accrues, but the time of accrual depends upon whether the claim is for breach of contract, breach of warranty, fraud or anticipatory repudiation. In some cases, the limitation period may be extended, but in no case for more than ten years after the cause of action accrues. In general, the cause of action accrues and the limitation period begins to run from the time the goods are "handed over" to the buyer.[2]

UCITA. Under UCITA § 805, actions must be commenced within the later of 1) four years after the right of action accrues, and 2) one year after the breach was or should have been discovered, but not later than five years after the right of action accrues. This rule is replicated in the proposed amendment to the UCC Article 2 statute of limitations (2–725). Under UCITA § 805, a right of action accrues when the breach occurs, and the breach occurs when tender of delivery of a copy or access to the information occurs, regardless of the aggrieved party's lack of knowledge of the breach. Where a warranty explicitly extends to future performance of information or a copy thereof, such as a warranty on software stating that there are no defects that will affect performance during the first ninety days after delivery, a right of action for breach of the warranty accrues only when "performance fails to conform to the

1. U. N. Doc. A/CONF.63/15, reprinted in I. L. M. 952 (1974).

2. For a summary, see Peter Winship, *The Convention on the Limitation Period in*

the International Sale of Goods: The United States Adopts UNICITRAL's First Born, 28 Intl. Law.1071 (1994).

warranty" (e.g., when a defect that affects performance appears during the ninety day warranty period). A "discovery" statute of limitations, however, is applied to a variety of specified rights of action: breach of warranty claims against third persons for infringement, misappropriation, libel, defamation or similar claims; breach of contract claims involving a party's disclosure or misuse of confidential information; and claims based on failure to provide indemnity or to perform another obligation to protect or defend against a third party claim. UCITA 805(d).

V. CONSUMER PROTECTION—MAGNUSON MOSS ET AL.

The drafters of the UCC are sometimes charged with deliberately avoiding the issue of consumer protection. It is true that the drafters rejected the idea of incorporating a comprehensive consumer protection dimension in the Code, but the fact that the issue was debated during the formative years of the Code in the 1940's and early 1950's demonstrates the drafters' precocious sensitivity to the plight of the consumer. As consumer legislation efforts in later decades would demonstrate, the goal of a uniform law protecting consumers in the late 1940's was impossible. The controversial discussions of consumer protection during the drafting of the UCC ended because the desperately-needed modernization of commercial law could have been much delayed or even doomed by an attempt to include major consumer protection provisions. The last four decades, however, have produced a flood of federal and state consumer protection legislation. Any attempt to summarize these efforts confronts a sobering reality described in the following introduction to a yeoman analysis:

> One looking for statutory provisions protecting consumers from abuses in consumer sales transactions might as well use a kaleidoscope as a telescope or a microscope. The much mottled picture is a virtual Jackson Pollock product of drippings from a wide variety of federal and state statutes, tinted with contrasting shades of judicial interpretations, and washed in parts by some peculiar disclosure provisions of the Magnuson–Moss Act. There is, of course, an appropriate place for abstract art. It is not, however, in an area of the law that applies so many times to so many people.[1]

Efforts at promoting uniform consumer legislation such as the Uniform Consumer Credit Code (the "U3C") were not successful. The National Consumer Act included a total ban on implied warranty disclaimers and remedy limitations in consumer transactions and was enacted in Massachusetts, Connecticut, Maine, Vermont, Maryland, West Virginia, Kansas, Mississippi, the District of Columbia and Alabama, the last of which limited its effect to personal injury actions.[2] The California Song–Beverly Act emphasized disclosure and consumer remedies, includ-

---

1. Donald F. Clifford, *Non-UCC Statutory Provisions Affecting Warranty Disclaimers and Remedies in Sales of Goods*, 71 N. C. L. Rev. 1011, 115 (1993).

2. *Id.*

ing double damages and attorney fees.[3] In some measure, this legislation was copied in Minnesota, New Hampshire, Oregon and Rhode Island. A number of states enacted "lemon laws" and statutes modeled on the Federal Trade Commission Act, which in Section 5 contains a general prohibition of unfair and deceptive sales practices. Other federal statutes and regulations, including the Consumer Credit Protection Act (of which the Truth in Lending Act is a part), added a national dimension to consumer-oriented legislation. Beyond the plethora of legislation and regulation, interpretation and construction issues add further complexity and war against uniformity.

Much consumer protection legislation takes the form of "disclosure" statutes that attempt to increase the information available to consumers concerning warranties and remedies. Whether such laws actually increase consumer awareness to any significant degree is doubtful. For example, the Magnuson–Moss Warranty Act, a federal statute explored in this section, requires that a written warranty on a consumer product "fully and conspicuously disclose in simple and readily understood language the terms and conditions of such warranty." Notwithstanding this laudable goal, most consumer warranties drafted since the statute took effect are hardly "simple and readily understood." Furthermore, it is unclear whether the typical consumer would pay great attention to warranties even if the language were comprehensible.

It is well beyond the scope of this book to attempt even a survey of the vast array of consumer protection laws. It is essential to consider specific state legislation in determining any special rights of the consumer. In this section we pursue an analysis of the Magnuson–Moss Warranty Act, which is often the basis for an added count in consumer actions for breach of warranty. President Gerald Ford signed the Magnuson–Moss Act into law on July 4, 1975. It grew out of Congressional efforts beginning as early as the Kennedy administration to provide federal regulation of consumer warranties. The Act itself was the result of more than four years of intense legislative haggling—a fact that accounts for the confusing legislative history mentioned in the *Skelton* case that follows this discussion.

The Magnuson–Moss Act does in fact enlarge consumer warranty protections, and it allows consumers to recover attorneys' fees in certain situations (see 110(d)(2) of the Act). The remedies it provides, however, are not readily accessible, and the substantive provisions of the Act involve only modest protection. The statute provides that implied warranties may not be totally disclaimed in consumer sales if the seller has given a "written warranty" as defined in the Act. The duration of implied warranties, however, may be severely limited, and exclusion of liability for consequential damages is still permitted. A reading of the Act

---

3. See, e.g., Barker v. Fleetwood Enterprises, 2002 WL 453931 (Cal.App.2002), which states, "Section 1794 provides that the amount of any civil penalty awarded for willful violations of the Song–Beverly Act 'shall not exceed two times the amount of actual damages.' (§ 1794, subd. (c).) This language focuses on the prevailing plaintiff's 'actual damages' as determined by the jury."

reveals that it is primarily a disclosure statute whose effectiveness depends on the energy and intelligence of consumers in using increased information.

If one compares the typical automobile warranty of today with the one-year, 12,000 mile provisions of the 1960's or 70's, it may be argued that Magnuson–Moss is having some effect. A causal relationship between the Act and expanded warranty protection for cars and other consumer products, however, is dubious. The principal cause of improvements in automobile warranties (which now generally cover three years or 36,000 miles of "bumper-to-bumper" protection, and may encompass "drive train" protection for seven years or more) may be found in increased competition among manufacturers of automobiles—particularly the effect of competition by makers from Japan and other foreign countries.

Notwithstanding the limitations of the Magnuson–Moss Act, it is important to understand its general operation since it often appears as a separate count in consumer warranty actions.

SKELTON v. GENERAL MOTORS CORPORATION

United States Court of Appeals for the Seventh Circuit, 1981.
660 F.2d 311, cert. denied 456 U.S. 974 (1982).

CUDAHY, J. Section 110(d) of Title I of the Magnuson–Moss Warranty–Federal Trade Commission Improvements Act ("Magnuson–Moss" or the "Act") creates a federal private cause of action for consumers damaged by the failure of a warrantor "to comply with any obligation under . . . a written warranty." 15 U.S.C. § 2310(d)(1) (1976). The issue on this interlocutory appeal is whether a "written warranty" actionable under § 110(d) is limited to the particular promises, undertakings or affirmations of fact expressly defined as "written warranties" by Congress in the Act. The district court held that § 110(d) provides a federal cause of action not merely for breach of a "written warranty" as defined in the Act but also for breach of "all written promises presented in connection with the sale of a formally warranted product." 500 F.Supp. 1181, 1190 (N.D.Ill.1980). We reverse.

Plaintiffs, purchasers of automobiles manufactured by defendant General Motors Corporation ("GM"), brought this action as a nationwide class action on behalf of all purchasers of GM automobiles manufactured from 1976 through 1979. In Count I of their amended complaint, plaintiffs allege that GM, through its "brochures, manuals, consumer advertising and other forms of communications to the public generally and to members of plaintiffs' class specifically," warranted and represented that 1976 through 1979 GM automobiles contained THM 350 (M38) transmissions, or "transmissions of similar quality and performance . . . and that [such transmissions] would meet a specified level of performance." Plaintiffs charge in Count I that contrary to these warranties and representations, GM substituted inferior

THM 200 transmissions for THM 350 (M38) transmissions in GM automobiles manufactured from 1976 through 1979. This undisclosed substitution is alleged to constitute a violation of written and implied warranties under § 110(d) of Magnuson–Moss. In Count II, plaintiffs claim that the substitution is actionable as a "deceptive warranty" under § 110(c)(2) of the Act, 15 U.S.C. § 2310(c)(2) (1976).

General Motors moved to dismiss both counts of plaintiffs' complaint for failure to state a claim upon which relief could be granted. On October 1, 1980, the district court granted this motion with respect to the "implied warranty" portion of Count I and the "deceptive warranty" claim in Count II, but denied GM's motion to dismiss the "written warranty" claim in Count I. 500 F.Supp. 1181 (N.D.Ill.1980). GM's interlocutory appeal from the district court's refusal to dismiss the "written warranty" claim was certified by the district court on October 31, 1980 and accepted by this court on December 4, 1980. Plaintiffs did not take timely interlocutory appeals from the district court's determinations against them with respect to the "implied warranty" and "deceptive warranty" claims.[1]

Magnuson–Moss is, in the main, a remedial statute designed to protect consumers from deceptive warranty practices. Its draftsmen believed that consumer product warranties often were too complex to be understood, too varied to allow meaningful comparisons and too restricted to provide meaningful warranty protection.[2] The Act's draftsmen sought to remedy these perceived ills by imposing extensive disclosure requirements and minimum content standards on particular types of written consumer product warranties. And, to promote enforcement of these warranties, the draftsmen devised a detailed remedial apparatus, which includes optional informal dispute settlement procedures as well as private and governmental judicial actions.

Although Magnuson–Moss does not require any manufacturer or seller to extend a warranty with its product,[3] any "written warranty"

1. This case is related to the much-publicized "engine interchange" litigation, a consolidated class action brought against GM on behalf of all purchasers of 1977 Oldsmobile automobiles equipped with engines produced by GM's Chevrolet division. That litigation has been before this court twice on questions concerning, first, the district court's approval of a subclass settlement, In re General Motors Corp. Engine Interchange Litigation, 594 F.2d 1106 (7th Cir.), cert. denied, 444 U.S. 870 (1979) and, second, the sufficiency of a notice which detailed an offer of settlement in individual subclass members, Oswald v. McGarr, 620 F.2d 1190 (7th Cir.1980). Nothing in our opinions or in the district court's orders in that case, however, directly addresses the issue before us here—namely, whether a warranty of description of an automobile component is actionable as a "written warranty" under § 110(d) of Magnuson–Moss.

2. The Report of the House Committee on Interstate and Foreign Commerce states a particular concern that appeared recurrently in legislative discussions of the Act: [T]he paper with the filigree border bearing the bold caption "Warranty" or "Guarantee" was often of no greater worth than the paper it was printed on. Indeed, in many cases where a warranty or guarantee was ostensibly given the old saying applied "The bold print giveth and the fine print taketh away." For the paper operated to take away from the consumer the implied warranties of merchantability and fitness arising by operation of law leaving little in its stead. H.R. Rep. No. 93–1107, 93d Cong., 2d Sess. 13, reprinted in (1974) U.S. Code Cong. & Ad. News 7706.

3. Not only does the Act not require the provision of warranties of any kind, it also bars the FTC from so requiring as well, in

offered with a consumer product is subject to the Act's regulatory requirements. The term "written warranty" is defined "for purposes of [the Act]" in § 101(6), which reads:

(6) The term written warranty means—

(A) any written affirmation of fact or written promise made in connection with the sale of a consumer product by a supplier to a buyer which relates to the nature of the material or workmanship and affirms or promises that such material or workmanship is defect free or will meet a specified level of performance over a specified period of time, or

(B) any undertaking in writing in connection with the sale by a supplier of a consumer product to refund, repair, replace, or take other remedial action with respect to such product in the event that such product fails to meet the specifications set forth in the undertaking,

which written affirmation, promise, or undertaking becomes part of the basis of the bargain between a supplier and a buyer for purposes other than resale of such product.

15 U.S.C. § 2301(6) (1976).

Sections 102 through 109 of the Act set forth the content and disclosure rules applicable to all "written warranties." Section 102 provides that "any warrantor warranting a consumer product to a consumer by means of a written warranty shall, to the extent required by the rules of the [Federal Trade] Commission, fully and conspicuously disclose in simple and readily understood language the terms and conditions of such warranty." 15 U.S.C. § 2302(a) (1976). Pursuant to this provision, the FTC has, by regulation, required that warrantors made detailed disclosures of information necessary to allow consumers to understand and enforce written warranties.[4] The FTC regulations also require, pursuant to § 102(b), that sellers of consumer products with written warranties make available to the consumer the text of such warranties prior to sale. 16 C.F.R. § 702.3 (1980).

Under § 103, warrantors must conspicuously designate written warranties as either "full" or "limited." If a warranty is designated as "full," § 104 provides that the warrantor must (1) remedy defects or malfunctions without charge and within a reasonable period of time; (2) make no limitation on the duration of any implied warranty on the product; (3) provide for no exclusion of limitation of consequential damages unless conspicuously stated, and (4) refund or replace the product if, after a reasonable number of attempted repairs, the supplier fails to remedy defects or malfunctions.

§ 102(b)(2), which reads: "Nothing in this title . . . shall be deemed to authorize the Commission . . . to require that a consumer product or any of its components be warranted." 15 U.S.C. § 2302(b)(2) (1976).

4. [Here, the court quotes Magnuson–Moss Warranty Act Regulations § 701.3(a).]

An additional obligation placed on suppliers extending written warranties is found in § 108, which provides that such suppliers may not disclaim, modify or limit the duration on implied warranties to a period shorter than the "duration of a written warranty of reasonable duration."[5]

The scope of the private action for breach of "written warranty" created by § 110(d) is the issue presented to us for resolution.[6] Section 110(d) provides in part that: "[A] consumer who is damaged by the failure of a supplier, warrantor, or service contractor to comply with any obligation under this title, or a written warranty, implied warranty, or service contract, may bring suit for damages and other legal and equitable relief [in any state court of competent jurisdiction or in an appropriate federal district court]." The district court properly rejected plaintiffs' argument that the Act's draftsmen intended in § 110(d) to create a federal private cause of action for breach of all written express warranties. None of the legislative history offered by plaintiffs in this record provides the clear evidence of Congressional intent necessary to overcome the "familiar principle governing the interpretation of statutes ... that if a statutory definition of a word is given, that definition must prevail, regardless of what other meaning may be attributable to the word." Evans v. Int'l Typographical Union, 76 F.Supp. 881, 887 (S.D.Ind.1948).[7] Indeed, we are less than confident that it is possible to

5. Any such limitation must be "conscionable and ... set forth in clear and unmistakable language and prominently displayed on the face of the warranty." The FTC has interpreted the phrase "on the face of the warranty" [in the Regulations at § 701.1(i)].

6. Plaintiffs' complaint alleged that GM had warranted that its automobiles contained THM 350 (M38) transmissions, or "transmissions of similar quality and performance ... and that [such transmissions] would meet a specified level of performance." The district court concluded that such a warranty did not fall within the § 101(6) definition of "written warranty," because it did not affirm that the transmission would "meet a specified level of performance over a specified period of time." This conclusion is consistent with the FTC's interpretation of § 101(6), which is set forth in its regulations at § 700.3(a). The district court noted that, by this reading of § 101(6), a representation that a "transmission would perform like a THM 350 transmission for the life of the transmission" would constitute a "written warranty," while the representation that a "transmission would perform like a THM 350 transmission" does not. The arbitrariness of this distinction is apparent, but a certain amount of arbitrariness is inevitable whenever a bright line must be drawn. And the need for a clearly circumscribed definition

in the statutory scheme before us is apparent since, to comply with the Act's obligations, manufacturers and suppliers must know in advance exactly which representations are subject to those obligations. Moreover, it is quite plausible that the Act's draftsmen defined "written warranty" in § 101(6) so as to exclude general descriptions of consumer products or their components from the reach of the Act, since it would be excessively cumbersome to impose the Act's disclosure rules on every advertisement containing a description of a product or its components. On this appeal, plaintiffs do not challenge the district court's conclusion that the warranties described in their complaint are not within the § 101(6) definition. 500 F.Supp. at 1185–86.

7. As a rule, there should be a strong presumption that a statutory term means what it is defined to mean, because, by the very act of including a definition in the statute, the statute's draftsmen have made a considered determination of the appropriate meaning of that term for the purposes of the particular statutory scheme they have created. Nothing offered by the plaintiffs is sufficient to suggest that Congress did not intend for the definition it ascribed to "written warranty" for purposes of the Act in § 101(6) not to apply to the phrase "written warranty" in § 110(d).

distill any unambiguous Congressional intent from the Act's legislative history. [At this point, the court considers arguments concerning the legislative history.]

[I]n arguing that § 110(d) provides consumers with a claim actionable in federal court for breach of any written express warranty, plaintiffs argue for a construction of § 110(d) that was not contemplated by either the House or the Senate.

The reports and proceedings of legislative bodies unquestionably lend themselves to the imagery of archaeology. But for better or worse, the papyrus scrolls or cuneiform tablets which survive such proceedings must count for more than the odd-shaped rocks, human skulls and miscellaneous artifacts scattered around the site. In its "archaeological dig" into legislative history, the district court tended to overlook the obvious but prosaic in favor of exotic "ambiguities" attributable more easily to drafting fatigue than to confusion of purpose.

CUNNINGHAM v. FLEETWOOD HOMES OF GEORGIA, INC.

United States Court of Appeals for the Eleventh Circuit, 2001.
253 F.3d 611.

Cox, J. In April of 1998, the Cunninghams purchased a new mobile home manufactured by Fleetwood from Ronnie Smith's Home Center, Inc.. The mobile home came with a manufacturer's warranty, and, as a part of the sales transaction, the Cunninghams executed an arbitration agreement with Ronnie Smith's [which expressly named Fleetwood as a third-part beneficiary].[1] Shortly after the purchase and installation of the home, the Cunninghams contacted Ronnie Smith's and Fleetwood with a variety of complaints about defects in the home. Unsatisfied with the response, the Cunninghams filed suit alleging [*inter alia*] violations of the Magnuson–Moss Warranty Act, 15 U.S.C. § 2301–2312. The district court, concluding that Fleetwood was a third-party beneficiary of the arbitration agreement but that the Magnuson–Moss Warranty Act precludes arbitration of the Cunninghams' written or express warranty claims, issued an order compelling arbitration of all claims except for the Magnuson–Moss claims for breach of written or express warranties. Fleetwood appeals.

Fleetwood notes that the Federal Arbitration Act (FAA) creates a presumption of validity for arbitration clauses, *see* 9 U.S.C. § 2, and argues that because Magnuson–Moss does nothing to disturb the FAA's

---

1. [The arbitration agreement read, in pertinent part:] Buyer and Seller agree, covenant and consent that any controversies or claims arising out of or in any way relating to the sale of the said mobile home and the negotiations leading up to the sale shall be settled solely by arbitration in accordance with the applicable Rules of the American Arbitration Association. It is further agreed by the parties that all rights, privileges and responsibilities under this agreement shall expressly inure to the benefit of the manufacturer of the said mobile home insofar as any claims may exist or thereafter arise against the manufacturer.

mandate, the arbitration agreement must be enforced according to its terms. The Cunninghams, on the other hand, argue that Magnuson–Moss and the rules promulgated by the Federal Trade Commission pursuant to Magnuson–Moss prohibit binding arbitration of warranty claims.

A. THE TEXT OF THE MAGNUSON-MOSS WARRANTY ACT

The Cunninghams note that 15 U.S.C. § 2310 (d) creates a statutory right of action for consumers "who are damaged by the failure of a supplier, warrantor, or service contractor to comply with any obligation under this chapter or under a written warranty, implied warranty, or service contract...." Also, in § 2310(a) Magnuson–Moss provides for the inclusion of informal dispute settlement mechanisms within written warranties, and delegates to the Federal Trade Commission the authority to establish minimum requirements for these mechanisms. The Cunninghams argue that Magnuson–Moss prohibits binding arbitration by making § 2310(a)'s informal dispute settlement mechanism the only exception to the right of action created by § 2310(d); no other mechanisms are permitted. In other words, in the Cunninghams' view Magnuson–Moss permits alternative dispute resolution, including arbitration, but only of the non-binding sort that fits the § 2310(a)(3) description and that complies with the rules promulgated by the Federal Trade Commission.

Fleetwood argues that § 2310(a)(1) only encourages inclusion of informal dispute resolution mechanisms in written warranties, and does not preclude enforcement of agreements to resolve claims by binding arbitration. Under Fleetwood's reading of Magnuson–Moss, the mechanism described by § 2310(a) is not the only method of alternative dispute resolution available to warrantors and consumers, and the statutory cause of action created by § 2310(d) merely confers a right that can be waived by express agreement. In support of this line of argument, Fleetwood notes that Magnuson–Moss expressly states that nothing in the Act shall invalidate or restrict any right or remedy of a consumer under any other federal law. 15 U.S.C. § 2311 (b). In Fleetwood's view, this provision necessarily includes the substantive portions of the FAA that protect the ability of contracting parties to enter into binding arbitration agreements.

B. THE LEGISLATIVE HISTORY OF THE ACT

Fleetwood argues that the legislative history of Magnuson–Moss does not express a clear intent to prohibit binding arbitration, but that at most, it evidences an intention to prohibit warrantors from including binding informal dispute resolution mechanisms in written warranties. Because the arbitration agreement at issue here was not in the manufacturer's warranty, but was instead a part of the sales transaction between the buyer and the seller, Fleetwood contends that legislative history indicating concerns with the content of written warranties is inapplicable.

In response the Cunninghams note that at the time of Magnuson–Moss's passage members of Congress indicated that use of the informal dispute resolution mechanism was intended as only a prerequisite, and would not be a bar to a later civil action on the warranty. In keeping with their construction of the text, the Cunninghams interpret this statement as an indication that Congress expected that all informal dispute resolution mechanisms would be non-binding, as they would otherwise violate the provisions of the Act. In support the Cunninghams cite the regulations promulgated by the Federal Trade Commission pursuant to the Act, which detail the particulars of the informal dispute resolution mechanism of § 2310(a), as well as the history of the regulations, which includes statements by the Federal Trade Commission rejecting industry calls for the incorporation of legally binding mechanisms. *See* 40 Fed. Reg. 60,168, 60,211 (1975) (stating "reference within the written warranty to any binding, non-judicial remedy is prohibited by the Rule and the Act."). Fleetwood's retort is to repeat that none of the above applies to arbitration agreements not in the written warranty.

C. The Purpose of the Act

Fleetwood locates the purposes of Magnuson–Moss in the section detailing the Act's disclosure requirements, which reads: "to improve the adequacy of information available to consumers, prevent deception, and improve competition in the marketing of consumer products." 15 U.S.C. § 2302 (a). Fleetwood submits that enforcing seller-consumer arbitration agreements that make warrantors third-party beneficiaries does not conflict with these purposes.

The Cunninghams note that the legislative history provides that Magnuson–Moss was passed at least in part to "provide the consumer with an economically feasible private right of action," *Wilson*, 954 F.Supp. at 1538 (quoting 119 CONG. REC. 972 (1973) (remarks of Congressman Moss)), and they argue that allowing Fleetwood to compel arbitration would force them to absorb costs that do not comport with the statutory policy of Magnuson–Moss. Additionally, the Cunninghams argue that because Magnuson–Moss's purpose is to require manufacturers to include all information relevant to the warranty in the warranty itself, allowing Fleetwood to compel arbitration as a third-party beneficiary of the Ronnie Smith's-Cunningham agreement defeats the express purpose of the Act. The Cunninghams also submit that the absence of language in the warranty referencing the arbitration agreement is itself a violation of the Act, as Magnuson–Moss and the Federal Trade Commission regulations require full and conspicuous disclosure of the terms and conditions of the warranty. *See* 15 U.S.C. § 2302; 16 C.F.R. § § 701.3, 703.2. Thus, the Cunninghams argue compelling arbitration on the basis of an arbitration agreement that is not referenced in the warranty presents an inherent conflict with the Act's purpose of providing clear and concise warranties to consumers.

The Federal Arbitration Act, 9 U.S.C. § 1, *et seq.,* "places arbitration agreements upon the same footing as other contracts." Congress enacted the Magnuson–Moss Warranty Act "to improve the adequacy of information available to consumers, prevent deception, and to improve competition in the marketing of consumer products." Magnuson–Moss does not require manufacturers to provide warranties, but instead creates specific duties and liabilities for manufacturers that choose to do so. 16 C.F.R. § 700.03. The Act focuses primarily on written warranties for consumer products.[2]

The most significant provisions in Magnuson–Moss pertain to the disclosure of written consumer product warranty terms and conditions, the pre-sale availability of written warranty terms, the authorization of consumer suits for damages and other legal and equitable relief, and the procedures for creating informal dispute settlement mechanisms. The Cunninghams argue that the text of these provisions evidences Congress's intention to prohibit or limit the waiver of judicial remedies for Magnuson–Moss claims. We turn first to § 2310, the civil action and informal dispute settlement mechanism section.

Section 2310 of Magnuson–Moss provides a statutory cause of action to consumers "damaged by the failure of a supplier, warrantor, or service contractor to comply with any obligation imposed by the Act or under a written warranty, implied warranty or service contract." *Id.* § 2310(d)(1). Suit may be brought in either state or federal court. The Act also permits class actions, and in an effort to encourage consumers to pursue claims, Magnuson–Moss allows prevailing consumer litigants to receive attorneys' fees and costs. *Id.* § 2310(d)(2), (e). The Act also places certain impediments in the way of litigation-minded consumers. First, prior to bringing suit for breach of warranty, a consumer must give persons obligated under the warranty a reasonable opportunity to "cure" the failure to comply with the obligations at issue. *Id.* § 2310(e). Second, in order to bring suit in federal court, the amount in controversy must be at least $50,000, exclusive of interests and costs. Additionally, there is a $25 per claim requirement and there must be 100 named plaintiffs for Magnuson–Moss class actions. Significantly, Magnuson–Moss also gives warrantors the ability to establish procedural prerequisites to a consumer's civil action.

To encourage the settlement of consumer disputes by means other than civil suits, § 2310 allows warrantors to include informal dispute settlement mechanisms in the warranty. *Id.* § 2310(a)(3). So long as the mechanism complies with the Act's requirements and the rules estab-

---

2. Magnuson–Moss defines "written warranty" as "any written affirmation of fact or written promise made in connection with the sale of a consumer product by a supplier to a buyer which relates to the nature of the material or workmanship and affirms or promises that such material or workmanship is defect free or will meet a specified level of performance over a specified period of time, or ... any undertaking in writing in connection with the sale by a supplier of a consumer product to refund, repair, replace or take other remedial action with respect to such product in the event that such product fails to meet the specifications set forth in the undertaking, which written affirmation, promise, or undertaking becomes part of the basis of the bargain between a supplier and a buyer for purposes other than resale of such product." 15 U.S.C. § 2301(6).

lished by the Federal Trade Commission, § 2310(a)(3)(B), and the written warranty contains the requirement that the consumer utilize the mechanism before pursuing a legal remedy, § 2310(a)(3)(C), warrantors can make the informal dispute settlement process a mandatory prerequisite to instituting a consumer suit in state or federal court.

The district court concluded that the informal dispute settlement procedure of § 2310(a)(3) is a non-binding mechanism, in that it serves at most as a prerequisite, and not a bar, to relief in court. We agree. The language of the section makes this clear when it states that, if a warrantor establishes a mechanism, "then ... the consumer may not commence a civil action ... unless he initially resorts to such procedure.". § 2310(a)(3). Congress's inclusion of the word "initially" in the proviso clause indicates that once a consumer has utilized the warrantor's conforming mechanism, a subsequent civil action is permissible—a possibility that binding arbitration does not anticipate. The legislative history buttresses this conclusion.

The Cunninghams contend, and the district court agreed, that the only permissible conclusion to be drawn from the text of § 2310 and the attendant legislative history is that Magnuson–Moss makes the non-binding § 2310 mechanism the sole exception to its guarantee of a consumer cause of action; these two alternatives eclipse the field of possibilities. Thus, binding arbitration agreements executed between buyer and seller that designate manufacturers as third-party beneficiaries violate the Act because they are binding, whether they are in the warranty or not, and they are therefore unenforceable. However, as Fleetwood notes, there is no explicit reference to binding arbitration in the statute, and a contrary conclusion is in fact permissible.

[T]he Supreme Court has revisited similar arbitration issues in a variety of contexts. A review of these cases convinces us that the district court was incorrect in concluding that, standing alone, the presence of the non-binding § 2310 mechanism in the statutory text requires the conclusion that Magnuson–Moss claims may not be the subject of binding arbitration agreements. Aspects of § 2310 of Magnuson–Moss resemble provisions in statutory schemes previously considered in the Supreme Court's FAA jurisprudence. However, while we are inclined to think that the presence of the non-binding § 2310 mechanism in the statutory text does not in and of itself mandate the conclusion that Magnuson–Moss renders binding arbitration agreements unenforceable, other key provisions of Magnuson–Moss, together with § 2310, cast considerable doubt on the propriety of the particular arrangement at issue here. These provisions include the requirements that significant conditions, limitations, and terms of the warranty be included in simple language in the warranty itself, and that the warranty must consist of a single, understandable document made available prior to sale to the consumer.

Magnuson–Moss provides rules governing the content of warranties "in order to improve the adequacy of information available to consumers, prevent deception, and improve competition in the marketing of consumer products." 15 U.S.C. § 2302 (a). The Act requires that any warrantor that chooses to provide a written warranty with a consumer product "shall ... fully and conspicuously disclose in simple and readily understood language the terms and conditions of such warranty." *Id.* The Act suggests the inclusion of thirteen items, among them: "a statement of what the warrantor will do in the event of a defect, malfunction, or failure to conform with the written warranty-at whose expense-and for what period of time," *id.* § 2302(a)(4); "a statement of what the consumer must do and expenses he must bear," *id.* § 2302(a)(5); "exceptions and exclusions from the terms of the warranty," *id.* § 2302(a)(6); "the step-by-step procedure which the consumer should take in order to obtain performance of any obligation under the warranty," *id.* § 2302(a)(7); "information respecting the availability of any informal dispute settlement procedure offered by the warrantor and a recital, where the warranty so provides, that the purchaser may be required to resort to such procedures before pursuing any legal remedies in the courts," *id.* § 2302(a)(8); and "the elements of the warranty in words or phrases which would not mislead a reasonable, average consumer as to the nature or scope of the warranty." *Id.* § 2302(a)(13). Magnuson–Moss delegates promulgation of specific disclosure requirements to the FTC, but requires that the terms of any written warranty be made available to the consumer or prospective consumer prior to sale. *Id.* § 2302(a), (b)(1)(A).

The disclosure requirements established by the FTC pursuant to Magnuson–Moss are codified at 16 C.F.R. § 701.3, and obligate warrantors to "clearly and conspicuously disclose warranty terms in a single document in simple and readily understood language." 16 C.F.R. § 701.3(a). Among these mandatory items, nondisclosure of which is a violation of both Magnuson–Moss and the Federal Trade Commission Act as an unfair or deceptive act or practice,[3] 15 U.S.C. § § 45 (a)(1), 2310(b), the FTC includes: "a statement of what the warrantor will do in the event of a defect, malfunction or failure to conform with the written warranty ..." 16 C.F.R. § 701.3(a)(3); "a step-by step explanation of the procedure which the consumer should follow in order to obtain performance of any warranty obligation ..." *id.* § 701.3(a)(5); and "information respecting the availability of any informal dispute settlement mechanism...." *Id.* § 701.3(a)(6). This last requirement is echoed in § 703.2, which requires the warrantor to disclose "clearly and conspicuously at least the following information on the face of the written warranty: ... a statement of the availability of the informal dispute settlement mechanism." *Id.* § 703.2(b)(1).

---

3. For purposes of an FTC-instituted action, a warranty is deceptive if it "contains an affirmation, promise, description, or representation which is either false or fraudulent, or which, in light of all of the circumstances, would mislead a reasonable individual exercising due care; or if the warranty fails to contain information which is necessary in light of all of the circumstances, to make the warranty not misleading to a reasonable individual exercising due care...." 15 U.S.C. § 2310 (c)(2).

The comprehensive disclosure requirements of Magnuson–Moss are an integral, if not the central, feature of the Act, perhaps eclipsing even the civil action and informal dispute resolution mechanisms in their importance to consumers. CURTIS R. REITZ, CONSUMER PROTECTION UNDER THE MAGNUSON–MOSS WARRANTY ACT 31 (1978). Prior to the passage of Magnuson–Moss, consumers had been inundated with problems concerning the complexity of warranties, complexity generated by the presence of misleading terms and incomplete disclosure on the part of warrantors. Magnuson–Moss's enactors anticipated that "one of the most important effects of this bill would be its ability to relieve consumer frustration by promoting understanding. [T]he purpose of this legislation is (1) to make warranties on consumer products more readily understood and enforceable".

Congress sought to remedy the situation by requiring that material terms be presented in clear language in a single document. The FTC, instructed to implement Congress's solutions to the perceived problems, crafted the disclosure requirements so that they might "inform the consumer of the full extent of his or her obligations under the warranty, and to eliminate confusion as to the necessary steps which he or she must take in order to get warranty performance." The single document rule reinforces these concerns by requiring warrantors to present all information relevant to the warranty in one place, where it might be easily located and assimilated by the consumer. Significantly, the FTC, bringing its regulatory experience to the task, recognized that the omission of relevant terms was as likely to foster erroneous assumptions as inclusion of misleading terms, because "the failure to disclose all conditions, limitations, and exclusions as to product warranties renders any affirmative claims about warranties deceptive."

Our preceding analysis commands the conclusion that Fleetwood's use of its third-party beneficiary status under the Ronnie Smith's-Cunningham agreement to compel arbitration where Fleetwood has failed to disclose in the warranty a term or clause requiring the Cunninghams to utilize an informal dispute resolution mechanism contravenes the text, legislative history, and purpose of the Magnuson–Moss Warranty Act. Fleetwood contends that neither Magnuson–Moss nor the rules promulgated by the FTC pursuant to Magnuson–Moss apply to agreements that are not incorporated into the terms of the written warranty, like the arbitration agreement here. Whether Fleetwood is correct in this contention or not, Magnuson–Moss and the rules do apply to the content of written warranties, including omissions, and Fleetwood can not "do by the surrogate or vicarious means" of the Ronnie Smith's-Cunningham arbitration agreement what Magnuson–Moss requires that it do directly: disclose in a single document all relevant terms of the warranty. Compelling arbitration on the basis of an arbitration agreement that is not referenced in the warranty presents an inherent conflict with the Act's purpose of providing clear and concise warranties to consumers.

[T]he propriety of Ronnie Smith's and the Cunninghams' agreement to arbitrate—the seller and buyer agreement—is not before us. We are not required to and do not decide whether Magnuson–Moss makes arbitration agreements unenforceable as to all Magnuson–Moss claims. Nor is it necessary for us to determine whether warrantors may include binding arbitration provisions in the warranty itself. The only issue we are presented with here, and thus decide, is whether Fleetwood can utilize its third-party beneficiary status under the Ronnie Smith's-Cunningham arbitration agreement to compel binding arbitration of the Cunninghams' breach of written or express warranty claims against Fleetwood when there is no reference to binding arbitration in the warranty. Because we conclude that Fleetwood's failure to disclose in the warranty a term or clause requiring the Cunninghams to utilize an informal dispute resolution mechanism runs afoul of the disclosure requirements of the Magnuson–Moss Warranty Act, we affirm the district court's order declining to compel arbitration of the written or express warranty claims.

AFFIRMED.

Problem 43

(a) A number of cases have found that parties failed to meet the $50,000 Federal Court jurisdictional threshold required by Magnuson–Moss (M/M). In *Gardynski–Leschuck v. Ford Motor Co.*, 142 F.3d 955 (7th Cir.1998), the plaintiff listed the following damages to activate M/M jurisdiction: Cost of vehicle: $18,491.99; Loss of use: $2,770; Aggravation/Inconvenience: $750; Reasonable attorneys' fees: $28,020. Total: $50,031.99. Does M/M apply in this case?

(b) In *Simmons v. Taylor Childre Chevrolet–Pontiac, Inc.*, 629 F.Supp. 1030 (M.D.Ga.1986), the court held that a statement on a seller's invoice describing an automobile as "new" may have created a UCC express warranty, but would not meet the requirements for a written warranty under M/M. Why not? Consider the definition of "written warranty" under M/M § 101(6) and 16 C.F.R. § 700.3.

(c) Before agreeing to purchase, the buyer of a diamond ring had received a written appraisal of the ring accompanied by an appraisal certificate which read as follows:

> We estimate the value of articles for insurance or other purposes at the current retail value, excluding taxes. In making this Appraisal we do not agree to purchase or replace the articles, nor is this Appraisal a guarantee that said articles will realize the Appraisal amount at any public, private or other sale. This Appraisal is made with the understanding that the Appraiser assumes no liability with respect to any action that may be taken in reliance on this Appraisal.

Does the appraisal constitute a "written warranty" under M/M?

(d) If a car dealer delivers the manufacturer's warranty to the buyer at the time of the sale of the new car, is the dealer "actually making" a written warranty and thereby subjecting itself to liability under M/M? See M/M § 110(f) and 16 C. F. R. § 700.4.

(e) For Magnuson–Moss purposes, a "consumer product" is defined in § 101(1) of the Act (15 USCA § 2301(1)). See also the M/M regulations at 16 C. F. R. § 700.1. With that background, identify which of the following involve a "consumer product" under M/M:

(i) Laura Richmond purchased a 27–inch Sony television set for her home.

(ii) Dr. Laura Richmond, an ophthalmologist, purchased a 27–inch Sony television set for the waiting room in her office.

(iii) Dr. Richmond is not only a very successful ophthalmologist but also a remarkably shrewd investor. To avoid the hassle of commercial flights to her island home on Providenciale, off Cuba, she has purchased a $3 million jet aircraft. The plane seats 5, cruises at 436 miles per hour, has a range of 1800 miles and is capable of landing on the short landing strip at the island's airport. Is the plane a "consumer product" under Magnuson–Moss?

(f) When he unpacked his newly purchased automatic coffee pot, George Hart found two documents: (a) a folded printed sheet containing, *inter alia*, a "limited warranty" warranting the pot against defects in materials and workmanship for a period of 90 days and limiting the implied warranty of merchantability to a like period; (b) a "warranty registration card" which stated that the buyer had to fill out the card and return it or the limited warranty would be void. George neglected to return the card. Thirty days after buying the pot George discovered a defect. Does he have a claim under M/M? See M/M § 108 and 16 C. F. R. § 700.7.

(g) Is a post-formation "written warranty" valid under M/M? What of a post-formation "service contract"? See M/M § 106 and C. F. R. § 700.11.

(h) Section 103 of M/M requires that every written warranty covered by M/M be labeled either "full" or "limited." The minimum standards that a "full" warranty must meet are listed in M/M § 104. Compare § 104(a)(2) and § 108(b). If a seller who gives written warranties wants to limit the duration of an implied warranty of merchantability in consumer sales, how should that seller proceed?

(i) Consider the kinds of terms that must be included or disclosed in a written warranty under M/M. See M/M § 102 and 16 C. F. R. § 701.3. Now consider M/M § 102(b)(1)(A). You represent a retail store that does not itself make written warranties but which sells products covered by manufacturers' written warranties. What are your client's obligations concerning the manufacturers' warranties? How should the manufacturers disclose the terms of their written warranties to retail consumers? See 16 C. F. R. § 702.3.

(j) You have a client that sells consumer products through its web site. The products are covered by written warranties within the meaning of M/M. How would you advise your client to comply with its disclosure obligations under M/M? Is 16 C.F.R. § 702.3(c) relevant?

Chapter 4

NONCONFORMING TENDER AND PROSPECTIVE NONPERFORMANCE

PART 1: THE RESPONSE TO TENDER

A. THE BUYER'S COURSES OF ACTION UPON RECEIPT OF GOODS UNDER UCC ARTICLE 2

1. Rejection, Acceptance, and Revocation of Acceptance Under Article 2: An Overview

To perform a contract of sale the seller must "tender" the goods—i.e., must offer delivery of the goods by putting and holding them at the buyer's disposal (2–503(1)). When a seller tenders (by, for example, having the goods delivered to the buyer's place of business) the buyer faces a decision. It can refuse the delivery, an action that article 2 calls *rejecting* the goods, or it can receive and retain the goods, a course that article 2 labels *acceptance* of goods.

The basic provision governing rejection of goods is 2–601, which authorizes the seller to reject "if the goods or the tender of delivery fail in any respect to conform to the contract." In other words, a buyer has the right to reject goods if they breach a warranty or if the seller's tender of delivery otherwise breaches the contract *"in any respect."* This so-called "perfect tender rule," however, is subject to a variety of limitations and conditions on the buyer's right to reject, all of which are explored in this Chapter. If the buyer rejects goods and the rejection is "rightful" (because the seller breached in a fashion that justifies rejection), it relieves the buyer of the obligation to pay the price. As we shall see, even a "wrongful rejection"—i.e., one where the buyer did not have the right to reject but did so anyway—may relieve the buyer of liability for the price, although such a buyer may be liable for damages.

The alternative to rejection is acceptance of the goods. Acceptance occurs if the buyer takes various affirmative actions with respect to tendered goods, or even if the buyer merely fails to reject the goods within a reasonable time after receiving them (2–606). Once the buyer accepts it can no longer reject and it becomes obligated to pay for the goods "at the contract rate" (2–607(1)), although it may still retain remedies (e.g., the right to recover damages) for any breaches by the seller (2–607(2)). In certain circumstances, however, the buyer who has accepted may be able to *revoke* its acceptance under 2–608. Revocation has the same effect on the parties' rights and obligations as rejection. See 2–608(3).

Thus suppose a law firm agreed to purchase a computer from a dealer but the machine that the seller delivered was defective. Also suppose the defects render the computer non-functional and constitute a breach of one or more warranties in the sales contract between the parties. Because the computer does not conform to the contract, the buyer has the right to reject the goods under 2–601. The buyer can reject by following the procedures in 2–602(1). If the buyer fails to reject the goods within a reasonable time after receiving them (because, e.g., it did not immediately discover the defects or it wanted the goods despite their problems) the buyer will have accepted them (2–606(1)(b)). In that case the buyer will have to pay the agreed price, 2–607(1), subject to the possibility of an offset for damages caused by the breach. The only way the buyer can escape the obligation to the pay the price and the other consequences of acceptance is to revoke its acceptance under 2–608.

If the buyer does properly reject or revoke acceptance, it can thrust the goods back on the seller and, absent an effective cure by the seller (2–508), discharge its contractual obligations. An analogous situation arises in non-sales transactions when one party's breach discharges the other party's duty to perform. Under the common law of contracts, such discharge generally occurs only if there is a *material* breach of contract, but the law of sales has traditionally had a different standard for discharge. Keep the common law background in mind as you work through the materials in this Chapter.

2. *Rejection*

Problem 44

Paley & Tologist ("P & T"), a law firm, agreed in writing to purchase 200 new IBX personal computers from Random Accessories, Inc., a computer dealer, for $200,000, delivery by November 1. Random warranted that the computers would be merchantable and that all components would be "100% original IBX equipment." On November 1, Random delivered 200 IBX computers to P & T's offices. After the Random truck departed, P & T's office manager noticed that all the computers were equipped with keyboards manufactured by Clonics, Inc. The Clonics keyboards, while cheaper than the standard IBX computer keyboard, are considered by many (but not all) to be superior to the IBX model. Does P & T have the right to reject the computers? Could P & T rightfully reject if only five computers had the Clonics keyboards and the other 195 came with the standard IBX keyboard?

Questions

(1) If P & T has the right to reject when only five computers have Clonics keyboards, may it reject all 200 computers? May it reject just the computers with Clonics keyboards? May it accept 100 computers and reject the remainder? Suppose P & T opts to accept the 195 conforming computers, becoming obligated under 2–607(1) to pay for them "at the contract rate." How much must it pay for the 195 computers? Consider comment 1 to 2–607.

(2) How should P & T go about rejecting the computers it does not wish to retain? Read 2–602. Suppose that on the day the computers were tendered P & T sent Random a letter stating, "We hereby reject all the computers you delivered." Is the letter a sufficient rejection? See 2–605. What are the consequences if a buyer's notice of rejection fails to identify a particular ascertainable and curable non-conformity?

(3) Suppose P & T properly rejects the computers. What should it do with them? See 2–602(2) and 2–603. See also 2–401(4).

Problem 45

One Saturday in April Sasha held a yard sale at her house. Among the items she offered for sale was her three year-old power lawn mower, which she had purchased (new) for $400 and which she priced at the garage sale at $50. Bert bought several items at Sasha's yard sale, including the mower. At the time of the purchase, Bert did not request and Sasha did not volunteer any information about the mower. When he got the mower home and tried to use it, Bert discovered that it did not run and would require extensive (and expensive) repairs to be put in working order. Does Bert have the right to reject the mower? See 2–106(2).

Problem 46

Return to the transaction in Problem 44 involving Random's sale of IBX computers to P & T for delivery on November 1. Now assume that, when Random delivered the computers on November 1, they were all equipped with standard IBX keyboards. When P & T's managing partner tried out several of the computers, she found the keyboards "stiff" and difficult to use. The operation of the keyboards on the computers tendered to P & T is normal for IBX models. Although articles in several computer magazines have complained about the "feel" and design of the standard IBX keyboard, IBX continues to ship millions of computers equipped with such keyboards and IBX personal computers equipped with the keyboards remain the best sellers in the industry. Can P & T rightfully reject the computers?

Questions

(1) Suppose P & T does not have a right to reject the computers, but it nevertheless sends Random notice of rejection and refuses to accept or pay for the goods. What are the consequences? Will a court ignore the improper rejection and treat P & T as having accepted (thus making P & T liable for

the price under 2–607(1) and 2–709(1)(a))? Or will a court give effect to the rejection but treat it as a breach? See the references to wrongful rejection in 2–602(3) and 2–703, and the discussion of wrongful but effective rejection in comment 3 to 2–602.

(2) Would your answer to Problem 46 change if Random had tendered the computers on November 2?

Note: Limitations on the Perfect Tender Rule

In Ramirez v. Autosport, 88 N.J. 277, 440 A.2d 1345 (1982), the New Jersey Supreme Court commented:

> Our initial inquiry is whether a consumer may reject defective goods that do not conform to the contract of sale. The basic issue is whether under the UCC, adopted in New Jersey as N.J.S.A. 12A:1–101 et seq., a seller has the duty to deliver goods that conform precisely to the contract. We conclude that the seller is under such a duty to make a "perfect tender" and that a buyer has the right to reject goods that do not conform to the contract....

> In the nineteenth century, sellers were required to deliver goods that complied exactly with the sales agreement.... That rule, known as the "perfect tender" rule, remained part of the law of sales well into the twentieth century. By the 1920's the doctrine was so entrenched in the law that Judge Learned Hand declared "[t]here is no room in commercial contracts for the doctrine of substantial performance." Mitsubishi Goshi Kaisha v. J. Aron & Co., Inc., 16 F.2d 185, 186 (2 Cir.1926).

> The harshness of the rule led courts to seek to ameliorate its effect and to bring the law of sales in closer harmony with the law of contracts, which allows rescission only for material breaches.... The chief objection to the continuation of the perfect tender rule was that buyers in a declining market would reject goods for minor nonconformities and force the loss on surprised sellers....

> To the extent that a buyer can reject goods for any nonconformity, the UCC retains the perfect tender rule. Section 2–106 states that goods conform to a contract "when they are in accordance with the obligations under the contract". N.J.S.A. 12A:2–106. Section 2–601 authorizes a buyer to reject goods if they "or the tender of delivery fail in any respect to conform to the contract". N.J.S.A. 12A:2–601. The Code, however, mitigates the harshness of the perfect tender rule and balances the interests of buyer and seller.

Ramirez v. Autosport, 440 A.2d at 1349.

Problems 45 and 46 suggest one way in which Article 2 "mitigates the harshness of the perfect tender rule." A buyer or lessee has the right to reject a tender only if "the goods or the tender of delivery fail ... to conform to the contract"—i.e., only if the seller or lessor breaches by, for example, delivering goods that do not conform to a warranty. Minor imperfections in the goods or the tender may not constitute a breach. For instance, the implied warranty of merchantability does not require flawless goods (unless the standards of the relevant trade or the requirements of ordinary use demand such). Another example involves delays in delivery by the seller or lessor. Unless the contract provides that time is of the essence, courts faced with delays that are only minor will sometimes treat delivery dates as "mere estimates" rather than contractually binding terms. There are, nevertheless, situations in which seemingly insignificant flaws in the goods or the tender clearly do constitute a breach, thus apparently permitting rejection of the goods under the perfect tender rule. Does Article 2 "mitigate[] the harshness of the perfect tender rule" in those circumstances? Consider the following.

Problem 47

The Lumber Region Corp., owner of a chain of home supply stores, agreed in writing to purchase 100,000 board feet of 2x8x10 No. 1 white oak boards from Northwestern Industries, Inc. for $.50 per foot ($50,000). When the goods arrived at Lumber Region's warehouse, 8,000 board feet graded as inferior No. 3 common white oak. Lumber Region rejected the entire shipment. Analyze whether the rejection was rightful in the following circumstances:

(a) The contract provided for replacement of any lumber that graded below No. 1, and stated that such replacement was the buyer's sole remedy. See 2–719(1).

(b) Alternatively, Northwestern proved there is a custom in the lumber industry allowing sellers to include up to 10% below-grade lumber in large shipments. Northwestern's invoice for the shipment reflected a price adjustment for the lower grade boards. See 1–303, 1–201(b)(3) & (12); North American Steel Corp. v. Siderius, 75 Mich.App. 391, 254 N.W.2d 899 (1977).

(c) Alternatively, Northwestern proved that in five previous transactions Lumber Region had accepted (with a price adjustment) shipments containing between 4% and 12% lower grade lumber. See Courtesy Enterprises, Inc. v. Richards Laboratories, 457 N.E.2d 572 (Ind.App.1983).

NEUMILLER FARMS, INC. v. CORNETT

Supreme Court of Alabama, 1979.
368 So.2d 272.

Shores, Justice. Jonah D. Cornett and Ralph Moore, Sellers, were potato farmers in DeKalb County, Alabama. Neumiller Farms, Inc., Buyer, was a corporation engaged in brokering potatoes from the growers to the makers of potato chips. The controversy concerns Buyer's rejection of nine loads of potatoes out of a contract calling for twelve loads. A jury returned a verdict of $17,500 for Sellers based on a breach of contract. Buyer appealed. We affirm.

From the evidence, the jury could have found the following:

On March 3, 1976, the parties signed a written contract whereby Sellers agreed to deliver twelve loads of chipping potatoes to Buyer during July and August, 1976, and Buyer agreed to pay $4.25 per hundredweight. The contract required that the potatoes be United States

Grade No. 1 and "chipt [sic] to buyer satisfaction." As the term was used in this contract, a load of potatoes contains 430 hundredweight and is valued at $1,827.50.

Sellers' potato crop yielded twenty to twenty-four loads of potatoes and Buyer accepted three of these loads without objection. At that time, the market price of chipping potatoes was $4.25 per hundredweight. Shortly thereafter, the market price declined to $2.00 per hundredweight.

When Sellers tendered additional loads of potatoes, Buyer refused acceptance, saying the potatoes would not "chip" satisfactorily. Sellers responded by having samples of their crop tested by an expert from the Cooperative Extension Service of Jackson County, Alabama, who reported that the potatoes were suitable in all respects. After receiving a letter demanding performance of the contract, Buyer agreed to "try one more load." Sellers then tendered a load of potatoes which had been purchased from another grower, Roy Hartline. Although Buyer's agent had recently purchased potatoes from Hartline at $2.00 per hundredweight, he claimed dissatisfaction with potatoes from the same fields when tendered by Sellers at $4.25 per hundredweight. Apparently the jury believed this testimony outweighed statements by Buyer's agents that Sellers' potatoes were diseased and unfit for "chipping."

Subsequently, Sellers offered to purchase the remaining nine loads of potatoes from other growers in order to fulfill their contract. Buyer's agent refused this offer, saying "... 'I'm not going to accept any more of your potatoes. If you load any more I'll see that they're turned down.' ... 'I can buy potatoes all day for $2.00.' " No further efforts were made by Sellers to perform the contract.

At the time of Buyer's final refusal, Sellers had between seventeen and twenty-one loads of potatoes unharvested in their fields. Approximately four loads were sold in Chattanooga, Tennessee; Atlanta, Georgia; and local markets in DeKalb County. Sellers' efforts to sell their potato crop to other buyers were hampered by poor market conditions. Considering all of the evidence, the jury could properly have found that Sellers' efforts to sell the potatoes, after Buyer's final refusal to accept delivery, were reasonable and made in good faith....

Section 7–2–703, Code of Alabama 1975 (UCC), specifies an aggrieved seller may recover for a breach of contract "Where the buyer *wrongfully* rejects ... goods ..." (Emphasis added). We must determine whether there was evidence from which the jury could find that the Buyer acted wrongfully in rejecting delivery of Sellers' potatoes.

A buyer may reject delivery of goods if either the goods or the tender of delivery fails to conform to the contract. § 7–2–601, Code of Alabama 1975. In the instant case, Buyer did not claim the tender was inadequate. Rather, Buyer asserted the potatoes failed to conform to the requirements of the contract; i.e., the potatoes would not chip to buyer satisfaction.

The law requires such a claim of dissatisfaction to be made in good faith, rather than in an effort to escape a bad bargain....

Buyer, in the instant case, is a broker who deals in farm products as part of its occupation and, therefore, is a "merchant" with respect to its dealing in such goods. § 7–2–104, Code of Alabama 1975. In testing the good faith of a merchant, § 7–2–103, Code of Alabama 1975, requires " ... honesty in fact and the observance of reasonable commercial standards of fair dealing in the trade."[1] A claim of dissatisfaction by a merchant-buyer of fungible goods must be evaluated using an objective standard to determine whether the claim is made in good faith. Because there was evidence that the potatoes would "chip" satisfactorily, the jury was not required to accept Buyer's subjective claim to the contrary. A rejection of goods based on a claim of dissatisfaction, which is not made in good faith, is ineffectual and constitutes a breach of contract for which damages are recoverable....

Affirmed.

Notes on Neumiller

(a) What proof was there in *Neumiller* that the seller had breached—i.e. that the goods or the tender of delivery were nonconforming? Did the buyer have the burden of proving such a breach? Consider 2–607(4).

(b) In Printing Center of Texas, Inc. v. Supermind Publishing Co., 669 S.W.2d 779 (Tex.App.1984), the court stated:

If the evidence does establish nonconformity in some respect, the buyer is entitled to reject if he rejects in good faith. Bus. & Com. Code Ann. § 1.203 provides that, "Every contract or duty within this Act imposes an obligation of good faith in its performance or enforcement."[2] Since the rejection of goods is a matter of performance, the buyer is obligated to act in good faith when he rejects the goods. Where the buyer is a merchant, his standard of good faith rejection requires honesty in fact and observance of reasonable commercial standards of fair dealing in the trade. Tex.Bus. & Com.Code Ann. § 2.103(2)....[3] Evidence of circumstances which indicate that the buyer's motivation in rejecting the goods was to escape the bargain, rather than to avoid acceptance of a tender which in some respect impairs the value of the bargain to him, would support a finding of rejection in bad faith. Neumiller Farms Inc. v. Cornett, 368 So.2d 272 (Ala.1979). Thus, evidence of rejection of the goods on account of a minor defect in a falling market would in some

1. [Ed. note] Under amended Article 1 and the proposed amendments to 2 of the UCC, the definition of "good faith" applicable to both merchants and non-merchants throughout the UCC (with the exception of Article 5) is found in 1–201(b)(20).

2. [Ed. note] Under amended Article 1 of the UCC, this provision is found at 1–304.

3. [Ed. note] Under amended Article 1 and the proposed amendments to 2 of the UCC, the definition of "good faith" applicable to both merchants and non-merchants throughout the UCC (with the exception of Article 5) is found in Section 1–201(b)(20).

instances be sufficient to support a finding that the buyer acted in bad faith when he rejected the goods.

(c) What are the consequences if a seller shows that a buyer rejected in bad faith? In Chandler v. Hunter, 340 So.2d 818 (Ala.Civ.App.1976), the buyer of a defective mobile home alleged, inter alia, that the seller failed to deal in good faith as required by UCC 1–203 (1–304 in the amended version of UCC Article 1). The court ruled that

> [f]ailure to act in good faith in the performance or enforcement of contracts or duties arising under [the U.C.C.] does not state a claim for which relief may be granted in Alabama. Nor have we been able to discover a jurisdiction which allows recovery of damages under this general provision of the Uniform Commercial Code. There is no indication, either in the text or the comments, that section 1–203 was intended to be remedial rather than directive. We conclude that the second count of [the buyer's] complaint does not state a claim for which relief can be granted.

340 So. 2d at 821. The approach in *Chandler* was expressly approved by the Alabama Supreme Court in Government Street Lumber Co. v. AmSouth Bank, 553 So.2d 68 (Ala.1989), and has been followed by several other courts (see, e.g., Management Assistance, Inc. v. Computer Dimensions, Inc., 546 F.Supp. 666 (N.D.Ga.1982)). In Reid v. Key Bank, Inc., 821 F.2d 9 (1st Cir.1987), however, the First Circuit Court of Appeals wrote:

> We reject the applicability of *Chandler* and the cases based on it for two reasons. First, a determination that no such cause of action exists would conflict with the clear meaning of section 1–203 of the U.C.C., particularly when read in conjunction with section 1–106(2).[4] We assume that the Maine courts would adhere to the plain language of these provisions, as well as to generally accepted modern contract principles. Secondly, the fact that numerous jurisdictions have allowed recovery on theories of breach of good faith refutes the empirical assumption upon which *Chandler* appears to have been based.

821 F.2d at 9–10 (citations omitted).

In a jurisdiction that followed the approach in *Chandler* and would not recognize a UCC cause of action for breach of the obligation of good faith, could a court hold that a bad faith rejection was "wrongful"? Ineffective?

Problem 48

Suppose the Problem 47 contract between Lumber Region and Northwestern Industries stated the price "FOB Northwestern Industries Sawmill." The contract also provided for shipment via truck by June 20. Truck transport to Lumber Region's warehouse would normally take 24 hours. Northwestern arranged for the lumber to be picked up by Eaton Wheeler, an independent trucker with a reputation for cheap but unreliable service. Wheeler loaded the lumber on June 20, although Northwestern did not

---

4. [Ed. note] Under amended Article 1 of the UCC, this provision is found at 1–305(b).

notify Lumber Region that shipment had occurred. Wheeler made various unscheduled stops and did not arrive at the Lumber Region loading dock until after closing on June 22. As a result, the goods could not be unloaded until the morning of June 23. Did Northwestern breach? If so, how? Is Lumber Region obliged to accept the tender? See 2–504.

Problem 49

Random Accessories, Inc. agreed in writing to sell 200 IBX computers to Paley & Tologist ("P & T") for delivery in five lots of 40 each. Random warranted that the computers would be merchantable and that all components would be "100% original IBX equipment." The first delivery was due November 1 with the remaining deliveries scheduled at two week intervals thereafter. P & T was to pay the entire contract price (covering all five deliveries) in a single payment due when it received the first delivery.

Before the first delivery was due a world-wide shortage of IBX components developed, making it almost impossible to obtain replacement IBX keyboards. When the November 1 delivery arrived it included five computers equipped with keyboards manufactured by Clonics, Inc. While cheaper, Clonics keyboards are generally rated equivalent or superior to the standard IBX keyboard in quality.

(a) Is this contract an "installment contract"? See 2–612(1).

(b) Does P & T have the right to reject the first delivery? See 2–601 & 2–612(2). How do you determine whether the nonconformity "substantially impairs the value of that installment"?

(c) What standard would P & T have to meet in order to justify canceling the remaining deliveries? See 2–612(3).

(d) Suppose that, because of bad experiences with non-IBX computer equipment, P & T had specifically negotiated for the clause requiring 100% IBX components? Does that effect whether P & T has a right to reject the first installment? Consider comment 4 to 2–612.

(e) Alternatively, suppose the clause requiring 100% IBX components was a standard clause included in the contract by Random (i.e., P & T did not have to negotiate for it). Because of its bad experiences with non-IBX equipment, P & T was happy about the clause, but no one mentioned to Random at the time of contracting that P & T strongly objected to non-IBX components. Can P & T reject the installment?

(f) Suppose P & T had specifically negotiated for the "standard IBX hardware only" clause and at the time of contracting had explained to Random that it would insist on strict compliance with the clause. P & T nevertheless accepted and paid for the first delivery, saying nothing about the five Clonics keyboards. P & T also accepted and paid for the second and third deliveries, both of which also contained a few computers equipped with Clonics keyboards. P & T, however, rejected the fourth delivery because three of the computers came with Clonics keyboards. Is the rejection rightful? Consider 2–208 (1–303 under amended Article 1).

Question

Why are there different standards for rejection in an installment contract as opposed to a single delivery contract? In other words, why should the standard for rejection in Problem 49 be different than the standard for rejection in Problem 44?

3. Cure

Problem 50

Return to the contract between Random Accessories and Paley & Tologist described in Problem 44—a single delivery contract for the sale of 200 computers equipped with IBX components to be delivered to the buyer (P & T) by November 1. Random tendered 200 computers on October 29, but five were equipped with Clonics keyboards and P & T rejected the entire delivery. When told of the rejection a Random representative told the P & T managing partner, "I'm surprised. Most of our customers are glad to get Clonics keyboards. But we'll take care of this matter." The P & T partner replied, "You guys had your chance. We're canceling our order." On November 1 Random re-tendered 200 computers, all equipped with IBX keyboards. P & T again refused to take delivery. Was the second rejection rightful? See 2–508(1).

Problem 51

Same facts as the previous problem, except Random did not make the original tender of delivery (which included five computers equipped with Clonics keyboards) until November 1. When P & T rejected the goods, Random could not re-tender 200 computers equipped with IBX keyboards until November 3. Can P & T properly reject the second tender? See 2–508(2). What precisely must Random show in order to require P & T to accept the second tender?

Note on the Requirements For Cure After The Date For Delivery

Under the pre-amendment version of 2–508(2), a seller who wants to have a "further reasonable time" beyond the contractual delivery date in which to cure a rejected tender must demonstrate that there had been "reasonable grounds to believe" that the buyer would accept the original rejected tender "with or without money allowance." The meaning of this requirement has generated controversy. See, e.g., T.W. Oil, Inc. v. Consolidated Edison Co., 57 N.Y.2d 574, 457 N.Y.S.2d 458, 443 N.E.2d 932 (N.Y.Ct. App.1982) (discussing disagreements among commentators as to whether a seller's lack of knowledge of nonconformities could provide the required "reasonable grounds to believe" that the original tender would be accepted). Proposed amended Section 2–508(2) would abandon the "reasonable cause to believe" requirement for cure after the contractual delivery date in favor of a requirement that cure be "appropriate and timely under the circumstances."

Is it easier for a seller to show that it is entitled to cure under the pre-amendment version of 2–508(2) or under the proposed amended version?

Problem 52

Fraim Mobile Home Sales contracted to sell a new mobile home to the Clarks. The contract, which was evidenced by a writing signed by both parties, did not specify a delivery date nor did Fraim disclaim the implied warranty of merchantability. The seller was responsible for transporting the mobile home to the Clarks' property—an expensive and time-consuming process. While delivering the mobile home to the Clarks' lot, employees of Fraim damaged an exterior corner panel of the trailer. The damage meant that the goods would not pass without objection in the retail mobile home trade as a "new" mobile home, but the damage could be completely repaired for approximately $75. Fraim offered to repair the damage and even sent employees to the Clarks' lot for that purpose. The Clarks, however, would not allow the employees on their land (where the mobile home was located). Instead the Clarks notified Fraim that they were rejecting the trailer because of the damaged panel, and they insisted that Fraim remove it from their property.

a) Did the buyers have the right to reject the mobile home because of the damaged panel?

b) Assuming the buyers had the right to reject the mobile home, did they perform the steps necessary to reject?

c) Assuming the answers to the previous two questions were yes, what obligations did the Clarks have with respect to the goods? See 2–602(2)(b).

d) Assuming the buyers properly rejected the goods, did the seller have a right to cure? Would that question be governed by 2–508(1) or by 2–508(2)? If the seller has a right to cure, does that preclude the buyer rejecting the goods? From canceling the contract? For the meaning of "cancellation," see 2–106(4).

e) Assuming the seller had a right to cure, could Fraim accomplish the cure by hauling the trailer back to its repair shop, making the needed repairs, then re-tendering the trailer (i.e., hauling it back to the Clarks' property)?

f) Is the procedure described in the previous question the only way for the seller to cure?

g) Did the Clarks act properly when they refused to permit the seller to repair the mobile home while it was on the Clarks' lot?

h) What are the legal consequences if a rejecting buyer improperly refuses to permit the seller to cure? Does the buyer thereby accept the goods, becoming liable for the price under 2–709(1)(a)? Or does the buyer commit a "wrongful" (but effective) rejection, incurring liability for the *difference* between the contract price and the resale or market price (see 2–706 and 2–708)?

Note on "Shaken Faith" and Cure by Replacement or Repair

Is repairing a defect in "new" goods an adequate cure, or must the seller offer a replacement? In Zabriskie Chevrolet, Inc. v. Smith, 99 N.J.Super. 441, 240 A.2d 195 (1968), the buyer took delivery of a new car which developed transmission problems within a mile of leaving the seller's dealership, and could be driven no faster than 10 m.p.h. The seller replaced the defective transmission with one removed from a car in its showroom, but the court held that the buyer's refusal to accept the repaired vehicle was proper under 2–508: "The 'cure' intended under the cited section of the Code does not, in the court's opinion, contemplate the tender of a new vehicle with a substituted transmission, not from the factory and of unknown lineage from another vehicle in plaintiff's possession." 240 A.2d at 205.

In Asciolla v. Manter Oldsmobile–Pontiac, Inc., 117 N.H. 85, 370 A.2d 270 (1977), the buyer's new car broke down soon after purchase. The mechanic who worked on the vehicle discovered ice chunks in the transmission, water in the trunk wells, and considerable rust on the underbody. He told the buyer that "the car appeared to have been flooded or submerged." Although the seller claimed that the defects in the car had been cured by repair, the court held that "any cure other than replacement of the automobile with a new one would, under the facts of this case, be insufficient to accomplish a conforming tender."

Other cases, in contrast, have permitted the seller to cure "new" goods by repairing them. In Wilson v. Scampoli, 228 A.2d 848 (D.C.Ct.App.1967), for instance, the court held that a buyer's refusal to permit the seller to cure by adjusting a new TV with a reddish picture tinge was improper: "While decided cases provide no mandate to require the buyer to accept patchwork goods or substantially repaired articles . . . , they do indicate that minor repairs or reasonable adjustments are frequently the means by which an imperfect tender may be cured." In Ramirez v. Autosport, 88 N.J. 277, 440 A.2d 1345 (1982), the court generalized as follows:

> In an age of assembly lines, we are accustomed to cars with scratches, television sets without knobs and other goods with all kinds of defects. Buyers no longer expect a "perfect tender." If a merchant sells defective goods, the reasonable expectation of the parties is that the buyer will return those goods and that the seller will repair or replace them.

How does one determine when repair will not be deemed an adequate cure? According to a comment to proposed amended Section 2–508, "[i]f the seller attempt to cure by repair, the cure would not be appropriate if it resulted in goods that did not conform in every respect to the requirements of the contract." In the *Zabriskie* case described earlier in this Note, the court justified the buyer's refusal to accept seller's tender of a repaired vehicle with the following:

> For a majority of people the purchase of a new car is a major investment, rationalized by the peace of mind that flows from its dependability and safety. Once their faith is shaken, the vehicle loses not only its real

value in their eyes, but becomes an instrument whose integrity is substantially impaired and whose operation is fraught with apprehension. The attempted cure in the present case was ineffective.

Courts continue to use this so-called "shaken faith" doctrine to limit a seller's right to cure, particularly in consumer cases. See Gappelberg v. Landrum, 666 S.W.2d 88 (Tex.1984). Could the buyer in Problem 52 invoke "shaken faith" to argue that the seller's attempt to cure was inadequate?

If the buyer's faith in the quality of all the seller's goods has been shaken, perhaps even replacement of the goods would not be an adequate cure. There are other situations where replacement is not sufficient to cure a non-conformity. For example, in David Tunick, Inc. v. Kornfeld, 838 F.Supp. 848 (S.D.N.Y.1993), the court held that a buyer who had revoked acceptance of a signed Picasso print with a forged signature did not have to accept a replacement print with a genuine signature, even if the replacement was from the same series as the print the buyer had purchased. The court noted that fine art prints, even from the same series, were each unique: their value would vary depending on subtle differences in the quality of the print, the signature, and the condition of the print; furthermore, a collector (like the buyer in the case) selected the print for aesthetic rather than utilitarian purposes—

> because he viewed it as uniquely beautiful, interesting, or well suited to his collection or gallery. Nothing else will satisfy that collector but that which he bought.... In this context it would be fundamentally unfair, and unsound policy, to impose on plaintiff a duty to accept another— inherently different print ... as a substitute for the one plaintiff actually viewed, bid for, and purchased.... Because prints are unique ... § 2–508 is not applicable to prints.

838 F.Supp. at 852.

Note on Cure by Price Adjustment

When a buyer objects to a nonconforming tender, the parties frequently attempt to deal with the situation by negotiating for a price adjustment. Can a seller require the buyer to accept nonconforming goods by offering such an allowance—i.e., cure by price adjustment? Comment 5 to 2–612 contemplates cure of a nonconforming installment in an installment contract by "an allowance against the price." The drafters of 2–508 apparently did not contemplate cure by price adjustment unless the contract (incorporating relevant trade usage and course of dealing) provided otherwise. McKenzie v. Alla–Ohio Coals, Inc., 29 U.C.C. Rep.Serv. 852 (D.D.C.1979), aff'd 610 F.2d 1000 (D.C.Cir.); 2 W. HAWKLAND, UNIFORM COMMERCIAL CODE SERIES § 2–508:04, at 703, & § 2–508:06, at 706 (1984). One treatise nevertheless argues in favor of cure by money allowance, "[d]espite the modest violence it does to the language of 2–508(2)," where the nonconformity is insubstantial. J. WHITE & R. SUMMERS, HANDBOOK OF THE LAW UNDER THE UNIFORM COMMERCIAL CODE § 8–5 at 338 (5th ed. 2000). Proposed amended Section 2–508 would, apparently, preclude cure by price adjustment. Under proposed amended

Section 2–508(2), for example, a seller would have to cure by making "a tender of conforming goods." A comment to the proposed amended provision states, "[t]he seller's cure under both subsection (1) and subsection (2) must be of conforming goods." This would appear to preclude cure by price adjustment.

Problem 53

Random Accessories, Inc. agreed in writing to sell 200 IBX computers to Paley & Tologist ("P & T") for delivery by November 1. Random warranted that all components would be original IBX equipment.

(a) Random tendered 200 perfectly conforming computers on November 2. P & T effectively rejected all 200 because of the late delivery. Can Random cure under 2–508? How would cure be accomplished?

(b) Suppose that on November 1 Random had tendered 200 computers, several of which were equipped with keyboards manufactured by Clonics rather than IBX. Assume Random reasonably believed this nonconforming tender would be accepted, but P & T rejected. After notifying P & T of its intentions, Random re-tendered 200 conforming computers on November 2. Must P & T accept? Is your answer consistent with your analysis of variation (a)? Do you think the drafters considered late tenders when they wrote 2–508. Would a contract clause providing that "time is of the essence" affect your responses?

KNIC KNAC AGENCIES v. MASTERPIECE APPAREL, LTD.

United States District Court, S.D. New York, 1999.
1999 WL 156379.

McKENNA, DISTRICT JUDGE. Plaintiffs seek a total of $1,613,494.52 in damages from defendants for breach of contract and failure to pay for goods manufactured, sold, and delivered. Plaintiffs' claims [include] ... a claim for $353,622.65 for the value of goods shipped to but allegedly rejected and/or abandoned by defendants....

* * *

From in or about July to December 1992, Masterpiece placed a total of 45 purchase orders with plaintiffs for garments to be manufactured in India and exported to the United States.

* * *

Although the first orders that Masterpiece placed with Plaintiffs were timely shipped and generally met its customers' specifications, relations between the parties soon soured. (Reich Aff. PP 10, 12). Masterpiece claims that plaintiffs began shipping goods before it had a chance to inspect them, delivering defective goods, and missing shipment deadlines. (Masterpiece 56.1 St. P 10). Specifically, upon opening some shipments, Logo 7 [one of Masterpiece's customers] found that labels were not sewn on properly and the stitching was such that the goods probably would not have made it through a washing machine cycle. (Reich Aff. P 12). Masterpiece's customers then directed it to instruct plaintiffs to make no further shipments and to cancel all unexecuted orders. (Id. P 13; Masterpiece 56.1 St. P 11). Accordingly, on February 24, 1993, Masterpiece sent a fax to Knic Knac [seller/plaintiff] stating:

> Please be advised that the quality of goods received by Logo 7 in your air shipments on LAB61 [and] LAB91 have be [sic] rejected due to very poor quality. At this point, Logo 7 will not accept any additional shipments from Knic Knac and will not accept documents for goods already shipped. (Proulx Aff. Ex. 27).

Two days later, 3M Global [which provided financing for the transactions] also notified Knic Knac by fax that:

> [T]here are extensive quality problems with goods shipped to Logo 7. As a result, we understand Logo 7 has canceled all orders for you. At the instructions of Masterpiece Apparel, please be advised that 3M Global Trading is hereby canceling all orders for Logo 7 goods and will not accept for payment documents against shipments of Logo 7 goods. (Reich Aff. Ex. 9).

* * *

The parties agree that New York law governs, as New York is the jurisdiction with the most significant interest in, and relationship to, the dispute. See Brink's Ltd. v. South African Airways, 93 F.3d 1022, 1030–31 (2d Cir.1996), cert. denied, 519 U.S. 1116 (1997). Specifically, because this case involves the sale of goods, it is governed by Article 2 of New York's U.C.C. See N.Y. U.C.C. § 2–102 (McKinney's 1993); Integrated Circuits Unlimited v. E.F. Johnson Co., 875 F.2d 1040, 1041 (2d Cir.1989).

* * *

5. Plaintiffs' Claim for $353,622.65 for Goods Rejected or Abandoned

Masterpiece moves for summary judgment as to this claim on the grounds that: (1) it effectively rejected and/or canceled these orders, thereby barring an action for the contract price regardless of whether the rejection was wrongful. . . . Plaintiffs maintain that there is an issue of material fact as to whether defendants accepted the goods, and alternatively, whether their rejection was either ineffective or wrongful.

Where the buyer has made a procedurally effective rejection, even if that rejection was substantively wrongful (i.e., the goods were conforming), the seller cannot maintain an action for the contract price under U.C.C. § 2–709. Integrated Circuits, 875 F.2d at 1042; Full–Bright Indus. Co. v. Lerner Stores, Inc., 1995 WL 413473, at *15 (S.D.N.Y. July 11, 1995); 1 James J. White & Robert S. Summers, Uniform Commercial

Code § 7–3, at 361–63 (4th ed.1995). A rejection is procedurally effective if it is made within a reasonable time after delivery or tender and the buyer seasonably notifies the seller. U.C.C. § 2–602. Masterpiece argues that it effectively rejected these goods and canceled future orders by its February 24, 1993 fax.[13]

As an initial matter, the Court rejects plaintiffs' argument that the transactions at issue in this suit are the subject of an installment contract and that defendants' right to reject was therefore restricted by U.C.C. § 2–612. An installment contract is defined as "one which requires or authorizes the delivery of goods in separate lots to be separately accepted...." U.C.C. § 2–612(1); see, e.g., Trans World, 769 F.2d at 904, 907 (contract calling for sale and delivery of 12,000 tons of aluminum to be delivered 1,000 tons per month for period of one year was installment contract). Here, in contrast, Masterpiece placed 45 purchase orders with the plaintiffs; each purchase order constituted a separate contract, with separate price, quantity, style, and delivery terms. Accordingly, these were single delivery contracts, with the buyer's right to reject governed by U.C.C. § 2–601 (the perfect tender rule), not § 2–612.[14]

Plaintiffs also assert that there is a question of fact as to whether defendants accepted the goods.[15] However, plaintiffs' evidence showing when they shipped the goods and when defendants may have taken possession of the goods (see Ahluwalia Aff. PP 98, 107–09 & Exs. 34, 35, 40) fails to raise a material issue of fact as to acceptance. Because acceptance does not occur until a buyer has had a reasonable time to inspect the goods, see U.C.C. § 2–606, the fact that a buyer takes temporary possession of the goods does not mean that he has accepted them. See Integrated Circuits Unlimited, Inc. v. E.F. Johnson Co., 691 F.Supp. 630, 634 (E.D.N.Y.1988), rev'd on other grounds, 875 F.2d 1040 (2d Cir.1989); 1 White & Summers § 8–2, at 429 ("[A]cceptance is only tangentially related to buyer's possession of the goods. Often the buyer will have had possession of the goods for some time before it has 'accepted' them...."). As long as defendants rejected the goods within a reasonable time after tender and seasonably notified plaintiffs of their defects and/or untimeliness, they effectively rejected the goods. See Texpor, 720 F.Supp. at 1110; Integrated Circuits, 691 F.Supp. at 634.

"What is a reasonable time for taking any action depends on the nature, purpose and circumstances of such action." U.C.C. § 1–204(2).

---

13. Defendants assert that plaintiffs actually had notice that there were problems with the Logo 7 goods as early as December 23, 1992, based on a series of faxes to Knic Knac notifying them of problems and missed shipment deadlines. (See Masterpiece Reply Br. at 5–6; Dunning Reply Aff. Exs. I–L).

14. Under § 2–601, the buyer is entitled to reject any goods or tender which "fail in any respect to conform to the contract."

15. Acceptance occurs when: (a) after a reasonable opportunity to inspect the goods, the buyer informs the seller that the goods are conforming or that he will retain them despite their non-conformity; (b) the buyer, after a reasonable opportunity to inspect, fails to make an effective rejection; or (c) the buyer does any act inconsistent with the seller's ownership. See U.C.C. § 2–606; Texpor Traders, 720 F.Supp. at 1109.

Here, plaintiffs' evidence shows that defendants may have taken possession of some goods as early as February 18, 1993; defendants formally rejected the Logo 7 goods and canceled future orders on February 24, 1993, at the latest. The Court finds as a matter of law that defendants' notice came within a reasonable time after tender. See Texpor, 720 F.Supp. at 1110–11 (notice was seasonable where shipment arrived on January 29, quality audits took place by Feb. 4, and by mid-February, buyer met with seller and stated that goods were defective and it would not accept them); D.C. Leathers Inc. v. Gelmart Indus., Inc., 509 N.Y.S.2d 161, 162–63 (3d Dep't 1986) (rejection was timely where it occurred within one month after receipt of goods).

However, defendants' rejection was ineffective as to several shipments for a different reason—the failure to particularize the defects found. U.C.C. § 2–605 provides:

> The buyer's failure to state in connection with rejection a particular defect which is ascertainable by reasonable inspection precludes him from relying on the unstated defect to justify rejection or to establish breach ... (a) where the seller could have cured it if stated seasonably.[16]

U.C.C. § 2–605; see also 1 White & Summers § 8–3, at 445–46 (noting that procedural requirements of effective rejection include obligation under § 2–605 to specify defects where ascertainable and seller could have cured). Where the time for performance has already passed, however, the buyer need not particularize the defects in order to make an effective rejection, since the seller would be unable to cure in any event. See Texpor, 720 F.Supp. at 1111 (rejection was not ineffective due to failure to particularize defects; seller could not have cured because shipments were already late).

Masterpiece's fax stated only that the Logo 7 goods were being rejected due to the "very poor quality" of specific shipments. (See Ahluwalia Aff. Ex. 36). 3M Global's follow-up fax was no more informative, referring only to "extensive quality problems with goods shipped to Logo 7." (Id. Ex. 37). Considering the nature of these goods, the alleged defects would have been readily ascertainable upon inspection by Masterpiece or its customers. Accordingly, Masterpiece's failure to particularize the defects in these goods renders its rejection ineffective, unless it would have been impossible for plaintiffs to cure because the shipments were already late. See Texpor, 720 F.Supp. at 1111.

The Court's review of the record reveals that most of the shipments were in fact made after the "latest ship date" stated in the final (November 20, 1992) amendment to L/C C6892963. (See Reich Aff. Ex. 10). Of the 23 invoices included in this claim (see Pls.' Response to Defs.' Interrog. No. 3, Maschio Aff. Ex. 16), 18 are for shipments that clearly were late ... Accordingly, Masterpiece did not have to particularize the

---

16. [Ed. note] The proposed amended version of Section 2–605 would make significant changes.

defects and its rejection of these shipments was effective, thereby precluding an action for the contract price under § 2–709.[17] Masterpiece is therefore granted summary judgment as to the claims based on these shipments.

As to the other five invoices, however, there is an issue of fact as to whether or not they cover shipments that were late.[18] If they were not late, then Masterpiece's failure to particularize rendered its rejection of them ineffective. Because an ineffective rejection is equivalent to an acceptance, see U.C.C. § 2–606, plaintiffs may maintain an action for the price of these shipments under § 2–709. See Miron, 400 F.2d at 117–19 (where buyer's rejection was ineffective, seller could sue for contract price without proving conformity). Accordingly, Masterpiece's motion is denied as to the claims based on these 5 invoices.

* * *

Note: Cure and Good Faith

There is an important link between the Code's cure provisions and the requirement that a buyer's rejection be in good faith. Several commentators have argued that prevention of bad faith rejection by buyers is the principal (if not exclusive) justification for the seller's right to cure. See J. WHITE & R. SUMMERS, HANDBOOK OF THE LAW UNDER THE UNIFORM COMMERCIAL CODE § 8–5 at 339 (5th ed. 2000) (2–508 "offers the possibility . . . of thwarting the chiseler who seeks to escape from a bad bargain"); Schwartz, *Cure and Revocation for Quality Defects: The Utility of Bargains*, 16 B. C. INDUS. & COMM. L. REV. 543, 545 (1975) ("a cure rule is defensible only because it may minimize buyer bad faith"); Travalio, *The U.C.C.'s Three "R's": Rejection, Revocation and (the Seller's) Right to Cure*, 53 U. CIN. L. REV. 931, 967–69 (1984) (2–508 is the only pragmatic way to police the good faith of a buyer's rejection). Thus when a buyer's rejection appears to be a pretext to escape a bad bargain or otherwise smacks of bad faith, courts are particularly solicitous to protect the seller's ability to cure. See, e.g., T.W. Oil, Inc. v. Consolidated Edison Co., 57 N.Y.2d 574, 457 N.Y.S.2d 458, 443 N.E.2d 932 (Ct.App.1982) (holding that buyer improperly rejected a second "curing" tender of the goods (crude oil) where buyer's rejection of the first nonconforming tender may have been motivated by the fact that market prices had fallen and oil was then available more cheaply than the contract price).

17. Plaintiffs have not claimed damages under any other measure. Notwithstanding that, because they are precluded from presenting evidence as to market price, and have not plead that these goods were resold, plaintiffs cannot show that they are entitled to any damages on this claim. See U.C.C. § 2–703.

18. According to the terms of the latest amendment to L/C C6892963, the orders covered by invoices KKA–59 and KKA–62 were to be shipped by January 15, 1993. (See Reich Aff. Ex. 10). Although the dates on the bills of lading are illegible, plaintiffs assert that they were timely shipped on December 31, 1992. (See Ahluwalia Aff. P 100 & Exs. 33, 34). For invoices TF–005, OI–013, and TD–059, the Court is unable to determine whether or not the shipments were late, because it is unable to determine the shipment deadlines for these orders.

4. *Acceptance and Revocation*

Problem 54

Return to the contract in which Paley & Tologist ("P & T") purchased 200 IBX computers, all warranted to be merchantable, from Random Accessories, Inc., to be delivered in a single delivery. Random tendered 200 properly equipped IBX computers on the contractual delivery date (November 1). P & T installed and tested the machines, after which it paid Random the purchase price. P & T used the computers for a month before one broke down. The service technician who was called in to make repairs discovered that the breakdown was caused by manufacturing defects in a major component, repairable only by replacing the component at considerable expense. Inspection of the other machines revealed that 55 of them contained the same defect. Assume the defects breach the implied warranty of merchantability.

(a) Has P & T accepted the computers? See 2–606.

(b) Assume P & T has accepted the computers and, despite the defects, would like to keep all 200. P & T, however, wants to hold Random responsible for the costs of repairing the defective computers and other damages it has suffered because of the defects. Should P & T take any actions to preserve its rights? See 2–607(3)(a).

(c) If P & T has accepted, is there any way it can return the 55 defective computers and get its money back? See 2–608. If P & T wants to revoke its acceptance, what requirements must it satisfy and how should it proceed? Did the nonconformity here substantially impair the value of the goods to P & T? Assuming P & T has the right to revoke, can it revoke its acceptance of all 200 computers, including the non-defective ones? See 2–105(5) & (6) (subsections (4) & (5) in the proposed amended version of Section 2–105). Could it revoke acceptance of four defective machines that, before their defects were discovered, had been severely damaged while being used by P & T's employees?

CISSELL MFG. CO. v. PARK

Court of Appeals of Colorado, 2001.
36 P.3d 85.

DAVIDSON, JUDGE. Defendant, Young Park, d/b/a Young's Equipment & Supplies (Park), appeals from the entry of partial summary judgment against him and the judgment of the trial court entered on a jury verdict in favor of plaintiff, Cissell Manufacturing Company. We affirm.

Park, a distributor for Cissell, bought 12 commercial clothing dryers from Cissell to lease to a laundromat owner. Park received and installed the dryers in April 1993, but never paid Cissell.

Difficulties with the dryers arose within days of installation, and Park alerted Cissell to the existence of these problems. After an unsuccessful attempt to meet with Cissell's representative in May 1993, Park and the laundromat owner sent a letter to Cissell on September 7, 1993, "rejecting and revoking acceptance" of the dryers under §§ 4–2–607 & 4–2–608, C.R.S.2000, of the Colorado Uniform Commercial Code (UCC). Ultimately, the dryers were removed and placed in storage.

Cissell sued Park to collect the purchase price. Park counterclaimed for breach of contract, [and] breaches of express and implied warranties. . . . The court granted partial summary judgment in favor of Cissell on its breach of contract claim and on Park's breach of contract counterclaim. . . . On the other counterclaims, the jury returned verdicts in favor of Cissell on all counts. Park's motion for new trial and for judgment notwithstanding the verdict was denied, and he now appeals.

I.

Park first argues that the trial court improperly granted Cissell's motion for summary judgment on Cissell's claim for payment and on Park's counterclaim for breach of contract. Park also argues that jury instructions based on the summary judgment ruling were incorrect. We agree. However, based on the jury verdicts on the remaining claims, we conclude that the errors were harmless.

* * *

On appeal, Park argues that the trial court erred in concluding that § 4–2–608 does not allow revocation of goods with latent defects after acceptance of the goods; that a buyer remains obligated to pay the entire price even after a successful revocation of acceptance of the goods under § 4–2–608; and that any purported attempt to revoke was invalid as a matter of law because the required notice was inadequate. We agree with Park.

* * *

Under the UCC, a buyer may either reject or accept delivered goods. Section 4–2–601, C.R.S.2000. . . . [O]nce a buyer accepts goods, he or she is precluded from rejecting them, § 4–2–607(2), C.R.S.2000, and is obligated to pay at the contract rate for goods accepted. Section 4–2–607(1), C.R.S.2000.

However, even after accepting, the buyer may revoke such acceptance:

[THE COURT QUOTED UCC 2–608]

Revocation of acceptance is a relatively new concept in the UCC, instituted to resolve the ambiguities of the common law doctrine of rescission. But for the fact that rejection is exercised before acceptance and revocation after, the two have the same legal effect. See W. Hawkland, Uniform Commercial Code Series § 2–608:1 (Art. 2) (1998).

In its complaint, Cissell asserted an entitlement to payment and interest on the goods delivered. See § 4–2–709, C.R.S.2000 (action for the price).

In such an action, the seller is entitled to recovery of the price of "goods accepted." Section 4–2–709(1)(a), C.R.S.2000. However, the UCC limits the definition of "goods accepted" to "only goods as to which there has been no justified revocation of acceptance, for such a revocation means that there has been a default by the seller which bars his rights under this section." Section 4–2–709 comment 5, C.R.S.2000.

Thus, a procedurally effective rejection or revocation "bars" acceptance, see J. White & R. Summers, Uniform Commercial Code § 7–3 (4th ed. 1995) (White & Summers), and revocation of acceptance, like rejection, allows the buyer to avoid the obligation to pay the price. See Hawkland, supra, § 2–608:1. To the extent the trial court determined otherwise in its summary judgment rulings, it was incorrect.

We also agree with Park that the trial court incorrectly determined that Park could not pursue a remedy under § 4–2–608 because he had not provided to Cissell a "formal" notice of rejection or revocation.

Contrary to the trial court's determination, there is no "formal notice of revocation" requirement under § 4–2–608, nor does it exist under § 4–2–607 (governing rejection). Indeed, § 4–2–608 does not require that a notice of revocation of acceptance assume any particular format, but rather that the content of the notice be determined by "considerations of good faith, prevention of surprise, and reasonable adjustment." Section 4–2–608 comment 5, C.R.S.2000; see also Allis–Chalmers Corp. v. Sygitowicz, 18 Wash.App. 658, 571 P.2d 224 (1977); R. Anderson, Uniform Commercial Code § 2–608:191, 194 (3d ed.1997). The notice of revocation, to be sufficient, should fairly apprise the seller that the buyer wants to give back the goods and receive a substitute or money in return. See Hawkland, supra, § 2–608:5.

Here, Park's September 1993 letter was adequate. The letter described in detail the dryers' alleged defects, attempted to "reject acceptance" of the dryers, demanded that Cissell remove the machines from the premises, and requested that damages be paid to Park and the laundromat owner.

* * *

Because the trial court erred in its grant of partial summary judgment on Cissell's claim for payment, we agree with Park that its instruction to the jury that Park had breached the contract by failing to pay was error. Similarly, the trial court erroneously refused to instruct the jury on Park's revocation of acceptance counterclaim. However, we are convinced that, even if the jury had been instructed properly, the verdict against Park would have been the same. Thus, the errors were harmless. See Dunlap v. Long, 902 P.2d 446 (Colo.App.1995).

As Cissell argues, to prove a valid revocation of acceptance, a buyer must show, inter alia, that the goods were nonconforming. Section 4–2–608(1). In this regard, revocation requires a greater showing than rejection: a buyer may reject goods if the tender fails "in any respect to conform to the contract," § 4–2–601, but, in order to revoke, a buyer must show, among other things, that the nonconformity of the goods substantially impairs their value to the buyer. Section 4–2–608 comment 2, C.R.S.2000; see also Hawkland, supra, § 2–608:2 (clarifying the policy that "it makes good sense to require more from a buyer who has accepted the goods than from one who has rejected them").

Determination of an item's nonconformity hinges on whether it "substantially impairs its value to [the buyer]." See Hawkland, supra, § 2–608:2; see also Keen v. Modern Trailer Sales, Inc., 40 Colo.App. 527, 578 P.2d 668 (1978) (although section 4–2–608 appears to create a subjective test in the sense that the requirements of the particular buyer must be examined and deferred to, impairment of the buyer's requirements must be substantial in objective terms). Whether goods are nonconforming requires reference to the terms of the contract and to the law of warranty. See § 4–2–106(2), C.R.S.2000 (goods are conforming when they are in accordance with the obligations under the contract); White & Summers, supra, § 8–4. In other words, if the goods are as contracted for and as warranted, they cannot be nonconforming.

Here, although Park's revocation of acceptance instruction was not presented to the jury, the jury was instructed on Park's remaining counterclaims for breach of express warranty, breach of implied warranty of fitness for a particular purpose, and breach of implied warranty of merchantability. Moreover, the evidence pertaining to the latter counterclaims was, as Park concedes, *90 identical to that which would have supported his claim of revocation of acceptance.

By special verdict, however, the jury found against Park on all three counterclaims. Specifically, the jury found that the dryers' features satisfied all of Cissell's express warranties as set forth in the parties' contract. The jury also found that Park had failed to prove that the dryers were "not suitable for the particular purpose for which they were warranted." See § 4–2–315, C.R.S.2000. Similarly, by rejecting Park's counterclaim of breach of implied warranty of merchantability, the jury found that the dryers were "of merchantable quality at the time of sale." See § 4–2–314, C.R.S.2000.

Thus, by finding that the goods were "as warranted," "suitable," and "merchantable," the jury necessarily rejected any purported claim of nonconformity. See §§ 4–2–106 & § 4–2–608; see also Gulfwind South, Inc. v. Jones, 775 So.2d 311 (Fla.Dist.Ct.App.2000) ("before the trial court could find a valid revocation of acceptance, it had to find that there was, in fact, a contractual or warranty provision setting a standard of conformity, and the facts demonstrated nonconformity with that standard").

Moreover, because of the manner in which the jury was instructed, the verdict on the warranty claims could not have been tainted, as Park argues, by the court's errors.

* * *

The judgment is affirmed.

RULAND and TAUBMAN, JJ., concur.

Questions

(1) In non-installment contracts where the parties have not agreed otherwise, the perfect tender rule applies. Why is revocation of acceptance governed by a different standard–"substantial impairment of value"?

(2) We saw previously that a buyer who lacked the right to reject (e.g., because the goods conformed perfectly to the contract) but who nevertheless sent a timely notice of rejection would not be deemed to have accepted the goods, and would escape the consequences of acceptance (such as liability for the full price) even though the improper rejection was a breach by the buyer. In other words a rejection can be "effective" but "wrongful." See the Questions following Problem 46 *supra*. Suppose a buyer lacks the right to revoke because the only nonconformity in the goods does not substantially impair their value. The buyer nevertheless sends a notice of revocation within a reasonable time after discovering the insubstantial nonconformity. Does the unjustified attempt to revoke "undo" the buyer's acceptance, thus requiring the seller to take back the goods and relieving the buyer of the consequences of acceptance (e.g., liability for the full price)? In other words, is there such a thing as an "effective" but "wrongful" revocation of acceptance? Does the *Cissell* case *supra* shed any light on this question? Under the proposed amended version of Article 2, a seller could treat a buyer's unjustified notice of revocation as effective by taking the goods back and seeking damages for wrongful revocation; but if the seller refused to take the goods back, the unjustified attempt to revoke would be ineffective.[1]

Problem 55

Return to the facts of Problem 54 in which, a month after receiving delivery of 200 computers from Random Accessories, P & T discovered that 55 of them contained a defect. Assume that P & T decides to revoke acceptance. To do so P & T must notify Random of the revocation. See 2–608(2). When must such notice be given? See 2–608(2) and comment 4 thereto. How does this compare with the rule governing the timing of notice of rejection? What should be in the notice of revocation? How do the requirements governing the contents of notice of revocation compare to the requirements for the contents of notice of rejection? See 2–605.

Problem 56

Suppose that, on the facts of Problem 54, Random opts to keep all 200 computers despite the defects in 55 of them.

---

1. See comment 2 to proposed amended Section 2–706 and comment 2 to proposed amended Section 2–708.

(a) P & T did not inform Random of the defects when they were discovered, but instead employed a third party repair service to fix the problems. A year after the computers had been delivered—well within the applicable statute of limitations (see 2–725) and approximately 11 months after discovering the defects—P & T served Random with papers for a lawsuit to recover the costs of repairing the defects. Random moves to dismiss the suit, alleging that P & T failed to give timely notice of the breach under 2–607(3)(a). What result? Under proposed amended Section 2–607(3)(a), Random would have to prove that it was "prejudiced" by the failure to receive timely notice. How could Random satisfy this requirement?

(b) Same facts as (a) except P & T served papers on Random within three weeks after the defects were discovered. Now what result?

(c) Suppose that P & T complained to Random as soon as the defects were discovered. P & T described the problem to Random, but it did not expressly claim that the defects constituted a breach of warranty, nor at that time did it threaten to sue or state the Random was responsible for damages. Indeed, P & T did not even demand that Random repair the defects, and several weeks later it purchased five additional computers from Random. When P & T eventually sued for breach of warranty, Random moved to dismiss for lack of timely notice of the breach. What result? Consider comment 4 to 2–607. Would it matter if the buyer had been an individual consumer who purchased a computer for home use? See comment 4 to 2–607.

(d) Suppose the computers Random delivered to P & T did not contain defects and were merchantable, but the delivery occurred six weeks after the delivery date required by the contract. Random, of course, was quite aware that delivery was late. If P & T wants to keep the computers and recover damages for the delay, should it give notice of breach under 2–607(3)(a)? See Eastern Air Lines, Inc. v. McDonnell Douglas Corp., 532 F.2d 957 (5th Cir.1976).

Note on the Purpose and Content of Buyer's Notice of Breach

The last two variations of Problem 55 raise two questions: 1) What does 2–607(3)(a) require as to the contents of the buyer's notice of breach? 2) Must a buyer give notice of breach when the seller is already aware of the defect? The answers to both questions must be derived from the purpose of the notice requirement. In Standard Alliance Industries, Inc. v. Black Clawson Co., 587 F.2d 813, 825–26 (6th Cir.1978), the court held that a buyer had to give notice of breach under 2–607(3)(a) even though the seller knew that its attempts to repair the goods had failed:

> The express language of the statute and the official comment mandate notice regardless whether either or both parties had actual knowledge of breach....
>
> An examination of the policy reasons which underlie 2–607 further support our view. Notice of breach serves two distinct purposes. First, express notice opens the way for settlement through negotiation between the parties.... Second, proper notice minimizes the possibility of prejudice to the seller by giving him "ample opportunity to cure the defect, inspect the goods, investigate the claim, or do whatever may be

necessary to properly defend himself or minimize his damages while the facts are fresh in the minds of the parties." Note, Notice of Breach and the Uniform Commercial Code, 25 U. Fla. L. Rev. 520, 522 (1973).... Compare 3 Williston on Sales (4th Ed.), § 22–11 and J. White & R. Summers, [Uniform Commercial Code 344 (1972)] which identify three policy reasons behind the notice requirement: 1) To enable the seller to make adjustments or replacement or to suggest opportunities for cure; 2) To enable the seller to prepare for negotiation or litigation; and 3) To give the seller peace of mind from stale claims.

See also Connick v. Suzuki Motor Co., 174 Ill.2d 482, 221 Ill.Dec. 389, 675 N.E.2d 584, 589 (1996) (seller's general knowledge of defects in goods it manufactured did not excuse buyer from giving notice of breach as to particular transaction).

Another issue is whether or not the buyer must convey that she deems the seller to be in breach in order to satisfy the notice requirement. The committee that first studied whether Article 2 should be revised had the following to say about this issue:

> A more important problem is the content of otherwise timely notice. Section 2–607(3)(a) says that the buyer must "notify the seller of breach." Comment 4, however, states, on the one hand, that the "content of the notification need merely be sufficient to let the seller know that the transaction is still troublesome and must be watched" and, on the other hand, that the "notification which saves the buyer's rights under this Article need only such as informs the seller that the transaction is claimed to involve a breach...." Some courts, taking a literal approach, have faulted a notice of problems that would arise if a breach occurred and a notice that identified existing problems without claiming a breach.

> Literal interpretations of the notice requirement should be rejected. Either the text of § 2–607(3)(a) or the comments should be revised to require only that the notice inform the seller that problems have arisen or continue to exist with regard to the accepted goods.

UCC PERMANENT EDITORIAL BOARD STUDY GROUP—UNIFORM COMMERCIAL CODE ARTICLE 2, PRELIMINARY REPORT 167–68 (1990).

Problem 57

Suppose that when the first of the defective computers in Problem 54 malfunctioned it caused a fire that injured one of P & T's employees. A year after the fire occurred, the employee sued Random to recover for her injuries on a breach of implied warranty theory (see 2–318 and 2–715(2)(b)). The employee gave no notice of breach before commencing suit. Should the suit be dismissed? Would it matter whether P & T had given Random notice of the defects in the computers? See 2–607(3)(a) and comment 5 thereto.

Given the substantial limitations placed on the perfect tender rule (e.g., by the cure provision) and the possibility of revoking acceptance, how important is it to determine whether a buyer or lessee has accepted the goods? Consider the following:

Problem 58

Morrow Department Store agreed to buy a custom designed 20–foot crystal Christmas tree for $35,000 (due on delivery) from American Glass Designers, Inc. (AGD). Morrow had one of its own trucks make the 100 mile trip to AGD's plant. The manager of Morrow's glass department accompanied the truck and had the opportunity to view the tree before it was disassembled, packed in boxes for shipment and loaded on the Morrow truck. The Morrow manager commented that the tree was "breathtaking" and "just the kind of thing we had in mind." After the manager delivered a $35,000 check to AGD, the Morrow truck was driven back to the Morrow store. The tree remained in the truck overnight until it could be unloaded the next morning (November 6). Jim Morrow, an internationally-known glass expert who had conceived of the tree project, became ill at this time and could not supervise the tree's re-assembly. In the meantime, the packages containing the disassembled tree were placed in a storage room.

On November 17 Jim returned to work and supervised erection of the tree in the Morrow glass department. When assembly was complete, Jim began a close inspection. He was startled to find an extremely fine crack running through the glass trunk. Although difficult to discern, the crack made the tree dangerous for display purposes and unusable by Morrow. In Jim's judgment, it will be virtually impossible to determine whether the crack existed when the tree was picked up or whether the trunk was damaged during transportation, storage or assembly. Jim has consulted you for advice. Can Morrow reject? See 2–606 and 2–607(2). If Morrow cannot reject, can it revoke acceptance? See 2–607(4). See also Miron v. Yonkers Raceway, Inc., 400 F.2d 112 (2d Cir.1968).

Note: Consequences of Acceptance

"The buyer's acceptance of goods, despite their alleged nonconformity, is a watershed. After acceptance, the buyer must pay for the goods at the contract rate; [UCC § 2–607(1)]; and bears the burden of establishing their nonconformity. [UCC § 2–607(4)]." Stelco Industries, Inc. v. Cohen, 182 Conn. 561, 563–64, 438 A.2d 759 (1980). After acceptance, the buyer may only avoid liability for the contract price by invoking the provision which permits revocation of acceptance. That provision, [UCC § 2–608(1)], requires proof that the "nonconformity [of the goods] substantially impairs [their] value to him."

Plateq Corp. of North Haven v. Machlett Laboratories, Inc., 189 Conn. 433, 456 A.2d 786 (1983).

Problem 59

Vince Vendee purchased a used Phord automobile from Perpetual Motors, Inc. for $5,000. The sales agreement included a 30–day warranty against defects. Vince paid $2,000 down and agreed to pay the balance in monthly installments. Consider the following scenarios:

(a) Vince took delivery of the car, but as he drove it home (a trip of three miles) it stalled several times, stopped functioning except in low gear, and would not exceed 10 m.p.h. When Vince finally reached home, he called Perpetual and described his problems, "canceled" the sale, and demanded his money back. Did Vince rightfully reject? Had he already accepted the car? Suppose the contract stated that Vince's exclusive remedy for breach of the 30–day warranty was repair of the defects or replacement of the defective parts. Would that affect your answer?

(b) Vince drove the car home without incident. The Phord worked fine for the first several days, when Vince used it only on city streets. When the weekend came and Vince attempted highway driving, however, he discovered the car would not exceed 40 m.p.h. Perpetual made several attempts to correct the problem, but had not succeeded by the end of the 30 day warranty period. At that point Perpetual refused to attempt further repairs. Vince then wrote a letter demanding that the sale be canceled and his down payment returned. Perpetual refused. Can Vince get his money back? Which provisions of the Code offer Vince his best argument?

(c) Same facts as (b). Two days after receiving Vince's "cancellation" letter, Perpetual sent an employee to pick up the car from Vince's garage. Vince refused to turn over the car before receiving a refund. Did Vince's refusal violate 2–602(2)(a) and/or (b)? See 2–711(3).

(d) Same facts as (b) with the following additions: because Vince had used all his savings for the down payment on the Phord he could not immediately buy a replacement vehicle. He therefore continued to commute in the Phord for the next two months, until he was able to buy a cheap but serviceable used car. After he purchased the replacement Vince continued to drive the Phord on errands approximately once a week "to keep the battery charged and the motor in operating condition." He eventually sued Perpetual to recover his down payment on the theory that he had either rejected or revoked his acceptance of the Phord. By the time of trial Vince had possessed the car for a year and had put 1350 miles on it—400 before canceling the sale, 700 during the following two months, and 250 after purchasing a replacement car. He can prove that the Phord's failure to run at higher speeds was due to a serious defect in the transmission. Perpetual argues that Vince's continued use of the car invalidated his "cancellation," citing 2–602(2)(a) and 2–606(1)(c). What result? Consider proposed amended Section 2–608(4).

LIARIKOS v. MELLO

Supreme Judicial Court of Massachusetts, 1994.
418 Mass. 669, 639 N.E.2d 716.

O'CONNOR, JUSTICE. A Superior Court jury, by special verdict, found that the defendant, Elliott P. Mello, was a partner with Michael W. Costa in the business of Pine Grove Auto Sales when that enterprise sold a Jaguar motor vehicle to the plaintiff, Kathleen F. Liarikos. The jury also found that Costa or Mello violated an express warranty to the plaintiff with respect to the odometer reading on the Jaguar at the time of the sale, and that Costa or Mello deceived and committed a fraud on the plaintiff. In addition, the jury found that the plaintiff made an effective revocation of the acceptance of the Jaguar to Pine Grove Auto Sales after discovery of the odometer change, and they assessed damages in the sum of $31,150. A judgment for that sum plus interest was entered.

* * *

Mello appealed to the Appeals Court, challenging ... the judge's instruction to the jury that continued use of an automobile may be consistent with a valid revocation of acceptance if special circumstances exist. We transferred the case here on our own initiative. We conclude ... that the instruction on continued use was correct....

The dispute that led to the litigation arose from the plaintiff's, Kathleen F. Liarikos, purchase of a 1984 Jaguar XJS automobile from Pine Grove Auto Sales in 1988. The plaintiff dealt almost exclusively with Michael Costa in regard to the purchase, although she asserted that Mello had made representations regarding the vehicle's low mileage. After experiencing various mechanical problems with the automobile, the plaintiff discovered in 1990 that the vehicle's odometer had been turned back. She sent a ... demand letter [under a consumer protection statute] to Pine Grove Auto Sales to which neither Mello nor Costa responded. The plaintiff asserts, and the defendant appears to agree, that the demand also served as the plaintiff's revocation of acceptance of the vehicle. The plaintiff continued to use the vehicle after the revocation.

* * *

The final issue argued by Mello raises a question not previously addressed by this court. In instructing the jury, the judge said:

"[T]he general rule of law is that a continued use after rejection does not permit this remedy of rescission or rejection unless there are some special circumstances that you as the jurors may consider for whatever considerations you want to give to them; whether or not there was any conduct by the plaintiff, in other words, inconsistent with her intent to reject it after she rejected it and if she did reject it."

Mello claims that this instruction was in error because continued use after revocation, if unexplained, constitutes an acceptance. Mello contends that only assurances of repair by the seller or an intent on the buyer's part to preserve the goods may explain continued use after revocation. After approximately one hour of deliberation, the jury asked the following question:

> "In reference to Question No. 5 [which read 'did the plaintiff make an effective revocation of the acceptance of the Jaguar to Pine Grove Auto Sales after discovery of the odometer change'] if the demand letter has been presented to the defendant and no response has been made to the demand can the plaintiff continue to use the vehicle until some resolution has been made to the demand?"

In response to the question, the judge replied:

> "Persons such as the plaintiff cannot continue to accept the vehicle and reject it at the same time. You cannot accept it and also reject.

> "Consistent[2] use after rejection of a motor vehicle or after being offered back to a dealer may be construed as continued acceptance unless the jury finds that there have been some special circumstances by reason of its continued use not inconsistent with rejection, but she must hold it in her possession with reasonable care after there has been a valid rejection, assuming there has been, so as to permit its availability to the seller to get possession of it; and consistent use may or may not be in conformity with that obligation, depending upon how the jury resolves the issue."

Mello objected again on the grounds that "special circumstances" are not an accepted explanation for continued use and that there was no evidence of "special circumstances" presented to the jury.

The judge's instruction and answer to the jury's question, although not as full as they might have been, were not erroneous. A buyer who has validly rejected goods or revoked acceptance has a duty to treat the goods in a manner not inconsistent with the seller's ownership. G.L. c. 106, §§ 2–602(2)(a) & 2–608(3) (1992 ed.). In interpreting identical provisions, a few courts have held that the continued use of an automobile after a valid revocation operates as a second or continuing acceptance, thereby invalidating the revocation. See, e.g., Bryant v. Prenger, 717 S.W.2d 242, 244 (Mo.Ct.App.1986) ("appellants continued to use the automobile as their own and not in a manner compatible with the attempted rescission ... [t]he effect was to nullify the prior revocation of acceptance"); Wendt v. Beardmore Suburban Chevrolet, Inc., 219 Neb. 775, 780, 366 N.W.2d 424 (1985) ("Logically, then, the Code requires that Plaintiffs' continued use of the automobile after their attempted rejection invalidates the revocation of acceptance," quoting Waltz v. Chevrolet Motor Div., 307 A.2d 815, 816 [Del. Super. Ct.1973]). Other

2. There are two places in the quoted language where the transcript reads "consistent," yet "continued" seems to be the appropriate word in the context of the instruction. It is unclear if the judge misspoke or the transcription is faulty.

courts have held, however, that "[a] blanket rule prohibiting a revoking buyer from continuing to use the goods would contravene the code's rule of reasonableness and its underlying purpose of modernizing commercial transactions." Johannsen v. Minnesota Valley Ford Tractor Co., 304 N.W.2d 654, 658 (Minn.1981). In reaching this conclusion, these courts "emphasize the practical consideration that an individual who buys an automobile ... may very well be unable, without extraordinary financial difficulty, to tender the automobile ... and do without it until the litigation concerning it is complete." Ex parte Stem, 571 So.2d 1112, 1114 (Ala.1990). We find this reasoning persuasive.

The continued reasonable use of an automobile should not as a matter of law prevent the buyer from revoking acceptance. See Ibrahim v. Ford Motor Co., 214 Cal. App. 3d 878, 897, 263 Cal. Rptr. 64 (1989), and cases cited. What constitutes reasonable use is a question of fact for the jury which must be decided under the circumstances of each case. The reasonableness of continued use has been based on the existence of so called special circumstances. See Wendt, supra 366 N.W.2d at 427–428. The judge in the instant case charged the jury using the special circumstances language. As demonstrated in the recitation of the judge's instruction above, the term "special circumstances" by itself does little to direct the jury's deliberations toward the determinations which will likely throw light on the reasonableness of the buyer's continued use. In the future, juries should be instructed that continued use, if reasonable, does not invalidate a revocation of acceptance. The jury should be further instructed that factors to consider on the issue of reasonable use are "the seller's instructions to the buyer after revocation of acceptance; the degree of economic and other hardship that the buyer would suffer if he discontinued using the defective goods; the reasonableness of the buyer's use after revocation as a method of mitigating damages; the degree of prejudice to the seller; and whether the seller acted in bad faith." Johannsen, supra at 658. See also Ozark Kenworth, Inc. v. Neidecker, 283 Ark. 196, 200–201, 672 S.W.2d 899 (1984).

In the present case, the jury would have been warranted in finding that the defendant ignored the plaintiff's request that he refund the purchase price and take back the automobile. Indeed, the evidence was not in conflict with respect to that point. In addition, the jury would have been warranted in finding, and again there was little controversy, that the plaintiff relied on her automobile to conduct her business and would have been harmed by lack of access to an automobile. Accordingly, while the judge's instruction was not optimal, it was sufficient in view of the evidence in this case, and the jury were warranted in finding that the plaintiff's continued use was reasonable. Mello's contention that continued use may only be explained by reliance on assurances of repair by the seller or as an attempt to preserve the value of the defective goods is an overly restrictive interpretation of reasonable continued use.

Judgment affirmed.

Notes

(a) In Design Plus Store Fixtures, Inc. v. Citro Corp., 131 N.C.App. 581, 508 S.E.2d 825 (Ct.App.1998), the court also applied the rule that a buyer's continued use of goods that have been rejected or whose acceptance has been revoked did not constitute acceptance, provided the buyer's use was "reasonable." The result, however, was different than in *Liarikos*. The buyer in *Design Plus*, a supplier of retail store fixtures, contracted to purchase store display tables that the buyer intended to re-sell to its primary customer. When the first two installments arrived, however, the tables had design defects that made them impossible to assemble, and the buyer properly notified the seller of rejection. The seller did not respond to the buyer's notice. In order to meet its customer's needs, the buyer drilled new holes in the tables to permit assembly and shipped them to its customer with the understanding that they would be replaced. Eventually (11 months later in the case of one installment, 19 months later in the case of the other installment) the buyer acquired replacement tables from another source, and it donated the original tables received from the seller to charity.

The seller argued, and the trial court found, that the buyer had accepted the tables by takings actions "inconsistent with the seller's ownership" under 2–606(c), and thus should be liable for the contract price (less an offset for damages caused by the defects). On Appeal, the North Carolina Court of Appeals agreed:

> A merchant buyer in possession of rejected goods, and without instructions from the seller, is in the somewhat difficult position of having a choice of reasonable options but no clear affirmative duties with respect to those goods, N.C.Gen.Stat. § 25–2–604 [UCC 2–604]; yet, the buyer must avoid acts "inconsistent with the seller's ownership" in order to avoid accepting the non-conforming goods. N.C.Gen.Stat. § 25–2–606(1)(c) (1995). The issue is whether [buyer's] actions constitute good faith steps toward "realization on or preservation of the goods," on the one hand, or "acts inconsistent with ownership" on the other. Compare, N.C.Gen.Stat. § 25–2–604 Official U.C.C. Comment (1995) and N.C.Gen.Stat. § 25–2–606(1)(c) (1995). Whether actions taken with respect to rejected non-conforming goods, beyond those suggested by statute, are "inconsistent with the seller's ownership," depends on the circumstances and the buyer's steps towards realization on or preservation of the goods in good faith.

> The repair and continued use of the non-conforming, rejected goods constitutes a reasonable good faith effort to preserve the goods while mitigating damages. . . .

>> Thus it has been frequently held that under certain circumstances a buyer rejecting goods or revoking his acceptance may continue to use the goods . . . particularly where such use is a direct result of the oppressive conduct of the seller . . . or where no prejudice is shown (citations omitted).

Frank's Maintenance & Engineering, Inc. v. C.A. Roberts Co., 86 Ill.
App.3d 980, 986–87, 42 Ill.Dec. 25, 408 N.E.2d 403, 408 (1980).

In this case, [seller] entered into the contract with the understanding that manufacturing and delivering the tables in a timely manner
was necessary to serve [buyer's] primary customer, Springmaid. [Seller]
delivered the tables late, and the tables were defective. According to the
trial court's findings of fact, the [buyer] "performed corrective measures" on the tables, and provided them to Springmaid with the understanding they would be replaced and "replacement of the tables could
not affect any of the scheduled store openings;" and, [seller] "offered
neither explanation nor solution." [Buyer] bore the expense of repairing
the tables for temporary use by Springmaid. [Seller] offered no instructions as to the disposal or return of the tables. Under these circumstances, we hold that repairing the tables and allowing Springmaid the
continued use of the tables were reasonable actions in good faith and did
not constitute acceptance of the tables.

However, after allowing Springmaid the reasonable continued use of
the repaired tables, [buyer] gave the nonconforming tables away, contending they had no market value. The trial court concluded, inter alia,
that "disposal of the tables after their replacement without notifying or
attempting to obtain the consent of [Defendant] Corporation constituted
acceptance of the goods under the code as acts inconsistent with Defendant's ownership." We agree.

As discussed above, reasonable repair and use of the tables to
temporarily satisfy a contract contemplated at the time of the transaction is not inconsistent with ownership; thus those actions did not
constitute an acceptance. However, discarding the tables without notifying [seller] is an unreasonable act, inconsistent with ownership, where
the tables had some salvageable value. Underlying the issue of acceptance, in this context, is the question of whether [buyer] acted inconsis-
tently, by rejecting the goods and then disposing of these goods as an
owner. Giving the tables to charity without notifying [seller] was such
an act of ownership . . . .

. . . . We therefore affirm the trial court's conclusion that [buyer]
accepted the Kansas and Oregon installments and its award of damages
to [seller] in the amount of the contract price for those goods, less an
offset for damages sustained by [buyer] by reason of the defects.
N.C.Gen.Stat. § 25–2–607(1) (1995).

(b) *Liarikos* and *Design Plus Store Fixtures* were decided under the pre-
amendment version of Article 2. The proposed amended version of Article 2
would explicitly address the effect of a buyer's continued use of goods after
rejection or revocation of acceptance. See proposed amended Section
2–608(4). Would the result in *Liarikos* and *Design Plus Store Fixtures* be the
same if proposed amended Section 2–608(4) applied?

Problem 60

Return to the facts of alternative (d) of Problem 59, where the buyer of a car (Vince Vendee) continued to use the vehicle after revoking his acceptance. Suppose Vince succeeds in a suit based on revocation of acceptance. Under 2–711(1), Vince would be entitled to recover payments he made to the seller, Perpetual Motors. Perpetual complains that it would be unfair to require a complete refund when Vince has had the use of the Phord for almost a year, and the value and condition of the car has depreciated over that time. What result? Consider proposed amended Section 2–608(4)(b). If the court decides to grant an offset for Vince's use of the car, how should the court determine the amount of the offset? Would the monthly rental rate for equivalent cars at consumer car rental agencies be an appropriate standard?

Questions

In some situations a buyer will use goods for a substantial period of time *before* revoking acceptance. Must the buyer pay for the value of such use? Under the pre-amendment version of Article 2, which does not explicitly address any aspect of a revoking buyer's liability for the value of using the goods, some courts permit sellers to offset the value of pre-revocation use against the sellers' liability to refund the price that the buyer had paid. See, e.g., North American Lighting, Inc. v. Hopkins Mfg. Corp., 37 F.3d 1253 (7th Cir.1994). Would that rule remain applicable under proposed amended Section 2–608(4), or is there a negative implication from the fact that the proposed amended provision apparently would authorize recovery only for the value of use *after* rejection or revocation? Note that, in leases of goods, UCC Article 2A explicitly allow a court to offset the value of pre-revocation use of goods against a lessor's liability for refunding rental payments a lessee has made. See 2A–508(1)(b) and comment 2 thereto.

Note: Revocation and the Circumstances of Acceptance

In order to revoke acceptance a buyer must show that she had a good reason for not rejecting the defective goods in the first place—i.e., she accepted either because she was reasonably unaware of the defects (they were difficult to discover or she had relied on the seller's "assurances") or because the seller promised to cure (but failed to do so). See 2–608(1)(a) & (b). Unless acceptance occurs in these circumstances, it cannot be revoked.

In Tai Wah Radio Manufactory Ltd. v. Ambassador Imports Ltd., 3 U.C.C.Rep.Serv.2d 117 (S.D.N.Y.1987), the buyer (a wholesaler of electronic goods) had taken delivery of, paid for, and resold one shipment of cassette recorders. It was awaiting delivery of a second order when it began receiving complaints from its customers concerning the quality of the recorders. When the second shipment arrived the buyer telexed the seller that it was taking possession of the shipment, but only as "collateral" against the seller's payment of compensation for losses caused by defects in the first shipment. The buyer repeatedly made it clear that it did not want the second shipment of recorders (which had the same defects as those in the first delivery), and would return them as soon as compensation for the first shipment was agreed upon. The seller sued for the purchase price of the second shipment (still in the buyer's possession) on the theory that the goods had been, and remained, accepted. See 2–607(1) and 2–709(1)(a). In granting partial summary judgment to the seller, the court commented:

> [A] buyer with knowledge that goods are defective when he accepts them does not lose his right to revoke the acceptance if the acceptance was based on the reasonable assumption that the nonconformity would be seasonably cured but the cure was not effected. In addition, acceptance may be revoked if the buyer, without discovering the nonconformity, was reasonably induced to accept the goods either by the difficulty of discovery before acceptance or by the seller's assurances. Neither of these exceptions is applicable to this case. When the defendant [buyer] accepted the second shipment of cassette recorders, it had knowledge of the recorder's allegedly defective nature. Defendant did not assume that plaintiff would cure this nonconformity. Thus, defendant did not have the right to revoke the contract [*sic*] for the second shipment.
>
> Although defendant may not have intended to keep the products when it took possession of the second shipment, this does not change the result. From the undisputed facts in this case, it is obvious that defendant was attempting to engage in a form of commercial "kidnapping" to compel plaintiff to resolve its differences with defendant. Defendant, instead of taking possession of the second shipment of recorders, should have rejected the second shipment. . . . Accordingly, it is apparent that plaintiff is entitled to payment for the second shipment.

CHAMPION FORD SALES, INC. v. LEVINE

Court of Special Appeals of Maryland, 1981.
49 Md.App. 547, 433 A.2d 1218.

THOMPSON, J. This case involves an appeal and a cross-appeal from a judgment entered in favor of Mr. and Mrs. Robert J. Levine, appellees and cross-appellants (buyers) against Champion Ford Sales, Inc. and Ford Motor Company, appellants and cross-appellees (sellers) in the Circuit Court for Baltimore County. The principal issues presented in the sellers' appeal are: (1) whether under the circumstances described below, the buyers justifiably revoked their acceptance, under Md.Com. Law Code Ann. § 2–608, of an automobile which had been purchased from Champion and manufactured by Ford; and (2) if revocation was justified, whether the damages awarded the buyers were proper. The only significant question presented in the buyers' cross-appeal is whether the trial judge erred in ruling that the Magnuson–Moss Warranty Act, 15 U.S.C. § 2301 et seq., was not applicable in the instant case and that the buyers were therefore not entitled to recover attorneys' fees under its provisions. For the reasons set forth below, we shall hold that the buyers' revocation of acceptance was justified . . . and that the trial judge erred in holding that the federal statute had no applicability.

On December 20, 1977, the buyers took delivery from Champion of a new 1978 Ford Granada. They had selected the Granada, which they intended to use for normal family transportation purposes, after considerable comparison shopping. With the car came a limited warranty[1] under which the manufacturer promised that "the Selling Dealer will repair, replace, or adjust free any parts, except tires, found to be defective in factory materials or workmanship within the earlier of twelve months or 12,000 miles." The buyers paid the purchase price of $5,446.35 in cash. Six days after delivery, when the car had been driven 109 miles, the engine became inoperable. After the car was towed to the dealer's service facility, an inspection revealed that a defective engine valve had broken and had fallen into a cylinder, destroying or damaging the engine block, the cylinder head, two pistons, a connecting rod, rings, and a number of gaskets. The defect had existed when the car was sold but could not have been discovered by any reasonable inspection. After the cause and extent of the damage was ascertained, the dealer informed the buyers that it would repair the engine and provided them with a "loaner" car. The buyers accepted the loaner vehicle, but after viewing their car while it was dismantled in the dealer's shop indicated that they did not want the engine repaired but rather desired replacement of either the engine or the car. It was their view that a vehicle with a shop-rebuilt engine was not comparable to one with a factory assembled engine. Both the buyers and the dealer's mechanic testified that certain equipment which Ford used in assembling engines in the factory and which it advertised as contributing to the quality of its engines was not available in the dealer's shop. A series of meetings with representatives of the dealer and the manufacturer followed, at which the buyers' requests for a new engine or car were refused. Following these refusals, on January 13, 1978 the buyers advised the dealer that they were revoking their acceptance of the car and demanded the return of the money they had paid. The dealer refused to refund the purchase price and proceeded to repair the car's engine. The repairs were performed by qualified mechanics at the dealer's service facility, at a cost of $889.69. The repairs were completed on February 10, 1978, at which time the car was test-driven by Champion personnel and found to operate satisfactorily. The buyers were then informed that their car was ready to be picked up. The buyers again advised the dealer that they had revoked their acceptance and declined to either inspect or accept the repaired car. On February 13, the buyers returned the loaner vehicle provided by the dealer. On April 10, 1978, when their money had not been refunded, they filed suit. In August 1978, the buyers purchased a replacement for the Granada, a used 1974 Ford Pinto, for which they paid $1,200.00.

On July 10, 1980, the buyers' action came to trial. Their amended declaration was in four counts. Count I sought return of the purchase price paid for the Granada, on the grounds that the buyers had revoked their acceptance; Count II set forth a claim for breach of the implied warranty of merchantability; Count III claimed violation of the Magnuson–Moss Act and breach of express warranties; and Count IV alleged

---

1. The sellers have not argued that the express warranty in any way limited the remedies available to the buyers. See Md. Com.Law Code Ann. § 2–719(1)(a).

wrongful breach of a guaranty in violation of Md.Com.Law Code Ann. § 14–401(k).[2] In each count, the buyers sought interest, costs, and attorneys' fees. At the close of the buyers' case, the trial judge directed a verdict for the sellers as to Counts III and IV. Counts I and II were submitted to the jury, which returned a verdict in favor of the buyers on each. The jury awarded damages in the amount of the purchase price of the Granada plus interest from the date acceptance was revoked.... The judge held that the Magnuson–Moss Act was not applicable and refused to award the buyers attorneys' fees. Appeals to this Court followed.

Md.Com.Law Code Ann. § 2–608 sets forth the circumstances under which a buyer may revoke his acceptance: [The court quoted § 2–608.]

At trial in the instant case, it was undisputed that the buyers accepted the car without knowledge of its defect, as the result of the practical impossibility of discovering the defect; that they revoked their acceptance within a reasonable time after discovery of the defect and before any substantial change in its condition, not the result of its own defect; and, that they gave adequate notice, within a reasonable time, to sellers: the only issue was whether, at the time they revoked acceptance, there existed a nonconformity which substantially impaired the value of the car to the buyers.

On this appeal, the sellers argue that the evidence was insufficient to permit the jury to find that such a nonconformity existed and that the buyers' revocation was justified. They contend that, although there was obviously a defect in the Granada when it was delivered, they had a right under § 2–608 to cure that defect and that the only competent evidence adduced showed that they did cure the defect; that the nonconformity which existed was eliminated by the repairs which were carried out and that the repaired vehicle "was like new." They further contend that, even if a nonconformity existed after the car was repaired, the evidence was insufficient to permit the jury to find that it substantially impaired the value of the car.

Under the Uniform Commercial Code, a seller is not expressly granted the right to cure when a buyer revokes acceptance, cf., § 2–508 (conferring the right to cure where a buyer rejects goods as nonconforming), although it may be inferred that such a right exists where the buyer accepts nonconforming goods with the expectation that the nonconformity will be remedied. See § 2–608(1)(a). Whether a general right to cure, applicable where a buyer accepts without knowledge of a nonconformity and thus without the expectation that it will be cured, is also to be inferred, has been the subject of considerable dispute and the decisions are in conflict. See, e.g., Conte v. Dwan Lincoln-Mercury, Inc., 172 Conn. 112, 374 A.2d 144, 149 (1976) (a seller has a right to cure, citing § 2–508 as authority); Werner v. Montana, 117 N.H. 721, 378 A.2d 1130, 1136 (1977) (no right to cure in revocation of acceptance situa-

2. Section 14–401(k) is part of the Maryland Consumer Products Guaranty Act, Md.Com.Law Code Ann. § 14–401 et seq. (1975, 1980 Cum.Supp.). The Act contains provisions similar to those found in the Magnuson–Moss Act.

tion).[4] We find it unnecessary to decide the issue. Even if we were to recognize that a seller has a right to cure where the buyer revokes acceptance, in order to be effective to bar revocation in a particular case, the seller plainly would be required to make a full and complete cure. In the instant case, the jury was instructed to determine whether the Granada, as repaired, contained a nonconformity which substantially impaired its value to the buyers; the jury in effect found that it did. Thus, the jury made an inferential finding that the sellers' repairs did not result in a fully conforming tender and did not constitute a cure. The only real issue is whether the evidence was sufficient to support that finding.

A nonconformity exists when the goods are not in accordance with the obligations under the contract. See Md.Com.Law Code Ann. § 2–106(2). The substantiality requirement bars revocation for defects which are trivial or easily corrected, Rozmus v. Thompson's Lincoln–Mercury Co., 209 Pa.Super. 120, 224 A.2d 782, 784 (1966), or for those which merely make the tender somewhat less than perfect, Rutland Music Service v. Ford Motor Co., 422 A.2d 248, 249 (Vt.1980). Whether a nonconformity substantially impairs the product's value to the buyer necessarily involves consideration of subjective factors, *i.e.*, the particular needs and circumstances of the individual buyer, yet proof of substantial impairment requires more than the buyer's subjective assertion that the value of the product to him was impaired; it requires evidence from which the trier of fact, applying objective standards, can infer that the needs of the buyer were not met because of the nonconformity. It is clear that the question of whether there exists a nonconformity which substantially impairs the value to the buyer is one of fact, to be decided by the jury on the facts and circumstances of each individual case.

* * *

Turning to the case before us, we are of the opinion that the evidence amply supported the jury's finding that the repaired Granada contained nonconformities which substantially impaired its value to these buyers and we therefore hold that the sellers failed to make a complete cure. The buyers purchased a new car with a new, factory-built and installed engine. They indicated that they chose that particular model, after careful comparison, because it was one in which they felt they could have confidence. What the sellers tendered was a repaired car with a shop-rebuilt engine. The members of the jury evidently perceived a difference between the two and they were completely justified in so doing; the goods tendered clearly did not conform to the contract. Nor

---

4. In the only Maryland decision to date which discusses § 2–608, Lynx, Inc. v. Ordnance Products, 273 Md. at 15, 327 A.2d 502, the Court stated, in dicta, that "the buyer cannot revoke his acceptance ... if following acceptance the seller in fact seasonably cured the nonconformity"; however it is unclear from the statement whether the cure, to be seasonable, must occur prior to the buyer's revocation. J. White and R. Summers, Uniform Commercial Code § 8–1 (2d ed. 1980), states: "The right to cure does not, however, limit revocation of acceptance"; the accompanying footnote reads in pertinent part: "Once a buyer has rightfully revoked acceptance many courts hold that the seller has no right to cure under 2–508."

was the evidence of substantial impairment any less compelling; the defect here was plainly neither trivial nor easily corrected, as the repairs required nearly four weeks and the replacement of a sizable number of engine components, at a cost of nearly $900. The buyers testified that because the car had undergone major repairs its value to them was substantially impaired. Certainly any consumer would consider the car the buyers contracted for to be considerably more valuable than that which they received, both monetarily and in terms of the degree of confidence with which it could be operated. . . .

The sellers requested that the jury be instructed that they were to determine whether any nonconformity found would substantially impair the value of the vehicle to an "average" buyer. The trial court properly declined to give the requested instruction. Section 2–608(1) clearly indicates that whether revocation of acceptance is justified is to be determined by judging the impairment of value to the particular buyer involved, not an average buyer. See Tiger Motor Co. v. McMurtry, 224 So.2d at 646; Jorgensen v. Pressnall, 545 P.2d at 1384.

The sellers object to the trial court's failure to instruct the jury that the sellers had a right to cure. The argument is without merit. Our review of the instructions given discloses that the judge consistently instructed the jury that they were to determine whether the engine, as repaired, impaired the value of the car. By so instructing the jury, the court presupposed a right to cure and the instructions were, if anything, more favorable to the sellers than they might have been. . . .

On their cross-appeal, the buyers contend that the trial judge erred in ruling that the Magnuson–Moss Warranty Act, 15 U.S.C. § 2301 et seq. had no applicability and that they were not entitled to recover attorneys' fees incurred in prosecuting their action against the sellers. We agree.

[THE COURT QUOTED PERTINENT PROVISIONS OF THE MAGNUSON-MOSS ACT.]

The Act thus permits recovery of attorneys' fees by a consumer who prevails in an action against the seller for breach of an implied warranty under state law provided the seller is afforded an opportunity to cure. In the instant case, the buyers prevailed in their action against the sellers for revocation of acceptance, which was based upon a nonconformity which breached the implied warranty of merchantability. As we have indicated above, the buyers, prior to instituting their action, afforded the sellers an opportunity to satisfactorily cure the nonconformity, *i.e.*, to replace the engine or the car. They therefore satisfied the requirements of the Act and were entitled to recover attorneys' fees, unless determined by the court to be inappropriate. We shall remand the case to the trial court for determination as to the amount of the buyers' attorneys' fees and for an award thereof, unless the court below, in its discretion, determines that such an award is inappropriate.

Judgment affirmed in part and reversed in part.

Notes and Questions

(1) As the *Champion* court notes, authorities are split on whether, under the pre-amendment version of Article 2, a seller has a right to cure following revocation of acceptance by the buyer. Compare Fitzner Pontiac–Buick–Cadillac, Inc. v. Smith, 523 So.2d 324, 328 n. 1 (Miss.1988) (recognizing a right to cure following revocation "[b]y analogy to [2–508] and in furtherance of the policy justification undergirding that statute and our common law doctrine of cure in contracts generally")[1] with, e.g., Gappelberg v. Landrum, 666 S.W.2d 88 (Tex.1984) (denying right to cure following revocation). Under proposed amended Section 2–508, a seller would be granted the right to cure following revocation, provided the buyer's original acceptance occurred because the buyer reasonably failed to discover the nonconformity (i.e., revocation under 2–608(1)(b)) rather than because the buyer relied on the seller's unfulfilled assurances of cure (i.e., revocation under 2–608(1)(a)). Under proposed amended Section 2–508, however, this right to cure following revocation would not apply in consumer sales contracts.

(2) Article 2 permits a buyer to revoke acceptance if there is a nonconformity that substantially impairs the value of the goods to the *particular* buyer or lessee. See 2–608(1). According to comment 2 to 2–608, the substantial impairment requirement should thus be analyzed from the buyer's "subjective" viewpoint—i.e., "the test [for substantial impairment of value] is not what the seller had reason to know at the time of contracting; the question is whether the non-conformity is such as will in fact cause a substantial impairment of value to the buyer though the seller had no advance knowledge as to the buyer's particular circumstances." Does the *Champion* court adopt a "subjective" approach to the substantial impairment question? On the facts of *Champion*, would it make any difference whether a subjective or and an objective approach was taken?

In Colonial Dodge, Inc. v. Miller, 420 Mich. 452, 362 N.W.2d 704 (1984), the buyer discovered that, "due to a nation-wide shortage caused by a labor strike," the new car he had just purchased lacked a spare tire. A majority of the Michigan Supreme Court held that the buyer could rightfully revoke acceptance.

> In this case, the defendant's concern with safety is evidenced by the fact that he ordered the special package which included special tires. The defendant's occupation demanded that he travel extensively, sometimes in excess of 150 miles per day on Detroit freeways, and often in the early morning hours. Mr. Miller testified that he was afraid of a tire going flat on a Detroit freeway at 3 a.m. Without a spare, he testified, he would be helpless until morning business hours. The dangers attendant upon a stranded motorist are common knowledge, and Mr. Miller's fears are not unreasonable.

> We hold that under the circumstances the failure to include the spare tire as ordered constituted a substantial impairment in value to Mr. Miller. . . .

---

1. See also Palmisciano v. Tarbox Motors, Inc., 39 U.C.C.Rep.Serv. (Callaghan) 146, 150–51 (R.I.Super.1984) (holding that 2–608(1) "explicitly" gives the seller an opportunity to cure following revocation).

A dissenting opinion, however, dismissed the problem as "a temporary deficiency easily remedied" which did not satisfy the statutory standard. Which approach better reflects the purposes of revocation of acceptance? Would an "objective" standard for substantial impairment change the result?

Note: Subjective vs. Objective Non–Conformity

While the revocation of acceptance provisions of the UCC permit proof of a "subjective" substantial impairment of value, they also require that the impairment result from a "non-conformity"—i.e., a breach of contract (see the definition of "conforming" in 2–106(2)). To what extent does the requirement of a nonconformity (as distinguished from the requirement of substantial impairment of value) import an "objective" element into the analysis? In other words, to prove a non-conformity (which in revocation situations will typically involve a breach of warranty) must a revoking buyer prove a violation of objectively manifested and reasonable (as opposed to merely subjective) expectations?

Consider Big Mac Mobile Homes, Inc. v. Cowgill, 31 U.C.C. Rep.Serv. (Callaghan) 1619 (Ark.Ct.App.1981). Within a month after moving into a mobile home purchased from the defendant, the plaintiff buyer (who had several allergy problems) "began experiencing an allergic reaction characterized by a sore throat, runny nose, and itching sensation of the eyes." When the reaction continued after the buyer thoroughly cleaned and aired out the home, she determined that it was caused by chemicals in the construction materials and carpeting of the home. She returned the home to the seller and, when she failed to receive a refund of the payments she had made, sued. A third party purchased the returned home from the seller and lived in it without any problems. A judgment for the buyer on a revocation of acceptance theory was reversed by the Court of Appeals, which commented as follows:

> While appellee appears to have allergic sensitivities to something, possibly in the mobile home, this does not make the mobile home defective or nonconforming. It is unfortunate that appellee possesses an apparent, peculiar sensitivity, or physical idiosyncrasy, in this regard. However, our Supreme Court has said, "the general rule seems to be that the manufacturer or employer is not required to foresee that someone might be affected because of his peculiar sensitivities to the substance causing the injury." Vanoven v. Hardin, 233 Ark. 301, 344 S.W.2d 340 (1961).

Since the trial court found that the mobile home produced an allergic reaction in the buyer, why was there no nonconformity? If there had been a nonconformity, would it have substantially impaired the value of the mobile home to the buyer?

Arguably, the fact that a substantial impairment of value can arise from the buyer's purely subjective and non-foreseeable reaction has no bearing on the separate requirement that revocation of acceptance be based on a nonconformity. As we have seen, where the perfect tender rule applies a buyer who wants to reject goods must show that the goods or the tender failed to "conform" to the contract, although there is no requirement that the nonconformity substantially impair the value of the goods. This nonconformity requirement means that rejection is permitted only if the seller has violated some *reasonable* expectation of the buyer (e.g., a warranty), and (as in the *Big Mac Mobile Homes* case) it is not satisfied by a purely "subjective," unforeseeable reaction by the buyer. It would be odd indeed to permit a buyer to revoke acceptance based on a "purely subjective" defect that would not justify rejection: by imposing a substantial impairment requirement on buyers who want to revoke acceptance but not on those who want to reject, the drafters of the UCC intended the requirements for revocation to be stricter than those for rejection.

Thus to revoke acceptance, the buyer must first establish that the seller violated a reasonable, objective expectation of the buyer (i.e., that the seller breached). In determining whether such breach was serious or harmful enough to justify revocation, however, a court should look to the particular buyer's "subjective" situation, taking into account consequences that the seller could not have foreseen. In other words, the existence of a "nonconformity" is determined from an objective standard, whereas the existence of a "substantial impairment of value" is determined subjectively.

Some courts, nevertheless, have gone far toward eliminating any "objective" nonconformity requirement for revoking buyers. In *Lanham v. Solar America of Cincinnati, Inc.*, 28 Ohio App.3d 55, 501 N.E.2d 1245 (1986), the Ohio Supreme Court affirmed a decision permitting buyers to revoke their acceptance of some solar energy units. The court reasoned as follows:

> In this case, we feel the statements made in the [written] warranties, whether breached or not, legitimately gave rise to certain expectations about the quality and performance of these solar units irrespective of whether the warranties were technically breached in any "objective" sense. . . .
>
> Notwithstanding appellant's argument that no objective proof of a warranty breach existed, [2–608] states a buyer is entitled to revoke acceptance where a product's non-conformity substantially impairs its value to him. Official Comment 2 to this section suggests that this is a subjective standard for the buyer. . . . We believe that [the problem experienced by the buyers] was justification for appellees to consider their solar unit's value to them to be substantially impaired irrespective of whether any warranty was actually breached.

For similar cases, see Blankenship v. Northtown Ford, Inc., 95 Ill.App.3d 303, 50 Ill.Dec. 850, 420 N.E.2d 167 (1981) and Frantz Lithographic Service, Inc. v. Sun Chemical Corp., 38 U.C.C. Rep.Serv. (Callaghan) 485 (E.D.Pa. 1984). Also see the discussion of non-conformity in the next case (*Seekings v. Jimmy GMC, Inc.*).

Consider also Hemmert Agricultural Aviation, Inc. v. Mid–Continent Aircraft Corp., 663 F.Supp. 1546 (D.Kan.1987). The plaintiff, a professional crop duster, purchased a model "Super 'B'" spray plane with a raised wing design different from the plane he previously used. When he flew the new plane, the buyer experienced "the sensation that the aircraft was 'falling out from under him.'" Four other crop dusting pilots who had never flown a Super "B" experienced similar sensations and complained of having to make wide turns when they flew plaintiff's plane. On the other hand, a professional flight tester with extensive experience with spray planes found that the plaintiff's aircraft "handled good and flew well." The flight tester also observed the buyer flying the plane and concluded that his problems were due to poor pilot technique. Another crop duster told the buyer that he too had been frightened when he first flew a Super "B," but that after 40–50 hours flying he became "accustomed" to the plane and after 75 hours "he loved his Super 'B.'" The buyer attempted to revoke acceptance of the plane, claiming he had lost confidence in it.

The court held for the buyer. It found several nonconformities: a breach of express warranties that the plane would be faster and more maneuverable than other models, and a breach of the implied warranty of merchantability because the plane "cannot pass without objection to its handling characteristics in normal turning maneuvers in spraying fields." As for the "substantial impairment" requirement:

> His [the buyer's] lost confidence in the Super "B" caused by its handling characteristics, which scare experienced pilots in making normal spraying maneuvers, amounts to a substantial impairment. A spray pilot's activities are considered dangerous in flying at very low altitudes and quickly maneuvering to apply sprays and to avoid obstacles. Undeniably a spray pilot's confidence in his plane is absolutely crucial.... A pilot's confidence and willingness to undertake dangerous spraying maneuvers in a plane is reasonably destroyed when the pilot consistently experiences the sensation that the plane is about to "fall out from under him" when making normal spraying turns.

Did the *Hemmert* court apply an objective or a subjective standard to the question of nonconformity? To the question of substantial impairment of value?

5. *Revocation for Breach of Manufacturers' Warranties*

SEEKINGS v. JIMMY GMC OF TUCSON, INC.

Supreme Court of Arizona, In Banc, 1981.
130 Ariz. 596, 638 P.2d 210.

Gordon, Justice. Plaintiffs/appellees/cross appellants [hereinafter appellees] Robert and Ida Seekings sued defendants/ appellants/cross appellees [hereinafter appellants]. They alleged breach of contract, breach of express warranty, breach of implied warranty, fraud, and consumer fraud.

On April 20, 1977, appellees went to appellant Jimmy GMC of Tucson, Inc. [hereinafter Jimmy GMC] to buy a motor home. They contracted to purchase a Four Winds motor home and traded in their Avco motor home for a $5,800.00 credit. When appellees later returned to pick up the Four Winds vehicle, it would not start. They refused to accept the Four Winds vehicle and demanded return of their trade-in.

Jimmy GMC told appellees that their trade-in had already been sold but that they could apply the credit to another motor home. On May 1,

1977, appellees agreed to purchase a motor home manufactured by appellant Beaver Coaches, Inc. [hereinafter Beaver]. Jimmy GMC had bought the vehicle from Beaver. Beaver expressly warranted the motor home against defects in workmanship and material. Jimmy GMC was Beaver's authorized agent for warranty work, but it disclaimed all express or implied warranties by itself. Some of the optional equipment added to the vehicle at appellees' request came with express warranties from the manufacturers, and appellees purchased a five-year power train warranty from Jimmy GMC.

The Beaver motor home had numerous problems. When appellees took their first trip in the vehicle, they discovered that the gas gauge and power generator did not work, the furnace would not start, the carburetor did not function properly, and the gas mileage was poor. Appellees returned the vehicle on May 23 to Jimmy GMC where it was worked on for five days. Apparently, not all of these problems were cured, and subsequently appellees complained that among other things, the passenger door was drafty, the motor stalled, the air conditioner malfunctioned, and sewage backed up into the bathtub. Appellees returned the motor home to Jimmy GMC for warranty work on June 1, June 16, and June 27.

Some of the defects were repaired, but others were not. Finally, on September 6, 1977, appellees' attorney sent a letter of revocation of acceptance[1] to Jimmy GMC; a similar letter was sent to Beaver on October 5, 1977. The letters detailed the remaining uncured problems, which included an engine that was difficult to start and would stall out at high altitudes, an improperly functioning power plant, and an improperly fitted passenger door. Appellees filed their complaint on December 12, 1977.

On April 6, 1978, appellants' representatives, with appellees' consent, went to appellees' home to inspect the motor home, apparently in an attempt to settle the dispute. After taking twenty-five to thirty minutes to get the vehicle started, appellants' representatives returned it to Jimmy GMC for more work. On May 15, 1978, appellant presented appellees with a list of defects which appellants attempted to cure. Appellees initialed the items they found cured but noted that a door shade was not yet satisfactory, the passenger door was still drafty, and the engine and auxiliary generator were still not functioning properly. When appellees drove the vehicle from Tucson to Phoenix in June, 1978, the dash air conditioner also failed.

The case was tried to the court alone. Before the case was submitted for decision, the trial judge ordered appellees to elect as a remedy either revocation of acceptance or damages for breach of warranty or contract.

---

1. Appellees' letters and their subsequent civil complaint requested "rescission" rather than "revocation of acceptance." The record of the proceedings is clear, however, that the parties here treated the complaint as a cause of action for revocation of acceptance under A.R.S. § 44–2371 rather than an action for common law rescission, which may still exist under A.R.S. § 44–2203. We will also treat the action as one for revocation of acceptance.

Appellees chose to press for revocation of acceptance. The trial judge then granted revocation against both appellants and awarded appellees $14,885.10 in incidental and consequential damages.

Appellants appealed to Division Two of the Court of Appeals and appellees cross-appealed. In reversing and remanding in 131 Ariz. 1, 638 P.2d 223, No. 2 CA–CIV 3638 (filed March 12, 1981), the Court of Appeals held that: (1) revocation of acceptance and incidental and consequential damages cannot be awarded against a manufacturer who has not sold directly to the purchaser; and (2) under the facts of this case, revocation could not be awarded against the seller. Appellees petitioned this Court for review to consider four issues:

(1) Is a purchaser entitled to revocation of acceptance of a product under A.R.S. § 44–2371 [UCC 2–608] against a manufacturer not in privity with the purchaser?;

(2) If the purchaser is not entitled to such revocation; [sic] is it bound by its election to sue for revocation?;

(3) Under the facts of this case, was revocation proper as against the seller?; and

(4) If appellees are entitled to revocation against either appellant, should the trial court have awarded loss of use damages? Taking jurisdiction pursuant to A.R.S. § 12–120.24 and Rule 23, Rules of Civil Appellate Procedure, we approve in part and vacate in part the opinion of the Court of Appeals. The case is remanded to the trial court for further proceedings consistent with this opinion.

Revocation Against the Manufacturer

Relying on *Durfee v. Rod Baxter Imports, Inc.*, 262 N.W.2d 349 (Minn.1977), appellees argue that the Court of Appeals erred in reversing the trial court's grant of revocation of acceptance against the manufacturer Beaver. The Durfee court, liberally administering the remedies of the Uniform Commercial Code [U.C.C.], see A.R.S. § 44–2206 [UCC 1–106, renumbered as 1–305 in amended Article 1], held that a manufacturer who indirectly profits from the sale of a product by its distributor can be sued for revocation of acceptance of that product. We believe Durfee is contra the plain meaning of the U.C.C.

The rights of aggrieved buyers under the U.C.C. are enumerated in A.R.S. §§ 44–2390 to 44–2396. All of the rights concern what the buyer is entitled to as against the "seller." A.R.S. § 44–2303(A)(4) [UCC 2–103(1)(d)] defines "seller" as "a person who sells or contracts to sell goods."

Beaver neither sold nor contracted to sell the motor home to appellees. Further, there was no evidence to support a finding that Jimmy GMC was an agent of Beaver for purposes of selling motor homes. Therefore, as Beaver was not in privity with appellees, appellees were not entitled to revocation against Beaver. The Court of Appeals was correct in so holding. *Accord Voytovich v. Bangor Punta Operations, Inc.*,

494 F.2d 1208 (6th Cir.1974); *Conte v. Dwan Lincoln–Mercury, Inc.*, 172 Conn. 112, 374 A.2d 144 (1976).

By holding that a manufacturer who does not sell to the purchaser cannot be liable for revocation and attendant damages, we follow the logic as well as the letter of the U.C.C. The remedies associated with revocation of acceptance are intended to return the buyer and seller to their presale positions. In general, the buyer is entitled to recovery of the purchase price plus all damages caused by the seller's failure to deliver conforming goods; the seller can recover the goods sold. But a manufacturer does not receive the buyer's purchase price and no longer has an ownership interest in the goods sold. In fact, in the instant case, Jimmy GMC made several modifications to the vehicle, at appellees' request, after it left Beaver's factory. Thus, the manufacturer logically cannot share the seller's burden or benefit in returning the contracting parties to their presale positions.

Election of Remedies

Appellees argue that if revocation of acceptance is unavailable against Beaver, then their election to sue for revocation was no election at all as to Beaver. They argue that they should now be permitted to sue Beaver for damages for breach of warranty. Beaver has not responded to this argument. We do not consider appellees' argument because we find even if the trial court erred in forcing appellees to make an election to sue either for revocation or for damages for breach,[2] appellees may no longer press the damages claim.

Our opinion in *Flory v. Silvercrest Industries, Inc.*, 129 Ariz. 574, 633 P.2d 383 (1981), precludes a U.C.C. warranty claim against Beaver for the same reason that a revocation of acceptance claim is precluded— Beaver is not in privity with appellees. But as we held in *Flory*, lack of privity between a manufacturer and retail purchaser does not preclude a claim outside the U.C.C. for breach of express warranty. A.R.S. § 44–2203 [UCC 1–103] would allow such a traditional action, and logic precludes rendering meaningless a manufacturer's express warranty to a retail purchaser.

We note, however, that appellees are not entitled to inconsistent or double recoveries. Because appellees have returned the vehicle and recovered the purchase money paid, they may not also receive damages for breach of warranty which are predicated on the buyer's retention of the nonconforming goods.

2. We observe that a plaintiff suing outside the U.C.C. for common law rescission and damages for breach of contract or warranty can be forced to choose either rescission or damages as a remedy. See *Beauchamp v. Wilson*, 21 Ariz.App. 14, 515 P.2d 41 (1973). This is not the rule under the U.C.C., however. Official Comment 1 to U.C.C. § 2–608 (A.R.S. § 44–2371) states: "[T]he buyer is no longer required to elect between revocation of acceptance and recovery of damages for breach. Both are now available to him. * * * The remedy under this section * * * is referred to simply as 'revocation of acceptance' of goods tendered under a contract for sale and involves no suggestion of 'election' of any sort." We do not decide at this time which rule to apply when a plaintiff may have both U.C.C. and non-U.C.C. claims.

Arguably, if due to any breach Beaver could be held jointly liable at common law for the incidental and consequential damages suffered by appellees, Beaver could still be sued for breach of an express non-U.C.C. warranty to recover these special damages. Beaver cannot be held liable for such damages, however. Beaver's express warranty contains this conspicuous clause: "Beaver Coaches, Inc. shall not be liable for consequential damages, including but not limited to loss of use of the unit, resulting from a breach of any written or implied warranty on any Beaver Coaches unit." Such a disclaimer of damages is valid under non-U.C.C. law as well as under the U.C.C.

At common law, "consequential" or "special" damages are those damages caused by a breach of contract or warranty that can reasonably be supposed to be within the contemplation of the parties at the time of the contracting.[3] *All American School Supply Co. v. Slavens*, 125 Ariz. 231, 609 P.2d 46 (1980); D. Dobbs, *Remedies* § 12.3 (1973). These are the type of incidental and consequential damages for which Jimmy GMC was held liable under A.R.S. § 44–2394. Because Beaver validly disclaimed liability for such damages, it cannot now be held jointly liable for them.[4] Therefore, even though appellees should not have been forced to abandon their breach of express warranty claim against Beaver, they are no longer entitled to recover anything as against Beaver.

REVOCATION AGAINST SELLER

Under A.R.S. § 44–2371(A) [UCC 2–608(1)], goods must have a nonconformity from what they are represented to be before revocation of acceptance is available. When it sold the Beaver motor home to appellees, Jimmy GMC conspicuously disclaimed in writing all express or implied warranties by itself, including the implied warranty of merchantability. The written disclaimer appeared in the purchase order and in the purchase money security agreement, both of which were signed by appellees. Generally, such a disclaimer is valid under A.R.S. § 44–2333 [UCC 2–316]. Jimmy GMC argued that because it disclaimed all warranties, it could not have sold nonconforming goods within the meaning of A.R.S. § 44–2371 [UCC 2–608] and, therefore, could not be liable for revocation of acceptance.

The trial court, however, found the disclaimer unconscionable, and, relying on A.R.S. § 44–2319(A) [UCC 2–302(1)],[5] refused to give it any

---

3. Thus, at common law, "consequential" damages has a broader meaning than under the U.C.C. because it included the U.C.C. definitions of both "incidental" and "consequential" damages. See A.R.S. § 44–2394. Because appellees could only bring a warranty suit under the common law and not the U.C.C., we give the term "consequential" damages its common law meaning. We find no contrary intent of the parties.

4. We do not at this time comment on whether Beaver has any liability to Jimmy.

We address only Beaver's liability to appellees.

5. "If the Court as a matter of law finds the contract or any clause of the contract to have been unconscionable at the time it was made the court may refuse to enforce the contract, or it may enforce the remainder of the contract without the unconscionable clause, or it may so limit the application of any unconscionable clause as to avoid any unconscionable result."

effect. The evidence tending to support unconscionability was that appellees did not have a chance to read the papers before signing them and Jimmy GMC forced the sale on appellees when it sold their trade-in and would only give them a credit towards a new motor home. The Court of Appeals reversed holding that: (1) the failure to read a contract before signing does not invalidate it in the absence of fraud, *see Apolito v. Johnson*, 3 Ariz.App. 232, 413 P.2d 291 (1966); and (2) although Jimmy GMC may have had a superior bargaining position, its actions were not unconscionable because it did not take advantage of its position.

> We believe the trial court reached the correct result but for an incorrect reason. Therefore, we will affirm the trial court's result in granting revocation against Jimmy GMC, *see Certified Collectors, Inc. v. Lesnick*, 116 Ariz. 601, 570 P.2d 769 (1977), and vacate the portion of the Court of Appeals' opinion reversing that result.

We agree with the Court of Appeals that the disclaimer was not unconscionable. Official Comment 1 to U.C.C. § 2–302 (A.R.S. § 44–2319) states:

"The basic test [for unconscionability] is whether, in the light of the general commercial background and the commercial needs of the particular trade or case, the clauses involved are so one-sided as to be unconscionable under the circumstances existing at the time of the making of the contract. * * * The principle is one of the prevention of oppression and unfair surprise * * * and not of disturbance of allocation of risks because of superior bargaining power." (Citations omitted.)

It is true that appellees were in an inferior bargaining position. Jimmy GMC had already sold appellees' trade-in and refused to give any compensation other than a $5,800 credit on another motor home. But we do not find that Jimmy GMC used their superior bargaining position to oppress or unfairly surprise appellees. There is no evidence that the disclaimer Jimmy GMC used in appellees' contract was different than the disclaimer Jimmy GMC used in all its sales contracts. As the Court of Appeals held, this allocation of risks should not be disturbed in the absence of overreaching by the party with superior bargaining power.

Nevertheless, we do not find that the disclaimer precludes the remedy of revocation of acceptance. The parties apparently believe that A.R.S. § 44–2371's [UCC 2–608's] reference to nonconformities refers only to failures to conform to an express or implied warranty. We do not read § 2371 [UCC 2–608] so narrowly. Had the drafters of the U.C.C., who pored over the code for years, meant for the remedy to apply only when a warranty is breached, they would have stated so expressly. Rather, we find that revocation may be available whenever goods sold fail to conform to the seller's representation of the goods if the nonconformity "substantially impairs" the value of the goods to the buyer.

What Jimmy GMC represented to appellees, at least impliedly, was that they would receive a new motor home warranted by the various manufacturers,[6] for which warranties Jimmy GMC was an authorized repair agent. Jimmy GMC did not represent that this was a motor home sold "as is" but rather was a vehicle that, after a reasonable time for authorized warranty repair work to cure any defects, would be "mechanically new and factory furnished, operate perfectly, and be free of substantial defects." *Zabriskie Chevrolet, Inc. v. Smith*, 99 N.J.Super. 441, 452, 240 A.2d 195, 202 (1968) (quoted in *Murray v. Holiday Rambler, Inc.*, 83 Wis.2d 406, 420, 265 N.W.2d 513, 520 (1978); *Orange Motors of Coral Gables, Inc. v. Dade County Dairies, Inc.*, 258 So.2d 319, 320 (Fla.Ct.App.1972)). Accord J. White and R. Summers, *Uniform Commercial Code* § 8 (3), at 264 (1972). This also was an allocation of the risks for which the parties freely bargained. Certainly, Jimmy GMC would not have received the price it did if appellees believed they were buying the vehicle "as is" in the sense that there was no guarantee that Jimmy GMC could effectively make all repairs covered by the warranties. Appellees were also not led to believe that they would have to take the vehicle for repairs to the manufacturers of the various components of the motor home. The express warranties guaranteed the vehicle could be made like new, and Jimmy GMC guaranteed it would perform all needed repairs. The disclaimer precludes a breach of warranty claim, but it does not avoid revocation if the vehicle does not conform to the representation that it can be made like new within a reasonable time.[7]

The question then becomes whether appellees proved they were entitled to revocation under A.R.S. § 44–2371 [UCC 2–608]. Revocation is proper where the buyer proves that the goods purchased: (1) have a nonconformity that substantially impairs their value to the buyer; and (2) were accepted either with knowledge of the nonconformity that the seller promised to cure but has failed to reasonably cure or without knowledge of the nonconformity where acceptance was induced by the difficulty of discovery or by the seller's assurances. A.R.S. § 44–2371(A) [UCC 2–608(1)].[8] Revocation is valid only if the buyer notifies the seller of it within a reasonable time after the buyer discovers or should have discovered the ground for revocation and before the condition of the

---

6. Jimmy GMC delivered or acknowledged the existence of an express warranty covering the work Beaver did in manufacturing the interior as well as warranties given by the respective manufacturers covering the roof and dash air conditioners, the power plant, the range and oven, and the furnace. In addition, Jimmy GMC sold appellees a five-year service contract covering the power train (motor, transmission, etc.)

7. If Jimmy GMC had sold the vehicle "as is," presumably revocation of acceptance would not be an available remedy. Jimmy GMC might also have tried to preclude revocation as a remedy by other express contractual terms. See A.R.S § 44–2398. In either of these cases the buyer would be on notice that revocation is not available as part of the bargain. In the instant case, the disclaimer of warranties gave no such notice; appellees did not freely bargain away revocation of acceptance as a remedy.

8. A.R.S. § 44–2371(A) provides:

"The buyer may revoke his acceptance of a lot or commercial unit whose non-conformity substantially impairs its value to him if he has accepted it:

"1. On the reasonable assumption that its non-conformity would be cured and it has not been seasonably cured; or

"2. Without discovery of such non-conformity if his acceptance was reasonably induced either by the difficulty of discovery before acceptance or by the seller's assurances."

goods substantially changes other than because of their own defect. A.R.S. § 44–2371(B) [UCC 2–608(2)].[9]

Jimmy GMC argues that there was no substantial nonconformity because it stood ready, willing, and able at all times to cure any defects in the motor home. The record shows, however, that Jimmy attempted to cure defects in the vehicle four times between May 23, 1977 and June 27, 1977. Nevertheless, when appellees sent their letter of revocation on September 6, the engine and power plant still functioned improperly and the passenger door did not fit correctly.[10]

> After the purchase of an automobile, the same should be put in good running condition; that is the seller does not have an unlimited time for the performance of the obligation to replace and repair parts. The buyer of an automobile is not bound to permit the seller to tinker with the article indefinitely in the hope that it may ultimately be made to comply with the warranty. 46 Am. Jur. Sales § 732; 77 C.J.S. Sales § 340. At some point in time, if major problems continue to plague the automobile, it must become obvious to all people that a particular vehicle simply cannot be repaired or parts replaced so that the same is made free of defect. *General Motors Corporation v. Earnest*, 279 Ala. 299, 184 So.2d 811 (1966).

Orange Motors of Coral Gables, Inc. v. Dade County Dairies, Inc., 258 So.2d 319, 320–21 (Fla.Ct.App.1972) (quoted in *Murray v. Holiday Rambler, Inc.*, 83 Wis.2d 406, 420–21, 265 N.W.2d 513, 521 (1978)). The evidence supports the trial court's finding that the value of the motor home was substantially impaired as to the appellees and the acceptance was induced by Jimmy GMC's assurance that the motor home was a conforming good.

Jimmy GMC also argues that appellees gave untimely notice of revocation because the revocation letter was sent some four months after the sale and two months after appellees had last complained about any defects. Appellees sent their letter of revocation to Jimmy GMC on September 6, 1977.

A.R.S. § 44–2371 requires notice of revocation within a "reasonable time" after the buyer discovers or should have discovered the basis for revocation. "What is a reasonable time for taking an action depends on the nature, purpose and circumstances of such action." A.R.S.

---

9. A.R.S. § 44–2371(B) states:

"Revocation of acceptance must occur within a reasonable time after the buyer discovers or should have discovered the ground for it and before any substantial change in condition of the goods which is not caused by their own defects. It is not effective until the buyer notifies the seller of it."

10. Months after appellees sent a notice of revocation, appellants performed more repairs on the vehicle. They spent a half hour at appellees' residence starting the vehicle, and then worked on it for another forty-eight days. Some defects were cured, but others were not. These repairs were an attempt to settle the case outside the court system. We strongly encourage such actions. But because these repairs occurred after revocation, they are relevant only to mitigation of damages and not the grounds for revocation. Although appellees continued to use the motor home during the course of these negotiations, the use was with appellant's consent and was not a waiver of revocation.

§ 44–2211(B). "The obvious policies behind the notice provisions are to give the seller an opportunity to cure, to permit the seller to assist the buyer in minimizing the buyer's losses, and to return the goods to seller early, before they have substantially depreciated." J. White and R. Summers, *Uniform Commercial Code* § 8 (3), at 261 (1972).

In the instant case, appellees gave Jimmy GMC several opportunities to cure defects in the two months after purchase. When a delay in notification is due to a series of complaints and attempted repairs, the delay is not unreasonable.

It is true that no complaints were made or repairs attempted in July and August of 1977. But we do not find this delay unreasonable, either, especially because it did not substantially prejudice Jimmy GMC. Two months is not an unreasonable time for consumers to decide a product's defects are incurable and to seek legal advice. Any substantial change in the condition of the vehicle during this period was due to its own defects. If Jimmy GMC had regained possession of the motor home during this period, its attempts to repair the vehicle for resale presumably would have been no more successful than the repairs it did attempt in an effort to settle this case in April and May of 1978. We find the trial court's decision on this issue supported by the evidence.

Therefore, the trial court was correct in granting revocation of acceptance against Jimmy GMC. Because incidental and consequential damages may be awarded in conjunction with revocation of acceptance, *Mobile Home Sales Management, Inc. v. Brown*, 115 Ariz. 11, 562 P.2d 1378 (App.1977), and the evidence supports the damages awarded, we affirm both the revocation and the damages awarded against Jimmy GMC. . . .

CONCLUSION

We approve the Court of Appeals' opinion to the extent it found as a matter of law that revocation of acceptance was not available against Beaver Coaches, Inc. Further, we approve the remand for a determination, in the trial court's discretion, of an award of costs and attorney's fees in favor of Beaver Coaches, Inc. We vacate the remainder of the Court of Appeals' opinion. We affirm the trial court's grant of revocation of acceptance and award of $14,885.10 in incidental and consequential damages against Jimmy GMC of Tucson, Inc. The case is remanded to the trial court with instructions to consider whether appellees proved loss of use damages against Jimmy GMC of Tucson, Inc.

The opinion of the Court of Appeals is approved in part and vacated in part, the actions of the trial court are affirmed in part and reversed in part, and the case is remanded to the trial court for further proceedings consistent with this opinion.

Notes

(1) New Sections 2–313A and 2–313B in the proposed amendments to Article 2 would expressly deal with manufacturers' warranties and other warranties made by a party other than the direct seller of the goods. Subpart (4) of each of those provisions address a "remote purchaser's" remedies for breach of such warranties. They would provide for the recovery of damages (see proposed amended Section 2–313A(4)(b) & (c) and proposed comment 9 thereto; proposed amended Section 2–313B(4)(b) & (c)), but they do not explicitly state whether the remote purchaser can reject or revoke acceptance for such breach.

(2) *Seekings* held that a buyer can revoke acceptance as to a seller who had disclaimed all warranties. This position has been criticized. One court stated that *Seekings*

> fought the express provisions of the UCC; to reach the desired result, it was necessary for the court to say that, although the disclaimer of the implied warranty of merchantability precluded a breach of warranty claim, it did not avoid revocation of acceptance "if the vehicle does not conform to the representation that it can be made like new within a reasonable time." [citation omitted] Although that rationale may be tempting, it is tantamount to saying that a seller may not disclaim all warranties, express and implied, which in our opinion is directly contrary to ORS 72.3160 [UCC 2–316]. Perhaps a seller should not be permitted to disclaim all warranties, but we believe the remedy is with the legislature. For example, the legislature may consider that the most appropriate solution is to permit revocation of acceptance (or the functional equivalent) from the manufacturer.

> Here ... the dealer disclaimed all warranties, express or implied. The only warranty was the limited one made by the manufacturer, not by the dealer. This truck conformed to the contract between plaintiffs and the dealer because plaintiffs got the vehicle that they had selected and had requested [the dealer] to obtain for sale to them.

Crume v. Ford Motor Co., 60 Or.App. 224, 228, 653 P.2d 564, 567 (1982).

(3) Courts have taken virtually every conceivable position on the question whether a buyer can revoke acceptance for breach of a manufacturer's warranty. For example, Oregon courts have held that a buyer cannot revoke acceptance against either the manufacturer who gave an express warranty but did not sell directly to the plaintiff, or the dealer who sold directly to the plaintiff but gave no warranties. Under this approach, the revocation remedy apparently would not generally be available for breach of a manufacturer's warranty. See Clark v. Ford Motor Co., 46 Or.App. 521, 612 P.2d 316 (1980); Crume v. Ford Motor Co., 60 Or.App. 224, 653 P.2d 564 (1982). But see Gaha v. Taylor–Johnson Dodge, Inc., 53 Or.App. 471, 632 P.2d 483 (1981) (particular facts demonstrated that car dealer was agent of manufacturer and thus manufacturer was "seller" against whom buyer could revoke acceptance).

On the other hand, several courts (in addition to *Seekings*) have permitted buyers (particularly consumer buyers) to revoke acceptance against a direct seller despite the fact that, in the court's view, the seller had disclaimed all relevant warranties. In other words, these courts have held that such a seller is liable under revocation of acceptance theory even though the seller apparently delivered goods that conformed to its sales contract with the buyer (i.e., the seller did not breach). See, e.g., O'Neal Ford v. Earley, 13 Ark.App. 189, 681 S.W.2d 414 (1985); Blankenship v. Northtown Ford, Inc., 95 Ill.App.3d 303, 50 Ill.Dec. 850, 420 N.E.2d 167 (1981). Cf. Fullerton Aircraft Sales & Rentals, Inc. v. Page Avjet Corp., 818 F.2d 28 (4th Cir.1987) (characterizing the Oregon courts' approach as a "novel interpretation of the UCC").

In addition, some courts have permitted a buyer to revoke acceptance against a distributor or manufacturer who did not sell directly to the buyer but who nevertheless warranted the goods to the buyer. See, e.g., Ford Motor Credit Co. v. Harper, 671 F.2d 1117 (8th Cir.1982) (permitting revocation against manufacturer) and Durfee v. Rod Baxter Imports, Inc., 262 N.W.2d 349 (Minn.1977) (permitting revocation against distributor where dealership that sold defective vehicle to the buyer was out of business). But see (in addition to *Seekings*, which denied revocation against the manufacturer) Voytovich v. Bangor Punta Operations, Inc., 494 F.2d 1208 (6th Cir.1974) (denying revocation).

Most courts, even those that forbid revocation against a party who did not sell directly to the aggrieved buyer, permit the buyer to recover damages from a manufacturer or distributor if the goods breached an express warranty that the manufacturer or distributor gave the buyer. See e.g., Kinlaw v. Long Mfg. N.C., 298 N.C. 494, 259 S.E.2d 552 (1979) ("the absence of contractual privity no longer bars a direct claim by an ultimate purchaser against the manufacturer for breach of the manufacturer's express warranty which is directed to the purchaser").[1] The buyer's damages provisions in the version of Article 2 applicable in *Seekings*, however, are phrased in terms of a breaching *seller*, and do not expressly address the liability of a remote manufacturer or distributor. See, e.g., 2–714(1) (buyer who has accepted may recover damages for loss resulting "from the seller's breach"). How does the *Seekings* court handle this?

For a survey of case law in this area and of the evolution of the relevant provisions of proposed amendments to Article 2 (as well as suggested solutions to the issues raised by manufacturers' warranties), see Harry M. Flechtner, *Breach of Remote Sellers' Warranties—Revocation, Refund and Remedy*, 31 UNIFORM COMMERCIAL CODE LAW JOURNAL 131 (1998) and *Enforcing Manufacturers' Warranties, "Pass Through" Warranties, and the Like: Can the Buyer Get a Refund?* 50 RUTGERS L. REV. 397 (1998).

(4) In many states, "lemon laws" explicitly allow purchasers of new vehicles to revoke acceptance against a non-privy manufacturer. The Penn-

---

1. Proposed amended Sections 2–313A(4) and 2–313B(4) expressly permit a buyer to recover such damages, although such a "remote purchaser" is precluded from recovering consequential damages for lost profits from the manufacturer or distributor, and the manufacturer or distributor is free to limit the remote purchaser's remedies under 2–719.

sylvania statute, for instance, requires a car manufacturer/distributor either to replace a defective vehicle or give a refund of the purchase price (less an allowance for the buyer's use) if substantial nonconformities cannot be repaired "after a reasonable number of attempts." Pa. Stat. Ann. tit. 73, § 1955 (Purdon Supp. 1990). Such lemon laws, however, generally apply only to a limited class of consumer goods (motor vehicles).

B. THE LESSEE'S COURSES OF ACTION UPON RECEIPT OF GOODS UNDER UCC ARTICLE 2A

1. Rejection, Acceptance and Revocation of Acceptance under Article 2A–in General

Except for special rules on finance leases, the provisions of Article 2A governing a lessee's rejection, acceptance, and revocation of acceptance of goods (2A–509 through 2A–517) are modeled closely on Article 2 and will presumably yield results analogous to those under the sales article. For example, 2A–509 states that a lessee can reject goods "if the goods or the tender of delivery fail in any respect to conform" to the contract, although (as under Article 2) there are a variety of exceptions and limitations on the right to reject. Article 2A also largely replicates the Article 2 rules governing the manner and effect of acceptance (2A–515 and 2A–516) and of rejection (2A–509(2), 2A–511, 2A–512 and 2A–514). Except in its treatment of finance leases, 2A–517 governing revocation of acceptance also generally follows its Article 2 analogues (2–608).

Problem 60A

Suppose that in Problems 44, 49 and 54 *supra*, P & T had leased rather than purchased the computers. How, if at all, would your analysis of those Problems change? See, inter alia, 2A–509, 2A–510, 2A–515, 2A–516 and 2A–517.

2. Rejection and Revocation in Finance Leases

In a finance lease, the lessee's warranty protection generally comes not from the other party to the lease contract (the "finance lessor"), but from a party further up the chain of distribution of the goods–the "supplier" who sold (or leased) the goods to the finance lessor. Thus rejection or revocation of acceptance of goods in a finance lease raises issues analogous to those that arise where a buyer of goods seeks to reject or revoke because the goods breached a manufacturer's warranty.

Problem 61

In a transaction that qualifies as a finance lease, Abel Corp. leased from Beta, Inc. equipment supplied by Canyon Company, the manufacturer of the equipment. The lease had a five year term. Neither the supply contract between Canyon and Beta nor the lease contract between Beta and Abel contained a disclaimer of implied warranties. Both the supply and the lease contracts stated that the equipment would be equipped with Stritton electric motors. Abel had insisted on Stritton motors because it had previously had a bad experience with Eastinghouse motors, resulting in costly litigation. Canyon shipped the equipment directly to Abel. Consider the following alternative scenarios:

(a) When the equipment arrived, Abel inspected it and determined that it was equipped with Eastinghouse rather than Stritton electric motors. Can Abel reject the equipment? See 2A–509.

(b) When the equipment arrived, Abel inspected it and determined that, although it was equipped with Stritton motors, it had defects which rendered it unmerchantable. Can Abel reject the equipment? Read 2A–509 carefully. Did Canyon warrant to Abel that the goods would be merchantable? See 2–314 and 2A–209(1). Did Beta warrant to Abel that the goods would be merchantable? See 2A–212(1). Did the goods "fail in any respect to conform to the lease contract" as required for rejection under 2A–509(1).[2] See 2A–103(1)(k) & (l).[3] In analyzing this problem, consider what would happen if the lessee could not reject. Could it refuse to pay the rent? See 2A–407. If it could not reject, would the lessee be without any remedy? See 2A–209 and the comments thereto as well as comment 1 to 2A–516. Do you think that the drafters of Article 2A intended the lessee to have a right to reject in these circumstances?

(c) Canyon delivered merchantable equipment equipped with Eastinghouse electric motors. Abel inspected the shipment when it arrived but failed to notice the brand of electric motors because they were mounted in the interior of the equipment. Abel signified its acceptance of the delivery. After using the equipment for two months, Abel discovered the Eastinghouse motors while doing routine maintenance. The electric motors on the equipment supplied by Canyon had been specially-designed and replacement with another brand would require expensive alterations. Abel would like to revoke its acceptance of the equipment. Can it? See 2A–517. If Abel cannot revoke can it refuse to pay rent? See 2A–407. If Abel cannot revoke, does it have any remedy against Beta? See comment 2 to 2A–407. Does it have a remedy against Canyon in these circumstances? If so, what is the remedy? See 2A–209 and comment 2 thereto, comment 5 to 2A–407, and comment 1 to 2A–516.

(d) Abel discovered the Eastinghouse motors during its original inspection. Abel decided to accept the shipment, however, when both Canyon and Beta promised that the Eastinghouse motors would be replaced. Canyon later informed Abel that replacing the motors was impossible. Can Abel revoke its acceptance under 2A–517?

(e) Before the goods were tendered Beta examined them at Canyon's plant and then told Abel that the equipment conformed to the supply

2. Under proposed amended Section 2A–509(1), rejection would be permitted if the goods "fail in any respect to conform to the contract."

3. These definitions would be renumbered to 2A–103(1)(s) & (t) in the proposed amended version of Article 2A.

contract. Upon delivery, therefore, Abel conducted only a cursory inspection and failed to discover the Eastinghouse motors. Can Abel revoke its acceptance if it discovers the Eastinghouse motors after using the machinery for two months?

Questions

Suppose Canyon delivered equipment with Stritton motors as per the contract, but the equipment had other defects that rendered it unmerchantable and dangerous. Abel would normally have discovered the defects upon delivery, but it failed to inspect because Beta had reported that the machinery conformed to the supply contract. After using the equipment for two months Abel discovered the problems. Abel would like to revoke its acceptance. Can it? Read the first paragraph of the "Purposes" section of the official comment to 2A–516. What is the meaning of the phrase "nonconformity with respect to the lease agreement, as opposed to the supply agreement . . ."?

Note—Finance Lessee's Notice of Revocation

In Cooper v. Lyon Financial Services, Inc., 65 S.W.3d 197 (Tex.Ct.App. 2001), a surgeon, Cooper, entered into a finance lease of a laser for use in plastic surgery. The finance lessor, Lyon Financial Services, acquired the laser from the supplier, Luxar Corp., which manufactured the laser. Lyon then leased it to the finance lessee, Cooper, who after accepting the goods became dissatisfied with the laser and stopped making payments. When Lyon sued, Cooper argued that he had revoked acceptance of the laser. Cooper submitted to the trial judge a proposed jury instruction on revocation of acceptance. The proposed instruction stated, *inter alia*, that "[r]evocation is not effective until the lessee notifies the lessor." The trial judge rejected the proposed instruction and, after losing in the trial court, Cooper appealed. The appeals court analyzed the situation as follows:

> Cooper, as a lessee under a finance lease, could revoke acceptance of the laser if the purported nonconformity substantially impaired the value of the laser and Cooper accepted the laser, "without discovery of the nonconformity if [Cooper's] acceptance was reasonably induced . . . by [the finance lessor's] assurances." Tex. Bus. & Com.Code Ann. § 2A.517(a)(2) (Vernon 1994). The lease agreement, however, provided that, in the event Cooper was not satisfied with the laser, he should "only look to entities other than [the finance lessor] such as the manufacturer." Under the Uniform Commercial Code ("UCC"), as well, Cooper's remedy for nonconformity of the laser—as opposed to the lease—was against Luxar [the supplier]. See Tex. Bus. & Com.Code Ann. § 2A.516 (cmt.1) (Vernon 1994). . . .

> To avail himself of this revocation defense, Cooper was required to notify both the lessor and the supplier. See Tex. Bus. & Com.Code Ann. § 2A.516(c)(1) (Vernon 1994). Because Cooper was complaining about a defect in the laser, essential notice was to the supplier. See Tex. Bus. & Com.Code Ann. § 2A.516 (cmt.1) (Vernon 1994). Cooper's instruction,

however, referred only to notice to Lyon. Cooper's instruction was not substantially correct. See Tex.R. Civ. P. 278.

63 S.W.3d at 205–06. The court rejected Cooper's appeal.

C. REFUSING COMPUTER INFORMATION UNDER UCITA

UCITA generally follows the structure of UCC Articles 2 and 2A in dealing with tender of a "copy" of computer information, although "rejection" is renamed "refusal." With one exception, however, UCITA adopts a "material breach" standard rather than a perfect tender rule— i.e., a party can refuse to perform its own duties only if the other side's breach is material. See UCITA § 601. The one situation in which UCITA adopts a perfect tender rule involves licenses of a single copy of information in a "mass-market transaction" (defined as a consumer transaction or other transaction in which the licensee acquires its rights at retail under standard terms). See UCITA §§ 601 and 704(b). An example of a "mass-market transaction" subject to UCITA's perfect tender rule would be the retail purchase of a piece of software for use on a home computer. Comments 2 and 3 to § 601 explain the position of the drafters of UCITA:

> .... Subsection (b) adopts the common law doctrine of material breach. A party's duty to perform is contingent on the absence of a prior material failure of performance by the other party. See *Restatement (Second) of Contracts* § 237.

> The concept of material breach is applied throughout contract law and has been for generations. It holds that a minor defect in performance does not warrant rejection or cancellation of a contract. While minor problems may constitute a breach, the remedy for that breach lies in recovery of damages. The common law policy underlying the idea of material breach is to avoid forfeiture for small errors. Often, truly perfect performance cannot be expected. If the parties desire to create a more stringent standard, they must do so by the terms of their agreement....

> The material breach standard does not apply to mass-market transactions involving mass market tender of delivery of a copy. Section 704(b). This follows Article 2 and Article 2A of the Uniform Commercial Code. These statutes stand alone in contract law in not using the material breach concept. Article 2 requires "conforming tender", but only in a single situation: a single delivery of goods not part of an installment contract. This Act creates a parallel rule for mass-market transactions.

> The "conforming [perfect] tender" rule is not a "perfect" tender rule even in Article 2. What is a conforming tender even in a single delivery context is hemmed in by legal considerations regarding merchantability, and interpretation principles including usage of

trade and course of performance. It is further limited by principles of waiver and a right to cure. As one leading treatise comments: "[we have found no case that] actually grants rejection on what could fairly be called an insubstantial non-conformity ... "

Are you convinced by the UCITA drafters' argument in favor of a material breach standard for most situations? Is their characterization of the perfect tender rule in Article 2 accurate? Why should there be an exception for "mass-market" computer information transactions?

UCITA provides for "acceptance" of a copy containing computer information (§ 609) and for "revocation of acceptance" (§ 708), with legal consequences similar to those under Article 2. UCITA also places a variety of limits on the right to refuse a copy that roughly parallel limitations on rejection in Article 2.

D. REFUSING GOODS UNDER THE CISG—AVOIDANCE OF CONTRACT

1. *Avoidance in General*

The CISG generally does not use the terms rejection, acceptance or revocation of acceptance to describe options available to an aggrieved buyer.[1] Under the Convention, if a buyer wishes to thrust tendered goods back upon the seller—to "reject" or "revoke acceptance" in UCC parlance—she must "avoid the contract." If the buyer instead is willing (in UCC terms) to "accept"—keep the goods, becoming liable to pay for them (subject to a remedy for any nonconformity)—she simply does not avoid the contract. Thus where a seller makes a non-conforming tender of goods, "avoiding the contract" under the CISG performs a function very similar to "rejecting" or "revoking acceptance" under the UCC, and failure to avoid has consequences resembling those for "accepting" under the UCC The materials that follow explore avoidance in these circumstances.

Before proceeding, however, you should be aware that the Convention's avoidance/"nonavoidance" procedure has a much broader scope and more far-reaching consequences than rejection, acceptance and revocation under UCC Article 2. The decision to reject, accept or revoke acceptance under the UCC is reserved for the buyer and arises only if the seller tenders delivery. The issue of avoidance or nonavoidance under the CISG, in contrast, confronts both buyers and sellers and can arise whether or not either party has tendered performance. An aggrieved party's decision to avoid or not to avoid invokes one of two distinct remedy systems provided by the CISG, and can involve remedial options

---

1. The term "reject" does appear in Article 86(1) & (2) of the CISG. These provisions impose an obligation to preserve goods on a buyer who exercises a right to "reject" them. The term "reject" here pre-

sumably refers to "avoiding the contract" after tender, as described in the text, or to demanding that the seller replace non-conforming goods with conforming substitute goods as permitted by CISG Article 46(2).

beyond those available under UCC Article 2. A full exploration of avoidance and its consequences under the CISG is reserved for the chapter on remedies. For the moment, consider the following materials in order to learn about the procedures governing a buyer's response to tender under the Convention. Compare the approach in the CISG with the UCC's rejection-acceptance-revocation system.

2. Avoidance for Fundamental Breach

Problem 62

Abel Manufacturing Corp., located in the United States, agreed to purchase six robots for use in an assembly line from Robotics Cie., located in France (a country that has ratified the CISG), delivery by December 1. Robotics shipped six machines in timely fashion. Upon their arrival, Abel inspected the robots and discovered that they could perform only seven of the eight functions required by the contract. Abel does not want the machines shipped by Robotics and would now prefer to purchase replacements from a different manufacturer. What should Abel do? See CISG Arts. 25, 26, 35, 45, 49(1)(a), 81 and 84.

DECISION OF APRIL 3, 1996, BUNDESGERICHTSHOF (SUPREME COURT), GERMANY, CASE NO. VIII ZR 51/95[1]

English Abstract from Unilex Data Base

A Dutch seller and a German buyer concluded several contracts for the sale of cobalt sulphate with specific technical qualities. The buyer declared the contracts avoided on the following grounds: the delivered cobalt was of a lower quality than that agreed to under the contracts; the cobalt was produced in South Africa and not in the UK as indicated in the contracts; the seller had delivered non conforming certificates of origin and quality. The seller denied the buyer's right to avoid and brought suit to recover the purchase price.

The Supreme Court [of Germany] held that the buyer had not validly avoided the contracts and awarded the seller the full price.

* * *

... [A]voidance was impossible also under Art. 49(1)(a) CISG. According to the Court, in the system of the Convention the remedy of avoidance for non conformity of the goods represents the last resort in respect to the other remedies available to the buyer, such as price

---

1. Reprinted with the permission of the Centre for Comparative and Foreign Studies—UNIDROIT, Rome, Italy. The Unilex English abstract of the decision, as well as the original German text, is available through the Unilex website, <*http://www.unilex.info*>. The full German text of this decision is also available online at <http:// www.jura.uni-freiburg.de/ ipr1/cisg/urteile/ text/135.htm>. An English-language summary of the case appears as Abstract No. 171 in Case Law on UNCITRAL Texts ((CLOUT), available online at <http://www.cisgw3.law.pace.edu/cases/ 960403g1.html>.

reduction or damages. In the case at hand the seller's delivery of non-conforming goods did not amount to a fundamental breach of contract. In determining whether the non conformity is fundamental, i.e. it deprives the buyer substantially of what it is entitled to expect under the contract (Art. 25 CISG), it is decisive whether the buyer can still make use of the goods or resell them in the usual commercial relationships without incurring any unreasonable difficulties. The fact that the buyer might be forced to resell the goods at a lower price is not to be considered in itself an unreasonable difficulty.

As to the alleged difficulties in exporting the goods due to the ten existing embargo against goods produced in South Africa, the Court held that the buyer should at least have proved unreasonable difficulties in trading the goods in Germany.

Likewise the fact that the defects of the goods cannot be repaired, as in the case at hand, is not in itself enough to determine that the breach is fundamental.

The Court, though admitting that the delivery of non conforming documents could amount to a fundamental breach, denied that this was so in the case at hand, since the buyer could have easily obtained the right certificates of origin by itself and the right certificate of quality through expert examination. Moreover, the non conformity of the documents did not prevent the buyer from taking delivery of the goods and disposing of them.

Notes and Questions on Buyer's Course of Action following Fundamental Breach

(1) Return to the facts of Problem 62. What happens if Abel successfully "avoids the contract?" According to Article 81(1), avoidance releases both parties from their contractual obligations. Thus upon proper avoidance Abel would not have to take and pay for the robots, and Robotics would be relieved of its obligation to transfer the contracted-for goods. Robotics, however, would remain subject to Abel's claim for damages. Under Article 81(2), furthermore, Abel would owe restitution of "whatever [Robotics] supplied ... under the contract"—i.e., the tendered machines—and would have to take reasonable steps to preserve the robots, Arts. 82, 86, 87 and 88. Compare UCC 2–602(2), 2–603 and 2–604 (rejection relieves buyer of all obligations beyond the duty to hold the goods with reasonable care at seller's disposition), as well as 2–711(1) (seller liable for damages if buyer rightfully rejects). Since rejection and avoidance are so similar, would anything change if the transaction in Problem 62 were governed by UCC Article 2?

(2) Assume the problems with the robots in Problem 62 constitute a fundamental breach. What must Abel do to avoid the contract and when must it act? See Arts. 26, 38–40, 44, and 49(2)(b)(i). Compare CISG avoidance procedures to the procedures for rejecting in UCC 2–602(1), 2–605 and 2–606. Suppose Robotics offered to repair the machines it had shipped.

Would that affect your answer in Problem 62? See Arts. 37 and 48. See also Art. 34. Compare these provisions to UCC 2–508. Under the CISG, must a seller notify the buyer of the intention to cure? What restrictions does the Convention place on a seller's right to cure before the time for performance? After the time for performance?

(3) Suppose that, rather than avoiding the contract, Abel decides to keep the goods and to seek damages (or repair by the seller) for the problems. How should Abel proceed? Consider Arts. 38–40. Compare the procedures under UCC Article 2 where a buyer chooses to accept and keep nonconforming goods.

Note on Retaining the Goods after Avoidance

Suppose Abel in Problem 62 had prepaid the entire price ($2 million) before the goods were shipped, and then had properly avoided the contract because of the defects in the tendered machines. Under Article 81(2) of the CISG, avoidance gives *both* parties a right to restitution of what each has "supplied or paid under the contract." Thus Robotics is entitled to return of the machines and Abel has a right to a refund of the prepayment (plus interest, under Art. 84(1)). If Robotics demands return of the robots, must Abel comply before getting its money back? The last sentence of Article 81(2) suggests that the answer is no: "If both parties are bound to make restitution, they must do so concurrently." An avoiding buyer who incurs expenses in preserving tendered goods, furthermore, can retain the goods until reimbursed for such expenses under Article 86(1). UCC 2–711(3) provides for similar results by giving a rejecting buyer "a security interest in goods in his possession or control for any payments made on their price and any expenses reasonably incurred in their inspection, receipt transportation, care and custody." The security interest permits a buyer to retain the rejected goods until the seller has made reimbursement for the specified items.[1]

If the seller refuses to make the required reimbursements, UCC 2–711(3) and 2–706(6) authorize the buyer to resell the goods *and* to retain the resale proceeds up to the amount of the expenses covered by the security interest. The CISG probably also authorizes an avoiding buyer to resell in such circumstances: given the right to "concurrent" restitution under Article 81(2), the seller's refusal to refund the buyer's payments may well constitute "an unreasonable delay ... in taking [the goods] back," giving the buyer a right to sell the goods for the seller's account under Article 88(1). In contrast to the UCC rule, however, it is not clear that the CISG allows the buyer to deduct payments for which the seller owes restitution from the proceeds of the sale. Article 88(3) provides only that a buyer can retain "an amount equal to the reasonable expense of preserving the goods and of selling them," and it explicitly requires the buyer to "account to the other party for the balance." Comments in the CISG's drafting history,

---

1. A UCC buyer's 2–711(3) security interest covers only "payments made on [the goods'] price" and certain incidental expenses (the cost of "inspection, receipt, transportation, care and custody" of the goods). Under the CISG, similarly, an avoiding buyer can retain goods only until she receives restitution of payments made (Art. 81(2)) and reimbursement for costs of preserving the goods (Art. 86(1)). Thus neither the Convention nor the UCC allow the buyer to withhold goods pending payment of other damage items, such as general or consequential damages.

however, suggest that parties selling goods under Article 88(3) retain offset rights that they would enjoy under domestic law.[2] Thus if U.S. law would apply under choice of law principles, the buyer might be able to invoke its right under UCC 2–706(6) to deduct payments on the price from resale proceeds. Because of ambiguities in this area, however, a buyer in a transaction governed by the CISG would do well to include a contract provision spelling out its right to resell goods and retain proceeds if the buyer avoids the contract.

Problem 63

Return to the contract in Problem 62. Robotics delivered six robots by December 1. Abel inspected the machines, was satisfied, and paid the price. It installed the robots in its plant and began using them. Several months later, one of the machines caught fire and was extensively damaged. Abel discovered that the blaze was caused by a defect which also existed in the other five machines. The problem made all the machines vulnerable to fire during normal use. During the period before Abel discovered the defect all the machines had undergone extensive (but quite normal) wear and tear, and three of them had been extensively altered. Abel wants to buy replacement robots from another manufacturer and to get its money back from Robotics. Can it do so? How should Abel proceed? See Arts. 25–26, 35, 38–40, 45, 49, 81–84, and 86–88.

Questions

(1) Would the wear and tear, the fire damage or the alterations to the robots prevent Abel from avoiding the contract in Problem 63? See Art. 82. If Abel were a robot broker who could not return the machines because it had resold them before discovering their defects, could Abel still avoid the contract under the CISG? See Arts. 82(2)(c) and 84(2). Could Abel revoke acceptance under UCC 2–608 in such circumstances? See comment 6 to 2–608. If Article 82 prevents Abel from avoiding has Abel lost all remedies? See Art. 83.

(2) Suppose the defect should have been discovered during Abel's original inspection. How (if at all) would that affect Abel's rights? See Arts. 38, 39, and 49(2). What impact would this fact have on Abel's power to revoke acceptance if UCC Article 2 applied? Suppose Abel's failure to discover the defect until the fire was reasonable, but the fire did not occur until 25 months after the robots were delivered. What result? See Art. 39(2).

Note: Compensation for Benefits From Goods

Although proper avoidance relieves the buyer of the obligation to pay for the goods, Article 84(2) of the CISG requires that an avoiding buyer "account to the seller for all benefits which he has derived from the goods or

---

2. Commentary on the Draft Convention on Contracts for the International Sale of Goods, Prepared by the Secretariat, Art. 77, ¶ 9, U.N. Doc. A/Conf.97/5 (1979), reprinted in J. HONNOLD, DOCUMENTARY HISTORY OF THE UNIFORM LAW FOR INTERNATIONAL SALES 453 (1989).

part of them." Thus in Problem 63 Abel must reduce its recovery or otherwise compensate Robotics in an amount equal to the value of the benefits Abel has derived from using or reselling the robots. The required compensation is presumably measured by the benefits buyer enjoyed rather than the effect on the value of the goods restored to the seller.

Compare the results under U.S. domestic sales law: although the pre-amendment version of UCC Article 2 does not explicitly require that a buyer who revokes acceptance after using the goods must compensate the seller for the value of such use, several courts have implied such an obligation, and proposed amended Section 2–608(4)(b) would expressly recognize the requirement.

Problem 64

For this problem, assume that the contract between Robotics and Abel described in Problem 62 required the six assembly line robots to be delivered in three installments (two robots per delivery). The first installment was delivered and the robots were put into production with no problems. When Abel received the second delivery, however, routine pre-installation testing revealed that one of the robots was seriously defective—a violation of Robotics' contract obligations. What are Abel's options as to avoidance?

(a) Can Abel avoid the contract as to the single defective machine while keeping the three conforming robots in its possession and retaining its rights to the final installment? See Art. 51(1).

(b) Does the defect in the one machine permit Abel to refuse the second installment while retaining the first two robots (as well as the right to the third installment)? See Art. 73(1).

(c) Can Abel avoid the entire contract? See Art. 51(2). Assuming Abel has the right to avoid the entire contract and that it properly exercises that right, what happens to the two machines in the first installment that Abel accepted?

(d) Suppose Abel properly avoided as to the second installment. Could it also avoid as to the undelivered third installment while retaining the robots from the first delivery? What must Abel show to justify doing so? See Art. 73(2). Contrast UCC 2–612(3) and comment 6 thereto. Other CISG provisions dealing with insecurity concerning future performance are explored in Part 2 Section B of this Chapter.

(e) Suppose the defective robot in the second installment was specially designed to work in tandem with the robots delivered in the first installment. Could Abel avoid as to the first and second installments while retaining its right to receive the final delivery? See Art. 73(3).

3. "Nachfrist" Avoidance

Problem 65

Return to the contract between Abel and Robotics in Problem 62 calling for delivery of six assembly-line robots by December 1. Suppose Robotics failed to deliver any machines by this date and failed to respond to Abel's repeated inquiries concerning the machines. Abel was quite anxious to acquire suitable robots for its plant. When Robotics still had not made delivery by December 8, Abel sent Robotics notice that it was avoiding the contract. Later that same day Abel contracted to purchase six substitute robots from a competitor of Robotics for a total price of $600,000 ($100,000 more than the price in the contract with Robotics). On December 10, Robotics tendered delivery of six robots, all of which met contract specifications. Was Abel's avoidance proper? Consider Article 25. Could Abel have done anything to strengthen its position? See Arts. 47 & 49(1)(b).

Notes and Questions

(1) The procedure outlined in Article 47 of the CISG, often called *Nachfrist* after the German legal doctrine from which it derived, is very useful in a late delivery situation like that in Problem 65. If Abel sends a *Nachfrist* notice specifying an additional period of "reasonable length" for Robotics to deliver and Robotics fails to deliver within that period, the buyer can avoid the contract under Article 49(1)(b) without worrying whether the delay has become a "fundamental breach" under Article 25. Once Abel properly avoids, it need not accept a subsequent tender by the seller. Clearly this can reduce the uncertainty facing a buyer who suffers a delay in delivery and who does not know whether the seller will eventually perform. By its terms, however, Article 47 is not limited to late-delivery or non-delivery situations. Apparently it could be used in response to any failure of performance. If a seller has delivered defective goods, would you advise the buyer to send a *Nachfrist* notice specifying an additional period for the seller to make a conforming tender? What would be the effect of such a notice? Read Articles 47 and 49(1)(b) carefully.

(2) If you were drafting a *Nachfrist* notice for the buyer in Problem 65, what would you include in it? What elements *must* such a notice include to satisfy the requirements of Article 47(1)? Would a letter demanding "immediate delivery" be adequate?[3] What factors should be considered in determining whether a deadline fixed in a *Nachfrist* notice is a "reasonable" period for performance?

Problem 66

Again take the contract described in Problem 62 in which Robotics agreed to sell Abel six industrial robots for delivery by December 1. An Abel representative consults you on December 8. She tells you that on December 1 Robotics delivered two of the six robots called for in the contract. Since that time Robotics has neither tendered the missing machines nor responded to inquiries from Abel. Can Abel use the *Nachfrist* procedure to avoid the contract as to the undelivered machines? See Arts. 47, 49 and 51. If Abel sends a *Nachfrist* notice and Robotics fails to deliver the four missing machines within the specified additional period, can Abel avoid the *entire* contract? See Art. 51(2).

---

3. For a discussion of this question, See J. Honnold, Uniform Law for International   Sales under the 1980 United Nations Convention § 289 (3rd ed. 1999).

Questions

Suppose the seller in an installment contract is late in making the first delivery, and the buyer sends a *Nachfrist* notice demanding the missing installment by a particular (reasonable) date. What rights does the buyer have if the seller fails to make the *Nachfrist* deadline? Can the buyer avoid the contract as to the first installment, keeping the remainder of the contract in force? Can the buyer avoid the entire contract? See Art. 73 and compare Art. 51.

Note

The *Nachfrist* procedure is explored further in Chapter 6 (Remedies).

4. Nonavoidance

Problem 67

Return to the facts of Problem 63, where Abel did not discover that the robots it received from Robotics were seriously defective until a fire occurred several months after delivery.

(a) It is a difficult and time-consuming process to install the robots in Abel's plant, and replacing the Robotics machines would shut down Abel's assembly line for two months. For this reason, Abel wants to have the defective robots repaired in place. Can Abel force Robotics to repair the machines? See Art. 46(3) of the CISG. Could Abel get a court order forcing Robotics to make repairs if UCC Article 2 governed the transaction?

(b) Alternatively, suppose the defect that caused the fire hazard was unrepairable. Apart from that defect, however, Abel has been very pleased with the Robotics machines and clearly prefers them over those manufactured by Robotics' many competitors. Can Abel force Robotics to supply replacement machines? See Art. 46(2) of the CISG. What are the prerequisites for a right to demand substitute goods? What should Abel do with the defective robots in its possession? See Arts. 82, 86–88. See also Art. 84(2). Would a court require Robotics to provide replacement machines if UCC Article 2 was the applicable law?

Note on Nonavoidance Remedies

To invoke the CISG's repair or substitute-goods remedies highlighted in Problem 67, a buyer need not—indeed, must not—avoid the contract. Avoidance "releases both parties from their obligations" under the avoided contract (Art. 81(1)), whereas the provision requiring a breaching seller to repair or provide substitute goods is premised on literal enforcement of the seller's obligations. The remedies in Article 46(2) and (3) are raised at this point because they apply when the buyer receives nonconforming goods, and they thus give the buyer an alternative to avoiding the contract and refusing to accept the seller's goods. These and other "nonavoidance remedies" will be explored in more detail in the chapter on remedies.

Under Article 46(3), a buyer can demand repair of nonconforming goods "unless this is unreasonable having regard to all the circumstances." Articles 46(2) and 82 provide that the buyer is entitled to replacement of nonconforming goods if the nonconformity is a fundamental breach and the buyer meets specified restitutionary obligations. Certain indirect restrictions further limit the availability of these and other "nonavoidance" remedies under the CISG. In particular, Article 28 permits a court to limit "a judgement for specific performance" to situations where such a remedy would be available under the court's domestic sales law. An order requiring a seller to repair or replace nonconforming goods would almost certainly be "a judgement for specific performance" under U.S. law. Thus despite Articles 46(2) and (3), a U.S. court in a jurisdiction that has adopted UCC Article 2 need issue an order requiring repair or replacement of defective goods only if the requirements for specific performance under UCC Article 2 are met.

PART 2: PROSPECTIVE NONPERFORMANCE

A. ADEQUATE ASSURANCES AND ANTICIPATORY REPUDIATION UNDER ARTICLE 2 OF THE UCC

Introductory Note

The materials in this section explore the legal rules applicable if, before the time for performance arrives, a party to a contract appears unable or unwilling to perform. Those rules should be designed to minimize the unfairness, futility and (in some circumstances) economic waste of requiring one side to await the other side's performance when it is clear that such performance will not occur. At the same time the rules must not allow the mere possibility of a future breach (which, after all, may never occur) to be used as a pretext for terminating contract obligations prematurely and unnecessarily. Traditionally, the common law of contracts tried to accommodate both concerns by treating a party's advance repudiation of its obligations as a present breach, but only if the repudiation was very clear, definite and unequivocal.[4]

Thus under pre-Code doctrine an ambiguous or hedged suggestion of future nonperformance by one party did not trigger any relief even if it undercut the other side's confidence in the contract and thus seriously impaired the purposes of the agreement. Indeed, even a clear repudiation could be retracted, subject to certain limitations. An unretracted and unambiguous repudiation, however, could be treated by the affected party as a present failure to perform. It could trigger consequences as severe as immediate rescission of the contract, coupled with liability for damages for total breach. The aggrieved party, however, generally had the alternative of ignoring the repudiation (at least for a time) and awaiting performance.

The treatment of prospective nonperformance in UCC Article 2 builds on the traditional common law approach while making some important changes and additions. Sections 2–610 and 2–611 represent a somewhat

---

4. According to an old Supreme Court opinion, a repudiation required "a positive, unconditional, and unequivocal declaration of fixed purpose not to perform in any event or at any time." Dingley v. Oler, 117 U.S. 490, 502 (1886).

modernized version of traditional doctrine. Section 2–609, on the other hand, contains a significant and influential contribution to the area—a procedure for demanding "adequate assurances" of future performance from a party who has created "reasonable grounds for insecurity" about such performance. Read the relevant provisions and their accompanying comments carefully before tackling the following materials.

NEPTUNE RESEARCH & DEVELOPMENT, INC. v. TEKNICS INDUSTRIAL SYSTEMS, INC.

Superior Court of New Jersey, Appellate Div., 1989.
235 N.J.Super. 522, 563 A.2d 465.

KING, JUDGE. This is a commercial dispute arising from the sale of a specialized manufacturing machine. This case turns on the issues of the seller's anticipatory breach and its later attempted retraction of that repudiation. We conclude that the buyer had the absolute right to cancel in view of the seller's repudiation. We affirm.

The buyer sued in the Law Division, demanding return of its $3,000 deposit plus interest and costs, alleging proper cancellation because the seller failed to make timely delivery. The seller answered and counterclaimed seeking the balance of a 15% contractually-established cancellation price. After a bench trial, Judge Russell found for the buyer and dismissed the counterclaim.

These are the facts. The evidence in this case consisted principally of the written contract and the testimony of Akos Sule, buyer's founder, president and majority shareholder, of Paul Ng, buyer's general manager and Sule's second-in-command, and of Dave Robertson, one of seller's owners. The facts were not in substantial dispute, although there was one minor difference of opinion.

Buyer manufactured solar-operated valves used in scientific instruments. The machine involved is a Model RC–520 triple access Precision Vertical Machining Center which is used to drill holes in components with the very high degree of accuracy required by buyer. Sule saw the machine advertised in a trade journal and, believing that it was ideal for buyer's needs, contacted seller in late March or early April 1986. Following negotiations with seller's president, Ed Shepler, and an inspection of seller's facility, Sule placed an order on April 22, 1986.

The purchase price was approximately $55,000. The parties agreed to a mid-June 1986 delivery date, Shepler believing at the time that the machine was then in transit from Japan. Although the writing specified a mid-June delivery date; there was no clause stating that time was of the essence of the contract. Each page of the contract had printed language stating: "Cancellation charge 15 percent of total purchase price." Sule was aware of this provision. Printed "boiler plate" language in the standard terms and conditions of the sale dealt with delivery terms. Among other things, paragraph 5 of the standard terms and conditions stated that shipping dates were approximate, and that the seller would not be liable for delays which were caused by circumstances beyond the seller's control, such as fire, flood, strikes, or acts of God.

In early June, Sule instructed Ng to call seller about the delivery date. Ng testified that from June onwards he made a number of telephone calls and got noncommittal or evasive responses. Robertson testified that after the sale was negotiated seller discovered a design deficiency in the machine and redesigned it in order to make a better product. However, there was no evidence that Robertson informed Sule or Ng of the alleged reasons for the delay.

By late August, buyer was in desperate need of the machine, although it is not clear whether this was communicated to seller. On August 29, Sule went to seller's place of business to examine the product, which was then in the process of being assembled. The machine was essentially the same as that ordered by Sule, except that it no longer had a linear ballbearing raise which Sule had thought was an attractive aspect.

Nonetheless, Sule agreed to take it. He, Shepler and Robertson agreed that seller would have the machine ready on September 5. Robertson promised to call Sule on September 3 so that Sule could have two days to arrange for his truckers to pick up the product.

Robertson did not call Sule on September 3. The next day, September 4, Sule told Ng to find out what was happening. Ng testified that he had three conversations with Robertson. According to Ng, during the first conversation Robertson told him that under "no circumstances" would seller be able to get the machine ready for pickup on September 5. Rather, the machine could be picked up at the earliest on September 9 or September 10. Ng reported this information to Sule, who then decided to cancel because he was "fed up" with the course of dealing and no longer had faith in seller. At Sule's direction, Ng telephoned seller and informed Robertson and the office manager, Lorraine Mercier, that buyer was cancelling the order and that the contract was void because of the extraordinary delay in delivery and seller's failure to be truthful with buyer. Ng also asked for the return of the deposit. The third phone call took place about an hour later, when Robertson stated that the machine could be ready by the next day. Ng responded, "Thank you, but no thanks."

Robertson testified that only two conversations occurred on September 4. During the first, Robertson advised Ng that the machine would not be ready the next day, but might be available about five days later. Ng responded that he would relate that information to Sule. Within an hour Ng called back and the following conversation took place:

> The second conversation, they had called me—Mr. Ng had contacted me back and had—we started discussing that he wanted an earlier delivery and at that point, we had discussed that for a Friday delivery and of the Friday delivery there, he says, well, I'll have to check with Mr. Sule because Mr. Sule at this point would like to cancel the machine.

So he had set the phone down and I assume he set it down, I could hear in the background Mr. Sule saying, no, I do not want the machine and then Mr. Ng had come back to the phone and had said that, no, Mr. Sule has decided he does not want the machine even if it is available for tomorrow and at that point, I'd indicated that may be a cancellation charge.

By letter dated September 4, 1986, addressed to seller's office manager, Sule confirmed that buyer no longer wanted the machine and expected the return of its $3,000 deposit. Robertson claimed that the machine was in fact ready to be picked up on September 5. The parties thereafter attempted to resurrect the transaction, but the terms proposed by buyer and its attorney were not acceptable to seller. Buyer then filed this law suit a few weeks later.

At trial, seller argued that, assuming Robertson's statements on September 4 amounted to an anticipatory breach, the breach was not material, and thus buyer could not cancel because the machine was, in fact, ready for delivery on the date promised, September 5. Buyer, on the other hand, contended that the agreed upon September 5 delivery date had to be viewed in the context of the original delivery date of mid-June. Buyer's counsel also theorized that the machine that was shown to Sule on August 29 was different enough so that the agreement to accept that machine amounted to a new contract.

Judge Russell interpreted the Uniform Commercial Code as requiring strict conformance with the time of delivery provisions in sales contracts, unlike other contracts in which untimely performance may or may not be a material breach. Thus, seller's failure to deliver the machine in mid-June 1986, as called for in the contract, entitled buyer to cancel. However, buyer agreed to accept a substitute machine provided it was delivered on September 5, 1986. According to the judge, the discussions on August 29 could be viewed either as a new contract or as an amendment to the prior contract. But the crucial fact, according to the judge, was that buyer cancelled after seller stated that delivery could not be made on September 5, and seller's subsequent attempt at agreement or to provide delivery on September 5 occurred after buyer had cancelled. Her precise findings on the critical point were that:

> There's a substantial dispute as to what happened on September 4th, various phone calls and so forth, but it's not disputed that in response to buyer's inquiry calls that the seller's employee represented the substitute machine could not be delivered on September 5th.

> Now, it's not disputed that upon the indication that it would not be timely delivered on September 5th that the purchaser rescinded. Purchaser was entitled to cancel and rescind at that time and was not obligated to accept nonconforming goods beyond the final of the original delivery date. [Emphasis supplied].

The judge found that upon seller's breach, buyer was entitled to the return of its deposit, and that seller could not collect the 15% cancellation charge sought by the counterclaim.

Seller contends that the trial judge mistakenly interpreted the Uniform Commercial Code. According to seller, § 2–508(1) of the Code allows a seller to cure any nonconformities. Seller contends that the same result follows under general contract law. According to seller, its announcement on September 4 that it could not deliver in time was not an anticipatory breach because it was not material. Seller contends that failure to timely perform is not ordinarily a material breach and a buyer cannot cancel on this basis.

Buyer contends that seller committed an anticipatory breach on September 4 by stating that it would not have the machine ready by the next day, as the parties had previously agreed. Buyer urges that the cure remedy was not available to seller because the goods had not been delivered and then rejected.

We disagree with seller that it had a right to cure. . . .

The express language of § 2–508 shows its inapplicability here. That provision speaks of a tender or delivery which is rejected because it is nonconforming. In other words, this section "specifies the extent to which a seller who has made a nonconforming tender which has been rejected may replace the original tender with a substitute tender within the original contract period, or within a reasonable time after the expiration of such period." 3 Anderson, Uniform Commercial Code (3 ed.1983), § 2–508:3 at 664. In the present case, buyer cancelled the contract before seller got around to tendering or delivering the goods. Buyer never rejected the machine. Buyer here simply claims that there was no contract in existence at the time seller was supposed to deliver.

What we then have is a repudiation by seller that allegedly amounted to an anticipatory breach, followed by a retraction. The Code prescribes specific rules for this kind of situation which are similar in many respects to the rejection-cure provisions, but which in some respects are different. N.J.S.A. 12A:2–610, entitled "Anticipatory Repudiation," states that when "either party repudiates the contract with respect to a performance not yet due the loss of which will substantially impair the value of the contract to the other, the aggrieved party may . . . resort to any remedy for breach." One of the remedies available to a buyer is cancellation, N.J.S.A. 12A:2–711(1), which occurs "when either party puts an end to the contract for breach by the other." . . . N.J.S.A. 12A:2–106(4). However, the Code permits a party to retract an anticipatory repudiation under some circumstances. Specifically, N.J.S.A. 12A:2–611(1) states:

> Until the repudiating party's next performance is due he can retract his repudiation unless the aggrieved party has since the repudiation cancelled or materially changed his position or otherwise indicated that he considers the repudiation final.

In our opinion, § 2–610 and § 2–611 govern here. The key questions are: (1) did seller in fact repudiate when Robertson stated that the machine could not possibly be ready by September 5, and (2) should seller be allowed to retract its repudiation because buyer did not change its position for the worse?

Implicated in the first question are whether a statement that the seller cannot deliver on time is a repudiation, and, on these facts, whether such a statement substantially impaired the value of the contract to buyer. The Uniform Commercial Code comment to § 2–610 states that the "most useful test of substantial value is to determine whether material inconvenience or injustice will result if the aggrieved party is forced to wait and receive an ultimate tender minus the part or aspect repudiated." Section 2–610 expresses preexisting New Jersey case law. See New Jersey study comment to N.J.S.A. 12A:2–610. There are some helpful, though not dispositive, extant cases.

Our Supreme Court offered a useful definition of anticipatory repudiation in Ross Systems v. Linden Dari–Delite, Inc., 35 N.J. 329, 173 A.2d 258 (1961), as follows:

> An anticipatory breach is a definite and unconditional declaration by a party to an executory contract—through word or conduct—that he will not or cannot render the agreed upon performance. [Citations omitted]. If the breach is material, i.e., goes to the essence of the contract, the non-breaching party may treat the contract as terminated and refuse to render continued performance. [Citation omitted; 35 N.J. at 340–341, 173 A.2d 258.]

We find no modern support for the trial judge's view that defendant's failure to make delivery in mid-June 1986 in itself constituted a repudiation, or material breach, and immediately entitled plaintiff to cancel. The contract had no "time-of-the-essence" clause and there was nothing in the surrounding circumstances to indicate that the initial time of performance was essential.

The Code leaves it to the parties to agree on time requirements; in the absence of an agreement the Code will imply a provision in the contract requiring delivery within a reasonable time. N.J.S.A. 12A:2–309(1). A court's function is to determine whether and when it was the intention of the parties to make timely performance a vital feature of the contract. If time was of the essence then the breach was material and plaintiff had a right to cancel.

A contract does not need to expressly state that time is of the essence in order for timely delivery to be deemed essential. A failure to deliver within the prescribed time may justify the buyer in cancelling. Likewise, an announcement by the seller to the buyer that he cannot deliver in time may be a repudiation under § 2–610.

While a seller's statement that delivery will be untimely may be a repudiation, it does not have to be. According to Ross Systems, the question is whether the breach is "material." 35 N.J. at 341, 173 A.2d

258. The Code uses different language, i.e., whether the repudiation substantially impairs the value of the contract, § 2–610, but it does not define that phrase and we think it reasonable to treat interchangeably that phrase and the materiality standard of Ross Systems. The Restatement sets forth flexible criteria for determining whether a breach is material, as follows:

(a) the extent to which the injured party will be deprived of the benefit which he reasonably expected;

(b) the extent to which the injured party can be adequately compensated for the part of that benefit of which he will be deprived;

(c) the extent to which the party failing to perform or to offer to perform will suffer forfeiture;

(d) the likelihood that the party failing to perform or to offer to perform will cure his failure, taking account of all the circumstances including any reasonable assurances;

(e) the extent to which the behavior of the party failing to perform or to offer to perform comports with standards of good faith and fair dealing.

[2 Restatement, Contracts 2d, § 241 at 237 (1981).]

We think under the circumstances here one could reasonably find that seller's repudiation went to the essence of the contract. Defendant had agreed to a mid-June delivery. Throughout the summer it not only failed to deliver, but it refused to explain its reasons for non-delivery or to give plaintiff adequate assurances that the machine would be delivered soon. Cf. N.J.S.A. 12A:2–609(1) (entitling a party to suspend performance under some circumstances if the other party fails to give adequate assurances). By late August buyer, according to Sule, was in desperate need of the machine. On August 29, Sule learned that the machine buyer bought was no longer available because seller had changed the design. We conclude that buyer readily could have cancelled at that point but it did not. Rather, Sule agreed to accept the modified machine but only on the express condition that seller have the product available by September 5.

While Sule did not expressly state to any of seller's representatives that time had now become of the essence, we conclude this condition can fairly be implied, from the surrounding circumstances. Buyer had already waited a long time, seller had not been candid with buyer, and Sule had good reason to believe that seller would not perform. In essence, the events of August 29 can be viewed as Sule giving seller "one last chance." Seller's failure to call buyer on September 3, as seller had promised to do, could have only deepened buyer's suspicion that seller was not going to perform. In light of these circumstances, Robertson's unequivocal statement on September 4, that under no circumstances would the machine be ready by the promised delivery date, September 5, was a repudiation going to the essence of the contract.

The factors set forth in § 241 of the Restatement are only illustrative. Those factors are "to be applied in the light of the facts of each case in such a way as to further the purpose of securing for each party his expectation of an exchange of performances." 2 Restatement 2d, at § 241, Comment (a) at 237–238. Factors (c), (d), & (e) are especially relevant here. Seller, the party which failed to perform, suffered no forfeiture as a result of plaintiff's cancellation, seller still has the machine. By September 4, buyer had every reason to believe that seller would not cure its failure. Finally, one has to question on this record whether seller acted in good faith between mid-June and September 4.

We conclude that Robertson's statement on September 4 constituted an anticipatory repudiation within the meaning of § 2–610. The remaining question is whether Robertson's offer later that day to make the machine available for delivery on the agreed-upon September 5 date amounted to an effective retraction of the repudiation within the meaning of § 2–611(1). That section allows a repudiating party to retract if performance is not yet due unless the nonbreaching party has "since the repudiation cancelled or materially changed his position or otherwise indicated that he considers the repudiation final."

The disjunctive language of § 2–611(1) is key. Pre–Code authority is somewhat ambiguous on whether a buyer must change his position for the worse in order to preclude a seller from retracting a repudiation. Williston is unclear. 11 Williston, Contracts (3 ed., 1968), § 1335 at 180–183. Corbin likewise is somewhat uncertain, but seems to hold that the nonbreaching party must change its position for the worse in order to preclude a retraction. 4 Corbin, Contracts (1951), § 980 at 935. Corbin states:

> In the case of the repudiation, it has sometimes been said that it becomes a final and irrevocable breach as soon as the other party expresses his assent to it as such. It is believed, however, that this statement is erroneous. In the cases in which such a dictum is found, either the court found that there had been no such expression of assent and proceeded to hold that there was no anticipatory breach, or the expression of assent by the injured party was accompanied by a material change of position on his part. The bringing of an action for damages is, of course, such a change of position. It is believed that, in spite of the mere words "I assent to your repudiation as final," the repudiator continues to have the power of retracting his repudiation as long as the other party's position has not been materially changed and as long as there has been no breach by actual non-performance at the time fixed for such performance by the contract. [Ibid.]

One pre-Code New Jersey case addresses the issue in dictum, and tentatively expresses the view that the standards might be different depending upon whether the nonbreaching party seeks damages or merely asks to rescind. Miller and Sons Bakery Co. v. Selikowitz, 8 N.J.Super. 118, 123, 73 A.2d 607 (App.Div.1950), states:

There is another rule relating to anticipatory breaches that has not been brought into the case by the pleadings, or request to charge, or otherwise, and which has not been argued before us but which we will mention in order not to seem to discard it by silence. An anticipatory breach is nullified as the basis of an action for damages, if the repudiation of the contract is withdrawn before the injured party brings his action or otherwise materially changes his position. [Citations omitted.] Whether it is nullified as the basis of rescission if the repudiation is not withdrawn until after the opposite party has manifested his election to rescind, is doubtful. [Citations omitted.]

We have found no helpful cases construing § 2–611(1), but we assume that the drafters intentionally used the disjunctive: that is, the breaching party loses the right to retract if the nonbreaching party materially changes his position or cancels. The cognate provision in the Restatement of Contracts states:

The effect of a statement as constituting a repudiation under § 250 or the basis for a repudiation under § 251 is nullified by a retraction of the statement if notification of the retraction comes to the attention of the injured party before he materially changes his position in reliance on the repudiation or indicates to the other party that he considers the repudiation to be final. [2 Restatement, Contracts 2d, § 256 at 293.]

The Comment explains:

Once the injured party has materially changed his position in reliance on the repudiation, nullification would clearly be unjust. In the interest of certainty, however, it is undesirable to make the injured party's rights turn exclusively on such a vague criterion, and he may therefore prevent subsequent nullification by indicating to the other party that he considers the repudiation final. [Id., Comment c. at 294–295.]

In the present case, buyer did not change its position for the worse prior to retraction, at least in the sense of either filing suit or getting a replacement machine. Buyer clearly had no time to do that, since seller attempted to retract its repudiation within an hour. The question before us is whether buyer's cancellation stands despite the absence of prejudice and seller's nearly immediate retraction. We can find no case which addresses a similar situation.

Under the facts before us, we give effect to buyer's cancellation. We reach this result for three reasons. First, the express language of § 2–611(1) permits cancellation and bars retraction even in the absence of prejudice. Second, the certainty interest expressed and found in the Restatement is, in this instance, persuasive. Third, we cannot ignore seller's previous, less-than-exemplary conduct. Corbin makes the point that if "substantial performance of the contract requires the maintenance of a relation of trust and confidence between the parties and the repudiation is of such a character as to shatter this relation beyond repair, the repudiation in itself creates such a change of position as to prevent retraction." 4 Corbin, § 980 at 932.

This was such a relationship. Seller was supplying an expensive, complex "high-tech" machine which, presumably, was important, if not essential, for the success of buyer's business enterprise. Seller was to supply installation services and train two operators as part of the contract. The machine was sold with express warranties. Such a machine would require periodic maintenance and repair, services which seller must perform under the terms of the express warranty. Indeed, the written contract itself contains a statement that seller looked forward to a "long and prosperous relationship." Seller's repudiation, which followed a series of deviations from the terms of the contract, was in a real sense "the straw that broke the camel's back." We find buyer reasonably concluded that it could no longer rely upon seller. The cancellation by buyer was justified.

Affirmed.

Notes and Questions

(1) The *Neptune Research* opinion emphasizes that, to trigger the remedies in 2–610, a repudiation must affect performance "the loss of which will substantially impair the value of the contract." In *Neptune*, however, the seller had originally promised to deliver the machine in mid-June. Thus on September 4, when the seller repudiated its obligation to deliver the next day, it was already some 2½ months late. Section 2–610 applies only to *anticipatory* repudiation—i.e., repudiation as to performance "not yet due." Actual failure to perform is a breach in its own right, outside the purview of 2–610. Why didn't the buyer prevail on the basis that the seller breached when it failed to deliver by mid-June, regardless of whether seller's statements on September 4 constituted a repudiation under 2–610? What was the trial's court's analysis of this question? The appeals court's?

Consider the following excerpt from the opinion:

We find no modern support for the trial judge's view that defendant's failure to make delivery in mid-June 1986 in itself constituted a repudiation, or material breach, and immediately entitled plaintiff to cancel. The contract had no "time-of-the-essence" clause and there was nothing in the surrounding circumstances to indicate that the initial time of performance was essential.

Although the failure to deliver in mid-June was clearly not a "repudiation," and as a breach it quite possibly was not "material," does UCC Article 2 require a material breach before the buyer can refuse delivery? Doesn't 2–601 (the perfect tender rule) offer "modern support" for the view that the seller's failure to make timely tender in this single-delivery contract would permit the buyer to cancel the contract, regardless of materiality? The *Neptune* court emphasizes the absence of a "time-of-the-essence" clause in the contract. Does that mean that the mid-June delivery date was not a contractually-binding promise at all? Or does it merely indicate that, although the seller was bound to deliver by mid-June, breach of that duty would not necessarily be material (if, for some reason materiality were relevant)?

(2) In *Neptune Research* the aggrieved buyer decided to cancel the contract almost immediately upon receiving the seller's repudiation. An alternative course available under 2–610(a) would have been to await the seller's performance "for a commercially reasonable time." Why did the buyer not wait in *Neptune*? Suppose the seller had continued to insist it could not deliver before September 10 but the buyer decided to await performance rather than cancel (e.g., because it was desperate for the machine and was not sure it could quickly obtain a substitute from another source). What should the buyer do if the contract required it to pay the balance of the purchase price by the close of business on September 4 (the day the seller repudiated)? See 2–610(c). If the buyer decides to wait and the seller in fact delivers on September 10, can the buyer recover damages caused by the delay? Cf. 2–607(2).

(3) How certain must an indication of nonperformance be in order to constitute a repudiation? In *Neptune Research* the seller told the buyer directly and without ambiguity or condition that the machine could not be delivered on the agreed date. Although it was not entirely clear whether the delay would substantially impair the value of the contract to the buyer, there was no doubt that the statement was otherwise a repudiation. Not all cases are so clear-cut: they may involve an ambiguous or uncertain threat of nonperformance. The pre-amendment version of Article 2 contains no statutory definition of the term "repudiation," although comment 1 to 2–610 states that "anticipatory repudiation centers upon an overt communication of intention or an action which renders performance impossible or demonstrates a clear determination not to continue with performance." See also comment 2 to 2–610. Proposed amended Section 2–610(2) would provide:

> Repudiation includes language that a reasonable party would interpret to mean that the other party will not or cannot make a performance still due under the contract or voluntary, affirmative conduct that would appear to a reasonable party to make a future performance by the other impossible.

A proposed comment to this provision indicates that, although it is based on Restatement (Second) of Contracts § 250, proposed amended Section 2–610(2) would codify the standard under pre-amendment Section 2–610. The proposed comment also indicates that proposed amended Section 2–610 merely "provides guidance" as to what constitutes a repudiation, and does not purport to be exhaustive.

Remember these materials, as well as the traditional common law position that repudiation requires an extremely clear indication of nonperformance, when dealing with the following.

Problem 68

In a transaction governed by UCC Article 2, Ceres Crofter agreed to sell 50,000 bushels of corn to Moody Elevator, Inc. for delivery by October 15. The written agreement required the corn to be grown on Crofter's own farm. Moody was to pay the $100,000 purchase price as follows: $5,000 upon signing the agreement on April 15, $25,000 on September 1, and the balance upon delivery of the corn. In which (if any) of the following alternative scenarios is there a repudiation that would permit the aggrieved party immediately to cancel the contract and enter into substitute arrangements with another party?

(a) In late August, Crofter called the manager of Moody Elevator to say that she did not like the manager's politics and would therefore not sell her corn to the elevator.

(b) In late August the manager of Moody Elevator drove past Crofter's farm and noticed that no corn had been planted.

(c) In late August the Moody manager heard from Crofter's seed supplier that Crofter had planted no corn on her farm. Because of the location and typography of the Crofter farm the manager could not personally confirm the seed supplier's story. Despite at least 15 attempts in five days, the manager has been unable to reach Crofter by telephone.

(d) Same facts as (c), but in addition the seed supplier has been involved in a dispute with Crofter concerning overdue payments for seed.

(e) On October 12 the manager of Moody Elevator learned that Crofter had not yet made good on a contract with a competitor to deliver 20,000 bushels of corn before the end of September. The price of corn has skyrocketed since Crofter and Moody entered into their contract.

(f) On September 5, Crofter sent Moody Elevator a letter stating that unless she received the balance of the entire purchase price before the end of September she would not deliver any corn in October.

(g) In the middle of August Crofter received a phone call from the manager of Moody Elevator. The manager explained that, because grain prices had been falling rapidly, the elevator was experiencing "temporary but severe cash flow difficulties" and would "almost certainly" not be able to make the $25,000 payment due September 1. The manager indicated that mid-September was a "more realistic" date for the payment. The manager also indicated that the elevator was depending on Crofter's corn and that all balances would be paid in full upon delivery—"or at least I hope so—nothing is certain when the wolves are at the door."

Questions

(1) Suppose there was a repudiation within the meaning of 2–610 on the facts of alternative (a) in Problem 68. Moody Elevator decides to suspend its $25,000 payment due September 1 and await Crofter's performance. See 2–610(a) & (c). Can the buyer sit back and wait until the end of October for Crofter to deliver? What (if any) additional information would you want? What would be a "commercially reasonable time" for the Elevator to await performance in alternative (b)? What exactly must Moody Elevator do within the commercially reasonable time specified 2–610(a)—i.e., how does it stop "awaiting?" What will happen if the elevator waits for more than a commercially reasonable time? See comment 1 to 2–610.

(2) What constitutes an adequate retraction of a repudiation? Re-read 2–611(2). If alternative (a) in Problem 68 involved a repudiation, what would

Crofter have to do to retract? Would the same retraction be adequate in alternative (b) (assuming Crofter had repudiated on those facts)? Suppose the buyer in *Neptune Research* had not cancelled before the third phone call on September 4, when the seller recanted and stated that the machine "could be ready by the next day." Would the seller's statement have been an adequate retraction?

Problem 69

Return to the transaction between Moody Elevator and Ceres Crofter in Problem 68. In late August the Elevator announced that it had ceased all operations, was going out of business permanently, and would not receive or pay for any more deliveries. Although she never mentioned it to the elevator, Crofter had not planted any corn. Can she treat the elevator's announcement as a repudiation and resort to her remedies for breach pursuant to 2–610(b)? See Gibbs, Nathaniel (Canada) Ltd. v. International Multifoods Corp., 804 F.2d 450 (8th Cir.1986).

Problem 70

Ceres Crofter consults you just after receiving the phone call from Moody Elevator described in alternative (g) of Problem 68 about delaying the $25,000 payment. Crofter wants to cancel the contract immediately and make substitute arrangements to sell the corn (see 2–706(1)). What are the consequences if you advise her to proceed as she planned and a court finds that the Elevator's statement was not a repudiation? If you are unsure about whether the elevator has repudiated should you advise Crofter to ignore the phone call and prepare to perform? Read 2–609 and outline precisely how you would proceed. Suppose that Crofter demands adequate assurances of future performance from Moody Elevator and the Elevator does not respond. What are the consequences?

UNIVERSAL RESOURCES CORP. v. PANHANDLE EASTERN PIPE LINE CO.

United States Court of Appeals, Fifth Circuit, 1987.
813 F.2d 77.

WOODWARD,* DISTRICT JUDGE.

FACTS

This is a diversity case arising out of the breach of a Gas Purchase and Sales Agreement between Universal Resources Corporation (URC) and Panhandle Eastern Pipe Line Company (Panhandle). URC is a nonoperating cotenant owner of gas wells in Oklahoma. URC, as seller, and Panhandle, as buyer, entered into a fifteen-year gas purchase and sales agreement (Agreement) in 1982. Under the Agreement, URC is required to tender for delivery a certain quantity of gas (Contract

---

* District Judge of the Northern District of Texas, sitting by designation.

Quantity)[1] to Panhandle at its pipeline connection. The Agreement also contains a standard "take-or-pay" clause obligating Panhandle to take gas, or pay for gas tendered for delivery but not taken. If, at the end of the Contract Year, Panhandle has not taken all the Contract Quantity, it must make deficiency payments for the difference between the Contract Quantity and the quantity actually taken. Panhandle may make up gas paid for but not taken during the succeeding five years of the Agreement.[2]

URC notified Panhandle of its deficiency quantity of 92,775 Mcf of gas and deficiency amount of $708,990.23 at the end of the 1983 Contract Year, and of the deficiency quantity of 119,388 Mcf of gas and deficiency amount of $919,168.21 at the end of the 1984 Contract Year. Panhandle refused to pay the deficiency amounts. URC brought suit in state court for breach of contract and Panhandle removed the case to federal court. The United States District Court for the Northern District of Texas rendered summary judgment in favor of URC and Panhandle brought this appeal. URC appeals only the award of prejudgment interest. We now affirm.

DISCUSSION

* * *

1. *Reasonable Insecurity Under § 2.609*

Panhandle argues that it was justified in refusing to make deficiency payments because URC failed to give adequate assurance that it had sufficient reserves to supply makeup gas in the future. After the execution of the Agreement, Panhandle conducted geological studies on the URC wells in the Fletcher Field which were dedicated to Panhandle and concluded that, based on the field reserves, specific well capabilities, and Panhandle's projected sales levels, it would be impossible for URC to supply both the Contract Quantity for the remaining term of the Agreement and makeup gas in sufficient quantities to permit full recoup-

---

1. Capitalized terms have the meanings given them in the Agreement. The Contract Quantity is calculated by a formula set out in ¶ 4.1 of the Agreement.

2. The applicable provisions, in pertinent part, read as follows:

"4.1 During each Contract Year, Seller agrees to sell and deliver to Buyer and Buyer agrees to buy and receive or failing to buy and receive, nevertheless to pay for from Seller's gas wells connected hereunder, a gas well Contract Quantity which shall be ... equal to 80 percent of each such well's maximum daily sustained capability....

"4.8 If, at the end of any Contract Year, Buyer's receipts of gas well gas, during said Contract Year were less than the Contract Quantity, and said volume was

tendered for delivery, then Buyer shall, within sixty (60) days thereafter, pay Seller for the deficiency at a price equal to the average of the prices in effect for such gas during the same Contract Year. Buyer during any of the five (5) ensuing Contract Years, or the balance of the term hereof, if less than five (5) Contract Years remain, may take volumes of gas, called 'make-up gas', equal to those paid for but not received; provided such volumes of 'make-up gas' shall be in excess of the Contract Quantity for any such year.

"For any 'make-up gas' received, Buyer shall pay Seller any difference in price between that in effect at the time of such make-up and that paid for such deficiency."

ment of deficiency payments. Affidavit and Supplemental Affidavit of Michael Knobloch, Record Vol. 1 at 108, 199. Panhandle then made written demand on URC for assurance that URC would either provide makeup gas or refund deficiency payments, and URC refused to give such assurance.

Article 2 of the Tex.Bus. & Com.Code Ann. (Vernon 1968), which governs the sale of goods, applies to gas purchase and sales agreements. E.g., Southern Natural Gas Co. v. Pursue Energy, 781 F.2d 1079, 1081 n. 3 (5th Cir.1986) (applying Mississippi law). Under Tex.Bus. & Com.Code Ann. § 2.609 a party may suspend performance without being in breach of the contract when certain conditions exist. That section provides

> (a) A contract for sale imposes an obligation on each party that the other's expectation of receiving due performance will not be impaired. When reasonable grounds for insecurity arise with respect to the performance of either party the other may in writing demand adequate assurance of due performance and until he receives such assurance may if commercially reasonable suspend any performance for which he has not already received the agreed return.

Before a party can suspend performance, however, he must have reasonable grounds for insecurity. The reasonableness of grounds for insecurity is determined by reference to commercial standards. Id. § 2.609(b). The trial court held,[3] and we agree, that Panhandle's fears of lack of makeup gas in the future did not rise to the level of reasonable insecurity as a matter of law.

First, there was no event occurring after the execution of the Agreement which could have given rise to a reasonable insecurity. There was no change in the reservoir capacity or in URC's ability to perform. The only "event" was Panhandle's evaluation of the Fletcher Field. Furthermore, as an experienced buyer of natural gas Panhandle is deemed to have known of the risk that it might not be able to recoup deficiency payments by taking makeup gas.

Second, Panhandle's alleged insecurity arose from purely subjective evaluations and projections and was not based on any objective, identifiable conduct of URC. URC properly tendered for delivery the Contract Quantity for the 1983 and 1984 Contract Years and has continuously maintained that it is willing and able to perform under the Agreement. Third, Panhandle's conclusion of insecurity is based upon some unsupported assumptions about the market for natural gas. URC's responsibility to supply makeup gas is only triggered when Panhandle has made deficiency payments in a preceding year, and Panhandle has taken the entire Contract Quantity for the year. Agreement ¶ 4.8. Panhandle assumes that in the five years following the years in which deficiency payments are made, the demand for gas will increase to the point that Panhandle will be able to take amounts of gas over and above the Contract Quantity. In fact, the demand for gas and Panhandle's ability

---

3. The trial court found that Panhandle had only a "mere suspicion" of a lack of makeup gas. Memorandum Opinion and Order, Record Vol. 2 at 267 n. 10.

to take the Contract Quantity has decreased, while Panhandle's deficiency quantities increased from 1983 to 1985 when this suit was filed. Record, Vol. 1 at 186–87. Panhandle cannot ignore its own obligations under the Agreement, assume that it will be able to take the Contract Quantity and more, and then demand that URC give adequate assurance that it can perform in Panhandle's hypothetical situation.

Because Panhandle did not have a reasonable insecurity regarding URC's future performance, URC was not required to give adequate assurance and its failure to do so does not excuse Panhandle from its obligation to make deficiency payments.

* * *

The judgment of the district court is AFFIRMED.

Problem 71

Q–Mart Inc., which operates discount general merchandise retail outlets throughout the United States, contracted to buy Model A–44 computerized cash registers from Jingo Sales Machinery Inc. The agreement provided that a single team of Jingo employees would install the machines in 50 specified Q–Mart stores (at an average of 10 machines per store) over a 50 week period. In return Q–Mart was to pay $200,000 for each store in which the registers were installed. Each $200,000 payment was due 30 days after installation in the store was complete. The contract also required Jingo to provide, at no additional cost, all service required by the machines for 12 months following installation.

Consider each of the alternative scenarios below and decide whether the situation involves a repudiation of the contract under 2–610, grounds for insecurity under 2–609, or neither. For every alternative in which you find reasonable grounds for insecurity, give a specific example of what would constitute "adequate assurances of future performance" sufficient to require the insecure party to proceed with the contract. See, *inter alia*, comments 3 & 4 to 2–609. If you believe the facts constitute a repudiation, describe what would be an adequate retraction of the repudiation.

(a) The Jingo team completed installation at the first store. Over the next 15 days the registers broke down repeatedly, in clear violation of a "performance warranty" given by Jingo. At the end of the 15 days Q–Mart sent Jingo a letter "rejecting or revoking acceptance of the cash registers." Q–Mart also wants to cancel the remainder of the contract. Consider comment 6 to 2–612 and comment 4 to 2–610.

(b) Same facts as (a) with the following addition: the Q–Mart executive in charge of the cash register project had been told by the president of another retailer that the Jingo Model A–44 registers she had put in 20 of her stores required constant attention and were out of service for extended periods. A member of the Jingo installation team also admitted to the Q–Mart executive that the Model A–44 was the first computerized register Jingo had built and was "kind of an experiment we hoped to learn from."

(c) Same facts as (a) with the following addition: another retailer had told Q–Mart that, after an initial period of several weeks to "adjust the bugs out," the Model A–44's she had installed in her 20 stores had proven extremely reliable.

(d) Alternatively, suppose Jingo completed work on 25 stores. Q–Mart has consistently been 10–15 days late in making the required payments. As Jingo knew when it entered into the contract, Q–Mart has a reputation as a financially solid company with a tendency to pay late. Can Jingo demand adequate assurances of future timely payments, suspend its own work, and cancel the remainder of the contract if Q–Mart fails to respond?

(e) Alternatively, suppose Jingo completed installation in the first 15 stores without any problems. At that point, a dispute arose between Jingo and Q–Mart concerning certain bar code scanning equipment that Q–Mart was buying from Jingo under a separate contract formed some eight months before the cash register agreement. Jingo is substantially behind the contract deadline for manufacturing and installing the bar code scanners. Can Q–Mart treat this situation as a repudiation or grounds for insecurity as to the cash register contract? See the second paragraph of comment 3 to 2–609.

(f) Alternatively, suppose that one week before installation work was to start Jingo's president heard rumors that Q–Mart was in financial difficulty. The source of the rumors had no direct dealings with Q–Mart, and had a reputation for spreading unfounded information. Jingo's president would normally have discounted the information but Jingo recently suffered an almost fatal financial blow when a customer went bankrupt. See the second paragraph of comment 3 to 2–609.

(g) Alternatively, suppose Jingo completed installation in several stores but Q–Mart complained that the cash registers frequently broke down and did not conform to the "performance warranty" given by Jingo. Q–Mart has therefore withheld payment for the installations, although it has not declared the contract canceled nor has it demanded adequate assurances that future installations will be conforming. Does Jingo have grounds for demanding adequate assurances of Q–Mart's future performance?

(h) Alternatively, suppose Jingo received reliable information that Q–Mart was in financial difficulty. At the time it received this information, Jingo was a week late in beginning installation of the cash registers in the first store, although it had planned to begin the work in the next two or three days. Can Jingo demand adequate assurances of payment from Q–Mart and suspend its own performance? Or must Jingo perform without such assurances?

Notes and Questions

(1) What must be included in a demand for adequate assurances? Nothing in the statute or the comments addresses this question. At the very least the demand should describe the grounds for insecurity (in order to permit the recipient to respond with assurances that are "adequate") and make it clear that serious consequences will flow from a failure to respond or from a response that is not prompt and adequate. In SPS Industries, Inc. v. Atlantic Steel Co., 186 Ga.App. 94, 366 S.E.2d 410 (1988), a buyer of

industrial equipment wrote the following letter to the seller, who had been late with the first delivery:

> It is imperative that you provide me with the information I requested on the subject orders during our telephone conversation last week. It would appear that the elapse [*sic*] of time since these orders were placed with your company would enable you to respond to delivery requests.... Your immediate response is expected.

The court held that the letter did not constitute a demand for adequate assurances under 2–609, but rather was a mere "request for information." Compare Cole v. Melvin, 441 F.Supp. 193 (D.S.D.1977) (buyer's letter mentioning possibility that seller might be "backing out on our contract" and requesting that seller "let me know what your plans are as soon as possible" was a sufficient demand for adequate assurances (dictum)).

The text of 2–609(1) says that a demand for assurances must be "in writing," and courts have sometimes refused to accept oral demands.[1] Several decisions, however, have approved non-written demands where they were unambiguously communicated and the recipient clearly understood their significance.[2]

(2) Frequently, the demand for assurances will call for a particular form of assurance. In Creusot–Loire Int'l, Inc. v. Coppus Engineering Corp., 585 F.Supp. 45 (S.D.N.Y.1983), for example, a buyer of industrial burners discovered that the same type of burner did not meet contractual performance specifications on other projects. The buyer demanded assurances in the form of an extension of the warranty period as well as the posting of a letter of credit to cover a refund of the purchase price should the burners prove inadequate. The court found that the demand was "reasonable," and that the seller's response—an assertion that the burners would work— constituted a repudiation under 2–609(4).[3] In demanding particular assurances, however, the insecure party must not overreach or demand assurances of performance not due under the contract. In United States v. Great Plains Gasification Assocs., 819 F.2d 831 (8th Cir.1987), the seller in a long-term gas supply agreement had the right to terminate the agreement provided it acted in good faith. The buyer demanded assurances that the seller would supply gas over the entire term of the contract. The court held that the buyer's demand was "invalid" because it sought more than the buyer was entitled to under the contract.[4]

1. Continental Grain Co. v. McFarland, 628 F.2d 1348, 29 U.C.C.Rep.Serv. (Callaghan) 512 (4th Cir.1980) (per curiam); Automated Energy Sys. v. Fibers & Fabrics of Ga., Inc., 164 Ga.App. 772, 298 S.E.2d 328 (1982). Proposed amended Section 2–609(1) would require that a demand for adequate assurances be "in a record."

2. AMF, Inc. v. McDonald's Corp., 536 F.2d 1167 (7th Cir.1976); Kunian v. Development Corp. of America, 165 Conn. 300, 334 A.2d 427 (1973).

3. See also Kunian v. Development Corp. of America, 165 Conn. 300, 334 A.2d 427 (1973) (buyer fell behind on payments for plumbing supplies; seller insisted that buyer put entire balance of purchase price into escrow before deliveries would resume; held—seller's proposal was a proper demand for adequate assurances).

4. See also, e.g., Scott v. Crown, 765 P.2d 1043 (Colo.App.1988) (seller's demand that buyer pay before date specified in the contract was an attempt to "forc[e] a modification" and thus was not a valid demand for assurances under 2–609).

If the insecure party specifies the form of assurance in the demand, can the other party provide different assurances as long as they are "adequate?" Demands for assurances frequently specify the time within which the insecure party requires a reply. Suppose the specified time is shorter than a full "reasonable time not exceeding thirty days" (see 2–609(4)). Does that invalidate the demand? If not, what result if the other side provides adequate assurances after the specified deadline but still within a "reasonable time?"

(3) Parties can eliminate some of the uncertainties surrounding the adequate assurances process by specifying in the contract itself what circumstances will justify a demand for assurances, what assurances will be adequate, and the time within which assurances must be given. See comment 6 to 2–609. It is difficult, however, to foresee all possible grounds for insecurity that could arise and the responses that would be reasonable in all circumstances. Thus care should be taken in drafting contractual "insecurity clauses" not to preempt completely the adequate assurances process in Article 2 unless that is truly what the parties intend.

Problem 72

Hirsute, Inc. had devised a radical new design for a home window air conditioner that was energy-efficient but did not use chemicals damaging to the environment. Hirsute planned to display a prototype of the machine at a trade show held September 15–18 by the Association of Cooling Technologists. This annual event, by far the largest gathering for the air conditioning industry, was traditionally a showcase for introducing new products. Hirsute had incurred substantial expenses (including the hiring of a public relations firm) preparing to debut its machine at the show. In order to produce the prototype in time, Hirsute had contracted out the production of one key component to Greasy Co. Because Hirsute itself planned to manufacture the component during normal production, the agreement required Greasy to deliver the finished component and to turn over all tools, dies, plans and specifications used in producing it in exchange for $20,000 payable 30 days after delivery. During negotiations Hirsute made it clear that delivery by the September 10 deadline specified in the contract was crucial in order to have the prototype ready for the trade show. The agreement itself provided that timely delivery was "of the essence."

Soon after Greasy began working on the component its president learned that Hirsute had fallen substantially behind in its account with two of its primary suppliers. At the same time she heard rumors that Hirsute was in financial distress. The president calls you for advice. She explains that if Greasy continues production of the component and does not get paid it will suffer a large loss, since no one but Hirsute would want either the component or the specialized tools and dies Greasy uses to produce the component. Greasy could cut its losses considerably by stopping production immediately. On the other hand, even the briefest interruption at this point would guarantee that Greasy could not meet the September 10 delivery date and would probably make it impossible to finish the component before the trade show ended. The president asks how to proceed. Advise her.

Problem 73

Same facts as Problem 72 except Greasy did not receive the information concerning Hirsute's uncertain financial condition until just before Greasy was to tender the goods. Does Greasy have any alternative to suspending its performance under 2–609? Consider 2–702(1) and 1–201(23).

Questions

Suppose that in Problem 73 Greasy did not receive the information on Hirsute's financial condition until the goods were en route to Hirsute's plant by rail carrier. Can Greasy do anything in these circumstances? See 2–705. When does Greasy's right to stop goods in transit end? If the rail carrier transporting the goods issued Greasy a "bill of lading" (see 1–201(6)), the answer to the last question might depend on the kind of bill of lading involved and what Greasy did with the bill. Bills of lading and other "documents of title" (see 1–201(16)) are discussed in the next chapter.

B. ADEQUATE ASSURANCES AND ANTICIPATORY REPUDIATION UNDER ARTICLE 2A OF THE UCC AND UCITA

Note on Prospective Nonperformance Under Article 2A

For leases subject to UCC Article 2A, the provisions governing anticipatory breach and adequate assurances are found in 2A–401 through 2A–403. Read these provisions and their accompanying comments, then compare the analogous Article 2 provisions (2–609 through 2–611). Do you detect any substantive difference between the treatment of prospective nonperformance in Article 2 and Article 2A? Would cases like *Neptune Research* and *Universal Resources* supra, both of which were decided under Article 2, be decided any differently if they involved leases governed by Article 2A? Do these Article 2 cases provide guidance on what constitutes a repudiation under 2A–402 or what are reasonable grounds for insecurity under 2A–401? See the discussion entitled "Relationship of Article 2A to Other Articles" at the end of the comment to 2A–101.

Note on Prospective Nonperformance Under UCITA

The provisions of UCITA governing anticipatory breach and adequate assurances are found in §§ 708 through 710. A careful reading of these provisions reveals that they closely track the analogous Article 2 provisions (2–609 through 2–611). Would cases like *Neptune Research* and *Universal Resources* supra, both of which were decided under Article 2, be decided any differently if they involved transactions governed by UCITA?

C. PROSPECTIVE NONPERFORMANCE UNDER THE CISG

Problem 74

On February 15 Industro Corp., a U.S. manufacturing concern, agreed to buy a specially designed machine tool to be custom built by Konsonanten

AG, located in Germany (a country that has ratified the CISG). Because Industro needed the machine tool to meet its own strict schedule of manufacturing commitments, the parties agreed that timely delivery by May 10 was "of the essence of the contract." On April 15, Industro executives heard through several reliable sources that Konsonanten was involved in a labor dispute that had shut down all its design and manufacturing facilities for the last 30 days. As a result, Industro believes that delivery of the machine tool will be delayed until the middle of June or later. Industro can buy a readily-available standard version of the machine tool from other sources. The standard version won't work as well in Industro's applications as the custom-designed tool ordered from Konsonanten, but it would allow Industro to minimize defaults to its own customers. The last thing Industro wants, however, is to end up obligated to buy two of the devices. The president of Industro consults you on April 18. Advise her how to proceed. See, *inter alia*, CISG Article 72. Suppose Konsonanten had written Industro a letter declaring that mid June was the earliest possible delivery date. How would that affect your advice?

Problem 75

Sawmill, Inc., located in Oregon, agreed to sell 10 million square feet of specially-manufactured one-half inch plywood to the State Construction Authority of the People's Republic of China (a Contracting State). The plywood had to meet particular requirements imposed by the Construction Authority. Sawmill was to deliver the plywood in five shipments of 2 million square feet each over a period of 10 months beginning in September, 1989. The purchase was part of a development project to be financed by a loan to the People's Republic by the World Bank.

In June, 1989, a domestic political crisis in the People's Republic precipitated a violent government crackdown on protest. The suppression of protest received international attention and caused major tension in relations between the People's Republic and other countries. Among the results was an announcement by the World Bank that it would not finance the development project. When this announcement was made, Sawmill was in the midst of manufacturing plywood for the first delivery under the contract.

A Sawmill representative consults you. She explains that the contract with the Construction Authority is the largest single order Sawmill has ever received and that the company planned to devote 80% of its facilities over the next 10 months to producing the plywood. If the contract falls through, Sawmill might end up in bankruptcy. On the other hand, Sawmill is extremely concerned that the failure of World Bank financing might cause the Construction Authority to default on its obligations, and Sawmill might find itself holding specially-manufactured plywood that would be difficult to sell elsewhere.

How do you advise Sawmill to proceed? In addition to CISG Article 72, consider Article 71.

Questions

(1) Suppose the World Bank had not rescinded its financing, but the People's Republic announced that it had canceled the development project. Would this change your advice?

(2) Compare the standards and procedures for suspending performance under Article 71 with those in UCC 2–609. Would it be easier to establish grounds for suspension under the UCC or under CISG? For instance, would rumors that a buyer is in financial difficulty permit the seller to suspend its performance under UCC 2–609? See the second paragraph of comment 4 to 2–609. Would those same rumors make it "apparent that the other party will not perform a substantial part of his obligations," and thus constitute grounds for the seller to suspend performance under CISG Article 71? Which approach deals better with threats of future non-performance? If you represented the seller in the example in this paragraph, which would you prefer? Would your answer change if you represented the buyer?

(3) Assume the facts of Problem 75 gave Sawmill grounds to suspend its performance under Article 71. What steps must Sawmill take if it wants to exercise that right? See Article 71(3). Suppose Sawmill gave notice of suspension and the People's Republic responded by revealing that it has obtained alternative financing for the development project. How should Sawmill proceed?

DECISION OF SEPTEMBER 30, 1992, LANDGERICHT BERLIN, GERMANY CASE NO. 99 0 123/92

English Abstract from Unilex Data Base[1]

A German shoe retailer ordered shoes from an Italian company to be delivered to the buyer's place of business four months later and to be paid for within 60 days of being charged. Between the date of signing of the contract and the date of performance, the German buyer failed to complete payment due under a prior contract between the parties. For this reason, the seller had reservations about the buyer's solvency and requested it to secure the payment of the price of the later contract within a week, announcing that otherwise it would exercise its right to resell the goods and claim damages. The buyer refused to give security, alleging that it had the right to refuse payment under the previous contract because of defects in the goods. The seller resold the shoes to a third party at a loss. It then commenced an action against the buyer, claiming recovery of the difference between the contract price and the price in the substitute transaction as well as sales commission, legal costs and interest.

The court held that the contract was governed by CISG as at the time of its conclusion the parties had their places of business in two contracting states (Art. 1(1)(a) CISG).

1. Reprinted with the permission of the Centre for Comparative and Foreign Studies–UNIDROIT, Rome, Italy. The Unilex English abstract of the decision, as well as the original German text, is available through the Unilex website, <http://www.unilex.info>.

The court stated that the seller had the right to declare the contract avoided under Art. 72(1) and (2) CISG, since even before the delivery of the shoes it was clear that the buyer would not pay the purchase price and thereby commit a fundamental breach of contract. The court held that the probability of a future breach of contract has to be very high and obvious to everybody, but did not require almost complete certainty. In the case at hand, there was reason to believe that the buyer would breach the later contract since at the time when delivery should have occurred the buyer had not yet performed under the prior contract.

The court held that the buyer was not authorized to suspend payment because it did not have the right to rely on a lack of conformity of the goods. According to the court, the buyer had not given notice of their non-conformity within a reasonable time in compliance with Art., 39 CISG, since it only gave notice more than three months after delivery, although generally defects of shoes can be easily recognized.

The court awarded damages to the seller pursuant to Arts. 74 and 75 CISG finding that the contract had been avoided and the seller had resold the goods in a reasonable manner and within a reasonable time after avoidance. The seller recovered the difference between the contract price and the price in the substitute transaction, which was payable in the currency in which the purchase price should have been paid (German Marks).

The seller recovered further damages arising from the buyer's breach of contract, including legal fees and interest paid for loans (Arts. 74 and 78 CISG). Damages did not include sales commission as this loss would have occurred even if the buyer had complied with its contractual obligations, and therefore it was not a consequence of the breach.

Note: Risks in Using Articles 71 and 72

When there are indications that one party to a sale will breach in the future, Articles 71 and 72 require the aggrieved party to make very difficult judgements—*i.e.*, she must decide whether "it is clear that [the other side] will commit a fundamental breach" or whether it is "apparent that the other party will not perform a substantial part of his obligations." Such determinations are easy to second guess. What happens if a party erroneously decides that the statutory standards are met and wrongfully attempts either to avoid the contract under Article 72 or to suspend performance under Article 71?

In the materials in Part 1 of this chapter we suggested that an unjustified notice of avoidance, presumably including one sent pursuant to Article 72, might itself constitute a repudiation of the sender's executory obligations and permit the recipient to avoid the contract under Article 72. It is less clear that an unjustified notice of suspension of performance under Article 71 would be deemed a repudiation, but that is possible. Alternatively, and with a nod to symmetry, a wrongful notice of suspension might be treated as grounds for the recipient herself to suspend performance under Article 71 and await adequate assurances by the sender. If a party who has given an unjustified Article 71 or Article 72 notice fails to perform when performance is actually due, of course, there is a clear breach of contract.

Problem 76

Return to the facts of Problem 75. On June 20, Sawmill gave the Construction Authority notice that it was suspending performance under Article 71, and it demanded adequate assurances. Sawmill heard nothing further from the People's Republic by the end of July. The Sawmill representative consults you once again. She tells you that it is already too late for Sawmill to produce enough plywood in time to meet the deadline for the first shipment. Sawmill is desperate to resolve the situation. It cannot await further developments, but must solicit other business to replace the China contract if it hopes to avoid bankruptcy. What is your advice? If UCC Article 2 applied to the transaction, what would be your advice?

Questions

(1) Suppose the People's Republic had given adequate assurances of its willingness and ability to accept and pay for all the plywood ordered. The assurances were given on July 15 and Sawmill immediately resumed manufacturing the plywood in accordance with Article 71(3). Because Sawmill had suspended production for almost a month, however, several of its deliveries were late. Assuming its suspension was proper under Article 71, has Sawmill breached the contract? What provisions of the Convention support your analysis?

(2) Suppose Sawmill had shipped the first installment of plywood before the events that precipitated the political crisis occurred. The shipment, however, had not arrived when the World Bank announced that it was withdrawing its financing for the development project. Suppose further that the Construction Authority was not required to pay for the plywood until 60 days after delivery. Assuming the World Bank's announcement would permit Sawmill to suspend performance under Article 71, what (if anything) could Sawmill do about the shipment in transit? See Article 71(2). Would your answer change if the shipment was covered by a negotiable bill of lading that Sawmill had already transferred to the Construction Authority? Compare a seller's right to stop goods in transit under UCC 2–705(2)(d).

Chapter 5

RISK ALLOCATION

A. BASIC OBLIGATIONS: A SURVEY

Consider the situation where a contract for the sale of goods has been formed and performance is about to occur. The basic contract of sale, repeated millions of times each day, imposes fundamental mutual obligations on the buyer and seller who have, through their bargain, agreed to exchange goods for money or other consideration. Section 2–301 of the UCC sets forth the parties' central responsibilities: "The obligation of the seller is to transfer and deliver and that of the buyer is to accept and pay in accordance with the contract." This simple directive, however, explodes into numerous specific Code sections adumbrating the performance obligations of the parties and the allocation of risk when something goes wrong.

Problem 77

Douglas Astair III, a handsome spendthrift, alcoholic, womanizer and nihilist had a luncheon appointment with the brilliant, beautiful and virtuous Allison DuPre. Allison had clawed her way from poverty to great wealth. She recently acquired a controlling interest in Amalgamated, Inc., formerly owned by the Astair family. Douglas Astair II, a widower, died several years ago of a heart attack and left his entire estate to his son. Douglas III did not live at the family mansion, preferring a townhouse in the city to pursue his lifestyle. He was now employed by Amalgamated in an inferior position which he feared would soon be terminated.

Douglas began the luncheon conversation with Allison by pledging sobriety, thrift and a virtual monastic existence. Allison said, "Listen, Dougie,"—a nickname she knew he despised—"you are free to attempt reformation if you choose. I want your father's Jaguar." Douglas was surprised. "That old thing. Why would you want that?" Allison had to hold back a tear as she answered, "Ten years ago my father was severely injured while working in the main Amalgamated plant. Your father refused to use that Jaguar to take my dad to the hospital. Your father worried he might get blood stains on the interior. My father died."

Even Douglas was shaken by this narrative. He attempted sympathetic words. "I'll give the car to you," he said. "No you won't," answered Allison. "I will pay the reasonable market value, which I have determined to be $20,000. And you can keep your job on the condition that you do it well." Douglas was contrite: "Whatever you say, Allison." Allison was not finished. "One more thing. I realize you may find it difficult, but from now on when you address or even refer to me you shall call me 'Ms. DuPre.' I, of course, shall continue to call you, 'Dougie.'" Douglas, being in no position to disagree, responded, "Of course, Ms. DuPre. Shall we say Saturday, 10 a.m. at my family's mansion to complete le transaction Jaguar (which Douglas pronounced JAG—OO—AR because he had spent six months at Oxford before being dismissed)?" Allison signed the country club luncheon check, then wrote the aforementioned terms on a napkin and signed it before pushing it in front of Douglas. Douglas signed. Allison grabbed the napkin and left without another word.

(a) What are the obligations of the parties to this contract as set forth in the UCC? See 2–201, 2–301, 2–308, 2–310, 2–319, 2–503, 2–504, 2–507 and 2–511.

(b) Suppose neither Allison nor Douglas appeared at the mansion on Saturday morning. Who has breached the contract?

(c) Suppose both parties appeared at the mansion at 10 a.m. on Saturday. The Jaguar was parked, legally, on the road in front of the Douglas estate. Allison presented a check for $20,000 to Douglas. Douglas handed Allison the keys to the car along with the title certificate properly completed to show the transfer to Allison. At that precise moment they heard a terrible crash. Looking out the window they saw the Jaguar in flames. Another car that had smashed into the Jaguar sped off and cannot be located. Allison stopped payment on the check. What result? Consider 2–509. [The proposed amendment would change § 2–509(3) to read as follows: "In any case not within subsection (1) or (2), the risk of loss passes to the buyer on buyer's receipt of the goods." This change eliminates any distinction between merchant and non-merchant sellers.]

(d) Suppose that Douglas had offered the keys and the title certificate to Allison but, before she took them or delivered the check to Douglas, the crash and fire occurred. What result? See 2–503. Suppose that Douglas had offered the keys and the title certificate to Allison who said, "Before I give you the check I want to go outside and look at the car." At that moment, the crash and fire occurred. Consider 2–509(3), 2–513 and Comment 1 to 2–310.

(e) (i) Suppose that Douglas could not sell the Jaguar to Allison at the luncheon because he had already sold it to a used car dealer, Jake North. Allison agreed to purchase it from North (with a 90 day warranty against defects) for $20,000. North noted the transfer on the certificate of title and offered it as well as the keys to Allison who declined to accept them saying that she wanted to look at the car before delivering the check which she had drafted to North. As Allison approached within 25 feet of the Jaguar on North's lot, a passing truck with an uninsured driver careened out of control, entered the used car lot and struck the Jaguar that was destroyed in the resulting fire. What result? See 2–509(3). Also consider 2–613.

(ii) Assume the same facts except that Allison had accepted the keys and the certificate of title from North, but had not delivered the check to North before the car was destroyed. See 2–509(3).

(iii) Assume the same facts as (ii) except that North had not yet prepared the certificate of title and only handed the keys to Allison. Analyze.[1]

(f) Assume the facts of (e)(iii) except that Allison's casualty insurance policy with the American Insurance Company covered the full value of all her personal property. Can Allison look to American Insurance to recover the value of the car? See 2–501 and 2–401.

(g) Assume that Douglas had agreed to sell the Jaguar to North, who agreed to pay the purchase price to Douglas within ten days. Douglas delivered the car to North but retained the certificate of title to the car. North then sold the car to Allison who paid for it and took delivery. North did not pay Douglas, who now seeks to replevy the car from Allison. Analyze. See 2–509(3) and 2–403(2) and (3).

B. DELIVERY TERMS AND RISK OF LOSS UNDER PRE–AMENDMENT UCC ARTICLE 2: BASIC CONCEPTS

Problem 78

(a) The Magnus Corporation (M) in Ann Arbor, Michigan, contracted to purchase five laser printers from Laser, Inc. (L) of Milwaukee, Wisconsin for a total price of $25,000. The written sales agreement signed by both parties included the following terms: "F.O.B. Milwaukee, Wisconsin" and "payment due 30 days after delivery." L chose Consolidated Freight Lines, a reputable carrier, to deliver the printers, and the printers were loaded on a Consolidated truck at L's plant. As the truck pulled away from the loading dock an ambulance speeding to a nearby hospital swerved to avoid striking a pedestrian and headed for the truck. The Consolidated driver turned sharply and the truck overturned. The driver was not seriously injured but the printers were destroyed. What are the rights of the parties? See, in particular, pre-amendment 2–319 as well as 2–504, 2–509 & 2–709.

(b) Assume the facts of (a) except that the F.O.B. term in the contract was "F.O.B. Ann Arbor, Michigan." What result? Consider pre-amendment 2–319 as well as 2–503 and 2–509.

(c) Suppose there was no F.O.B. term in the contract. The contract simply stated the address of the buyer in Ann Arbor, Michigan. Analyze. See the comments to 2–503.

(d) Assume the original facts of (a) except that the laser printers were not destroyed. They suffered a few dents and scratches, but would still function properly. What are the rights of the parties? See 2–601 and 2–613.

---

1. Proposed amended Section 2–509(3) would eliminate the distinction between merchants and non-merchants. Under the amendment, where the case is not within 2–509(1) or (2), the risk of loss passes to buyer upon *receipt* of the goods regardless of whether the seller is a merchant.

Problem 79

Harris, Ltd. agreed to sell four sets of office furniture to Miller, Miller & Dane, architects. The contract, which was governed by the pre-amendment version of Article 2, contained an "F.O.B. shipment" term, and Harris chose a reasonable carrier, Martin Van Lines, to deliver the furniture. Harris employees placed the furniture on the loading dock to await the Martin truck. When the truck arrived the driver and his helper indicated they were ready to load the furniture, and the Harris shipping manager told them to do so. The Martin driver completed a bill of lading (see 1–201(b)(6) and (15)) and handed it the shipping manager. Before the furniture could be loaded, however, a freak fire (not the fault of Harris) destroyed everything on the loading dock. The next day Harris billed Miller, Miller & Dane for the purchase price of the furniture. The architectural firm refuses to pay. What result? Consider 2–709 as well as all other sections discussed to this point.

C. OTHER DELIVERY TERMS UNDER PRE–AMENDMENT UCC ARTICLE 2: F.O.B. VESSEL—F.A.S.—C.I.F.

Problem 80

Consolidated Beverages, Inc. (C) of Los Angeles agreed to sell certain used bottling equipment to Jack's, Inc. (J) for $20,000. J agreed to give C two weeks notice before sending a truck to pick up the equipment. The written contract, which was governed by pre-amendment UCC Article 2, included the term "F.O.B. purchaser's truck." After notifying C, J sent its truck for the equipment. The truck arrived safely at C's warehouse despite the riot occurring in that section of Los Angeles. The J truck pulled up to the loading dock where the bottling equipment was stacked. At that moment rioters attacked the warehouse and damaged the equipment. When order was restored the J driver refused to take the damaged machinery. C brings an action against J for the price of the equipment which, because of the damage, cannot be resold. What result? See pre-amendment 2–319 as well as 2–503, 2–509.

Problem 81

(a) A sales contract governed by pre-amendment UCC Article 2 contains a term specifying that delivery will be "F.A.S. SS Houston, Galveston Texas, U.S.A." What are the seller's obligations under such a term? When does the risk of loss pass to the buyer? See 2–319(2).

(b) GM Industries, located in New Jersey, contracted to sell certain equipment to Le Mer, Ltd, located in France. The parties agreed that pre-amendment UCC Article 2 rather than the CISG would control the transaction. Their written contract stated that "the equipment will be shipped to 13 Rue Madelaine, Paris, France," and it stated the price as "$80,000 (U.S.) C.I.F." The contract contained no F.O.B. or other such delivery term. GM arranged to ship the goods from the port of New York. When the goods were loaded on the ship, the shipper gave GM a bill of lading for the equipment. GM immediately sent the bill of lading to Le Mer. The equipment was destroyed when the ship carrying it caught fire en route to France. GM demands the $80,000 purchase price from Le Mer. What result? In addition to provisions previously studied, consider 2–320.

(c) Suppose the goods in (b) were on a loading dock in New York harbor, but had not yet been put on the ship. The shipper handed a bill of lading covering the shipment to a GM employee, who accepted it. Before the equipment could be loaded, however, lightning struck the dock causing a fire that destroyed the equipment. Analyze.

D. DELIVERY TERMS UNDER AMENDED UCC ARTICLE 2; INCOTERMS

Proposed Amendments to Article 2 would repeal the definition of shipping and delivery terms in 2–319—2–324 because those definitions are seen as out of date with modern commercial practice. While the amendments suggest no substitute, earlier drafts of revisions to Article 2 recommend that delivery terms be viewed in the light of trade usage, course of performance and course of dealing. **INCOTERMS**, produced by the International Chamber of Commerce and frequently used in international sales, were mentioned favorably.

INCOTERMS are a set of international rules for the interpretation of the most commonly used trade terms in foreign trade. INCOTERMS are designed to eliminate, or at least lessen, the uncertainties of different interpretations of such terms in different countries. First published in 1936, the most recent version is INCOTERMS 2000. While they are occasionally enacted as part of the domestic law (Spain and Iraq), they may be recognized as trade customs (e. g., France and Germany). They also may be specifically referenced in a given contract, as by a phrase stating that a delivery term is being used "as defined in INCOTERMS 2000." Consider the following INCOTERMS:

"Ex Works": Under this term, seller delivers the goods when it makes them available to buyer at seller's premises—factory, "works," warehouse, etc. The buyer bears all costs and risks involved in taking the goods from the seller's premises.

FCA (Free Carrier): seller delivers when it hands the goods over to the carrier at the named place or point. The term may be used for any mode of carriage (e. g., truck, ship, rail). Risk of loss passes from seller to buyer when goods are delivered to the carrier.

FAS (Free Alongside Ship): seller delivers when the goods are placed alongside the vessel at the named port of shipment. The term can only be used when the goods will be transported by boat or ship. Risk of loss passes from seller to buyer when the goods are placed alongside the vessel for loading.

FOB (Free on Board): seller delivers when the goods have passed over the ship's rail at the named port of shipment. FOB should be used only when the goods will be transported by boat or ship. FOB means that the risk of loss passes from seller to buyer when the goods pass over the ship's rail in the process of being loaded.

CFR (Cost and Freight): another term to be used for water transport, under "CFR" seller pays the costs and freight necessary to bring the good to the named port of destination. The risk of loss, however, continues to pass as under "FOB"—when the goods move over the ship's rail.

CIF (Cost, Insurance and Freight): again designed for water transport, this term imposes the same obligations and risk of loss consequences on the seller as "CFR" with the additional requirement that the seller must obtain marine insurance on the goods.

CPT (Carriage Paid To): the equivalent of "CFR" except designed for use with any kind of transport, under this term seller must pay the freight to the named destination and the risk of loss passes to the buyer when the goods have been delivered into the custody of the carrier.

CIP (Carriage and Insurance Paid To): the equivalent of "CIF" except designed for use with any kind of transport, it imposes the same obligations and risk of loss consequences on the seller as CPT with the additional requirement that the seller must obtain cargo insurance.

DAF (Delivered at Frontier): seller must make the goods available, cleared for export, at the named point and place at the frontier, but before the customs border of the adjoining country. Risk of loss does not pass to buyer until the goods are so delivered, so that risk while the goods are in transit to the frontier remains on seller.

DES (Delivered Ex Ship): seller must make the goods available on board the ship uncleared for import at the named port of destination. Risk of loss does not pass to the buyer until the goods are so delivered.

DEQ (Delivered Ex Quay—duty paid): seller's obligation is fulfilled when it makes the goods available to the buyer on the quay (wharf) at the named port of destination, cleared for importation. The seller must bear all risks and costs including taxes, duties and other charges for such delivery.

DDU (Delivered Duty Unpaid): the seller performs its obligation to deliver by making the goods available at the named place in the country of importation and bearing the costs and risks involved in that delivery but *excluding* taxes, duties and other official charges payable upon importation.

DDP (Delivered Duty Paid): same meaning as "DDU" except that the seller must bear the risks and costs of delivery *including* taxes, duties and other charges of delivery, and must clear the goods for importation.

ST. PAUL GUARDIAN INSURANCE COMPANY v. NEUROMED MEDICAL SYSTEMS & SUPPORT

United States District Court for the Southern District of New York, 2002.
2002 WL 465312.

STEIN, J. Plaintiffs St. Paul Guardian Insurance Company and Travelers Property Casualty Insurance Company have brought this action as subrogrees of Shared Imaging, Inc., to recover $285,000 they paid to Shared Imaging for damage to a mobile magnetic resonance imaging system ("MRI") purchased by Shared Imaging from defendant Neuromed Medical Systems & Support GmbH ("Neuromed"). [Neuromed moved to dismiss the complaint on the ground that it failed to state a claim.]

Shared Imaging, an American corporation, and Neuromed, a German corporation, entered into a contract of sale for a Siemens Harmony 1.0 Tesla mobile MRI. The MRI was loaded aboard the vessel "Atlantic Carrier" undamaged and in good working order. When it reached its destination of Calmut City, Illinois, it had been damaged and was in need of extensive repair, which led plaintiffs to conclude that the MRI had been damaged in transit. Both parties [had] engaged various entities to transport, insure and provide customs entry service for the MRI. Plaintiffs originally named those entities as defendants, but the action has been discontinued against them by agreement of the parties. Neuromed is the sole remaining defendant.

The one page contract of sale contains nine headings, including: "Product;" "Delivery Terms;" "Payment Terms;" "Disclaimer;" and "Applicable Law." Under "Product" the contract provides, the "system will be delivered cold and fully functional." Under "Delivery Terms" it provides, "CIF New York Seaport, the buyer will arrange and pay for customs clearance as well as transport to Calmut City."

Under "Payment Terms" it states, "By money transfer to one of our accounts, with following payment terms: US $93,000—down payment to secure the system; US $744,000—prior to shipping; US $93,000—upon acceptance by Siemens of the MRI system within 3 business days after arrival in Calmut City." In addition, under "Disclaimer" it states, "system including all accessories and options remain the property of Neuromed till complete payment has been received." Preceding this clause is a handwritten note, allegedly initialed by Raymond Stachowiak of Shared Imaging, stating, "Acceptance subject to Inspection."

Neuromed contends that because the delivery terms were "CIF New York Seaport," its contractual obligation, with regard to risk of loss or damage, ended when it delivered the MRI to the vessel at the port of shipment and therefore the action must be dismissed because plaintiffs have failed to state a claim for which relief can be granted. Plaintiffs respond that the generally accepted definition of the "CIF" term as defined in INCOTERMS 1990, is inapplicable. Moreover, plaintiffs suggest that other provisions of the contract are inconsistent with the "CIF" term because Neuromed, pursuant to the contract, retained title subsequent to delivery to the vessel at the port of shipment and thus, Neuromed manifestly retained the risk of loss.

The parties concede that pursuant to German law, the U.N. Convention on Contracts for the International Sale of Goods ("CISG") governs this transaction because (1) both the U.S. and Germany are Contracting States to that Convention, and (2) neither party chose, by express provision in the contract, to opt out of the application of the CISG. The CISG aims to bring uniformity to international business transactions, using simple, non-nation specific language. To that end, it is comprised of rules applicable to the conclusion of contracts of sale of international goods.

Germany has been a Contracting State since 1991, and the CISG is an integral part of German law. Where parties, as here, designate a choice of law clause in their contract—selecting the law of a Contracting State without expressly excluding application of the CISG—German courts uphold application of the Convention as the law of the designated Contracting state.

"CIF," which stands for "cost, insurance and freight," is a commercial trade term that is defined in INCOTERMS 1990, published by the International Chamber of Commerce ("ICC"). The aim of INCOTERMS, which stands for international commercial terms, is "to provide a set of international rules for the interpretation of the most commonly used trade terms in foreign trade." These "trade terms are used to allocate the costs of freight and insurance" in addition to designating the point in time when the risk of loss passes to the purchaser. INCOTERMS are incorporated into the CISG through Article 9(2) which provides that,

> The parties are considered, unless otherwise agreed, to have impliedly made applicable to their contract or its formation a usage of which the parties knew or ought to have known and which in international trade is widely known to, and regularly observed by, parties to contracts of the type involved in the particular trade concerned.

CISG, art. 9(2), reprinted in 15 U.S.C.A. App.

At the time the contract was entered into, INCOTERMS 1990 was applicable. INCOTERMS define "CIF" (named port of destination) to mean the seller delivers when the goods pass "the ship's rail in the port of shipment."The seller is responsible for paying the cost, freight and insurance coverage necessary to bring the goods to the named port of destination, but the risk of loss or damage to the goods passes from seller to buyer upon delivery to the port of shipment. Further, "CIF" requires the seller to obtain insurance only on minimum cover.

Plaintiffs' legal expert contends that INCOTERMS are inapplicable here because the contract fails to specifically incorporate them. Nonetheless, he cites and acknowledges that the German Supreme Court (Bundesgerichtshof [BGH])—the court of last resort in the Federal Republic of Germany for civil matters—concluded that a clause "fob" without specific reference to INCOTERMS was to be interpreted according to INCOTERMS "simply because the [INCOTERMS] include a clause 'fob'."

Conceding that commercial practice attains the force of law under section 346 of the German Commercial Code, plaintiffs' expert concludes that the opinion of the BGH "amounts to saying that the [INCOTERMS] definitions in Germany have the force of law as trade custom." As encapsulated by defendant's legal expert, "It is accepted under German law that in case a contract refers to CIF-delivery, the parties refer to the INCOTERMS rules...."

The use of the "CIF" term in the contract demonstrates that the parties "agreed to the detailed oriented [INCOTERMS] in order to enhance the Convention." Thus, pursuant to CISG art. 9(2), INCOTERMS definitions should be applied to the contract despite the lack of an explicit INCOTERMS reference in the contract.

Plaintiffs argue that Neuromed's explicit retention of title in the contract to the MRI machine modified the "CIF" term, such that Neuromed retained title and assumed the risk of loss. INCOTERMS, however, only address passage of risk, not transfer of title. Under the CISG, the passage of risk is likewise independent of the transfer of title. See CISG art. 67(1). Plaintiffs' legal expert mistakenly asserts that the moment of 'passing of risk' has not been defined in the CISG. Chapter IV of that Convention, entitled "Passing of Risk," explicitly defines the time at which risk passes from seller to buyer pursuant to Article 67(1),

> If the contract of sale involves carriage of the goods and seller is not bound to hand them over at a particular place, the risk passes to the buyer when the goods are handed over to the first carrier for transmission to the buyer in accordance with the contract of sale. If the seller is bound to hand the goods over to a carrier at a particular place, the risk does not pass to the buyer until the goods are handed over to the carrier at that place.

CISG, art 67(1), reprinted in 15 U.S.C.A. App.

Pursuant to the CISG, "the risk passes without taking into account who owns the goods. The passing of ownership is not regulated by the CISG according to art. 4(b)." Article 4(b) provides that the Convention is not concerned with "the effect which the contract may have on the property in the goods sold." CISG art. 4(b). Moreover, according to Article 67(1), the passage of risk and transfer of title need not occur at the same time, as the seller's retention of "documents controlling the disposition of the goods does not affect the passage of risk." CISG art. 67(1).

Had the CISG been silent, as plaintiffs' expert claimed, the Court would have been required to turn to German law as a "gap filler." There again, plaintiffs' assertions falter. German law also recognizes passage of risk and transfer of title as two independent legal acts. In fact, it is standard "practice under German law to agree that the transfer of title will only occur upon payment of the entire purchase price, well after the date of passing of risk and after receipt of the goods by the buyer." Support for this proposition of German law is cited by both experts. They each refer to section 447 of the German Civil Code, a provision dealing with long distance sales, providing in part—as translated by plaintiff's expert—that "the risk of loss passes to the buyer at the moment when the seller has handed the matter to the forwarder, the carrier or to the otherwise determined person or institution for the transport.

Accordingly, pursuant to INCOTERMS, the CISG, and specific German law, Neuromed's retention of title did not thereby implicate retention of the risk of loss or damage.

Plaintiffs next contend that even if the "CIF" term did not mandate that title and risk of loss pass together, the other terms in the contract are evidence that the parties' intention to supercede and replace the "CIF" term such that Neuromed retained title and the risk of loss. That is incorrect.

Citing the "Delivery Terms" clause in the contract, plaintiffs posit that had the parties intended to abide by the strictures of INCOTERMS there would have been no need to define the buyer's obligations to pay customs and arrange further transport. Plaintiffs' argument, however, is undermined by INCOTEERMS 1990, which provides that "it is normally desirable that customs clearance is arranged by the party domiciled in the country where such clearance should take place." The "CIF" term as defined by INCOTERMS only requires the seller to "clear the goods for export" and is silent as to which party bears the obligation to arrange for customs clearance. The parties are therefore left to negotiate these obligations. As such, a clause defining the terms of customs clearance neither alters nor affects the "CIF" clause in the contract.

2.   "PAYMENT TERMS"

Plaintiffs also cite to the "Payment Terms" clause of the contract, which specified that final payment was not to be made upon seller's delivery of the machine to the port of shipment, but rather, upon buyer's acceptance of the machine in Calumet City. These terms speak to the final disposition of the property, not to the risk for loss or damage. INCOTERMS do not mandate a payment structure, but rather simply establish that the buyer bears an obligation to "pay the price as provided in the contract of sale." Inclusion of the terms of payment in the contract does not modify the "CIF" clause.

3.   THE HANDWRITTEN NOTE

Finally, plaintiffs emphasize the handwritten note, "Acceptance upon inspection." Based upon its placement within the contract and express terms, the note must serve to qualify the final clauses of the

"Payment Terms," obliging buyer to effect final payment upon acceptance of the machine. As defendant's expert correctly depicts, "A reasonable recipient, acting in good faith, would understand that the buyer wanted to make sure that receipt of the GOOD should not be construed as the acceptance of the buyer that the GOOD is free of defects of design or workmanship and that the GOOD is performing as specified. This addition does not relate to the place of delivery." Accordingly, despite plaintiffs' arguments to the contrary, the handwritten note does not modify the "CIF" clause; it instead serves to qualify the terms of the transfer of title.

The terms of the contract do not modify the "CIF" clause in the contract such that the risk of loss remained with Neuromed. The fact remains that the CISG, INCOTERMS, and German law all distinguish between the passage of the risk of loss and the transfer of title. Thus, because (1) Neuromed's risk of loss of, or damage to, the MRI machine under the contract passed to Shared Imaging upon delivery of the machine to the carrier at the port of shipment and (2) it is undisputed that the MRI machine was delivered to the carrier undamaged and in good working order, Neuromed's motion to dismiss for failure to state a claim is hereby granted.

———————

Note

In **Skandia Ins. Co. v. Star Shipping, AS**, 173 F.Supp.2d 1228 (S.D.Ala.2001), the plaintiff (SCA) sought recovery of the value of reels of printing paper that it agreed to sell and deliver to World Color Press (WCP) in Dyersburg, Tennessee. The goods were damaged by a 1998 hurricane in Mobile, Alabama. The terms of the sale were "DDP," an INCOTERM for "Delivered Duty Paid," which means that title to the paper and risk for its loss or damage would not transfer to the buyer until the goods were put at the buyer's disposal at their destination–i.e., seller bears all risks of the goods during the whole transport. Thus the risk had not transferred from SCA to WCP when the paper was damaged because the goods had not been delivered to WCP in Dyersburg. For an illustration of the effect of the INCOTERM "Ex Works," see **Claudia v. Olivieri Footwear, Ltd.**, 1998 WL 164824 (S.D.N.Y.1998).

In **Paul Blum Co. v. Daewoo Int'l (America) Corp.**, 2001 WL 1537687 (S.D.N.Y.2001), the parties had agreed to the purchase and sale of cement "CFR" (cost and freight). Under the INCOTERMS definition of CFR, the seller must pay the costs and freight to transport the goods to the delivery port, but title and the risk of loss pass to the buyer when the cargo is loaded on board the vessel at the port for shipment. The court found the results under UCC 2–320 and its comments to be similar—title and risk of loss pass to the buyer upon delivery of the goods to a carrier if the seller has properly fulfilled its obligations. UCC 2–320, cmt. 1. Thus if the goods are damaged or lost during transport, the buyer is responsible for paying the price to the seller and must seek a remedy against the carrier or insurer.

JASON'S FOODS, INC. v. PETER ECKRICH & SONS, INC.

United Stated Court of Appeals for the Seventh Circuit, 1985.
774 F.2d 214.

POSNER, J. Section 2–509(2) of the Uniform Commercial Code as adopted in Illinois (whose law, the parties agree, governs the diversity suit) provides that where "goods are held by a bailee to be delivered without being moved, the risk of loss passes to the buyer ... (b) on acknowledgment by the bailee of the buyer's right to possession of the goods." Ill. Rev. Stat. ch. 26, [P] 2–509(2). We must decide whether acknowledgment to the seller complies with the statute. There are no reported cases on the question, either in Illinois or elsewhere. Three commentators have opined that acknowledgment must be to the buyer, but without discussion. The defendant submitted in the district court an affidavit from a professor of commercial law (Professor Clovis), who also concluded, also without elaboration, that acknowledgment must be to the buyer. The plaintiff did not question the admissibility of expert testimony on a pure issue of domestic law—though well it might have. An alternative procedure would have been for the district judge to invite a disinterested expert on commercial law to submit a brief as amicus curiae. See Code of Judicial Conduct for United States Judges, Canon 3 (A) (4) and commentary thereto.

On or about December 30, 1982, Jason's Foods contracted to sell 38,000 pounds of "St. Louis style" pork ribs to Peter Eckrich & Sons, delivery to be effected by a transfer of the ribs from Jason's account in an independent warehouse to Eckrich's account in the same warehouse—which is to say, without the ribs actually being moved. In its confirmation of the deal, Jason's notified Eckrich that the transfer in storage would be made between January 10 and January 14. On January 13 Jason's phoned the warehouse and requested that the ribs be transferred to Eckrich's account. A clerk at the warehouse noted the transfer on its books immediately but did not mail a warehouse receipt until January 17 or January 18, and it was not till Eckrich received the receipt on January 24 that it knew the transfer had taken place. But on January 17 the ribs had been destroyed by a fire at the warehouse. Jason's sued Eckrich for the price. If the risk of loss passed on January 13 when the ribs were transferred to Eckrich's account, or at least before the fire, Jason's is entitled to recover the contract price; otherwise not. The district judge ruled that the risk of loss did not pass by then and therefore granted summary judgment for Eckrich.

Jason's argues that when the warehouse transferred the ribs to Eckrich's account, Jason's lost all rights over the ribs, and it should not bear the risk of loss of goods it did not own or have any right to control. Eckrich owned them and Eckrich's insurance covered any ribs that it owned; Jason's had no insurance and anyway, Jason's argues, it could not insure what it no longer owned. (The warehouse would be liable for the fire damage only if negligent. Cf. Refrigeration Sales Co. v. Mitchell–Jackson, Inc., 770 F.2d 98 (7th Cir.1985).) Finally, Jason's points out that the draftsmen of the Uniform Commercial Code were careful and deliberate. Both Subsections (a) and (c) of section 2–509 (2)—the subsections that surround the "acknowledgment" provision at issue in this case—provide that the risk of loss passes to the buyer on or after "his receipt" of a document of title (negotiable in (a), nonnegotiable in (c)). If the draftsmen had meant that the acknowledgment of the buyer's right to possession of the goods—the acknowledgment that is subsection (b)'s substitute for a document of title—must be to the buyer, they would have said so.

Eckrich argues with great vigor that it cannot be made to bear the loss of goods that it does not know it owns. But that is not so outre a circumstance as it may sound. If you obtain property by inheritance, you are quite likely to own it before you know you own it. And Eckrich's position involves a comparable paradox: that Jason's continued to bear the risk of loss of goods that it knew it no longer owned. So the case cannot be decided by reference to what the parties knew or did not know; and neither can it be decided, despite Jason's urgings, on the basis of which party could have insured against the loss. Both could have. Jason's had sufficient interest in the ribs until then. You do not have to own goods to insure them; it is enough that you will suffer a loss if they are lost or damaged as, of course, Jason's would if the risk of loss remained on it after it parted with title. Section 2–509(2) separates title from risk of loss. Title to the ribs passed to Eckrich when the warehouse made the transfer on its books from Jason's' account to Eckrich's but the risk of loss did not pass until the transfer was "acknowledged."

Thus, as is usually the case, insurability cannot be used to guide the assignment of liability. (The costs of insurance might sometimes be usable for this purpose, as we shall see, but not in this case.) Since whoever will be liable for the loss can insure against it, the court must determine who is liable before knowing who can insure, rather than vice versa. If acknowledgment to the seller is enough to place the risk of loss on the buyer, then Eckrich should have bought insurance against any losses that occurred afterward. If acknowledgment to the buyer is necessary (we need not decide whether acknowledgment to a third party may ever suffice), Jason's should have bought insurance against any losses occurring until then.

The suggestion that the acknowledgment contemplated by subsection (b) can be to the seller seems very strange. What purpose would it serve? When Jason's called up the warehouse and directed that the transfer be made, it did not add: and by the way, acknowledge to me when you make the transfer. Jason's assumed, correctly, that the transfer was being made forthwith; and in fact there is no suggestion that the warehouse clerk ever "acknowledged" the transfer to Jason's. If the draftsmen of subsection (b) had meant the risk of loss to pass when the transfer was made, one would think they would have said so, and not complicated life by requiring "acknowledgment."

A related section of the Uniform Commercial Code, section 2–503 (4)(a), makes acknowledgment by the bailee (the warehouse here) a method of tendering goods that are sold without being physically moved; but, like section 2–509 (2)(b), it does not indicate to whom acknowledgment must be made. The official comments on this section, however, indicate that it was not intended to change the corresponding section of the Uniform Sales Act, section 43(3). See UCC comment 6 to § 2–503. And section 43 (3) had expressly required acknowledgment to the buyer. Rules on tender have, it is true, a different function from rules on risk of loss; they determine at what point the seller has completed the performance of his side of the bargain. He may have completed performance, but if the goods are still in transit the risk of loss does not shift until the buyer receives them, if the seller is a merchant. See UCC § 2–509 (3) and UCC comment 3 to section 2–509. In the case of warehouse transfers, however, the draftsmen apparently wanted risk of loss to conform to the rules for tender. For comment 4 to section 2–509 states that "where the agreement provides for delivery of the goods as between the buyer and seller without removal from the physical possession of a bailee, the provisions on manner of tender of delivery apply on the point of transfer of risk." And those provisions apparently require (in the case where no document of title passes) acknowledgment to the buyer. The acknowledgment need not, by the way, be in writing, so far as we are aware. Jason's could have instructed the warehouse to call Eckrich when the transfer was complete on the warehouse's books. That is why Jason's case is not utterly demolished by the fact that the document of title—that is, the warehouse receipt—was not received by Eckrich till after the fire. Acknowledgment in a less formal manner is authorized; indeed, section 509(2)(b) would have no function if the only authorized form of acknowledgment were by document of title, whether negotiable or non-negotiable.

The second sentence of comment 4 to section 509 is also suggestive: "Due delivery of a negotiable document of title covering the goods or acknowledgment by the bailee that he holds for the buyer completes the 'delivery' and passes the risk." The reference to a document of title is to subsections (a) and (c); and in both of those cases, of course, the tender involves notice to the buyer. It would be surprising if the alternative of acknowledgment did not.

All this may seem a rather dry textual analysis, remote from the purposes of the Uniform Commercial Code, so let us shift now to the plane of policy. The Code sought to create a set of standard contract terms that would reflect in the generality of cases the preferences of contracting parties at the time of contract. One such preference is for assignments of liability—or, what amounts to the same thing, assignments of the risk of loss—that create incentives to minimize the adverse consequences of untoward events such as (in this case) a warehouse fire. There are two ways of minimizing such consequences. One is to make them less painful by insuring against them. Insurance does not prevent a loss—it merely spreads it—but in doing so it reduces (for those who are risk averse) the disutility of the loss. So if one of the contracting parties can insure at lower costs than the other, this is an argument for placing the risk of loss on him, to give him an incentive to do so. But that as we have seen is not a factor in this case; either party could have insured (or have paid the warehouse to assume strict liability for loss or destruction of the goods, in which event the warehouse would have insured them), and so far as the record shows at equal cost.

The other method of minimizing the consequences of an unanticipated loss is through prevention of the loss. If one party is in a better position than the other to prevent it, this is a reason for placing the risk of loss on him, to give him an incentive to prevent it. It would be a reason for placing liability on a seller who still had possession of the goods, even though title had passed. But between the moment of transfer of title by Jason's and the moment of receipt of the warehouse receipt by Eckrich, neither party to the sale had effective control over the ribs. They were in a kind of limbo, until (to continue the Dantesque image) abruptly propelled into a hotter region. With Jason's having relinquished title and Eckrich not yet aware that it had acquired it, neither party had an effective power of control.

But this is not an argument for holding that the risk of loss shifted at the moment of transfer; it is just an argument for regarding the parties' positions as symmetrical from the standpoint of ability either to prevent or to shift losses. In such a case we have little to assist us besides the language of subsection (b) and its surrounding subsections and the UCC comments; but these materials do point pretty clearly to the conclusion that the risk of loss did not pass at the moment of transfer.

When did it pass? Does "acknowledgment" mean receipt, as in the surrounding subsections of 2–509(2), or mailing? Since the evidence was in conflict over whether the acknowledgment was mailed on January 17 (and at what hour), which was the day of the fire, or on January 18, this could be an important question—but in another case. Jason's waived it. The only theory it tendered to the district court, or briefed and argued in this court, was that the risk of loss passed either on January 13, when the transfer of title was made on the books of the warehouse, or at the latest on January 14, because Eckrich knew the ribs would be transferred at the warehouse sometime between January 10 and 14. We have discussed the immateriality of the passage of the title on January 13; we add that the alternative argument, that Eckrich knew by January 14, that it owned the ribs, exaggerates what Eckrich knew. By the close of business on January 14 Eckrich had a well-founded expectation that the ribs had been transferred to its account; but considering the many slips that are possible between cup and lips, we do not think that this expectation should fix the point at which the risk shifts. If you were told by an automobile dealer from whom you brought a car that the car would be delivered on January 14, you would not take out insurance effective that day, without waiting for the actual delivery.

Finally, Jason's argument from trade custom or usage is unavailing. The method of transfer that the parties used was indeed customary but there was no custom or usage on when the risk of loss passed to the buyer.

Affirmed.

Note

Proposed amended Sections 2–503(4)(a) and 2–509(2)(b) would make it clear that the bailee's acknowledgment must be made to the *buyer* in order for risk of loss to pass, in accordance with the holding and rationale in *Jason's Foods* case.

Problem 82

(a) Allen Family Foods, Inc. (Allen) delivered a large quantity of chicken backs to US Cold Storage, Inc. (Storage) in February of 1998. Subsequently, Albus Trading, Inc. (Albus) purchased the chicken backs from Allen. The chicken was delivered by Storage to Albus on May 14, and Albus shipped the chicken to a buyer in Romania on that date. Upon arrival in Romania, the chicken was discovered to be infected with salmonella, which required that it be destroyed. Albus brought an action against Allen to recover the purchase price of the chicken which Albus argued was infected with salmonella prior to its delivery to Albus. Allen produced documents from a USDA inspector that the chicken evidenced no salmonella contamination on May 14. It also produced an affidavit from its quality control officer that salmonella contamination is impossible when the chicken is stored below 44 degrees, Fahrenheit. Another affidavit from Storage stated that the chicken was frozen when received and thereafter stored at 0 degrees Fahrenheit. Allen moved for summary judgment. Analyze. See 2–509(2)(b).

(b) Bander, Inc. (B) contracted to purchase 100,000 gallons of antifreeze from the Zerone Corporation (Z). The contract authorized delivery by an independent carrier. Z chose Export Van Lines (E), a reliable trucking company. On Friday morning, an E truck was loaded with the antifreeze and had driven just a few blocks when the driver noticed a transmission problem. He carefully drove back to the Z plant and requested that the loaded truck remain at the plant until Monday, when it could be repaired. There was ample time under the contract for timely delivery despite the delay. Z agreed to allow the truck to remain in a secure area at its plant over the weekend. On Sunday an earthquake damaged the truck, causing the antifreeze to leak out. Can Z recover the price of the antifreeze from B?

Problem 83

(a) Just before she finished work on Friday afternoon, Danielle Simmons received notice that she had been promoted to executive vice president of the Mainline National Bank. Ecstatic about her new position (and salary), she visited the local Cadillac dealership on her way home. The sales manager, Biff Roberts, greeted Danielle and insisted that she test drive a new model that Cadillac was introducing. Danielle was impressed with the performance and quality of the car. After much haggling, Biff finally quoted a price that Danielle thought reasonable. While she leaned toward purchasing the car, she still worried whether the Cadillac was "right" for her. "Why don't you take it home for the weekend" Biff suggested. "If you decide not to buy it, you don't even have to drive it back. You're right around the corner and we'll send somebody to pick it up."

Danielle agreed and drove the car (with dealer's plates attached) to her home. Her friends and neighbors all admired the vehicle. At noon on Sunday, Biff telephoned Danielle. "I'm not pressuring you," he said, "but I wanted to know if you've come to a decision." Danielle replied, "I don't see how I can give this car up. It's wonderful. Do I have to bring it back before its mine?" Biff replied, "Don't worry about it. We'll get the paper work prepared and you can come in Monday to sign. Congratulations on becoming the owner of a new Cadillac."

On Sunday evening a drunken uninsured motorist "totaled" the Cadillac while it was parked in Danielle's driveway. Danielle had mistakenly assumed that her employer provided auto insurance for all personnel at the rank of vice-president and higher. The dealership's insurance policy covered all goods "owned" or "held for sale" by the dealer. What are the rights of the parties? In addition to 2–509, see 2–326 and 2–327.

(b) Suppose Danielle had decided to buy the Cadillac at the dealership on Friday. After the certificate of title had been completed naming her as owner, Danielle mentioned that she was about to go on vacation for two weeks. She asked if she could leave the car at the dealership until she returned. Biff agreed. A week later the car was destroyed without any fault by the dealership. Analyze. See Martin v. Melland's, Inc., 283 N.W.2d 76 (N.D.1979).

E.   BREACH OF CONTRACT AND RISK OF LOSS (2–510)

Problem 84

(a) Bromley Mills, Inc. (B) in Philadelphia, Pa., contracted to produce a special order of 1,000 yards of carpeting at $40 per yard for the new Nestle Hotel (N) in Philadelphia. B manufactured the carpet and shipped it to N. The manager of the hotel, Albert Simmons, inspected the shipment and concluded that the pattern of the finished carpeting did not match the description in the contract. He immediately sent B a fax explaining the problem and demanding that the carpet be taken back. That evening, a fire destroyed the hotel and the carpeting without the fault of N or its employees.

(i) Assume Simmons was correct that the carpet did not match the pattern specified in the contract. Must N pay for the carpet?

(ii) Assume Simmons was incorrect about the carpet pattern—i.e., the carpeting matched the contract specifications and was perfect in every way. What are the rights of the parties?

(iii) Suppose Simmons was correct that the carpet did not match the contract specifications, but the hotel burned before Simmons had a chance to notify B of the defect. What are the rights of the parties?

(b) Suppose B produced carpet that conformed precisely to the contract description. The carpet was packed into rolls and designated for shipment to the buyer N. Before it could be delivered, however, Albert Simmons (the manager of N) telephoned B and "cancelled" the order, explaining that the carpeting N had ordered would "just not go with our new decor." Later that same day, a flash flood of unprecedented proportions ruined the N carpet sitting in B's warehouse. What are the rights of the parties? Consider the following opinion.

MULTIPLASTICS, INC. v. ARCH INDUSTRIES, INC.

Supreme Court of Connecticut, 1974.
166 Conn. 280, 348 A.2d 618.

BOGDANSKI, J. The facts may be summarized as follows: The plaintiff, a manufacturer of plastic resin pellets, agreed with the defendant on June 30, 1971, to manufacture and deliver 40,000 pounds of brown polystyrene plastic pellets for nineteen cents a pound. The pellets were specially made for the defendant, which agreed to accept delivery at the rate of 1000 pounds per day after completion of production. The defendant's confirming order contained the notation "make and hold for release. Confirmation." The plaintiff produced the order of pellets within two weeks and requested release orders from the defendant. The defendant refused to issue the release orders, citing labor difficulties and its vacation schedule. On August 18, 1971, the plaintiff sent the defendant the following letter: "Against P. O. 0946, we produced 40,000 lbs. of brown high impact styrene, and you have issued no releases. You indicated to us that you would be using 1,000 lbs. of each per day. We have warehoused these products for more than forty days, as we agreed to do. However, we cannot warehouse these products indefinitely, and request that you send us shipping instructions. We have done everything we agreed to do." After August 18, 1971, the plaintiff made numerous telephone calls to the defendant to seek payment and delivery instructions. In response, beginning August 20, 1971, the defendant agreed to issue release orders but in fact never did.

On September 22, 1971, the plaintiff's plant, containing the pellets manufactured for the defendant, was destroyed by fire. The plaintiff's fire insurance did not cover the loss of the pellets.

The trial court concluded that the plaintiff made a valid tender of delivery by its letter of August 18, 1971, and by its subsequent requests for delivery instructions; that the defendant repudiated and breached the contract by refusing to accept delivery on August 20, 1971; that the period from August 20, 1971, to September 22, 1971, was not a commercially unreasonable time for the plaintiff to treat the risk of loss as resting on the defendant under General Statutes § 42a–2–510 (3); and that the plaintiff was entitled to recover the contract price plus interest.

General Statutes § 42a–2–510, entitled "Effect of breach on risk of loss," reads, in pertinent part, as follows: "(3) Where the buyer as to conforming goods already identified to the contract for sale repudiates or is otherwise in breach before risk of their loss has passed to him, the seller may to the extent of any deficiency in his effective insurance coverage treat the risk of loss as resting on the buyer for a commercially reasonable time."[1] The defendant contends that § 42a–2–510 is not applicable because its failure to issue delivery instructions did not constitute either a repudiation or a breach of the agreement. The defendant also argues that even if § 42a–2–510 were applicable, the period from August 20, 1971, to September 22, 1971, was not a commercially reasonable period of time within which to treat the risk of loss as resting on the buyer. The defendant does not claim that the destroyed pellets were not "conforming goods already identified to the contract for sale," as required by General Statutes § 42a–2–510 (3), nor does it protest the computation of damages.

The trial court's conclusion that the defendant was in breach is supported by its finding that the defendant agreed to accept delivery of the pellets at the rate of 1000 pounds per day after completion of production. The defendant argues that since the confirming order instructed the plaintiff to "make and hold for release," the contract did not specify an exact delivery date. This argument fails, however, because nothing in the finding suggests that the notation in the confirming order was part of the agreement between the parties. Since, as the trial court found, the plaintiff made a proper tender of delivery, beginning with its letter of August 18, 1971, the plaintiff was entitled to acceptance of the goods and to payment according to the contract.

The remaining question is whether, under General Statutes § 42a–2–510 (3), the period of time from August 20, 1971, the date of the breach, to September 22, 1971, the date of the fire, was a "commercially reasonable" period within which to treat the risk of loss as resting on the buyer. The trial court concluded that it was "not, on the facts in this case, a commercially unreasonable time," which we take to mean that it was a commercially reasonable period. The time limitation in § 42a–2–510 (3) is designed to enable the seller to obtain the additional requisite insurance coverage. Although the finding is not detailed, it supports the conclusion that August 20 to September 22 was a commercially reasonable period within which to place the risk of loss on the defendant. As already stated, the trial court found that the defendant repeatedly agreed to transmit delivery instructions and that the pellets were specially made to fill the defendant's order. Under those circumstances, it was reasonable for the plaintiff to believe that the goods would soon be taken off its hands and so to forgo procuring the needed insurance.

1. Risk of loss in the absence of breach passes, under the contract involved in this case, to the buyer upon his receipt of the goods if the seller is a merchant. General Statutes § 42a–2–509(3).

We consider it advisable to discuss one additional matter. The trial court concluded that "title" passed to the defendant, and the defendant attacks the conclusion on this appeal. The issue is immaterial to this case. General Statutes § 42a–2–401 states: "Each provision of this article with regard to the rights, obligations and remedies of the seller, the buyer, purchasers or other third parties applies irrespective of title to the goods except where the provision refers to such title." As one student of the Uniform Commercial Code has written: "The single most important innovation of Article 2 [of the Uniform Commercial Code] is its restatement of . . . [the parties'] responsibilities in terms of operative facts rather than legal conclusions; where pre-Code law looked to 'title' for the definition of rights and remedies, the Code looks to demonstrable realities such as custody, control and professional expertise. This shift in approach is central to the whole philosophy of Article 2. It means that disputes, as they arise, can focus, as does all of the modern law of contracts, upon actual provable circumstances, rather than upon a metaphysical concept of elastic and endlessly fluid dimensions." Peters, "Remedies for Breach of Contracts Relating to the Sale of Goods under the Uniform Commercial Code: A Roadmap for Article Two," 73 Yale L.J. 199, 201.

There is no error.

Note

The principal case involves a rare example of the application of 2–510(3). Consider the elements that must be met for that provision to apply: (a) identification of the goods to the contract (2–501); (b) repudiation; (c) deficiency in the seller's insurance coverage, and (d) a commercially reasonable time has not expired. As contrasted with the principal case, if a buyer notifies a seller that the buyer will not accept the goods, the "commercially reasonable" time to allow the seller to obtain insurance coverage will be relatively short.

Question

Why should risk of loss depend upon whether a party has effective insurance coverage? See comment 3 to 2–510.

Problem 84A

(a) The Kauffman Corporation (K) ordered 1000 model 365 telephones from Motorola (M). The model 365 is the only cellular phone on the market that can be used for intercontinental transmissions on a new network to be opened in the near future. Because of this feature, the 365's are much more expensive than other cell phones models. M delivered 1000 telephones and a K official, Margo White, inspected them. She concluded that the wrong model had been shipped because she saw nothing in the accompanying literature about the intercontinental feature. White immediately notified M that K rejected the telephones because they were the wrong model. M personnel checked the shipment and determined that the phones were the correct model. They attempted to convey this information to White or other K personnel, but the telephone lines to K's offices were not operating because of an electrical problem. Unknown to anyone at K or M, the shipment of model 365 telephones contained other defects. These defects, it is stipulated, could have been remedied immediately by an M representative located in the building next to K, where the phone lines were working. Before M succeeded in contacting anyone at K, the electrical problem that had disrupted telephone service to K caused a fire that destroyed the M telephones. M seeks the contract price of the telephones and K resists. Analyze. In addition to 2–510, see 2–605.

(b) The Phillips Corporation (P) contracted to purchase 5,000 tons of a specified type of steel from Steel, Ltd. (S). The steel was delivered and P inspected it using methods standard in the steel trade. The shipment appeared to conform to the contract and P informed S that the steel "is fine." Two days later, one of P's new young scientists subjected the steel to a new test which she had just created. The test revealed that the steel had a carbon content that did not conform to the contract description. The steel was otherwise a usable commercial grade, although it was not suitable for P's purposes. P immediately faxed S notice of the situation. Three hours later, an aircraft crashed into the P plant, destroying all the steel manufactured by S. What are the rights of the parties? Do you need further information?

F. RISK OF LOSS UNDER THE CISG (ARTICLES 66–70)

Problem 85

(a) The Bayer Corporation (B) in Germany agreed to ship 6000 units of a certain chemical to the Frank Corporation (F) in Gary, Indiana, USA. Bayer arranged for a German trucking company, Allgemein Träger (T), to deliver the goods to a Liberian vessel (the "Star of the Sea"), which would carry the chemical to New York where Excel Freight Lines (E) would pick them up for transport to F in Gary. What are the rights of the parties if the goods are destroyed without the fault of the carrier while in the possession of E? See CISG Article 67(1). What result if the casualty occurred while the goods were on board the "Star of the Sea?" While being transported by T?

(b) Same facts as a) except the contract provided that the goods would be delivered "DDP (delivered duty paid) as per INCOTERMS 2000." What result?

(c) Same facts as a) except that B shipped the goods on its own trucks and ship. The goods were destroyed in transit. Which provision of the CISG governs, and what is the result?

(d) Same facts as a) except that F used its own trucks and ship to pick up the goods from B in Germany and transport them to its storage facility in Gary. Which provision of the CISG governs, and what is the result?

(e) Suppose F contracted with B to purchase the chemical after B had already shipped the goods and while they were in transit on a Liberian freighter headed for New York. F's purchase covered 25% of the total amount of the chemical that B had in transit on the freighter. Thereafter, a leak in the freighter ruined the chemical shipment before the freighter reached New York. What result? What result if the leak ruined only half the chemical shipment on the freighter? What result if the leak occurred before F contracted to purchase the chemical, but neither B nor the carrier was aware of the problem at the time the contract with F was formed? Suppose it is not clear exactly when the leak and the damage occurred?

G. RISK OF LOSS UNDER UCC ARTICLE 2A

Problem 86

The Hilton Corporation (H) of Chicago, Illinois, wanted to acquire an isotope spectrometer for use in Hilton's advanced research facility. The spectrometer Hilton wanted was manufactured by the Darson Corporation (D) of Cambridge, Massachusetts. In order to finance the acquisition, H arranged for Milner Finance Co. (M) to purchase the equipment from D subject to H's approval of the sales contract. H then leased the equipment from M. Consider the rights of the parties under 2A–219 and 2A–220 in each of the following situations:

(a) Both the lease contract (between H and M) and the sales contract (between M and D) stated that the equipment would be delivered by independent carrier to H's research facility in Chicago, "FCA Cambridge, as per INCOTERMS 2000." The equipment was destroyed en route without fault of the carrier. Must H pay M for the destroyed equipment? Must M pay D the purchase price for the equipment?

(b) The contracts, which were governed by the pre-amendment versions of Articles 2 and 2A, provided for shipment "F.O.B. Chicago," and the equipment was destroyed en route without fault of the carrier. Must H pay M for the equipment? Must M pay D the purchase price?

(c) The equipment was destroyed en route without fault of the carrier. Neither contract contained any delivery term (i.e., no "FCA" or "F.O.B." term or the like) or any other provision relating to risk of loss. Must H pay M? Must M pay D?

(d) Assume the facts of (c) except H had leased the spectrometer directly from D rather than through M. Must H pay D for the destroyed equipment? Suppose the lease between H and D included the following: "Lessee will assume risk of loss for all leased equipment." What result?

(e) Return to the original three-party arrangement involving H, M and D, and assume the contracts included the term in (b) ("F.O.B. Chicago," as defined in pre-amendment Article 2). The equipment arrived safely but it did not conform to the lease agreement. Before H had a chance to inspect the equipment, however, it was destroyed in a fire at H's facility. The fire was not the fault of H. Given the F.O.B. term, is the time when risk of loss passes "not stated?"

(f) The equipment arrived safely and was put into use by H. After several weeks H discovered defects in the equipment that could not be discovered before that point. H notified M and D that it was "returning the spectrometer." Before it could be returned, however, it was destroyed in H's facility without the fault of H. What result? Do you need further information?

(g) Suppose the date for shipping the spectrometer had not yet arrived when H repudiated the lease. The equipment was then destroyed at D's plant without the fault of D. What result? Do you need further information? Would your answer change if H had leased the equipment directly from D and the lease said nothing about risk of loss?

Problem 86A

The Crane Corporation (C) provided cranes of various sizes under leases. Jarvis Corporation (J) required a 75 foot crane to remove a smoke stack from a building J had contracted to refurbish. C agreed to lease J a crane meeting its requirements. J planned to close an adjacent street when it removed the smoke stack, and C was informed that delays in delivering the crane would result in substantial difficulty and loss to J. The crane nevertheless did not arrive on the day specified in the lease. J telephoned C and was told that the crane C "had in mind" for J had been vandalized the evening before (without the fault of C), and no other suitable crane would be available for another two weeks. In fact, C had other 75 foot cranes that would have been adequate, but C did not want to lease them out because they were not covered by insurance. It took J another week to lease a 75 foot crane from a different supplier, and the delay cost J $20,000. J seeks to recover that amount from C, who defends by citing 2A–221. What result?

H. RISK OF LOSS UNDER UCITA

Note

UCITA Risk of Loss. "Computer information" is defined in Section 102(10) as "information in electronic form which is obtained from or through the use of a computer, or which is in a form capable of being processed by a computer. The term includes a copy of information and any documentation or packaging associated with the copy." Section 614 deals with risk of loss of a copy. A copy can be transferred in tangible form or electronic form. If the copy is electronic, the risk of loss passes to the licensee upon receipt. If the copy is tangible, the same rule applies unless the contract terms indicate that it is a "shipment" contract (under which the risk of loss passes to the licensee upon delivery to the carrier) or a "destination" contract (where the risk passes to the licensee upon tender of the copy at the particular destination).

I. IDENTIFICATION AND CASUALTY TO IDENTIFIED GOODS

Problem 87

(a) Bart and Tricia Adams went to their local Sears store to purchase a new refrigerator. They chose the Kenmore model 435, which Bart preferred because it had a device on the door to dispense cool water and either crushed or cubed ice. The model 435 was on sale for $1195.00. The salesperson noted that the "display model" which the couple had inspected was priced at only $1100.00. Delighted to save almost $100, the couple decided to buy the display model and they arranged for delivery in three days. That night, without the fault of Sears, a fire in the Sears store destroyed the display model. What are the rights of the parties? Consider, inter alia, 2–501, 2–509 & 2–613.

(b) Assume the facts of (a) except that Bart declared that he wanted a "new" refrigerator, not the floor model. Frowning, Tricia agreed. The salesperson dutifully completed an order slip for a model 435 to be shipped from the Sears warehouse in southern Louisiana, where Sears maintained its entire inventory of model 435's. Two days later, before the Adams' refrigerator had been shipped, all the refrigerators in the Louisiana warehouse were destroyed by hurricane Andrew. What are the rights of the parties? Is the contract avoided under 2–613?

(c) Assume the facts of (b) except that the hurricane did not destroy all the refrigerators at the Louisiana warehouse. A refrigerator with Adams' order slip stapled to the carton was sitting on the warehouse loading dock when the hurricane struck. That refrigerator and approximately 30 others on the loading dock were destroyed. The rest of Sears' inventory of approximately 1000 Model 435's was untouched. What result?

(d) The Heinz Company purchases tomatoes for its catsup and other products from growers all over the world. This year Heinz has contracted to purchase the entire tomato output of 457 individual farmers. It has also contracted with several tomato brokers for the remainder of its tomato requirements. Heinz does not know where the brokers procure their tomatoes. One hundred of the individual farmers notify Heinz that, because of adverse weather, their tomato crops are a total loss. Five of the brokers also notify Heinz that they have been unable to procure sufficient tomatoes to meet their contract obligations. The 100 individual farmers and the brokers all claim that their respective contracts are avoided under 2–613. What results? Also consider 2–501 and comment 9 to 2–615.

(e) The new Saturn automobile is the best selling car introduced by a United States manufacturer in many years. General Motors Saturn plants cannot make cars fast enough to satisfy the demand. Buyers must wait up to 12 weeks for delivery. George Archer and his son Tom each wanted a new Saturn but they would not wait 12 weeks. Barbara Sims owned Sims Motors, a Saturn dealership. Barbara was eager to please the Archers because they were on Barbara's bowling team. Sims informed the Archers that two Saturns were en route from South Carolina to her dealership on a truck owned by Car Carrier Freight, Inc. (CCFI). The cars were identical in features and color, and each sold for $11,000. The Archers signed contracts to purchase the two Saturns. After the contracts were signed, Sims and the Archers went bowling and had "some beer." Afterwards, Tom Archer drove the three bowlers back to the dealership to allow Sims to get her car. As they approached the dealership, Tom's foot slipped from the brake pedal. A truck swerved to avoid the bowlers' car, jackknifed and plummeted over a hillside. The truck happened to be the one transporting the Saturns, which were destroyed in the accident. The truck driver was miraculously uninjured. What are the rights of the parties?

J. COMMERCIAL IMPRACTICABILITY

As students of contract law will recall, doctrines defining an excuse for nonperformance of a contract include impossibility of performance and frustration of purpose as well as the concept of commercial impracticability. The early common law was inclined to enforce the literal terms of a contract in all circumstances, but courts began to recognize exceptions in obvious cases. The general rule required performance as promised with certain exceptions. The classic exceptions included the death or injury of the promisor, performance prevented by operation of law, and destruction of the subject matter of the contract without the fault of the promisor.[1]

The last of the listed exception was established in the classic nineteenth-century case, *Taylor v. Caldwell,* 3 B. & S. 826, 32 L.J., Q.B. 164 (1863), where performance of a contract to rent a music hall was excused when the hall was destroyed without the fault of the promisor. The court based its holding on

> . . . the principle that where, from the nature of the contract, it appears that the parties must from the beginning have known that it could not be fulfilled unless when the time for fulfillment of the contract arrived some particular specified thing continued to exist, so that, when entering into the contract, they must have contemplated such continuing existence as the foundation of what was to be done; there in the absence of any express or implied warranty that the thing shall exist, the contract is not to be construed as a positive contract, but as subject to an *implied condition* that the parties shall be excused in case, before breach, performance becomes impossible from the perishing of the thing without default of the contractor.

About 100 years later, the drafters of the UCC articulated a crisp, generalized restatement of the "principle" first enunciated in *Taylor v. Caldwell*. Section 2–615 excuses a seller's delay in delivery or nondelivery of goods "if performance as agreed has been made impracticable by the occurrence of a contingency the non-occurrence of which was a basic assumption on which the contract was made." The modern doctrine applies easily to the facts of *Taylor*. Certainly, it was a "basic assumption" that the music hall would continue to exist—i.e., it was assumed that its destruction would not occur. There was a "contingency"—the destruction of the music hall which the parties assumed would not occur but which unexpectedly did occur. The expectation of the music hall's continuing existence, which *Taylor* called the "foundation" of the contract, would be labeled a "basic assumption" in the terminology of 2–615. When that foundation or basic assumption turned out to be

---

1. For a modern statement of these exceptions, see RESTATEMENT (SECOND) OF CONTRACTS 36 §§ 261–263.

untrue, the *Taylor* court found an "implied condition" excusing the promisor. The UCC wisely rejects the "implied condition" notion,[2] stating simply that upon failure of a basic assumption the promisor is excused—provided the failure of the assumption rendered the promisor's performance extremely difficult ("impracticable").

In fact, the tests in 2–615 and *Taylor v. Caldwell* are at bottom almost indistinguishable, and the Code drafters knew it. As comment 3 to 2–615 states, "basic assumption" was designed as a "familiar" test, although the Code deliberately substituted "commercial impracticability" for the traditional "impossibility" and "frustration" standard "to call attention to the commercial character of the criterion chosen by this Article."[3]

Several "classic" cases in which courts have struggled with the UCC impracticability doctrine have arisen from events that disrupted global commerce on a fairly massive scale. A cluster of cases arose from the closure of the Suez Canal during unrest in the Middle East. In one, the closure had forced a ship carrying goods to Iran to re-route around the Cape of Good Hope, thereby substantially enlarging the distance and expense of the journey. In a famous opinion, Judge Skelly Wright refused to award the carrier extra compensation, finding that the original contract terms were not excused by the closure. *Transatlantic Financing Corp. v. United States,* 363 F.2d 312 (D.C.Cir.1966). Sudden, sharp increases in the price of oil and other fuels during the 1970's brought a new series of cases in which energy suppliers facing skyrocketing costs sought to be excused from long-term supply contracts.[4] In all these cases, the courts were eager to remind us of the admonition of comment 4 to 2–615: "Increased cost alone does not excuse performance unless the rise in cost is due to some unforeseen contingency which alters the essential nature of the performance." The comment's reference to the foreseeability concept ("unforeseen contingency") is crucial,[5] although it raises questions. In one sense, almost anything is foreseeable raising the question of whether the standard should be "unexpected" rather than "unforeseen."[6]

Even if an unexpected/unforeseen contingency has occurred, the consequences of the event will excuse performance only if they are severe enough to render performance "impracticable." Thus in *Westinghouse*

---

2. Courts tend to invoke a concept like "implied condition" in conclusory fashion, as a substitute for cogent analysis.

3. It is often suggested that the first pre-Code case establishing a general excuse for impracticability was Mineral Park Land Co. v. Howard, 172 Cal. 289, 156 P. 458 (1916), but even that opinion speaks in terms of a recognized exception to the usual rule requiring literal performance.

4. See, e.g., Iowa Elec. Light & Power Co. v. Atlas Corp., 467 F.Supp. 129 (N.D.Iowa 1978), rev'd on other grounds, 603 F.2d 1301 (8th Cir.1979).

5. See also comment 8 to 2–615: "Thus the exemptions of this section do not apply when the contingency in question is sufficiently foreshadowed at the time of contracting to be included among the business risks which are fairly to be regarded as part of the dickered terms, either consciously or as a matter of reasonable, commercial interpretation from the circumstances."

6. See the discussion of foreseeability in the *Transatlantic* case, 363 F.2d at 318–19.

Elec. Corp. Uranium Contracts Litigation, 517 F.Supp. 440 (E.D.Va. 1981), an energy supplier whose costs had risen markedly was denied excuse because it failed to prove that the contract as a whole was unprofitable. In *Missouri Pub. Serv. Co. v. Peabody Coal Co.*, 583 S.W.2d 721 (Mo.App.1979), the court refused relief in part because the contingency that caused the supplier's costs to soar (the oil embargo) also created an offsetting increase in the value of another asset—the supplier's coal reserves. Claims of impracticability also raise the issue of *causation*. Even if the promisor can establish a sufficiently unexpected event and a huge (greater than material) loss in performing the contract, the entire loss may not be attributable to the contingency. If the loss is attributable to the promisor's own actions, inactions or decisions, he should hardly be excused from performing on the ground that performance has become impracticable.[7]

Given the onerous requirements of 2–615 and its counterparts in general contract law, it is not remarkable that, except in rare cases of dubious precedential value,[8] promisors have been notoriously unsuccessful in their attempts to escape contract obligations by claiming impracticability. The excuse has typically been invoked when a long-term supply contract proves highly unfavorable to one of the parties. Courts are particularly loathe to permit the supplier to escape its obligations under such a contract because the whole point of the arrangement is to shield the parties from price fluctuations. Granting excuse because of an increase or decrease in the market price of the goods involved, even when changes are very large and reflect severe cost changes, could undermine the utility of contracts as risk allocation plans. On the other hand, if an unanticipated contingency fits into one of the traditional "exceptions" recognized at common law, courts are quite willing to excuse performance under 2–615. In short, the impracticability provision of Article 2 has caused surprisingly little change in judicial attitudes toward excusing performance based on events occurring after contract formation.[9]

SPECIALTY TIRES OF AMERICA, INC.
v. THE CIT GROUP, INC.

United States District Court for the Western District of Pennsylvania, 2000.
82 F.Supp. 2d 434.

D. BROOKS SMITH, DISTRICT JUDGE. In this case, Specialty Tires, Inc. ("Specialty") has sued the CIT Group/Equipment Financing, Inc.("CIT") for breach of contract arising out [of] CIT's failure to deliver eleven tire presses that it had previously contracted to sell to Specialty.

---

7. See *Iowa Elec. Light & Power Co. v. Atlas Corp.*, 467 F.Supp. 129 (N.D.Iowa 1978), rev'd on other grounds, 603 F.2d 1301 (8th Cir.1979).

8. See *Aluminum Co. of Amer. v. Essex Group, Inc.*, 499 F.Supp. 53 (W.D.Pa.1980).

9. For more on traditional excuse doctrine and the Code approach to such issues, see J. MURRAY, MURRAY ON CONTRACTS §§ 112–115 (4th ed. 2001).

CIT, in turn, has filed a third-party complaint against Condere Corporation arising out of the latter's alleged wrongful refusal to permit those presses to be removed from its factory. CIT has moved for full summary judgment on the ground that its performance was excused under the doctrine of impossibility or commercial impracticability.

In December 1993, CIT, a major equipment leasing company, entered into a sale/leaseback with Condere for eleven tire presses located at Condere's tire plant in Natchez, Mississippi, under which CIT purchased the presses from Condere and leased them back to it for a term of years. CIT retained title to the presses, as well as the right to possession in the event of a default by Condere. In May 1997, Condere ceased making the required lease payments and filed for Chapter 11 bankruptcy in the Southern District of Mississippi. In September 1997, Condere rejected the executory portion of the lease agreement, and the bankruptcy court lifted the automatic stay as to CIT's claim involving the presses.

CIT thus found itself, unexpectedly, with eleven tire presses it needed to sell. Maurice "Maury" Taylor, the CEO of Condere, stated his desire that the presses be removed quickly and advised CIT on how they might be sold. Later, CIT brought two potential buyers to Condere's Natchez plant, where representatives of Condere conducted them on a tour of the facility. Subsequently, Taylor and CIT negotiated concerning Condere's purchase of the presses, but negotiations fell through, after which Taylor again offered his assistance in locating another buyer.

CIT decided to advertise the presses. Specialty, a manufacturer of tires which sought to expand its plant in Tennessee, responded, and in early December 1997, representatives of Specialty, CIT and Condere met to conduct an on-site inspection of the equipment. Condere's representative discussed with CIT's personnel and in the presence of Specialty's agents the logistics concerning the removal of the presses. At that meeting, Condere's representative told CIT and Specialty that CIT had an immediate right to possession of the tire presses, and the right to sell them. At no time did any representative of Condere express any intent to oppose the removal of this equipment. The negotiations proved fruitful, and, in late December 1997, CIT and Specialty entered into a contract for the sale of the presses for $250,000. CIT warranted its title to and right to sell the presses.

When CIT attempted to gain access to the presses to have them rigged and shipped to Speciality, Condere refused to allow this equipment to be removed from the plant. This refusal was apparently because Condere had just tendered a check to CIT for $224,000, without the approval of the bankruptcy court, in an attempt to cure its default under the lease. This unexpected change in position was rejected by CIT, which promptly filed a complaint in replevin to obtain possession It became clear at that juncture that Specialty was not going to obtain its tire presses expeditiously.

CIT then advised Specialty that the presses were subject to the jurisdiction of the bankruptcy court and suggested that Specialty either withdraw its claim to the equipment and negotiate with CIT for a sum of liquidated damages or make a bid for the presses at any auction that might be held by that court. Specialty, as was its right, rejected both suggestions and affirmed the existing contract, demanding performance. To date, Condere has refused to surrender to CIT, and CIT has failed to deliver to Specialty, the tire presses.

Subsequent to the briefing of these motions, the replevin court has issued findings of fact and conclusions of law to the effect that Condere wrongfully retained possession of the presses and that CIT is entitled to remove them immediately. Although Condere may appeal this ruling, CIT has informed Specialty that it is still willing to deliver the presses as soon as it gains possession, and Specialty has indicated its interest in accepting them, in "partial" settlement of its claims.

In the overwhelming majority of circumstances, contractual promises are to be performed, not avoided: pacta sunt servanda, or, as the Seventh Circuit loosely translated it, "a deal's a deal." Waukesha Foundry, Inc. v. Industrial Eng'g, Inc., 91 F.3d 1002, 1010 (7th Cir.1996) (citation omitted); see generally John D. Calamari & Joseph M. Perillo, The Law of Contracts § 13.1, at 495 (4th ed. 1998). This is an eminently sound doctrine, because typically "a court cannot improve matters by intervention after the fact. It can only destabilize the institution of contract, increase risk, and make parties worse off.... Parties to contracts are entitled to seek, and retain, personal advantage; striving for that advantage is the source of much economic progress. Contract law does not require parties to be fair, or kind, or reasonable, or to share gains or losses equally." Industrial Representatives, Inc. v. CP Clare Corp., 74 F.3d 128, 131–32 (7th Cir.1996) (Easterbrook, J.). Promisors are free to assume risks, even huge ones, and promisees are entitled to rely on those voluntary assumptions. Calamari & Perillo, supra § 13.16, at 522.

Even so, courts have recognized, in an evolving line of cases from the common law down to the present, that there are limited instances in which unexpectedly and radically changed conditions render the judicial enforcement of certain promises of little or no utility. This has come to be know[n], for our purposes, as the doctrines of impossibility and impracticability.[1] Because of the unexpected nature of such occurrences, litigated cases usually involve, not interpretation of a contractual term, but the judicial filling of a lacuna in the parties agreement. See 2 E. Allan Farnsworth, Farnsworth on Contracts § 9.5, at 603 (2d ed. 1998); 1 James J. White & Robert S. Summers, Uniform Commercial Code § 3–10, at 169 (4th ed. 1995). Such "gap-filling," however, must be understood for what it is: a court-ordered, as opposed to bargained-for,

---

1. The reported cases on this topic, unfortunately, are not characterized by either consistency or clarity of expression. As one respected treatise puts it, "Students who have concluded a first year contracts course in confusion about the doctrine of impossibility and have since ... found that the cases somehow slip through their fingers when they try to apply them to new situations[] may take some comfort in knowing that they are in good company." 1 White & Summers, supra § 3–10, at 164.

allocation of risk between the parties. Albert M Greenfield & Co. v. Kolea, 475 Pa. 351, 380 A.2d 758, 760 (Pa. 1977); John E. Murray, Jr., Murray on Contracts § 112, at 635–36 (3d ed. 1990). As such, it must be applied sparingly. Dorn v. Stanhope Steel, Inc., 368 Pa. Super. 557, 534 A.2d 798, 812 (Pa.Super.Ct.1987).

Traditionally, there were three kinds of supervening events that would provide a legally cognizable excuse for failing to perform: death of the promisor (if the performance was personal), illegality of the performance, and destruction of the subject matter; beyond that the doctrine has grown to recognize that relief is most justified if unexpected events inflict a loss on one party and provide a windfall gain for the other or where the excuse would save one party from an unexpected loss while leaving the other party in a position no worse than it would have without the contract.[2] Thus, the Second Restatement of Contracts expresses the doctrine of impracticability this way:

> Where, after a contract is made, a party's performance is made impracticable without his fault by the occurrence of an event the non-occurrence of which was a basic assumption on which the contract was made, his duty to render that performance is discharged, unless the language or the circumstances indicate the contrary.

Restatement (Second) of Contracts § 261 (1981).

Article 2 of the U.C.C., which applies to the sale of goods presented by the case sub judice, puts it similarly:

> Delay in delivery or non-delivery in whole or in part by a seller ... is not a breach of his duty under a contract for sale if performance as agreed has been made impracticable by the occurrence of a contingency the non-occurrence of which was a basic assumption on which the contract was made....

U.C.C. § 2–615(1) (codified at 13 Pa. C.S. 2615(1)).

The principal inquiry in an impracticability analysis, then, is whether there was a contingency the non-occurrence of which was a basic assumption underlying the contract. It is often said that this question turns on whether the contingency was "foreseeable," 2 Farnsworth, supra § 9.6, at 616, on the rationale that if it was, the promisor could have sought to negotiate explicit contractual protection.[3] This, however, is an incomplete and sometimes misleading test. Anyone can foresee, in some general sense, a whole variety of potential calamities, but that does not mean that he or she will deem them worth bargaining over. See

---

2. The second of these two grounds is what economists deem a "Pareto-optimal" move; that is, an adjustment that makes some parties better off and none worse off than they were initially. For an economic analysis of the law of impossibility, see Hon. Richard A. Posner, Economic Analysis of Law § 4.5 (5th ed. 1998).

3. Indeed, this rationale can be traced down to the root of the impossibility doctrine at common law as expressed by Paradine v. Jane, Aleyn 26, 82 Eng. Rep. 897 [1647]. See Murray, supra § 112, at 634.

Calamari & Perillo, supra § 13.18, at 526; Murray, supra, § 112, at 641 ("If 'foreseeable' is equated with 'conceivable', nothing is unforeseeable."). The risk may be too remote, the party may not have sufficient bargaining power, or neither party may have any superior ability to avoid the harm. 2 Farnsworth, supra, § 9.6, at 617. As my late colleague Judge Teitelbaum recited two decades ago in a famous case of impracticability:

> Foreseeability or even recognition of a risk does not necessarily prove its allocation. Parties to a contract are not always able to provide for all the possibilities of which they are aware, sometimes because they cannot agree, often because they are too busy. Moreover, that some abnormal risk was contemplated is probative but does not necessarily establish an allocation of the risk of the contingency which actually occurs.

Aluminum Co. of Am. v. Essex Group, Inc., 499 F.Supp. 53, 76 (W.D.Pa. 1980) (applying Indiana law) (quoting Transatlantic Fin. Corp. v. United States, 124 U.S. App.D.C. 183, 363 F.2d 312 (D.C.Cir.1966) (Skelly Wright, J.)); accord Opera Co. v. Wolf Trap Found., 817 F.2d 1094, 1101 (4th Cir.1987) (also quoting Transatlantic).

So, while the risk of an unforeseeable event can safely be deemed not to have been assumed by the promisor, the converse is not necessarily true. See Restatement (Second) of Contracts § 261 cmt. c. Properly seen, then, foreseeability, while perhaps the most important factor,

> is at best one fact to be considered in resolving first how likely the occurrence of the event in question was and, second, whether its occurrence, based on past experience, was of such reasonable likelihood that the obligor should not merely foresee the risk but, because of the degree of its likelihood, the obligor should have guarded against it or provided for non-liability against the risk.

Wolf Trap, 817 F.2d at 1102–03 (quoted in Farnsworth, supra § 9.6, at 617–18).[4]

It is also commonly said that the standard of impossibility is objective rather than subjective—that the question is whether the thing can be done, not whether the promisor can do it. 2 Farnsworth, supra § 9.6, at 619. This too is more truism than test, although Pennsylvania courts have couched their decisions in this rhetoric. Indeed, the First Restatement took such an approach, see Calamari & Perillo, supra § 13.15, at 521, but the Second simply applies "the rationale ... that a party generally assumes the risk of his own inability to perform his duty." Craig Coal, 513 A.2d at 439 (quoting Restatement (Second) of Contracts § 261 cmt. e). This holds particularly when the duty is merely to pay money. It is therefore "preferable to say that such ["subjective"]

---

4. Another respected text defines the unforeseeable as "an event so unlikely to occur that reasonable parties see no need explicitly to allocate the risk of its occurrence, although the impact it might have would be of such magnitude that the parties would have negotiated over it, had the event been more likely. Calamari & Perillo, supra, § 13.18, at 526.

risks as these are generally considered to be sufficiently within the control of one party that they are assumed by that party." 2 Farnsworth, supra § 9.6, at 619–20. It is, of course, essential that the impossibility asserted by the promisor as a defense not have been caused by the promisor. Id. § 9.6, at 613–14; Dorn, 534 A.2d at 812; Craig, 513 A.2d at 440.

Generally speaking, while loss, destruction or a major price increase of fungible goods will not excuse the seller's duty to perform, the rule is different when the goods are unique, have been identified to the contract or are to be produced from a specific, agreed-upon source. In such a case, the nonexistence or unavailability of a specific thing will establish a defense of impracticability. Murray, supra, § 113, at 649. § 263 of the Second Restatement recites:

> If the existence of a specific thing is necessary for the performance of a duty, its failure to come into existence, destruction, or such deterioration as makes performance impracticable is an event the non-occurrence of which was a basic assumption on which the contract was made.

Moreover, the Supreme Court of Pennsylvania has interpreted this section's predecessor in the First Restatement to apply to, in addition to physical destruction and deterioration, interference by third parties with a specific chattel necessary to the carrying out of the agreement. Greenfield, 380 A.2d at 759 (quoting West v. Peoples First Nat'l Bank & Trust Co., 378 Pa. 275, 106 A.2d 427 (Pa. 1954)). [Here, the court cites and discusses other cases].

The situation presented here is in accord with these cases. CIT contracted to supply specific tire presses to Specialty. This was not a case of fungible goods; Specialty inspected, and bid for, certain identified, used presses located at the Natchez plant operated by Condere. All parties believed that CIT was the owner of the presses and was entitled to their immediate possession; Condere's representatives stated as much during the inspection visit. Neither Specialty nor CIT had any reason to believe that Condere would subsequently turn an about-face and assert a possessory interest in the presses. The most that can be said is that CIT had a course of dealings with Condere, but nowhere is it argued that there was any history of tortious or opportunistic conduct that would have alerted CIT that Condere would attempt to convert the presses to its own use.

Thus, whether analyzed traditionally in terms of foreseeability, as courts apply that term, or by the risk-exposure methodology outlined supra, it is clear that this is not the sort of risk that CIT should have expected to either bear or contract against. In economic terms, which I apply as a "check" rather than as substantive law, it cannot be said with any reliability that either Specialty or CIT was able to avoid the risk of what Condere did at a lower cost. It was "a bolt out of the blue" for both parties. On the other hand, Specialty was in a better position to know what consequences and damages would likely flow from nondelivery or delayed delivery of the presses. This suggests that Specialty is the appropriate party on which to impose the risk, See Posner, supra § 4.5, at 118; Calamari & Perillo, supra § 13.2, at 498. Moreover, judicial discharge of CIT's promise under these circumstances leaves Specialty in no worse a position than it would have occupied without the contract; either way, it would not have these presses, and it has only been able to locate and purchase three similar used presses on the open market since CIT's failure to deliver. On the other hand, CIT is relieved of the obligation to pay damages. Accordingly, excuse for impracticability would appear to be a Pareto-optimal move, note [2] supra, increasing CIT's welfare while not harming Specialty. This too is a valid policy reason for imposing the risk of loss on Specialty. See Calamari & Perillo, supra § 13.1, at 496. Thus, economic analysis confirms as sound policy the result suggested by the case law discussed supra.

Plaintiff makes much of the argument that there was no "basic assumption" created by Condere upon which Specialty and CIT based their contract, stating that it relied upon CIT's representations alone. This is specious. As a matter of both law and logic, a basic assumption of any contract for the sale of specific, identified goods is that they are, in fact, available for sale. Accordingly, I reject this contention and conclude that the actions of Condere in detaining the presses presents sufficient grounds on which to base an impracticability defense.

Plaintiff also argues that this is a case only of subjective impossibility, presumably because Condere—which has been holding the presses essentially hostage—could deliver them up to Specialty. Thus, plaintiff contends that only CIT is incapable of performing and therefore should not be excused. This proves too much; in theory, at least, any hold-out party can be brought to the table if the price is high enough, including the parties in the cases discussed supra. Certainly, if CIT offered Condere $3 million to surrender the presses, there is little doubt that they would comply, but the law of impracticability does not require such outlandish measures. This is simply not a case in which CIT became insolvent and could not perform, or in which the market price of tire presses spiked upward due to a shortage, making the contract unprofitable to CIT. While CIT did assume the risk of its own inability to perform, it did not assume the risk of Condere making it unable to perform by detaining the presses, any more than CIT assumed the risk that thieves would steal the presses from Condere before the latter could deliver them. In sum, this risk was not "sufficiently within the control of [CIT] that [it should be inferred that it was] assumed by that party." 2 Farnsworth, supra § 9.6, at 619–20. It was completely within the control of Condere.

Accordingly, I conclude on this record that CIT has made out its defense of impracticability. The ruling of the replevin court, however, indicates that CIT's performance is impracticable only in the temporary sense. Temporary impracticability only relieves the promisor of the obligation to perform as long as the impracticability lasts and for a reasonable time thereafter. Once it receives possession of the presses,

CIT asserts that it stands ready and willing to perform its contract with Specialty. That issue is not ripe for adjudication and must await a separate lawsuit if CIT should fail to perform after obtaining possession. Suffice it to say that, to the extent Specialty seeks damages for nondelivery of the presses to date, CIT is excused by the doctrine of impracticability and is entitled to full summary judgment.

Problem 88

The MR Corporation required an assured supply of antimony oxide which it had been purchasing from the same supplier for several years. A worldwide shortage of the product led MR's supplier to refuse to assure future supplies and MR sought such assurances elsewhere and found a broker, Hess, who promised to deliver 140,000 pounds to MR at $1.80 per pound. Delivery was delayed on successive occasions with Hess informing MR that the shipment was "on the water" coming from another country. Finally, Hess admitted that the shipment would not arrive because his Chinese source of supply failed. MR found the product elsewhere at $2.65 per pound and brought an action against Hess for the difference between the contract price and the "cover" price. Hess raised a 2–615 defense. Analyze. See, in particular, comment 5 to 2–615.

Note

Failure of Supply. Where a defendant claimed commercial impracticability as an excuse in a contract to supply school buses because its source of supply failed, a court found that where such a seller fails to make the contract expressly contingent on adequate supply, courts are reluctant to excuse the seller who could have insisted upon a clause excusing the seller if that identified source of supply failed. See *Alamance County Bd. Of Educ. v. Bobby Murray Chevrolet, Inc.*, 121 N.C.App. 222, 465 S.E.2d 306 (1996).

CLIFFSTAR CORPORATION v. RIVERBEND PRODUCTS, INC.

United States District Court for the Western District of New York, 1990.
750 F.Supp. 81.

CURTIN, J. Riverbend processes and sells tomato paste and frozen citrus products. It has processing plants in Visalia, California and Yuma, Arizona. On July 14, 1988, Cliffstar ordered 3.2 million pounds of tomato paste from Riverbend. In the same order, Cliffstar attempted to purchase an option on an additional 500,000 pounds of paste. Delivery of the paste was to be spread over the following year, until June 30, 1989. Riverbend accepted the order in writing on July 25, 1988. Riverbend's Director of Sales, rejected Cliffstar's requested option, however, writing: "at this time I am unable to give any options for any additional quantities due to the uncertainty of the incoming tonnage. I will keep you advised as the season progresses."

Between October and December 1987, Riverbend had forecast sales for the 1988 tomato crop of approximately 53 million pounds of tomato paste. In January and February of 1988, Riverbend's field department contracted with growers in Arizona and California to supply 170,000 tons of raw tomatoes. The field department also projected purchasing additional tons of raw tomatoes on the spot market. By combining firm contracts with spot buys, Riverbend planned to acquire sufficient numbers of raw tomatoes to support its sales forecast. Thereafter, Riverbend received oral and written orders for approximately 78 million pounds of tomato paste. It remains disputed, however, whether Riverbend accepted these orders, and thus entered into contracts to supply this amount.

About the time the Cliffstar–Riverbend contract was formed, and into the early fall, a shortage developed in the tomato crop in Arizona and California. Weather conditions in Arizona caused the crop, normally harvested over an eight to nine week stretch in June and July, to "bunch" (i.e., ripen at the same time), and thus last only five to six weeks from June 1 until mid-July. The California crop experienced similar bunching, causing an accelerated harvest concluding in late September. When the harvest is accelerated in this fashion, processors cannot process all of the crop as it becomes ready and growers are forced to plow under some of the crop, thus creating a shortage.

The combined 1988 Arizona and California tomato harvest was about 8.45% less than early season estimates. However, Riverbend's contract growers delivered only 95–100,000 tons of the 170,000 tons of tomatoes Riverbend had contracted for, or about 56–58%. Shortages developed in other parts of the country as well. Riverbend became aware of the Arizona shortage by August 1, 1988, and of the California shortage in September, 1988, when its processing plants had completed canning the shortened supply.

Based on the shortages it was experiencing, Riverbend failed to deliver the 3.2 million pounds of paste. Instead, Riverbend chose to allocate its available supply among its customers. Riverbend first notified Cliffstar by letter of September 27, 1988, that all contracts would have to be reevaluated.[1] Riverbend notified Cliffstar by letter of November 21, 1988, that Cliffstar would be allocated one million pounds of paste. Riverbend did not allocate to each of its customers an equal percentage of their orders.

Between November 21, 1988, and January 23, 1989, Riverbend and Cliffstar engaged in oral and written settlement-modification negotiations. The parties dispute whether Cliffstar agreed to an allocation, or

---

1. This letter, from Dale Seal at Riverbend to David Diodato at Cliffstar, said in part:

We have been forced to re-evaluate all contracts and shipping schedules due to the 1988 short-crop. We fully expected to fulfill all preseason and post-season contracts, but unfortunately our two plants produced only a percentage of our original field projections due to force majeure and other factors beyond our control. We will do our very best to provide you with updated information concerning the tomato paste situation and the disposition of the remaining product.

otherwise modified the initial contract with Riverbend. In any event, Riverbend delivered substantially less than one million pounds of paste to Cliffstar. Cliffstar demanded its full contract amount and this lawsuit ensued.

Plaintiff Cliffstar has moved for summary judgment. In order to prevail on its motion, Cliffstar must show "that there is no genuine issue as to any material fact and that [it] is entitled to a judgment as a matter of law." Fed. R. Civ. P. 56(c).

Plaintiff bases its cause of action on the fact that (1) it ordered 3.2 million pounds of tomato paste on July 14, 1988 for delivery over the next year, (2) this order was accepted by defendant on July 25, 1988, and (3) the tomato paste was not forthcoming. Riverbend defends under N.Y.U.C.C. Law § 2–615. [Here the court quotes UCC 2–615.]

Summary judgment largely hinges on whether defendant has complied with this section.

To prevail under this defense, Riverbend must establish that: "(1) a contingency has occurred; (2) the contingency has made performance impracticable; and (3) the nonoccurrence of that contingency was a basic assumption upon which the contract was made." Waldinger Corp. v. CRS Group Eng'rs, Inc., 775 F.2d 781, 786 (7th Cir.1985). In addition, Riverbend must show that its allocation to Cliffstar was "fair and reasonable," N.Y.U.C.C. § 2–615 (b), and that it "seasonably" notified Cliffstar of its need to allocate and the amount Cliffstar was to receive under this allocation. N.Y.U.C.C. § 2–615 (c). Riverbend also has the burden of proof on each element of this defense.

Under § 2–615, the first question is whether the 1988 tomato crop shortage was "a contingency the non-occurrence of which was a basic assumption on which the contract was made." N.Y.U.C.C. § 2–615 (a). This question, in turn, hinges on whether the crop shortage was foreseeable at the time the contract was made. "If a contingency is foreseeable, it and its consequences are taken outside the scope of U.C.C. § 2–615, because the party disadvantaged by fruition of the contingency might have protected himself in his contract." Eastern Air Lines, 415 F.Supp. at 441. However, non-foreseeability is not an absolute requirement. "After all, as Williston has said, practically any occurrence can be foreseen but whether the foreseeability is sufficient to render unacceptable the defense of impossibility is 'one of degree'...." Opera Co. of Boston v. Wolf Trap Foundation for the Performing Arts, 817 F.2d 1094, 1101–02 (4th Cir.1987).

Plaintiff argues that Mr. Seal at Riverbend was aware of the bunching of the 1988 Arizona tomato crop as early as June 1, 1988, or in any event no later than mid-July when it had been fully harvested. Plaintiff further argues that Mr. Seal knew of the shortfall in the California crop at the end of July, 1988. Plaintiff also points out that, in his letter accepting Cliffstar's 3.2 million pound order, Mr. Seal advised Cliffstar that "the uncertainty of the incoming crop" prevented him from giving Cliffstar an option for additional tomato paste. Thus, plaintiff claims, Riverbend could have foreseen the crop shortage by July 25, 1988, when it confirmed Cliffstar's order. Riverbend's failure to protect itself against this contingency bars application of § 2–615, plaintiff concludes.

Defendant admits that on July 25, 1988, the Arizona harvest had just concluded, but argues Mr. Seal was not aware that Riverbend's Arizona processing plant had processed only 50% of its expected tonnage until August 1, 1988. Riverbend also notes that the much larger California harvest did not conclude until mid-to-late September. Until that time, Riverbend remained hopeful that the California harvest would make up the shortfall caused by the bunching in the Arizona crop. Indeed, the Food Institute Report ("FIR") had increased its estimate of California production from 6.9 million tons on March 26, 1988 to 7.1 million tons by July 16, 1988, and held to this production estimate as late as September 10, 1988. It was not until its issue of September 17, 1988, that the FIR noted that "[h]ot temperatures in California have reduced crop prospects in that state." Id.

Under these facts, the court finds that there is a genuine issue of material fact as to whether the crop shortage was foreseeable at the time the contract was made.

Plaintiff's second argument is that Riverbend's failure to deliver the tomato paste was not caused by the 1988 crop shortfall but by oversale of its contracted-for supply. "To successfully assert the affirmative defense of commercial impracticability, the party must show that the unforeseen event upon which excuse is predicated is due to factors beyond the party's control." Roth Steel Products v. Sharon Steel Corp., 705 F.2d 134, 149–50 (6th Cir.1983). Defendant may not have caused the event that prevents performance. In Roth Steel, the court barred an impracticability defense where the "record indicated that Sharon continued to accept an unprecedented amount of purchase orders during the first half of 1973 even though it knew that raw materials were in short supply." Roth Steel, 705 F.2d at 150.

Both parties agree that by early 1988, Riverbend had projected sales of approximately 53 million pounds of tomato paste. Riverbend then contracted with local growers in Arizona and California to receive 170,000 tons of raw tomatoes. Riverbend also planned to purchase an additional 30,000 tons of raw tomatoes on the spot market. Thereafter, Riverbend received orders for approximately 78 million pounds of paste. These facts are not disputed.

The dispute between the parties centers on the validity of Mr. Seal's assertion in his May 31, 1990 affidavit that "although I received orders for approximately 78 million pounds of tomato paste, I did not enter into contracts to sell that amount." Defendant devotes five pages of its brief arguing that this assertion does not contradict Mr. Seal's deposition testimony.[2] Defendant argues first that [a certain exhibit contains] only

2. Mr. Seal, in his deposition of September 21, 1989, stated:

a list of purchase orders, not contracts, for 1988 tomato paste received by Riverbend. Defendant further argues that Mr. Seal, a layperson, meant "orders" when he said "contract" during his deposition testimony. "Further, many of the orders were standing orders from year to year pursuant to which various buyers requested Riverbend to ship as much tomato product as possible up to a certain maximum quantity, and then during the year that figure [would be] adjusted by both parties depending upon price and availability of product."

Plaintiff argues that Mr. Seal's testimony, and the purchase orders speak for themselves. Plaintiff further argues that Mr. Seal should not be able to raise an issue of fact merely by contradicting his prior testimony.

After thorough examination, the court concludes that Mr. Seal's testimony and the attached documents are not without some ambiguity. Moreover, the question to be decided is whether Riverbend's shortages were the result of factors outside its control. It must be noted that Riverbend was only able to deliver 41,924,097 pounds of 1988 tomato paste through May 1, 1989. Yet Riverbend had contracted to receive a quantity of raw tomatoes sufficient to process approximately 53 million pounds of paste. And it must be taken as true for purposes of this motion that the farmers Riverbend had contracted with were able to provide only 56–58% of this raw tomato supply. These facts thus raise a material issue of fact whether the tomato crop shortage forced Riverbend to allocate its available supply of tomato paste under § 2–615.

[Plaintiff argues] that Riverbend has failed under § 2–615(b) to make a "fair and reasonable" allocation of the shortfall. Plaintiff admits that in making its allocation Riverbend considered such factors as customer loyalty, past performance, needs, the relationship between Riverbend and the customer, and Riverbend's projections of potential future sales to the customer. Plaintiff argues, however, that Riverbend did not treat it equally. Riverbend does not contest this. Riverbend argues instead that § 2–615 does not require equal allocation. See N.Y.U.C.C. § 2–615 comment 11 (1964) ("this section seeks to leave

Mr. Seal: The discrepancy between the 78,300,000 pounds, and our forecasted tonnage of 53 million pounds was the difference between spot-buy tonnage, which we felt was going to be available, finished product which we could purchase from other processors, such as Ragu, Del-Monte, which was purchased in the past, as well as imports which we planned on purchasing.

Mr. Bloomberg: All right. You told me that your sales forecast was to sell 53 million pounds of paste?

Mr. Seal: Correct.

Mr. Bloomberg: And yet you took orders to sell 78 million pounds of paste?

Mr. Seal: Yes.

Mr. Bloomberg: And is it your testimony then that you thought Riverbend would be able to buy finished products, imports and spot-buys sufficient to make up the 25 million—

Mr. Seal: Yes.

Mr. Bloomberg:—pounds of paste difference?

Mr. Seal: Yes.

Mr. Bloomberg: Certain documents are attached as tab 46. Are those all of the written documents relating to purchase orders for product out of the '88 tomato crop?

Mr. Seal: Yes. I might rephrase. These are what we had contract for sale.

every reasonable business leeway to the seller"). See also Intermar, Inc. v. Atlantic Richfield Co., 364 F.Supp. 82, 99 (E.D.Pa.1973) ("The fact that plaintiff, under the allocation formula, receives less than its marketing needs is the result of its lack of sales history in 1972 rather than the result of any arbitrary and discriminatory conduct by the defendant....."); J. White & R. Summers, Uniform Commercial Code § 3–9 (1988).[3]

The court finds that the question whether Riverbend's allocation to Cliffstar was "fair and reasonable" is one of fact to be decided by the jury.

Finally, plaintiff argues that Riverbend failed to "seasonably" notify it of its allocation amount. N.Y.U.C.C. § 2–615 (c). Riverbend sent a letter on September 27, 1988 informing Cliffstar they were being forced by the crop shortage to reevaluate all contracts. Riverbend did not, however, inform Cliffstar of its allocation quota at that time. This did not take place formally by letter until November 21, 1988.

Although plaintiff is correct that § 2–615 (c) requires notification not only of the facts of delay or non-delivery but also, where allocation is contemplated, of the estimated quota that will be delivered to buyer, as a practical matter, a seller may not be able to provide this notice instantaneously. As one hornbook notes:

> In any given case, however, it may be difficult to know whether the excusing contingency will merely cause a delay in delivery or absolutely preclude it. In that circumstance the seller faces a problem as to what kind of notice he must give and whether and when he should begin a plan of allocation. The seller should be protected if he gives seasonable notice of the delay and indicates in good faith that he is uncertain as to whether the delay will ripen into nondelivery and that he will keep the buyer informed of developments as they unfold. Of course, the seller must, thereafter, make good on his promise to keep the buyer informed, and as soon as the seller knows that nondelivery will occur he must notify the buyer of this fact.

3 W. Hawkland, Uniform Commercial Code Series § 2–615:13.

3. Professors White and Summers offer a lengthy note about the factors that may be properly considered in a fair allocation:

> One should note that a direction to allocate pro rata is far from an explicit and rigid set of allocation rules. Seller may choose to prorate based upon historic deliveries, historic contract amounts, current needs, current contract amounts and possibly other contract grounds. By choosing one or another scheme to establish his proration, the seller may be able to favor one set of customers over another to a considerable extent. Moreover if we allow further deviations in the pro rata scheme based upon appropriate priority rules either because of the social utility of certain uses or because of the more serious injuries that some buyers would suffer if they did not receive more than a pro rata share, we leave the seller with a great deal of flexibility. We believe that the seller should have considerable flexibility and that courts will not often improve things by putting their own oar in. The seller's selfish long-term interest in maintaining a cadre of customers will usually sufficiently induce him to treat his customers as he should.

UNIFORM COMMERCIAL CODE § 3–9, at 182.

In this case, Mr. Seal at Riverbend was not fully aware of the extent of the tomato crop shortage until mid-to-late September. A short time later, Mr. Seal informed Cliffstar that it would have difficulty filling the order completely. Thereafter, Riverbend was in regular contact with Cliffstar discussing the tomato paste contract. Although its final, formal notification of the amount Cliffstar would be allocated did not come until November 21, 1988, the court does not agree with plaintiff that, as a matter of law, this notice was unseasonable.

[T]he motion for summary judgment on behalf of Cliffstar is denied.

Force Majeure Clauses—Contracting For Excusable Non–Performance. Section 2–615 begins, "Except so far as a seller may have assumed a greater obligation. . . ." Thus a party may agree to assume greater risks than those allocated under 2–615, but such an assumption would be unusual. It is not, however, unusual for parties to include a "force majeure" clause to describe events beyond the control of the parties that make performance impossible or impracticable, i. e., instead of relying on 2–615 or a comparable common law impracticability concept, the parties may attempt to reallocate risks according to their express intention. Section 2–615, therefore, constitutes a "default" term that will govern in the absence of the parties own reallocation of risks. Events such as war, riots, natural disasters such as floods, hurricanes or other "Acts of God" are invariably included in force majeure clauses. Terrorists attacks have become staples in recent drafts. The clause typically includes other events such as labor strikes and any other event beyond the control of the parties.

Problem 89

In a contract governed by UCC Article 2, Chromatic, Ltd. (C) agreed to sell 10 tons of a certain mineral to Edwards Industries (E). The written contract signed by both parties contained the following *force majeure* clause:

> The parties hereby agree that performance by the seller hereunder is subject to acts and events beyond the control of the seller, including but not limited to Acts of God such as floods, tornados, hurricanes and other natural disasters, as well as wars, embargoes, acts of government whether pursuant to statute, regulation or executive authority, and riots, terrorist attacks, or other civil disturbances which cause delay or impracticability in delivery of the goods described herein. Seller shall not be liable for any failure to meet its obligations hereunder that result from such causes. By this agreement, the parties do not intend to restrict the scope of commercial impracticability permitted by the Uniform Commercial Code. Buyer also agrees that, in the event of delay in delivery caused by any such event as described herein, expressly or by implication, buyer will stand ready to take delivery whenever seller is no longer excused from delivery by such circumstances.

After the contract was formed, C notified E that it could not deliver the mineral because of certain new export restrictions imposed by a foreign government. E believed that C could ship at least half the quantity specified in the contract. E therefore demanded that C make a 50% shipment by the original delivery date, which was within 30 days of E's demand. C ignored E's demand and failed to deliver any of the mineral by the delivery date. E arranged for a "cover" purchase of 10 tons from a substitute supplier, Zex Corporation (Z). Seven months later, C notified E that the export restrictions had been eased and, pursuant to the terms of their contract, C would now ship all 10 tons of the mineral.

(a) Assume that E was correct in assuming that C could have shipped 50 percent of the chemicals on time. What result?

(b) Assume that E was incorrect in its assumption—i.e., C could not have shipped any amount on time, although seven months later it was capable of shipping the entire amount. What result? In addition to 2–615, see 2–616.

Note

By its literal terms, 2–615 provides an excuse only to sellers. The impracticability section of the Restatement (Second) of Contracts, § 261, however, refers simply to a "party." Notwithstanding the literal language of UCC 2–615, several courts have concluded that the principles of 2–615 apply to buyers as well as sellers. See, e.g., Lawrance v. Elmore Bean Warehouse, 108 Idaho 892, 702 P.2d 930 (1985). Proposed amended Section 2–615 would replicate its predecessor with only minor language changes.

Courts require that "force majeure" events be beyond the control of the party seeking to be excused and be "unforeseeable." May parties contract to allocate foreseeable risks that may be within the control of the excused party? Consider the following case.

PERLMAN v. PIONEER LIMITED PARTNERSHIP

United States Court of Appeals for the Fifth Circuit, 1990.
918 F.2d 1244.

Per Curiam. William Perlman (Perlman) filed this diversity suit for a declaratory judgment against Pioneer Limited Partnership (Pioneer) and Kendrick Cattle Company (Kendrick) seeking to have an oil and gas lease and a surface lease declared unenforceable due to an alleged occurrence of a force majeure. He claimed that his performance of the contract had been hindered by state regulations in Wyoming and Montana. Pioneer entered into an Oil and Gas Lease (the Lease) with Perlman to "explore, drill, prospect and operate" for oil and gas on acreage located in Montana and Wyoming. In return for these rights, Perlman agreed to (1) pay Pioneer $137,676.65 in initial rent, and (2) spend $1,500,000 in exploring and developing the acreage or, alternatively, to pay Pioneer the difference between $1,500,000 and the amount he spent. Perlman also obtained from Kendrick the right of access to and use of land in Wyoming and Montana overlying and adjoining Pioneer's acreage (the Surface Agreement) and in exchange, agreed to pay Kendrick $60,000. Incorporated into the Lease was a "force majeure" clause which states in pertinent part:

> 14. FORCE MAJEURE ... This lease shall not be terminated ... nor Lessee held liable in damages ... if compliance [with covenants in lease] ... is prevented or hindered by an act of God, of the public enemy, adverse field, weather or market conditions, labor disputes, inability to obtain materials in the open market or transportation thereof, *inability to obtain governmental permits or approvals necessary or convenient to Lessor's operations* ... such circumstances of events being hereafter referred to as "force majeure".... Lessee shall notify Lessor in writing ... within fifteen (15) days of any force majeure which prevents or hinders any compliance, activity or event hereunder.... Lessee shall use all reasonable efforts to remove such force majeure ...

Perlman concluded unilaterally that the actions of the Wyoming regulators hindered his performance under the contract. He also unilaterally concluded that because Montana regulated its water similarly or more stringently than Wyoming, he would also be hindered there. On the basis of such unilateral decisions, Perlman invoked the force majeure clause taking the position that he was no longer bound to perform under the Lease or the Surface Agreement. He notified Pioneer and Kendrick in December 1987 of the purported occurrence of the force majeure and filed this suit for declaratory judgment in April 1988.

At trial, the district court held that under the doctrine of force majeure Perlman's performance was not excused because the event complained of was within Perlman's control and was entirely foreseeable. The court also determined that Perlman could have performed because performance had not been rendered impossible or untenable. The district court rested its holding on the general principle that "a force majeure clause is to relieve [a] lessee from harsh termination due to circumstances beyond [his] control that would make performance untenable or impossible." *Edington v. Creek Oil Co.*, 213 Mont. 112, 690 P.2d 970 (1984). As Perlman aptly argues, however, the district court erred in using the "doctrine of force majeure"[4] to interject terms into

---

4. Force majeure is a phrase coined primarily for the convenience of contracting parties wishing to describe the facts that create a contractual impossibility due to an "Act of God." *See* 6 A. Corbin, *Corbin on Contracts*, § 1324 (1962). As Corbin points out, this term is outmoded and serves no useful purpose as a test of responsibility, and the question of the promisor's discharge would be better approached by looking to (1) the terms of the contract, (2) the custom of businessmen in like cases, and (3) prevailing opinion of public welfare as evidenced by the judicial decisions. *Id.* "Force

majeure" is therefore, not a fixed rule of law that regulates the content of all force majeure clauses, but instead is a term that describes a particular type of event, i.e., an "Act of God" which may excuse performance under the contract. That a party labels a condition or event a "force majeure" in a contract does not make that event a force majeure in the traditional sense of the term. Therefore, courts should not be diverted by this "red herring." Instead, they should look to the language that the parties specifically bargained for in the contract to determine the parties' intent

the contract that were not contemplated by the parties. Therefore, he urges, control and foreseeability are not at issue. The only issue in this instance, insists Perlman, is whether he was hindered by governmental regulations in his efforts to fulfill the contract.

Perlman is correct that this case is essentially one of contract interpretation. The language in the force majeure clause in the Lease is unambiguous and its terms were specifically bargained for by both parties. Therefore, the "doctrine" of force majeure should not supersede the specific terms bargained for in the contract. When the terms of a contract are unambiguous, the courts must give effect to the intentions of the parties expressed by the language they employ. Because the clause labeled "force majeure" in the Lease does not mandate that the force majeure event be unforeseeable or beyond the control of Perlman before performance is excused, the district court erred when it supplied those terms as a rule of law. But even under the terms of the Lease, Perlman's performance would not be excused unless he was hindered by the regulatory process in Wyoming or Montana.

Perlman argues that because the Wyoming officials refused to commit to permitting a gas well using Perlman's process once they received the hydrology and other expensive studies, and because the regulatory process itself might prevent his meeting the six-month drilling deadline, he was "hindered" by his "inability to obtain governmental permits or approvals necessary or convenient to [his] operations." Perlman's sole basis for this argument is his interpretation of the October 26 meeting between his representative and the officials from the Wyoming Gas and Water Commissions. Perlman's interpretation is that the Wyoming officials would refuse to permit any well that drew as much water as could a well using his process. But, as the district court found, the state officials never refused to permit Perlman's operations; they merely required advance studies of the use, quantity, drainage and quality of the water Perlman's process would affect. This requirement was apparently standard, or at least not unusual, for anyone likely to use substantial amounts of water in Wyoming. Furthermore, the amounts of water that would be produced on the Pioneer/Kendrick land using the Perlman process was not a certainty; neither was it known whether the wells might not show beneficial use under the Wyoming water regulations. And, significantly in this case, Perlman's obligation was not limited to use of his patented process.

From the evidence it is clear that no actual hindrance resulted from the regulations or the regulators in Wyoming because Perlman made no effort whatsoever to obtain the appropriate permits or to begin drilling the wells. Consequently, Perlman's self-serving conclusion that a force majeure condition existed was at best merely speculation as to what might have happened had he attempted to drill the wells as planned.

concerning whether the event complained of excuses performance. *See, e.g., PPG In-*   *dustries v. Shell Oil Company,* 919 F.2d 17, slip op. at 1161 (5th Cir. Nov. 6, 1990).

[The court affirmed the judgment of the trial court for damages in excess of $1.7 million.]

K. EXEMPTION UNDER CISG ARTICLE 79

Problem 90

In a transaction governed by the CISG, (C) agreed to sell 10 tons of a certain mineral to (E). The written contract signed by both parties contained the same *force majeure* clause as Problem 89. After the contract was formed, C notified E that it could not deliver the mineral because of new export restrictions imposed by its government. E believed that C could ship at least half the quantity specified in the contract and therefore demanded that C make a 50% shipment by the original delivery date, which was within 30 days of E's demand. C ignored E's demand and failed to deliver any of the mineral by the delivery date. E then purchased the mineral from a substitute supplier. Seven months later, C notified E that the export restrictions had been eased and, pursuant to the terms of their contract, C would now ship all 10 tons of the mineral.

(a) Assume that E was correct in assuming that C could have shipped 50 percent of the chemicals on time. What result?

(b) Assume that E was incorrect in its assumption—i.e., C could not have shipped any amount on time, although seven months later it was capable of shipping the entire amount. What result?

L. EXCUSE FOR NON–PERFORMANCE UNDER ARTICLE 2A

Problem 90A

Parsons Corporation (P) agreed to lease 25 fork lift trucks from the Fork Corporation (F). Before delivery of the trucks was due, F notified P that a new government regulation required the addition of certain safety devices to all fork lift trucks, and that complying with this regulation would prevent F from meeting the agreed delivery schedule. P then learned that F was supplying some fork lifts to other customers. Is P entitled to any trucks under the lease with F? See 2A–405.

M. EXCUSE FOR NON–PERFORMANCE UNDER UCITA

UCITA Section 615 provides an excuse provision that very closely tracks the language of UCC 2–615, except that the UCITA provision expressly makes the doctrine available to either "party." Some thought was given to including buyers as well as sellers in 2–615, but the *proposed amendment* to 2–615 makes only the most minor language changes with no mention of buyers.

N. THE DOCUMENTARY TRANSACTION

Many commercial sales are made on open credit—i.e., the seller simply ships the goods to the buyer and waits for payment at some agreed later date. Such arrangements are common where the seller trusts the buyer because of past dealings, where the amounts involved do not justify a more elaborate approach, or where open credit is the industry standard. Sometimes, however, sellers are reluctant to part with their products merely on the strength of the buyer's promise to pay, particularly where the buyer is located at some distance or has not dealt with the seller in the past. The seller's concerns are particularly acute in international transactions. Recall the sale of equipment by an American manufacturer to a French buyer in Problem 81(b). Suppose the equipment had arrived unharmed in Paris, but the buyer claimed the goods were defective. The buyer's claim might be honest, or it might be operating in bad faith to extract a "discount" from the seller. In either case, the seller will find itself in a transnational dispute with limited bargaining power since the buyer has control of the goods. If the buyer rejects the equipment, the American seller must try to dispose of goods located thousands of miles away in a locale where the seller may have no agents and no customers.

Even where there is no dispute concerning conformity of the goods, the unpaid seller may discover that the buyer is insolvent. The seller must then pay for lawyers' advice to the effect that "You can't get blood from a stone" and similar unhelpful observations. If the UCC is the governing law, 2–702 suggests the possibility of reclaiming the goods from an insolvent buyer.[1] The seller's right to reclaim goods, however, is subject to the rights of buyers in ordinary course, good faith purchasers and, in some jurisdictions, lien creditors.[2] A seller trying to reclaim goods may also find itself in a contest with the buyer's secured creditors.[3]

One method for dealing with the problems that arise from long-distance sales is the so-called *documentary transaction*. Documentary transactions require the use of a "document of title," defined in 1–201(b)(16) as a "document which in the regular course of business or financing is treated as adequately evidencing that the person in possession of it is entitled to receive, hold and dispose of the document and the goods it covers." The most common documents of title are the **bill of lading** (1–201(b)(6)) and the **warehouse receipt** (1–201(b)(42)), which are discussed in more detail below. Other documents of title include dock warrants, dock receipts and delivery orders (7–102(1)(d)).

---

1. 2–702(2) requires that the buyer has received goods on credit while insolvent. The seller, however, must demand reclamation within ten days after buyer's receipt of the goods unless the buyer had made a written misrepresentation of solvency within three months before delivery. *Proposed Amended Section 2–702(2)* would remove the artificial ten-day and three month limitations and substitute a requirement that the seller's demand to reclaim the goods be "made within a reasonable time after buyer's receipt of the goods." If the buyer is in bankruptcy at the time of the reclamation, however, the seller must comply with Section 546(c) of the Bankruptcy Code, which requires that reclamation be demanded within 10 days.

2. See 2–702(3), which originally listed lien creditors along with buyers in ordinary course and good faith purchasers as parties who prevail against a reclaiming seller. The UCC Permanent Editorial Board amended the provision in 1966 to remove the reference to lien creditors, but not all states have adopted the amendment. "Lien creditor" is defined in 9–102(52).

3. A reclaiming seller's rights under 2–702 as against the buyer and various third parties claiming an interest in the goods through the buyer (such as creditors of the buyer holding a security interest in the goods under UCC Article 9) are explored in Chapter 6.

As the last sentence of 1–201(b)(16) indicates, the goods covered by a document of title are held by a **bailee**. A bailment arises whenever an owner of goods voluntarily transfers possession but not ownership of the goods to another party. Every bailment has a particular purpose. If you take your clothes to a dry cleaner, you (the bailor) transfer possession of (but not title to) the clothes to the cleaner (the bailee) for the particular purpose of having the clothes cleaned. The cleaner issues a receipt that evidences the bailment. When a seller such as GM Industries in Problem 81(b) delivers goods to an independent carrier (truck, railroad, airline or other carrier), the carrier—a bailee who has received the goods for the particular purpose of transporting them—issues a receipt called a bill of lading to the bailor/seller. The bill of lading, however, is much more than a receipt for the goods. It is a document of title that controls the goods: the carrier is legally bound to deliver the goods only to a "holder" of the bill of lading or to the party named as the "consignee" in the bill. See 7–403(1), (3) & (4). The typical bill of lading identifies the carrier, the shipper, the consignor (i.e., the owner of the goods shipped) and the consignee. The goods are described and the particular vehicle that will carry them is identified by number. The bill is signed by the agent of the carrier. The original bill is given to the consignor—i.e., the seller if the goods are being transported as part of a sale. The reverse side of the typical bill of lading is usually covered with virtually illegible boilerplate that the carrier hopes will protect it from liability if the goods are lost or damaged while in its possession.

When a party stores goods in a bonded warehouse (where billions of dollars worth of commodities and other goods are stored), the warehouseman (bailee) issues a warehouse receipt to the owner-bailor. Like a bill of lading, a warehouse receipt is a document of title that controls the right to receive the goods from the bailee. And as with a bill of lading, a warehouse receipt usually includes barely legible boilerplate attempting to protect the warehouseman in time of need.

Article 7 of the U.C.C., a revised and consolidated successor to the old Uniform Warehouse Receipts Act and the Uniform Bills of Lading Act, governs documents of title. Article 7, however, does not control where federal or other state law preempts it. See 7–103. For this reason, bills of lading for interstate shipments—a large proportion of all shipping—are governed by federal law, specifically the Federal Bills of Lading Act (49 U.S.C. §§ 81–124)[4] and the Carmack Amendment to the Interstate Commerce Act (49 U.S.C. § 20(11) & (12)). Warehouse receipts covering agricultural products stored for interstate or foreign commerce are governed by the United States Warehouse Act of 1916 (7 U.S.C. §§ 241–273). Other federal statutes also preempt Article 7's coverage of warehouse receipts and bills of lading.[5] In general, however, there are great similarities between Article 7

---

4. According to § 81 of the Federal Bills of Lading Act, "Bills of lading issued by any common carrier for the transportation of goods in any Territory of the United States, or the District of Columbia, or from a place in a State to a place in a foreign country, or from a place in one State to a place in another State, or from a place in one State to a place in the same State through another State or foreign country, shall be governed by this Chapter."

5. See, for example, the Perishable Agricultural Commodities Act, 7 U.S.C. § 499a–s, the Harter Act, 46 U.S.C. §§ 190–195, and the Carriage of Goods by Sea Act, 46 U.S.C. §§ 1300–1315.

and other statutes regulating documents of title. The distinctions that do exist have typically not caused great difficulty for courts, although specific differences can loom large in a given situation.[6] Article 7 is generally consistent with other legislation affecting documents of title because the UCC provisions reflect common law standards that the other statutes also incorporate. Thus, it is not unusual for a court to rely on Article 7 as analogous authority even when the UCC is technically inapplicable.[7]

Differences in the traditional rules applicable to bills of lading on the one hand and warehouse receipts on the other precluded a totally unified treatment of these documents of title in Article 7. As a result, part 2 of Article 7 contains special rules for warehouse receipts while the provisions of part 3 apply only to bills of lading. The other parts of Article 7 apply to both types of documents.

Litigation concerning documents of title often focuses on the bailee's duty of care and attempts to limit liability. Consider the following case.

I.C.C. METALS, INC. v. MUNICIPAL WAREHOUSE CO.

Court of Appeals of New York, 1980.
50 N.Y.2d 657, 431 N.Y.S.2d 372, 409 N.E.2d 849.

GABRIELLI, J. In the autumn of 1974, plaintiff, an international metals trader, delivered three separate lots of an industrial metal called indium to defendant commercial warehouse for safekeeping. The parties have stipulated that the three lots of indium, which had an aggregate weight of some 845 pounds, were worth $100,000. When the metal was delivered to defendant, it supplied plaintiff with warehouse receipts for each lot. Printed on the back of each receipt were the terms and conditions of the bailment, as proposed by defendant. Section 11 of those terms and conditions provided as follows:

> Limitation of Liability—Sec. 11. The Liability of the warehouseman as to all articles and items listed on the face of this warehouse receipt is limited to the actual value of each article and item, but the total liability of the warehouseman shall not exceed in any event for damage to any or all the items or articles listed on this warehouse receipt the sum of fifty ($50.00) dollars; provided, however, that such liability may, on written request of the bailor at the time of signing this warehouse receipt or within twenty (20) days after receipt of this warehouse receipt, be increased on part or all of the articles and items hereunder, in which event, increased rates shall be charged based upon such increased valuation, but the warehousemen's maximum liability shall in no event exceed the actual value of

---

6. See the note following the next principal case (*I.C.C. Metals*), discussing the differences between Article 7 and federal law (the Carmack Amendment) concerning the enforceability of a limitation of liability clause in a document of title.

7. See, E.G., David Crystal, Inc. v. Cunard Steam–Ship Co., 223 F.Supp. 273 (S.D.N.Y.1963), *aff'd* 339 F.2d 295 (2d Cir. 1964), *cert. denied*, 380 U.S. 976 (1965), where the court saw no reason why the admiralty rule should not be the same as the rule in Article 7 and other uniform acts.

any or all of the articles and items in question. In no case shall the liability be extended to include any loss of profit.

Plaintiff did not request any increase in defendant's contractual liability, nor did it inform defendant of the value of the metal.

For almost two years, defendant billed plaintiff for storage of each of the three lots by means of monthly invoices that specifically identified the stored metal, and plaintiff duly paid each invoice. Finally, in May of 1976, plaintiff requested the return of one of the three lots of indium. At that point defendant for the first time informed plaintiff that it was unable to locate any of the indium. Plaintiff then commenced this action in conversion, seeking to recover the full value of the indium. In response, defendant contended that the metal had been stolen through no fault of defendant's and that, at any rate, section 11 of the terms printed on each warehouse receipt limited plaintiff's potential recovery to a maximum of $50 per lot of indium.

Special Term granted summary judgment to plaintiff for the full value of the indium. The court found that plaintiff had made out a prima facie case of conversion by proffering undisputed proof that the indium had been delivered to defendant and that defendant had failed to return it upon a proper demand. As to defendant's contention that the metal had been stolen, the court concluded that this allegation was completely speculative and that defendant had failed to raise any question of fact sufficient to warrant a trial on the issue. Finally, Special Term held that the contractual limitation upon defendant's liability was inapplicable to an action in conversion. The Appellate Division affirmed the judgment in favor of plaintiff and we granted defendant leave to appeal to this court. We now affirm the order appealed from.

Absent an agreement to the contrary, a warehouse is not an insurer of goods and may not be held liable for any injury to or loss of stored property not due to some fault upon its part (Uniform Commercial Code, § 7–204, subd. [1]). As a bailee, however, a warehouse is required both to exercise reasonable care so as to prevent loss of or damage to the property and, a fortiori, to refrain from itself converting materials left in its care (see Prosser, Torts [4th ed.], § 15). If a warehouse does not convert the goods to its own use and does exercise reasonable care, it may not be held liable for any loss of or damage to the property unless it specifically agrees to accept a higher burden. If, however, the property is lost or damaged as a result of negligence upon the part of the warehouse, it will be liable in negligence. Similarly, should a warehouse actually convert stored property to its own use, it will be liable in conversion. Hence, a warehouse which fails to redeliver goods to the person entitled to their return upon a proper demand, may be liable for either negligence or conversion, depending upon the circumstances (see, generally, White & Summers, Uniform Commercial Code [2d ed.], § 20–3).

A warehouse unable to return bailed property either because it has lost the property as a result of its negligence or because it has converted the property will be liable for the full value of the goods at the time of the loss or conversion unless the parties have agreed to limit the warehouse's potential liability. It has long been the law in this State that a warehouse, like a common carrier, may limit its liability for loss of or damage to stored goods even if the injury or loss is the result of the warehouse's negligence, so long as it provides the bailor with an opportunity to increase that potential liability by payment of a higher storage fee. If the warehouse converts the goods, however, strong policy considerations bar enforcement of any such limitation upon its liability. This rule, which has now been codified in subdivision (2) of section 7–204 of the Uniform Commercial Code,[1] is premised on the distinction between an intentional and an unintentional tort. Although public policy will in many situations countenance voluntary prior limitations upon that liability which the law would otherwise impose upon one who acts carelessly, such prior limitations may not properly be applied so as to diminish one's liability for injuries resulting from an affirmative and intentional act of misconduct such as a conversion. Any other rule would encourage wrongdoing by allowing the converter to retain the difference between the value of the converted property and the limited amount of liability provided in the agreement of storage. That result would be absurd. To avoid such an anomaly, the law provides that when a warehouse converts bailed property, it thereby ceases to function as a warehouse and thus loses its entitlement to the protections afforded by the agreement of storage. In short, although the merely careless bailee remains a bailee and is entitled to whatever limitations of liability the bailor has agreed to, the converter forsakes his status as bailee completely and accordingly forfeits the protections of such limitations. Hence, in the instant case, whether defendant is entitled to the benefit of the liability-limiting provision of the warehouse receipt turns upon whether plaintiff has proven conversion or merely negligence. Plaintiff has proffered uncontroverted proof of delivery of the indium to defendant, of a proper demand for its return, and of defendant's failure to honor that demand. Defendant has failed to make a sufficient showing in support of its suggested explanation of the loss to defeat plaintiff's motion for summary judgment. Its unsupported claim that the metal was stolen does not suffice to raise any issue of fact on this point.[2] Upon this record, it is beyond cavil

1. We find no merit to defendant's suggestion that the term "conversion to his own use" as used in subdivision (2) of section 7–204 means something more than a simple conversion.

2. The explanation proffered by the warehouse in such a case must be supported by sufficient evidence and cannot be merely the product of speculation and conjecture. "The explanation must show with reasonable certainty how the loss occurred, as, by theft or fire * * * It is not enough to show that defendant-bailee used reasonable care in its system of custody if mysterious disappearance is the only 'explanation' given" (PJI 4:93, at pp. 1090–1091; see Dalton v. Hamilton Hotel Operating Co., 242 N.Y. 481, 488–489). In the instant case, defendant offered proof of the following facts in support of its claim that the indium had been stolen: "(1) the storage of the indium in three different locations in two different buildings, and the absence of any indication in [defendant] Municipal's records that the indium was moved, negate the possibility of misdelivery; (2) the storage of the indium without special precautions, because [plaintiff] ICC failed to advise Municipal of its true value, supports the likelihood of theft; (3) the form of the indium (small bars) would have facilitated removal without detection; (4) a recently discharged employee was experienced in 'weighing and sampling' and thus presumably was aware of the val-

that plaintiff would be entitled to judgment had it elected to sue defendant in negligence. We now hold that such a record also suffices to sustain plaintiff's action in conversion, thereby rendering inapplicable the contractual limitation upon defendant's liability.[3]

The rule requiring a warehouse to come forward with an explanation for its failure to return bailed goods or be cast in damages in negligence is based upon practical necessity. As is noted above, a warehouse may only be held liable for loss of or damage to bailed goods if the loss or damage is due to the negligence of the warehouse or if the warehouse has converted the property. Hence, in order to recover damages for lost or damaged goods, a bailor must prove either that the warehouse was negligent or that it converted the goods. Since bailed property is in the possession of and under the sole control of the warehouse at the time of injury or loss, however, it is the warehouse which is in the best, if not the only, position to explain the loss of or damage to the property. Indeed, such information normally will be exclusively in the possession of the warehouse and will not be readily accessible to the bailor. Because of this, the law properly refuses to allow a warehouse, which has undertaken for a fee to securely store goods belonging to another, to avoid liability by simply pleading ignorance of the fate of the stored merchandise. To allow the warehouse to so easily escape its responsibilities would be to place the bailor in an untenable position and would serve to encourage both dishonesty and carelessness. Clearly, the temptation to convert stored property would be significantly increased could the warehouse then avoid all civil liability by simply denying all knowledge of the circumstances of the loss and placing upon the bailor the well nigh impossible burden of determining and proving what happened to his property while it was hidden from sight in the depths of the defendant's warehouse. Similarly, such a rule would reward those warehouses with the least efficient inventory control procedures, since they would be most able to honestly plead ignorance of the fate of goods entrusted to their care.

---

ue of indium; (5) there was a series of alarms, any one of which could have been caused by a theft; (6) Municipal promptly reported the loss to the police; and (7) ICC reported the loss to its insurers as a theft and continued to employ Municipal's services, thus negating any suspicion that Municipal had misappropriated the indium or had been grossly negligent in its care." Viewed most favorably to defendant, this evidence would indicate at most that theft by a third party was one possible explanation for the defendant's failure to redeliver the indium to plaintiff. This is simply insufficient, since the warehouse is required to show not merely what might conceivably have happened to the goods, but rather what actually happened to the goods. Defendant proved only that theft was possible, and presented no proof of an actual theft.

Hence, the proffered explanation was inadequate as a matter of law.

3. We emphasize at this point that we do not suggest by our holding in this case that proof of negligence will support a recovery in conversion. Rather, our holding is limited to those situations in which the warehouse fails to provide an adequate explanation for its failure to return stored goods. If the warehouse comes forward with an explanation supported by evidentiary proof in admissible form, the plaintiff will then be required to prove that the loss was due to either negligence or conversion, depending on the circumstances. For plaintiff to recover in conversion after the warehouse has established a prima facie explanation for its failure to deliver, the trier of facts must find all the traditional elements of conversion.

To prevent such absurd results, the law has long placed upon the warehouse the burden of advancing an adequate explanation of the reasons for its failure to properly return stored property. This does not mean that the warehouse is required to prove that it acted properly, nor does this doctrine shift the burden of proof to the warehouse. Rather, the warehouse must come forward and explain the circumstances of the loss of or damage to the bailed goods upon pain of being held liable for negligence. If the warehouse does provide an explanation for the loss or damage, the plaintiff then must prove that the warehouse was at fault if he is to recover. A few illustrations of this principle may be of some assistance. Where the warehouse simply refuses to return bailed property upon a legitimate demand and does not advance any explanation for that refusal, the plaintiff will be entitled to recover without more. Similarly, where the warehouse does suggest an explanation for the loss but is unable to proffer sufficient evidentiary support for that explanation to create a question of fact, as in this case, the plaintiff will be entitled to recover without more. Where, however, the warehouse proffers sufficient evidence supporting its explanation to create a question of fact, the jury must be instructed that if it believes that explanation, the plaintiff must be denied any recovery unless he has proven that the warehouse was at fault (Uniform Commercial Code, § 7–403, subd. [1], par. [b]). In other words, if the jury is persuaded that the goods were accidentally mislaid or destroyed in a fire or accident or stolen by a third party, the plaintiff cannot recover unless he has proven that the loss or the fire or the accident or the theft were the proximate result of either a purposive act or a negligent commission or omission by the warehouse.

Although it has long been settled that this is the rule in an action in negligence, there has been considerable inconsistency and uncertainty as to the application of this principle to an action in conversion. Thus, although we have on occasion declared that a bailor establishes a prima facie case of conversion by simply proving delivery to the bailee and an unexplained failure to return the stored goods upon demand, we have at other times indicated that something more is needed to maintain an action in conversion and that a plaintiff will be required to provide positive evidence of an intentional act by the warehouse inconsistent with the plaintiff's interest in the property. We now conclude that there exists no sound reason to apply a different rule to the two types of action where, as here, the bailee comes forward with insufficient proof of its explanation for the loss of the bailed goods. The same policy considerations which prevent a warehouse from avoiding liability in negligence by a declaration of ignorance appear equally applicable to an action in conversion. Indeed, as a practical matter, a bailor will be even less able to prove conversion by a warehouse than he would negligence, since a warehouseman who actually converts stored property will generally strive mightily to prevent knowledge of his malfeasance from coming to light. The possibility of fraud is obvious, for a dishonest warehouseman might well be encouraged to convert bailed property if he could then obtain the benefit of a contractual limitation of liability by the simple expedient of professing ignorance as to the fate of the goods. The rule requiring a warehouse to explain the loss of or damage to the goods lest it be held liable would be severely undermined could a warehouse avoid the bulk of potential liability in such a case by means of a contractual provision.

We note, moreover, that the requirement that a warehouse provide an explanation for loss of property entrusted to it is certainly not overly harsh, nor does it impose a heavy burden upon the warehouse. The warehouse must only offer proof of what actually happened to the goods and need not show that it was free from fault, for once the warehouse makes the initial required showing, the burden of proving the warehouse to be at fault will fall squarely upon the plaintiff. No greater duty of care is created by this rule, nor does it establish any sort of strict liability. Certainly a warehouse may reasonably be required to keep track of goods entrusted to it and to supply an accurate explanation of any loss to the bailor.

Finally, where a warehouse does not explain the cause of the loss, it would appear as reasonable to assume that this profession of ignorance is due to the fact that the warehouse has converted the goods as to presume that it is due to the fact that the warehouse has been negligent. Indeed, one who commits an intentional wrong is more likely to attempt to cover his tracks than one who has been at most negligent, especially in light of the disparity in potential liability created by the insertion of a limitation of liability clause. For all these reasons, we conclude that plaintiff was entitled to summary judgment in its action in conversion. Quite simply, plaintiff proved delivery of the indium to defendant warehouse and defendant's subsequent failure to return the metal, whereas defendant has not come forward with adequate evidentiary proof in admissible form to support its suggested explanation of that failure. That being so, the limitation on liability was inapplicable, and plaintiff was entitled to recover the actual value of the missing indium.

Accordingly, the order appealed from should be affirmed, with costs.

Notes

Warehouse Liability. Perhaps the best-known case on the liability of a warehouse for failure to deliver bailed goods is Procter & Gamble Distributing Co. v. Lawrence American Field Warehousing Corp., 16 N.Y.2d 344, 266 N.Y.S.2d 785, 213 N.E.2d 873 (1965), where millions of pounds of soybean oil were supposedly stored in a warehouse which had issued warehouse receipts for the oil. The oil mysteriously disappeared. In an action for conversion, the plaintiff was granted summary judgment because the warehouse failed to sustain its burden of explaining why the oil disappeared.

The principal case involves a warehouse receipt with a clause that attempts to limit the bailee's liability for lost or damaged goods. Bills of lading typically include similar clauses limiting the carrier's liability to a stated value of the goods. Section 7–309(2) permits such limitations if the consignor is afforded an opportunity to declare a higher value. Higher valuations carry an additional fee to cover the greater risk of liability assumed by the carrier. The last portion of 7–309(2), however, renders a limitation of liability in a bill of lading ineffective if the carrier has converted the goods to its own use.

The result in the principal case depends on a presumption of conversion that arises when a warehouse does not provide a reasonable explanation for loss or damage to goods covered by a warehouse receipt. In Art Masters Assoc. v. United Parcel Service, 153 A.D.2d 41, 549 N.Y.S.2d 495 (1989), rev'd 77 N.Y.2d 200, 566 N.Y.S.2d 184, 567 N.E.2d 226 (1990), the New York Appellate Division applied a similar presumption in a case involving a bill of lading. The court held that a clause in the bill of lading limiting the carrier's liability was not enforceable where the defendant (UPS) could not explain the loss of certain paintings valued at $27,000. UPS had argued that the controversy was governed by federal law, under which a common carrier's failure to explain loss of or damage to bailed goods does not raise a presumption of conversion, i.e., under federal law the plaintiff would have to prove an actual conversion by the carrier. The Appellate Division, however, applied state law because the shipment in question was wholly intrastate (from Buffalo to Brooklyn). The court cited warehouse cases like the principal case that established a presumption of conversion in the absence of explanation for a loss.

On further appeal the New York Court of Appeals reversed because it refused to extend the presumption of conversion in the warehouse cases to motor carriers. The Court held that, although state law applied to the controversy, the state law governing motor carriers must be interpreted in accordance with federal law (the Carmack Amendment to the Interstate Commerce Act) and an actual conversion had to be shown. The bailor's failure to prove actual conversion made the limitation of liability clause enforceable, thereby reducing the bailor's recovery to just under $1000. *Art Masters Assoc. v. United Parcel Service,* 77 N.Y.2d 200, 566 N.Y.S.2d 184, 567 N.E.2d 226 (1990).

O.   NEGOTIABLE OR NON–NEGOTIABLE

Both bills of lading and warehouse receipts may be negotiable and or non-negotiable. Bills of lading, warehouse receipts and other documents of title are forms of "commercial paper." Modern law school courses on "payment systems" focus on "money paper"—commercial documents importing a money obligation, such as checks, promissory notes, certificates of deposit and the like. Bills of lading and warehouse receipts are "commercial paper" but they are not "money paper"; rather they are "commodity paper," since they typically represent commodities in storage (warehouse receipts) or goods being transported (bills of lading).

A document of title is *negotiable* if it meets the requirements of U.C.C. 7–104(1)—i.e., if it provides for the goods to be delivered "to bearer or to the order of a named person." These are the "magic words" of negotiability. The importance of negotiability may be easier to understand with respect to a form of "money paper". If you look at your checkbook you will see printed on every check, "Pay to the order of...." If I issue that check to Mildred White by filling in her name on the blank following "Pay to the order of," I have instructed my bank to pay the amount of the check to Mildred White or those to whom Mildred White properly transfers ("negotiates") the check. If Mildred White wants to "cash" the check or deposit it in an account at her bank she must indorse it (sign it on the back, though there are various kinds of indorsements) because only Mildred can transfer it.

Suppose I issued a $200 check to Mildred because I purchased her CD player. Mildred takes my check, indorses it, and gives it to her plumber, Abe Rosenthal, to pay for $200 worth of work Abe has just completed on her house. If Abe takes that check in good faith, for value, and without notice of any defenses that I might have against Mildred, Abe is much more than a mere transferee or assignee of Mildred's right to payment from me; he is a *holder in due course* of a negotiable instrument. A mere assignee stands in the shoes of the assignor. All defenses to payment that would be good against the assignor are also good against the assignee. Because Abe is *a holder in due course of a negotiable instrument*, however, he *takes free of most defenses that could be asserted against his transferor*.[1]

Suppose I discovered something wrong with the CD player I purchased from Mildred, and suppose the defect breaches an express warranty Mildred gave me. I stop payment on my check. Unaware of the dispute over the CD player, Abe presents the check to my bank for payment. The bank refuses payment. Abe has no claim against my bank, which has simply followed the instructions of its customer to refuse payment—something the bank promised it would do under my deposit contract with the bank. Abe, however, still has a right to enforce the obligation created by the check against me, and because Abe is a "holder in due course" of the check, I may not assert my breach of warranty defense against him, although it would be effective against Mildred who transferred the check to Abe. Again, as a holder in due course, he took the check free of such a defense against him.

The purpose of the rules protecting holders in due course of negotiable documents is to make commercial paper (in our example, "money paper" in the form of a check) freely transferable. Abe would be reluctant to accept the check if the rights it represents were subject to all defenses good against Mildred, especially since Abe is unlikely to know about those defenses. Although some relatively rare defenses against the transferor are available against a holder in due course, Abe's status will shield him from many common defenses—including my breach of warranty claim against Mildred.

The rules for checks are similar to those governing *negotiable* documents of title such as a negotiable bill of lading or negotiable warehouse receipt. Thus a *"holder"* to whom a negotiable document of

---

1. Section 3–302 sets forth the requirements for becoming a holder in due course. Section 3–305 lists the special rights of a holder in due course.

title has been "duly negotiated" is more than a mere assignee or transferee. Such a holder may acquire more rights than the document's transferor had—in particular, the right to enforce the document free of many defenses the bailee could assert against the transferor. See 7–502 and the comment to 7–104. There is, however, one major difference between money paper (like checks) and commodity paper. A check or other negotiable instrument does not by itself convey rights over particular funds, but a negotiable document of title gives the holder a right to receive, hold and dispose of the document and the particular (identified) goods it covers. This is sometimes referred to as the "merger" of the goods in the document.

Even if a document of title does not contain the magic words to make it negotiable under 7–104(1)(a) (i.e., delivery "to bearer" or "to the order of" a named person), it will still be negotiable if the document is recognized as negotiable in overseas trade because it "runs to a named person or assigns" (7–104(1)(b)). If the document of title fails to qualify as negotiable under either branch of 7–104(1), it still has utility as evidence of transfer. Non-negotiable bills of lading and other documents of title are frequently used in commerce. The transferee of a non-negotiable document of title, however, does not receive the special status of a *holder*. Thus the transfer of a non-negotiable document is merely the assignment of the rights of the transferor. As a result the transferee succeeds only to the rights that the transferor had, and is subject to defenses good against the transferor.

Problem 91

(a) Korsecka Ltd. (K), an Austrian firm, contracted to sell a large quantity of raw plastic to the Parker Corporation (P) in New York. K, who had never dealt with P before, did not want to extend open credit to P. To make sure that it would receive payment for the plastic, K insisted upon a "documentary transaction." P insisted that the contract be governed by Article 2 of the UCC, and K agreed. K shipped the plastic via United Cargo Corporation (U), an ocean freight carrier. U issued a negotiable bill of lading to K which named a New York bank as consignee. K sent the bill of lading through banking channels (starting with K's own bank in Austria) to the New York bank. Along with the bill of lading K sent a "draft" for the purchase price of the plastic. The draft, which operated rather like a check, was "drawn on" P—i.e., it ordered P to pay the amount of the draft to a named payee. The payee whom P was supposed to pay in this case was K itself, and this particular draft was a "sight draft" payable immediately upon presentation to P.[1]

---

1. Both checks and drafts are "three-party paper." A check, in fact, is a particular kind of "draft"—one payable on demand and "drawn on" a bank. See UCC 3–104(f). If you take out your checkbook and "write" a check, you are, in UCC terms, *drawing* the check. You are the *drawer*. Your check *orders* your bank (the *drawee*) to pay the amount of the check "to the order of" a third party, the *payee*. Similarly, you can draw a *draft* on a party that is not a bank, ordering the drawee to pay a specified amount to a named payee. With respect to the sight draft in the problem, the drawer is

If it had worked as it was intended, the documentary transaction between K and P would have unfolded as follows: When the New York bank received the bill of lading with sight draft attached it would notify P, who would come to the bank and pay the amount of the draft (the price of the plastic), perhaps by arranging a loan from the bank. In exchange for payment of the draft, the bank would indorse and transfer ("duly negotiate") the negotiable bill of lading to the buyer. The negotiable bill of lading is critical because the carrier who issued the document is obligated to deliver the goods only to the party who holds the bill of lading and surrenders it upon taking delivery of the goods (7–403). After receiving P's payment, the New York bank, working through banking channels, would pay the amount of the draft into K's account at its Austrian bank. If P later became insolvent or claimed that the goods were defective, K would be in the strong position of having already received payment. By combining a negotiable bill of lading, which controls who is entitled to receive the goods from the carrier, with the sight draft, which permits payment to be made through banking channels, K would be assured of payment before giving up control of the goods. The arrangement would also be acceptable to P, who would take over effective control of the goods (through the negotiable bill of lading) immediately upon payment. This, again, was the way the transaction was *intended* to work.

In this case, however, P never went to the New York bank to pay the sight draft, and thus the bank never negotiated the bill of lading to P. As was proper in these circumstances, the bank transferred the bill of lading back to K. This would normally have allowed K to control disposition of the goods. This time, however, the carrier (U) delivered the goods to P without requiring surrender of the negotiable bill of lading as required by 7–403(3). P is now unable to pay for the plastic. K brings an action against U, which defends on the basis that a New York agent of K waived the rule requiring surrender of the bill of lading and authorized delivery of the plastic to P. K seeks summary judgment. What result and why? See 7–403(1) and (4).

(b) Assume that P went to the New York bank and fraudulently represented that it had substantial assets elsewhere. P promised to pledge those assets as collateral if the bank would lend it the money to satisfy the sight draft. The bank agreed to the loan, surrendered the bill of lading to P, and paid the amount of the draft to K. The carrier (U) then delivered the plastic to P in exchange for the bill of lading. Has U acted properly? When the bank discovers P's fraud will it have any claim against U?

(c) Assume the facts of (b) except P did not take delivery of the plastic. Instead, P indorsed and duly negotiated the bill of lading to another user of plastic, Dreadnought, Inc. (D), which paid P the current market value of the plastic covered by the bill of lading. The bank has discovered P's fraud and claims that it is entitled to the plastic. As between D and the bank, who is entitled to the plastic from the carrier (U)? Suppose U delivered the plastic

the seller (K) who is ordering the buyer (P) to pay the amount of the draft (the price of the goods) to a payee. The payee is also K. The drawing of a draft to pay one's self is not unusual. You can (and perhaps have) drawn a check on your bank naming yourself as payee—i.e., you have written a check to yourself. Note that the mere drawing of a check or draft on a drawee does not mean that the drawee will pay. If your checking account has insufficient funds to cover a check, your bank will probably *dishonor* it. So too, a non-bank drawee of a draft may (rightfully or not) refuse to honor the draft.

to P even though P did not have the bill of lading. The bank and D each claim the plastic in the hands of P. What result? Remember the definition of "document of title" in 1–201(b)(16).

(d) Assume the facts of (a) except that the bill of lading was non-negotiable. [Non-negotiable bills of lading are commonly used in domestic transactions.] The seller (K), who was the consignor, also named itself as the consignee in the bill. By naming itself as consignee, K retained control of the goods covered by the bill. An authorized agent of K instructed the carrier (U) to deliver the plastic without demanding surrender of the non-negotiable bill. Should the carrier follow that instruction? See 7–303 & 7–403.

P. LETTERS OF CREDIT

1. What Is a "Letter of Credit"?

The purpose of a documentary transaction such as the one in problem 91(a) is to allow the seller to retain control over goods being delivered to a distant buyer until the seller has been paid. It protects the seller from the problem of retrieving goods from the possession of a buyer who refuses to pay. Korsecka (K) took the precaution of making delivery by means of a negotiable bill of lading with sight draft attached. This certainly provided K with more security than a sale on open credit.

Unfortunately, such precautions do not offer complete protection to a seller such as K. In Problem 91(a), the buyer Parker (P) refused to pay the sight draft after the draft (and the attached bill of lading) arrived at the New York bank. Perhaps P had discovered a better price for raw plastic from another supplier. Maybe P could not raise the funds to pay the sight draft, or perhaps P honestly believed that K has breached the contract in some fashion. Whatever the reason, P's refusal to pay puts K in a tough spot. Even if the carrier United Cargo (U) acts properly and refuses to deliver the goods except upon surrender of the negotiable bill of lading, the plastic will end up sitting on a dock in New York or accruing storage charges in a warehouse while K in Austria tries to decide what to do. The bill of lading will almost certainly keep the goods out of P's hands, a real advantage in this situation, but it cannot help K dispose of a commodity located on another continent. K may have a cause of action against P for breach of contract, but K's immediate problem is to do something about the plastic.

To avoid this dilemma and to enhance its ability to collect the price, K could have bargained for a contract term requiring P to supply a *letter of credit*. To comply with such a term, P would arrange for its bank in New York, in exchange for a fee, to transmit to K a written undertaking obliging the bank to pay K the purchase price of the goods if K met specified conditions. Those conditions would probably include presenting to the bank a negotiable bill of lading covering the goods along with a draft drawn on the bank for the price. Under Article 5 of the UCC, which deals with letters of credit, the written undertaking by the bank qualifies as a letter of credit (or simply "credit"), and the parties associated with the letter of credit are identified as "issuer" (the New York bank), "beneficiary" (K), and "applicant" (P). See 5–102. *[Note: section numbers in the text and problems are from the revised Article 5 (1995). Article 5 section numbers in the judicial opinions in this section, however, refer to the earlier version. With respect to citations to the former Article 5, the student should consult the Table of Disposition of Sections (comparing sections in the former and revised versions of Article 5), which appears near the beginning of the revised Article 5 in various statutory compilations.]*

Such a letter of credit would give K an independent right to demand payment of the price from the bank upon satisfying the conditions of the credit. See 5–108(a) & (f)(1), 5–109(a). To invoke this right, K would obtain a negotiable bill of lading from the carrier and indorse it to the New York bank, attach a draft for amount of the price naming the New York bank as drawee and K (or its Austrian bank) as payee,[1] and transmit the documents to the New York bank through banking channels. If the documents comply with the terms of the letter of credit, their arrival at the New York bank will trigger that bank's obligation to pay the draft. K can depend on payment by the bank (probably a solvent and reliable party), and need not rely entirely on P.

2. *"Commercial" and "Standby" Letters of Credit*

The foregoing discussion focused on the typical "commercial" letter of credit that has been traditionally used, particularly in international sales transactions. In recent years a variation—the so-called "standby" letter of credit—has arisen. It is used in a variety of situations to reinforce or guarantee other obligations. Its distinguishing feature is that the conditions to the issuer's duty to pay are ones that will not be met as a matter of course. In other words, the issuer must "stand by"—ready to pay—although it may never be called upon to do so.

For example, in construction projects the builder may be obligated to supply a standby letter of credit in lieu of a performance bond to assure the builder's performance of its contract. The issuer's obligation to pay under such a letter of credit will be triggered only if the builder defaults and if specified documentation of the default is presented to the issuer. Even in construction projects where a traditional performance bond is issued, the surety (bonding company) might feel insecure and ask the builder to have its bank issue a standby letter of credit naming the surety as beneficiary. If the builder defaults and the bonding company must pay under its performance bond, the bonding company can look to the letter of credit for reimbursement.

---

1. The analogy to the ordinary check is clear. When you sign one of your checks, you are the "drawer." You draw the check on your bank (the "drawee"). You are ordering the bank to pay the check from your checking account. The "payee" is the party to whom you are ordering the bank to "pay to the order of." Thus, checks are "three-party paper" where the drawee is a bank.

"Drafts" are three-party paper with the same three parties except that the drawee is not a bank. Commercial "money" paper involving only two parties is illustrated by a promissory note where the party issuing the note has promised to pay. It becomes "negotiable" if it meets the formal requisites of negotiability.

The standby letter of credit is now widely used. It even appears in sales transactions, as the next case (*Benetton Services*) illustrates. The standby letter of credit has become so popular that the Comptroller of the Currency issued regulations to make them subject to lending limits prescribed by Federal Law.[2] We mention "standby" letters of credit to acquaint the student with them and to distinguish them from the "commercial" letter of credit traditionally used in sales transactions.

3. *Law Governing Letters of Credit*

Before the uniform commercial code appeared, the rules governing letters of credit derived almost exclusively from case law that was uncertain and non-uniform. In response to these problems, The International Chamber of Commerce in 1929 promulgated the *Uniform Customs and Practice for Commercial Documentary Credits* (The "Uniform Customs," or simply the UCP), which became very influential. Even after enactment of article 5 of the UCC dealing with letters of credit, the UCP continued its influence. This was due in part to a non-uniform amendment to the scope provision of Article 5 adopted by New York (the most significant letter of credit jurisdiction) and three other states, which allowed the UCP to displace Article 5.[3] While the UCP and Article 5 of the code are very similar, there are some differences in substance and coverage. Article 5 itself provides that it is "far from comprehensive" and that, particularly with respect to standards of performance, "it is appropriate for the parties and the courts to turn to customs and practices such as the uniform customs and practice for documentary credits." 5–103 comment 2. With certain exceptions, Article 5 sections may be varied by agreement (5–103(c)). Thus if a letter of credit provides that it will be subject to the UCP, the UCP terms will supercede conflicting Article 5 sections unless the Article 5 provisions may not be varied by agreement.

A comprehensive treatment of letter of credit law under the UCP and Article 5 is beyond the scope of this book. The following materials are designed to acquaint the student with some of the basic issues that arise in connection with letters of credit.[4]

BENETTON SERVICES CORPORATION v. BENEDOT, INC.

Supreme Court of Alabama, 1989.
551 So.2d 295.

SHORES, J. Benetton Services Corporation ("Benetton"), an Italian clothing manufacturer and distributor, appeals from an order enjoining

2. See 12 C.F.R. § 32.2.

3. Alabama, Arizona and Missouri joined New York in adding the following subsection (4) to original 5–102: "Unless otherwise agreed, this Article 5 does not apply to a letter of credit or a credit if by its terms or by agreement, course of dealing or usage of trade such letter of credit or credit is subject in whole or in part to the Uniform Customs and Practice for Commercial Documentary Credits fixed by the Thir-

teenth or by any subsequent Congress of the International Chamber of Commerce." Because New York City is our dominant financial center, this Amendment effectively precludes the application of Article 5 to most letters of credit.

4. For more on letters of credit, see Chapter 20 of J. WHITE & R. SUMMERS, UNIFORM COMMERCIAL CODE (5th ed. 2000).

it from drawing on an irrevocable letter of credit issued by Southland Bank of Dothan ("Southland") on behalf of Benedot, Inc. ("Benedot").

Benedot was formed for the purpose of selling Benetton clothing at retail. The agreement between Benedot and Benetton provided that Benedot would sell only Benetton clothing. Benedot opened a retail outlet in Dothan and one in Auburn.

Benedot placed several orders with Benetton over a period of approximately 36 months. All the orders were delivered late, and all contained some non-conforming merchandise. Benedot's account with Benetton became past due in the amount of approximately $140,000, although the exact past due amount was disputed by Benedot.

Benedot was told by Benetton that Benetton had made changes in personnel, and that future orders would be conforming and would be delivered on time. Benedot placed a "spring/summer 1988" order with Benetton.

As a condition to shipping Benedot's order, Benetton required Benedot to pay $20,000, and to have issued to Benetton an irrevocable letter of credit in the amount of $61,000. Pursuant to Benedot's request, Southland issued an irrevocable letter of credit to Benetton. The letter of credit provided:

> Southland Bank of Dothan opens its Irrevocable Standby Letter of Credit in favor of Benetton Services Corp. for the account of Benedot, Inc. in the following manner and on the following terms:
>
> 1. Purpose. This credit is available and drafts must be drawn hereunder for the account of Benedot, Inc., Dothan, Alabama 36303.
>
> 2. Drafts. Benetton Services Corp. drawn on Southland Bank of Dothan at sight which must be negotiated on or before February 28, 1989 but not prior to December 30, 1988 and each of which must state upon its face 'Drawn under Standby Letter of Credit #8 dated July 26, 1988 of the Southland Bank of Dothan' [sic].
>
> 3. Documentation. Drafts, when presented for negotiation, must be accompanied by the following instruments:
>
> > (a) Official invoice statement from Benetton, S.P.A and/or Benetton Manufacturing Corporation for the account of Benedot, Inc. showing unpaid balance sixty (60) or more days past due, indicating unpaid amounts, plus freight and duty (if due), plus reasonable attorney's fees and collection expenses (if applicable), for merchandise shipped and received after the date of this Letter of Credit.
>
> > (b) Statement signed by an official of Benetton Services Corp. certifying that the account of Benedot, Inc. is sixty (60) or more days past due and remains unpaid as of the date of the draft.

4. Notation. This is a notation of credit. Each draft hereunder must be endorsed herein, each draft or an attached writing must indicate that such notation has been made, and this Letter of Credit must be attached to the last draft when the credit is exhausted.

5. Total. The sum or sums of all drafts drawn under this Letter of Credit must not exceed $61,000.00.

6. Expiration. This Letter of Credit expires at our counters in Dothan, Alabama on February 28, 1989.

7. Obligation of Issuer. Southland Bank of Dothan agrees with the drawers, endorsers, and bona fide holders of drafts drawn and negotiated in compliance with the terms of this Letter of Credit that such drafts will be duly honored upon due presentation to this bank.

8. Other Provisions. Partial drawings are permitted. All charges in connection with this Letter of Credit are for the account of Benedot, Inc.

This credit is subject to the Uniform Customs and Practice of Documentary Credits 1983 Revision, International Chamber of Commerce, Paris, France, Publication #400 and engages us in accordance with the terms thereof.

The spring/summer 1988 order was delivered late and it contained nonconforming goods. Benedot accepted the shipment, as it had accepted the earlier orders, notwithstanding its nonconformity.

Benedot explained that it had accepted the merchandise because it was very difficult and expensive to return the goods to Italy and that Benetton had requested that Benedot sell the goods.

When Benedot's account regarding the spring/summer 1988 order became 60 days past due, Benetton drew a draft against the letter of credit. On February 28, 1989, Benetton presented the draft and the required documentation to Southland in compliance with the terms of the letter of credit. Southland refused to pay Benetton under the terms of the letter of credit and advised it that a temporary restraining order had been issued pursuant to Rule 65(b), A. R. Civ. P., enjoining Southland from making payment thereunder. A hearing was held, and the trial court granted a preliminary injunction enjoining Benetton from drawing upon, and Southland from honoring, the letter of credit. The trial court further ordered Southland to pay the amount of the drafts into court within seven days of the order granting the injunction. Benetton appeals.

Payment under an irrevocable letter of credit, upon compliance with its terms, is independent of the underlying contract. The issuer of a letter of credit must honor a draft drawn thereunder that complies with the terms of the letter of credit, regardless of whether the goods or documents conform to the underlying contract. Code 1975, § 7–5–114.

Because the letter of credit represents an independent obligation of the issuer to the beneficiary, payment under an irrevocable letter of credit may not be enjoined absent evidence of forgery or fraud in the issuance of the letter or fraud in the underlying transaction for which the letter of credit was issued.

In order for one to succeed on a fraud claim, he must establish that a false representation of a material existing fact was made, that he detrimentally relied upon it, and that he was damaged as a proximate result. If the fraud claim is based upon a promise to perform a future act, the party must also prove that the promisor, at the time of the alleged misrepresentation, did not intend to do the act promised and had an intent to deceive.

Benedot has failed to prove fraud. Benetton promised that, upon receipt of the $20,000 and a letter of credit, it would ship conforming goods and that delivery would be timely. This is clearly a promise to do an act in the future; to base a fraud claim on that promise, Benedot had to prove that Benetton, when it made the agreement, did not intend to comply with its terms. Also, Benedot had to prove that, at the time that promise was made, Benetton had an intent to deceive. The record is devoid of any such evidence. The evidence would support, at most, a finding that the promise was recklessly made and a reckless misrepresentation cannot support a fraud action where that misrepresentation relates to a future act. Furthermore, the failure to perform a promised act is not in itself evidence that the defendant, at the time the promise was made, intended to deceive.

Ala. Code 1975, § 7–5–103(1)(a), defines a letter of credit as: "an engagement by a bank ... made at the request of a customer ... that the issuer ... will honor drafts or other demands for payment ... upon compliance with the conditions specified in the [letter of] credit."

It is a contract between the issuer and the beneficiary of the letter of credit. The obligation of the issuer is independent of the underlying contract between the customer and the beneficiary and runs directly to the beneficiary.... See J. Dolan, The Law of Letters of Credit: Commercial and Standby Credits para. 2.02 at 2–3 (1984).

In Bank of the Southeast v. Jackson, 413 So.2d 1091, 1099 (Ala. 1982), this Court expressly recognized that the contract between the issuer and the beneficiary was independent, and not derivative of, the contract between the customer and the beneficiary. There, we said:

> The letter is quite independent of the primary agreement between the party for whose account it is issued and the beneficiary, or any underlying transactions. Neither the issuing nor the confirming bank has any obligation, and is not permitted, to go behind the terms of the letter and the documents which are required to be presented, and to enter controversies between the beneficiary and the party for whose account the letter was opened concerning any other agreements or transactions....

Likewise, rulings of the Comptroller of the Currency provide: "(d) The bank's obligation to pay should arise only upon the presentation of a draft or other documents as specified in the letter of credit, and the bank must not be called upon to determine questions of fact or law between the account party ... and the beneficiary...." 12 C.F.R. § 7–7016 (1988). Accord, Ala. Code 1975, § 7–5.114.

The trial court's order granting the preliminary injunction is, therefore, due to be reversed, and the case is remanded with instructions to release the funds due and owing to Benetton pursuant to the letter of credit issued by Southland.

Note

The *"Independence Principle"* is fundamental to letter of credit law. To understand that principle, one must unravel the various strands of a typical transaction involving a letter of credit. A commercial letter of credit involves two contracts in addition to the letter of credit itself.[1] For example, suppose S agrees to sell goods to B but insists on a documentary transaction with a letter of credit. B agrees. The buyer now has a contractual obligation to arrange for a letter of credit to be issued by a reputable bank or other financing agency (UCC 2–104(2)); a buyer who fails to arrange for a required letter of credit breaches the sales contract. See 2–325(1). Thus one contract involved in our commercial letter of credit transaction is the underlying sales contract between S and B. When B arranges for its bank to issue the letter of credit in exchange for a fee,[2] a second contract (the "issuing" contract) will be formed between B as "applicant" (5–102(a)(2)) and the bank as "issuer" (5–102(a)(9)).

The bank issues the letter to S, the "beneficiary." 5–102(a)(3). Traditional contract law might move us to think of S as a third party beneficiary of the issuing contract between the bank and its customer B, but that would be misleading. As a third party beneficiary under contract law, S's rights would be derivative of B's—i.e., the bank could assert against S any defenses that the bank had against B. Under letter of credit law, however, S is *not* subject to such defenses. For example, neither lack of consideration in the issuing contract nor B's breach of that contract would prevent S from enforcing the letter of credit against the bank. See 5–105 & 5–106. And as the *Benetton* case illustrates, S's rights against the bank are also unaffected by claims or defenses (other than fraud) that *B* might have based on the underlying sales contract. If S breached that contract by shipping nonconforming goods, the bank would, absent fraud by S, still have to honor a demand for payment that complied with the conditions of the letter of credit. 5–108. "[T]he bank's obligation to the beneficiary is *independent* of the beneficiary's performance on the underlying contract [with the customer]."[3]

Neither is the letter of credit a "guarantee" or "surety" promise. Consider *Hamada v. Far East National Bank*, 291 F.3d 645, 650 (9th Cir.2002), where the court explains,

---

1. We might even call the letter of credit a contract, although the classification limps. The credit is a commitment by the issuer upon which the beneficiary may rely, but it involves no exchange between the issuer and the beneficiary.

2. The bank also receives a right of reimbursement against B for any amounts the bank pays under the credit. 5–108(i)(1).

3. J. White & R. Summers, Uniform Commercial Code § 20–1c. (5th ed. 2000) (emphasis supplied).

"The key distinction between letters of credit and guarantees is that the issuer's obligation under a letter of credit is primary whereas a guarantor's obligation is secondary—the guarantor is *only* obligated to pay if the principal defaults on the debt the principal owes." *Tudor Dev. Group, Inc. v. United States Fidelity & Guaranty Co.*, 968 F.2d 357, 362 (3d Cir.1992). A bank issuing a letter of credit, unlike a guarantor, is not obligated "until after its customer fails to satisfy some obligation, [and] it is satisfying its own absolute and primary obligation to make payment rather than satisfying an obligation of its customer." *Id.* Thus, as opposed to the guaranty given by a surety, in a letter of credit transaction the bank's obligation under the letter of credit is independent of the underlying contract. *Id. See also San Diego Gas & Elec. Co. v. Bank Leumi*, 42 Cal.App.4th 928, 50 Cal.Rptr.2d 20, 24 (Cal.Ct.App.1996) (discussing the "independence principle" as the primary characteristic of letters of credit).

In short, issuers of letters of credit are not "liable with" the debtor on the obligation owed to the creditor; therefore, letter of credit issuers are not eligible under § 509 for statutory subrogation in this context. *Slamans v. First Nat'l Bank & Trust Co. (In re Slamans)*, 69 F.3d 468, 475–76 (10th Cir.1995) (letter of credit issuer does not satisfy the plain language requirements of § 509).

Thus, because of the independence principle, a letter of credit bestows upon the beneficiary a unique set of legal rights. The rationale for this arrangement in the context of a sales transaction is quite simple: insulating the beneficiary's rights from problems connected with the underlying sales contract or the issuing contract is what makes letters of credit useful. A seller whose right to payment is supported by a letter of credit need not worry about the buyer's solvency or the prospect of a dispute arising after the goods have been shipped to the buyer's location. These are the very risks that the seller sought to avoid by demanding a letter of credit.

If the issuer does not get involved with the underlying sale, how does it decide whether or not to honor drafts for the price of the goods? Here is another fundamental principle of letter of credit law: the issuer deals strictly in *documents,* i.e., a demand for payment under a letter of credit is a "paper transaction." If the documents required by the letter are presented, the issuer must (in the absence of fraud) honor a draft or demand for payment even if the underlying contract was breached. How does one determine if the documents meet the requirements of the letter of credit? As a comment to 5–108 indicates, UCC Article 5 requires "strict compliance" (rather than mere "substantial compliance") with the terms of the letter of credit, although "[s]trict compliance does not mean slavish conformity to the terms of the letter of credit." 5–108 comment 1. Thus whether documents do or do not comply with the terms of the letter of credit is a matter of case-by-case adjudication. The following case confronts this question.

COURTAULDS NORTH AMERICA, INC.
v. NORTH CAROLINA NAT. BANK

United States Court of Appeals for the Fourth Circuit, 1975.
528 F.2d 802.

BRYAN, SENIOR CIRCUIT JUDGE. A letter of credit with the date of March 21, 1973 was issued by the North Carolina National Bank at the request of and for the account of its customer, Adastra Knitting Mills, Inc. It made available upon the drafts of Courtaulds North America, Inc. "up to" $135,000.00 (later increased by $135,000.00) at "60 days date" to cover Adastra's purchases of acrylic yarn from Courtaulds. The life of the credit was extended in June to allow the drafts to be "drawn and negotiated on or before August 15, 1973."

Bank refused to honor a draft for $67,346.77 dated August 13, 1973 for yarn sold and delivered to Adastra. Courtaulds brought this action to recover this sum from Bank.

The defendant denied liability chiefly on the assertion that the draft did not agree with the letter's conditions, viz., that the draft be accompanied by a "Commercial invoice in triplicate stating [inter alia] that it covers ... 100% acrylic yarn"; instead, the accompanying invoices stated that the goods were "Imported Acrylic Yarn."

Upon cross motions for summary judgment on affidavits and a stipulation of facts, the District Court held defendant Bank liable to Courtaulds for the amount of the draft, interest and costs. It concluded that the draft complied with the letter of credit when each invoice is read together with the packing lists stapled to it, for the lists stated on their faces: "Cartons marked:—100% Acrylic." After considering the insistent rigidity of the law and usage of bank credits and acceptances, we must differ with the District Judge and uphold Bank's position.

The letter of credit prescribed the terms of the drafts as follows:

Drafts to be dated same as Bills of Lading. (Drafts) to be accompanied by:

1. Commercial invoice in triplicate stating that it covers 100,000 lbs. 100% Acrylic Yarn, Package Dyed at $1.35 per lb., FOB Buyers Plant, Greensboro, North Carolina Land Duty Paid.

2. Certificate stating goods will be delivered to buyers plant land duty paid.

3. Inland Bill of Lading consigned to Adastra Knitting Mills, Inc. evidencing shipment from East Coast Port to Adastra Knitting Mills, Inc., Greensboro, North Carolina.

The shipment (the last) with which this case is concerned was made on or about August 8, 1973. On direction of Courtaulds bills of lading of that date were prepared for the consignment to Adastra from a bonded warehouse by motor carrier. The yarn was packaged in cartons and a packing list referring to its bill of lading accompanied each carton. After the yarn was delivered to the carrier, each bill of lading with the packing list was sent to Courtaulds. There invoices for the sales were made out, and the invoices and packing lists stapled together. At the same time, Courtaulds wrote up the certificate, credit memorandum and draft called for in the letter of credit. The draft was dated August 13, 1973 and drawn on Bank by Courtaulds payable to itself.

All of these documents—the draft, the invoices and the packing lists—were sent by Courtaulds to its correspondent in Mobile for presentation to Bank and collection of the draft which for the purpose had been endorsed to the correspondent.

This was the procedure pursued on each of the prior drafts and always the draft had been honored by Bank save in the present instance. Here the draft, endorsed to Bank, and the other papers were sent to Bank on August 14. Bank received them on Thursday, August 16. Upon processing, Bank found these discrepancies between the drafts with accompanying documents and the letter of credit: (1) that the invoice did not state "100% Acrylic Yarn" but described it as "Imported Acrylic Yarn," and (2) "Draft not drawn as per terms of [letter of credit], Date [August 13] not same as Bill of Lading [August 8] and not drawn 60 days after date" [but 60 days from Bill of Lading date 8/8/73]. Since decision of this controversy is put on the first discrepancy we do not discuss the others.

On Monday, August 20, Bank called Adastra and asked if it would waive the discrepancies and thus allow Bank to honor the draft. In response, the president of Adastra informed Bank that it could not waive any discrepancies because a trustee in bankruptcy had been appointed for Adastra and Adastra could not do so alone. Upon word of these circumstances, Courtaulds on August 27 sent amended invoices to Bank which were received by Bank on August 27. They referred to the consignment as "100% Acrylic Yarn", and thus would have conformed to the letter of credit had it not expired. On August 29 Bank wired Courtaulds that the draft remained unaccepted because of the expiration of the letter of credit on August 15. Consequently the draft with all the original documents was returned by Bank.

During the life of the letter of credit some drafts had not been of even dates with the bills of lading, and among the large number of invoices transmitted during this period, several did not describe the goods as "100% Acrylic Yarn." As to all of these deficiencies Bank called Adastra for and received approval before paying the drafts. Every draft save the one in suit was accepted. The factual outline related is not in dispute, and the issue becomes one of law. It is well phrased by the District Judge in his "Discussion" in this way: "The only issue presented by the facts of this case is whether the documents tendered by the beneficiary to the issuer were in conformity with the terms of the letter of credit."

The letter of credit provided: "Except as otherwise expressly stated herein, this credit is subject to the 'Uniform Customs and Practice for Documentary Credits (1962 revision), the International Chamber of Commerce, Brochure No. 222'." Finding of fact 6.

Of particular pertinence, with accents added, are these injunctions of the Uniform Customs:

> Article 7.—Banks must examine all documents with reasonable care to ascertain that they appear on their face to be in accordance with the terms and conditions of the credit.

> Article 8.—In documentary credit operations all parties concerned deal in documents and not in goods.

* * *

> If, upon receipt of the documents, the issuing bank considers that they appear on their face not to be in accordance with the terms and conditions of the credit, that bank must determine, on the basis of the documents alone, whether to claim that payment, acceptance or negotiation was not effected in accordance with the terms and conditions of the credit.

* * *

> Article 9.—Banks ... do [not] assume any liability or responsibility for the description, ... quality, ... of the goods represented thereby....

* * *

> The description of the goods in the commercial invoice must correspond with the description in the credit. In the remaining documents the goods may be described in general terms.

Also to be looked to are the North Carolina statutes, because in a diversity action, the Federal courts apply the same law as would the courts of the State of adjudication. Here applied would be the Uniform Commercial Code—Letters of Credit, Chap. 25 G.S.N.C. Especially to be noticed are these sections:

> § 25–5–109. Issuer's obligation to its customer.

> (1) An issuer's obligation to its customer includes good faith and observance of any general banking usage but unless otherwise agreed does not include liability or responsibility

>> (a) for performance of the underlying contract for sale or other transaction between the customer and the beneficiary; or

* * *

>> (c) based on knowledge or lack of knowledge of any usage of any particular trade.

> (2) An issuer must examine documents with care so as to ascertain that on their face they appear to comply with the terms of

the credit but unless otherwise agreed assumes no liability or responsibility for the genuineness, falsification or effect of any document which appears on such examination to be regular on its face.

In utilizing the rules of construction embodied in the letter of credit—the Uniform Customs and State statute—one must constantly recall that the drawee bank is not to be embroiled in disputes between the buyer and the seller, the beneficiary of the credit. The drawee is involved only with documents, not with merchandise. Its involvement is altogether separate and apart from the transaction between the buyer and seller; its duties and liability are governed exclusively by the terms of the letter, not the terms of the parties' contract with each other. Moreover, as the predominant authorities unequivocally declare, the beneficiary must meet the terms of the credit—and precisely—if it is to exact performance of the issuer. Failing such compliance there can be no recovery from the drawee. That is the specific failure of Courtaulds here.

Free of ineptness in wording the letter of credit dictated that each invoice express on its face that it covered 100% acrylic yarn. Nothing less is shown to be tolerated in the trade. No substitution and no equivalent, through interpretation or logic, will serve. Harfield, Bank Credits and Acceptances (5th Ed. 1974), at p. 73, commends and quotes aptly from an English case: "There is no room for documents which are almost the same, or which will do just as well." Equitable Trust Co. of N.Y. v. Dawson Partners, Ltd., 27 LLOYD'S LIST LAW RPTS. 49, 52 (1926). Although no pertinent North Carolina decision has been laid before us, in many cases elsewhere, especially in New York, we find the tenet of Harfield to be unshaken.

At trial Courtaulds prevailed on the contention that the invoices in actuality met the specifications of the letter of credit in that the packing lists attached to the invoices disclosed on their faces that the packages contained "cartons marked:—100% acrylic". On this premise it was urged that the lists were a part of the invoice since they were appended to it, and the invoices should be read as one with the lists, allowing the lists to detail the invoices. But this argument cannot be accepted. In this connection it is well to revert to the distinction made in Uniform Customs, supra, between the "invoice" and the "remaining documents", emphasizing that in the latter the description may be in general terms while in the invoice the goods must be described in conformity with the credit letter.

The District Judge's pat statement adeptly puts an end to this contention of Courtaulds: "In dealing with letters of credit, it is a custom and practice of the banking trade for a bank to only treat a document as an invoice which clearly is marked on its face as 'invoice' ".

This is not a pharisaical or doctrinaire persistence in the principle, but is altogether realistic in the environs of this case; it is plainly the fair and equitable measure. (The defect in description was not superficial but occurred in the statement of the quality of the yarn, not a frivolous concern.) The obligation of the drawee bank was graven in the credit. Indeed, there could be no departure from its words. Bank was not expected to scrutinize the collateral papers, such as the packing lists. Nor was it permitted to read into the instrument the contemplation or intention of the seller and buyer. Adherence to this rule was not only legally commanded, but it was factually ordered also, as will immediately appear.

Had Bank deviated from the stipulation of the letter and honored the draft, then at once it might have been confronted with the not improbable risk of the bankruptcy trustee's charge of liability for unwarrantably paying the draft moneys to the seller, Courtaulds, and refusal to reimburse Bank for the outlay. Contrarily, it might face a Courtaulds claim that since it had depended upon Bank's assurance of credit in shipping yarn to Adastra, Bank was responsible for the loss. In this situation Bank cannot be condemned for sticking to the letter of the letter.

Nor is this conclusion affected by the amended or substituted invoices which Courtaulds sent to Bank after the refusal of the draft. No precedent is cited to justify retroactive amendment of the invoices or extension of the credit beyond the August 15 expiry of the letter.

Finally, the trial court found that although in its prior practices Bank had pursued a strict-constructionist attitude, it had nevertheless on occasion honored drafts not within the verbatim terms of the credit letter. But it also found that in each of these instances Bank had first procured the authorization of Adastra to overlook the deficiencies. This truth is verified by the District Court in its Findings of fact:

> 42. It is a standard practice and procedure of the banking industry and trade for a bank to attempt to obtain a waiver of discrepancies from its customer in a letter of credit transaction. This custom and practice was followed by NCNB in connection with the draft and documents received from Courtaulds.

> 43. Following this practice, NCNB had checked all previous discrepancies it discovered in Courtaulds' documents with its customer Adastra to see if Adastra would waive those discrepancies noted by NCNB. Except for the transaction in question, Adastra waived all discrepancies noted by NCNB.

> 44. It is not normal or customary for NCNB, nor is it the custom and practice in the banking trade, for a bank to notify a beneficiary or the presenter of the documents that there were any deficiencies in the draft or documents if they are waived by the customer.

This endeavor had been fruitless on the last draft because of the inability of Adastra to give its consent. Obviously, the previous acceptances of truant invoices cannot be construed as a waiver in the present incident.

For these reasons, we must vacate the decision of the trial court, despite the evident close reasoning and research of the District Judge, Courtaulds North America, Inc. v. North Carolina N.B., 387 FS 92 (M.D.N.C.1975). Entry of judgment in favor of the appellant Bank on its summary motion is necessary. Reversed and remanded for final judgment.

Note

The "strict compliance" view espoused by the court is clearly the dominant view, although a few cases adopt a "reasonable compliance" or an ambiguous "substantial performance" standard. The principal case also states the prevailing view that the contents of one document presented to the issuer cannot cure defects in other required documents. Even the "strict compliance" view, however, should not allow an issuer to dishonor drafts where the error in a presented document is so trivial that no one could possibly be misled. The basic concept is to allow the issuer to examine the documents and determine, on their face, whether they comply with the letter. Thus if it is clear beyond peradventure that the discrepancy should not mislead the issuer, allowing dishonor would open the door to bad faith. Indeed, 5–109(a) provides that, even where the issuer can prove that a required document is fraudulent, the obligation to honor a demand for payment that conforms on its face to the requirements of the letter of credit will only be excused if the fraud is "material," i.e., "the fraudulent aspect of the document [must] be material to a purchaser of that document or … the fraudulent act [must] be significant to the participants in the underlying transaction." 5–109 comment 1.

Even if the documents are perfect in form and content, the beneficiary must present them within the *time* specified in the letter of credit. On this, the courts are absolutely uniform. Once the time for presentment has expired, the issuer's obligation is discharged and the subsequent presentment of perfect documents will not cure this deficiency. This is true even if the delay was the fault of the medium of transmission. No matter how reliable the chosen medium normally is (e.g., the postal service), the risks of delays in transmission are on the beneficiary.

The Article 5 *statute of limitations* requires actions to enforce any claim arising under a letter of credit to be "commenced within one year after the expiration date of the relevant letter of credit or one year after the [claim for relief] [cause of action] accrues, whichever occurs later. A [claim for relief] [cause of action] accrues when the breach occurs, regardless of the aggrieved party's lack of knowledge of the breach." 5–115.

Problem 92

The National Bank of Cleveland sent the following letter to Charles Haller, who had agreed to lend $100,000 to Edward Palermo.

Dear Mr. Haller:

This letter evidences our permanent commitment to you that the National Bank of Cleveland will assume the obligation arising from a note signed by Edward Palermo in the amount of $100,000. We will honor this commitment 60 days after the date of the note upon notice to us that the loan has not been paid by Edward Palermo.

The letter was signed by George Avery, a vice president of the National Bank of Cleveland.

(a) Does this writing constitute a letter of credit as defined in 5–102(a)(10)?

(b) If this writing is deemed to be a letter of credit, is it revocable or irrevocable? See 5–106(a) and comment 1 to that section. What difference does it make? See 5–106(b). Which approach is better? See comment 1 to 5–106: "Given the usual commercial understanding and purpose of letters of credit, revocable letters of credit offer unhappy possibilities for misleading the parties who deal with them." If a sales contract requires the buyer to furnish a letter of credit but does not specify whether the credit is to be revocable or irrevocable, what is the buyer's obligation? See 2–325(3).

(c) Suppose Charles Haller relied upon the letter of credit in this problem. Would that affect your analysis of the revocability of the credit?

(d) If Haller, Palermo and the bank wanted to modify the letter, could they do so? How? See 5–104 and 5–106(b).

(e) What are the time limits for an issuer to honor drafts presented under a letter of credit? See 5–108(b). See also 5–106(c) & (d).

(f) Suppose Palermo defaulted on his note. Haller properly presented a draft complying with the letter of credit to the National Bank of Cleveland, but the bank wrongfully refused to pay the draft. What are Haller's rights against the bank? See 5–111.

Chapter 6

REMEDIES

A. REMEDIES UNDER UCC ARTICLE 2—IN GENERAL

Introduction—Underlying Principles

According to a provision in Article 1 of the UCC, Code remedies are to "be liberally administered to the end that the aggrieved party may be put in as good a position as if the other party had fully performed...."[1] This statement of the fundamental principle underlying UCC remedies—protection of an aggrieved party's expectation interest—clearly applies to the remedy provisions of Article 2. In studying the materials in this chapter, it is vital to remember this fundamental concept and to return to it when the waters become murky.

The availability of particular Article 2 remedies depends on the factual situation. For example, certain kinds of damages are available only if the buyer does not end up with the goods—e.g., if the buyer rejects the goods, or if the seller fails to deliver. That makes sense, since any attempt to award damages that will put the aggrieved party into the position it would have been in had the other side not breached must take into account whether or not the buyer retains the goods. In studying the materials that follow, it is important to focus on the factual and procedural prerequisites for an aggrieved party to invoke particular remedies.

Beyond the expectation principle, certain other fundamental remedial concepts appear in the remedy provisions of Article 2. Thus 2–715(2)(a) forbids the recovery of consequential damages for losses that an aggrieved buyer could have avoided by taking reasonable actions—the mitigation principle—and for losses that were not foreseeable consequences of breach at the time the contract was entered into.[2] Be aware of the way these principles are expressed in and influence the remedies studied in this chapter.

---

1. UCC 1–106, moved to Section 1–305 in the Amended version of Article 1.

2. The mitigation and foreseeability principles also appear in the provision gov-

erning an aggrieved seller's consequential damages in the proposed amended version of Article 2 (proposed amended Section 2–710(2)).

B. UCC REMEDIES WHEN THE BUYER DOES NOT RECEIVE OR RETAIN THE GOODS

1. *Buyers' Damages Measured by Substitute Transactions or Market Prices*

Problem 93

On October 1, the law firm Paley & Tologist ("P & T"), located in Chicago, agreed in writing to purchase 200 IBX computers from Seattle-based Random Accessories, Inc., which was selling off its inventory of computers because it was getting out of the computer business. The contract price was $600,000 ($3,000 per computer). The contract required Random to deliver the computers to P & T's offices on Random's own trucks by November 1. P & T prepaid $10,000 of the purchase price on October 10. Random failed to deliver by November 1. At the close of business on November 1, P & T's purchasing manager called Random to inquire about the missing computers and was told that Random had no plans to ship the goods. P & T's purchasing manager then told Random that the contract was canceled. Market prices for the kind of computers involved in the transaction had begun rising soon after the parties entered into their agreement. On November 1 the market price was $3,500 per computer in Chicago and $3,450 in Seattle. Because she was exceptionally busy with other matters, P & T's purchasing manager waited until November 9 to buy replacements for the missing computers. By that time market prices had risen to $3,900 per computer in Chicago, and $3,850 in Seattle. On November 9, P & T contracted with a Chicago supplier to purchase 200 replacement computers for $800,000 ($4,000 per computer).

P & T sues Random seeking to recover the $10,000 it had prepaid on the price, as well as $200,000 in damages calculated as the difference between the amount P & T paid for replacement computers and the price in the contract with Random. Is P & T entitled to these amounts? Consider 2–711 and 2–712. What requirements must P & T satisfy in order to recover the $200,000 damages it seeks? Suppose P & T's purchase of replacement computers did not satisfy the requirements for proper cover. What damages (if any) could it recover? See 2–712(3) and 2–713, as well as 2–723 and 2–724. What damages (if any) could P & T recover if it did not even attempt to cover? Would any of your answers change if the contract between Random and P & T had provided for delivery by an independent trucking company "FCA Seattle, as per INCOTERMS 2000?"

DANGERFIELD v. MARKEL

Supreme Court of North Dakota, 1979.
278 N.W.2d 364.

ERICKSTAD, CHIEF JUSTICE. This appeal arises as a result of our decision in Dangerfield v. Markel, 252 N.W.2d 184 (N.D.1977), in which we held that Markel, a potato grower, breached a contract with Dangerfield, a potato broker, to deliver potatoes, thus giving rise to damages under the Uniform Commercial Code. On remand the district court awarded Dangerfield $47,510.16 in damages plus interest and costs less an award to Markel of $3,840.68 plus interest. Markel appeals contending, among other things, that the district court made an erroneous award of damages to Dangerfield, and Dangerfield cross-appeals for an additional $101,675 in incidental and consequential damages. We affirm the district court judgment.

The facts in this case are stated in detail in two previous appeals to this court. By contract dated June 13, 1972, Markel (seller) contracted to sell Dangerfield (buyer) 25,000 cwt. of chipping potatoes during the 1972–1973 shipping season.[2] The seller allegedly breached the contract by refusing to deliver 15,055 cwt. of potatoes during the contract period and the buyer was allegedly forced to purchase potatoes on the open market to fulfill a contract with potato processors.

* * *

The primary issue on this appeal is whether or not the trial court made an erroneous award of damages to the buyer under the Uniform Commercial Code. The trial court in essence found that the buyer was entitled to damages pursuant to Section 41–02–91, N.D.C.C. (§ 2–712, U.C.C.) for the amount expended by the buyer to purchase the 15,055 cwt. of potatoes still due under the contract:

It appears to the Court that the Defendant (seller) ... should be liable for the difference in price including freight, if any, between the quantity of the potatoes remaining to be delivered under the ... contract after February 10, 1973 (date of breach), and the price including freight, if any, that the plaintiff (buyer) actually paid for potatoes to "cover" the supply that the plaintiff, Dangerfield, had a right to expect to be delivered ... under ... (the) contract during the remainder of the 1972–73 potato shipping season.

The court determined that the buyer completed "covering" the contract on March 21, 1973, which was 38 days after the date of breach. During the first eighteen days of this cover period, the buyer's purchases averaged $4.41 per cwt. During the remaining twenty days, the buyer's purchases averaged over $5.41 per cwt., with many purchases made at $6.00 per cwt.

Seller argues in substance that thirty-eight days for the buyer to cover in a rapidly rising market is improper under Sections 41–02–90 and 41–02–91, N.D.C.C. (§§ 2–711 and 2–712, U.C.C.); therefore, he submits that Section 41–02–92, N.D.C.C. (§ 2–713, U.C.C.) should have been used to compute damages.

---

2. The contract provided in part for the sale and purchase of 20,000 cwt. storage and 5,000 cwt. field "Kennebec & /or Norchip chipping potatoes at the following prices F.O.B. Red River Valley:

FIELD	$1.25
Nov.	$1.60
Dec.	$1.65
Jan.	$1.80
Feb.	$1.90
March	$2.00
April	$2.15
May	$2.30"

The contract did not specify a monthly delivery date nor a specific quantity to be delivered each month.

* * *

The seller submits that the market price at the time of the breach was between $3.75 and $4.25 per cwt. He argues that a proper measure of damages pursuant to Section 41–02–92, N.D.C.C. [UCC 2–713], would be an average of $4.00 per cwt. minus the contract price at the time of the breach ($1.90), or damages of $31,615.50 as opposed to the present award of $47,510.16, a reduction of $15,894.66.

The buyer responds that due to the perishable nature of the product involved in this case and the installment nature of the contract, the cover period was not unreasonable pursuant to Section 41–02–91, N.D.C.C. [UCC 2–712]; therefore, the damages are correct.

The pre-code measure of damages for a breach of contract for the sale of goods was to allow the aggrieved party the difference between his bargain (contract price) and the market price. Although this worked reasonably well in the majority of cases, practical problems arose in determining the market price as well as the related questions of "as of when" and "where." After the seller's breach, the buyer faced a dilemma, *i.e.* to ensure that he would be fully compensated for the seller's breach, the buyer had to make a substitute purchase that the finder of fact would later determine to be at the "market value". This "20–20 hindsight approach" by the factfinder produced questionable results. Therefore, Section 2–712, U.C.C., (Section 41–02–91, N.D.C.C.) was added to the buyer's arsenal of remedies. This section allows the buyer to make a substitute purchase to replace the goods that were not delivered by the seller and the damages are measured by the difference between the cost of the substitute goods and the contract price. See J. White & R. Summers, Handbook of the Law Under the Uniform Commercial Code 175–180 (1972); R. Nordstrom, Handbook of the Law or Sales 439–44 (1970); T. Quinn, Uniform Commercial Code Commentary and Law Digest, 2–445–2–448 (1978).

The official comment to Section 2–712, U.C.C., states that "the test of proper cover is whether at the time and place the buyer acted in good faith and in a reasonable manner, and it is immaterial that hindsight may later prove that the method of cover used was not the cheapest or most effective."

In order for Section 2–712, U.C.C., to apply, the buyer must make a reasonable purchase in good faith without unreasonable delay. If a buyer fails to cover or covers improperly, *e.g.* waits an unreasonable length of time or buys in bad faith, he may still be entitled to some relief.

The seller argues that the buyer's purchases did not satisfy the criteria of Section 2–712, U.C.C.; therefore, he is limited to the traditional measure of damages. Specifically, the seller argues that the buyer was obligated to purchase the entire cover on the date of the breach or shortly thereafter in order to mitigate his damages.

* * *

The record indicates that the buyer could not cover the balance of the contract on the date of the breach:

Q. Once you learned you were not going to receive any more potatoes from Mr. Markel in February of 1973, did you attempt to buy potatoes to cover the shortage on the contract?

A. I did.

Q. Were you able to go out right at that time on February 12th or 13th, and buy quantity to cover the remaining balance on the contract?

A. No, I was not able to.

Q. Why was this?

A. Well, we were continuing on rising market, no one wanted to commit more than one or two loads at any one time, so would load on basis whatever day they got car, they would accept whatever market was at that day.

Q. If I understand what you are saying correctly, is that potatoes that were available at that time had to be bought and you would have to take delivery and ship them, that what you mean?

A. That's correct.

Q. That's correct?

A. Right.

Q. You were not able to buy potatoes in February for delivery in May?

A. No.

Q. Were you able to buy potatoes in middle of February for delivery say a month or two later?

A. No.

Q. Did you try to do this?

A. Yes.

Furthermore, the trial court was obviously of the opinion that the buyer acted in good faith under the circumstances:

Based upon the foregoing facts and the Uniform Commercial Code as quoted above, the Court is of the opinion that the plaintiff having elected to "cover" the defendant's breach was not obliged to purchase the entire cover as of the date of the breach since this contract called for installment deliveries over a period of months during the 1972, 1973 potato shipping season. In the absence of a showing of plaintiff so as to increase his damages against the defendant, the Court will view as reasonable a course of purchases of cover stocks from time to time. This ruling is particularly called for in this case where the subject of the contract is a bulky perishable commodity and the quantities must be warehoused at carefully controlled temperatures to avoid freezing or undue deterioration in holding. It would be unreasonable under these circumstances to hold the covering buyer to a February 10, 1973, market price date for immediate delivery of the entire amount of cover necessary to complete the contract of sale. This is particularly true where, as here, the quantity and bulk of goods in question is large and where the goods normally would flow into commerce upon delivery rather than into storage.

It is generally accepted that if the buyer complies with the requirements of Section 2–712, U.C.C., his purchase is presumed proper and the burden of proof is on the seller to show that cover was not properly obtained. Kiser v. Lemco Industries, Inc., supra at 589; Laredo Hides Co., Inc. v. H & H Meat Products Co., Inc., 513 S.W.2d 210, 221 (Tex.Civ.App.1974).

* * *

In Farmer's Union Co-op Co. of Mead v. Flamme Bros., 196 Neb. 699, 245 N.W.2d 464 (1976), the Supreme Court of Nebraska was presented with a similar situation in which the seller argued that the buyer should not have been allowed to cover a breached corn contract over a 15–day–period in a rising market.

The Nebraska court rejected the argument:

In the case at bar, the appellee did not go into the market and buy corn specifically to cover the contracts, but appellee did continue buying corn from its members, as was its normal practice until the three contracts were fulfilled. The trial court determined, as inherent in its verdict and judgment for appellee, that appellee did "cover" the contract "without unreasonable delay," and under all the circumstances of this case, we affirm the trial court's judgment. Appellee did between the dates of January 2 and January 15, 1974, purchase over 111,000 bushels of corn and applied such purchases to the unfulfilled contracts. The comment following section 2–712, U.C.C., is particularly applicable to this case. That comment states, in part: "2. The definition of "cover" under subsection (1) envisages a series of contracts or sales, as well as a single contract or sale; * * * and contracts on credit or delivery terms differing from the contract in breach, but again reasonable under the circumstances. The test of proper cover is whether at the time and place the buyer acted in good faith and in a reasonable manner, and it is immaterial that hindsight may later prove that the method of cover used was not the cheapest or most effective.

The offended party is not bound by hindsight, and the practice used by appellee might have resulted in lower damages if the price over the time period had declined. Instead, the price fluctuated and the net result was that the damages were slightly higher than if the entire volume of corn had been purchased on January 2, 1974, at the

$2.32 price. Appellee acted in good faith and made the 'cover' purchases without unreasonable delay, within the meaning of the Uniform Commercial Code. 196 Neb. at 706, 245 N.W.2d at 468.

. . . . We are mindful of the Code's basic remedial message in Section 41–01–06, N.D.C.C., (§ 1–106, U.C.C.) to put the aggrieved party in the position performance would have. White and Summers, in their Hornbook series on the Uniform Commercial Code, comment on Sections 1–106 and 2–712:

> If 2–712 is to be the remedy used by more aggrieved buyers than any other remedy, then the courts must be chary of finding a good faith buyer's acts unreasonable. The courts should not hedge the remedy about with restrictions in the name of reasonableness that render it useless or uncertain for the good faith buyer. Indeed, one may argue that the courts should read very little substance into the reasonableness requirement and insist only that the buyer proceed in good faith. A question a lawyer might put to test his client's good faith under 2–712 is this: "How, where, and when would you have procured these goods if you had not been covering and had no prospect of a court recovery from another?" If the client can answer truthfully that he would have spent his own money in the same way, the court should not demand more. J. White & R. Summers, Handbook of the Law under the Uniform Commercial Code, at p. 178.

We do not feel that the seller met his burden of showing that cover was improperly obtained in this case or that the district court's findings were clearly erroneous. Consequently, we affirm the district court judgment on this issue.

* * *

The district court's judgment is affirmed in all respects.

SAND, PAULSON, PEDERSON AND VANDE WALLE, JJ., concur.

Notes on Dangerfield

According to *Dangerfield*, the purpose of cover damages is to allow an aggrieved buyer to make a good faith and reasonable substitute purchase and be assured that its expectation interest will be protected—i.e., after recovering damages it will end up paying no more than the original contract price. The cover remedy also serves other functions. In McGinnis v. Wentworth Chevrolet Co., 295 Or. 494, 668 P.2d 365 (1983), the Oregon Supreme Court reversed a lower court decision holding that a buyer's rental of a car to replace the vehicle she had rejected constituted "cover." The court commented:

> The Court of Appeals' opinion evinces a misconception as to the purpose and function of the UCC's "cover" remedy. . . .

> The UCC's "cover" alternative was intended to enable the buyer to "obtain the goods he needs" by allowing the disappointed buyer to reenter the market place and make a reasonable purchase of substitute

goods. See UCC § 2–712, Comment 1. This remedy also can obviate the often difficult calculation of the market price of the goods. See generally White and Summers, Uniform Commercial Code §§ 6–3, 6–4 (1972). . . .

Given the "cover" remedy's purpose in providing certainty for the calculation of the buyer's loss-of-bargain, while also allowing the buyer to obtain the needed goods, we conclude that the UCC's "cover" remedy [under Article 2] generally is not intended to apply to a rental. Rather, the remedy is limited only to those situations where the buyer has purchased or contracted to purchase goods as an actual replacement for the agreed-upon goods. . . . Rental costs are not readily translatable into a comparable value figure for computation of the loss-of-bargain and, therefore, viewing temporary rentals as "cover" would defeat the remedy's intended purpose.

Thus, as *McGinnis* emphasizes, an important purpose of the cover remedy under Article 2 is to eliminate the difficulties of proving market price. *McGinnis* also teaches, however, that the remedy is available only when the cover price is in fact an appropriate way to measure the buyer's lost bargain.

Problem 94

Odin Inc. makes components for heavy construction equipment. It uses, on average, 20,000 tons of raw steel per month. It acquires the steel from a variety of sources by contracts calling for delivery in 30 days. On July 1 Odin contracted in writing to purchase 1,000 tons of steel at $100 per ton from Thor Metals Company, delivery by July 31. Odin intended to use the steel to make drive shafts for one of its customers. When the steel arrived on July 31 Odin rightfully rejected it because it failed to conform to the contract. Thor refused to cure. To make the drive shafts for its customer, Odin substituted steel which it had previously purchased on July 3 at $105 per ton. In the first week of August Odin entered into the following contracts to purchase steel from other suppliers for delivery in 30 days:

August 2:	750 tons at $120 per ton
August 3:	1,250 tons at $130 per ton
August 5:	2,500 tons at $125 per ton
August 6:	1,000 tons at $115 per ton

Although this pattern and pace of purchasing steel was not unusual, Odin argues that it purchased an extra 1,000 tons of steel during the first week of August to rebuild its inventory after the default by Thor. None of the purchases during that period, however, was designated at the time as replacement for the Thor steel. All purchases were reasonable given market conditions when they were made.

Has Odin "covered" within the meaning of 2–712, or is that term reserved for a purchase made with the specific intent of fixing the amount of the seller's damages? If Odin has "covered," how should damages be measured? Should you use the July 3 transaction ($105 per ton) which produced the steel that was in fact used to replace the missing Thor steel in the drive shaft project? Or should you use a purchase or purchases entered into after the breach (if so, which ones)?

Note: Equivalency of Substitute Purchase for Purposes of Cover Damages

In order to qualify for cover damages under UCC Article 2, an aggrieved buyer must purchase substitute goods that are more or less equivalent to those it should have received from the seller, on terms that are at least roughly comparable to those in the breached contract. As comment 2 to 2–712 states, cover "envisages ... goods not identical with those involved but commercially usable as reasonable substitutes under the circumstances of the particular case; and contracts on credit or delivery terms differing from the contract in breach, but again reasonable under the circumstances."[1] Thus in Problem 93, if the replacement computers P & T purchased were significantly different in quality, features or capacity from the machines it had contracted to purchase from Random, P & T might not be able to recover cover damages measured by the substitute purchase. In such a case, the purchase of quite different goods does not stand as a good surrogate for the breached contract: allowing the buyer to acquire markedly better (or worse) substitute goods for the price in the original breached contract (which is the effect of awarding cover damages) would not put P & T in the position it would have been in had Random properly performed. In that case, P & T would be relegated to its market price remedy under 2–713.

Problem 95

Return to the transaction in Problem 93 involving the sale of 200 computers by Random Accessories to the law firm of Paley & Tologist ("P & T") for delivery by November 1 at a price of $3,000 per computer. Random fails to deliver the computers. On November 1 the market price for the computers in question is $3,500 per computer. On November 2 the market price begins to fall. On November 5 P & T makes a good faith and reasonable cover purchase for $3,200 per computer. P & T sues for market price damages under 2–713. Random argues that P & T should be limited to the smaller cover damages. What result? Consider 1–106[2], comment 5 to pre-amendment 2–713.[3]

Problem 96

Dura–Wood, which manufactured treated timbers for use in landscaping projects, received a special order for a large number of timbers. To avoid disrupting shipments to its regular customers, Dura–Wood decided to fill part of this special order by acquiring timbers from other manufacturers. For this purpose, it contracted to purchase a quantity of timbers from Century Products at $5 per timber. When Century repudiated this contract,

---

1. The substance of this language is found in comment 4 to proposed amended Section 2–712.

2. This provision appear as 1–305 in the amended version of Article 1.

3. According to comment 7 to proposed amended Section 2–713, "[a] buyer that has covered may not recover the contract market difference under this section."

Dura–Wood decided to manufacture the necessary timbers itself at a cost of $6 per timber. Dura–Wood then sued Century. Can Dura–Wood recover the difference between the contract price and its costs of manufacturing replacement timbers as "internal cover" damages under 2–712? Would it matter if, before deciding to make the necessary timbers itself, Dura–Wood had solicited price quotes from other timber suppliers and the cheapest had come in at $7 per timber? Alternatively, would it matter if substitute timbers were not available from other suppliers?

Note: Measuring Buyer's Market Price Damages when Seller Repudiates

Suppose that, in a contract requiring the goods to be delivered on November 1, the seller repudiates the contract (e.g., unequivocally declares it will not perform) on October 1. As of what date should the buyer's market price damages be measured? If market prices are volatile, the answer can make a large difference in the amount of damages the buyer can recover. Under the pre-amendment version of 2–713(1), which requires market price damages to be measured "when the buyer learns of the breach" and has no special rule dealing with repudiation situations, this issue has caused considerable controversy. In Cosden Oil & Chemical Co. v. Karl O. Helm Aktiengesellschaft, 736 F.2d 1064 (5th Cir.1984) the court declared that the question was "one of the most difficult interpretive problems of the Uniform Commercial Code." The *Cosden* court also noted that "[c]ourts and commentators have identified three possible interpretations of the phrase 'learned of the breach' [in 2–713]. If seller anticipatorily repudiates, buyer learns of the breach: (1) When he learns of the repudiation; (2) When he learns of the repudiation plus a commercially reasonable time; or (3) When performance is due under the contract."

Proposed amended Section 2–713(1) would include changes that impact this issue. The amended section states two different rules regarding the time for measuring market price for purposes of awarding damages to an aggrieved buyer. In non-repudiation situations (i.e., when the seller wrongfully fails to deliver or the buyer rightfully rejects or justifiably revokes acceptance), proposed amended Section 2–713(1)(a) measures market prices "at the time for tender under the contract." rather than at the time the buyer learned of the breach. Where the seller has repudiated, however, proposed amended Section 2–713(1)(b) measures market prices "at the expiration of a commercially reasonable time after the buyer learned of the repudiation, but no later than the time [for tender under the contract]." How does one determine the end of a "commercially reasonable time" after repudiation? What factors are relevant? Under the pre-amendment version of Article 2, courts have held that a "commercially reasonable time" expires on the same day as the buyer learned of the repudiation if the repudiation was "unequivocal," cover was readily available in an easily accessible market, and the market price was rising at the time. First National Bank of Chicago v. Jefferson Mortgage Co., 576 F.2d 479 (3d Cir.1978); Oloffson v. Coomer, 11 Ill.App.3d 918, 296 N.E.2d 871 (1973). Would such decisions remain good law under the amended version of 2–713? Comment 4 to proposed amended Section 2–713 states that the "commercially reasonable time" rule applicable in repudiation situations "approximates the market price at the time the buyer would have covered even though the buyer has not done so...."

2. Buyers' Recovery of the Goods

Introductory Note on Buyers' Right to Reach the Goods under the UCC

Rather than pursuing damages, a buyer who has not received the goods that it contracted for may desire to seize the goods from the seller, or to compel the seller to deliver them. Allowing such relief is consistent with the remedial goal of protecting the aggrieved party's expectation interest.

UCC Article 2, in line with the common law's traditional preference for damage remedies over specific relief, puts significant limits on a buyer's right to recover the goods themselves (as opposed to damages) from a seller who is unwilling to deliver voluntarily. Nevertheless, Article 2 contains three provisions, each with a distinct purpose, theory and history, that permit a buyer to reach goods in the seller's control:

(1) In certain circumstances, 2–502 permits a buyer who has pre-paid all or part of the price to recover identified goods from a seller who has become insolvent within ten days after receiving the first install-ment of the price. See 2–502. The purpose of the provision is to protect a buyer when the seller's financial condition renders a mere right to money damages ineffective. Where the buyer is a consumer, proposed amended Section 2–502 would eliminate the requirement that the seller become insolvent, thus greatly expanding a consumer buyer's right to recover goods on which it has pre-paid.[1]

(2) A buyer who has not received delivery may have a right of replevin (or other similar action) for identified goods if "after reasonable efforts" the buyer is unable to effect cover for the goods, or an attempt to cover would be "unavailing" in the circumstances. See 2–716(3). Before the UCC was enacted, a buyer could replevy goods from a seller only if the buyer had title. See Uniform Sales Act § 66. This property-orientation resulted in complicated and confusing rules having little connection to the policy issues underlying the replevin remedy. As codified in the UCC, the right of replevin has undergone fundamental conceptual changes in keeping with the Code's de-emphasis on title (see 2–401).

(3) Under 2–716(1), a buyer may in some circumstances claim specific performance. As an equitable remedy, specific performance (in contrast to the legal action of replevin) was traditionally available only if the remedy "at law" (i.e., money damages) was inadequate. To satisfy this requirement in the context of a sales contract, a buyer generally had to prove that the goods involved were literally "unique"—e.g., a one-of-a-kind work of art. In such cases damages would be inadequate both because the value of a unique item is extremely difficult to measure and because the buyer literally could not replace the goods. Under the UCC, specific performance is still granted when the goods are "unique,"

---

1. This change is in line with recent amendments to Article 9 of the UCC.

but it is also available "in other proper circumstances." The drafters' comments suggest that they intended to expand the number of situations in which specific performance is available, although the extent of the intended expansion is unclear.

Problem 97

Plebian Power Inc. ("PPI"), a public utility, agreed to purchase a complex piece of pollution control equipment from Ecologistics Corp. for $10 million. The largest and most important components of the equipment were of standard design, but many of the smaller parts were to be specially built for PPI. The manner in which the components were to be assembled once they had all been built, furthermore, was custom-designed for PPI's generating plant. PPI paid $2 million upon signing the contract. The remainder of the price was due upon installation, which Ecologistics was to supervise and which was to be completed 14 months after contract execution.

Several days after the contract was signed federal environmental regulators unexpectedly announced new air pollution controls for electrical generating plants. Only equipment made by Ecologistics and two other manufacturers could be used to meet the new standards. As a result of the announcement of the new regulations, market prices for the equipment immediately doubled. Even at the advanced prices, demand far exceeded the capacity of Ecologistics and the two other producers. Within a week of signing the contract with PPI and before any substantial work under that agreement had begun, Ecologistics announced it was repudiating the arrangement unless PPI raised the contract price by $8 million to be paid immediately. PPI has come to you for advice.

(a) Can PPI specifically enforce the contract against Ecologistics under 2–716? Does it matter that Ecologistics has yet to manufacture some components and has not assembled the final product? Under § 68 of the old Uniform Sales Act, specific performance was available only if the contract was for "specific or ascertained goods." Read comment 2 to 2–716. Consider how you would draft the order PPI would want issued. Could a court easily administer your proposed order? Suppose that after lengthy litigation a court issued an order for specific performance against Ecologistics. Could PPI also recover damages for delay in the delivery and installation of the equipment?

(b) Could PPI claim specific enforcement if equipment from the other two manufacturers was readily available at the increased market prices? See comment 2 to 2–716. See also Duval & Co. v. Malcom, 233 Ga. 784, 214 S.E.2d 356 (1975) (specific performance not available even though the market price of the commodity covered by the contract had skyrocketed; "[t]he mere fact that plaintiff might be compelled to pay an unreasonable price . . . is not a ground for equitable relief but rather relates to the amount of his damages at law"). Suppose PPI's financial condition and/or regulated rate structure made it difficult or impossible to finance the higher price. Is that relevant? See Stephan's Machine & Tool, Inc. v. D & H Machinery Consultants, Inc., 65 Ohio App.2d 197, 417 N.E.2d 579 (1979).

(c) Suppose PPI was an equipment broker who had contracted to resell the equipment, and that breaching its resale contract would subject PPI to huge liability for consequential damages. Do these facts justify awarding specific performance? See Ace Equipment Co. v. Aqua Chem, Inc., 20 U.C.C. Rep.Serv. (Callaghan) 392 (Pa.Com.Pl.1975).

(d) Suppose the contract between PPI and Ecologistics contained a clause providing that, if the seller unjustifiably refused to deliver the equipment, PPI could obtain specific performance. Should a court enforce the clause? Is the clause enforceable if PPI could readily obtain substitute equipment at a reasonable price? Proposed amended Section 2–716(1) would include the following: "In a contract other than a consumer contract, specific performance may be decreed if the parties have agreed to that remedy.".[2] Comment 3 to that provision states that "[t]he parties' agreement to specific performance could be enforced even if legal remedies are entirely adequate."

SEDMAK v. CHARLIE'S CHEVROLET, INC.

Missouri Court of Appeals, 1981.
622 S.W.2d 694.

SATZ, JUDGE. This is an appeal from a decree of specific performance. We affirm.

In their petition, plaintiffs, Dr. and Mrs. Sedmak (Sedmaks), alleged they entered into a contract with defendant, Charlie's Chevrolet, Inc. (Charlie's), to purchase a Corvette automobile for approximately $15,000.00. The Corvette was one of a limited number manufactured to commemorate the selection of the Corvette as the Pace Car for the Indianapolis 500. Charlie's breached the contract, the Sedmaks alleged, when, after the automobile was delivered, an agent for Charlie's told the Sedmaks they could not purchase the automobile for $15,000.00 but would have to bid on it.

The trial court found the parties entered into an oral contract and also found the contract was excepted from the Statute of Frauds. The court then ordered Charlie's to make the automobile "available for delivery" to the Sedmaks. . . .

[T]he record reflects the Sedmaks to be automobile enthusiasts, who, at the time of trial, owned six Corvettes. In July, 1977, "Vette Vues," a Corvette fancier's magazine to which Dr. Sedmak subscribed, published an article announcing Chevrolet's tentative plans to manufacture a limited edition of the Corvette. The limited edition of approximately 6,000 automobiles was to commemorate the selection of the Corvette as the Indianapolis 500 Pace Car. The Sedmaks were interested in acquiring one of these Pace Cars to add to their Corvette collection. In November, 1977, the Sedmaks asked Tom Kells, sales manager at Charlie's Chevrolet, about the availability of the Pace Car. Mr. Kells said he did not have any information on the car but would find out about it.

2. The next sentence of proposed amended Section 2–716(1) would provide that a contract clause permitting specific enforcement is not enforceable "if the breaching party's sole remaining contractual obligation is the payment of money."

Kells also said if Charlie's were to receive a Pace Car, the Sedmaks could purchase it.

On January 9, 1978, Dr. Sedmak telephoned Kells to ask him if a Pace Car could be ordered. Kells indicated that he would require a deposit on the car, so Mrs. Sedmak went to Charlie's and gave Kells a check for $500.00. She was given a receipt for that amount bearing the names of Kells and Charlie's Chevrolet, Inc. At that time, Kells had a pre-order form listing both standard equipment and options available on the Pace Car. Prior to tendering the deposit, Mrs. Sedmak asked Kells if she and Dr. Sedmak were "definitely going to be the owners." Kells replied, "yes." After the deposit had been paid, Mrs. Sedmak stated if the car was going to be theirs, her husband wanted some changes made to the stock model. She asked Kells to order the car equipped with an L82 engine, four speed standard transmission and AM/FM radio with tape deck. Kells said that he would try to arrange with the manufacturer for these changes. Kells was able to make the changes, and, when the car arrived, it was equipped as the Sedmaks had requested.

Kells informed Mrs. Sedmak that the price of the Pace Car would be the manufacturer's retail price, approximately $15,000.00. The dollar figure could not be quoted more precisely because Kells was not sure what the ordered changes would cost, nor was he sure what the "appearance package"—decals, a special paint job—would cost. Kells also told Mrs. Sedmak that, after the changes had been made, a "contract"—a retail dealer's order form—would be mailed to them. However, no form or written contract was mailed to the Sedmaks by Charlie's.

On January 25, 1978, the Sedmaks visited Charlie's to take delivery on another Corvette. At that time, the Sedmaks asked Kells whether he knew anything further about the arrival date of the Pace Car. Kells replied he had no further information but he would let the Sedmaks know when the car arrived. Kells also requested that Charlie's be allowed to keep the car in their showroom for promotional purposes until after the Indianapolis 500 Race. The Sedmaks agreed to this arrangement.

On April 3, 1978, the Sedmaks were notified by Kells that the Pace Car had arrived. Kells told the Sedmaks they could not purchase the car for the manufacturer's retail price because demand for the car had inflated its value beyond the suggested price. Kells also told the Sedmaks they could bid on the car. The Sedmaks did not submit a bid. They filed this suit for specific performance.

[The court affirmed the trial court's holding that a contract to purchase the vehicle had been formed, and that such contract was enforceable under the Article 2 Statute of Frauds (UCC 2–201).]

* * *

Finally, Charlie's contends the Sedmaks failed to show they were entitled to specific performance of the contract. We disagree. Although it has been stated that the determination whether to order specific performance lies within the discretion of the trial court, Landau v. St. Louis Public Service Co., 273 S.W.2d 255, 259 (Mo.1954), this discretion is, in fact, quite narrow. When the relevant equitable principles have been met and the contract is fair and plain, "specific performance goes as a matter of right." Miller v. Coffeen, 280 S.W.2d 100, 102 (Mo.1955). Here, the trial court ordered specific performance because it concluded the Sedmaks "have no adequate remedy at law for the reason that they cannot go upon the open market and purchase an automobile of this kind with the same mileage, condition, ownership and appearance as the automobile involved in this case, except, if at all, with considerable expense, trouble, loss, great delay and inconvenience." Contrary to defendant's complaint, this is a correct expression of the relevant law and it is supported by the evidence.

Under the Code, the court may decree specific performance as a buyer's remedy for breach of contract to sell goods "where the goods are unique or in other proper circumstances." § 400.2–716(1) RSMo 1978 [UCC 2–716(1)]. The general term "in other proper circumstances" expresses the drafters' intent to "further a more liberal attitude than some courts have shown in connection with the specific performance of contracts of sale." § 400.2–716, U.C.C., Comment 1. This Comment was not directed to the courts of this state, for long before the Code, we, in Missouri, took a practical approach in determining whether specific performance would lie for the breach of contract for the sale of goods and did not limit this relief only to the sale of "unique" goods. Boeving v. Vandover, 240 Mo.App. 117, 218 S.W.2d 175 (1949). In Boeving, plaintiff contracted to buy a car from defendant. When the car arrived, defendant refused to sell. The car was not unique in the traditional legal sense but, at that time, all cars were difficult to obtain because of war-time shortages. The court held specific performance was the proper remedy for plaintiff because a new car "could not be obtained elsewhere except at considerable expense, trouble or loss, which cannot be estimated in advance and under such circumstances (plaintiff) did not have an adequate remedy at law." Id. at 177–178. Thus, Boeving, presaged the broad and liberalized language of § 400.2–716(1) and exemplifies one of the "other proper circumstances" contemplated by this subsection for ordering specific performance. § 400.2–716, Missouri Code Comment 1. The present facts track those in Boeving.

The Pace Car, like the car in Boeving, was not unique in the traditional legal sense. It was not an heirloom or, arguably, not one of a kind. However, its "mileage, condition, ownership and appearance" did make it difficult, if not impossible, to obtain its replication without considerable expense, delay and inconvenience. Admittedly, 6,000 Pace Cars were produced by Chevrolet. However, as the record reflects, this is limited production. In addition, only one of these cars was available to each dealer, and only a limited number of these were equipped with the specific options ordered by plaintiffs. Charlie's had not received a car like the Pace Car in the previous two years. The sticker price for the car was $14,284.21. Yet Charlie's received offers from individuals in Hawaii and

Florida to buy the Pace Car for $24,000.00 and $28,000.00 respectively. As sensibly inferred by the trial court, the location and size of these offers demonstrated this limited edition was in short supply and great demand. We agree, with the trial court. This case was a "proper circumstance" for ordering specific performance.

Judgment affirmed.

___

Question

Suppose that in *Sedmak* there had been a written contract with a clause providing that, if the seller failed to deliver, the buyer's sole remedy would be a refund of the deposit paid ($500). Would that change the result in the case?

Note: Proof Problems and Specific Performance

Sometimes proof problems can prevent an aggrieved buyer from recovering damages—for example, if the amount of the buyer's losses is speculative. Does this situation constitute "other proper circumstances" justifying an award of specific performance under 2–716(1)? According to one frequently-cited pre-Code case, "[t]he adequate remedy at law, which will preclude the grant of specific performance of a contract by a court of equity, must be as certain, prompt, complete, and efficient to attain the ends of justice as a decree of specific performance." National Marking Mach. Co. v. Triumph Mfg. Co., 13 F.2d 6, 9 (8th Cir.1926). The Supreme Court of New Mexico invoked this principle in affirming an award of specific performance in a long-term fixed-price contract for fabricated nuclear fuel:

> In this case, there is substantial evidence to support the conclusion that damages are an inadequate remedy. The evidence shows that no seller was willing to make a long-term contract with [buyer] on any basis other than the market price at the time of delivery. Because fixed price contracts for future delivery were unavailable, there was no way to predict the price [buyer] might have to pay. Thus specific performance was a proper remedy, even though the goods involved are not "unique" in the traditional sense of that term.

United Nuclear Corp. v. General Atomic Co., 96 N.M. 155, 162, 629 P.2d 231, 238 (1980). In contrast, the court in Copylease Corp. of America v. Memorex Corp., 408 F.Supp. 758 (S.D.N.Y.1976), noted that "California law does not consider a remedy at law inadequate merely because difficulties may exist as to precise calculation of damages."

Note on Specific Performance in Requirement and Output Contracts

Comment 2 to UCC 2–716 states that output and requirement contracts constitute the "typical" modern situation calling for specific performance. What features of output and requirements contracts make them likely candidates for specific enforcement? In Laclede Gas Co. v. Amoco Oil Co., 522 F.2d 33 (8th Cir.1975), rev'd on other grounds, 531 F.2d 942 (8th Cir.1976), Laclede had entered into a long term contract to purchase from Amoco the propane gas requirements of specified housing developments. The contract required Amoco to maintain storage and delivery facilities to which Laclede would attach its distribution pipeline for each development. When Amoco attempted to "cancel" the agreement, Laclede sued. The appeals court held that the contract should be specifically enforced:

> As Amoco points out, Laclede has propane immediately available to it under other contracts with other suppliers. And the evidence indicates that at the present time propane is readily available on the open market. However, this analysis ignores the fact that the contract involved in this lawsuit is for a long-term supply of propane to these subdivisions. The other two contracts under which Laclede obtains the gas will remain in force only until March 31, 1977 and April 1, 1981, respectively; and there is no assurance that Laclede will be able to receive any propane under them after that time.... Additionally, there was uncontradicted expert testimony that Laclede probably could not find another supplier of propane willing to enter into a long-term contract, such as the Amoco agreement, given the uncertain future of worldwide energy supplies. And, even if Laclede could obtain supplies of propane for the affected developments through its present contracts or newly negotiated ones, it would still face considerable expense and trouble which cannot be estimated in advance in making arrangements for its distribution to the subdivisions.

Are the factors highlighted in this analysis more likely to be present if the contract in question is an output or requirements contract rather than a fixed-quantity agreement?

An order of specific performance for an output or requirements contract may require careful monitoring over extended periods of time, increasing the potential for disputes after the order has issued. Concerns about the administrability of specific relief and excessive demands on scarce court resources have been cited to justify the traditional preference for a damages remedy. The *Laclede* opinion, however, dismissed such concerns:

> While a court may refuse to grant specific performance where such a decree would require constant and long-continued court supervision, this is merely a discretionary rule of decision which is frequently ignored when the public interest is involved.... Here the public interest in providing propane to the retail customers is manifest, while any supervision required will be far from onerous.

Not all courts have been so cavalier about the problems of administering specific relief in output or requirements contracts:

> .... [I]t will be necessary to reconcile California's policy against ordering specific performance of contracts which provide for continuing acts or an ongoing relationship with § 2–716 of the Code.... Output and requirements contracts, explicitly cited [in the official comments] as examples of situations in which specific performance may be appropriate, by their nature call for a series of continuing acts and an ongoing relationship. Thus the drafters seem to have contemplated that at least

in some circumstances specific performance will issue contrary to the historical reluctance to grant such relief in these situations. If, at the hearing, [the buyer] makes a showing that it meets the requirements of § 2–716, the sensible approach would be to measure, with the particulars of this contract in mind, the uniqueness or degree of difficulty in covering against the difficulties of enforcement which have caused courts to refrain from granting specific performance.

Copylease Corp. of America v. Memorex Corp., 408 F.Supp. 758, 760 (S.D.N.Y.1976).

Problem 98

Return to the facts of Problem 97. Could PPI use 2–502 to recover the equipment that Ecologistics contracted to provide? Consider, inter alia, the definition of "insolvent" in 1–201(23). Could PPI replevy the equipment using 2–716(3)?

Problem 99

Same facts as Problem 97 except that Ecologistics did not repudiate the contract until the equipment had been manufactured, packed and labeled for shipment to Plebian Power ("PPI") in preparation for installation. Do these changes alter the result with respect to specific performance? Replevin? Recovery under 2–502?

Question

Is 2–502 the *exclusive* means for a buyer to recover the goods from an insolvent seller, or could a buyer argue that, because a damage award against an insolvent seller is uncollectible, the seller's insolvency creates "other proper circumstances" for awarding specific performance? See Proyectos Electronicos, S.A. v. Alper, 37 Bankr. 931 (E.D.Pa.1983); but see J. WHITE & R. SUMMERS, UNIFORM COMMERCIAL CODE § 6–6 at 274 (3rd ed. 1988) (criticizing the *Proyectos* decision).

Problem 100

Again take the sale of pollution control equipment by Ecologistics to Plebian Power ("PPI") described in Problem 97, but now assume that, despite the new regulations and their effect on the market for its products, Ecologistics did not repudiate its agreement with PPI. Instead, Ecologistics manufactured, assembled and installed the equipment within the time required by the contract. The newly-installed equipment, however, failed to function as designed. Without the Ecologistics equipment, PPI's facility could be brought up to the new federal air pollution guidelines only by additional chemical treatment of emissions that was not only extremely expensive but also controversial. Indeed, the chemical treatment is currently under regulatory review, and many experts predict it will be outlawed within the next five years. The expected useful life of the Ecologistics equipment, which was warranted to bring the PPI plant within federal air pollution guidelines without the use of chemical treatment, was 25 years. Only Ecologistics has the expertise necessary to repair the defective equipment, and PPI wants to obtain a court order requiring the seller to do so. Under what provision of UCC Article 2 should PPI proceed and what would it have to prove to obtain the relief? See Colorado–Ute Electric Ass'n v. Envirotech Corp., 524 F.Supp. 1152 (D.Colo.1981).

---

3. *Seller's/Lessor's Damages Measured by Substitute Transactions or Market Prices*

Problem 101

On October 1 Random Accessories, Inc., located in Seattle, contracted to sell 200 computers to the law firm of Paley & Tologist ("P & T"), located in Chicago, for $600,000 ($3,000 per computer). On the contractual delivery date (November 1) Random sent its trucks to deliver 200 perfectly conforming computers, but P & T wrongfully rejected the goods. P & T had prepaid $10,000 on the purchase price of $600,000 ($3,000 per computer), but it refused to make any further payments. Market prices for the computers in question had been falling, so that their market value on November 1 was $2,500 per computer in Chicago and $2,450 in Seattle. By November 9 market prices had fallen to $2,150 per computer in Chicago and $2,100 in Seattle. On that day Random sold the computers it had intended to ship to P & T to another buyer in Seattle for $2,000 per computer ($400,000 total).

Random sued P & T for breach of the sales contract and seeks to recover "resale damages" measured by the difference between the price in its contract with P & T ($600,000) and the price at which it was able to resell the computers ($400,000). What result? See UCC 2–706. What requirements must Random satisfy in order to recover resale damages? Should the calculation of Random's damages take into account the fact that, under the resale contract, Random does not have to transport the computers from Seattle to Chicago? Suppose Random's resale of the computers did not satisfy the requirements of 2–706. What damages, if any, could Random recover? See 2–708(1). If Random attempts to recover market price damages, at what time and place should the market price of the goods be measured? Would your answers change if the contract between Random and P & T had provided for delivery by an independent trucking company, although without specifying any delivery term (i.e., no "FOB" or similar term)?

Problem 102

In a situation governed by UCC Article 2, Cudahy wrongfully repudiated a contract to purchase 3,000 tons of barley from Coast Trading Co. for $130 per ton. After giving Cudahy notice, Coast resold the barley to one of its wholly-owned subsidiaries—Merchandisers, Inc.—for $100 per ton, which was five dollar less than the market price at the time. Five days after the resale, at a time when the market price for barley had risen to $115 per ton,

Merchandisers sold the 3,000 tons of barley back to Coast for $100.25, which immediately resold the barley to an unrelated party for $115 per ton. Cudahy sues to recover damages measured by the difference between the contract price and the price in the resale to Merchandisers—$30 per ton ($90,000 total). How should the court rule? Would it matter whether the resale to Merchandisers was a private sale or a public sale meeting the requirements of 2–706(4)? See Coast Trading Co. v. Cudahy Co., 592 F.2d 1074 (9th Cir.1979).

Note: Types of Resales and Notice of Resale

An aggrieved seller can qualify for resale damages under 2–706 by reselling the goods in a "public sale" or in a "private sale." See 2–706(2). No matter which type of resale is chosen, however, "every aspect" of the resale "including the method, manner, time, place, and terms must be commercially reasonable." In addition, public sales are subject to particular regulations in 2–706(4). What is the difference between a public resale and a private resale? See comment 4 to 2–706 (comment 5 to proposed amended Section 2–706). The seller must give the buyer notice of both public and private resales, although notice of a public sale is not required if the goods "are perishable or threaten to decline in value speedily." See 2–706(3) & (4)(b). What is the purpose of requiring the seller to notify the buyer of resale? Consider comment 8 to 2–706. Many cases have held that failure to give the required notice means that the seller cannot recover resale damages under 2–706 (i.e., the seller is relegated to market price damages under 2–708(1)).

Problem 103

Belcher contracted to buy 48,000 barrels of No. 2 heating oil from Apex. When a ship containing the oil arrived at Belcher's terminal, Belcher wrongfully rejected the shipment. Anxious to avoid further shipping charges, Apex immediately arranged for the heating oil on the ship to be delivered to another customer, Cities Service, in fulfillment of a preexisting contract. The price in the Cities Service contract was higher than the contract price with Belcher. A short time later, and after notifying Belcher of its intentions, Apex sold 48,000 barrels of No. 2 heating oil to a third party—Gill & Duffus—for several thousand dollars less than the contract price with Belcher. How should Belcher's direct damage be measured? Should Belcher receive resale damages measured by the sale to Gill & Duffus (resulting in several thousand dollars in damages)? Should Belcher receive resale damages measured by the sale to Cities Service (resulting in no damages)? Should Belcher recover market price damages under 2–708(1)? See Apex Oil Co. v. Belcher Co. of New York, Inc., 855 F.2d 997 (2d Cir.1988).

4. Sellers' Lost Profit Recovery

Problem 104

Terri Crane decided to buy a new automobile from Total Autosource, Inc. (TAI). Because it was the start of a new model year, TAI insisted that Terri pay the full sticker price for the vehicle she chose—$28,000—even though TAI could obtain any number of similarly-equipped cars from the manufacturer for the dealer's wholesale price of $22,000 each. Since she had no real alternative (all dealerships refused to bargain down from the sticker price of the model Terri wanted at this time of year), Terri finally gave in. She signed all the necessary papers to buy the car for $28,000 and agreed to take delivery on September 3. Late on September 2, however, Terri called to "cancel" the order without any justification.

(a) TAI sold the car to another buyer on September 4 for the sticker price of $28,000. What damages can the seller recover under 2–706?

(b) Alternatively, TAI sued for damages under 2–708(1). What are the seller's damages under that provision?

(c) Do your answers in (a) and (b) comport with the mandate of 1–106(1) (found in 1–305(a) in amended Article 1)—i.e., do they put the TAI into the position it would have been in had Terri performed her end of the contract?

(d) Can TAI invoke 2–708(2)? Consider comment 5 to proposed amended Section 2–708. Would the measure of damages in 2–708(2) protect TAI's expectation interest?

KENCO HOMES, INC. v. WILLIAMS

Court of Appeals of Washington, 1999.
94 Wash.App. 219, 972 P.2d 125.

MORGAN, JUDGE. Kenco Homes, Inc., sued Dale E. Williams and Debi A. Williams, husband and wife, for breaching a contract to purchase a mobile home. After a bench trial, the trial court ruled primarily for Williams. Kenco appealed, claiming the trial court used an incorrect measure of damages. We reverse.

Kenco buys mobile homes from the factory and sells them to the public. Sometimes, it contracts to sell a home that the factory has not yet built. It has "a virtually unlimited supply of product," according to the trial court's finding of fact.

On September 27, 1994, Kenco and Williams signed a written contract whereby Kenco agreed to sell, and Williams agreed to buy, a mobile home that Kenco had not yet ordered from the factory. The contract called for a price of $39,400, with $500 down.

* * *

On or about October 12, Williams gave Kenco a $600 check so Kenco could order an appraisal of the land on which the mobile home would be located. Before Kenco could act, however, Williams stopped payment on the check and repudiated the entire transaction. His reason, according to the trial court's finding of fact, was that he "had found a better deal elsewhere."

When Williams repudiated, Kenco had not yet ordered the mobile home from the factory. After Williams repudiated, Kenco simply did not place the order. As a result, Kenco's only out-of-pocket expense was a minor amount of office overhead.

On November 1, 1994, Kenco sued Williams for lost profits. After a bench trial, the superior court found that Williams had breached the contract; that Kenco was entitled to damages; and that Kenco had lost profits in the amount of ... $6,720 on the mobile home.... The court further found, however, that Kenco would be adequately compensated by retaining Williams' $500 down payment....

* * *

Under the Uniform Commercial Code (UCC), a nonbreaching seller may recover "damages for non-acceptance" from a breaching buyer. The measure of such damages is as follows:

[The court quoted 2–708]

... [T]he statute's purpose is to put the nonbreaching seller in the position that he or she would have occupied if the breaching buyer had fully performed (or, in alternative terms, to give the nonbreaching seller the benefit of his or her bargain). A party claiming damages under subsection (2) bears the burden of showing that an award of damages under subsection (1) would be inadequate.

In general, the adequacy of damages under subsection (1) depends on whether the nonbreaching seller has a readily available market on which he or she can resell the goods that the breaching buyer should have taken. When a buyer breaches before either side has begun to perform, the amount needed to give the seller the benefit of his or her bargain is the difference between the contract price and the seller's expected cost of performance. Using market price, this difference can, in turn, be subdivided into two smaller differences: (a) the difference between the contract price and the market price, and (b) the difference between the market price and the seller's expected cost of performance.

So long as a nonbreaching seller can reasonably resell the breached goods on the open market, he or she can recover the difference between contract price and market price by invoking subsection (1), and the difference between market price and his or her expected cost of performance by reselling the breached goods on the open market. Thus, he or she is made whole by subsection (1), and subsection (1) damages should be deemed "adequate." But if a nonbreaching seller cannot reasonably resell the breached goods on the open market, he or she cannot recover, merely by invoking subsection (1), the difference between market price and his or her expected cost of performance. Hence, he or she is not made whole by subsection (1); subsection (1) damages are "inadequate to put the seller in as good a position as performance would have done;" and subsection (2) comes into play.

The cases illustrate at least three specific situations in which a nonbreaching seller cannot reasonably resell on the open market. In the first, the seller never comes into possession of the breached goods; although he or she plans to acquire such goods before the buyer's breach, he or she rightfully elects not to acquire them after the buyer's breach.[14] In the second, the seller possesses some or all of the breached goods, but they are of such an odd or peculiar nature that the seller lacks a post-breach market on which to sell them; they are, for example, unfinished, obsolete, or highly specialized.[15] In the third situation, the seller again possesses some or all of the breached goods, but because the market is already oversupplied with such goods (i.e., the available supply exceeds demand), he or she cannot resell the breached goods without displacing another sale.[16] Frequently, these sellers are labeled "jobber," "components seller," and "lost volume seller," respectively;[17] in our view, however, such labels confuse more than clarify.

To illustrate the first situation, we examine Copymate Marketing v. Modern Merchandising,[18] a case cited and discussed by both parties. In that case, Copymate had an option to purchase three thousand copiers from Dowling for $51,750. Before Copymate had exercised its option, it contracted to sell the copiers to Modern for $165,000. It also promised Modern that it would spend $47,350 for advertising that would benefit Modern. It told Dowling it was exercising its option, but before it could finish its purchase from Dowling, Modern repudiated. Acting with commercial reasonableness, Copymate responded by canceling its deal with Dowling and never acquiring the copiers. It then sued Modern for its lost profits and prevailed in the trial court. Modern appealed, but this court affirmed. Because Copymate had rightfully elected not to acquire the copiers, it had no way to resell them on the open market; subsection (1) was inadequate; and subsection (2) applied. Thus, Copymate recovered

14. Copymate Marketing, Ltd. v. Modern Merchandising, Inc., 34 Wash. App. 300, 660 P.2d 332 (1983); Nobs Chemical, U.S.A., Inc. v. Koppers Co., Inc., 616 F.2d 212 (5th Cir.1980); Blair Int'l, Ltd. v. LaBarge, Inc., 675 F.2d 954 (8th Cir.1982); see RCW 62A.2–704(2).

15. Copymate, 34 Wash. App. 300, 660 P.2d 332; Coast Trading Co. v. Parmac, Inc., 21 Wash.App. 896, 909 n. 5, 587 P.2d 1071, 1079 n. 5 (1978).

16. R.E. Davis Chemical Corp. v. Diasonics, 826 F.2d 678 (7th Cir.1987); Islamic Republic of Iran v. Boeing Co., 771 F.2d 1279 (9th Cir.1985), cert. dismissed, 479 U.S. 957, 107 S.Ct. 450, 93 L.Ed.2d 397 (1986) (applying Washington law); Teradyne, Inc. v. Teledyne Ind., Inc., 676 F.2d 865 (1st Cir.1982); Nederlandse Draadindustrie NDI B.V. v. Grand Pre–Stressed Corp., 466 F.Supp. 846 (E.D.N.Y.1979); Autonumerics, Inc. v. Bayer Ind., Inc., 144 Ariz. 181, 696 P.2d 1330 (App.1984); Unique Designs, Inc. v. Pittard Machinery Co., 200 Ga.App. 647, 409 S.E.2d 241, 243 (1991); Neri v. Retail Marine Corp., 30 N.Y.2d 393, 334 N.Y.S.2d 165, 285 N.E.2d 311 (N.Y.1972); Vanderwerff Implement, Inc. v. McCance, 561 N.W.2d 24, 25 (S.D. 1997). In passing, we observe that this lost volume situation can be described in several ways. Focusing on the breached unit, one can say that due to a market in which supply exceeds demand, the lost volume seller cannot resell the breached unit without sacrificing an additional sale. Focusing on the additional unit, one can say that but for the buyer's breach, the lost volume seller would have made an additional sale. Focusing on both units, one can say that but for the buyer's breach, the lost volume seller would have sold both units. Each statement is equivalent to the others.

17. E.g., WHITE & SUMMERS at 384, 387, 389, 398.

18. 34 Wash. App. 300, 660 P.2d 332 (1983).

its contract price with Modern ($165,000), minus the expected cost of performing its contract with Modern ($51,750 for Dowling, $47,350 for advertising, and $180 for a miscellaneous import fee), for a total of $65,720.

To illustrate the second situation, we again examine Copymate. Based on substantial evidence, the Copymate trial court found that after Modern's repudiation, Copymate had "no active or reasonably available market for the resale of the ... copiers."[19] One reason was that the copiers had been in storage in Canada for nine years; thus, they seem to have been obsolete. Again, then, Copymate could not resell the copiers on the open market; subsection (1) was inadequate; and subsection (2) provided for an award of "lost profits."

To illustrate the third situation, we examine R.E. Davis Chemical Corp. v. Diasonics.[20] In that case, Davis breached his contract to buy medical equipment from Diasonics. Diasonics was in possession of the equipment, which it soon resold on the open market. Diasonics then sued Davis for "lost profits" under subsection (2), arguing that "it was a 'lost volume seller,' and, as such, it lost the profit from one sale when Davis breached its contract."[21] The trial court granted summary judgment to Davis, but the appellate court reversed and remanded for trial. Other courts, the appellate court noted, "have defined a lost volume seller as one that has a predictable and finite number of customers and that has the capacity either to sell to all new buyers or to make the one additional sale represented by the resale after the breach."[22] This definition, the appellate court ruled, lacks an essential element: whether the seller would have sold an additional unit but for the buyer's breach.[23] On remand, then, Diasonics would have to prove (a) that it could have produced and sold the breached unit in addition to its actual volume, and (b) that it would have produced and sold the breached unit in addition to its actual volume.[24]

In this case, Kenco did not order the breached goods before Williams repudiated. After Williams repudiated, Kenco was not required to order the breached goods from the factory; it rightfully elected not to do so; and it could not resell the breached goods on the open market. Here, then, "the measure of damages provided in subsection (1) is inadequate to put [Kenco] in as good a position as [Williams'] performance would have done;"[26] subsection (2) states the applicable measure of damages; and Kenco is entitled to its lost profit....

19. 34 Wash. App. at 302, 660 P.2d 332.

20. 826 F.2d 678 (7th Cir.1987).

21. 826 F.2d at 680.

22. 826 F.2d at 683. In essence, then, these courts hold that a lost volume seller is one who proves at trial that his or her supply of product exceeds the demand for such product on the relevant market.

23. 826 F.2d at 684; accord, WHITE & SUMMERS, § 7–9, at 386.

24. 826 F.2d at 684; accord, WHITE & SUMMERS, § 7–9, at 386.

26. RCW 62A.2–708(2).

* * *

Reversed with directions to enter an amended judgment awarding Kenco its lost profit. . . .

Note: The "Lost Volume Seller" and Other Theories for Sellers to Recover Lost Profits

The court in *Kenco Homes* notes that courts have awarded an aggrieved seller lost profits under 2–708(2) in three situations: 1) where the seller is a "jobber" or middleman who never acquires the goods because of the buyer's breach; 2) where the seller is a "components seller" who does not complete manufacturing or assembling the goods because of the buyer's breach; and 3) where the seller is a "lost volume seller." Comment 5 to proposed amended Section 2–708 states explicitly that a lost profits recovery is available in these three situations. In R.E. Davis Chemical Corp. v. Diasonics, Inc., 826 F.2d 678 (7th Cir.1987), discussed in the Kenco Homes opinion, the court explained the "lost volume seller" theory for recovering lost profits under 2–708(2) as follows:

> Diasonics [the aggrieved seller in the case] claims the § 2–708(1) does not provide an adequate measure of damages when the seller is a lost volume seller. To understand Diasonics' argument, we need to define the concept of the lost volume seller. Those cases that have addressed this issue have defined a lost volume seller as one that has a predictable and finite number of customers and that has the capacity either to sell to all new buyers or to make the one additional sale represented by the resale after the breach. According to a number of courts and commentators, if the seller would have made the sale represented by the resale whether or not the breach occurred, damages measured by the difference between the contract price and market price cannot put the lost volume seller in as good a position as it would have been in had the buyer performed. The breach effectively cost the seller a "profit," and the seller can only be made whole by awarding it damages in the amount of its "lost profit" under § 2–708(2).

826 F.2d at 683 (citations omitted). Another court has elaborated as follows:

> Clearly a "lost volume seller" is not in as good a position as if there had been no breach, if he is confined to the § 2–708(1) formula. Under that formula, he would first take the contract/market differential, which would be less than the profit he expected. If that is added to the resale profit [i.e., the profit seller made by reselling the goods that the breaching buyer failed to take], he would make only one total profit, rather than the two profits he would have earned had there been no breach.

Snyder v. Herbert Greenbaum & Assoc., 38 Md.App. 144, 380 A.2d 618, 624 (1977) (citations omitted).

The "lost volume seller" theory for applying 2–708(2), or at least the idea that lost volume situations always require a lost profit recovery, has been criticized by some scholars. See, e.g., Goetz & Scott, *Measuring Sellers' Damages: The Lost–Profits Puzzle*, 31 STAN. L. REV. 323 (1979); Shanker, *The Case for a Literal Reading of UCC Section 2–708(2) (One Profit for the Reseller)*, 24 CASE W. RES. L. REV. 697 (1973). Despite the criticism, the lost volume seller theory for applying 2–708(2) has been very widely accepted by courts and, as mentioned above, is expressly adopted in comment 5 to proposed amended Section 2–708.

Problem 105

On September 1 Handel Corp., a gasoline broker, contracted to sell 10 million gallons of gasoline to Elgar Inc. for $1 per gallon, delivery on October 1. Handel planned to cover this commitment using gasoline which it had contracted to buy from one of its regular suppliers for 90 cents per gallon. On September 23 the market price for gasoline plummeted to 70 cents per gallon, and the next day Elgar repudiated its contract with Handel. Handel sued and claimed damages of 30 cents per gallon under 2–708(1). Elgar admitted the breach, but argued that Handel's damages should be limited to 10 cents per gallon under 2–708(2), citing 1–106 (§ 1–305(a) in amended Article 1). What result? Would it matter if Handel had been released *gratis* from its obligation to purchase gasoline from its supplier at 90 cents per gallon? Suppose Handel had paid its supplier $500,000 to be released from the contract? Compare Nobs Chemical, U.S.A., Inc. v. Koppers Co., 616 F.2d 212 (5th Cir.1980) with Trans World Metals, Inc. v. Southwire Co., 769 F.2d 902 (2d Cir.1985).

Note on Accounting for the Proceeds of Resale in a Lost Profits Recovery

In Problem 104, the aggrieved seller (TAI) resold the car for the same amount as the price in the breached contract. Under the pre-amendment version of 2–708(2), a seller recovering lost profits must give the breaching buyer "due credit for payments or proceeds of resale." Applying that language literally in a situation like Problem 104 would result in the seller recovering no damages and would thus defeat the purpose of the lost profit recovery. One court commented on this problem:

> The literal language of § 2–708(2) requires that the proceeds from resale be credited against the amount of damages awarded which, in most cases, would result in the [lost volume] seller recovering nominal damages. In those cases in which the lost volume seller was awarded its lost profit as damages, the courts have circumvented this problem by concluding that this language only applies to proceeds realized from the resale of uncompleted goods for scrap.

R.E. Davis Chemical Corp. v. Diasonics, Inc., 826 F.2d 678, 684 (7th Cir.1987). The problematic language in 2–708(2) would be dropped under proposed amended Section 2–708(2).

5. Sellers' Right to Specific Performance

Problem 106

On December 1 Scrivener & Quire ("S & Q"), a Philadelphia law firm, contracted to purchase 500 cartons of paper embossed with the firm's letterhead from Foolscap Industries, Inc., a paper wholesaler located in a Philadelphia suburb. The price was $100 per carton and delivery was due December 15. When Foolscap's truck attempted to deliver the paper, all of which conformed to the contract, S & Q unjustifiably refused to allow the cartons to be unloaded. The truck returned to Foolscap's warehouse with its load intact.

(a) Can Foolscap recover the price under 2–709(1)(b)? What precisely must Foolscap show to do so? Suppose S & Q can prove that Foolscap did not seek alternative buyers for the paper. Would that prevent Foolscap from recovering the price? If Foolscap succeeds in obtaining an order requiring S & Q to pay the price, what should Foolscap do with the paper? See 2–709(2).

(b) Suppose that, before the trial of Foolscap's law suit started, a paper recycler offered to buy the 500 cartons of S & Q letterhead paper for 50 cents per carton. If Foolscap refuses this offer can it recover the price under 2–709(1)(b)? If Foolscap accepts the offer and gives S & Q any required notice, can Foolscap recover the difference between the contract price ($100 per carton) and the resale price (50 cents per carton) as damages under 2–706?

Note on Seller's Specific Performance

A seller's right under 2–709 to recover the price in a situation like Problem 106 has been called "seller's specific performance" because it forces the buyer to perform its contractual duty of paying for the goods, thus also creating a strong incentive for the buyer to perform its contractual duty of taking delivery. Under the pre-amendment version of Article 2, however, the provision that grants a right to what is actually labeled "specific performance" (2–716) is limited to buyers. Under proposed amended Section 2–716, "specific performance" would be available to sellers "if the goods . . . are unique or in other proper circumstances." It remains to be seen whether making 2–716(1) available to sellers expands in any significant way on the seller's right to compel performance by means of a price recovery under 2–709(1)(b).

C. UCC ARTICLE 2 REMEDIES WHEN THE BUYER RETAINS THE GOODS

1. Aggrieved Buyers' Damages When Goods Remain Accepted

Problem 107

Natural Monopolies Inc. ("NMI"), a Midwestern electric utility, agreed to purchase its requirements of coal for one of its Missouri generating plants from Newcastle Minerals Corp. The contract, which had a five year term and was evidenced by a writing, required "sweet" coal with a sulphur content below specified levels. For a two month period during the third year of the contract, however, Newcastle delivered coal with a sulphur content that substantially exceeded contract specifications. Although NMI immediately pointed out the sulphur problem to Newcastle, the utility had little choice but to take delivery (by paying the freight charges) and use the coal—which it did. When deliveries of normal quality coal resumed, NMI consulted you. In response to your incisive questioning, NMI revealed that the contract price was $100 per ton "FCA (Free Carrier) Big Rock, Colorado as per INCOTERMS 2000." (Big Rock, Colorado was the location of one of Newcastle's large coal mines.) NMI also indicated that Newcastle delivered 1000 tons of high sulphur coal during the two months in question. The market price of coal had risen after the contract with Newcastle was entered into. During the two months in question, sweet coal of the kind required by the contract has been selling for $150 per ton in Colorado and $170 per ton in Missouri. Even high sulphur coal like that delivered by Newcastle sold for $85 per ton in Colorado and $95 per ton in Missouri during that period. NMI wants to know how much it owes Newcastle for the high sulphur coal it used. Advise how NMI should proceed and what it should expect to recover. Consider UCC 2–607, 2–714 and 2–717.

Note: Buyer's Damages for Non–Conforming Goods that Are Accepted

The UCC provisions dealing with damages for accepted goods contain several subsections. Section 2–714(1) provides a general rule for measuring damages where the buyer accepts goods and does not revoke the acceptance: the buyer is entitled to damages measured by "the loss resulting in the ordinary course of events from the seller's breach as determined in any manner which is reasonable." This general rule is frequently applied when the buyer seeks damages for late delivery. Section 2–714(2) contains a specific rule applicable to the most common and important type of breach that an accepting buyer suffers–breach of warranty: a buyer who chooses (or is forced) to retain goods despite a breach of warranty can recover the difference between the value of the goods if they had conformed to the warranty and the value of the non-conforming goods that the buyer actually received.

General damages for breach of warranty are illustrated by Kee v. Campbell, 8 Kan.App.2d 561, 661 P.2d 831 (1983), where the seller sued to recover for the price of an oil field pump it had sold and delivered to the buyer, and which remained in the buyer's possession. The buyer defended by claiming a breach of warranty. Reviewing the trial court's judgment for defendant buyer, the appeals court stated:

> The trial court found that plaintiff had breached an express warranty by improperly advertising the pump as a mud pump and entered judgment

for defendant. . . . Having neither rejected the pump nor timely revoked his acceptance, defendant's remedy was a claim for damages for breach of warranty under [UCC 2–714 (2)]. All the evidence indicated the pump was worth $2,000 less than if it had been as advertised. Hence . . . plaintiff . . . was entitled to the $6,500 price less defendant's damages of $2,000 or a net of $4,500. The breach of warranty entitled defendant to damages but was not a complete defense.

The formula for breach-of-warranty damages is phrased in terms of the "value" of goods, not their price—i.e., the difference between the "value" of the goods if they had been as warranted and the "value" of the non-conforming goods accepted. As the North Dakota Supreme Court stated in Carlson v. Rysavy, 262 N.W.2d 27, 31 (1978): "With respect to the value of the goods as warranted [for purposes of calculating 2–714(2) damages], contract price offers strong evidence of such value, although not conclusive." In other words, proof of the contract price may establish a prima facie case for the value of goods if they had been as warranted, but it can be rebutted by proof that conforming goods would in fact have been worth more or less than the contract price.

For example, in Melody Home Manufacturing Co. v. Morrison, 502 S.W.2d 196, 202–03 (Tex.Civ.App.1973), the plaintiffs had purchased a mobile home for a cash price of $5300. When the home proved nonconforming, the buyers kept it but sued for breach of warranty. The trial court awarded damages on the basis that the "value" of a mobile home that conformed to the contract would have been $6,000. The appeals court affirmed:

> Under § 2.714(b) of the Business & Commerce Code [UCC 2–714(2)], the trial court properly utilized the actual cash market value of the mobile home instead of the base contract price, even though the base contract price may have been a lesser sum. See Ash v. Beck, 68 S.W. 53 (Tex.Civ.App., 1902, n.w.h.); and 51 Tex Jur 2d (rev), part 1, Vol 51, Sales 354, p 144, footnote 9, with reference to the Business & Commerce Code, § 2.714(b) wherein it is stated:
>
> > It might be noted that the measure is based on "value" rather than "price." Thus, if the buyer purchases for $100 a machine that would be worth $200 if it answered its warranties, but is worth only $50 as the result of a breach of warranty, the UCC provision might permit the buyer to recover $150, rather than merely $50, which would be the amount if "price" were the criterion.

In Continental Sand & Gravel, Inc. v. K & K Sand & Gravel, Inc., 755 F.2d 87, 91–92 (7th Cir.1985), the court noted:

> [I]t is not unusual for damages in a breach of warranty case to exceed the purchase price of the goods. . . . This result is logical, since to limit recoverable damages by the purchase price, as defendants suggest, would clearly deprive the purchaser of the benefit of the bargain in cases in which the value of the goods as warranted exceeds that price.

This point was dramatically illustrated in Chatlos Sys., Inc. v. N. C. R. Corp., 670 F.2d 1304 (3d Cir.1982), where the court found that a computer system purchased for $45,000 would have been worth $208,000 if it had conformed to the contract; the court awarded the buyer difference-in-value damages of $202,000, calculated as the value of the computer as warranted, less the $6,000 value of the non-conforming system actually delivered.

Problem 108

Financial Forecasters Inc. purchased a new photocopier from Office Machines Corp. ("OMC"). In the nine months following delivery the copier broke down 40 times and was in operating condition less than 60% of the time. Neither OMC nor several other copier repair services that Forecasters consulted could diagnose or correct the underlying problem. At last, Forecasters sued OMC. One count of the complaint seeks damages under 2–714 for breach of the implied warranty of merchantability. How should Forecasters go about proving the difference between the value of the copier as warranted and its value in its defective delivered condition? Describe specifically the kind of evidence that would be adequate and practicable. Would testimony by one of Forecasters' officers that the defective copier had no value to the firm be sufficient to establish that the value of the machine as accepted was $0? See Wharton, Aldhizer & Weaver v. Savin Corp., 232 Va. 375, 350 S.E.2d 635 (1986). If Forecasters had resold the machine, would the resale price establish the copier's actual value for 2–714(2) purposes?

HOLDEN MACHINERY v. SUNDANCE TRACTOR & MOWER

United States Bankruptcy Court for the Middle District of Georgia, 1998.
218 B.R. 247, 36 U.C.C. Rep.Serv.2d 709.

WALKER, JAMES D. JR., BANKRUPTCY JUDGE.... Holden, a company based in England, and Sundance, a company based in the United States, had a business relationship where Holden would sell used farm equipment to Sundance which would resell the equipment to consumers in the United States. As a result of financial difficulties, Sundance filed this bankruptcy case. In response, Holden filed a Motion To Terminate Financing Agreement, To Obtain Possession Of Consigned Goods, And For An Accounting. Sundance alleged that the amount of Holden's claim should be offset by certain repair costs it incurred to correct defects in fourteen items of equipment it had purchased from Holden.

* * *

EVIDENCE OF REPAIRS

Holden questions the sufficiency of the evidence presented at trial on the issue of damages for breach of warranty. In Georgia, "[t]he measure of damages for breach of warranty is the difference at the time and place of acceptance between the value of the goods accepted and the value they would have had if they had been as warranted, unless special circumstances show proximate damages of a different amount." O.C.G.A.

§ 11–2–714(2). In its ruling, the Court determined that evidence regarding the cost of repairs was relevant and persuasive on the question of the difference "between the value of the goods accepted and the value they would have had if they had been as warranted." Holden disagrees with this conclusion, stating that Sundance failed to meet its evidentiary burden to establish the value of the goods accepted because, under Georgia law, repair cost figures are not sufficient for this purpose. The Court disagrees and reaffirms its conclusion that the reasonable repair cost figure of $7,292.87 is the proper measure of damages for Holden's breach of implied warranties.

At the hearing, Holden argued that repair costs are an inappropriate measure of damages because, in some cases, they would allow the buyer a windfall. Citing the example of an automobile collision where the repair costs exceed the value of the vehicle, Holden explained that, in such a situation, the proper measure of damages would be the value of the vehicle before the accident rather than the cost of repairs. Otherwise, the owner of the vehicle would profit from the accident. In factual scenarios analogous to the one noted by Holden, repair costs might be an inappropriate measure of damages for breach of warranty. If the cost of repairs exceeded the value of the equipment sold, the Court would not award such costs as damages. In fact, in this case, the Court concluded that some of the repair costs needed to be adjusted to make them reasonable.[3] The theory presented by Holden does not discredit the probative value of the evidence of adjusted repair costs presented by Sundance to show the measure of damages in this case.

Holden's reference to an award of repair costs confuses the issue in the case. Simply stated, Holden is correct that repair costs are not recoverable as a measure of damages. However, such a simple statement ignores the factual context of this case. Using Holden's example of an automobile, consider the case of the sale of a collector's item, such as Elvis Presley's Cadillac, on display in Memphis, Tennessee. If the car's engine did not run, its buyer would expect little success in a claim for offset based on repair costs. The value of that item lies in its worth as an exhibition and is not likely to be affected by the performance characteristics of its engine. The required proof of damages in that setting would be vastly different from this case.

Here, Holden's claim is based on sales of numerous items of farm equipment, each one intended by both parties to be resold by Sundance in a retail market. Unlike Elvis Presley's Cadillac, the mechanical condition of each of these items is an important element of their value.

---

3. The Court reduced some of the labor costs from $45 per hour to $25 per hour. Apparently, the $25 per hour rate was initially utilized by Sundance to calculate the repair costs. However, after some "bad blood" had developed between the parties, Sundance increased the labor cost to $45 per hour. The Court found this rate increase to be unreasonable, and, therefore, required that all repair cost figures be recalculated at the lower rate. A general principle of the commercial statutes in Georgia is that the aggrieved party be put in "as good a position as if the other party had fully performed." O.C.G.A. § 11–1–106(a). Implicit in this policy is the idea that no party should be put in a better situation than it would have been absent breach.

In determining the reasonable repair costs of each item, the Court also considered whether it was necessary to make the repairs for Sundance to realize the value of the items as warranted. If the cost of repairs had exceeded the purchase price of any item or if the cost of repair had not appeared to correspond on a dollar for dollar basis to the value of the items as warranted, the award of such costs would not have been appropriate.

* * *

Unfortunately, because of the factual variations in the various written opinions cited by the parties and as well as those located by the Court's own research, there is no controlling case authority. It does appear, however, that the basic rule followed by Georgia courts is that the measure of damages for breach of warranty is to be determined by the formula in O.C.G.A. § 11–2–714(2). The question of whether repair costs can satisfy that proof requirement depends entirely on the sufficiency and reliability of the evidence presented in the context of the case at hand. One treatise explained this concept well by stating the following:

> While repair and replacement provide useful methods for determining damages in most warranty cases, it must be kept in mind that costs of repair or replacement are not the test of damages but only provide evidence of what the ordinary damages are. The test in all cases is the difference between the value of the goods as accepted and the value they would have had if they had been as warranted, unless special circumstances show proximate damages of a different amount. Repair and replacement costs provide evidence to prove the difference between the value of the goods as accepted and the value they would have had if they had met the warranty, and this evidence will be relatively strong or weak depending on the circumstances surrounding repair or replacement. Obviously, a repair or replacement made in a commercially reasonable manner is entitled to much more weight than one that is not so made.

William D. Hawkland, Uniform Commercial Code Series § 2–714:04 (1996).

In this case, Sundance provided evidence of costs of repairs to the equipment it purchased from Holden. The Court considered this evidence and found the reasonable costs of repair to be $7,292.87. This amount was determined to be sufficient proof of the difference between the value of the goods as accepted and the value that they would have had if they had been as warranted. The Court reaffirms that holding.

* * *

Note on Using Repair Costs to Measure
Damages for Breach of Warranty

In Continental Sand & Gravel, Inc. v. K & K Sand & Gravel, Inc., 755 F.2d 87, 92 n. 5 (7th Cir.1985), the court stated:

> [G]enerally, damages based on cost of repair are recoverable [under 2–714] regardless whether the repairs are actually undertaken. Presumably, if the repairs are not made, the potential market value of the goods is reduced by an amount equivalent to the value which would have been added by repair.

See also Carlson v. Rysavy, 262 N.W.2d 27, 31 (S.D.1978):

> [Seller] contends, and it is generally held, that a useful objective measurement of the difference in value as is and as warranted is the cost of repair. However, there are many cases in which the injury will be irreparable and therefore the cost of repairs will not serve as a yardstick of the buyer's damage. In such cases the court will have to determine by some other measure the value of the goods as warranted and the value of the goods accepted. . . .

Question

Suppose that in Problem 108 OMC had delivered a merchantable copier, but did so six weeks after the delivery date called for in the sales contract. What remedy is available to Forecasters if it decides to accept the machine? See 2–714(1) & (3). What information would you seek from Forecasters in order to determine its claim for damages?

2. Sellers' Right to the Price for Accepted Goods

Problem 109

On December 1 Scrivener & Quire ("S & Q"), a Philadelphia law firm, orally ordered 500 cartons of standard size typing paper at $50 per carton from Foolscap Industries, Inc., a paper wholesaler located in a Philadelphia suburb. Pursuant to the order, Foolscap delivered the paper on December 15. S & Q put the 500 cartons into its supply room. Just as it had always done in the parties' previous dealings, Foolscap sent S & Q an invoice requiring payment of the purchase price ($25,000) within 30 days of delivery. It is now the end of February. S & Q has not paid the invoice nor has it responded to letters and phone calls demanding payment. Can Foolscap recover the full price from S & Q? See 2–709. Also consider 2–201.

Question

Suppose the contract in Problem 109 had called for S & Q to pay for the paper by transferring to Foolscap certain computer equipment the law firm owned. After receiving the paper, S & Q refused to convey the computer equipment. If Foolscap succeeds in establishing its right to the price under 2–709, what should it recover? Consider 2–304(1).

SIEMENS ENERGY & AUTOMATION, INC. v. COLEMAN ELECTRICAL SUPPLY CO.

United States District Court, E.D. New York, 1999.
46 F.Supp. 2d 217.

TRAGER, DISTRICT JUDGE. This is an action for monies owed for goods sold and delivered on an open account.... Plaintiff has moved for summary judgment....

Plaintiff, Siemans Energy and Automation Inc. ("Siemans"), manufactures electrical products. Defendant, Coleman Electrical Supply Co., Inc. ("Coleman"), purchased and distributed electrical supplies.... [Siemans shipped electrical supplies to Coleman on credit.]

In 1998, after losing one of its major clients, Coleman began experiencing financial difficulties and started to fall behind in payments on its outstanding bills. In an attempt to lessen its debt, Coleman offered to return some of the unpaid goods to Siemans for resale. Siemans refused the returns and demanded payment of the outstanding debt....

* * *

.... Defendants first contend that Siemans had a duty to mitigate defendants' damages by accepting Coleman's offer to return the unsold goods. Siemans counters that the inventory which Coleman offered to return was subject to the financing lien of Coleman's secured lender, CIT, and that, therefore, if Siemans had accepted the inventory it would have subjected itself to the possibility of an action for conversion by CIT. See Decl. of Douglas J. Kramer in Reply to Def. Opp. to Pl. Mot. for Sum. J., citing Aff. of Kenny Kirsh, dated 1/21/99.

Since the present case concerns the sale of goods, the duty to mitigate question is governed by § 2–709 of the Uniform Commercial Code ("U.C.C."). See N.Y. U.C.C. § 2–709 (McKinney's 1999). Specifically, § 2–709(1)(a) provides, in pertinent part, that "[w]hen the buyer fails to pay the price as it becomes due the seller may recover, together with any incidental damages ... the price of goods accepted." Id. Clearly, since it is undisputed that Coleman accepted the goods shipped by Siemans, Siemans has the right to seek the amount due under the contract. While § 2–709(1)(b) provides that a seller may recover the price "of goods identified to the contract if the seller is unable after reasonable effort to resell them at a reasonable price," this section applies only to goods that have been identified but not actually shipped or accepted. Id. at § 2–709(1)(b). Thus, § 2–709(1)(b) is not applicable in this case, and there is no obligation under § 2–709 on the part of the seller to accept a return of previously accepted goods.

The distinction between subdivisions (a) and (b) of § 2–709, with respect to the duty to mitigate, is clearly displayed in Industrial Molded Plastic Products, Inc. v. J. Gross and Son Inc., 263 Pa. Super. 515, 398 A.2d 695 (Pa.Super.Ct.1979), a case concerning a buyer who purchased 5,000,000 clothing clips from a manufacturer, but wrongfully failed to take possession of or pay for 4,228,000 of the clips. Because, in that case, the buyer had repeatedly given assurances that it intended to accept the clips, the court held that the clips had been deemed accepted. The Pennsylvania Superior Court, interpreting U.C.C. § 2–709(1)(a), held that although a duty exists to mitigate when dealing with goods that have merely been identified, "a seller of goods is [] entitled to recover the contract price due *for goods accepted by the buyer*." Id. at 522, 398 A.2d at 699 (emphasis added). Specifically, the court held that, "[u]nder the code, a buyer's acceptance of goods occurs, inter alia, when, after a reasonable opportunity to inspect the goods, the buyer fails to make an effective rejection of them. To preserve his rights, the seller is only obligated to tender the goods in accordance with the terms of the contract. The seller is under no obligation to resell accepted goods in order to maintain his action for price." Id. at 522, 398 A.2d at 699 (citations omitted) (emphasis added). Furthermore, in Unlaub Co., Inc. v. Sexton, 568 F.2d 72 (8th Cir.1977), a case involving a contract for the sale of coal screen units, the Eighth Circuit, also interpreting U.C.C. § 2–709(1)(a), held that once the coal screen units had been accepted, the seller was entitled to recover the unpaid balance of the contract price and was "under no obligation to attempt a resale of accepted goods." Id. at 76 n. 3.

* * *

Furthermore, as noted, defendants have not cited, nor has research disclosed, any common law case holding that, in the absence of a prior agreement, a manufacturer is under a duty to mitigate its losses by accepting a return from its distributor of goods which have already been sold and delivered. To the contrary, Reforestacion Cafetalera Agro—Industrial S.A. v. Campesino Food Corp., 97 Civ. 5553, 1999 WL 4964 (S.D.N.Y. Jan.6, 1999), explicitly held, without relying on the U.C.C., that a coffee seller is under no duty to mitigate its damages by accepting from a buyer the return of coffee that had been sold, delivered, and accepted. Accordingly, Siemans' duty to mitigate its damages did not involve an obligation to accept the return of already shipped products. As Coleman accepted the delivered goods without objection and, subsequently, failed to pay the price of the goods as it became due, Siemans had an unquestionable right to recover the price of the accepted goods.

* * *

For the forgoing reasons, plaintiff's motion for summary judgment is granted. . . .

Problem 110

Same facts as Problem 109, except the parties signed a written contract and S & Q claims that the paper Foolscap delivered contains defects that violate the implied warranty of merchantability (which was not disclaimed). S & Q notified Foolscap of the alleged defects on the day of delivery, and told the seller to remove the paper, which Foolscap did. If the goods were in fact defective, can Foolscap recover the price? Suppose S & Q was mistaken and there were no defects in the goods. Can Foolscap recover the price? Suppose Foolscap had insisted (correctly) that the goods were not defective and had refused to take the goods back. S & Q kept the paper in storage and continued to insist that Foolscap take the goods back. Can Foolscap recover the full price?

Note on Ineffective vs. Wrongful Rejection

In analyzing Problem 110, consider the following:

The seller's remedies for a rejection of goods which is "ineffective" because the buyer failed to follow proper procedures are distinct from the remedies for a rejection which is "wrongful" because it was unjustified. . . .

Section 2–709 allows an action for the price only if the goods have been "accepted" (or are lost, damaged, or non-resalable, none of which are true in this case). Section 2–606, in turn, defines acceptance as "failure to make an *effective* rejection." (emphasis added). It is cross-referenced to 2–602(1), which provides that a rejection of goods must be made "within a reasonable time after their delivery or tender," and is "*ineffective* unless the buyer seasonably notifies the seller" (emphasis added). Thus, the remedy for an ineffective rejection—one which is procedurally defective under 2–602(1)—is an action for the price.

By contrast, a *wrongful* rejection may still be an effective rejection, and does not in itself entitle the seller to the price. Since an ineffective rejection constitutes an acceptance, by negative inference any effective rejection—whether or not it is justified—bars acceptance and protects the buyer from 2–709 damages. Subsection (3) of 2–602, which is *not* cross-referenced to the 2–606 definition of acceptance as ineffective rejection, makes separate mention of goods "wrongfully" rejected. It provides that the remedies in cases of wrongful rejection are contained in 2–703, entitled "Seller's Remedies in General." Subsection (e) of 2–703 states that the measure of damages for goods wrongfully rejected is the difference between the contract price and the market price (2–708), or "in a proper case the price" under 2–709. Thus a seller whose goods have been wrongfully rejected will be entitled to the price only if that measure of damages is "proper" under 2–709 because the rejection was also procedurally ineffective.

Integrated Circuits Unlimited, Inc. v. E.F. Johnson Co., 691 F.Supp. 630, 633 (E.D.N.Y.1988). Even if a buyer has a right to reject (because the seller's tender was non-conforming), the attempt to reject may be ineffective (if she failed to promptly notify the seller).

Questions

(1) Return to the contract in Problem 110, but suppose S & Q originally accepted the goods and now claims that the alleged defects appeared only after the paper had been removed from the carton and exposed to the air for 30 days. S & Q complained to Foolscap as soon as it learned of the alleged defects, and demanded that Foolscap remove the unopened cartons of paper, which Foolscap did. If the goods were in fact defective, is S & Q liable for the price of those cartons? Would your answer change if S & Q was mistaken and there were no defects in the goods? Suppose Foolscap had insisted (correctly) that the goods were not defective and had refused to take the goods back. S & Q kept the paper in storage and continued to insist that Foolscap take the goods back. Can Foolscap recover the full price? According to comments to the proposed amended version of Article 2, a seller can treat a buyer's unjustified notice of revocation as effective by taking the goods back and seeking damages for wrongful revocation; but if the seller refuses to take the goods back, the unjustified attempt to revoke is ineffective.[4]

(2) Alternatively, suppose S & Q discovered serious and real defects in the paper on the day of delivery, but it did not complain to Foolscap or ask that the defective paper be removed until 60 days later. Is S & Q liable for the price? What remedies, if any, does S & Q have for the defects? See, inter alia, 2–607.

Problem 111

The Senior Circuitry Appliance Store, located in Washington, D.C., contracted in writing to purchase 100 Compact Disk players from Blunt Electronics, Inc. in St. Louis for $10,000. The goods were to be shipped in two installments of 50 each "FCA (Free Carrier) St. Louis as per INCO-TERMS 2000." On March 4, Blunt shipped the first 50 CD players via independent trucker. Later that day, while en route to Washington, the truck crashed, destroying the CD players. Can Blunt recover the price of the 50 CD players if they conformed to the contract? Would it matter if the goods breached a warranty in the contract? What result if the breach was extremely minor and easily repairable? In addition to 2–709, consider 2–510 and 2–612.

Problem 112

Suppose the CD players in Problem 111 conformed to the contract and arrived undamaged in Washington. Senior Circuitry, however, wrongfully rejected the shipment. Blunt arranged for the goods to be stored in a warehouse in Washington. The warehouse burned, destroying the 50 CD players. Can Blunt recover their price? Would it matter if the warehouse fire

---

4. See comment 2 to proposed amended Section 2–706 and comment 2 to proposed amended Section 2–708.

occurred five months after the buyer's rejection? What would you have advised Blunt to do with the goods following the rejection?

3. *Reclamation by Sellers*

Problem 113

In a transaction governed by Article 2 of the UCC, the law firm of Paley & Tologist ("P & T") purchased 200 computers from Random Accessories, Inc. The written sales contract permitted P & T to pay the purchase price in 12 monthly installments of $50,000 beginning on the first of the month following delivery. Random delivered the computers on time and they were accepted by the buyer. P & T, whose practice was flourishing, made the first three monthly payments but then got into a dispute with Random over other matters and began to withhold the payments for the computers. P & T is now four months behind on its payments, and Random would like to take back the computers. Can Random do so? If your answer is yes, point to the specific Article 2 provision(s) you would rely on and identify what requirements the seller must satisfy.

Note on Sellers' Right to Recover Delivered Goods

With two somewhat narrow exceptions, nothing in UCC Article 2 permits a seller to reclaim goods that have been accepted by the buyer. The seller's usual UCC remedy in this situation is an action for the unpaid price. In general, if the seller want to be able to reclaim the goods because the buyer has failed to complete payment for them (a particularly useful right if the buyer is insolvent or for some other reason a money judgment is uncollectible), the seller must contract for an additional set of rights in the goods called a "security interest." The process of taking a security interest in goods sold so that they act as collateral for the buyer's obligation to pay the price is governed by Article 9 of the UCC and explored in courses on secured transactions. If a seller fails to take a security interest in goods sold on credit, it usually cannot reclaim the goods if the buyer defaults. The two exceptions to this rule in UCC Article 2 are explored in the following materials.

Problem 114

On October 5, Teeville Oil Co. agreed in writing to sell 20,000 gallons of home heating oil to Northeast Heating Supply Inc. for delivery by November 1. The agreement required Northeast to pay the purchase price ($15,000) within thirty days after delivery. On November 1 Teeville delivered the oil to Northeast, which stored it in a 20,000 gallon tank located at Northeast's loading facilities. Five days later Teeville learned that Northeast had stopped paying its bills and was rumored to be going out of business. Teeville wants to get the oil back—it believes a money judgment would be useless because Northeast is insolvent and thus "judgment proof." What are Teeville's rights and how should it proceed? See 2–702(2) & (3).

(a) Suppose that on November 3 Northeast resold the oil to Vulture Bros. Petroleum. Can Teeville recover the oil under 2–702(2)? Would it matter if the oil remained stored in Northeast's tank pending delivery to Vulture Bros.? Suppose Vulture Bros. had paid for the oil with a check which Northeast had not yet cashed. Could Teeville claim the check under 2–702? Would Teeville's rights change if Northeast had not resold the oil to Vulture until *after* Teeville had demanded reclamation? According to comment 4 to proposed amended Section 2–702, "[t]he amendments take no position on the seller's claims to proceeds of the goods. Courts have disagreed on the seller's rights to proceeds of goods that would have been subject to reclamation had they not been resold."

(b) Suppose that Northeast had previously granted a security interest in all its oil inventory, including after-acquired inventory, to Penultimate National Bank to secure a large loan. Northeast has defaulted on its loan payments to Penultimate, which wants to foreclose on its collateral. The oil and other property securing the loan from Penultimate will be insufficient to cover the unpaid balance of the loan. Can Teeville reclaim the oil? Consider 2–702(3).

(c) Suppose that Northeast had stored the oil delivered by Teeville in a 100,000 gallon tank in which it had already deposited 70,000 gallons of home heating oil from other suppliers. The day after the delivery from Teeville Northeast withdrew 30,000 gallons of oil from the tank. Two days later Teeville deposited 25,000 gallons purchased from other suppliers. What are Teeville's reclamation rights under 2–702(2)?

(d) Suppose that immediately after receiving the oil Northeast treated it with expensive additives. The additives, which cannot now be removed, increased the value of the oil by at least 15%. Can Teeville reclaim the oil? Would your answer change if Northeast had not blended in the additives until *after* Teeville demanded reclamation?

(e) Suppose that Teeville did not discover Northeast's financial problems until November 15. Can Teeville reclaim the oil? Would it matter if, at the beginning of October, Northeast had given Teeville a financial report falsely depicting Northeast's financial condition as sound? What if the financial report were dated June 30? What if no one from Teeville had read the financial report until after the oil had been delivered to Northeast? Note that the pre-amendment version of 2–702(2) requires that the seller demand reclamation of the goods within ten days of the time the buyer received them, although this limitation does not apply if a written misrepresentation of the buyer's solvency was made to the seller within three months before delivery. Proposed amended Section 2–702(2) would eliminate the 10 day limitation (as well as the exception thereto if there was a written misrepresentation of solvency), and would only require that the demand for reclamation be made "within a reasonable time after the buyer's receipt of the goods."

Questions

(1) Suppose that in Problem 114 Teeville successfully reclaimed the oil from Northeast under 2–702(2). After notifying Northeast of its intentions, Teeville resold the oil for $12,000—a reasonable price at the time. Can Teeville now recover damages measured by the difference between the

$15,000 contract price and the resale price? See 2–702(3) and comment 3 thereto.

(2) Suppose Teeville discovered Northeast's financial problems on October 27, before the oil was shipped. How should Teeville proceed? What should Teeville do if the oil had been handed over to an independent trucker on October 26 and was en route to Northeast's storage facility? What advice if the independent trucker had issued a non-negotiable bill of lading covering the shipment? Would it matter if the bill of lading was negotiable? What if Teeville had indorsed and forwarded the bill of lading to Northeast on October 26? See 2–702(1) and 2–705.

Problem 115

Return to the facts Problem 114 except that, rather than giving Northeast 30 days to pay, the agreement required the buyer to pay in full upon delivery. On November 1 Northeast tendered to Teeville a check for $15,000, whereupon Teeville delivered the oil. Teeville deposited the check in its bank account on November 5. On November 12 the bank notified Teeville that Northeast's check had been returned for "insufficient funds"—i.e., the check "bounced." Can Teeville use 2–702(2) to reclaim the oil? Can Teeville reclaim under any other provisions of the pre-revision version of Article 2? Consider 2–507 and 2–511. See also comment 3 to the pre-amendment version of 2–507. Proposed amended Section 2–507(2) would codify the doctrine permitting "cash sellers" to reclaim the goods if payment fails, provided the seller demands reclamation "within a reasonable time after the seller discovers or should have discovered that payment was not made."

Questions

(1) Suppose that in Problem 115 Teeville succeeded in reclaiming the goods as a cash seller whose payment was defeated. Could Teeville also recover damages, such as the difference between the contract price and the resale price of the oil? Recall 2–702(3). Why is a reclaiming credit seller treated differently than a reclaiming cash seller in this regard?

(2) Suppose that in Problem 115 the agreement required Northeast to pay 10% of the purchase price upon delivery with the balance due 30 days after delivery. Northeast gave Teeville a check for $1500 upon delivery, but the check was dishonored. Can Teeville reclaim the oil as a "cash seller"? Would it matter to your answers if the initial payment was 25% of the purchase price? 50%? 90%?

Note: Sellers' Reclamation Rights and Bankruptcy

The circumstances that give a seller the right to reclaim goods (i.e., a credit buyer receiving goods while insolvent or a cash buyer paying with a "rubber check") are also circumstances in which the buyer is likely to enter bankruptcy proceedings. While UCC Article 2 grants a seller certain reclamation rights against her buyer, those rights are not necessarily valid against the buyer's trustee in bankruptcy. The trustee represents those with claims against the bankrupt buyer. The trustee therefore has rights and powers beyond those the buyer itself enjoyed. These rights, known as a trustee's "avoiding powers," might defeat a seller who seeks or has obtained reclamation from a buyer who enters bankruptcy, although a provision of the Bankruptcy Code (11 U.S.C. § 546) preserves some—but not necessarily all—of the seller's reclamation rights. The stakes are high. A seller who fails to reclaim goods or who must disgorge already reclaimed goods usually ends up with a mere unsecured claim for the price of the goods—a claim for which the seller will likely receive much less than full payment in the buyer's bankruptcy. In most bankruptcies, the seller would be far better off if it could recover the goods themselves.

D. OTHER REMEDIES UNDER UCC ARTICLE 2

1. *Incidental and Consequential Damages*

Introductory Note

Under UCC Article 2, an aggrieved buyer (and others entitled to sue the seller because of the demise of privity barriers) can recover consequential damages, provided the losses meet the requirements imposed by the definition of consequential damages in 2–715(2), *and* provided the parties have not agreed to exclude liability for consequential damages under 2–719(3). An aggrieved buyer is also entitled to incidental damages as defined in 2–715(1). The buyer's recovery of incidental and consequential damages is in addition to any direct or general damages (i.e., cover damages, market price damages, or damages for accepted goods) to which it is entitled. See 2–712(2), 2–713(1) and 2–714(3). Indeed, an award of incidental or consequential damages can be included in a decree of specific performance if the court deems such relief "just." See 2–716(2). In many situations, including those involving products liability claims for personal injuries, consequential damages may be the dominant or even exclusive remedy sought, and can involve very large sums. Under the pre-amendment version of Article 2, an aggrieved seller can recover incidental damages (in addition to resale damages, market price damages, lost profit or price recovery) but is not authorized to recover consequential damages. See 2–706(1), 2–708(1) & (2), 2–709(1) and 2–710; see also 1–106(1) (renumbered as 1–305(1) in amended Article 1). In the proposed amended version of Article 2, in contrast, a seller is allowed to recover consequential damages except in consumer contracts. See proposed amended Sections 2–706(1), 2–708(1)(a) & (b), 2–708(2), 2–709(1) and 2–710(2) & (3).

The meaning of the terms "incidental damages" and "consequential damages" under the UCC, and how these types of damages are distinguished from each other and from "direct damages," is a matter of some controversy, as the following materials demonstrate. What is clear is that the fundamental remedial principles mentioned at the very beginning of this chapter—the expectation principle, the mitigation principle, and the foreseeability limitation on damages—have some of their most important applications (as well as their most difficult challenges) with respect to incidental and consequential damages.

The following materials explore the rules in UCC Article 2 governing incidental and consequential damages, beginning with the damages available to aggrieved buyers.

Problem 116

In early June, Pluckett Poulterers Co. agreed to purchase 5,000 processed fresh Grade A tom turkeys, average of 20 pounds per bird (100,000 pounds total), for delivery on the Monday before Thanksgiving, at a price of 25 cents/lbs. ($25,000 total). The seller was Rosemary County Turkey Packers, Inc. ("RCTP"). During the rest of the summer, turkey prices rose steadily on fears that a bad grain harvest would keep poultry supplies tight. In late August, Pluckett agreed to resell the turkeys to Bag 'n Buy, Inc., which operates a chain of grocery stores, for 50 cents/lbs. ($50,000 total). Soon thereafter it became clear that the grain harvest would be better than anticipated and turkey prices fell. On the Monday before Thanksgiving, RCTP tendered 5,000 turkeys. Upon inspection, however, Pluckett discovered that the birds did not meet grade A standards, and it immediately rejected them. Pluckett could not purchase replacement turkeys so close to Thanksgiving, so it informed its customer Bag 'n Buy that it would not deliver the turkeys it had contracted to sell.

The wholesale market price throughout the United States for large fresh grade A tom turkeys during Thanksgiving week was 35 cents per pound ($35,000 for 100,000 pounds). Pluckett had spent $500 inspecting the turkeys it rejected. Pluckett would have spent $1,000 to deliver the turkeys to Bag 'n Buy. In a suit against RCTP based on its rightful rejection of the turkeys, what are Pluckett's general damages under 2–713? Can it recover any incidental or consequential damages as defined in 2–715? Would your analysis change if there were alternative supplies of turkeys (even so close to Thanksgiving), but Pluckett chose not to take advantage of them?

CITY NATIONAL BANK OF CHARLESTON v. WELLS

Supreme Court of Appeals of West Virginia, 1989.
181 W.Va. 763, 384 S.E.2d 374.

MILLER, JUSTICE. [In September, 1982, after informing defendant car dealership that he needed a truck for his stonemasonry business, plaintiff Leonard Wells bought a new Toyota truck from the dealership for $8,520. Wells paid $1,000 down and financed the balance of the price with a bank. Problems with the truck soon developed. Following nine months of unsuccessful attempts to repair the vehicle, Wells revoked his acceptance and stopped making payments to the bank on the note. In September, 1983 the bank repossessed the vehicle, sold it, and applied the proceeds to Wells' debt, leaving a deficiency of $1,329.57 for which he was responsible. Wells eventually settled with the bank and sued the dealership for breach of express and implied warranties under the U.C.C.

and the Magnuson–Moss Act. The jury awarded Wells $10,333.00 in damages.]

* * *

The defendant also contends that the trial court erred in allowing the jury to consider evidence that the plaintiff's credit rating was impaired following his default on the note. The defendant argues that this is not a proper element of consequential damages recoverable by the buyer under the UCC.

As a general rule, a buyer who justifiably revokes his acceptance of nonconforming goods is entitled to recover any incidental and consequential damages flowing therefrom. W.Va.Code, 46–2–711(1); W. Va. Code, 46–2–713(1). Consequential damages are described in W. Va. Code, 46–2–715(2):

[The Court Quoted 2–715(2)]

It is recognized that this provision is broad enough to encompass a variety of losses, including lost profits, interest and finance charges, and extra overhead, labor and expenses incurred as a result of the seller's breach. "To recover consequential damages, the buyer must establish: (1) causation, (2) foreseeability, (3) reasonable certainty as to amount, and (4) that he is not barred by mitigation doctrines." [1 J.] White & [R.] Summers, [UNIFORM COMMERCIAL CODE] at 309 [(3rd ed. 1988). The burden of proving consequential damages is on the buyer.

The plaintiff here sought consequential damages pursuant to W. Va. Code, 46–2–715(2)(a). The evidence at trial showed that in July, 1985, a St. Albans bank had refused to finance the plaintiff's purchase of an automobile for personal use. The notice from the bank listed "Delinquent credit obligations" and "Insufficient Equity" as reasons for the refusal, based on information received in a report from the Credit Bureau of Charleston, a consumer reporting agency. When the plaintiff inquired further, he learned that his default on the loan for the Toyota truck had been made a part of his credit history. The plaintiff testified that he filed a letter of rebuttal, explaining the circumstances of the default, with the Credit Bureau and was subsequently able to obtain financing from a bank which did not require a credit check.

In June, 1986, however, the plaintiff applied for a loan to purchase earth-moving equipment for use in his business. The plaintiff testified that he was refused the loan because of his damaged credit rating. The plaintiff testified that he needed the equipment immediately for a job he had contracted to do and was forced to pay other contractors with appropriate equipment $3,000.00 to perform the work until he was able to obtain financing one month later.

The defendant contends that any loss sustained by the plaintiff was attributable either to the Bank's action in reporting the default to the Credit Bureau or to the plaintiff's own conduct in defaulting on the obligation. Consequently, the defendant argues that any loss suffered was not the proximate result of any breach on its part. The defendant further asserts that the plaintiff failed to mitigate his losses by either continuing to make the payments or by returning the truck to the defendant for repairs.

In ACME Pump Co., Inc. v. National Cash Register Co., 32 Conn. Supp. 69, 337 A.2d 672 (1974), the purchaser of a bookkeeping machine sued the seller for breach of warranty when the machine proved defective. The plaintiff had financed the transaction through a lease arrangement with a third party, Granite Equipment Leasing Corporation (Granite). When it became apparent that the machine was defective, the plaintiff ceased making payments. Granite repossessed the unit and obtained a deficiency judgment against the plaintiff. In its breach of warranty action against the seller, the plaintiff sought to recover the amount of the deficiency judgment as consequential damages.

In ruling that the plaintiff was entitled to recover on this claim, the court in ACME Pump, 32 Conn.Supp. at 76, 337 A.2d at 677, stated:

> In this case, the defendant's breach of warranty was the proximate cause of the Granite lawsuit. The judgment obtained by Granite ... was in a reasonable amount. It could not have been avoided by any reasonable or prudent effort on the part of the plaintiff. Obviously, it would have been unfair to compel the plaintiff to continue payments on a machine which was wholly defective. The plaintiff's resulting default led to the repossession by Granite....
>
> "If a breach of contract is the cause of litigation between the plaintiff and third parties that the defendant had reason to foresee when the contract was made, the plaintiff's reasonable expenditures in such litigation are included in estimating his damages." Restatement, 1 Contracts § 334. Since the defendant helped to arrange the lease between the plaintiff and Granite, the defendant had reason to anticipate that if the machine were defective, the plaintiff might breach its lease with Granite and Granite thereafter might sue the plaintiff.

See Lycos v. Gray Mobile Home Sales, Inc., 76 Mich. App. 165, 256 N.W.2d 63 (1977).

We conclude that this approach is correct.[10] Except insofar as we have already addressed the issue in Section I of this opinion, the defendant here does not contest that the plaintiff justifiably revoked his acceptance of the Toyota truck under W. Va. Code, 46–2–608. The plaintiff was, therefore, entitled to cancel the contract of sale. W. Va. Code, 46–2–711. Thus, the defendant's breach of warranty was the proximate cause of the plaintiff's default on the obligation held by the Bank. That, in turn, produced the bad credit which ultimately required the plaintiff to incur the expense of hiring additional men and equip-

---

10. There is authority elsewhere to the contrary. In Chaney v. General Motors Acceptance Corp., 349 So.2d 519 (Miss.1977), the Supreme Court of Mississippi rejected the rationale of ACME Pump and concluded that any damage suffered by the defaulting plaintiff was proximately caused by his failure to make payments and not by any breach of warranty on the part of the seller.

ment when he was turned down on another loan. As we have already noted, such expenses are recognized as a loss for which consequential damages may be awarded. . . .

In addition, there was evidence that the loss was foreseeable within the meaning of W. Va. Code, 46–2–715. The plaintiff advised the defendant when he purchased the truck that he intended to use it in his business. The defendant was intimately involved in the financing arrangement and, thus, had reason to know that if the vehicle were defective, the plaintiff might legitimately refuse to make any further payments. In such circumstances, it is not unreasonable to assume that the plaintiff might suffer an impaired credit rating and incur additional business expenses. The amount of those expenses was reduced to a reasonably certain sum.

Nor do we find any failure on the part of the plaintiff to mitigate damages which would warrant reversal of the judgment. The buyer's duty to mitigate damages does not require him to undertake undue or oppressive burdens. As we have already stated, the plaintiff here justifiably revoked his acceptance of the defective truck and had no obligation to afford the defendant yet another opportunity to repair it. Moreover, the plaintiff's testimony indicates that he was financially unable to pay for two vehicles at once. In these circumstances, we cannot say that the plaintiff's failure to allow the defendant an opportunity to cure or refusal to continue payments on the defective vehicle constituted an unreasonable failure to mitigate damages.

In sum, we conclude that the plaintiff's evidence of losses due to an impaired credit rating satisfies all the requirements of consequential damages recoverable under the UCC. W. Va. Code, 46–1–106(1), provides that "[t]he remedies provided by this chapter shall be liberally administered to the end that the aggrieved party may be put in as good a position as if the other party had fully performed. . . ." Accordingly, we conclude that the issue of whether the plaintiff could recover consequential damages for the alleged impairment of his credit rating was properly submitted to the jury, and we find no grounds for reversing the judgment of the circuit court.

* * *

Problem 117

Apex Enterprises, Inc. ("AE") is a U.S. corporation formed to manufacture an advanced portable x-ray machine designed by AE's founder and principle shareholder Emily Apex. Using funds supplied by investors and borrowed from banks, AE began to put together a manufacturing facility and to assemble the inventory needed to produce the machines. A key component of the machine was an elaborate thin lead sheet. AE agreed to buy its requirements of the lead sheets from Helter Smelters, Inc., located in

Pennsylvania. The written contract required Helter Smelters to commence deliveries in nine months. The timing was coordinated with AE's plant construction schedule and designed to give Helter Smelters time to do the exacting design and tooling work needed to produce the sheets.

When the first shipment of lead sheets arrived, however, AE discovered serious defects. It rightfully rejected the tender and, because Helter Smelters refused to acknowledge or correct the problem, canceled the remainder of the deliveries. Because alternative sources could not begin to supply the lead sheets for at least nine months, and because it was already fully extended financially, AE had no choice but to sell its assets (at a very considerable loss) and cease active business. Can AE recover damages for the profits it would have earned in the x-ray machine venture under UCC Article 2? Could AE choose to recover, in lieu of lost profits, the investment it made in plant and inventory (less the amount for which it resold those assets)? Would recovery of such amounts put AE in the position it would have been in had Helter Smelters performed?

Problem 118

Overstreet is a practicing veterinarian who raises thoroughbred horses on his farm. He became concerned about an outbreak of a viral disease—equine rhinopneumonitis—which causes pregnant mares to abort. A sales agent for Norden Labs, a pharmaceutical company, called upon Overstreet and left pamphlets promoting "Rhinomune," a new drug which the pamphlets asserted would prevent the disease. After reading the pamphlets, Overstreet purchased Rhinomune and administered it to his horses. During the spring, six mares inoculated with the drug contracted rhinopneumonitis and aborted. Overstreet sued Norden under UCC Article 2 for breach of warranty, claiming as consequential damages the market value of the aborted foals. Norden defended by arguing that, because there existed no effective alternative drug to immunize horses against rhinopneumonitis, the failure of Rhinomune to live up to its warranties did not cause Overstreet's losses. Unless Overstreet could prove that his purchase of Rhinomune induced him to forego some other effective means of preventing the disease, Norden reasoned, he could not show that the use of Rhinomune caused the loss of the foals. What result? If the court denies recovery for the lost foals, will Overstreet be put in the position he would have been in had Norden fulfilled its warranty?

Problem 119

Molly Turbo, a professional race car driver, ordered a custom-designed engine part from Nipper Auto Racing Resources, Inc., explaining to the Nipper representative that she needed the part to participate in an important upcoming race—the Bradenton 500. Nipper delivered the part two days before the race. Defects in the part caused it to fail during preliminary time trials. The defects breached Nipper's warranty obligations. Because a new part could not be manufactured in time and there were no alternative suppliers, Molly could not race and she forfeited the $5,000 race entry fee she had paid. Can Molly recover as consequential damages the prize money she would have received had she won the race? Suppose there were nine other drivers entered in the race. Could Molly recover 10% of the first prize money? Alternatively, can Molly recover the lost entry fee as consequential damages? Suppose Nipper argues that Molly cannot recover the fee because it is money she would have spent even if the part had not been defective and she had participated in the race. Is Nipper's argument sound? Would awarding Molly the forfeited fee put her in the position she would have been in had there been no breach?

INDIANA GLASS COMPANY v. INDIANA MICHIGAN POWER COMPANY

Court of Appeals of Indiana, 1998.
692 N.E.2d 886.

GARRARD, JUDGE. Indiana Glass Company ("Indiana Glass") appeals the trial court's grant of summary judgment in favor of Indiana Michigan Power Company ("I & M") on Indiana Glass's claim for attorney's fees as incidental or consequential damages under the Indiana Uniform Commercial Code (the "UCC"). We affirm.

ISSUE

Whether a buyer may recover attorney's fees as incidental or consequential damages under the UCC for breach of the implied warranties of merchantability and fitness for a particular purpose.

FACTS

Indiana Glass is an Indiana corporation that manufactures glassware at its plant located in Dunkirk. I & M contracted to supply electricity to Indiana Glass pursuant to a written agreement. On several occasions between January 25, 1989, and September 25, 1990, I & M allegedly supplied electricity to Indiana Glass's Dunkirk facility at a diminished or an increased voltage which caused damage to Indiana Glass's manufacturing processes. Accordingly, on January 23, 1991, Indiana Glass filed its complaint against I & M and alleged that I & M was negligent, or in the alternative, that I & M breached the UCC's implied warranties of merchantability and fitness for a particular purpose when it sold and delivered "defective" electricity. Indiana Glass sought damages for lost machine hours, extraordinary maintenance costs, the cost of repairing machinery which was damaged due to voltage fluctuations, and for "all other just and proper relief."

Following a motion for partial summary judgment filed by Indiana Glass, on November 18, 1993, the trial court entered partial summary judgment in favor of Indiana Glass and concluded, as a matter of law, that electricity is a "good" under the UCC and that I & M had not disclaimed the UCC implied warranties of merchantability and fitness for a particular purpose in the parties' agreement. Thus, the trial court determined that Indiana Glass could pursue its UCC claims against I & M.

The parties thereafter entered into a confidential settlement agreement resolving all issues between the parties except Indiana Glass's claim for attorney's fees as incidental or consequential damages under the UCC. The parties filed cross-motions for summary judgment asking for a determination, as a matter of law, on the issue of whether Indiana Glass would be entitled to recover attorney's fees as incidental or consequential damages under the UCC in the event Indiana Glass could establish I & M's breach of the implied warranties. Following a hearing, the trial court granted summary judgment in favor of I & M and concluded that Indiana Glass could not recover attorney's fees as incidental or consequential damages under the UCC. Indiana Glass appeals that determination of law.

DISCUSSION AND DECISION

* * *

Attorney's Fees as Incidental or Consequential Damages

In this appeal, we are asked to resolve a pure question of law. Indiana Glass contends that the trial court erred when it concluded, as a matter of law, that a buyer may not recover attorney's fees as incidental or consequential damages under Indiana's UCC. The parties agree that the issue presented is one of first impression in Indiana.

We begin with our well-settled rule that each party to litigation is responsible for his or her own attorney's fees absent statutory authority, agreement, or rule to the contrary. Crowl v. Berryhill, 678 N.E.2d 828, 831 (Ind.Ct.App.1997). The contract between I & M and Indiana Glass makes no provision for the recovery of attorney's fees in the event of breach.[1] Accordingly, we address Indiana Glass's argument that Indiana Code § 26–1–2–715 [UCC 2–715] provides statutory authority for its proposition that a buyer is entitled to recover attorney's fees in the event of the seller's breach of the implied warranties. . . .

Although no Indiana court has had occasion to address this statutory argument under Indiana law, we have encountered this argument under Kentucky law. In Landmark Motors v. Chrysler Credit Corp., 662 N.E.2d 971, 976–77 (Ind.Ct.App.1996), this Court considered whether attorney's fees were recoverable as incidental or consequential damages pursuant to Kentucky Revised Statutes § 355.2–715, a provision identical to Indiana Code § 26–1–2–715. We held that Kentucky law did not provide for the recovery of attorney's fees as incidental or consequential damages. Specifically, we relied on the Kentucky Court of Appeals decision in Nick's Auto Sales, Inc. v. Radcliff Auto Sales, Inc., 591 S.W.2d 709, 711 (Ky.Ct.App.1979).

1. There is no merit to Indiana Glass's claim that the contract's silence as to the recovery of attorney's fees by either party in the event of a breach creates an ambiguity in the contract to be construed in its favor. We find silence to be the simplest way to draft a contract to indicate that no such fees are contemplated by the parties.

In Nick's Auto Sales, the court addressed the question of whether attorney's fees should be included as incidental or consequential damages under the UCC and held that, in accordance with the overwhelming weight of authority from other states, attorney's fees are not recoverable under § 2–715. Nick's Auto Sales, 591 S.W.2d at 711.[2] The Kentucky Court of Appeals went on to note that White and Summers, a leading authority on the UCC, has suggested that "[t]he recovery of legal fees is probably available in rare circumstances only." Id. (quoting JAMES J. WHITE AND ROBERT S. SUMMERS, HANDBOOK OF THE LAW UNDER THE UNIFORM COMMERCIAL CODE at 302 n. 57 (1972)).

Despite the overwhelming weight of authority from other jurisdictions indicating that attorney's fees are not recoverable under § 2–715, Indiana Glass urges us to review the specific language of that section and hold differently. First, Indiana Glass points to § 2–715(1) which provides that incidental damages include "any other reasonable expense incident to the delay or other breach." Indiana Glass argues that this language indicates that the legislature contemplated broad recovery on the part of the buyer in the event of the seller's breach, and that such recovery should include attorney's fees. Contrary to Indiana Glass's position, the commentary to subsection (1) indicates that incidental damages are the reasonable expenses incurred by the buyer in connection with the handling of rightfully rejected goods or goods whose acceptance may be justifiably revoked, or those expenses incurred in connection with effecting cover where goods are non-conforming or have not been delivered. Ind. Code § 26–1–2–715(1), cmt. 1. Attorney's fees were clearly not contemplated as recoverable under this subsection.

Next, Indiana Glass points us to the use of the broad term "any loss" in subsection (2)(a) [of UCC 2–715] to describe what is included in a buyer's consequential damages resulting from a seller's breach. Ind. Code § 26–1–2–715(2)(a). Again, there is no indication in the official commentary that the legislature intended for attorney's fees to be recoverable as consequential damages. Moreover, as noted by the Supreme Court of Tennessee, courts consistently have held that, despite the use of the broad language "any loss," the Code makes no change in the general rule that, regardless of the outcome of litigation, each party must bear its own legal expenses. Kultura, Inc. v. Southern Leasing

---

2. In support of its decision, the Kentucky Court of Appeals cited: Empire Realty Co. v. Fleisher, 269 Md. 278, 305 A.2d 144 (1973); Certain–Teed Products Corp. v. Goslee Roofing and Sheet Metal, Inc., 26 Md. App. 452, 339 A.2d 302 (1975); Universal C.I.T. Credit Corp. v. State Farm Mut. Auto. Ins. Co., 493 S.W.2d 385 (Mo.Ct.App. 1973); Equitable Lumber Corp. v. IPA Land Dev. Corp., 38 N.Y.2d 516, 381 N.Y.S.2d 459, 344 N.E.2d 391 (1976); Hardwick v. Dravo Equip. Co., 279 Or. 619, 569 P.2d 588 (1977); Modine Mfg. Co. v. North East Indep. Sch. Dist., 503 S.W.2d 833 (Tex.Civ.

App.1973); Murray v. Holiday Rambler, Inc., 83 Wis.2d 406, 265 N.W.2d 513 (1978).

In addition to the cases cited by the Kentucky Court of Appeals see Jacobs v. Rosemount Dodge–Winnebago South, 310 N.W.2d 71 (Minn.1981); Kultura, Inc. v. Southern Leasing Corp., 923 S.W.2d 536 (Tenn.1996); Devore v. Bostrom, 632 P.2d 832 (Utah 1981); but see Cady v. Dick Loehr's, Inc., 100 Mich. App. 543, 299 N.W.2d 69 (1980); Osburn v. Bendix Home Sys., Inc., 613 P.2d 445 (Okla.1980).

Corp., 923 S.W.2d 536, 540 (Tenn.1996) (citing 2 Roy Ryden Anderson, Damages Under the Uniform Commercial Code § 11.34, p. 132 (1992)).

Although we understand Indiana Glass's reliance on the language of Indiana Code § 26–1–1–106(1) which provides that the remedies provided by the UCC "shall be liberally administered to the end that the aggrieved party may be put in as good a position as if the other party had fully performed," we are also cognizant of § 1–103 which specifically states:

> Unless displaced by the particular provisions of IC 26–1, the principles of law and equity, including the law of merchant and the law relative to capacity to contract, principal and agent, estoppel, fraud, misrepresentation, duress, coercion, mistake, bankruptcy, or other validating or invalidating cause, shall supplement the provisions of IC 26–1.

Ind. Code § 26–1–1–103. As noted by the official commentary, this section emphasizes the continued applicability to commercial contracts of all supplemental bodies of law except insofar as they are explicitly displaced by the provisions of the UCC. Ind. Code § 26–1–1–103, cmt. 1. Section 2–715 does not explicitly provide for the recovery of attorney's fees as incidental or consequential damages and, thus, that section was not intended to abrogate the common law in Indiana regarding the recovery of attorney's fees.

We agree with the Kentucky Court of Appeals in Nick's Auto Sales, as well as the majority of our sister states, that attorney's fees are not recoverable as incidental or consequential damages under the UCC § 2–715.[3] The trial court properly entered summary judgment in favor of I & M.

Affirmed.

HOFFMAN and DARDEN, JJ., concur.

Problem 120

Amy Acquiz agreed to buy a new Phord from Perpetual Motors, Inc. for $20,000. To finance the transaction, Acquiz borrowed $15,000 from Middle National Bank. She paid Perpetual the loan proceeds (along with $5,000 of her own savings) when the car was delivered. Six months later, serious defects appeared in the Phord's engine. Perpetual failed to correct the problems and Acquiz validly revoked her acceptance. In her subsequent suit against Perpetual, Acquiz demanded a refund of the entire purchase price.

---

3. We note that attorney's fees have been permitted when incurred by the buyer in third-party litigation, a situation not presented here. See Alterman Foods, Inc. v. G.C.C. Beverages, Inc., 168 Ga. App. 921, 310 S.E.2d 755 (1983) (buyer could recover from seller attorney's fees incurred in defense of personal injury action brought by third-party consumer); Universal C.I.T. Credit Corp. v. State Farm Mut. Auto. Ins. Co., 493 S.W.2d 385 (Mo.Ct.App.1973) (indemnitee in breach of implied warranty action could recover attorney's fees incurred in defense of suit brought by third-party).

She also sought, as consequential damages, the finance charges (loan interest) imposed by Middle National Bank from the time the loan was made until such time as Perpetual would refund the price (enabling Acquiz to repay the loan). Assuming her revocation was rightful, can Acquiz recover for the finance charges? Would it matter if Perpetual helped Acquiz arrange the bank loan? See, e.g., Carl Beasley Ford, Inc. v. Burroughs, 361 F.Supp. 325 (E.D.Pa.1973); Distco Laminating, Inc. v. Union Tool Corp., 81 Mich. App. 612, 265 N.W.2d 768 (1978). Would recovering the finance charges protect Acquiz's expectation interest?

Note on Recovering Finance Charges

In Aubrey's R.V. Center, Inc. v. Tandy Corp., 46 Wash.App. 595, 731 P.2d 1124 (1987), the court upheld an award of finance charges in a revocation of acceptance case. In doing so it distinguished an earlier decision that had denied recovery of finance charges to a buyer who had not revoked acceptance but who sought damages for breach under 2–714. Consider the following excerpt. Do you agree?

> The focus of [2–714's] basic measure of damages, i.e., the difference between the value of goods as accepted and the value of goods as warranted is based on the rationale a buyer should only be given the benefit of his or her bargain and nothing more. Consequently, the buyer's measure of recovery is limited to the difference in value, plus incidental and consequential damages foreseeably *arising from* the breach of warranty.... The inclusion of finance charges within § 2–714's basic measure of damages overcompensates the buyer. Likewise, finance charges are not includable as incidental or consequential damages as they do not result from or arise incident to the breach.

> The objective behind awarding damages to a buyer who justifiably revokes acceptance is different. There, the buyer is not merely seeking the benefit of his or her bargain. Rather, the buyer seeks to be restored to the position he or she would have been in if the contract had never been entered into. Thus the objective of this remedy is primarily restitution. The measure of damages used to achieve this goal entitles the buyer not only to the return of the purchase price ... but also any expenses incurred by the buyer in reasonable reliance upon the contract, plus incidental and consequential damages arising from the breach....

> A buyer is not returned to the "precontract" position if he or she is not allowed, in a proper case, to claim any additional amount he or she has incurred in reliance on the contract. If held otherwise, the buyer, here, not only does not have the goods, but remains liable for finance charges.... Although compensated for the contract price of the goods, the buyer suffers out-of-pocket damages in the amount of interest paid to the financier. We conclude the court properly awarded [the buyer] Aubrey's not only the contract price, but also the finance charges less any amount saved if [the buyer's financier] releases Aubrey's from future finance charges.

Problem 121

S contracted to supply B six very large custom-designed and manufactured doors for a dam that B was building. The written contract between the parties included a schedule specifying when the doors were to be delivered—an important matter because B had to complete the dam before a necessary government permit expired. In addition, the contract included the following clause: "In no event shall S be liable for any incidental or consequential damages." S failed to deliver the doors by the dates specified on the delivery schedule, delaying B's completion of the dam (although B did manage to finish the project before its government permit expired). B had no choice but to accept the doors, which could not readily be obtained elsewhere. The delay caused B to incur increased expenses of two types: 1) extra compensation paid to employees and subcontractors during the period of the delay, and 2) extra interest charges for money B had borrowed to finance the project, which could not be repaid until the project was complete and B itself received payment. B sues S for damages under UCC 2–714(1) and seeks to recover the extra expenses caused by the delay. S argues that those expenses are incidental or consequential damages precluded by the contract. What result? See McNally Wellman Co. v. New York State Electric & Gas Corp., 63 F.3d 1188 (2d Cir.1995). See also Wright Schuchart, Inc. v. Cooper Industries, Inc., 40 F.3d 1247 (9th Cir.1994).

Problem 122

BGG, Inc., a corporation engaged in producing freeze dried flowers, purchased a new "floral freeze dryer" from Rose Electronic Supply for $15,000. The machine carried a warranty from its manufacturer, Southstar Industries, that it was free of defects in materials and workmanship and would operate continuously if properly maintained. Soon after the purchase BGG began to experience problems and breakdowns with the machine as a result of a faulty compressor. BGG also discovered that the machine would not operate continuously. As a result, the machine produced only half the freeze dried flowers that BGG had expected. BGG sued Southstar for breach of warranty and claimed as damages the costs of repairing the compressor and lost profits. What result if BGG's purchase of the freeze dryer is governed by the pre-amendment version of Article 2? See Beyond the Garden Gate, Inc. v. Northstar Freeze–Dry Mfg., Inc., 526 N.W.2d 305 (Iowa 1995). What would be the result if proposed new Sections 2–313A and 2–313B applied?

Remedies for Breach of Warranty to a "Remote Buyer" under Proposed Amended Article 2

New Sections 2–313A and 2–313B in the proposed amended version of Article 2 would govern warranties and remedial promises (defined in proposed amended Section 2–103(1)(p)) made by a manufacturer or other seller to a "remote purchaser"—i.e., a purchaser (like BGG in Problem 122) who does not acquire the goods directly from the seller making the warranty or remedial promise.[1] Under proposed Sections 2–313A(4)(c) and 2–313B(4)(c), a remote purchaser who has suffered a breach of such obligations can recover as damages "the loss resulting in the ordinary course of events as determined in any manner that is reasonable"—language that is derived from 2–714(1) on buyer's damages for accepted goods. In addition, under proposed Sections 2–313A(4)(b) and 2–313B(4)(b) the remote purchaser can recover incidental and consequential damages as defined in 2–715, except for lost profits. [Quaere—why should a remote purchase be denied damages for lost profits?] Comment 9 to proposed Section 2–313A states:

> As a rule, a remote purchaser may recover monetary damages measured in the same manner as in the case of an aggrieved buyer under Section 2–714, including incidental and consequential damages to the extent they would be available to an aggrieved buyer. Subsection (4)(c) parallels Section 2–714(1) in allowing the buyer to recover for loss resulting in the ordinary course of events as determined in any manner which is reasonable. In the case of an obligation that is not a remedial promise, the normal measure of damages would be the difference between the value of the goods if they had conformed to the seller's statements and their actual value, and the normal measure of damages for breach of a remedial promise would be the difference between the value of the promised remedial performances and the value of the actual performance received.

Note on Sellers' Incidental and Consequential Damages

As was noted earlier, the pre-amendment version of UCC Article 2 permits an aggrieved seller to recover incidental damages but does not expressly authorize a seller to recover consequential damages. See 2–706, 2–708, 2–709 and 2–710. In addition, 1–106(1) (renumbered as 1–305(a) in amended Article 1) states that consequential damages cannot be recovered under the UCC "except as specifically provided" in the statute. As a result, courts addressing the issue have uniformly held that an aggrieved seller cannot recover consequential damages in a transaction governed by the pre-revision version of Article 2, although at least one commentator has disagreed.[2] In this context, distinguishing between incidental and consequential damages becomes critical for an aggrieved seller.

The proposed amended version of Article 2 would authorize an aggrieved seller to recover consequential damages in non-consumer cases. See proposed amended Section 2–710. Nevertheless, distinguishing between incidental and consequential damages can still be important for both buyers and seller if,

---

1. Proposed amended 2–313A governs so-called "pass-through" warranties–i.e., warranties and remedial promises made to a remote purchaser that are created in "a record packaged with or accompanying the goods" (proposed amended Section 2–313A(2)). Proposed amended 2–313B governs warranties and remedial promises to a remote purchaser when they are created by "advertising or similar communication to the public" (proposed amended Section 2–313B(2)).

2. Anderson, *In Support of Consequential Damages for Sellers*, 11 J.L. & Com. 123, 148–153 (1992).

e.g., the contract validly excludes liability for consequential (but not incidental) damages.

Problem 123

Perquisite Inc. contracted in writing to purchase a new "Cordelia Executive" model jet airplane from its manufacturer, the Seznah Corporation, for $1 million. After equipping the plane with certain features ordered by Perquisite, including a specially configured passenger compartment decorated in a "pinstripe" motif, Seznah tendered delivery of the jet. Perquisite, however, wrongfully rejected the plane. Seznah was able to resell the jet to another customer for $800,000, but only after suffering a considerable delay and spending $10,000 converting the passenger compartment to a more conventional configuration and appearance. In its suit against Perquisite, Seznah claimed resale damages under 2–706. It also claimed damages for the $10,000 spent to re-do the passenger compartment and for the following additional items: $500 spent to fly the jet back to the Seznah plant after rejection; $1,500 in sales commissions and other added expenses associated with the resale; $2,000 in finance charges incurred during the period after rejection on funds borrowed to finance construction of the plane; and $1,000 spent insuring the plane after rejection. Seznah also claimed that, since it was the exclusive source for many parts used in the Cordelia Executive jet, it would have earned additional profits of at least $15,000 by selling Perquisite replacement parts required for normal maintenance of the plane.

(a) Which of the damage items claimed by Seznah are incidental damages within the meaning of 2–710? Which are "consequential" damages unrecoverable by a seller under the pre-revision version of Article 2? Does the following passage help you?

> While the distinction between [incidental and consequential damages] is not an obvious one, the Code makes plain that incidental damages are normally incurred when a buyer (or seller) repudiates the contract or wrongfully rejects the goods, causing the other to incur such expense as transporting, storing or reselling the goods. On the other hand, consequential damages do not arise within the scope of the immediate buyer-seller transaction, but rather stem from losses incurred by the non-breaching party in its dealings, often with third parties, which were a proximate result of the breach, and which were reasonably foreseeable by the breaching party at the time of contract.

Petroleo Brasileiro, S.A., Petrobras v. Ameropan Oil Corp., 372 F.Supp. 503, 508 (E.D.N.Y.1974).

(b) Suppose Seznah could not recover resale damages under 2–706 because it had not given proper notice of the resale. Could Seznah nevertheless recover the expenses of the resale (e.g., sales commissions) as incidental damages, provided such expenses were reasonable? See Lee Oldsmobile, Inc. v. Kaiden, 32 Md.App. 556, 363 A.2d 270 (1976).

Question

Suppose the parties' contract provides that the seller can recover consequential damages resulting from the buyer's breach. Is the provision enforceable under the pre-amendment version of Article 2? In analyzing this question you may want to consider the materials in the next section on liquidated damages.

2. *Liquidated Damages*

KVASSAY v. MURRAY

Court of Appeals of Kansas, 1991.
15 Kan.App.2d 426, 808 P.2d 896.

WALKER, DISTRICT JUDGE, ASSIGNED: Plaintiff Michael Kvassay, d/b/a Kvassay Exotic Food, appeals the trial court's finding that a liquidated damages clause was unenforceable and from the court's finding that damages for lost profits were not recoverable. Kvassay contends these damages occurred when Great American Foods, Inc., (Great American) breached a contract for the purchase of baklava. Great American and Albert and Deana Murray, principals of Great American, cross-appeal the trial court's ruling that Kvassay could pierce Great American's corporate veil to collect damages awarded at trial.

On February 22, 1984, Kvassay, who had been an independent insurance adjuster, contracted to sell 24,000 cases of baklava to Great American at $19.00 per case. Under the contract, the sales were to occur over a one-year period and Great American was to be Kvassay's only customer. The contract included a clause which provided: "If Buyer refuses to accept or repudiates delivery of the goods sold to him, under this Agreement, Seller shall be entitled to damages, at the rate of $5.00 per case, for each case remaining to be delivered under this Contract."

Problems arose early in this contractual relationship with checks issued by Great American being dishonored for insufficient funds. Frequently one of the Murrays issued a personal check for the amount due. After producing approximately 3,000 cases, Kvassay stopped producing the baklava because the Murrays refused to purchase any more of the product. . . .

In April 1985, Kvassay filed suit for damages arising from the collapse of his baklava baking business. Great American counterclaimed and, in May 1988, the trial court sustained a defense motion to bifurcate the case. The court conducted bench hearings on the validity of the liquidated damages clause and the question of piercing the corporate veil. The trial court ruled that liquidated damages could not be recovered and that Great American's corporate veil could be pierced by Kvassay. The court also held "as a matter of law" that Kvassay would not be able to recover damages for lost profits in the action because they were too "speculative and conjectural."

* * *

Kvassay first attacks the trial court's ruling that the amount of liquidated damages sought by him was unreasonable and therefore the liquidated damages clause was unenforceable.

Kvassay claimed $105,000 in losses under the liquidated damages clause of the contract, representing $5 per case for the approximately 21,000 cases of baklava which he was not able to deliver. The trial court determined that Kvassay's use of expected profits to formulate liquidated damages was improper because the business enterprise lacked duration, permanency, and recognition. The court then compared Kvassay's previous yearly income (about $20,000) with the claim for liquidated damages ($105,000) and found "the disparity becomes so great as to make the clause unenforceable."

Since the contract involved the sale of goods between merchants, the Uniform Commercial Code governs. See K.S.A. 84–2–102 [UCC 2–102]. "The Code does not change the pre-Code rule that the question of the propriety of liquidated damages is a question of law for the court." 4 Anderson, Uniform Commercial Code § 2–718:6, p. 572 (3d ed. 1983). Thus, this court's scope of review of the trial court's ruling is unlimited.

Liquidated damages clauses in sales contracts are governed by K.S.A. 84–2–718, which reads in part:

> (1) Damages for breach by either party may be liquidated in the agreement but only at an amount which is reasonable in the light of the anticipated or actual harm caused by the breach, the difficulties of proof of loss, and the inconvenience or nonfeasibility of otherwise obtaining an adequate remedy. A term fixing unreasonably large liquidated damages is void as a penalty.

To date, the appellate courts have not interpreted this section of the UCC in light of facts similar to those presented in this case. In ruling on this issue, the trial court relied on rules governing liquidated damages as expressed in U.S.D. No. 315 v. DeWerff, 6 Kan. App.2d 77, 626 P.2d 1206 (1981). DeWerff, however, involved a teacher's breach of an employment contract and was not governed by the UCC. Thus, the rules expressed in that case should be given no effect if they differ from the rules expressed in 84–2–718.

In DeWerff, this court held a "stipulation for damages upon a future breach of contract is valid as a liquidated damages clause if the set amount is determined to be reasonable and the amount of damages is difficult to ascertain." 6 Kan.App.2d at 78, 626 P.2d 1206. This is clearly a two-step test: Damages must be reasonable and they must be difficult to ascertain. Under the UCC, however, reasonableness is the only test. K.S.A. 84–2–718. K.S.A. 84–2–718 provides three criteria by which to measure reasonableness of liquidated damages clauses: (1) anticipated or actual harm caused by breach; (2) difficulty of proving loss; and (3) difficulty of obtaining an adequate remedy.

In its ruling, the trial court found the liquidated damages clause was unreasonable in light of Kvassay's income before he entered into the manufacturing contract with Great American. There is no basis in 84–2–718 for contrasting income under a previous unrelated employment arrangement with liquidated damages sought under a manufacturing contract. Indeed, the traditional goal of the law in cases where a buyer breaches a manufacturing contract is to place the seller "in the same position he would have occupied if the vendee had performed his contract." Outcault Adv. Co. v. Citizens' Nat'l Bank, 118 Kan. 328, 330–31, 234 P. 988 (1925). Thus, liquidated damages under the contract in this case must be measured against the anticipated or actual loss under the baklava contract as required by 84–2–718. The trial court erred in using Kvassay's previous income as a yardstick.

Was the trial court correct when it invalidated the liquidated damages clause, notwithstanding the use of an incorrect test? If so, we must uphold the decision even though the trial court relied on a wrong ground or assigned an erroneous reason for its decision. To answer this question, we must look closer at the first criteria for reasonableness under 84–2–718, anticipated or actual harm done by the breach.

Kvassay produced evidence of anticipated damages at the bench trial showing that, before the contract was signed between Kvassay and Great American, Kvassay's accountant had calculated the baklava production costs. The resulting figure showed that, if each case sold for $19, Kvassay would earn a net profit of $3.55 per case after paying himself for time and labor. If he did not pay himself, the projected profit was $4.29 per case. Nevertheless, the parties set the liquidated damages figure at $5 per case. In comparing the anticipated damages of $3.55 per case in lost net profit with the liquidated damages of $5 per case, it is evident that Kvassay would collect $1.45 per case or about 41 percent over projected profits if Great American breached the contract. If the $4.29 profit figure is used, a $5 liquidated damages award would allow Kvassay to collect 71 cents per case or about 16 ½ percent over projected profits if Great American breached the contract.

An examination of these pre-contract comparisons alone might well lead to the conclusion that the $5 liquidated damages clause is unreasonable because enforcing it would result in a windfall for Kvassay and serve as a penalty for Great American. A term fixing unreasonably large liquidated damages is void as a penalty under 84–2–718.

A better measure of the validity of the liquidated damages clause in this case would be obtained if the actual lost profits caused by the breach were compared to the $5 per case amount set by the clause. However, no attempt was made by Kvassay during the bench trial to prove actual profits or actual costs of production. Thus, the trial court could not compare the $5 liquidated damages clause in the contract with the actual profits lost by the breach. It was not until the jury trial that Kvassay attempted to prove his actual profits lost as part of his damages. Given the trial court's ruling that lost profits were not recoverable and could not be presented to the jury, it is questionable whether the court would have permitted evidence concerning lost profits at the bench trial.

The trial court utilized an impermissible factor to issue its ruling on the liquidated damages clause and the correct statutory factors were not directly addressed. We reverse the trial court on this issue and remand for further consideration of the reasonableness of the liquidated damages clause in light of the three criteria set out in 84–2–718 and our ruling on recoverability of lost profits which follows.

* * *

The trial court's decisions with respect to liquidated damages and lost profits are reversed and the case is remanded for a new trial on those issues. The trial court's decision on piercing the corporate veil is affirmed.

Notes and Questions on *Kvassay*

(1) Compare the non-UCC doctrine applied by the trial court in determining the enforceability of the liquidated damages clause in *Kvassay* with the UCC tests in 2–718(1). Can you describe the differences precisely? Think of an example of a situation in which the result would be different under the two approaches. Proposed amended Section 2–718(1) would omit consideration of "the difficulties of proof of loss" and "the inconvenience or nonfeasibility of otherwise obtaining an adequate remedy" as factors in evaluating the reasonableness of liquidated damages, except in consumer contracts. The proposed amended provision would also omit the phrase stating that "[a] term fixing unreasonably large liquidated damages is void as a penalty" because that language is, according to comment 1(b), "unnecessary and capable of causing confusion."

(2) Suppose the liquidated damages clause in *Kvassay* provided that $5 for each undelivered case was a *minimum* recovery, and that the seller could recover his actual damages if they exceeded that amount. Would that affect the validity of the clause? See Stock Shop, Inc. v. Bozell & Jacobs, Inc., 126 Misc.2d 95, 481 N.Y.S.2d 269 (1984) (denying enforcement to liquidated damages clause). Compare Baker v. International Record Syndicate, Inc., 812 S.W.2d 53 (Tex.Ct.App.1991) (enforcing apparently identical liquidated damages clause).

(3) As we saw in the previous section, the pre-amendment version of UCC Article 2 does not authorize a seller to recover consequential damages. Could an aggrieved seller nevertheless use consequential losses to show that a liquidated damages clause was "reasonable in the light of the anticipated or actual harm" as per 2–718(1)?

Problem 124

In March, 1996 C & H, Inc., a large-scale sugar processor, contracted with Sun Ship Co. to purchase, for $25 million, an ocean-going cargo ship.

The ship was an innovative design combining two large components, one to be constructed by Sun and the other to be built by another shipbuilding firm, Halter Marine Inc. Sun was responsible for joining the two components and delivering the finished ship. The written contract that was negotiated by the teams of lawyers representing both parties required Sun to deliver the ship to C & H by June 30, 1998, and a contract clause labeled "liquidated damages" required Sun to pay C & H $20,000 for each day that delivery was delayed beyond that date. Halter Marine was almost seven months late in delivering its component. That, however, did not effect Sun who was even later in finishing its component. Sun did not deliver the completed ship until the end of April 27, 1999. During the delay, as it turned out, C & H managed to arrange for substitute shipping at extremely low rates, the lowest in 20 years, because of an excess of commercial cargo ship capacity. C & H sued Sun to collect the agreed damages for the 300 day delay in delivering the ship—$6 million. Sun countered that, because Halter Marine was late in completing its part of the contract, C & H would have suffered almost the same delay even if Sun had not breached. Sun also argued that C & H suffered no harm from the delay, and thus should be precluded from receiving a $6 million windfall. What result under 2–718(1)? See also California and Hawaiian Sugar Co. v. Sun Ship, Inc., 794 F.2d 1433 (9th Cir.1986), opinion amended, 811 F.2d 1264 (1987); Lind Building Corp. v. Pacific Bellevue Developments, 55 Wash.App. 70, 776 P.2d 977 (1989) (non-UCC case).

Note on "Take-or-Pay" Contracts

A common arrangement for long-term natural gas supply contracts is the "take-or-pay" contract, which obligates the buyer to pay for a specified minimum quantity of gas per given time period whether or not the buyer actually takes delivery of that quantity during the period. If the buyer fails to take the minimum amount and has to pay for gas it did not receive, the take-of-pay clause typically allows the buyer to arrange for "make-up" deliveries of gas in later periods. Nevertheless, if the buyer's "takes" fall sufficiently below the minimum or if unfavorable market conditions persist, the buyer may never receive gas for which it must pay under the take-or-pay clause. For this reason, defaulting buyers have sometimes attacked take-or-pay provisions as, in effect, unenforceable penalty clauses designed to coerce performance.

The reported cases suggest that the buyers' argument seldom prevails. Most decisions addressing the issue have held that take-or-pay clauses do not constitute attempts to liquidate damages, and thus are not subject to the requirements of the liquidated damages provision of UCC Article 2. Consider the following (from a court whose jurisdiction includes areas of significant natural gas production):

> [The buyer] alleges the take-or-pay provisions operate as a penalty or liquidated damages provision and are unenforceable pursuant to [2–718(1)] because the amount of the deficiency sought by plaintiff bears no reasonable relationship to plaintiff's actual damages and the amount of actual damages is not impracticable or extremely difficult to determine.

[The seller] asserts that the payment obligation under a take-or-pay contract is a promise or obligation, not a punishment for breach, and that payment pursuant to such contract provision constitutes performance thereof, not payment for breach of the contract of an amount stipulated as damages. Thus, plaintiff asserts that the payment obligation is neither a penalty nor a liquidated damages provision....

The court agrees with plaintiff and with the United States District Court for the Northern District of Texas that "[t]he take-or-pay provisions ... specifies a contractual obligation rather than dictates damages upon breach." Accordingly, the take-or-pay provision, or more particularly the payment provision, cannot constitute a penalty for failure to perform or a liquidated damages provision specifying damages for breach of the "take" obligation.

Sabine Corp. v. ONG Western, Inc., 725 F.Supp. 1157 (W.D.Okl.1989). See also, e.g., Prenalta Corp. v. Colorado Interstate Gas Co., 944 F.2d 677 (10th Cir.1991) (take-or-pay provision creates alternative modes of performance rather than liquidated damages; hence take-or-pay clause cannot be an invalid penalty). But see Lake River Corp. v. Carborundum Co., 769 F.2d 1284 (7th Cir.1985) (non-UCC case holding that take-or-pay clause in a contract for services was an invalid penalty; dicta suggests different result for natural gas take-or-pay contracts).

---

3. Restitution for Breaching Buyers

Problem 125

On Monday Andrew agreed in writing to buy Emily's 3–year old Miasma 4–door sedan for $7,000. Emily was to deliver the car (with necessary title papers) on Friday. Andrew paid a $2,000 deposit on signing the contract, with the balance due five days after delivery. On Friday morning Andrew called Emily to explain that he had changed his mind and would "most certainly *not* be buying the car." He demanded his $2,000 back. Emily, of course, has held on to the car.

(a) Must Emily give Andrew a refund? See 2–718(2). Under proposed amended Section 2–718(2), the seller would not have an automatic right to retain the smaller of $500 or 20% of the total price.

(b) Would your answer change if, after giving Andrew notice, Emily had sold the car to another buyer for $5,000—a reasonable price in the circumstances? Consider 2–718(3).

Problem 126

Take the facts of problem 125, but suppose Andrew had not repudiated on Friday morning. Emily delivered the car on time. Although he lacked the right to do so, Andrew immediately gave notice that he was rejecting the car. He refused to return the vehicle to Emily until she refunded his $2,000 down payment, and he has put the car in storage. Is Andrew entitled to a refund under 2–718(2)? Has Emily "withheld delivery" of the goods?

E. REMEDIES UNDER UCC ARTICLE 2A

1. *Overview of Article 2A Remedies*

The remedy provisions of UCC Article 2A, like all remedy provisions in the UCC, are subject to the general principle in Article 1 that Code remedies are to "be liberally administered to the end that the aggrieved party may be put in as good a position as if the other party had fully performed. . . ."[3] Other remedial principles found in Article 2–specifically the mitigation of damages principle, the requirement that losses be foreseeable in order to give rise to recoverable damages, and a preference for substitutional relief (damages) over remedies requiring actual performance of contractual obligations (specific performance)–also appear in Article 2A. Because UCC Articles 2 and 2A share these foundational principles, their remedy provisions are quite similar. Indeed, most Article 2A remedy sections were derived from provisions of Article 2. There are, of course, some differences in the details and particulars of these shared remedies, and even some Article 2A remedies that have no counterpart in Article 2. The materials that follow will highlight both the common aspects and the differences in the remedy systems of these laws.

2. *Lessees' Remedies under Article 2A*

Problem 127

On October 1, the law firm Paley & Tologist ("P & T"), located in Chicago, agreed in writing to a three-year lease of 200 IBX computers from Seattle-based Random Accessories, Inc. The lease term began on November 1, and the monthly rent was $20,000 ($100 per computer). The contract required Random to deliver the computers to P & T's offices on Random's own trucks by November 1. When November 1 arrived, Random failed to deliver and shortly thereafter declared it would not deliver any computers under the lease. On November 1 the market rent per month for the computers was $125 per computer in Chicago and $120 per computer in Seattle. On November 9 (by which point the market rent had risen to $135 in Chicago and $130 in Seattle) P & T leased 200 replacement computers for three years at a rent of $140 each per month. P & T sues to recover (1) one month's rent it had prepaid, and (2) damages in the amount of the difference between the present values of the rent in the replacement lease ($28,000 per month for three years) and the rent in the original lease with Random ($20,000 per month for three years). [For the "present value" aspect of the calculation, see "Note: Present Value Damages" *infra*.] What result? See UCC 2A–508(1)(b) and 2A–518. What requirements must P & T satisfy in order to recover the damages it seeks? Suppose that P & T's substitute lease did not satisfy the requirements for proper cover, or that P & T did not attempt to lease replacement computers. What damages (if any) could it

---

3. UCC 1–106, moved to Section 1–305 in the Amended version of Article 1.

recover? See 2A–518(3), 2A–519(1) & (2), and 2A–507(2). If P & T had suffered incidental or consequential losses, could it recover damages for them?

Note: Equivalency of Substitute Lease for Purposes of Cover Damages

As was noted earlier (see "Note: Equivalency of Substitute Purchase for Purposes of Cover Damages" *supra*), the cover damages provisions of UCC Article 2 (2–712) requires that the terms and features of an aggrieved buyer's substitute purchase of goods must be roughly equivalent to those in the breached sales contract in order for the substitute purchase to qualify as "cover" and be used to measure the buyer's damages. Contractual terms and features of leases tend to be even more variable than those in sales. For this reason, Article 2A adds a requirement that the substitute lease be "substantially similar to the original lease agreement" before it can be used to measure cover damages. See 2A–518(2). Comments 4 and 5 to 2A–518 describe factors to consider in dealing with the "substantially similar" requirement:

> First, the goods subject to the new lease agreement should be examined [to see if they are similar to the goods in the original lease]. . . . Second, the various elements of the new lease agreement [e.g., options to purchase, warranties, service provisions] should also be examined. . . . If the differences between the original lease and the new lease can be easily valued, it would be appropriate for a court to adjust the difference in rental to take account of the difference between the two leases, find that the new lease is substantially similar to the old lease, and award cover damages under this section.

Problem 128

Return to the contract in Problem 127 involving P & T's lease of 200 computers from Random, Inc., but suppose Random delivered the computers on November 1. P & T inspected the computers and discovered that each was missing a component that was supposed to be included with the computers. P & T informed Random of the problem, but decided to accept the computers anyway. P & T decided to purchase the missing components from another supplier, and paid a total of $5000 to do so. The first post-delivery rental payment of $20,000 is now due, and P & T wants to know if it has to pay the full amount. Consider 2A–519(3) & (4), along with 2A–508(6) (renumbered in proposed amended Section 2A–508 as subsection (5)).

Note: Lessees' Right to Recover Leased Goods from the Lessor

The provisions of Article 2A governing a lessee's right to recover goods from a lessor that has not delivered closely track the provisions in Article 2 governing a buyer's right to recover goods from a seller that has failed to deliver. The changes in these provisions made in the proposed amended version of Article 2A also closely follow the changes made in the proposed amended version of Article 2. Read the Article 2A provisions on "Lessee's Right to Goods on Lessor's Insolvency" (2A–522), and on specific performance and replevin (2A–521—moved to 2A–507A in the proposed amended version), then compare the "Introductory Note on Buyers' Right to Reach the Goods under the UCC" *supra*.

Note: Present Value Damages under UCC Article 2A

Article 2A mandates that damages be discounted to "present value." Section 2A–519(1), for example, defines an aggrieved lessee's market rent damages as "the present value, as of the date of the default, of the then market rent minus the present value as of the same date of the original rent." The other Article 2A damages provisions also mandate that damages be discounted to present value. The adjustment to present value is designed to account for the time-value of money—i.e., the fact that, because money can be invested and earn a return, a dollar in damages received today covers more than one dollar in future losses.

To illustrate the principle on which this is based, suppose someone owed you $100. The debtor told you that she was willing to pay either immediately or at the end of one year. Suppose further that your bank paid simple (i.e., not compounded) 10% annual interest on savings accounts. If you received immediate payment you could deposit the $100 in your savings account and (ignoring complicating factors like taxes) earn an additional $10 in one year's time. The $100 paid immediately would have turned into $110 at the end of one year. Thus you would be better off taking an immediate payment rather than waiting a year. Indeed, because you can earn a 10% return in one year you would be better off taking an immediate $100 payment even if the debtor had offered to pay $108 a year from now. Only if the debtor offered $110 at the end of one year would you be indifferent between payment in the future and an immediate $100 payment.[1] In other words, if you can earn a 10% simple annual rate of return, the "present value" to you of $110 to be received after one year is $100. Similarly, if your debtor could also earn a 10% simple annual return on funds, the "present value" to her of $110 to be paid after one year would be $100: by investing the $100 that otherwise would have been paid immediately she can earn $10 in interest and make the deferred $110 payment at year's end. Thus with a 10% simple rate of return the present value of a $110 payment to be made one year in the future is $100.

The rate of return on investments assumed in this scenario is a critical factor. If the highest annual return you could earn on money was only 8%, then the present value of $110 in one year's time would be *more* than $100. In other words, with an 8% annual rate of return you would prefer that your debtor defer payment for one year and pay an extra ten dollars because you could earn only $8 by investing $100 for one year. Conversely, your debtor would prefer to pay $100 now rather than $110 in one year's time because she could earn only $8 by deferring payment and investing the $100 for one year. Thus with an 8% interest annual rate, the present value of $110

---

1. This assumes there is no chance your debtor will lose the ability to pay during the year in which payment was deferred. Otherwise you would need an even larger payment at year's end to make up for the risk.

payable one year in the future is greater than $100—in fact it is $101.85. The amount of time before the future payment must be made is also crucial. Even assuming only an 8% annual rate of return, the present value of $110 to be received *two* years in the future is *less* than $100 because a $100 investment will earn more than $10 over a two year period. One thing, however, always remains true: the present value of a future payment is less than the amount of the future payment. How much less will depend on the rate of return available on investments (called the "discount rate") and how far in the future the payment will occur.

To see how "present value" comes up in the calculation of damages under Article 2A, assume that a lease of equipment had a term of 3 years and called for annual rental payments of $1,000 due at the end of each year of the lease. The lessor, who was supposed to deliver the equipment on June 1, repudiated. The lessee covered by leasing equivalent equipment from another supplier starting June 1. The terms of the new lease were identical to those in the repudiated lease, except that the new rent was $1,100 per year. If the substitute lease qualifies under 2A–518(2), the lessee can recover the difference between the rent for the three-year term of the substitute lease ($3,300 total) and the rent under the defaulted lease ($3,000 total). Before calculating the difference, however, the statute requires that the rental payments in the original and the cover lease be "discounted" to their "present value, as of the date of the commencement of the term of the new lease agreement." In other words, the amount awarded must be adjusted to reflect the fact that the extra $300 the lessee must pay for the equipment under the cover lease is spread over the three years following the start of the substitute lease. If the lessee recovered the full $300 on June 1 it would be overcompensated because it could invest and earn a return on the money until it had to make the extra payments on the cover rental.[2]

"Present value" is defined in § 2A–103(1)(u) as "the amount as of a date certain of one or more sums payable in the future, discounted to the date certain." To calculate the present value of rental payments in order to compute general damages under Article 2A, you need to know the amount and timing of each payment, the date as of which present value is to be calculated, and the discount rate to be applied. In the example in the previous paragraph, the cover lease requires the lessee to pay $1,100 one year after the lease commenced, $1,100 two years after commencement, and $1,100 three years after commencement. The original lease, on the other hand, required $1,000 due one year after the commencement of the cover

---

2. The date as of which Article 2A requires present value to be calculated (*e.g.,* the date a cover lease commences, the date of default, the date the lessor repossesses) will normally be earlier than the date damages will actually be paid by the breaching party. Damages so discounted will not fully compensate an aggrieved party, who does not have the use of the damage award until it is actually paid. Theoretically, damages discounted to present value as of a date earlier than the time they are paid should be adjusted upward to reflect lost interest from the earlier date. Article 2A, however, does not itself authorize the payment of pre-or post-judgment interest on damage awards. The extent to which other law authorizes such interest varies from jurisdiction to jurisdiction. Even when prejudgment interest *is* authorized, it may be limited to a "legal rate" different from the discount rate used for Article 2A present value calculations. See generally Bergkamp v. Carrico, 108 Idaho 476, 481, 700 P.2d 98, 103 (App.1985); Benfield *Lessor's Damages Under Article 2A After Default by the Lessee As to Accepted Goods,* 39 ALA. L. REV. 915, 930–31 nn. 36 & 37 (1988).

lease, $1,000 two years after that commencement date, and $1,000 three years after the commencement date. The payments under the original lease and the cover lease must now be adjusted according to a discount rate which reflects the return the aggrieved party could expect on investments. The further into the future a payment is to be made, the more it will be discounted and the lower the present value of that payment will be. Similarly, the higher the discount rate, the lower the present value of a future payment.

Assuming a 10% discount rate, the present value of three annual payments of $1,100 (the rent under the cover lease) commencing one year in the future is $2,735.54.[3] In other words this amount, if invested immediately at a 10% annual rate of return, would cover the three annual $1,100 payments. The present value of three annual payments of $1,000 (the rent under the original lease) starting one year in the future is $2,486.85. Lessees' cover damages recoverable under 2A–518 are calculated by subtracting the discounted rent in the original lease from the discounted rent in the cover lease—resulting in damages of $248.69 in this case. If the discount rate were 20%, the present value of the three cover rental payments of $1,100 would be $2,317.13 and the present value of the three original rental payments of $1,000 would be $2,106.48, yielding only $210.65 in cover damages.

The discount rate used in calculating present value is a key variable. It should be the rate of return someone in the position of the aggrieved party can earn on risk-free investments. The discount rate thus reflects the extent to which a given damage award paid on a specified date will, if the proceeds are invested, compensate for a larger amount of loss to be suffered at a later time. According to 2A–103(1)(u), a court is to apply "a commercially reasonable rate that takes into account the facts and circumstances of each case at the time the transaction was entered into." In cases not governed by Article 2A courts have applied a variety of rates and approaches, including the "legal" rate of interest applicable by law to judgments,[4] a discount rate used by an expert witness and not challenged by opposing counsel,[5] and a rate dictated by a complicated formula designed to factor out the effects of inflation.[6] What discount rate to apply is a question of fact to be resolved in

---

3. This number is calculated by determining the present value of each of the three annual payments, then adding the results. The present value (PV) of each payment can be obtained by applying the formula $PV = FV/(1 + r)^t$, where FV is amount of the future payment, r is the discount rate for a given period, and t is the number of such periods before the payment will be made. Thus with a 10% annual discount rate, the present value of the $1100 payment to be made after one year is $1100/1.1, or $1000; the present value of the $1100 payment due after two years is $1100/1.1^2, or $909.09; and the present value of the $1100 payment due in three years is $1100/1.1^3, or $826.45. Adding the results yields a present value for all three payments of $2735.54. Where you are deal-

ing with equal amounts payable at equal intervals (as in the problem at hand), a short cut is available: you can calculate the present value of the entire stream of payments (called an "annuity") by applying the formula $PV = FV \, [1 - (1 + r)^{-n}]/r$.

4. E.g., Look v. Werlin, 590 S.W.2d 526, 528 (Tex.Civ.App.1979) (applying the postjudgment interest rate of 9%).

5. Admae Enterprises, Ltd. v. 1000 Northern Blvd. Corp., 104 A.D.2d 919, 480 N.Y.S.2d 537, 538 (1984) (applying a 10% discount rate).

6. "Said discount rate of 21/2 is derived by dividing the average interest rate of 1.0867 (8.67%) by a 6% inflation rate, expressed as 1.06%." Sam & Mary Housing Corp. v. Jo/Sal Market Corp., 121 Misc.2d

the same fashion (and with the same delays and expense) as other litigated issues.[7] If the parties have specified an interest rate in their agreement, courts must use it as the discount rate unless it was "manifestly unreasonable at the time the transaction was entered into." See 2A–103(1)(u).[8]

Once the variables (the discount rate, the amount of the future payments, the time at which those payments will occur) have been determined, the calculation of present values involves somewhat complex formulas. See footnote 3 *supra*. Luckily, computer programs and financial calculators can perform the task. For those who prefer to calculate without machines, present value tables—which state discount factors for various combinations of time periods and discount rates—are available, although they frequently are not designed for the monthly (as opposed to annual) payments typically involved in a lease. Whether or not you are asked to calculate present values in this course, you must be aware of and understand the reasons for Article 2A's mandate to discount prospective general damages to present value as of an earlier date. Remember that, even if you dislike working with numbers, you may very well be called upon to do present value calculations in practice.

3. Lessors' Remedies under Article 2A

Problem 129

Random Accessories, Inc., located in Seattle, leased 200 computers to the law firm of Paley & Tologist ("P & T"), located in Chicago, for $600,000 ($3,000 per computer). Random was liquidating its inventory of computers, and planned to sell its residual interest in the computers to a third party. When Random tendered delivery, P & T wrongfully rejected the goods. Random then re-leased the computers to another customer and sought to recover damages measured by the present value of the rent in the lease with P & T less the present value of the rent in the subsequent lease. See 2A–527 and "Note: Present Value Damages" *infra*. What requirements would Random have to satisfy in order to qualify for this measure of damages? Must Random notify P & T that it is leasing the goods to someone else? If Random did not re-lease the computers or its re-lease did not satisfy the requirements for recovering damages measured by a substitute lease, what measure of damages would be available to Random? See 2A–528(1). If Random had suffered incidental or consequential losses, could it recover damages for them?

434, 444 n. 6, 468 N.Y.S.2d 294, 301 n. 6 (1983).

7. W.L. Scott, Inc. v. Madras Aerotech, Inc., 103 Idaho 736, 653 P.2d 791, 798 (1982) ("We hold that the discounting rate is a question of fact and must be determined by the trier of fact"). Lawyers and judges calculating present value damages under Article 2A can presumably seek guidance from the practice in other areas. In tort cases, for example, damages for lost future earnings are often discounted to present value. The parties frequently introduce expert testimony as to an appropriate rate of discount, the claimant arguing for a lower discount rate (to minimize the effect of the discount) and the defendant urging a high rate of discount (to minimize the present value of the future losses).

8. An interest rate higher than that permitted under a jurisdiction's usury laws might represent a "manifestly unreasonable" rate.

Questions

(1) Suppose Random was not getting out of the computer leasing business, and in fact had a large inventory of computers as well as the ability to acquire whatever computers it needed from manufacturers. Suppose also that Random managed to re-lease the computers rejected by P & T for the same rent as in its lease with P & T. What is the measure of Random's recoverable damages? Consider 2A–528(2).

(2) Alternatively, suppose the computers had been specially and irreversibly modified for B & B, and as a result could not be leased or sold to anyone else except for scrap. What should Random recover? Consider 2A–529(1)(b). Would Random be entitled to specific performance under proposed amended Section 2A–507A?

Problem 130

Random Accessories, Inc., located in Seattle, leased 200 computers to the law firm of Paley & Tologist ("P & T"), located in Chicago. Random delivered the computers on time and they were accepted. P & T, whose practice was flourishing, made the first three monthly rental payments but then got into a dispute with Random over other matters and began to withhold the rent for the computers. P & T is now four months behind on the rent, and Random would like to take back the computers. Can Random do so? If your answer is yes, point to the specific Article 2A provision(s) you would rely on and identify what requirements the lessor must satisfy.

Note on Lessors' Right to Repossess

If a lessee commits certain kinds of defaults, a lessor is entitled to repossess the leased goods before the end of the lease term. This right, which can even be exercised without going to court if repossession can be effected "without breach of the peace," arises out of the fact that the lessor remains the owner of leased goods: the lease transfers to the lessee only a temporary right to possess and use the goods for the lease term; the lessor retains title, which it can assert when the lessee forfeits its lease rights by breaching. The right to repossess upon the lessee's default is the most important remedy that a lessor has. It is governed by 2A–525(2) & (3), which grant the right to repossess if the lessee commits the kinds of defaults specified in 2A–523(1) & (3)(a). Those defaults include wrongful rejection and revocation, failure to make a payment when due, repudiation, and any other default that "substantially impairs the value of the lease contract to the lessor." The lease agreement can also authorize the lessor to repossess for other defaults. The lessor's right to repossess the leased goods is quite robust, for (with one minor exception) it takes precedence over the rights of the lessee's creditors. See 2A–307. The lessor's right to repossession is generally good even if the lessee has entered bankruptcy proceedings, although the lessor may have to seek permission of the bankruptcy court before exercising its right and may even have to forego repossession if the bankruptcy estate cures the defaults as permitted by the Bankruptcy Code (11 U.S.C. § 365).

Note on Lessor's Recovery of the Full Rent

Article 2A permits a lessor to recover the unpaid rent for the entire lease term, discounted to present value, if the lessee has accepted the goods and has not rightfully revoked acceptance. See 2A–529(1)(a). The right to the full rent, however, is good only if the lessor has not repossessed the goods and the lessee has not offered to return the good to the lessor before the end of the lease term. If the lessor does repossess or the lessee offers to return the goods, the lessor is only entitled to the rent up to the time of repossession or tender of return (or, alternatively, the commencement of a "substantially similar" substitute lease); for the balance of the lease term, the lessor generally cannot recover the full rent, but is limited to damages measured by the *difference* between the rent in the breached lease and either the rent in a "substantially similar" substitute lease of the goods (2A–527) or the market rent for the goods (2A–528).

Section 2A–529(1)(a) also authorizes a lessor to recover the full rent for the entire lease term, discounted to present value, if the goods are lost or damaged within a commercially reasonable time after risk of loss passes to the lessee. Recall, however, that except in a finance lease or where the parties agree otherwise, the lessee does not bear risk of loss.

Finally, 2A–529(1)(b) authorizes a lessor to recover the full rent for the entire lease term, discounted to present value, if "the lessor is unable after reasonable effort to dispose of them at a reasonable price or the circumstances reasonably indicate that effort will be unavailing...."

4. Liquidated Damages under Article 2A

Note on Liquidated Damages under Article 2A

The provision governing liquidated damages clauses in Article 2A (2A–504(1)) states that the reasonableness of the amount fixed in a liquidated damages clause is to be evaluated by reference to only one factor—the harm that, at the time the liquidated damages clause was agreed to, could be anticipated to arise from breach or default. According to the comments to 2A–504, the elimination of other considerations that are found in the Article 2 provision governing liquidated damages (e.g., the difficulty of proving losses, or the non-feasibility of otherwise obtaining an adequate remedy) was designed to create "greater flexibility" in dealing with liquidated damage clauses in leases, because "[t]he ability to liquidate damages is critical to modern leasing practices." In other words, 2A–504(1) is supposed to make it easier and more likely for courts to enforce liquidated damage provisions in leases. The question that inevitably arises is, how far has Article 2A gone in liberalizing the rules governing the validity of liquidated damage?

Problem 131

McRentals Home Center leased a collection of living room furniture to Sandra Smith. The lease term was 24 months and the monthly rent was $100. Two months into the lease Sandra's employer "downsized" her out of her job. She stopped paying the rent and McRentals repossessed the furniture with 20 months remaining on the lease. The written lease contract Sandra had signed included a provision stating that, if lessee defaulted, McRentals would incur a variety of costs, administrative expenses and lost profits that were difficult to anticipate or prove. The provision then gave McRentals the right, upon lessee's failure to comply with any term of the agreement, to repossess the goods and recover the following: a) any accrued and unpaid past rent at the time of repossession; b) the full accelerated amount of all future rent to the end of the lease term, without present value discount; c) interest on the amounts in a) and b) from the date of default to the date of actual payment at the rate of 20% (or, if less, the highest rate permitted by applicable usury laws); d) an additional payment equal to 50% of the combined amounts in a), b) and c). Is Sandra liable for the amounts stated in the lease contract? If you say no, specify the changes that would make the provision described above enforceable.

F.   REMEDIES UNDER THE CISG

1. *Overview of CISG Remedies*

There is a consensus that the expectation principle underlies the remedy provisions of the CISG. Other concepts underlying CISG remedies include the mitigation of damages principle and the limitation of recoverable damages to losses that were foreseeable when the contract was formed. Since these principles also underlie UCC remedies, it is not surprising that the CISG includes remedy provisions that bear a striking resemblance to those in UCC Article 2. Because the CISG represents an international legal regime strongly influenced by non-U.S. legal systems and remedial concepts, however, aspects of the Convention's remedy system depart notably from the approach in U.S. domestic sales law. The following materials explore both the familiar and the unfamiliar in CISG remedies.

2. *Buyers' Remedies Under the CISG*

Problem 132

On October 1, the law firm of Boyze & Barry ("B & B"), located in Toronto, Canada (a country that has ratified the CISG), contracted to purchase 200 IBX computers from Random Accessories, Inc., located in Seattle, Washington. The contract price was U.S. $600,000 (U.S. $3,000 per computer). The contract required Random to deliver the computers to B & B's offices on Random's own trucks by November 1. B & B prepaid $10,000 of the purchase price on October 10. Random failed to deliver by November 1 and shortly thereafter declared it would not deliver any computers under the contract. On November 5, B & B emailed Random that the contract was avoided. The going prices for the kind of computers involved in the transaction had begun rising soon after the parties entered into their agreement. On November 1 the price was U.S. $3,500 per computer in Toronto and U.S. $3,450 in Seattle. By November 5, those prices had risen to U.S. $3700 in Toronto and U.S. $3650 in Seattle. Prices continued to rise, and by November 10 had reached U.S. $3,900 per computer in Toronto and U.S. $3,850 in Seattle. On that day B & B contracted with another supplier to purchase 200 replacement computers for U.S. $800,000 (U.S. $4,000 per computer).

B & B sues Random seeking to recover the $10,000 it prepaid on the price, as well as $200,000 in damages calculated as the difference between the amount B & B paid for replacement computers and the price in the contract with Random. Is B & B entitled to these amounts? See CISG Arts. 49(1), 81 and 75. What requirements must B & B satisfy in order to recover the $200,000 it seeks? Suppose that B & B's substitute purchase did not satisfy the requirements of Article 75, or that it did not attempt to purchase replacement computers. What damages (if any) could it recover? See Art. 76. Would any of your answers change if the contract provided for delivery by an independent trucking company "FCA Seattle, as per INCOTERMS 2000." If B & B suffered any incidental or consequential damages, such as lost profits or extra expenses, between November 1 and the time it was able to acquire replacement computers, could it recover damages to cover them? See Art. 74. Also see Art. 77.

Problem 133

Alumitique is a mining concern in Guinea—a country that has ratified the CISG. On March 15 Alumitique contracted to sell a specified quantity of bauxite (an aluminum ore) to Complete Fabrications, Inc., a corporation organized and located in the United States. The price was $10 million to be paid thirty days following delivery. The bauxite was shipped from Conakry in Guinea and arrived in Newport News, Virginia in late June, as per the contract. The material delivered, however, tested at a lower grade than that specified in the contract. Fabrications has decided to keep the lower-grade bauxite, which at current market prices is worth $6 million as opposed to the $12 million that contract-grade bauxite would now be worth.

(a) What can Fabrications recover as damages? Consider CISG Art. 74. Suppose it will be difficult if not impossible for Fabrications to prove the extra costs of processing the lower-grade ore. Does Article 74 permit Fabrications to recover damages measured as they would be under UCC 2–714(2)—the difference between the value of conforming goods and the value of the lower-grade bauxite? What are Fabrications' damages under this standard?

(b) What price would Fabrications owe if it invokes CISG Article 50? Compare the result if Fabrications claims damages under Article 74 measured by the difference between the value of conforming bauxite and the ore actually delivered, and then offsets those damages from the price. Perform similar comparisons between the results under Articles 50 and 74 for the following alternative scenarios (amounts refer to market values at the time of delivery):

(i) Lower grade ore = $4 million; contract grade ore = $8 million.

(ii) Lower grade ore = $5 million; contract grade ore = $10 million.

Note on Calculating Price Reduction under CISG Article 50

CISG Article 50 permits a buyer who has received non-conforming goods to reduce the price of the goods "in the proportion as the value that the goods actually delivered had at the time of the delivery bears to the value that conforming goods would have had at that time." The calculation required by this rather difficult passage can be accomplished by the following two-step process: first, divide the value of the nonconforming goods at the time of delivery (*not* the time of contracting) by the higher value that conforming goods would have had at that time; next, take the result (a fraction) and multiply it by the original contract price. The result is the reduced price authorized by Article 50. Applying this procedure to an example, suppose non-conforming goods with a contract price of $5.2 million were worth only $2.5 million at the time of delivery, while conforming goods would have been worth $5.0 million at that time. First divide the $2.5 million value (at the time of delivery) of the actual non-conforming goods by the $5.0 million value of conforming goods, yielding a fraction of ½. Now multiply that fraction by the contract price of $5.2 and you arrive at the reduced price of $2.6 million. In short, Article 50 would permit the buyer in this example to cut the original contract price in half because, as measured at the time of delivery, the goods delivered were worth only half of what conforming goods would have been worth.

The Article 50 formula presents some difficult valuation questions. How does one determine the value of the "goods actually delivered" for Article 50 purposes? There may well be no established market for defective goods and thus no market price. Could one use the value of non-defective goods less the cost of repair? Determining the "value that conforming goods would have had" at the time of delivery also raises issues. Clearly contract price is not the same thing as "value," but can one use the contract price as *evidence* of value?

Problem 134

Genau A.G. is a business concern located in Germany, a country that has ratified CISG. Genau is one of at least a dozen makers of computer-controlled precision metal cutting machines. It contracted to sell one of its machines to Militus Co., a U.S. corporation, for $5.2 million. Delivery to a specified U.S. port was due June 15. After world prices for precision machine tools climbed steeply, Genau informed Militus on May 21 that the ordered machine would not be delivered. Although several other manufacturers make cutting machines that would meet its needs, Militus strongly prefers the Genau product because it has a reputation for superior performance.

(a) Can Militus force Genau to deliver? See Arts. 45 & 46. If Militus wants to force delivery under Article 46(1) would you advise it to sue in a U.S. court? See Art. 28.

(b) Suppose Militus would lose $10,000 each day that it did not have a precision metal cutting machine. It will take at least 15 months to obtain a court order requiring Genau to deliver. Equivalent machines are readily available for immediate delivery from other sources. Does Militus have any alternative to seeking an order requiring Genau to deliver? Suppose Militus persisted in pursuing an order requiring delivery and eventually obtained one after 15 months. Can it recover the profits it lost during the 15 months? See Arts. 45(2), 74 & 77.

Problem 135

Same facts as the previous problem except that on June 15 Genau delivered one of its metal-cutting machines to Militus at the designated U.S. port. Upon inspection, Militus discovered the machine had substantial defects that breached contractual representations and that seriously impaired the machine's performance. Militus still strongly prefers Genau products, but it cannot use the tendered machine in its defective condition.

(a) What must Militus prove in order to obtain an order requiring Genau to deliver a replacement machine under Article 46(2)? If it wants to pursue that remedy, what should it do to secure its rights? See Arts. 38–40, 82–83 & 86–88.

(b) What must Militus prove in order to obtain an order requiring Genau to repair the machine under Article 46(3)? How should it proceed? See Arts. 38–40. Suppose Genau has no U.S. operations or offices, so that to repair the machine it would have to send personnel from Germany. There are several firms in the U.S. who are capable of performing the needed repairs at considerably smaller expense. Can Militus procure an order requiring Genau to repair? If Militus pays a U.S. firm to repair the machine, can Militus recoup the cost from Genau? See Arts. 45 & 74. See also Art. 44.

(c) If Militus decides to sue in the United States rather than in Germany, what will it have to prove in order to obtain a decree requiring Genau to replace the defective machine? To repair the machine? See Art. 28 and Problem 100 *supra*. If Militus cannot obtain such orders from a U.S. court, what remedies remain available? What remedies would Militus have if UCC Article 2 applied?

3. Sellers' Remedies Under the CISG

Problem 136

Random Accessories, Inc., located in Seattle, contracted to sell 200 computers to the law firm of Boyze & Barry ("B & B"), located in Toronto, Canada (a country that has ratified the CISG). Random, which was getting out of the computer business and liquidating its computer inventory, delivered the computers on its own trucks, but B & B unjustifiably refused the delivery. After notifying B & B that the contract was avoided, Random resold the computers to another party. Can Random recover damages measured by the difference between the price in its contract with B & B and the price at which it was able to resell the computers? See CISG Art. 75. What requirements must Random satisfy in order to recover damages measured by the price in its resale contract? See Arts. 64(1) and 75. Must Random give B & B notice that it is reselling the goods? Suppose Random's resale of the computers did not satisfy the requirements of Article 75. What damages (if any) could Random recover? See Art. 76. If Random attempts to recover damages under Article 76, at what time and place should the "current price" of the goods be measured? Would your answers change if the contract between Random and B & B had provided for delivery by an independent trucking company "FCA Seattle, as per INCOTERMS 1990"? If Random suffered any incidental or consequential losses, such as added expenses for trucking the computers back after B & B refused them, can Random recover damages to cover them? See Art. 74. Also see Art. 77.

Question

Suppose Random was not getting out of the business of selling computers, and could acquire as many computers as it needed from manufacturers. Suppose too that the price at which Random resold the computers that B & B refused was the same as the contract price with B & B, and it was also the current price for the goods at the time of avoidance. What damages can Random recover? Could it recover the profits it lost on the sale to B & B, as it might if UCC 2–708 applied to the transaction? Consider Article 74.

Note: Avoidance of Contract under the CISG Compared to Cancellation under the UCC

In order to recover damages measured by a substitute transaction under CISG Article 75, or damages measured by the current (market) price under Article 76, both aggrieved buyers *and* aggrieved sellers must first avoid the contract. As we saw in Chapter 4, when an aggrieved buyer avoids a contract because of a breach by the seller, the avoidance releases both parties from their obligations to perform under the contract (although it does not release the breaching party from liability for damages), and it obliges both parties to make restitution of whatever the other side has "supplied or paid under the contract." See Art. 81. Avoidance has the same effect when an aggrieved seller avoids a contract because of the buyer's breach. The requirements for an aggrieved seller to avoid a contract are also equivalent to those applicable to an aggrieved buyer. Thus in order for a seller to avoid a sales contract the buyer must have committed a "fundamental breach" or have failed to perform its basic obligations (to take delivery of the goods and pay the price) within a deadline established in a *Nachfrist* notice. See Article 64(1). The seller must also give the buyer notice of avoidance within time periods established in Article 64(2).

"Cancellation" is the UCC concept that comes closest to avoidance of contract under the CISG. According to the definition in UCC 2–106(4), cancellation occurs when an aggrieved party puts an end to the contract because of the other side's breach. Cancellation under the UCC, however, only discharges executory (unperformed) obligations under the canceled contract. See 2–106(3) & (4). CISG avoidance, in contrast, releases the parties even from contractual duties that have already been performed—i.e., upon avoidance each party must make restitution of what the other side has already "supplied or paid" under the contract. See CISG Art. 81. Cancellation plays a far more modest role in the UCC remedy scheme than does avoidance in the CISG remedial system. Whereas under the CISG avoidance is a prerequisite to the buyer's right to return non-conforming goods to the seller and to either party's right to recover damages measured by a substitute transaction or the current price of the goods, under the UCC little appears to turn on whether an aggrieved party has canceled the contract. For example, 2–711(1), an index of buyer's remedies, expressly provides that those remedies apply whether or not the buyer has canceled. That does not mean cancellation has no significance under the UCC. A buyer or seller seeking relief from executory contract obligations because of an existing repudiation or breach by the other party can use the cancellation mechanism. Thus a party who has accepted non-conforming performance under an installment contract but who wishes to escape the unperformed remainder of the contract must give seasonable notice of cancellation. See 2–612(3). Under 2–611(1), furthermore, the right to retract a repudiation ends when the aggrieved party cancels the contract.

DECISION OF SEPTEMBER 22, 1992, OBERLANDESGERICHT HAMM, GERMANY

Case Number 19 U 97/91.

ENGLISH ABSTRACT FROM UNILEX DATA BASE[1]

A German company entered into negotiations with an Italian company for the purchase from the latter of 200 tons of bacon to be delivered in 10 instalments. The offer contained a request that the bacon be delivered wrapped. The reply by the Italian company stating that the bacon would be delivered unwrapped, was accepted by the German company in writing with no objections. The buyer, after taking delivery of the first four instalments, refused to take delivery of the last 6 instalments. The seller resold the goods for approximately 25% of the contract price and commenced action to recover damages pursuant to Art. 74 CISG.

The court held that the contract was validly concluded since the seller's reply to delivery the bacon unwrapped constituted a counter-offer according to Art. 19 CISG, which the buyer accepted in writing without any objection.

The buyer alleged that the parties had orally agreed that in case of complaints by the veterinary department and the custom's office about

---

1. Reprinted with the permission of the Centre for Comparative and Foreign Studies—UNIDROIT, Rome, Italy. The Unilex English abstract of the decision, as well as the original German text, is available through the Unilex website, <*http://www.unilex.info*>.

the condition of bacon, the buyer would be entitled to refuse the goods. While admitting that under the CISG, in principle, oral agreements could contradict a written contract term, the court held that in the case at hand the buyer had failed to prove the existence of such oral agreement.

According to the court the seller was entitled to avoid the contract (Art. 64(1)(a) CISG) insofar [*sic*—because?] the buyer's failure to take delivery of more than half of the goods constituted a fundamental breach.

The court stated that following Art. 77 CISG and the principle of mitigation of damages therein laid down, the seller was not only entitled but even obliged to resell the goods in accordance with Art. 75 CISG. However, since the seller was able to recover only about 25% of the contract price, there was no resale "in a reasonable manner" as required by Art. 75 CISG; therefore the court granted damages in accordance with the criteria set forth in Art. 76 CISG.

Finally, the court held that the seller was entitled to interest on the unpaid price (art. 78 CISG). The rate of interest was determined by applying German private international law rules, which led to the Italian statutory interest rate.

Problem 137

Dassa, an import/export concern operating out of Syria (a country that has ratified CISG), contracted to purchase 5000 metric tons of wheat from Garkill, Inc., a United States grain merchant. The wheat was to be shipped by freighter from New Orleans to the Syrian port of Latakia, to arrive by November 1. The price was $500 per ton ($2.5 million total). Before Garkill shipped the wheat, Dassa repudiated the contract. The wheat is readily resalable to other buyers for the prevailing market price ($490 per ton). Can Garkill obtain an order requiring Dassa to take delivery and pay for the wheat?

Note on a Seller's Right to the Price under the CISG

In a situation like that in the preceding problem, CISG Article 62 appears to authorize a seller to obtain a judicial order requiring the buyer to take delivery and pay the full price for the goods—relief that would be unavailable on these facts under UCC Article 2 (do you see why?). CISG Article 62 reflects the influence of civil law countries (including much of continental Europe) whose remedy systems characteristically emphasize requiring actual performance of contractual obligations, as opposed to the emphasis on "substitutional relief" (i.e., damages) that is characteristic of common law systems like the U.S. We also encountered the civil law's influence on the CISG when we explored a buyer's right to specific performance. At any rate, Article 62 authorizes a seller to force the buyer to take delivery and pay the full price "unless the seller has resorted to a remedy which is inconsistent with this requirement." A remedy inconsistent with requiring the buyer to receive and pay for the goods would be avoidance of the contract, which releases both parties from their executory obligations.

A seller's very broad right to the price under Article 62 is, however, subject to extremely significant limitations. The most important is Article 28, which provides that "a court is not bound to enter a judgement for specific performance unless the court would do so under its own law in respect of similar contracts of sale not governed by this Convention." An order requiring the buyer to take delivery of and pay for goods it has not voluntarily accepted is almost certainly an order for "specific performance." Thus, according to Article 28, a U.S. court would not have to issue such an order unless, under the facts before it, it would do so under our domestic sales law–i.e., Article 2 of the UCC

A seller's ability to require the buyer to take delivery and pay the full price may also be limited by the seller's obligation under CISG Article 88(2) to resell goods in certain circumstances. If the goods are resold, the seller must "account" to the buyer for all proceeds beyond the costs of preserving and reselling the goods (Art. 88(3)). Thus when forced to resell under Article 88(2), the seller is in effect limited to recovering the difference between the contract price and the resale price, as under Article 75. Resale is required by Article 88(2) when "the goods are subject to rapid deterioration or their preservation would involve unreasonable expense." Requiring resale in such circumstances—and thus in effect precluding an action for the full price— conforms to the mitigation of damages principle announced in Article 77. Indeed, the Convention's mitigation policy may limit the availability of the price remedy in a variety of other situations in which forcing the buyer to take and pay for goods would entail "needless waste and hardship." See JOHN HONNOLD, UNIFORM LAW FOR INTERNATIONAL SALES UNDER THE 1980 UNITED NATIONS CONVENTION § 419 (3rd ed.1999).

Problem 138

Return to the contract in Problem 137, but assume that Dassa did not repudiate. Garkill shipped the wheat by freighter from the port of New Orleans, but the freighter carrying the goods sank while crossing the Atlantic and the wheat was lost. Can Garkill recover the $2.5 million price from Dassa? Suppose the contract stated that the goods would be delivered "F.O.B. New Orleans." Alternatively, suppose the delivery term was "DDU (Delivered Duty Unpaid) Latakia, Syria, as per INCOTERMS 2000." Alternatively, suppose the contract did not include a delivery term.

Problem 139

On December 1 Scrivener & Quire ("S & Q"), a Philadelphia law firm, orally ordered 500 cartons of standard size typing paper at $50 per carton from Foolscap Industries, Inc., a paper wholesaler located in Toronto, Canada. Pursuant to the order, Foolscap delivered the paper on December 15. S & Q put the 500 cartons into its supply room. Just as it had always done in the parties' previous dealings, Foolscap sent S & Q an invoice requiring payment of the purchase price ($25,000) within 30 days of delivery. It is now the end of February. S & Q has not paid the invoice nor has it responded to letters and phone calls demanding payment. Can Foolscap recover the full price from S & Q? See CISG Art. 62.

Question

Suppose that, on the facts of Problem 139, S & Q sent Foolscap a notice stating that the buyer was avoiding the contract. Assuming the goods conformed fully to the contract and the buyer did not have a basis for avoiding, must the seller take the goods back and be relegated to the damages available to it upon avoidance? In other words, can a buyer "wrongfully but effectively" avoid a contract under the CISG? Should your answer depend on the jurisdiction in which litigation is brought? Cf. Art. 28.

Problem 140

Return to the facts of Problem 139, but assume that Foolscap would prefer to recover the goods from S & Q rather than to attempt to collect the price. Can it do so?

Note: Sellers' Right to Recover Delivered Goods under the CISG

Under the CISG, a seller who has delivered the goods to the buyer can avoid the contract if the seller either suffers a fundamental breach or fails to receive payment within the deadline established in a valid *Nachfrist* notice. See CISG Art. 64(1). Upon avoidance, the seller become entitled to restitution of the goods (as well as obligated to give restitution of whatever the buyer has paid). See Art. 81(2). Thus by the mechanism of contract avoidance, an aggrieved seller can become entitled to reclaim delivered goods under the CISG. This reclamation right, however, may not be good against creditors of the buyer who have seized or asserted rights in the goods. The scope of the CISG is limited to the rights of the buyer and the seller: it does not govern the question of the seller's rights vis-a-vis third parties like the buyer's creditors. See Art. 4. The question of the *priority* of an avoiding seller's claim for restitution as against other claims on the goods is thus left up to the national law applicable under choice of law principles. Under that law, the seller may well find that its right to reclaim the goods is subordinated to the rights of others, such as the buyer's trustee in bankruptcy.

---

4. *Incidental, Consequential and Liquidated Damages Under the CISG*

DELCHI CARRIER SpA v. ROTOREX CORP.

United States Court of Appeals for the Second Circuit, 1995.
71 F.3d 1024.

WINTER, CIRCUIT JUDGE. Rotorex Corporation, a New York corporation, appeals from a judgment of $1,785,772.44 in damages for lost profits and other consequential damages awarded to Delchi Carrier SpA following a bench trial before Judge Munson. The basis for the award was Rotorex's delivery of nonconforming compressors to Delchi, an Italian manufacturer of air conditioners. Delchi cross-appeals from the denial of certain incidental and consequential damages. We affirm the award of damages; we reverse in part on Delchi's cross-appeal and remand for further proceedings.

BACKGROUND

In January 1988, Rotorex agreed to sell 10,800 compressors to Delchi for use in Delchi's "Ariele" line of portable room air conditioners. The air conditioners were scheduled to go on sale in the spring and summer of 1988. Prior to executing the contract, Rotorex sent Delchi a sample compressor and accompanying written performance specifications. The compressors were scheduled to be delivered in three shipments before May 15, 1988.

Rotorex sent the first shipment by sea on March 26. Delchi paid for this shipment, which arrived at its Italian factory on April 20, by letter of credit. Rotorex sent a second shipment of compressors on or about May 9. Delchi also remitted payment for this shipment by letter of credit. While the second shipment was en route, Delchi discovered that the first lot of compressors did not conform to the sample model and accompanying specifications. On May 13, after a Rotorex representative visited the Delchi factory in Italy, Delchi informed Rotorex that 93 percent of the compressors were rejected in quality control checks because they had lower cooling capacity and consumed more power than the sample model and specifications. After several unsuccessful attempts to cure the defects in the compressors, Delchi asked Rotorex to supply new compressors conforming to the original sample and specifications. Rotorex refused, claiming that the performance specifications were "inadvertently communicated" to Delchi.

In a faxed letter dated May 23, 1988, Delchi canceled the contract. Although it was able to expedite a previously planned order of suitable compressors from Sanyo, another supplier, Delchi was unable to obtain in a timely fashion substitute compressors from other sources and thus suffered a loss in its sales volume of Arieles during the 1988 selling season. Delchi filed the instant action under the United Nations Convention on Contracts for the International Sale of Goods ("CISG" or "the Convention") for breach of contract and failure to deliver conforming goods. On January 10, 1991, Judge Cholakis granted Delchi's motion for partial summary judgment, holding Rotorex liable for breach of contract.

After three years of discovery and a bench trial on the issue of damages, Judge Munson, to whom the case had been transferred, held Rotorex liable to Delchi for $1,248,331.87. This amount included consequential damages for: (i) lost profits resulting from a diminished sales level of Ariele units, (ii) expenses that Delchi incurred in attempting to remedy the nonconformity of the compressors, (iii) the cost of expediting shipment of previously ordered Sanyo compressors after Delchi rejected the Rotorex compressors, and (iv) costs of handling and storing the rejected compressors. The district court also awarded prejudgment interest under CISG art. 78.

The court denied Delchi's claim for damages based on other expenses, including: (i) shipping, customs, and incidentals relating to the two shipments of Rotorex compressors; (ii) the cost of obsolete insulation and tubing that Delchi purchased only for use with Rotorex compressors; (iii) the cost of obsolete tooling purchased only for production of units with Rotorex compressors; and (iv) labor costs for four days when Delchi's production line was idle because it had no compressors to install in the air conditioning units. The court denied an award for these items on the ground that it would lead to a double recovery because "those costs are accounted for in Delchi's recovery on its lost profits claim."

. . .

On appeal, Rotorex argues that it did not breach the agreement, . . . that the calculation of the number of lost sales was improper, and that the district court improperly excluded fixed costs and depreciation from the manufacturing cost in calculating lost profits. Delchi cross-appeals, claiming that it is entitled to the additional out-of-pocket expenses and the lost profits on additional sales denied by Judge Munson.

DISCUSSION

The district court held, and the parties agree, that the instant matter is governed by the CISG, reprinted at 15 U.S.C.A. Appendix (West Supp.1995), a self-executing agreement between the United States and other signatories, including Italy.[1] Because there is virtually no caselaw under the Convention, we look to its language and to "the general principles" upon which it is based. See CISG art. 7(2). The Convention directs that its interpretation be informed by its "international character and . . . the need to promote uniformity in its application and the observance of good faith in international trade." See CISG art. 7(1); see generally John Honnold, Uniform Law for International Sales Under the 1980 United Nations Convention 60–62 (2d ed. 1991) (addressing principles for interpretation of CISG). Caselaw interpreting analogous provisions of Article 2 of the Uniform Commercial Code ("UCC"), may also inform a court where the language of the relevant CISG provisions tracks that of the UCC. However, UCC caselaw "is not per se applicable." Orbisphere Corp. v. United States, 726 F.Supp. 1344, 1355 (Ct.Int'l Trade 1989).

* * *

Under the CISG, "[t]he seller must deliver goods which are of the quantity, quality and description required by the contract," and "the

---

1. Generally, the CISG governs sales contracts between parties from different signatory countries. However, the Convention makes clear that the parties may by contract choose to be bound by a source of law other than the CISG, such as the Uniform Commercial Code. See CISG art. 6 ("The parties may exclude the application of this Convention or . . . derogate from or vary the effect of any of its provisions.") If, as here, the agreement is silent as to choice of law, the Convention applies if both parties are located in signatory nations. See CISG art. 1.

goods do not conform with the contract unless they ... [p]ossess the qualities of goods which the seller has held out to the buyer as a sample or model." CISG art. 35. The CISG further states that "[t]he seller is liable in accordance with the contract and this Convention for any lack of conformity." CISG art. 36.

Judge Cholakis held that "there is no question that [Rotorex's] compressors did not conform to the terms of the contract between the parties" and noted that "[t]here are ample admissions [by Rotorex] to that effect." We agree. . . .

Under the CISG, if the breach is "fundamental" the buyer may either require delivery of substitute goods, CISG art. 46, or declare the contract void, CISG art. 49, and seek damages. With regard to what kind of breach is fundamental, Article 25 provides:

> A breach of contract committed by one of the parties is fundamental if it results in such detriment to the other party as substantially to deprive him of what he is entitled to expect under the contract, unless the party in breach did not foresee and a reasonable person of the same kind in the same circumstances would not have foreseen such a result.

CISG art. 25. In granting summary judgment, the district court held that "[t]here appears to be no question that [Delchi] did not substantially receive that which [it] was entitled to expect" and that "any reasonable person could foresee that shipping non-conforming goods to a buyer would result in the buyer not receiving that which he expected and was entitled to receive." Because the cooling power and energy consumption of an air conditioner compressor are important determinants of the product's value, the district court's conclusion that Rotorex was liable for a fundamental breach of contract under the Convention was proper.

We turn now to the district court's award of damages following the bench trial. . . .

The CISG provides:

> Damages for breach of contract by one party consist of a sum equal to the loss, including loss of profit, suffered by the other party as a consequence of the breach. Such damages may not exceed the loss which the party in breach foresaw or ought to have foreseen at the time of the conclusion of the contract, in the light of the facts and matters of which he then knew or ought to have known, as a possible consequence of the breach of contract.

CISG art. 74. This provision is "designed to place the aggrieved party in as good a position as if the other party had properly performed the contract." Honnold, supra, at 503.

* * *

Rotorex contends ... that the district court improperly awarded lost profits for unfilled orders from Delchi affiliates in Europe and from sales agents within Italy. We disagree. The CISG requires that damages be limited by the familiar principle of foreseeability established in Hadley v. Baxendale, 156 Eng.Rep. 145 (1854). CISG art. 74. However, it was objectively foreseeable that Delchi would take orders for Ariele sales based on the number of compressors it had ordered and expected to have ready for the season. The district court was entitled to rely upon the documents and testimony regarding these lost sales and was well within its authority in deciding which orders were proven with sufficient certainty.

Rotorex also challenges the district court's exclusion of fixed costs and depreciation from the manufacturing cost used to calculate lost profits. The trial judge calculated lost profits by subtracting the 478,783 lire "manufacturing cost"—the total variable cost—of an Ariele unit from the 654,644 lire average sale price. The CISG does not explicitly state whether only variable expenses, or both fixed and variable expenses, should be subtracted from sales revenue in calculating lost profits. However, courts generally do not include fixed costs in the calculation of lost profits. See Indu Craft, Inc. v. Bank of Baroda, 47 F.3d 490, 495 (2d Cir.1995) (only when the breach ends an ongoing business should fixed costs be subtracted along with variable costs); Adams v. Lindblad Travel, Inc., 730 F.2d 89, 92–93 (2d Cir.1984) (fixed costs should not be included in lost profits equation when the plaintiff is an ongoing business whose fixed costs are not affected by the breach). This is, of course, because the fixed costs would have been encountered whether or not the breach occurred. In the absence of a specific provision in the CISG for calculating lost profits, the district court was correct to use the standard formula employed by most American courts and to deduct only variable costs from sales revenue to arrive at a figure for lost profits.

In its cross-appeal, Delchi challenges the district court's denial of various consequential and incidental damages, including reimbursement for: (i) shipping, customs, and incidentals relating to the first and second shipments—rejected and returned—of Rotorex compressors; (ii) obsolete insulation materials and tubing purchased for use only with Rotorex compressors; (iii) obsolete tooling purchased exclusively for production of units with Rotorex compressors; and (iv) labor costs for the period of May 16–19, 1988, when the Delchi production line was idle due to a lack of compressors to install in Ariele air conditioning units. The district court denied damages for these items on the ground that they "are accounted for in Delchi's recovery on its lost profits claim," and, therefore, an award would constitute a double recovery for Delchi. We disagree.

The Convention provides that a contract plaintiff may collect damages to compensate for the full loss. This includes, but is not limited to, lost profits, subject only to the familiar limitation that the breaching party must have foreseen, or should have foreseen, the loss as a probable consequence. CISG art. 74; see Hadley v. Baxendale, supra.

An award for lost profits will not compensate Delchi for the expenses in question. Delchi's lost profits are determined by calculating the hypothetical revenues to be derived from unmade sales less the hypothetical variable costs that would have been, but were not, incurred. This figure, however, does not compensate for costs actually incurred that led to no sales. Thus, to award damages for costs actually incurred in no way creates a double recovery and instead furthers the purpose of giving the injured party damages "equal to the loss." CISG art. 74.

The only remaining inquiries, therefore, are whether the expenses were reasonably foreseeable and legitimate incidental or consequential damages.[2] The expenses incurred by Delchi for shipping, customs, and related matters for the two returned shipments of Rotorex compressors, including storage expenses for the second shipment at Genoa, were clearly foreseeable and recoverable incidental expenses. These are up-front expenses that had to be paid to get the goods to the manufacturing plant for inspection and were thus incurred largely before the nonconformities were detected. To deny reimbursement to Delchi for these incidental damages would effectively cut into the lost profits award. The same is true of unreimbursed tooling expenses and the cost of the useless insulation and tubing materials. These are legitimate consequential damages that in no way duplicate lost profits damages.

The labor expense incurred as a result of the production line shutdown of May 16–19, 1988 is also a reasonably foreseeable result of delivering nonconforming compressors for installation in air conditioners. However, Rotorex argues that the labor costs in question were fixed costs that would have been incurred whether or not there was a breach. The district court labeled the labor costs "fixed costs," but did not explore whether Delchi would have paid these wages regardless of how much it produced. Variable costs are generally those costs that "fluctuate with a firm's output," and typically include labor (but not management) costs. Northeastern Tel. Co. v. AT & T, 651 F.2d 76, 86 (2d Cir.1981). Whether Delchi's labor costs during this four-day period are variable or fixed costs is in large measure a fact question that we cannot answer because we lack factual findings by the district court. We therefore remand to the district court on this issue.

* * *

CONCLUSION

We affirm the award of damages. We reverse in part the denial of incidental and consequential damages. We remand for further proceedings in accord with this opinion.

---

2. The UCC defines incidental damages resulting from a seller's breach as "expenses reasonably incurred in inspection, receipt, transportation and care and custody of goods rightfully rejected, any commercially reasonable charges, expenses or commissions in connection with effecting cover and any other reasonable expense incident to the delay or other breach." UCC § 2–715(1) (1990). It defines consequential damages resulting from a seller's breach to include "any loss resulting from general or particular requirements and needs of which the seller at the time of contracting had reason to know and which could not reasonably be prevented by cover or otherwise." UCC § 2–715(2)(a).

ZAPATA HERMANOS SUCESORES, S.A. v. HEARTHSIDE BAKING CO.

United States District Court, N.D. Illinois, 2001.
2001 WL 1000927.

MEMORANDUM OPINION AND ORDER

SHADUR, SENIOR DISTRICT J. After having prevailed in principal part before the jury that heard the litigants' major commercial dispute, Zapata Hermanos Sucesores, S.A. ("Zapata") has moved for an award of attorneys' fees....

In an unsuccessful effort to "make the worse appear the better reason,"[1] Lenell's counsel lay heavy stress on the facts that Zapata has sued Lenell in a United States court and that the well-known "American Rule" calls for litigants to bear their own legal expense. But in so doing, Lenell's counsel present their arguments in a way that impermissibly seeks to draw attention away from an exception that is built into the American Rule itself[2]—an exception that their Memorial itself quotes from F.D. Rich Co. v. United States f/u/o Industrial Lumber Co., 417 U.S. 116, 126 (1974) (internal quotation marks and citation omitted, but with appropriate emphasis added):

> The so-called "American Rule" governing the award of attorneys' fees in litigation in the federal courts is that attorneys' fees are not ordinarily recoverable *in the absence of a statute or enforceable contract providing therefor*.

Accord, such cases as Alyeska Pipeline Serv. Co. v. Wilderness Soc'y, 421 U.S. 240, 257 (1975).

There is a reason of course that the doctrine on which Lenell seeks to rely is called the American Rule: This country is in the minority of commercial jurisdictions that do not make prevailing parties truly whole by saddling their adversaries with the winners' legal expenses—an omission that does not (as does the vast majority of other jurisdictions' fee-shifting approach) put the winners in contract disputes into the same economic position as if the breaching parties had performed their required obligations under the contracts.... In this instance two stipulations in which Lenell has joined bury its efforts to escape liability via the American Rule:

> 1. Both sides have agreed all along that their claims and counterclaims are governed by a treaty to which the United States is a signatory, the Convention on the International Sale of Goods

---

1. John Milton, Paradise Lost, bk. II, ll. 113–14, likely drawn from Diogenes Laertius, Socrates 5.

2. As this opinion explains, that sleight-of-hand effort—better suited to a shell game along the midway of a state fair than to a legal memorandum—serves to obscure the true simplicity of the current inquiry.

("Convention"). And here is the controlling provision of Convention Art. 74 ("Article 74") (emphasis added):

Damages for breach of contract by one party consist of a sum equal to the loss, including loss of profit, suffered by the other party as a consequence of the breach. Such damages may not exceed the loss which the party in breach foresaw or ought to have foreseen at the time of the conclusion of the contract, in light of the facts and matters of which he then knew or ought to have known, as a possible consequence of the breach of contract.

2. Before trial the litigants entered into a June 8, 2001 Stipulation that provided in relevant part (again with emphasis added):

1. As of the dates when Lenell issued its purchase orders for the tins described in the invoices attached as Group Exhibit A to Zapata's Complaint in this case, Lenell foresaw or should have foreseen that if Lenell failed to pay for the tins that it ordered, received and accepted, Zapata would incur litigation costs *including attorneys fees*, to seek payment of the invoices for said tins.

2. The Court shall determine if *attorney's fees* are recoverable as a matter of law.

3. The amount of litigation costs, *including attorneys' fees*, to be assessed as consequential damages in this case, if any, will be for the Court to determine on a fee petition, rather than for the jury to decide.

There is no room to question the source of law to which this Court is to look to make the determination called for by the last-quoted Stipulation.... [T]he Convention—a treaty—[controls] the relationship between Mexican seller Zapata and United States purchaser Lenell.... And a treaty, occupying international scope as it does and (as in this case) defining the relationships between nationals of different signatory countries, calls for uniformity of construction. Although written about a different provision of the Convention, the analysis in MCC–Marble Ceramic Ctr., Inc. v. Ceramica Nuova d'Agostino, S.F .A., 144 F.3d 1384, 1391 (11th Cir.1998) applies with equal force to mandate universality rather than a purely home-town rule as to the awardability of attorneys' fees under the Convention.

One of the primary factors motivating the negotiation and adoption of the CISG was to provide parties to international contracts for the sale of goods with some degree of certainty as to the principles of law that would govern potential disputes and remove the previous doubt regarding which party's legal system might otherwise apply. See Letter of Transmittal from Ronald Reagan, President of the United States, to the United States Senate, reprinted at 15 U.S.C. app. 70, 71 (1997). Courts applying the CISG cannot, therefore, upset the parties' reliance on the Convention by substituting familiar principles of domestic law when the Convention requires a different result. We may only achieve the directives of good faith and uniformity in contracts under the CISG by interpreting and applying the plain language of article 8(3) as written and obeying its directive to consider this type of parol evidence.

It is therefore wholly misleading for Lenell to contend as it does for the parochial application of the American Rule.... Although the norm in our own judicial system is for each litigant in a purely United States-based dispute to bear the burden of its own legal expense, that does not at all equate to the notion that public policy (or anything else) forbids a federal court's judicial enforcement of a different rule that is appropriately brought into play—indeed, the earlier-quoted language from F.D. Rich expressly contemplates such enforcement where there is a statute (and a treaty calls for an a fortiori application of that notion) that instead establishes a "loser pays" regime.

It surely cannot be said that Zapata opted for the application of Illinois substantive law (or for the American Rule as such) just by having sued Lenell in a jurisdiction that did not pose serious problems of the nature that would have been generated by an attempt to sue at Zapata's own home base in Mexico—that is, by selecting a forum where Lenell could not assert any otherwise available challenge to in personam jurisdiction and where a favorable judgment for Zapata would be directly enforceable and capable of execution. And when purely parochial considerations are put aside (quite properly so), it cannot be gainsaid that the normal unstrained reading of Article 74 coupled with the above-quoted Stipulation calls for Zapata's recovery of its attorneys' fees as foreseen consequential damages.

When the searchlight of analysis is thus properly focused on the language of the Convention without any inappropriate overlay from the American Rule, the question becomes a simple one. As n.2 has said, it truly smacks of a shell game for Lenell to have entered into the commitments to which it has stipulated and yet to urge that Zapata's admittedly foreseeable legal expense ("which the party in breach [Lenell] foresaw or ought to have foreseen," in the language of Article 74) was not "suffered by the other party [Zapata] as a consequence of the breach" (again the language of Article 74). It is totally unpersuasive for Lenell's counsel to contend instead that those commitments and Lenell's admissions do not equate to saying that attorneys' fees are "consequential damages" recoverable under the Convention.[3]

---

3. As hackneyed as the reference has become, it is hard to resist repeating the familiar quotation from Lewis Carroll's Alice Through the Looking–Glass ch. 6:

"When I use a word," Humpty Dumpty said, in rather a scornful tone, "it means just what I choose it to mean—neither more nor less."

"The question is," said Alice, "whether you can make words mean so many different things."

"The question is," said Humpty Dumpty, "which is to be master—that's all."

For the reasons explained here, Lenell and its counsel will not be permitted to emulate Humpty Dumpty—except of course for their sharing the ultimate fate of having a great fall.

That distorted reading of the language is clearly refuted by the decisions cited at Zapata Mem. 4 from other countries' courts and arbitral tribunals. Obviously unable to counter directly, Lenell attempts to draw an inference from cases that decide the applicable interest rate under the Convention—not the right to the payment of interest, which the Convention admittedly calls for—under local law. But that effort to equate those issues really misses its mark, for the following explanation demonstrates that such interest-rate-related rulings really support Zapata's position rather than Lenell's.

Look at the situation of the injured seller of goods and what is required to make it whole. There is of course no near-universal rate of interest on unpaid obligations, and the drafters of the Convention took note of the fact that some sellers injured by nonpayment for their goods would be made whole by applying the interest rates at their homes, while others would need prejudgment interest to be paid at the rate applicable at their buyers' locales to provide full relief (see Peter Schlechtriem, Uniform Sales Law—The UN–Convention on Contracts for the International Sale of Goods 98–99 (Manz, Vienna 1986). For that reason the Convention's drafters called for the payment of prejudgment interest (which every unpaid seller needs for full recovery), but compromised by leaving the interest rate open for decision on a case-by-case basis (id.)—so that the injured seller's make-whole expectations are met by compensating it for its own cost of delayed payment as well as recovering the payment itself.

Now look at the situation of the same injured seller in terms of the other component of being made whole. Exactly as with prejudgment interest, that result is assured only by freeing its damages recovery from the burden of attorneys' fees. Little wonder, then, that the award of such fees is nearly universal among commercial nations.... And surely in this instance, the make-whole expectations of the injured seller—a Mexican company–are best met by conforming to Mexico's own adherence to that nearly universal rule.

In sum, the award of attorneys' fees has really been agreed to, although Lenell does not now acknowledge it,[4] by the combination of Lenell's stipulation and Article 74. Because the amount of the fee award

---

4. Lenell has studiously sought to avoid the fact that its own Amended Counterclaim filed January 3, 2000 (comprising a whole set of claims arising out of asserted late deliveries and other alleged nonperformance by Zapata) sought not only compensatory damages of some $225,000 but also, as part of its requested judgment on that counterclaim (emphasis added):

In favor of Lenell and against Envases, awarding Lenell its interest, costs, disbursements, consequential damages, *attorneys fees* and other and further relief as this Court deems just and proper.

But now that the shoe is on the other foot, Lenell's position has mysteriously become that the attorneys' fees that it specifically sought under the Convention are somehow nonrecoverable by Zapata because of the American Rule. Leaving aside the level of hypocrisy (or perhaps even estoppel or "mend the hold" principles) raised by Lenell's stance, it need scarcely be added that whether under the Convention or otherwise, the case for attorneys' fees sought by a prevailing party from Mexico (where local law awards them) necessarily has to be stronger, if anything, than a like claim by an Illinois party (where local law does not).

remains to be resolved, a status hearing is set for 9 a.m. September 5, 2001, to discuss the procedure and timing for that purpose.

* * *

Notes

On appeal, the Seventh Circuit reversed the district court's interpretation of the term "loss" in CISG Article 74 as permitting a prevailing plaintiff to recover attorney fees. Zapata Hermanos Sucesores, S.A. v. Hearthside Baking Co., 313 F.3d 385 (7th Cir.2002). Judge Posner's opinion for the Seventh Circuit states:

> There is no suggestion in the background of the Convention or the cases under it that "loss" [in Article 74] was intended to include attorneys' fees, but no suggestion to the contrary either. Nevertheless it seems apparent that "loss" does not include attorneys' fees incurred in the litigation of a suit for breach of contract. . . .

> The Convention is about contracts, not about procedure. The principles for determining when a losing party must reimburse the winner for the latter's expense of litigation are usually not a part of a substantive body of law, such as contract law, but a part of procedural law. For example, the "American rule," that the winner must bear his own litigation expenses, and the "English rule" (followed in most other countries as well), that he is entitled to reimbursement, are rules of general applicability. They are not field-specific. There are, however, numerous exceptions to the principle that provisions regarding attorneys' fees are part of general procedure law. For example, federal antidiscrimination, antitrust, copyright, pension, and securities laws all contain field-specific provisions modifying the American rule (as do many other field-specific statutes). An international convention on contract law could do the same. But not only is the question of attorneys' fees not "expressly settled" in the Convention, it is not even mentioned. And there are no "principles" that can be drawn out of the provisions of the Convention for determining whether "loss" includes attorneys' fees; so by the terms of the Convention itself the matter must be left to domestic law (i.e., the law picked out by "the rules of private international law," which means the rules governing choice of law in international legal disputes).

> U.S. contract law is different from, say, French contract law, and the general U.S. rule on attorneys' fee shifting (the "American rule") is different from the French rule (loser pays). But no one would say that French contract law differs from U.S. because the winner of a contract suit in France is entitled to be reimbursed by the loser, and in the U.S. not. That's an important difference but not a contract-law difference. It is a difference resulting from differing procedural rules of general applicability.

The interpretation of "loss" for which Zapata contends would produce anomalies, which is another reason to reject the interpretation. On Zapata's view the prevailing plaintiff in a suit under the Convention would (though presumably subject to the general contract duty to mitigate damages, to which we referred earlier) get his attorneys' fees reimbursed more or less automatically (the reason for the "more or less" qualification will become evident in a moment). But what if the defendant won? Could he invoke the domestic law, if as is likely other than in the United States that law entitled either side that wins to reimbursement of his fees by the loser? Well, if so, could the plaintiff waive his right to attorneys' fees under the Convention in favor of domestic law, which might be more or less generous than Article 74, since Article 74 requires that any loss must, to be recoverable, be foreseeable, which beyond some level attorneys' fees, though reasonable ex post, might not be? And how likely is it that the United States would have signed the Convention had it thought that in doing so it was abandoning the hallowed American rule? To the vast majority of the signatories of the Convention, being nations in which loser pays is the rule anyway, the question whether "loss" includes attorneys' fees would have held little interest; there is no reason to suppose they thought about the question at all.

For these reasons, we conclude that "loss" in Article 74 does not include attorneys' fees,

For further discussion of the recovery of attorney fees under CISG Article 74, see Harry M. Flechtner, *Recovering Attorneys' Fees as Damages under the U.N. Sales Convention (CISG): The Role of Case Law in the New International Commercial Practice, with Comments on Zapata Hermanos v. Hearthside Baking,* 22 NORTHWESTERN J. INT'L L. & BUS. [] (2002).[1]

Note on Liquidated Damage Clauses under the CISG

The CISG contains no provision addressing liquidated damages or their enforceability. Does that mean that, in international sales governed by the CISG, liquidated damage clauses are always enforceable, even if they provide for unreasonable liquidated damages? Recall that Article 4 of the CISG states that the Sales Convention "is not concerned with (a) the validity of the contract or of any of its provisions. . . ." Unconscionability is an example of a "validity" doctrine beyond the scope of and not pre-empted by the CISG. Thus a liquidated damages clause that was unconscionable under the national law applicable according to choice of law principles could not be enforced. The provisions of UCC Article 2 that render unreasonable liquidated damages unenforceable may also be deemed rules of validity. If so, they remain applicable even in transactions subject to the CISG, provided choice of law rules lead to the application of a jurisdiction that has enacted Article 2.

---

1. A draft of this article is posted on the Internet at <http://www.cisg.law.pace.edu/   cisg/biblio/flechtner4. html#iv>.

G. REMEDIES UNDER UCITA

Note on UCITA Remedies

Comment 2 to UCITA § 801 identifies protection of the aggrieved party's expectation interest as the basis for UCITA remedies. Other UCITA provisions adopt the mitigation of damages principle (§ 807(a)), the principle that only foreseeable losses should be compensated for by damages (§ 102(a)(14)), and the principle that specific performance should be available only in exceptional circumstances (§ 811). These remedial purposes and principles are also found in UCC Article 2 and 2A, and it should not be surprising that the remedy provisions of UCITA are often similar to (and, in fact, many were derived from) the remedy provisions of Articles 2 and 2A of the UCC

For example, in a computer information transaction governed by UCITA, an aggrieved licensee who has not received (or who has properly refused or revoked acceptance of) performance by the licensor can recover the following: restitution of the payments it has made for the performance (§ 809(a)(1)(B)(i)); damages measured either by "the market value of the performance less the contract fee" (§ 809(a)(1)(B)(ii)) or by "the cost of a commercially reasonable substitute transaction less the contract fee under the breached contract" (§ 809(a)(1)(B)(iii));[2] and, in addition, incidental and consequential damages (§ 809(a)(2)). These remedies are strikingly similar to that are available to an aggrieved buyer or lessee under UCC Articles 2 and 2A, and the cited UCITA remedy provision were in fact derived from UCC Article 2A. Similarly, an aggrieved licensor under UCITA can invoke remedies that parallel the remedies available under the UCC to an aggrieved seller or lessor of goods, including (when the breaching licensee has not accepted the licensor's performance) recovery of damages measured by a substitute transaction, market value, or lost profits (UCITA § 808(b)(1)(B) & (C)). The UCITA provision on specific performance (UCITA § 811) also closely tracks the approach in UCC Articles 2 and 2A.

However, the nature of the transactions covered by UCITA, as well as their subject matter, sometimes were deemed to require special remedy provisions that do not have close analogues in the law governing sales or leases. Thus the right of an aggrieved licensee to continued access and use of licensed information (absent cancellation of the license) is provided for in UCITA § 813, and the right of an aggrieved licensor to discontinue the licensee's access to information under an "access contract" if the licensee has materially breached is specified in UCITA § 814. In addition, UCITA § 816 regulates the use of "electronic self-help" (e.g., use of hidden electronic disabling programs) by an aggrieved licensor that wishes to deny a breaching licensee use of licensed information.

---

2. UCITA § 809(a)(1)(B)(iii) permits an aggrieved licensee of computer information to measure its damages against a substitute transaction only if the substitute transaction covers "substantially similar information with the same contractual use restrictions" as in the breached contract. This "substantially similar" requirement is derived from the "cover" damages provision of UCC Article 2A (2A–518).

UCITA § 807(e) requires that damages relating to events that will occur after the date a judgement is issued must be reduced to their present value on the judgement date. For discussion of discounting damages to present value, see "Note: Present Value Damages under UCC Article 2A" *supra*.

INDEX

References are to Pages

ACCEPTANCE OF GOODS
Generally, 236–237,
Actions constituting, 254
Acts inconsistent with seller's ownership, 262–269
Article 2A (leases), 288–291
Consequences of, 261
Damages for accepted goods, 421–427
Failure to make effective rejection, 253, 261
Finance leases, 291–293
Ineffective rejection or revocation, 237, 246, 430–432
Inspection of goods, 249–253
Notice of breach, 259–260
Price recovery by seller, 427–432
Rejection, 236–245
Revocation of acceptance, 254–288
UCITA, 291–292
U.N. Sales Convention (CISG), 292–293

ACCEPTANCE OF OFFERS
Generally, 35–37
Battle of the forms, 37–50
Mirror image rule, 36
Notice of acceptance, 36–37

ADEQUATE ASSURANCES
See also Prospective Nonperformance; Reasonable Grounds for Insecurity; Repudiation
Generally, 300–319
Article 2A, 319
Demand for, 316–318
Failure to provide, 312–315
Form of, 316–318
Grounds for, 313–316
Suspension of performance, 318–319
UCITA, 319

AGREEMENT
See also Contract of Sale
Defined, 35
Modification, 73–80
Offer and acceptance, 35–37
Open terms, 35–36, 99–103

ANTICIPATORY REPUDIATION
See Repudiation

ARTICLE 2A
See Leases and Leasing

"AS IS"
See Disclaimer of Warranties

ATTORNEY'S FEES
Recovery under Magnuson–Moss Warranty Act, 222

AVOIDANCE OF CONTRACT
See also United Nations Convention on Contracts for the International Sale of Goods (CISG)
And cure, 294–295
Fundamental breach, 293–296
Installment contracts, 297
"Nachfrist," 297–299, 467–469
Notice of, 467
Rejection/revocation (UCC) compared, 292–293
Remedies, 467–469
Use of goods, 295–297

BAD FAITH
See Good Faith

BAILEES
Loss of goods in bailee's possession, 346–348, 370–376
Risk of loss, 335–340

BANKRUPTCY
And seller's right of reclamation, 434–435
Recovery of goods by buyer/lessee, 405–407
Recovery of goods by seller, lessor, 432–434

BASIS OF BARGAIN
See Express Warranty

BATTLE OF THE FORMS
Amended 2–207, 51–52
Article 2, 37–50
Article 2A, 53
"Battle of the Records," 53–54
Mirror image rule, 36
Post-sale terms, 54–61
UCITA, 53–54
U.N. Sales Convention (CISG), 52–53

BILL OF LADING
See Documents of Title

BREACH
See also Nonconformity/Nonconforming
    Goods or Tender; Remedies
Cure, 245–253, 269–275
Effect on risk of loss, 340–344
Notice of, 259–260
Repudiation, 300–312
Wrongful rejection/revocation, 430–432

BREACH OF WARRANTY
    See also Nonconformity/Nonconforming
        Goods or Tender; Remedies
Damages, 413–421
Economic loss, 206–207
Non-privy warrantor, 195–205, 207
Notice of, 207–208

BUYER'S REMEDIES
See also Remedies
Accepted goods, 421–427
Consequential damages, 435–446
Cover, 396–404
Economic loss damages, 206–207
Insolvent seller, 405
Limitations on recoverable damages,
    185–195
Liquidated damages, 449–453
Market price damages, 396–402
Recovery of goods, 405–413
Rejection, 236–245
Replevin, 405
Repudiation, 404–405
Restitution of payments, 454
Revocation of acceptance, 254–288
Specific performance, 405–413
U.N. Sales Convention (CISG), 463–466,
    467–469, 471–482

CANCELLATION OF CONTRACT
    Generally, 467–468
Upon repudiation, 301–312

CARRIAGE OF GOODS
See Risk of Loss

CASUALTY TO GOODS
See Excuse/Impracticability; Risk of Loss

CHARACTERIZATION OF TRANSACTION
Mixed goods and services (hybrid), 13–20
Sale vs. lease, 21–26
Security interest vs. "true lease," 21–26

C.I.F.
See Risk of Loss

CISG
See United Nations Convention of Con-
    tracts for the International Sale of
    Goods (CISG)

COMMENTS TO THE UCC
See Uniform Commercial Code (UCC)

COMMERCIAL IMPRACTICABILITY
See Excuse/Impracticability

CONSEQUENTIAL DAMAGES
    Generally, 435–436
Accepted goods, 436
Agreement to exclude liability, 185–195
Article 2A (leases), 455–456
Causation, 436–441
Economic loss, 206–207
Finance charges, 444–445
Foreseeability, 436–441
Lost profits, 435–436,
Mitigation, 436–441
Reliance damages, 439–445
Seller's, 447–449
Speculative, 439–440
U.N. Sales Convention (CISG), 471–476

CONSUMER PROTECTION
        See also Magnuson–Moss Warranty
            Act
    Generally, 221–223

COMPUTER INFORMATION
See Electronic Contracting; Uniform Com-
    puter Information Transactions Act
    (UCITA)

CONTRACT OF SALE
    See also Agreement
Defined, 35–36
Formation, 36–37
Good faith obligation, 35–36
Statute of Frauds, 67–70

CONTRACTUAL REMEDY PROVISION
    Generally, 185–195

COURSE OF DEALING
        See also Course of Performance;
            Trade Usage
    Generally, 83–90
And parol evidence rule, 80–91
Article 2A (leases), 99
U.N. Sales Convention (CISG), 91–98

COURSE OF PERFORMANCE
        See also Course of Dealing; Trade
            Usage
    Generally, 80–91
And Statute of Frauds, 67–69
Article 2A (leases), 99
As modification, 90–91
U.N. Sales Convention (CISG), 91–98

COVER DAMAGES
    Generally, 396–403
Article 2A (leases), 456
Calculation, 402
Good faith, 396–402
Internal cover, 404
Purpose of, 402–403
Reasonableness, 396–402

COVER DAMAGES—Cont'd
Recovery of market price damages despite cover, 396–397
Requirements, 396–402
U.N. Sales Convention (CISG), 467–468
What constitutes, 401–403

CURE
Adequate cure, 245–248
After rejection, 245–246
After revocation of acceptance, 269–277
After time for performance, 249–253
And perfect tender rule, 245–248
Article 2A (leases), 288–291
Before time for performance, 245
Good faith, 253
Late delivery, 245
Notice of intent to cure, 245
Price adjustment, 248–249
Reasonable grounds to believe tender is acceptable, 245–246
Refusal to permit, 245–248
Repair, 247–249
Replacement, 247–249
Repudiation, 247–249
Seller's knowledge of nonconformity, 245–253
Shaken faith, 247–249

CURRENT PRICE
See Market Price/Rent Damages

DAMAGES
See Remedies

DEFECTS/DEFECTIVE GOODS
See Nonconformity/Nonconforming Goods or Tender

DELIVERY
Installments, 100–101
Time and place, 100–103

DESTINATION CONTRACT
See Risk of Loss

DISCLAIMERS OF WARRANTY
Generally, 146–155
And Magnuson–Moss Warranty Act, 221–223, 234–235
Article 2A (leases), 153
Computer information transactions, 155
Express warranty, 146–152
Fitness for particular purpose warranty, 146–152
Inspection of goods, 147–148
Limitation of remedies compared, 104–105
Merchantability warranty, 146–152
Title warranty, 162–164
U.N. Sales Convention (CISG), 153–154

DOCUMENTARY TRANSACTION
See also Documents of Title
Generally, 367–370
Drafts, use of, 370–376

DOCUMENTS OF TITLE
Generally, 367–370
Bailees, liability of, 370–376
Bill of lading, 368–370
Function of, 367–370
Negotiability, 376–378
Obligation to deliver goods, 368–369
Transaction involving, 378–380
Warehouse receipt, 367–370

ECONOMIC LOSS
Damages for, 206–207

ELECTRONIC CONTRACTING
See also Uniform Computer Information Transactions Act (UCITA); Uniform Electronic Transactions Act (UETA)
Generally, 7–9, 26–27
History, 7–9
Statute of Frauds, 72

ENTRUSTMENT
See Title

E–SIGN
Generally, 64–68

ESSENTIAL PURPOSE, FAILURE OF
See Failure of Essential Purpose

EXCUSE/IMPRACTICABILITY
Generally, 348–350
Allocation of goods, 351–363
Article 2A (leases), 367
Casualty to identified goods, 326–328, 346–348
Force majeure, 363–367
Government regulations, 363–364
Impracticability, 350–363
Partial impracticability, 357–363
UCITA, 367
U.N. Sales Convention (CISG), 367

EXPRESS WARRANTY
Generally, 104–119
And parol evidence rule, 112
Article 2A (leases), 119
Basis of the bargain, 108–118
Computer information transactions, 119
Creation, 108–118
Disclaimers, 146–152
Finance Leases, 139–146
Opinion, value, commendation and puff, 105–108
Post-sale warranties, 117–118
Proposed Amended, 116–117
Puffery, 105–108
Reliance, 108–116
Samples/models, 118
U.N. Sales Convention (CISG), 119
What constitutes, 108–116

FAILURE OF ESSENTIAL PURPOSE
See Limitation of Remedies

F.A.S.
See Risk of Loss

FINANCE LEASES
    Generally, 139–146
Defined, 139–146
"Hell or high water" obligation of lessee, 145–146
Lessee as beneficiary of warranties in supply contract, 139–146
Rejection, 288–290
Remedies, 320–321
Revocation of acceptance, 288–291
Warranties, 139–146

FITNESS FOR PARTICULAR PURPOSE
See Implied Warranty of Fitness for a Particular Purpose

F.O.B.
See Risk of Loss

FORCE MAJEURE
See Excuse/Impracticability

FORMS
Contract formation, 36–50

FULL WARRANTY
See Magnuson–Moss Warranty Act

FUNDAMENTAL BREACH
And avoidance of contract, 293–296

GOOD FAITH
    Generally, 35–36
Cover damages, 396–402
Cure, 253
Output and requirements contracts, 410–412
Resale remedy, 413–415

GOODS
Defined, 11–19
Scope of Article 2, 11

"HELL OR HIGH WATER" OBLIGATION
See Finance Leases

IDENTIFICATION OF GOODS
    Generally, 325
And recovery of goods by buyer, 405–410
And risk of loss, 346–348
Excuse for casualty to goods, 346–348

IMPLIED TERMS
    Generally, 99–102

IMPLIED WARRANTY OF FITNESS FOR A PARTICULAR PURPOSE
    Generally, 126–129
Article 2A (leases), 129
Computer information transactions, 133
Disclaimers, 147–153
Finance leases, 139–146

IMPLIED WARRANTY OF FITNESS FOR A PARTICULAR PURPOSE—Cont'd
U.N. Sales Convention (CISG), 129–133

IMPLIED WARRANTY OF MERCHANTABILITY
    Generally, 119–120
Article 2A (leases), 123
Computer information transactions(UCITA), 124–126
Disclaimers, 103–105
Finance leases, 147–153
Merchant requirement, 119–120
Standards, 119–122
U.N. Sales Convention (CISG), 123–124
UCITA, 123–124

IMPOSSIBILITY
See Excuse/Impracticability

IMPRACTICABILITY
See Excuse/Impracticability

INCIDENTAL DAMAGES
    Generally, 435–436
Buyer's, 435–436
Distinguished from consequential damages, 448
Seller's, 447–449

INCOTERMS
    Generally, 328–329

INDEFINITENESS
Enforceability of contract, 99–101

INFRINGEMENTS, WARRANTY AGAINST
Generally, 165–171
Disclaimer, 170
Proposed Amendments, 170–171
U.N. Sales Convention (CISG), 172–173
UCITA, 173

INSECURITY
See Adequate Assurances; Reasonable Grounds for Insecurity

INSTALLMENT CONTRACTS
Cancellation, 244
Rejection, 244
Substantial impairment, 244
U.N. Sales Convention (CISG), 297–298

INSURABLE INTEREST
See Identification of Goods

INTERNATIONAL SALES
    See also United Nations Convention on Contracts for the International Sale of Goods (CISG)
Statute of Limitations, 220

LEASE REMEDIES
    Generally, 455
Accepted goods, 455–456
Consequential damages, 455–456, 460
Cover damages, 456
Effect of bankruptcy, 434–435

LEASE REMEDIES—Cont'd
Liquidated damages, 462
Lost profits by lessor, 461
Market rent damages, 457
Mitigation of damages, 456
Present value damages, 457–460
Recovery of goods by lessee, 456–457
Re-lease damages, 457–460
Rent, action for, 462
Repossession of goods by lessor, 461
Specific performance, 461

LEASES AND LEASING
See also Finance Leases; Lease Remedies; Quiet Possession, Warranty of; Revision of Article 2A
Generally, 5, 22–26
Characterization of transactions, 22–26
Defined, 22
Disclaimers of warranties, 153
Finance leases, 139–146
Parol evidence rule, 99
Products liability, 219–221
Rejection of goods, 288
Revocation of acceptance, 288
Risk of loss, 345–346
Scope of Article 2A, 22–26
Security interest distinguished, 22–26
Statute of Frauds, 71–72
Statute of Limitations, 220
"True lease," 22–26
Warranties, 119, 123, 129

LETTER OF CREDIT
Generally, 380–382
Compliance with terms, 388–394
Conformity of documents, 388–394
Establishment, 393–394
Form, 393–394
Fraud, 382–386
Independence from underlying contract, 382–387
Irrevocability, 394
Law governing, 382
Modification, 387
Standby letter of credit, 381–382
Strict compliance rule, 388–384

LIMITATION OF LIABILITY
Generally, 185–194

LIMITATION OF REMEDIES
Generally, 104
Article 2A (leases), 194
Consumer protection law, 221–223
Disclaimers of warranties compared, 104–105
Exclusion of consequential damages, 185–194
Failure of essential purpose, 185–194
UCITA, 195

LIMITED WARRANTY
See Magnuson–Moss Warranty Act

LIQUIDATED DAMAGES
Generally, 449–454
As limit on recovery, 453–454
Reasonableness of amount, 452–454
Relation to actual harm, 452–454
"Take or pay" contracts, 453–454

LOST PROFITS
See Profits

MAGNUSON-MOSS WARRANTY ACT
Generally, 221–223
Arbitration under, 227–23
Attorney's fees, 222
Consumer product, 222–223
Disclaimer of implied warranties, 221–223, 234–235
Duration of warranties, 221–223,2334–235
Express warranties and written warranties, 223–227
Full warranties, 225
Limitation of remedies, 221–223
Limited warranties, 225
Scope, 234–235
Written warranties, 223–227, 230–234

MARKET PRICE/RENT DAMAGES
Generally, 413–414, 457
Article 2A (leases), 457
Calculation, 457–460
Current price, 457–460
Limited by lost profits, 352–353
Recovery despite cover, 456
Repudiation by seller, 404–405
Time and place for measuring, 457–460
U.N. Sales Convention (CISG), 467–468

MERCHANTABILITY, WARRANTY OF
See Implied Warranty of Merchantability

MISSING TERMS
Gap fillers under Article 2, 35–36, 99–102

MODELS
See Express Warranty

MODIFICATION OF CONTRACT
Generally, 73–74
And parol evidence rule, 80–82
And statute of frauds, 73–79
Article 2A (leases), 79–80
U.N. Convention on Contracts for the International Sale of Goods (CISG), 79–80

"NACHFRIST"
See U.N. Convention on Contracts for the International Sale of Goods (CISG)

NEGOTIABILITY
See Documents of Title

NONAVOIDANCE OF CONTRACT
See also United Nations Convention on Contracts for the International Sale of Goods (CISG)

NONAVOIDANCE OF CONTRACT—Cont'd
Generally, 299–300

NONCONFORMITY/NONCONFORMING GOODS OR TENDER
Cure, 245–253
Damages for, 421–427
Delivery, 238–240
Failure to notify of shipment, 243–244
Installment contracts, 244–245
Perfect tender rule, 236–239
Rejection, 236–245
Revocation of acceptance, 196–233
Substantial impairment, 244
Tender, 238–240

NOTICE
Acceptance of offer, 36–37
Avoidance of contract, 467
Breach of warranty, 207–208
Intent to cure, 245
Rejection, 249–253
Particularizing defects in goods, 259–260

OFFER
See Acceptance of Offers; Agreement; Contract of Sale

OPEN AND IMPLIED TERMS
See Implied Terms

OUTPUT CONTRACTS
Generally, 72–73
Quantity of goods, 72–73
Specific performance, 410–412

PAROL EVIDENCE RULE
Generally, 83–99
Article 2A (leases), 99
Course of dealing, 83–90
Course of performance, 91
Trade usage, 83–90
United Nations Convention on Contracts for the International Sale of Goods (CISG), 91–98

PAYMENT
Buyer's payment obligations, 324–326
Documentary transaction, 367–370
Letter of credit, 380–394
Time for payment, 99–102

PERFECT TENDER RULE
See also Rejection of Goods
Generally, 236
Cure, 243–245
Exceptions, 243–245
Good faith, 240–242
Nonconforming goods or tender, 236–240

PERFORMANCE
Generally, 324–326
Adequate assurances, 300–319
Insecurity concerning, 300–319
Repudiation, 300–323

POST-SALE TERMS
Generally, 54–61

PRESENT VALUE DAMAGES
Generally, 457–460

PRICE/RENT RECOVERY BY SELLER/LESSOR
See also Lease Remedies; Remedies
Accepted goods, 421–427, 455–456
Article 2A (leases), 457, 462
Specific performance, 405–413, 421, 461
U.N. Sales Convention (CISG), 469–470

PRICE TERM, IMPLICATION
Generally, 99–101

PRIVITY OF CONTRACT
Economic loss damages, 206
Products liability, 195–205
Revocation of acceptance, 277–288

PRODUCTS LIABILITY
Generally, 195–220
Article 2A (leases), 219–221
Defective vs. unmerchantable product, 214–218
Economic loss damages, 206–207
Privity of contract, 195–205
Proposed Amendments, 209–210
Restatement (2d) Torts § 402A, 206–207
Statute of limitations, 208–210
UCITA, 219–221
United Nations Convention on Contracts for the International Sale of Goods (CISG). 219–221

PROFITS
Generally, 419–420
As limit on market price damages, 420
Calculation, 420
Consequential damages, 373–374
Lost volume seller, 419–420
Unfinished goods, 419–420

PROSPECTIVE NONPERFORMANCE
See also Adequate Assurances; Repudiation
Generally, 300–323
Article 2A (leases), 319
U.N. Sales Convention (CISG), 319–323
UCITA, 319

QUALITY OF GOODS
See Warranties

QUANTITY OF GOODS
Output and Requirements Contracts, 72–73

QUIET POSSESSION, WARRANTY OF
Generally, 156–164

REASONABLE EXPECTATIONS DOCTRINE
Generally, 62–63

REASONABLE GROUNDS FOR INSECURITY
See also Adequate Assurances
Effect, 312–315
What constitutes, 312–315

RECLAMATION
See Recovery of Goods by Seller/Lessor

RECOVERY OF GOODS BY BUYER/LESSEE
Generally, 405, 456–457
Article 2A (leases), 456–457
Insolvent seller, 405
Replevin, 405
Specific performance, 405–413, 421
U.N. Sales Convention (CISG), 471

RECOVERY OF GOODS BY SELLER/LESSOR
And bankruptcy, 434–435
Article 2A (leases), 456–457
Cash sales, 434–435
Identified goods, 325
Insolvent buyer, 434–435
Third party claims to goods, 432

REDUCTION OF PRICE
U.N. Sales Convention (CISG), 465

REJECTION OF GOODS
Generally, 236–237
Article 2A (leases), 288
Cure, 245–253
Failure to particularize defects, 249–253
Finance leases, 288–290
Good faith, 240–243
Installment contracts, 244–245
Limitation of remedy, 261–262
Nonconformity, 236–240
Notice of, 249–253
Perfect tender rule, 236–240
Security interest for amounts buyer paid, 261–262
Substantial impairment, 244
U.N. Sales Convention (CISG), 292–293
Use of goods following, 261–262
Wrongful vs. ineffective, 246, 430–432

RELIANCE DAMAGES
As consequential damages, 439–445

REMEDIES
Generally, 395–396
Accepted goods, buyer's damages for, 421–427
Article 2A (leases), 455–463
Cancellation, 467–468
Consequential damages, 435–439, 441–445
Cover damages, 396–403
Economic loss damages, 206–207
Incidental damages, 435–439, 441–445
Limitation of damages, 185–194
Liquidated damages, 449–454
Lost profits, 419–420
Market price/rent damages, 413–414, 457

REMEDIES—Cont'd
Modification/limitation of remedies, 185–194
Present value damages, 457–460
Price/rent recovery, 421–427, 455–456
Reclamation of goods by seller/lessor, 432–435
Recovery of goods by buyer/lessee, 405
Recovery of finance charges, 444–445
Reduction of price, 465
Reliance damages, 439–445
Replevin, 405
Repudiation, 404–405
Resale/re-lease damages, 413–419
Restitution of buyer's payments, 454
Specific performance, 405–413, 421
Stoppage of goods in transit, 433
Tort damages distinguished, 195–211
UCITA, 483–484
U.N. Sales Convention (CISG), 463

REPAIR OR REPLACE REMEDY
See Limitation of Remedies

REPLEVIN
By buyer, 405

REPUDIATION
See also Adequate Assurances; Prospective Nonperformance; Reasonable Grounds for Insecurity
Generally, 300–323
Actions constituting, 311–312, 316–319
And buyer's market price damages, 396–405
Common law, 300
Retraction, 300–310
Substantial impairment, 244

REQUIREMENTS CONTRACTS
Generally, 72–73
Quantity of goods, 72–73
Specific performance, 467–468

RESALE/RE-LEASE DAMAGES
Notice, 414
Profit on resale, 419–420
Public vs. private resale, 414
Reasonableness, 414
Recovery of market price damages despite resale, 413–414
Requirements, 419–420
What constitutes, 414

RESTITUTION
Avoidance of contract, 464
Buyer's payments, 454

REVOCATION OF ACCEPTANCE OF GOODS
Generally, 254–288
Against disclaiming seller, 277–288
Against non-privy warrantor, 277–288
Article 2A (leases), 288–291
Circumstances of acceptance, 268–287
Cure, 269–273

REVOCATION OF ACCEPTANCE OF GOODS—Cont'd
Finance lease, 288–291
Limitation of remedy, 261–262
Security interest for amounts paid, 261–262
Subjective impairment, 275–277
Substantial impairment, 269–275
U.N. Sales Convention (CISG), 292–293
Use of goods by buyer, 262–268
Wrongful vs. ineffective, 258

RISK OF LOSS
Generally, 324
Absence of breach, 324–326
Acceptance of goods, 340–344
Bailees, 335–339
Carriage of goods, 326–328
C.I.F. term, 330–334
Destination contracts, 327–329
Effect of breach, 340–344
F.A.S. term, 326–329
Finance lease, 345–346
F.O.B. term, 326–328
Goods sold in transit, 340–341
Implied term, 101–102
Incoterms, 328–329, 331–
Price recovery by seller, 421–427
Receipt, 324–326
Shipment contracts, 326–328
Tender of delivery, 324–326
Title, effect on, 20–21
Transit risk, 326–329, 330–334, 346–348
U.N. Sales Convention (CISG), 330–334, 344–345

SALE
Battle of the forms, 37–50
Contract formation, 36–37
Defined, 35–37
Parol evidence rule, 83–99
Statute of Frauds, 67–70
Transaction in goods, 11–19
Vs. services transaction, 13–20

SAMPLES
See Express Warranty

SCOPE OF CISG
Generally, 9–10
Contracting States, 9–10, 33–34
Goods, 11–19
Mixed goods and services, 28–29
Parties in different states, 29–34
Validity issues, 28–29

SCOPE OF UCC ARTICLE 2
Generally, 11–19
Goods, 11–19
Goods and real property, 11–19
Mixed goods and services, 13–19
Sale, 20
Secured transactions, 21–22

SCOPE OF UCC ARTICLE 2A
Generally, 19–23

SCOPE OF UCC ARTICLE 2A—Cont'd
Security interest distinguished, 22–26

SECURED TRANSACTIONS
See Security Interest

SECURITY INTEREST
Applicability of Article 2, 22–26
Applicability of Article 2A, 22–26
Definition of, 23–25
Disguised security interest, 22–26
"True lease" distinguished, 22–26

SELLER'S REMEDIES
See also Remedies
Accepted Goods, 427–430
Consequential damages, 447–449
Incidental damages, 447–449
Liquidated damages, 449–454
Lost profit recovery, 415–420
Market price damages, 413
Price, recovery of, 421–427
Reclamation, 432–435
Resale damages, 414
U.N. Sales Convention (CISG), 466–471

SHIPMENT CONTRACT
See Risk of Loss

SPECIFIC PERFORMANCE
See Recovery of Goods by Buyer/Lessee

STANDBY LETTER OF CREDIT
See Letter of Credit

STATUTE OF FRAUDS
Generally, 66–70
Admission exception, 68–69
Article 2A (leases), 71–72
Computer information transactions, 72
Confirmation exception, 68–69
Intangibles, 66–68
Modifications, 73–79
Part Performance, 69–70
Proposed Amendments, 70–71
Quantity term, 68–69
Receipt of goods or price exception, 68–69
Scope, 67
Specially-manufactured goods exception, 69–70
Sufficient writing, 67–68
U.N. Sales Convention (CISG), 72
UCITA, 72

STATUTE OF LIMITATIONS
Computer information transactions, 220
International sales, 220
Leases, 220
Products liability, 216–220
Tort claims, 219–220

STRICT LIABILITY
See Products Liability

SUBSTANTIAL IMPAIRMENT
Installment contracts, 244
Revocation of acceptance, 275–277

SUBSTANTIAL IMPAIRMENT—Cont'd
Subjective vs. objective, 269–275

SUPPLY CONTRACT
See also Finance Lease
Defined, 145–146
Warranties and finance lessee, 145–146

TAKE OR PAY CONTRACT
As liquidated damages, 453–454

TENDER OF DELIVERY
Time and place, 100–103

TENDER OF PAYMENT
Time and place, 99–102

TITLE
See also Title, Warranty of
   Generally, 152–162
Effect of passage of title, 20–21
Fraud, 156
Good faith purchase, 156–157
Passage under the U.C.C., 20–21
Risk of loss, 20–21
Secured party's rights, 156–157
Stolen goods, 156–163
Void and voidable, 158–162

TITLE, WARRANTY OF
   See also Infringements, Warranty
     Against
   Generally, 153–173
Claims of prior owners, 163
Disclaimers, 162–164
Third party's superior title, 163
U.N. Sales Convention (CISG), 171–173
UCITA, 173

TORTS
See Products Liability

TRADE USAGE
   See also Course of Dealing; Course of
     Performance
   Generally, 80–91
And parol evidence rule, 80–91
Article 2A (leases), 99
U.N. Sales Convention (CISG), 91–98

"TRUE LEASE"
See Characterization of Transaction

UNCONSCIONABILITY
   Generally, 173–185
And merchants, 174
Contract of adhesion, 175–177
Exclusion of consequential damages, 178–184
Fine print, 178–184
Lack of choice, 175–176
Modification or limitation of remedies, 178–184
Procedural, 175–176, 185
Substantive, 175–176, 185
Time for determining, 175–176
Unequal bargaining power, 174–175

UNCONSCIONABILITY—Cont'd
Unexpected terms, 174–175

UNEQUAL BARGAINING POWER
See Unconscionability

UNFORESEEN CIRCUMSTANCES
See, Excuse/Impracticability

UNIFORM COMMERCIAL CODE (UCC)
   Generally, 3–6
Background, 2–3
Comments, weight in construing UCC, 6
Enactment by states, 2–3
History, 2–3
Interpretation, 4–5, 27–28
Overview, 3–6
Purposes, 3–6
Supplementation by common law, 4–5

UNIFORM COMPUTER INFORMATION TRANSACTIONS ACT (UCITA)
   Generally, 7–8, 26–27
Battle of the forms, 53–54, 61–62
Disclaimers of warranties, 155
Excuse, 291–292
Express warranties, 119
Implied warranty of merchantability, 124–125
Material breach, 185–186
Products liability, 219–221
Remedies, 483–484
Risk of loss, 346
Scope, 26–27
Statute of Frauds, 72
Statute of Limitations, 220

UNIFORM ELECTRONIC TRANSACTIONS ACT (UETA)
   Generally, 8–9

UNITED NATIONS CONVENTION ON CONTRACTS FOR THE INTERNATIONAL SALE OF GOODS
   Generally, 9–10
Adequate Assurances, 319–321
Adoption, 29–33
Applicability, 29–33
Attorneys' fees, recovery of, 477–482
Avoidance of contract, 292–296
Battle of the forms, 52–53
Choice of law, 29–33
Consequential damages, 471–476
Contract formalities, 72
Contract formation, 52–53
Cover damages, 467–468
Cure, 293–295
Disclaimers, 153–154
Excuse, 367
Fundamental breach, 293–296
History, 9–10
Liquidated damages, 471–476, 482
Lost profit damages, 467–469
Market (current) price damages, 467–468
Mitigation of damages, 468–469
Modifications, 79–80

UNITED NATIONS CONVENTION ON CONTRACTS FOR THE INTERNATIONAL SALE OF GOODS—Cont'd
"Nachfrist," 297–299, 467–469
Nonavoidance of contract, 299–300
Parol evidence rule, 91–98
Preservation of goods, 295–297
Price, recovery by seller, 469–470
Prospective nonperformance, 319–321
Remedies generally, 463–482
Repudiation, 319–322
Resale damages, 468–469
Risk of loss, 330–334, 344–345
Scope, 27–34
Specific performance, 471
Statute of Frauds, 72
Substitute goods,
Use of goods, 295–297
Validity issues, 29–33
Warranty, 119, 123–124, 129–132
Writing requirements, 72

USAGE OF TRADE
See Trade Usage

WAREHOUSE RECEIPT
See Document of Title

WAREHOUSEMAN
Conversion, liability for, 370–375
Delivery of goods against documents, 367–370
Duty of care, 370–376

WARRANTY
See also Express Warranty; Implied Warranty of Fitness for a Particular Purpose; Implied Warranty of Merchantability; Infringements, Warranty Against; Quiet Possession, Warranty of; Title, Warranty of
Generally, 104–105
Article 2A (leases), 119, 123, 129
Cumulation and conflict, 133–139
Disclaimers, 146–155, 162–164
Express, 105
Finance lease, 139–146
Implied, 119–129
Infringements, 165–171
Magnuson–Moss Warranty Act, 221–223
Quiet Possession, 156–164
Title, 156–173
U.N. Sales Convention (CISG), 119, 123–124, 129–132

WARRANTY DISCLAIMERS
See Disclaimers of Warranty

WARRANTY OF TITLE
See Title, Warranty of

WRITING REQUIREMENT
See Statute of Frauds

WRITTEN WARRANTY
See Magnuson–Moss Warranty Act

†